A S H L E Y

ASHLEY

*Portrait
of a village...*

*...in an
age of change*

Conversations with David Ellington

HOUGH GREEN
PUBLICATIONS

First published 2001 by Hough Green Publications
6 Hough Green, Ashley, Altrincham, Cheshire WA15 0QS

British Library Cataloguing-in-Publication Data
Ellington, David
Ashley: portrait of a village in an age of change
1. Ashley (England) - Social life and customs - 20th Century
I. Title
942.7'1'0859
ISBN 0 9540354 0 2

Cover design by Les Burgess
Cover photographs by Brian Gee and author
Typeset by Focus Marketing, Holmes Chapel
Printed and bound by Deanprint Ltd., Stockport

HOUGH GREEN
PUBLICATIONS

From Ashley People
to
the People of Ashley
to mark a new Millennium

ACKNOWLEDGEMENTS:

Thanks above all to those featured on these pages, without whom
there would be no book;

to Messrs Hamish Hamilton for permission to quote the excerpt from
The Plague by Albert Camus, translated by Stuart Gilbert, on page x;

to Messrs. Faber and Faber for permission to quote the line from
T.S.Eliot's *Four Quartets* on page xii;

to Mr Stan Hibbert and the Musicians' Union for permission to quote on page 71
part of his tribute to the late Brian Fitzgerald which appeared in the
Manchester Branch Bulletin of 11th September, 1994;

and to Christine, who lit the fuse and suffered the consequences.

CONTENTS

Insofar as there is any significance in the order that follows, I have taken, very rough-ly, a sweep though the village as an imaginary line would move starting from where Castle Mill Lane leaves the Wilmslow Road, approximately to the South and East, and moves towards its exit, West of Ashley Road on the boundary of Hale, roughly to the North. The main point of this was to give the impression of moving from the outer edges with their farms and more isolated dwellings, in towards the centre with the post office, Egerton Moss and Hough Green at the heart of the village, and then out again towards the more isolated members on the other side.

Because I want to emphasize the kaleidoscopic charm of the community as a whole rather than draw attention to the more sensational aspects of a few individuals, I have tried to edit each conversation down to a similar length. Some, however, have more detailed stories or issues to air and I was unwilling to leave them out. These have been collected into an Appendix at the end and they include memories of the war or national service - for some their only experience of a wider world; farming seemed to merit a section on its own; and so did the institutions which form a significant part of the community's structure. I hope Mr Randle Brooks will not mind being described as an institution! but as the current owner of the Tatton Estate he is landlord of near-ly all the agricultural property as well as much else in the village, and so his attitude and influence directly affects the character of the place. A portrait of Ashley would have been incomplete without a word with him, and I am grateful to him for his entering into the spirit of the enterprise.

The cast, in order of appearance, is as follows:

APPENDICES

PREFACE

This is a portrait of Ashley through the medium of conversations held during 1999 for the most part. The date is important because some conversations include discussion, speculation and rumour about issues that concerned us at that time but which have now moved on, rendering what is said here either irrelevant or misleading, or both. Much of it never had any firmer anchorage in fact than village gossip ever has, and what little it had is further weakened by the passage of time; but that is what people were saying in 1999, and as such it forms part of our story. On the immediate future of the school, for instance: when the earlier conversations were recorded an official enquiry was under way to consider the possibility of closing the school on the grounds that it was too small to be viable. These conversations reflect people's fears. Before I was halfway through the book the authorities had decided that the school was viable, and should stay open. Subsequent conversations reflect the community's relief and expectations in the light of that judgement. Again, a good deal is said about the air-port, including speculation about any possible plans they might have for building a third runway. Since then the airport has categorically denied having any plans for a third runway. Any fears or speculations about this should be understood in the light of what was known at the time, much of which is rendered obsolete and irrelevant by this later announcement. The significance of these earlier views is purely historical.

The book is composed of almost verbatim excerpts transcribed from the tapes of these conversations, which means that it is written as people speak. Had I rewrit-ten it as literature we would have here a much smaller, but probably rather boring book: I want the reader to be able to hear the voices of people as they speak, to catch those subtle little expressions and intonations which help to define character. For this is essentially a book about character - or rather characters: the idea came from my suddenly realising how incredibly rich a mix of characters we have here in Ashley, and the beauty of it is that the place is small enough for everyone to be encompassed with-in the covers of one book.

This is not meant to be a reference book, it is meant to be a portrait - or, if you prefer it, a tableau, a time-capsule. This is how we were in the NOW that has been captured in each conversation. We are not like that anymore: some have died, some have moved away, others have moved in; all of us are a year or two older. This is our verbal photograph album. It was originally conceived as nothing much more than that, something we could share with each other now, and with our children and grandchil-dren in the future, to show that this is how we were at the turn of the Millennium. As the conversations got under way, however, themes began to emerge which are of more than local interest: situations and dilemmas, joys and fears, which are shared by most people engaged in the curious adventure of human life. Words written by Albert Camus in his novel *The Plague* seem to be confirmed here:

> *Perhaps the easiest way of making a town's acquaintance is to ascertain how the people in it work, how they love, and how they die . . .*

Being placed where we are, much of the way people work is bound up with farming - so much so that I have given it an appendix of its own, although there is still plenty about farming in the main section as well. And the more I heard about the problems facing farmers who, more than anyone else, have defined the shape of this community until now, the more I was reminded of the coal miners two decades ago, as they and their communities passed through fires more ferocious, but essentially the same, as those scorching the fringes of the farming communities now (this, be it noted, before the Foot-and-Mouth epidemic of 2001). And, to return to Camus, on every page evidence of how people love, and how much they love. And there is dying, and bereavement somehow lived through, and life's threads somehow picked up again.

I have felt humbled often and sometimes inspired as I listen to these stories. I only hope some of this is conveyed in the pages that follow. Somewhere here are most of the issues facing most people as we move into a new Millennium.

Welcome to Ashley!

David Ellington
Hough Green, Ashley.
April, 2001.

History is now and England.
T.S.Eliot

Chris Frankland. Hillside

D.   Chris, how long have you lived here?

C.   Three years.

D.   How did you come to move here?

C.   Through wanting to find a place in Ashley. My parents were having to leave Broussa Kindergarten School. Phillipa and I were living in the flat at the top of the school. My parents were not able to carry on running the school, and then that was brought to a decision-making point by my father's death. Mother carried on for a while, and then we all started looking more seriously for a place to live. Ashley was always where I'd like to have lived if I could because it linked up more realistically with the tree business than Hale.

D.   Can I go back a bit? You were living in Hale: how long had you lived there?

C.   My parents came back from working abroad. When I was three-and-a-half they landed at Liverpool. Father got a job teaching at Norris Road in Sale: Hale was on the route home. So he ended up buying a house in Gilbert Road. A few years later my parents took over Broussa Schools. Our family moved into the flat above Broussa Kindergarten. My parents ran Big Broussa on Broomfield Lane for nineteen years until John Connor took it over and changed its name to Hale Prep. Shortly after my father's death mother sold Broussa Kindergarten to the Stopfords and Currans.

D.   So were they both teaching, your parents?

C.   Both teaching, yes. As Father was a priest he had other duties: weddings, funerals, interregnums, etc., so he knew many of the local parishes.

D.   Not just interregnums, but holidays and things like that. I owe several holidays to him! So you've been in Hale from your very early childhood?

C.   Since leaving Sierra Leone, West Africa.

D.   And from where you'd been living in Hale you'd got to know Ashley?

C.   Not initially, other than as a kid I used to come out and look in ponds on cycle rides. Then as I got older I used to come on runs, to train for squash. And then, as the tree business took over, it was the obvious place to try and find somewhere to be based.

D.   How did the tree business start?

C.   When I was in primary school it's what I always wanted to do. But if you do well in an academic subject in school, you tend to get pushed that way. So I ended up teaching Maths and Physics: first of all abroad, and then at Sale Grammar. And then, being single, I had evenings, weekends and holidays, with no sport to run because they'd all been stopped due to the teacher dispute at the time. So my childhood ambition took over, and I started doing tree work. I ended up being an approved contractor on the Trafford list while I was still a Maths teacher at Sale Grammar.

D.   How interesting that you came back to your first love. Because when you were talking just now, the way you said it made me feel as if you were viewing your ten years' teaching almost as a diversion.

C.   It was a sort of diversion, but it was something that I really enjoyed doing. But in order to go into it in such a committed way I had to stop teaching.

D.   So you don't have any regrets about the years you spent teaching?

C.   No. Ultimately I'd like to get more involved in teaching, but about trees. Either directly, or through organizations, associations, etc. But I've got a long way to go yet.

D.   By this time of course you're married with a family?

C.   Philly and I met on a Trafford Schools ski trip. We got engaged twelve days later: we had a lot of similar interests. Less than three months after we met we were married and Philly moved in to Warwick Road. I handed my notice in just after the Hurricane in '89. I thought that if I couldn't get enough work here I could always go down south. It was a good opportunity to start. But I only ever managed to get a few weekends down there, as a favour, because I was so busy up here, right from the start. I handed my notice in at the November half-term, and ended up, over two weeks, going from being a single Maths teacher, to being a full-time tree contractor and engaged. Slight change!

D.   I'd just love to have seen your father's face as these things were happening!

C.   Also, in the same fortnight, I was offered a Deputy Headship in the school in Barbados where I was teaching before. Philly wondered what this guy was, that had just left Maths teaching, gone into "trees", and was refusing a job in Barbados!

D.   This had been growing in you for quite some time.

C.   Oh, it had always been there. Even when I was working in Barbados, we converted much of the school grounds, from being an overgrown jungle: and we ended up planting palm trees, fruit trees and all sorts of bits and pieces round the school grounds, for the kids to supplement their school food.

D.   So can you explain what the attraction has been, in trees?

C.   I suppose it's the little boy inside. You can get paid for playing - climbing trees. But then physically it's very demanding: but as things have gone on it's been more intellectually challenging, to try and make the business efficient, and provide a service. To learn about what is involved in tree contracting, which is a combination of a vast number of hugely varied skills and disciplines. The perception of the outsider is that you're just going along the road cutting trees; without the consideration that you're also the health-and-safety manager, the business manager, the book-keeper/accountant, the transport manager, the maintenance manager, the personnel manager, the insurance expert, the legal expert, the MD. And the list goes on - before you even touch on the tree.

D.   I suspect what is closest to your heart is the tree, and where the tree's just come from.

C.   Apart from people, yes that's right. Trees stir up a huge variety of emotions in most people. If you asked five people why they think trees were important you might get twenty five different answers. The subject is huge but our knowledge is relatively poor. Even the basics - very few people can identify the common Ash. We just know we like them, so long as they don't threaten our drains or foundations, and give us shade when - and only when! - we want it. Oh, and they must not make a mess. Another problem is that people perceive that knowledge about trees is automatic if you buy a chainsaw and put "Tree Specialist" on your vehicle.

D.   You've touched on another thing I was wondering about, which is, how do you learn this business? If a ten-year-old boy was reading this, and he thought, Oh I'd like to do that! How does he start?

C.   There's many different ways that people have "got into trees". I've always learned by watching, talking, asking - and trying out myself. So my main source of information was from contractors and tree officers: people within the industry, who were prepared to pass on their knowledge. Then later through seminars, books and the trade press.

D.   And how long is it now, since you left that teaching post?

C.   Eleven-and-a-half years.

D.   How has the business developed in that time?

C.   I started off with a Volvo and trailer. I soon realised that I needed to get a brush-wood chipper. And then the next improvement, and so on. The business has gradually grown, and I've wanted to keep it that way. I could always have expanded faster, but I didn't want to lose control. We've got five men full-time, on-site. Phillipa helps in the office, behind the scenes and does most of the planting, and we have part-time help in the office.

D.   May I go on to this, because it's been a revelation coming here, to where you've been living for the past three years: can you say something about what you've got here? It's an absolute medley.

C.   It's very hard to take a nice piece of timber, and just bin it. We've spent years trying to find positive uses: for example, since we moved here we extended. A friend advised us to put Ash flooring down. As a result our floor here is Ash that used to grow next to the precinct car park in Hale Barns. And the stump is still there, with a bird table on it.

D.   So we're walking around on what used to be on the edge of that precinct?

C.   Yes. One big Ash tree that died because of the way it had been hacked in the past. The timber is more interesting because it's not commercially grown, and it has the natural staining from fungal infections, giving darker figuring.

D.   So even diseases in trees have their uses?

C.   Oh yes. They increase the staining and figuring.

D.   What other timber have you got here? Practically everything I can see here is wood.

C.   Most of the wood has a local story behind it.

D.   And outside there are all sorts of structures. I saw somebody lounging on a hammock in a . . .

C.   Philly said, You're processing people's trees and offering it back, suggesting that they can build something with their own tree. Why don't we do something here? So last summer I made a playhouse for the girls. And we've made timber storage shelters out of our own timber, and we have plans to do many more projects, trying to use as much of our own timber as possible. When I say Our own timber, local timber that we cut, from gardens as opposed to forests.

D.   So that's the recycling aspect. But the other thing I noticed is masses of trees that you've planted.

C.   We're trying to teach ourselves a lot of the things that modern living takes away from one. Last November Philly planted nine Apple trees of varieties with a Cheshire history, as grown by the old Clibrans Nursery on Bankhall Lane in Hale. So we've nine of those. We've planted Damsons, Cherries, Plums, Pears and a Mulberry. Then we have a fruit cage, which Philly planted up last year. This year digging it has been easier as the sand and woodchip is loosening up the clay soil. We have the various piles of timber in the field. And of course there's the five chickens.

D.   So my impression is that what's happening here is a re-establishment of native England, as it was.

C.   Well not quite. More of a marriage of some of the best from the past with some of the best from the new. Because we're in a job where we have far greater opportunities than the average person to do things like this, it seemed something we should do: but from a selfish point of view, it's a load of fun. It's satisfying, eating your own eggs, and eating your own vegetables, and building using timber that would otherwise be put on a bonfire; making charcoal; heating the house and water from timber you have cut yourself. But it's difficult to find a use for the poor quality wood. Chester Zoo, for example, have used some of our large logs - rotting or interestingly shaped - for habitat. They have also used a large number of heavy rustic benches. The sad thing is that it is often cheaper to burn it.

D.   The other thing that I'm wondering if you have any views about: your business is obviously mainly to do with bringing trees down; what about re-planting programmes?

C.   We have a small nursery here so that we can replace trees for people. Whenever we get the opportunity to encourage a client to replace trees we try to do so but we can only advise or encourage, we cannot insist. There are so many issues to do with trees that it is very difficult always to do the right thing. We aim to advise good tree management but we cannot always avoid removing trees that we believe should stay. Occasionally we are able to help a tree owner use their own dead or dangerous tree by arranging its planking so that they can use the timber on their own property.

D. Chris, I think we're running out of time: I just wondered, How was it for you actually moving into Ashley, having been looking at Ashley for some time?

C. It's wonderful. We'd been looking at Ashley for some time, but we knew Ashley quite well, because I'd been working out of Stock Farm for about ten years. I think one of the joys of living here is that we've got a rare opportunity to live the kind of life that we feel we should be living. We have the opportunity through the work we do, to actually be in a position to prove that it's possible to recycle urban timber by putting it back into a building. This is one of the few countries in the world where that is a novelty. It makes one question how "developed" we are.

D. When you think of our past I suppose, as well, in connection with trees: I'm thinking that almost every county has its ancient forest. And that we were a maritime nation, moving about in oak trees. So that the tree must have been absolutely central.

C. It was because of the navy that we have the hedgerow Oak. Every farmer in the country was ordered to plant oaks in his hedgerows because they were running out of good shipbuilding timber. But then steel took over. Things moved on, and many of our old skills disappeared.

D. And the culture with it, and the whole connection with . . .

C. With the planet.

D. And with this particular part of the planet, trees, which have always carried so much symbolical power. Just because we've lost the physical connection.

C. The difficulty with the tree in modern society is that the tree is not compatible with impatient people. Modern society as a whole is very impatient. If we want some screening we'll put up something that will give fast results. Hence the success of the Leyland Cypress. We do it here as much as anybody, I suppose, but what we're trying to do is teach ourselves another way. Getting closer to our planet has huge cross-generation educational value that gives passion a chance to breathe. We had six teenage girls from the youth group in Hale spent a night camping here. And on the Saturday morning I said, We'll make some charcoal so we can barbecue on Sunday. The immediate reaction of one of the girls was, *Oh you should have said, I could have brought some.*

Rebecca Page and John Swan. Barleywell Cottage

D.   How did you get to be in Ashley?

J.   We moved in just over a year ago. It's rented accommodation, and it's quite a long story, really. Basically, I'm separated from my wife, with two children. I moved in with Rebecca six months prior to our moving here, or rented this place together, essentially to be convenient because the kids live about three miles away, down the road. That's why we're in Ashley. It wasn't any desire to live in Ashley. At the time, we'd never even been to Ashley. It was rented through one of the estate agents in Hale. In actual fact the landlady is the daughter of the old lady who used to live here.

D.   Did you choose the decor? because it looks so beautiful.

R.   Oh, thank you. The walls and everything were just painted cream, and we put all the bits in.

D.   And they're your pictures? It's lovely.

R.   Thank you. This is my favourite room. I like it because it's little. Cosy. It's nice.

D.   So basically it was the convenience of it which brought you here?

R.   Convenience, but also I love the countryside. I lived in Mossley, in Lancashire, it was beautiful. It was a mill that was built in 1639, I think. It was then converted into a church. And I lived up in the attic part of it, it was beautiful. It had all the original beams, and overlooked all the fields, didn't it? So I stipulated that I didn't want to live in the city. So it was incredibly convenient that Ashley existed, for me.

D.   It must have been, because that's quite a lot to leave, by the sound of it.

J.   It was a very small place we had there. And I went out there and I was convert-ed to country living. Having never lived in anything other than a built-up area. But would favour this, in the future. It's quite incredible, though. You drive out of Hale and drive down to here, and it's like a new world. Especially, because I do a lot at dusk. So with the sunsets . . . I've even started mowing the lawn!

R.   Not often! My only criticism is that sadly the city appears to be encroaching.

J.   It's halfway, it's a halfway stage. We're already talking about where we're going to live next. And we've been a little further south into Cheshire, where they'll resist urbanisation a little way out. This isn't doing such a bad job. I mean, it's half a mile to our nearest paper.

R.   And there's this, as well: John does have two children, a little boy and a little girl, and we only have two bedrooms. It's OK for them for the time being because they're still only young. But they'll need separate bedrooms. So we would have to move any-way, eventually.

D.   How do the children like it?

J.   They love it.

R.   Matthew loves the garden, because it's like a field, and he's got his goal posts. So it's just like a football field. And our friends who live in North Manchester, they love to come, don't they? They always say that they would love to live here.

J.   It's a great garden for them. Four or five times bigger than the garden they used to have. And it's a great place to play. We could just do with more sunshine and less rain! Manchester rain.

R.   Why did I ever move north?!

D.   Did you move north?

R.   Well my parents live in Gloucestershire. So that's where I lived from being about eight, until I came to Manchester to train as a nurse. So I lived in Gloucestershire. And the difference in weather is quite incredible. Even in terms of temperature. Even in the winter, when it's cold in Gloucestershire, it's a few degrees colder here. And it's always raining! I always used to remember my journeys home from Gloucestershire, and the nearer to Manchester, the darker the sky got. It really does.

D.   So did you choose Manchester for your nursing training? Which hospital?

R.   North Manchester General. At Crumpsall. I came initially to do my children's training, my paediatric training, and then there were problems with Booth Hall, they were looking to shut Booth Hall Children's Hospital. It changed Health Authorities. So North Manchester no longer offered the paediatric training course. So I was asked to train as an adult nurse, and then I could change halfway through. Well as it happened I didn't like my children's nursing placement at all, and so ended up being an adult nurse. So I'm now a Cardiac Rehabilitation nurse. But I work in Liverpool now. So again Ashley's quite handy because, having said I don't like the motorway, it's actually very useful. My journey is made easy because it's close to the motorway.

D.   So you have to drive in and out of Liverpool?

J.   It takes about as long as I take to get to Manchester.

D.   Where are you, John?

J.   North Manchester.

D.   Crumpsall? How long have you been there?

J.   Five years. Seems like forever. I came up from London. I trained in Manchester, then went to London to do cardiology training, then came back up here.

D.   Cardiology: does that embrace both medical and surgical treatment?

J.   No. It's a medical specialty. There's a little bit of overlap in Cardiology, because of the investigations required. Basically we would work on a patient to make a decision as to whether an operation is required. By-pass surgery is the most typical, but it might be valve replacement, or whatever. And then, at that stage, you bring in a surgeon, as a technician, to do the operation. And then we get the patient back afterwards for the longer term preventive management. So it's a medical specialty, but we do end up sticking tubes into people, and doing relatively minor surgery, like pacemakers, while the surgeons go dealing with the complicated matters. But we regard the surgeons as mere technicians to do the job.

D.　Yes, I can hear that!

R.　You're going to get hung, drawn and quartered by the surgeons!

J.　You haven't got any of the heart surgeons living here?

D.　No, funnily enough!

R.　I actually do the best job, though. Out of all of them.

D.　What do you do?

R.　Well my job basically is to look after patients. I go and see patients in hospital who've just had a heart attack. Immediately, a couple of days after the heart attack, I go and give them advice regarding their lifestyle: risk factors, things like smoking and things like that. And then also provide support and advice when they go home. And then bring them back to a rehabilitation programme.

J.　I think it probably is one of the most important things.

R.　Cardiac rehabilitation is looked at actually in terms of four phases: the first phase being when they're in hospital immediately after their heart attack; unfortunately now phase two would have been something like a home visit, but we don't do that anymore. The patients are always encouraged to phone the hospital. And then at four weeks they come back to the hospital for an appointment anyway. And we see them again, and then bring them back to the rehabilitation programme. Or an education programme, depending on whether they have . . . They might be waiting for surgery, in which case exercise wouldn't be appropriate.

D.　This takes place at the hospital?

R.　At the hospital, yes. They come back to the hospital. But also we do have - they are advised that they can phone us at any time.

D.　That's terribly important, because every little thing that might happen causes near-panic.

R.　And understandably so. You don't have time as a cardiologist to say . . . So this is why we have rehabilitation nurses who do that, and continue to support people.

J.　The Liverpool Centre is miles ahead of the game. We don't offer anything like this sort of comprehensive service. There's nothing that I'm aware of quite as advanced as this. A lot of us are moving in that direction. That's why I said it's very important. But for a variety of reasons, both logistical and financial, it's not developed to this extent in most of the hospitals.

R.   I'm only on a year's contract, and hoping that it will be . . . I've been quite lucky.
I've only been qualified for three years, but I managed to get a sister's post. It's actually a sister's grade. But I'm actually only on a year's contract to cover maternity leave
at the moment. But the hospital is looking for funding from the British Heart
Foundation to set up another post. And they would try and keep me in that post if
they get funding. The government have got a number of standards, in terms of the services that should be offered to patients who've had heart attacks. Which is great for
somebody like me, because it means they will continue to need more nurses to do
these kind of jobs.

J.   It's only being given priority as long as it's cost neutral. It's just a lot of hype really. You have to go elsewhere - the British Heart Foundation. I have pharmaceutical
companies funding my coronary prevention unit. You can't get money out of the
NHS. At the moment.

D.   Is that the situation all over the NHS?

J.   Yes, I think I'm restricting what I say about the NHS for the purposes of this
interview to, It is a chronically under-funded institution. And, working in it, it's strikingly obvious. The pressure's on to improve service without any increased cost. I'm
sure that's the same in most public service industries. But nevertheless it's particularly obvious, and a major problem for the NHS.

D.   And where does it hurt most?

J.   Well if you stick to cardiology, then the most strikingly obvious thing is the waiting list for by-pass operations. We need more surgeons, more cardiologists, more
operating time.

D.   But if you suddenly had money . . . ?

J.   No, that's not the answer is it? I mean you can have short-term waiting list ini-
tiatives, where you pay surgeons to work in their spare time, to clear a waiting list. But
you can't do that long-term, because people won't be prepared to work like that.

D.   I think this might be quite an important point, for people who don't know the
ins and outs of the Health Service. Because that is to say that, in this particular field
anyway, nobody can promise to improve the waiting list situation in the next two or
three years.

J.   The implication there is that we can all work harder. You can't do that. The surgical waiting list, from when I decide they need an operation to actually getting one,
at the moment, for my patients on the North side of Manchester, is eighteen months.
They've already waited up to twelve months for my investigations, and up to six
months to see me, so that's three years isn't it: potentially three years from the GP first
thinking a patient should have a by-pass operation, to getting one.

D.   My immediate wonder is, How many of them actually last long enough to get
one?

J.   In general, a by-pass operation's not a life-saving operation, it's to relieve you of symptoms. There's a small group of patients who'll live longer because they've had the operation, but because that group is very small, then we get away with long waiting lists, because statistically you can't prove that being on the waiting list is detrimental, in terms of killing you. It's the unseen, psychological morbidity. Because if you have chest pains all the time, -

D.   You can hardly do anything. I suppose.

R.   So that's interesting, because the new programme that we're looking at setting up at Fazakerley is looking at patients who do have very severe angina, and either are on a waiting list for surgery, or have already had surgery but unfortunately are still very poorly: looking at running a propramme for them which involves a psychologist, and helping them to cope with their pain, and helping them to deal with the fact that they have angina, and looking at the psychological side of it, helping them to learn how to cope with that. Which is a big thing isn't it, for patients with heart disease. So that's actually a new thing that hopefully we'll be looking to set up at Fazakerley. To help patients like that.

J.   You know the best research came out of France? Proving that red wine . . .

R.   Which is why we're drinking it!

J.   It's very important to drink at least half a bottle a day!

R.   We had a lovely Christmas Day, didn't we? Last Christmas Day, because that was actually the first Christmas that we'd been together, and we had John's children on Boxing Day, and Christmas Day we had a really nice time, we were here together, and while the Christmas dinner was cooking we went to The Greyhound, with an old-fashioned game that John bought me for Christmas, called *Shut the Box*. And we took it to The Greyhound, and the landlord thought it was fascinating. As soon as he could get any space he'd come and stand over our shoulder and watch. But that was really lovely, Christmas. It was very special. John and Matthew used to go in and play dominoes, didn't you? So the children love The Greyhound as well. We often go there for Sunday lunch.

J.   I want to talk about Manchester City.

R.   Oh yes, John wants to get his Manchester City Football fan bit in, don't you? Before the end.

J.   Maybe we could start a fan club. Perhaps you could put in that I'd be quite interested in founding the Ashley Branch of the Manchester City Fan Club. Regular trips to Wembley from now.

Irene Daniel and Ian. Higher Thorns Green Farm

D.   Irene, could you tell us how you come to be in Ashley in the first place?

I.   I married Bill, in 1950. When first we were married we lived in the farm house, in two rooms, at the back. And we built Orchard House, my father-in-law built Orchard House for us. And we moved in there in June '52 and Jean was born in the September. I had all my other children in there, Margaret and the three boys, Edward, Andrew and Ian. And they all went to Ashley School and were in the church choir, they were all in the choir in turn. I don't say they were very good, I used to hear funny stories, you know, about playing noughts and crosses, as Mr. Henshall used to say. They used to play noughts and crosses in the choir. Jean and Margaret were both Rose Queens. You know, they've been very involved in the village, all along, the children.

D.   So she'd have been Rose Queen, Jean, in about the mid sixties?

I.   Sixty six.

D.   How long had it been going by then, that Rose Queen fête?

I.   Oh dear! I think it started when Jean was about - well Jean first joined in when she was four.

D.   So it was already well-established.

I.   Yes it was. It used to be held at Ashley Hall.

D.   I hadn't realised that the fête had moved so much - from Ashley Hall to the Old Vicarage, to Midways. And to the school now. So this is its fourth venue.

I.   Yes, that's right. But they didn't have the Rose Queen when it was at Ashley Hall. It was just a Garden Party. The Church Garden Party.

D.   And you, Ian. How did you find it, going to school here?

Ian. Going to school here? It was OK. A lot of people there were my neighbours. I'd grown up with them, hadn't I? Went to primary school, secondary school. When we left Ashley we went to Bradbury, in Hale. A lot of my neighbours, a gang of my group were a similar age. Nigel Wright, Robert Davies. Malcolm Norbury. We were all the same age. There was Katherine Lamont, Arthur's daughter. We were all in the same class, in the same year.

D.   Was it automatic that if you went to the school you were in the church choir?

Ian. Oh no.

D.   How were they selected?

Ian. We were told to go, I think.

(Laughter)

11

D.   Yes! I wondered! And what happened after Bradbury?

Ian.   Went for a short time day release at college at South Trafford. It moved to Hartford, one day a week. Spread over five years. Just learning agriculture. After that came back to work on the farm.

D.   And do you get any spare time to do other things off the farm?

Ian.   Yes, I've got quite a busy social life. Well, most nights. Busy Crown Green bowling at the minute. Once or twice, or even three times a week sometimes. My home Green actually is fourteen miles away, in Comberbach. But I'm in the Knutsford League, and we can bowl anywhere around Knutsford. It's like a NFU team, a farmers' team, really.

D.   What else do you do? You're on this Millennium Committee. Go to the pub.

Ian.   Go to quizzes at the pub. Occasionally play golf. Watch football in the pub.

I.   Everything revolves round the pub!

Ian.   But I do other things. Play squash. Badminton.

D.   Where do you go for those?

Ian.   Either Knutsford, or Altrincham Leisure Centre.

D.   I associate your family with ploughing. Do people still plough, or is that something from the days of horses? When there were ploughing matches and so forth?

Ian.   Yes, we've all been to ploughing matches with tractors. Don't do it much now.

D.   Who organises the ploughing match, the Cheshire Ploughing Match?

I.   That's the Cheshire Ploughing Match Society, isn't it? It's Ted Bowen, isn't it?

D.   So it's more an individual than an actual organisation?

Ian.   It's a small committee.

I.   But they are all farmers. Well the main one who runs it, he's turned eighty. He's retired, but he still carries on in charge of it, sort of thing. He used to be one of our friends. Well, he still is a friend. He was in the Young Farmers when my husband Bill was in the Young Farmers. And he's just carried on, and he still does it.

D.   It's just that it sounds like an absolute institution, the ploughing match. Wherever I go people mention it.

Ian.   It's still popular, because you go to that, and it's ninety-nine per cent farming people go to it. Whereas the Cheshire Show, which used to be an Agricultural Show, has gone the other way, ninety per cent non-farming people. The agriculture is a very small part of it now.

D.   Yes, that's interesting. Nobody else has made that sort of comment. That must have changed the character of the Cheshire Show enormously? Quite a different sort of thing from what it was.

I.   Well they cater more for the townspeople, don't they?

D.   Well, I suppose it's all down to money, isn't it?

I.   Of course it is. The stands, a lot might be for cars. All sorts of things. Double glazing. The Cheshire Ploughing Match is all farming. Typical farmers' thing.

D.   The other thing that I associate with this room, but it's disappeared now, was a mural of a fox hunt going on all over the wall.

I.   It was that wall over there. Yes. Oh, it was heart-breaking. It had to come off. Because we had a lot of trouble with the chimney, and the whole of the chimney breast, everything, had to come down and be rebuilt. So there were a terrible decision day. This painting had to come off. We did take some photographs of it.

D.   Oh, good! Who'd done it?

I.   Originally? It was the chap who'd been decorating the room. And it was when there used to be the old-fashioned fireplace here, you know, a black range with a mantelpiece. Well your grandma, she wanted the fireplace taken out and this one put in. But of course there was a big bare patch there, what were we going to do with it? And the chappy who was decorating, he said, I could paint you a picture on it. So she says Oh could you? And he says Yes, what would you like? So Granddad says, Oh, I want a horse on it. So that's what it was. Anyway, he couldn't do a heavy horse, but he'd do a hunter, he said. And it was, and it had the dogs on as well, hadn't it? It was sad when it had to go, it was heart-breaking. It was a big job as well, it was an expensive job! They had to re-line it completely, didn't they?

D.   Sad. I've never seen anything like it anywhere else.

I.   I know, it was quite different.

D.   And what are your interests, Irene?

I.   Well I've always been very interested in the WI. Over the years I've been president and secretary, and all sorts.

D.   How did you get started?

I.   Well my mother-in-law was in the WI when I got married. She was a member. And Mrs Johnson came, she must have been on the committee at that time. Do you remember the Johnsons, who lived on Back Lane? And I hadn't been back off my honeymoon many days, and she came to ask me to join the WI. And, I mean, she'd got in before my mother-in-law, sort of thing - she said, *Well I was going to have brought her!* So that was a long time ago, in 1950. And there was a little period when I didn't go, when the children were all small. But then I got back again, and I've been a member ever since. And I do enjoy it. I support it very much.

D.   When you started, how was the age balance?

I.   Well, there was nobody younger than us. I joined along with Joan Erlam, who used to be at the next farm, and they were all older than us, really. I think you always get that with the Women's Institute, don't you? There was quite a lot of my age at that time, which I must have been in my late twenties. But of course there wasn't a lot else.

D.   No. But it goes on. And it's very interesting to listen, because almost everyone - which is why I asked you, really - was taken along by their mother-in-law!

I.   Oh yes, you'd got to be done properly you see, you had to be invited to come, and then you had to be proposed. There was no business of you just coming and you joined, you know. It was all a bit of a palaver.

D.   Is it still getting some of the younger . . . ?

I.   Not really. No, we could do with some, you want new blood in it, really. But I think it is dwindling a bit all over the country, I think the membership is going down. Because there are so many other attractions. And another thing I think with people, the younger people: they do more things with their husbands and their families, don't they? Rather than the ladies just go out once a month on their own. There are so many other things they can do as a family, aren't there, nowadays.

D.   That certainly seems to be more what people choose to do if they go out. Would you say that the WI might have an image problem? That it's not at all like its image may suggest?

I.   Yes, that's true. We keep trying to say this. We try to make it as pleasant and as interesting as you can for people. I enjoy it, anyway.

D.   How do you see Ashley's future? Is the character of the community changing?

Ian.   It is, slowly. Yeah. Like Hough Green Farm, that's been sold, hasn't it?

I.   Fred Erlam's.

Ian.   Buildings derelict, and the house been sold separate now. It's going to keep going that way, I think. Farms doing less, and being bought up by business people.

D.   Part of this must be to do with the estate. They used not to sell. I'm thinking of all those the other side, around Stock Farm and Birkin Farm, which were pretty well derelict, and eventually they got tenants who themselves refurbished it, practically rebuilt them in a lot of cases. But tenants. And that somehow seems to make a bit of a difference.

Ian.   I think we've got a good community in Ashley, haven't we? I'd like to see that continue.

"The chappie who was decorating, he said, I could paint you a picture on it."
(Photograph courtesy of Mrs Irene Daniel)

John and Mary Heathcock. Middle Cottage

D.   John, tell me about your connection with Ashley.

J.   It goes back to when I was a child, really. Ashley's always been, so to speak, on our doorstep. I was born in Cavendish Road, Bowdon, and if I wanted to go out anywhere as a child, on my bicycle, I'd come to Ashley. I used to swim in Castle Mill. And so naturally, I think, when it came towards retirement, the place I wanted to retire to was Ashley.

D.   Do you want to fill in any of that, between being born and retiring?

M.   No!

D.   Just give us a quick potted account of your life!

J.   Right. I was born, as I say, in Cavendish Road. This you will not believe, but when I was four I went to Culcheth Hall School for Girls! Which, I would emphasize, in those days had a Kindergarten. I then went to Altrincham Prep. School on Langham Road. And that only lasted a term, because I just didn't seem to get on with them, and they didn't get on with me. So then I went to Wadham House School, in Hale; which funnily enough was where Herbie Hope went. And then from Wadham House I went to St Edward's, Oxford. Then I went for national service in the Gunners. Went out to Egypt and Malta. Came back to UK, met Mary, married, -

D.   How did you meet Mary?

J.   One of the crowd, really.

M.   Thanks!

J.   There was a crowd of us, boys and girls. Actually I was taking out at the time her cousin, and she said, You must meet this very beautiful cousin of mine, she's absolutely lovely! I saw Mary, and I thought, I don't know what she's raving about! Anyway, so there you are. To cut a long story short I eventually realised there was something in it. So we very happily got married.

M.   You can cut that bit out for a start!

J.   Initially we went to live in Brooklands because we couldn't afford the property prices in Bowdon. But after about five years in Brooklands we bought a house in St Margaret's Road, in Bowdon, and we lived there for twenty-odd years, had two children, were very very happy. And then, when the children moved away and did their own thing, we moved to The Boundary: the bungalow next to the Bowdon Cricket and Hockey Club. I was closely involved with the club all my life. I played hockey there as well as cricket, although cricket to a lesser extent. And squash. And I've been on the committee and on the council, you name it. It was just ideal, and I was living right next door to the club. But unfortunately, as the years advanced, my interest in hockey was obviously declining, and I was preparing to retire, and I didn't think that The Boundary would sufficiently absorb me when I had more free time, because there was very little I could do to it, or the garden. So the opportunity to acquire Middle

Cottage came along, and it was just where I've always wanted to be, so we grabbed it, and moved.

D.   I can remember, when you were in St Margaret's Road, every Saturday was sacrosanct to the garden.

J.   Oh I love gardening, always have loved gardening. It's one of my greatest hobbies. I mean here, another reason for moving, is we grow all our own vegetables here. Rabbits permitting! In fact this place, if you come in, is a bit like Boot Hill, in that if you look you'll see that we have fenced in an enclosure over there, and another one there, rather like the old graveyard at the top of Boot Hill. And the thing is, that's the only rabbit-proof area in the garden. Also, when I did retire, I was asked to take on the chairmanship of Bowdon Cricket, Hockey and Squash Club which was in trouble at the time, they had financial problems and there was a lack of momentum, things were going wrong. So I did that for five years. Just preparatory to having a heart attack, unfortunately. But there you go.

D.   All this was since you moved here?

J.   Yes, correct. All this since I moved here. And that was very time-consuming. There was a lot of work involved in that. Also I was still working as a consultant in Manchester. I was doing three days a week as a consultant. So it's been a very busy period actually, hasn't it?

D.   When did you actually come here?

J.   About eleven years ago. Twelve. So that would make it, what? 1988? Something like that.

D.   And where are the children now?

J.   Well James is running his own business, landscape gardening and garden maintenance. And he lives in Mobberley. He's got a wife, Lizette, and two children, Cassie aged ten, and Sasha aged eight. Very happily married, doing very well. Very pleased. Elizabeth, she's a qualified beauty therapist, but she doesn't practise. She had her two years off, when she went as a hotel courier, and she worked for Intasun, in Gibraltar, and then in Turkey. She had a wonderful time. Came back. Met this chap who'd come over from South Africa. It was love at first sight, and within almost weeks they were engaged, and within just over twelve months they were married. And they were married from Middle Cottage. They had a hundred and twenty, hundred and thirty people here, and it was a wonderful setting. And she's very happily married, she's got two children: Leanne is six and Vaughan is three.

D.   So Ashley has been on your doorstep all your life, as a place you were very familiar with, you used to come swimming at Castle Mill and things like that: how was it, coming actually to live here?

J.   It was almost like coming home. You see I do feel that, whereas in my youth Bowdon was on the extremities of suburbia, Bowdon is now in the midst of suburbia. And therefore if I'm going to try and recapture that which I enjoyed when I was young, I have to move further out. Ashley was a natural place to come to. And now we're on the edge of suburbia. I think it's tragic, the way that Hale, Hale Barns and Bowdon have been turned into cities of flat-dwellers.

D. Yes, I remember our discussing this twenty five years ago, when you lived in St Margaret's Road.

J. Yeah. All the development now, it's ribbon development from Bowdon almost out to Mere. It's getting worse.

D. So what do you think about Ashley's future?

J. Yes. I confess that I'm concerned about it. Maybe I'm being over-pessimistic, but you will recall that there was a proposition that Runway 2 would come here. In which case we were demolished. If you look at the map: logically, the M56 bends round, and to have put Runway 2 through Ashley, the whole of the area between the M56 and the existing runway would be encompassed by the airport, and they could put up half a dozen terminals, with fantastic access. They could operate two runways independently. Right. Now I think the airport authorities realised that that data was too hot. Therefore they went for the option which they considered would be acceptable, and it has been. Now that it's a fact, and thousands of acres of land have been swallowed up, I think that their long-term plan will be to go back to this one. In which case Ashley as you and I know it will cease to exist.

D. So you see that as more of a threat than encroaching suburbia?

J. Yes. That's not going this way, I don't think it's going this way. The Bollin is the demarkation. It's going towards Bucklow Hill, that way.

D. What have you done, in twelve years, with a garden like this? I can't imagine you've left it as you found it. What have you been up to?

J. When we came, at the back there was no terrace as such. And the back faces North, so if we were going to enjoy the privacy of our own garden I had to extend the terrace. There's now a huge terrace at the back. We've also built a water feature, which you can't see from where you are sitting. There was virtually nothing here, at all. Nothing.

M. The oak trees.

J. The oak trees were about all that was here.

D. So you built all that - I can see the water feature now, with a wall round one side, and a rockery on the other. All these vast rocks: did you bring them all in?

J. Well I didn't, James did.

D. Oh yes of course. And then you've got another pond down the other side.

J. Over there? That was there, yes. You can see the moorhen now.

D. Yes, I can see it standing there, thinking about spring.

J.   We usually have a hatch on that pond. Providing it's sensible enough to build it near the middle, because the fox goes and drinks there every night. And of course we've got dogs. We've got a greyhound which we rescued, it was abandoned in a field. We've got a rough collie. And we seem to inherit Elizabeth's dog for long periods of time, which is a golden retriever. So the three of them are huge, and I take those for a walk every day. I play golf, at Hale. So. I just don't know when I had time to work. What do you do now? Write books?

D.   I do things like this, yes! Pry into other peoples business, and then type it all out.

J.   You don't do anything with the church then? Not even to stand in as a locum?

D.   No, I don't dare preach anymore. I think I've got too muddled as to what I believe and what I don't believe. I hadn't intended to when I retired, but after about five years in retirement I suddenly came across a school of psychotherapy, Psychosynthesis, and that had a quite extraordinary effect on me. I was so intrigued by this, because it seemed to connect up with the same sort of thing that made me think I was meant to be working with the church in the first place.

J.   Psychotherapy?

D.   Yes. So I wanted to find out more about this psychosynthesis, and the only way I could find out more, which was entirely for my own interest, was to go into train-ing, to start training to be a psychotherapist. So I did that for two years. And I think the experience moved me so far away from orthodox church teaching that I decided I wasn't safe to be let loose in a pulpit anymore. Without a health warning, anyway!

J.   The interesting thing is that going back many years, you were never over-enam-oured with parish work. What you really wanted to do was to take the church into industry and commerce, remember?

D.   Yes, yes. In those days that's what I wanted to do.

J.   But it never really took off, did it?

D.   No. I got epilepsy, that's basically what happened. I was all set to move, had a place, was buying a house, and had a successor coming in to our house: and all of a sudden - in connection with buying the house, actually, it was the medical for the insurance to cover the mortgage - the medical uncovered this thing and nobody knew quite what it was, and then they decided it was epilepsy. And, being over thirty . . . You're supposed to develop epilepsy, if you're going to get it, before you're thirty. So if it starts after thirty they start thinking thoughts like . . .

J.   Is it something else? What's caused it?

D.   That's right. So I was taken in, and it was at that stage that I decided, if there was some question of there being a brain tumour it was no time to move the family away from all our friends. So we stayed where we were. And luckily St John's was looking for a temporary - would you believe? - not wanting another vicar, but look-ing for a temporary caretaker. So I was shuffled - to make room for my successor who was due to move into our house - I was shuffled sideways, to the parish next door. It just happened to be free.

J.   How did you get involved with Ashley then? With St Elizabeth's?

D.   After seven years at St John's I took some time out and went to live on The Downs, doing nothing - well actually, trying to write another book. It was about 1980, I think. And Ted Harris, the vicar here at the time, started having trouble with his heart. So I used to come out from time to time, to take services; and it just developed from there. Eventually he had to retire, and by that time I'd become a familiar figure on the scene here, and I moved in. But, again, on a temporary basis. I was given a five-year contract on the understanding that it was a rehabilitation move for me - because this must have been the smallest parish in the Church of England I should think. So the Bishop said, you can have it for five years, but this is to get you back on your feet, and after that I shall expect you to move to a job where you earn your living. So five years and a different Bishop later, I was summoned to discuss where I should go to earn my living. And by then it was clear that I hadn't been able to hold down Ashley, never mind a normal-sized parish. So I had to say I couldn't possibly take on a bigger job. And we were left staring at the wall seeing the word Redundant written in invisible letters all over it. And he screwed himself up, as if he was going to say something I didn't want to hear, and said You've never ever thought of *taking early retirement*, have you? And I went into orbit. I mean, I'd never for long thought of anything else, more or less since the day I started work, but only in my dreams! I didn't tell him that, I just said Yes, but how? He said, Go and see your doctor. I'd no idea I was eligible for being invalided out, but that's what happened. And life started for me, then.

M.   Darling, are you going to pour some drinks out?

D.   Yes let's stop this, shall we? We were supposed to be talking about you, not about me!

J.   Well the only thing is that business-wise, as you know, David, I was a marine underwriter in Manchester, with my own family company. When I retired it was the largest underwriting office outside London. But I'm so pleased I've retired, because the whole industry has changed totally. Heathcocks now, as a company, which had been going almost a hundred years: within twelve months of my retirement, ceased to exist. And it is like all industry and commerce in the country today: people are tending to buy companies to eliminate the competition. They asset-strip them, and close them down. When they say asset-stripping . . . we were bought by the Norwich Union, who sold us to the Maritime, which is a specific underwriter office. The Maritime bought Heathcocks off the Norwich Union, took all the best accounts into the Maritime, got rid of the ones they didn't want, got rid of the staff they didn't want, and closed it down.

D.   End of story.

J.   End of story. Right, let's switch off now, David. It's time for a drink!

Steve and Ruth Evason. Primrose Hill Farm

S.   We bought the farm in May 1996, at an auction which was held at The George Hotel, in Knutsford. We'd seen the property very briefly, for ten minutes. I mean, we usually take longer to buy a pair of trousers from Marks and Spencers! I was working in Knutsford at the time, on a job, and remembered that the auction was being held. So I said to my partner, Right, we'll go to the job, then we'll go and have lunch, and go to the auction, see what this farm goes for. So off we popped, and we found ourselves sat in The George at three o'clock and, carried along on the euphoria of the occasion, I started bidding. We bought it on the hammer. And immediately Buyer's Remorse set in, as I thought what were the consequences of my actions, not least having to tell my wife.

D.   I was going to ask about that!

S.   Who knew very little about it. In fact we came straight here to just refresh my memory about what the place looked like, because I couldn't remember. And I know the only thing that cheered me up was my partner, as we walked up the drive, said, Well if you don't want it I'll have it. So from that, I had to deal with the thorny question of telling my wife what I'd done. And my mobile phone rang on the way home, and this little voice said, Well what did the farm go for? So I said, Well, it went for what I paid for it. To which she said, No! You didn't! I said Yes, I did. No you didn't! Yes I did! No you didn't! This went on for some minutes before I said, Well talk to Phil. So I passed the phone over to my partner, who proceeded to say, Yes, he has. Yes he has. Yes he has. And her closing words were, But I don't want it! Having paid ten per cent deposit, I walked into the kitchen of our house in Salford, to find very gloomy faces, and the children looking very stern, and a wife who looked shell-shocked to say the least. My son Sebastian said We're not going there! So I had some convincing to do. However Ruth came round to the conclusion fairly quickly, I think, that it was Fate that was driving this situation, and things came together very quickly. We hadn't sold our old house but we did, and in the month before we had to complete we managed to get a mortgage and things - because I didn't know if I could get a mortgage on a 350-year-old house with a flag roof.

R.   And you did actually say, one thing you did say which was supposed to convince us, was that it was going to take two months before it was habitable.

S.   Well, being in the building trade, I was able to convince them to look at the potential of the place, and not the place as it was. I mean, although it was very clean and tidy internally, it was absolutely devoid of all, shall we say, the mod. cons. There was no central heating, it hadn't been rewired for fifty years, there was no plumbing in copper. So we really had to start from scratch. New roof. We moved into a terraced house in Salford whilst we did the work. Luckily we were doing it over the summer months, so it made my job quite pleasant, because first thing Saturday morning I packed my sandwiches and my flask, and off I came up here, and I'd work away all weekend. Saturday afternoons with a couple of cans of beer, and we'd sit in the sunshine and meditate, and imagine what it was going to be like when it was finished. It needed a big imagination though, at the beginning! Because it was a big task, and it took six months. We haven't changed the house. In fact what we tried to do was take it back into its original state. So all the rendering that had been put on the front of the place in the 1920s was taken off, and the brickwork was all re-pointed and cleaned. A matching roof was put on. We had to replace some of the timbers. But apart from that we've kept as many of the original features as we can, and you can see the wattle and daub, and the beautiful oak beams. The original bits and pieces. It's smashing.

D.   Ruth, should I be asking for your version of all this?

R.   Probably, yes! He did sort of say, I'm going to the auction. But we didn't believe him. And we didn't believe him at all when he said he'd bought it. And then we'd get conned. A month! He actually said, A month. And then he said two months. And it took six. And we moved in on the 6th December 1996. It was a lot of hard work.

S.   But it was such a cataclysmic change. We've lived in Salford all our lives. I've lived in the same area, Ruth's lived in the same house for much of her life, in Worsley. And we were very city-orientated, suburban. We came here for a change of lifestyle, and a challenge.

D.   Was it sudden? Or had you been thinking about it?

R.   No, we'd been looking. The reason we were looking was, Victoria was about to change schools. And we were thinking about moving so that she could go to Altrincham Grammar. And that was the catalyst really. As luck would have it, we moved in just a month or so before the cut-off point for her to be in Altrincham. And the same year that they went grant-maintained, and changed the boundaries. So we are literally two hundred yards within the boundary.

S.   So the dice were cast. The bones had been shaken. We were definitely fated to arrive here.

D.   Is this a pattern in your life? Because you sound so cool about it!

S.   I do believe that there are people who God looks on a little more favourably. But there again, you make your own luck. Fortune favours the brave, doesn't it? And so many times in my life I've had fortuitous circumstances. But the thing is, none of us had really any inkling of what we were getting into, in terms of village life, or country life. So many of the Cheshire out-of-town areas now are suburbs of Manchester. Ashley's quite different, I think. Ashley's still -. It doesn't support a lot of what I call Trophy Houses. It still has a very strong farming-linked community. We were quite - not fearful, that's not the word - but reticent: how and if we'd be accepted because, you know, we were outsiders.

D.   And how have you found it?

S.   We've been wonderfully and pleasantly surprised by the friendship that we've found round here. John, our next-door neighbour, you couldn't find a nicer bloke. And when we arrived he had two children the same age as ours. They struck up quite strong friendships. It certainly made the transition here much easier. When we actually got here they'd gone, but the fact that they'd been here made everybody feel a lot more comfortable about the move. But since that time, in these three years, we've - we knew the Martins, who came from the same neck of the woods as ourselves.

R.   We came in December, and Victoria was in her last year at school in Eccles. And Seb was there. So I didn't want to move her. So I used to take them there every day on my way to work, which was a long round trip, just until they finished. And then she went straight to Altrincham, and Sebastian went to Bowdon Church School. Which he did not like when he first went there, at all.

D.   He'd have been, what, nine?

R.   He was nine. And it was tough. It was a term before he made friends. And since then he's fine.

D.   What about Victoria?

R.   Oh, she's thoroughly enjoyed being at Altrincham. I can remember her first day. And you watch them go in, and you're slightly apprehensive. She didn't bat an eyelid. Marched straight in. She didn't know anybody at the school, but she wasn't fazed.

S.   We've got the biggest nightclub in North Cheshire in our barn.

R.   That's another story!

S.   My fortieth birthday, I'll tell you about that in a minute. When we came we had an idea of how we would develop the place. And horses: well, my daughter rode, and Ruth had had a long interest in horses, so about two years ago, twelve months after moving in, we bought Victoria a pony. And then Ruth has got herself a huge hunter charger cum Shire horse cum carthorse, who's a sweet thing, but big enough to pull a house down. So a lot of the time now revolves around horses and horse management. Much to my chagrin, but . . .

D.   I wondered why I was supposed to be keeping you off horses!

S.   Well, it's the cost, David, it's the cost.

R.   If he didn't have that to complain about it would only be something else, so. . .

D.   Did you already ride?

R.   I did as a child.

D.   Did it take long to get back?

R.   Oh no. I'd always ridden on and off. It wasn't as if it was something new. Obviously it's idyllic, really, if you have them on your doorstep.

S.   And now we've built the sand school. We had hamsters when we lived in Salford. Now we've got two dogs, two horses, two children; it's like Noah's Ark.

D.   Do you pine for hamsters?

S.   It's surprising. We wouldn't be without the dogs now. Ruth was dead against them, but they live quite happily here, and we wouldn't be without them. It's become

Evasons, Animals, Children, Etc. But yeah, the plan for the place is developing. And last year was my fortieth birthday. So I decided that - We had a barn that previously had been a shippon that had about forty stalls for cows. And I had rashly promised anybody that would listen to me that I was going to hold my fortieth birthday in this barn. And as the day approached -

R.   Which is December.

S.   The middle of December. I decided that I had to get my backside into gear, so to speak. So last September we started work converting this barn into the biggest nightclub in North Cheshire. Six weeks and about two thousand man-hours later, we now have a barn with a stage, dance floor, bar, gallery; and on the night, was fitted out with a lighting rig that wouldn't have shamed the Rolling Stones, I think. It was quite a night. A hundred and sixty people. And we managed to keep it warm by various tactics, filling the place full of hot air, but it was a big logistical exercise. We got away with it.

R.   You see the pattern again now? He's promised he's going to do something, and finds he's always bitten off more than he can chew.

S.   Yeah, but we always get there, David! We always get there! And everybody that came said it was the best thing they'd ever been to! Evason rides again! You make your luck.

D.   I heard you were at the Town Hall, Ruth, but how did you get there?

R.   I've worked for the City Council in Manchester since just after Victoria was born. I work in the Marketing Department. I tend to specialise in event management, and promotion of the City Centre.

D.   Now here's my ignorance coming out: What sort of things would you be handling, then?

R.   Anything, everything. Last week we had the Homecoming. United had said they weren't going to do a parade. And, obviously, were then shamed into having to do one. So the decision was actually made finally on the Tuesday morning, to do it on the Thursday evening -

D.   So you're another one that tends to work rather fast!

R.   I then have to coordinate all the safety arrangements for the services, and how those all integrate, and cooperate with the police.

D.   In two days flat. But I hadn't realised United had been reluctant.

R.   Oh, very. Very. They didn't want to take responsibility for safety, because I mean it was absolutely heaving. And the cost. I mean that's one aspect of it. But I do all sorts of things. One of the big ones I've done, probably is, I did the V.E. Day celebration in Manchester. Which was just a great big street party in Albert Square. And, you know, cultural festivals, sporting events. You name it. Nothing too small or too large.

D. Is it a big department?

R. No. No, there's ten of us. No, we're not a large department at all. We take on a lot of freelance staff from agencies from time to time. But we do have a very wide-ranging remit.

D. Do you enjoy it?

R. I do enjoy it.

S. You little liar! You keep telling me you want to give up work! She wants to be a Lady Who Hunts.

D. So have you started hunting, Ruth?

R. No, no, no, no. Haven't got time at the moment. I think if I do, it will just be drag hunting. Not anything more than that. But my intention is to do more, now that we've got the horse box, and also for Victoria to do more. Because without that it's been very difficult. You can't ride anywhere very easily.

Enter Sebastian, with Peter Martin.

D. And what was it like for you, Seb, coming here? Because you were a bit fed up, weren't you, when you heard you were moving here? So what was it like, when you got here?

Seb. It was quite nice, really. But I didn't really like it when we first came. It was all tatty. The kitchen was blue. Flowery wallpaper. Old-fashioned curtains.

D. So that was the house. And no neighbours?

Seb. Oh, I had neighbours. And their son, James, moved away, when we moved into our house.

D. That was tough, wasn't it? A pity. So what sort of things were you doing when you got here?

Seb. I don't know. Playing about, really.

D. Who were your friends?

Seb. I had Peter. And another Peter, he's moving. And somebody called John. And Christian.

D. Are they from school? Schoolfriends? Because you two are at the same school, aren't you?

Both. Yeah.

D. So you did that for a bit, played around, making dens. What are you interested in doing now?

Seb. Cycling, and on a mountain bike.

D.   Do you do that at all, Peter?

P.   I'm not a big fan of it like Seb is, but I do quite a lot of biking.

D.   But Seb is a really big fan of it, is he? How did you get into that, Seb?

Seb. My mum was organising this bike day at work. And she said, Do you want to come? and I said, Yeah, OK. And there was this obstacle course there, and you were timed. The fastest time. And I was the fastest. And then, after that, you got into this final, and then it was the improved final thing. And it was the National Finals, skills and time trials.

D.   Where was that?

Seb. That was at the belladrome in Manchester.

D.   Oh, they had it in Manchester, the National Finals? So how did you do in that?

Seb. Well I came thirtieth in my class. I didn't do too well, because it was my first race. But I came fourth in the time trial. And I came about tenth in the skills course.

D.   My goodnesss! Fourth in the whole country.

S.   He's done better than that. He's now . . .

Seb. Won the hill-climbing champion, North West.

D.   Well thank you very much for talking to me, it was very nice to hear about that. I shall look forward to hearing about all your future bicycling.

John Erlam. Sugar Brook Farm

J.   I was born at Hough Green Farm in 1953. Jeff Warburton was born the same time of year. Steve Blackburn and Mike Davies were born the same year I think. I can always remember The Green being there. I can only just remember the cottages opposite the Garage. They got knocked down, what was it? '60.

D.   What are your memories as a child in Ashley, growing up at Hough Green Farm?

J.   Well it was a lovely life. The one unfortunate thing about Hough Green Farm was that you had the house on the one side of the road, and the farm on the other side of the road. So as a small child you were banned from going across the road, unless you were with someone who was taking you. My earliest memory is sitting on top of a pile of pea haum silage, and the milk lorry coming. I don't know why I remember that. I must have climbed myself up there, and I was waiting for the milk lorry to come.

D.   You mention the road, this is of course the Mobberley Road: was that road as bad as it is now? Because it's a terrible road now.

J.   Nothing like as bad as it is now then, but it was still considered a danger.

D.   And brothers and sisters?

J.   One sister, Christine. She's younger, but Jeff Warby and I lived in trepidation of Christine. She used to beat us up! So we lived under her thumb most of our lives. Although Jeff was probably three times the size of her! She totally dominated us.

D.   Well it will be interesting to hear Christine's version of that! What happened about school?

J   I didn't go to Ashley School. And I regret not going to Ashley School, because I think it's a good way of getting to grow up and be with the people you've got around you. You develop relationships early on in life. But I went to Altrincham Prep. School. But with Jeff Warby, so I still had a local.

D.   But you felt that put a distance between you and other children in the village?

J.   Yeah. Like the Danielses, the Davieses. You only got to know them as you got older, and probably mobile yourself, and met them again through Young Farmers. So it was quite a long time. We didn't particularly have any friends right on the doorstep.

D.   And while that was going on, was your heart in the farm all the time?

J.   No. When I was at school I did not show very much interest in farming. I think that again was principally because of the split. I think as a child you develop this interest in farming if you've got it all there, but because you were almost banned from going on the farm because you couldn't cross the road, my interest developed in other areas, and I wanted to go into medicine really. I took A levels, made a hash of them, took them again and I could have gone into dentistry. But then I can remember my father saying to me, You must always remember I can make £100 a week out of this job easily. At the time he was farming and contracting. And he says, 'You've got to think, whatever job you go into is going to make more than that.' And I thought about it, and I got an offer of a free place at Newcastle University. And I thought this is just clicking in. So I didn't take up the dentistry, and I took up the place at Newcastle.

D.   And what did you read?

J.   Agriculture. But I went and got to Newcastle, and didn't like the place at all. I opted out within three months and then went on to agricultural college, where I was much happier. I did quite well at college, and I also had met a girl at college. And we got married as soon as I left college, and I came back and I did day release. I came back working for my dad on the farm. But I'd had an insight into how other farming was done. And Judy and I - Judy I suppose was my first girlfriend - we got married and we went to live at Rostherne, at Jasmine Cottage. And Mr and Mrs Gardner, who'd been neighbours, were living at Sugar Brook, and they'd only had a daughter, and they were thinking of retiring. And when the opportunity came up I was offered Sugar Brook. At really what was a very young age, at twenty-three. And it was quite a big responsibility. It was sixty acres here at Sugar Brook then, and we got offered it in a farming partnership with Mr Brooks, the landlord. And we went into pigs. Which didn't please my father at all, because he didn't like pigs. But I made money out of pigs, pigs went well for me. And more land came in. Barnshaw Farm came in, and then Parkside Farm came in. And so it seemed that I was amassing more and more land. And then my father died in 1986 - quite early on, he was only sixty-four - and the opportunity for having Hough Green land came in too. But arable farming went through a depression up to '91. So I gave up. The estate offered me the tenancy on either Hough Green or Sugar Brook. I've missed out quite a lot of personal detail now, because Judy and I, our marriage lasted ten years then we separated. My father was very ill, and I'd met Viv. And we got married the November before my father died. And we had two children very quickly, James and Jessica, they were born within a year of each other. We were already living at Sugar Brook, and I felt it would be far less of an upheaval although Hough Green's a beautiful house. I also felt that with the children growing up this was much more of an adventure playground for them here. Not got the road to cross, which had been a bugbear of my life. I thought well this is going to get rid of all that sort of hassle; they've got the brook down to play in, they've got no end of adventures there, to play at. And so it worked out.

D.   And what about the land? Did you take in any of the Hough Green land?

J.   Yes. The tenancy of Hough Green had been 112 acres. So the estate gave me a tenancy. Sugar Brook had only originally had sixty-odd. It now was made up to 112 acres and made on a full-term tenancy. I kept the Barnshaw land and the Parkside land on a farm business tenancy.

D.   Coming back to the village, John. You say you always remember Hough Green?

J.   Yes, I always remember Hough Green. And I think one of the fortunate things is that we've not become built on. There's very little extra building gone on.

D.   It's interesting to hear from you that it's the better for not having got any bigger. Lots of other people have said that, but they're mainly people who've come here for the sake of getting into a place like this, away from town.

J. I'd like to see more houses to support the school in some respects.

D. As I go round listening to people, the great fear is that it would be the thin end of the wedge. Everyone agrees that a few more houses would be a good idea, because it would just make the difference between insecurity and security for the school, that sort of thing. But mention the idea that half-a-dozen houses may be built, and most people go into a sort of panic mode: Where will it stop? Sooner or later there'll be no spare land between us and Hale, we'll just become part of South Manchester suburbia. There's a great fear about it.

J. It's very pleasant. You get over that Bollin Bridge, and you're in the countryside. It's opened up. I'm very conscious that I'd like - you don't want Ashley to remain the same, but you do want the basis of the village to remain the same. We've got the shop, we've got the pub, we've got the church, we've got the school.

D. But apart from the pub, I imagine that's secure, but it's interesting you see: shop, church, school; they're only just keeping their heads above water. And the policeman didn't. And you wonder what might go next. If the community was that little bit larger it would make a lot of difference to the security of places like the shop and the post office. I don't know what the answer is, but it's quite interesting that the conflict is not resolved, or I've not heard it resolved: it would be nice to have just a few more people, but then on the other hand as soon as you hear about any building plans, Whoah, Whoah back! It's going to be turned into a part of Hale. Would this be the point to move on to the conclusion, to try to round it off?

J. How would I like to see Ashley in another hundred years' time? How do I see it developing? I would hate to think that the land which has been farmed in Ashley since 1840 by the Erlams would end up under concrete, certainly during my lifetime. And I would hope not for the next century.

D. Can I go back to something that came up earlier? I hadn't realised that you had a significant section here that is to do with horses and leisure. It's quite a big thing in Ashley, looking after people's horses, and part of Ashley's income must be from that particular leisure pursuit: and yet people who keep their horses here don't have anywhere to ride. They're hacking along these awful roads. Do you see any way of changing that at all, or is that all that we can offer?

J. No. I've tried to put in a cross-country - not a cross-country but a similar sort of thing. But the estate wouldn't have it.

D. Really? I didn't know that.

J. Other people have agreed to the idea. All the farmers would be quite happy if we could sort something out, have a Pay-for-Ride scheme or something. I don't know whether the estate had the idea of doing something similar themselves at Peover at one time, and they thought whether it might just tread on their toes, but it got a No when I asked about it. I'm not very horsey-minded, I don't like horses particularly, but you've got to accept that they're here, and they're a way of making some money. And so you try to keep them as low key, so that people don't really notice them. You hate to think that you've just got a farm overrun by horses. But nearly every farmer I could mention in the village has got horses.

Kevan Gibbons. Arden Lodge

K.   I came to Ashley when I was about four or five years old. But previously to that my mother was an Ashley person. I think they'd moved out just after the war. My mother was born in Ashley and that is basically how we've come to be in the village. Originally my granddad was the blacksmith at the Smithy Garage, which is now obviously a main agent garage, but at one time it was just where all the horses were shod. In those days there were no cars, it was just all horses.

D.   This is your grandfather Watson?

K.   Grandfather Watson, yeah. They moved there, I can't remember the dates, but just after the war some time. And the family lived at the - the house is still there, if you have a look at the - . The showroom, that's the original house, and then the buildings at the back are where the smithy was. That was basically where the family originate from. And then they moved to the shop in the fifties some time.

D.   Again, it was your grandmother who first got the shop?

K.   My grandmother ran the shop, yeah, and my mum and her four sisters lived at the shop. When Gran wanted to retire, in the early seventies, we took over and moved in, in '73 I think.

D.   And at that stage you were four or five?

K.   About five maybe. I'd started school in Altrincham. And obviously moved on to Ashley, with my brother, my elder brother Mark.

D.   Were there rules for you? I mean, about the shop? Were there places where you weren't supposed to go?

K.   Well we weren't supposed to go in the shop when it was open, really. When we were younger. But as we got older I was helping out, stacking shelves and working in there. Because it was a family-run thing. My mum and my aunty ran it, and my gran still worked in there a couple of days a week, so it was a family-run thing. But Dad and my brother really didn't have much to do with it at all.

D.   But you were interested, so you were able to contrive to see what was going on?

K.   Yeah, I was always interested in what was going on, because I was sort of like intrigued by . . . just being nosey really, I didn't like to miss anything, all the gossip, you know! So that's the main reason I was always in the shop, stacking shelves or whatever. Just intrigued by having people coming into your front door, sort of thing, all the time. That's how it felt to me, you know.

D.   Had your football already started?

K.   Football had already started, yeah, I'd been playing football since I'd - with my father, on the beach in Blackpool, from the age of about two and three. And the place where we lived in Altrincham, all my cousins were round there, and they were a lot older, so we were playing football at a very early age. So when we moved to Ashley, at break time or at dinner time, it was Where's the football? *Football? Don't have footballs here*. So we brought the football in, and started kicking it around in the playground, and got a few people interested in football. And that's been my life really, David, football. I mean, I've built my business on contacts through football. It's been a big part of my life really.

D.   Lots of people of a slightly older generation than yours talk about playing football opposite the post office there. Was that still going on?

K.   Yeah. I mean right opposite. I forget what it's called now, the little estate. Egerton Moss, it's called, yeah. The land was owned by Greenall's Brewery. We had a bit of a football field on there, a couple of goal posts, so we used to play on there.

D.   So what was your next stage in football?

K.   I was already playing on a Saturday morning, in Altrincham. With Stamford Lads. On Stamford Park. On a Saturday morning we used to have a game. I was playing competitive football from like the age of eight or nine, really. Mainly I played all my football in Altrincham as a youngster. Up until the age of like fourteen or fifteen really. And then a team from Cheadle approached me to play for them. Which was a very good side, quite a bit higher standard than what I was already playing. So I ended up going to Cheadle on a Sunday morning. But Father was working and we only had one car, so I used to have to ride my bike to Altrincham, leave my bike in Altrincham at my aunty's, and catch two buses to go and play football, so that's how keen I was. It was a bit of an early start on a Sunday morning to get to Cheadle for half ten, but I enjoyed it, and I had two or three years there. Then obviously that took me to seventeen and I was driving, so I could drive there in the end. Then I started playing for Knutsford at seventeen, eighteen. Knutsford Town, which is like a semi-professional standard of football. And I've been there fifteen years at Knutsford now, fifteen years.

D.   And are you still playing?

K.   Still playing. Still trying to play! Not as often as in the past. Injuries have taken toll, and this that and the other. It's a nice little club, and done well over the years, so - like I say, I've done my business round contacts through football, so you feel like you need to put a little bit more back into it.

D.   What league is it?

K.   It's called The Cheshire League, which is on what they call the F.A. Pyramid. They have a pyramid. The top of the pyramid is obviously the Premiership, and then it comes down and you've got all your feeder leagues. And it's on the bottom rung of what they call the Pyramid. So in effect, if your ground was up to standard and your team was up to standard, and you had some money, you could go all the way. It's promotion all the way, sort of thing. We've also played a lot of football on a Sunday morning. I played for quite a successful side in Manchester, I used to go down to Manchester on a Sunday morning and play. And that's quite a successful side. Won Manchester County Cups and all sorts with those. I mean we've won things with Knutsford on a Saturday, but we've won quite a lot on a Sunday morning. Used to play in Chorlton.

D.   So you played twice a week?

K.   Yeah. Played twice a week for fifteen years. As I say the injuries are taking a toll a bit now.

D.   And mid-week training of any sort?

K.   Yeah. I always trained twice a week. I'm still training twice a week now.

D.   Kev, you've mentioned the business: how did this come to be started? Perhaps we ought to go back. I seem to remember you went off to Australia at some stage. Was this after leaving school?

K.   No. Immediately after leaving school I served an apprenticeship at Quick's in Hale. The Ford main agents. And then when I came out of my time it all seemed to fit in nicely. When I got to twenty-one and came out of the apprenticeship, the garage closed down. So they wanted me to move to Timperley, which I didn't really want to do. So I decided to leave, because I'd got my apprenticeship, and I thought, Well I've always fancied going to Australia, and it seemed like an ideal time. So I finished work on the Friday, went and bought myself a round-the-world air ticket on Monday, and went about three or four weeks later. Just took off and went to Australia. To see, basically, whether it was worth going and living out there, or whatever.

D.   This was definitely a possibility?

K.   It was there in my mind, yeah. And I also took my football boots with me, hopefully to play a few games of football out there. Which I did do, I played football out there. But it was just the enormity of the place. You know. You couldn't get over it. To go anywhere it was like a five or six hour drive. To go anywhere, you know. Everything was so vast, and you just couldn't comprehend how big it was. So I stuck it for about eight or nine months, then decided to come home, but came home via America and Canada, and places like that. So I was away twelve months altogether.

D.   You came back, anyway. So what was the next step? You had to find work: did you know what you were going to do?

K.   Well, I knew I had a trade behind me, so basically that wasn't a problem. I could have got a job anywhere, in any garage. I had thought of maybe getting out of the motor trade, but . . . I went working for a friend of mine, driving a van around for a while. But I thought, I've got this trade, I might as well make use of it, so I went and got a job in a garage, but didn't particularly like that, and then I decided I'd give it a go on my own. And that was in 1991, and I've been on my own ever since. First of all started working in Nigel's at Ashley Mowers, we shared the workshop there. But Nigel quickly found a niche in the market with lawn mowers, and grew very quickly. So I had to get out of there, and approached Andrew Erlam about moving here, and he wasn't against it. Been here six months and the Council got to find out I was here, and tried to close me down. Because it turned out, I'd thought it was somebody locally had complained about my working here, but it turned out it was Ashley Smithy Garage complained about my working here. Unfair competition, they said. So they tried to get me closed down. One day I was working here, and a man just arrived with a suitcase, with a briefcase, arrived and said, I'm from Macclesfield Borough Council.

You've not got permission to be working here. This is a farm in our eyes, and you're running a garage from here. Basically, I've come to close you down. But, he said, don't panic. Sign this form. You've got a stay of execution for six months while - basically you're signing this form to appeal against their decision. So I then had to go through all the rigmarole of applying for change of use for the buildings, from being a farm building to being a garage. Eventually I got it.

D.   And now, I presume, you can reckon that you're pretty secure?

K.   Well, yeah. If I wanted to take it one step further I could have a big sign outside advertising the fact that I'm here, but I don't want to do that, David, you know. All I ever wanted to do from the start was earn myself a living. I don't want to change, deface the place.

D.   You mentioned this time when your mother died, and I wondered if you'd like to tell us more about that, because it must have been an enormous upheaval for the whole family?

K.   Yeah, at the time when it happened. We're going back to 1990 now, it's a long time ago. It's still very fresh in my mind. I'd gone to watch United actually, I was in Scotland when it actually happened. It was a Wednesday. Mum and Dad had gone to Chester because it was half-day closing at the shop. And they were on their way back from Chester and got involved in a car accident and Mum was killed instantly. But at the time I was in Scotland, I was watching United, up Ibrox Park, which is where Rangers play. And you're stood there watching the game, and you hear it thousands of times watching football games, it comes over the tannoy, you know. And I heard my name over the tannoy. I said to my mate, That's my name over the tannoy. It's as clear now as what it was then, I can hear . . . It's sort of like a double-take, you think, I'm sure . . . They say you've got to go to the local security place. I went, and they'd obviously told all the police, they said, Oh they want you downstairs. And there's a big grand hall there, at this football stadium, with a big wooden staircase. And I can see it now. And we walked in, and we had to go into this little room, and there's this policeman there. As you're sat there now, I can picture him, you know what I mean? He just said, Your mum's been killed in a car accident. I thought - it's just - you don't believe it, you know. So quickly we had to get home. And it was just dreadful, David, really. Just dreadful.

D.   Mark had already gone to live in Birmingham?

K.   Mark was in Birmingham. Everyone was round at my aunty's house, and he was already there, he'd been called and he was there. And I was the last one to get there. Because I was coming from Scotland. Yeah, the next twelve months were very very difficult. We had a decision to make about the shop, were we going to keep it on, were we going to sell it? We thought the best thing was not to upheave. So me and Sally decided to take the shop on. Sally agreed to take the shop on, so she had to learn all the post office. She did very well, she did OK, and helped the family out tremendously by keeping it going a couple of years. And then it was decided that it was probably time, and best to move on really, sell the business off. And I think we actually sold it about '93, '94. We kept it going for two or three years, I think. My dad moved to Knutsford, and that was probably the best thing for him, you know, moving out and moving to Knutsford, not far from his brother and his sister, and no pressures of the shop or this, that and the other. In a way the two or three years that me and Sally had the shop was good for him. But it was time to move on. Unfortunately. I felt a great deal of sadness, because I'd always loved the shop ever since I'd moved there, you know. It was like twenty-two years of my life. It was a great upheaval really. But sometimes you've got to move on for the better, haven't you?

D. Yes, but it's a lot to leave behind, isn't it?

K. Yes. But thankfully, twelve months after we lost the shop I got the opportunity to move back into the village anyway, by getting a house on Tatton Estate. And then unfortunately, twelve months after we'd got the house, Sally decided she wanted to move out and do whatever. So I'm left there on my own. But it's my ideal house. I used to ride past there when I was a kid, going picking potatoes for John Erlam next door, and in those days, in the seventies, the guy that had it looked after it, and it always looked white, and all the flowers out, it always looked immaculate. And I always used to say to my brother, I'd love to live in that house. And my dream came true. So as far as I'm concerned, David, I'll never move from there. It's my ideal house, it's where I want to live. I'm happy to be back in the village. I feel that I belong in the village. And it's nice that the family have got somebody who's still in the village, so we can still say there is a part of us still in the village.

D. Of course! There was a family wedding, wasn't there?

K. The family wedding on Saturday, yeah. So, although he's living in America, my cousin Christopher, he's come back to Ashley and got married. Which is tremendous really. But that just shows you what a bonding the family has with the village. It's great really. Although there's only me actually living in the village now.

D. Well I think it's quite important for the village, as well as for the family.

K. Yeah. We've still got a footing in the village, if you like, really. Which, after losing the shop, we could quite easily have lost that, really. But I was determined to get back to Ashley at some stage in my life. It's just where I want to be David, I feel that Ashley's my place. I'm working here, I'm happy here, and I know a lot of people and get on with ninety-nine per cent of them, and like I say, hopefully, I'm here for the rest of my life.

Douglas and Alice Raven. Lower House Farm

Da.   How did you come to be in Ashley?

Do.   It's best to call it "drawing pins". Because we were looking for a bigger farm.

Da.   Where were you before?

Do.   We were at a place called Southwaite. Between Penrith and Carlisle. We were looking for a bigger farm, really. I was at that age where I wanted more acres.

Da.   Was that where you were born and bred?

Do.   Yes I was from that area, yes. And we looked at farms, as everyone does who's in the same circumstances. And you could say that's how we arrived here. But we looked at other farms, didn't we? Before we came to Ashley.

Da.   Did you expect to have to look so far afield? It seems such a long way to come.

A.   We were looking far afield, weren't we? We were even looking down in Evesham. And Devon.

Da.   All over the country, really?

Do.   It's not a big country. Not really. When you think of my people, on mum's side: came down from Ayrshire. And it was all just on the railway. And buses and carts. So I mean, I think today, with transportation the way it is, distances are small really. So you can move around. Easily.

A.   We came down in '67. Angela was fourteen, Judy eleven, and Peter nine.

Da.   Was it a similar type of farming you were doing in Cumbria?

Do.   Yes. It was a mixed farm.

Da.   Did you bring your stock and equipment with you? You brought it all down?

Do.   Yes, we did. Transferred it all down.

A.   You had a couple of days a week, didn't you, for a few weeks beforehand, bringing things down.

Da.   And how did you find it, the settling in process here?

A.   Well I think with farming it's easy really, isn't it? Once you've found your way to different places. We had to find out where Chelford was, for your farm supplies. Things like that. And they're funny little roads, aren't they, to Chelford. It's a case of finding your way.

Do. It's not easy . . . It's not easy finding your way to Chelford. Now if you're drunk . . . ! Or finding your way back!

Da.   And do neighbours make a difference, welcoming?

A.   Oh, yes. Betty and Fred Erlam were just fantastic. And they had children the same age as ours. And they did everything, lots of things together. And we went out quite a bit with them, we went dancing. It was very good.

Do.   That's how you come to settle. Because you get to know more people.

A.   And then we also found we were middle-of-the-road, in middle position, for relatives. Because those living a hundred miles north, in Cumbria, and then you had brothers and sisters living down Devon and South London. And so everybody used to meet up with us here.

Da.   So this became the sort of gathering place?

Do.   We are in the middle of the country here.

Da.   And how was it for the children? Because they had to move schools.

A.   Oh here? They went to Culcheth Hall. And Peter was at boarding school, he was at Seascale. Quite a lot of the sons around us went to Seascale, and he had about a year and a half. But we decided when we came down here, it was very devious to get out onto the west coast of Cumbria, and so he came and went to Altrincham Prep.

Da.   Yes. So, you got down here.

A.   Well we came down and . . . I came down with my mother and the two girls, to get them settled into school, because we came in May. But there was no grass here, was there? Because the previous farmer had had sheep on it a lot, on the place all winter. And we had a lot of rye grass. So I left him up there with the cattle, and we were down here. And you came about two or three weeks after.

Do.   Giving the grass a chance to recover, you see.

A.   I came down, and I had two horses, and I had the bull, and there were some heifers, weren't there? There was cattle in each field. As long as I could see them I could settle. And then you came down with three wagonloads of cattle. They all came on the same day.

Do.   I don't know how many cattle there were altogether. Top side of a hundred, I think.

Da.   How does a move like that affect cattle?

A.   Well they don't get a drink, do they? That's the main thing.

Do.   There was another factor which was to consider, and that was the aircraft. The noise of the aircraft. And then, in those days, there weren't these fighters, which there are today, flying low through the Lake District. And so I asked the NFU, and they said No, no need to insure against anything. Your cattle will be so tired when they get down there, that they'll step out of those wagons, and all they'll want to do is graze.

A.   Drink.

Do.   And sleep. And by that time quite a lot of aircraft will have flown over them, they'll have got used to them. And that is what happened. That's how it turned out. So they settled in fairly well. And we milked, with the old milking parlour. We'd had Fulwoods in and they'd gone right through it, and brought it up to date, put a new tank in and such like. So we could go straight into gear, you see.

Da.   Did that all come down with you?

Do.   No, they'd done that previous to us coming, you see. Fulwoods had done it. So it was all prepared and ready. So therefore, you see, we could just carry on.

Da.   That sounds remarkably smooth.

A.   Yes, it was. It was. It was well organised.

Do.   As well as it could be.

Da.   How have things developed in the thirty years you've been here? I mean, there must have been a lot of changes in that time?

Do.   When we first arrived here there was labour to be had everywhere. Now, you see, over these years we've been here, we've watched labour drift off the land, because other people could offer them more money, and for less hours. So people - . You see, you're right here on the south of Manchester. There's an awful lot of competition for your labour. Here. You're not out in the sticks, where people have got to stay with farming because there's nothing else.

A.   But there again, things have been mechanised, haven't they? So you don't need the people.

Do.   Yes but we've watched this change. And we've watched it get very competitive, to get labour on the farms, over the years.

A.   Well the whole concept of the farm labourer has changed, hasn't it? They are an extremely well-paid man who knows his job. Must do.

Do.   That's right. You see, if you have a cowman, you've got a man who is working with a milking parlour that's cost anything from twenty to fifty thousand pounds, which he's got to look after. He's got to look after. Then he's got a herd of cattle as well. So what's your value then? So these men, they're very responsible people, really. They're not like they used to be. Likewise, if you haven't got a dairy herd and you're an arable man, and you put a man on a tractor: a tractor costs thirty thousand. Fifty. That's for one tractor. So they've got to be pretty responsible, these people. You can't just put anybody on them. So yes, that's how it's changed.

John Williams. Thorns Green Farm

J.   I started working for Eric Warby. I'd be twenty. So that's thirty-five years ago. Came out as an agricultural fitter. I was an engineer before that. I was an an engineer in my father's engineering works, in Dukinfield. He had a foundry as well. I'd worked in there. So I was brought up in engineering, so it was quite easy to adapt. As I've had to do. I started work there, and I lived at Lane End Cottages. And then we bought a house in Timperley, and then this came up. So we decided to come out here.

D.   And when was that?

J.   I'd been with Eric about two years. Two to three years. Seems a long time when you're young. I think the estate wanted somebody on agricultural repairs, so they said, Yes, go ahead with it. So we sold the house we'd bought in Timperley. Fortunately we'd picked a good time, we bought it for three thousand and sold it for nine. So that gave us a bit of cash. Came in here to do my wagon repairs here, for probably two to three years. Then the Council came round and said, *Right! That's enough.* You know. *You'll have to find somewhere.* And they found me a garage in Macclesfield. The Council found that, and they got the planning cleared for me. They wanted me to stop doing wagon repairs here.

D.   They didn't want wagon repairs here? They didn't mind nice agricultural things?

J.   Yeah they were happy with that, but they didn't like the wagons. So they found me this garage, and I went and bought that. So I did all my repairs up there and lived here.

D.   And this, for the time being, was just your home?

J.   Yeah. So that was quite nice. Then I started doing horses, before Heather got married. That was just a sideline, wasn't it? Just something to keep the fields tidy.

D.   How many fields? I mean, how much is there here?

J.   There's twenty acres here. That's Tatton's though.

D.   So the horses were half sideline, half sort of Heather's?

J.   It was good for the kids, and it was like a nightclub. For the kids. Because they didn't need to go out, did they? Her friends came here, and there was a bit of a club in there, set up. Sit around and talk. It saved the kids going away. There's always kids here. So it was quite nice.

D.   So what was the history of the Macclesfield site?

J.   I built a house for Sherril up there, for us. A big one. On site, alongside the canal, it was a nice site. That was my first experience of building. But fortunately one of my fitters was a builder, and when I first started he was helping me. So we started, and got it up to first floor level, and then that's when I had my accident. Flywheel dropped off a wagon and broke my leg. I was working on my own anyway then, because I'd let most of the garage off in units. So at that point I let it all off. And for six years I retired. About thirty-five to forty. I just collected my rents. So I had five or six years out, doing very little.

D.   How was that for you? How did you like that?

J.   Brilliant! Put a lot of weight on. So I've had five years' retirement already. I built the swimming pool, and did a lot of work round here. And then I finished the house off, in between. So I thought, Right, we'll get something done here. Finished the house off, and then she decided, because I was letting the garage at that time, and things were altering: We'll make this into an office block. And I let that. The actual design of the house lends itself to offices. It was still a bare shell anyway, so it was quite handy. And that sorted that job out. And then I let it for - ten, fifteen years? After I'd been retired for five years I started doing a bit of building. Built Barker's in Timperley, that florist's. Did Wright's extension. Did one or two big extensions in Hale.

D.   How many of you were you?

J.   Me. I got labourers on it in Timperley, couldn't have done it otherwise. I enjoyed that. And that got me set up in building. The house in Bollington, I finished that on my own. I had to keep going round building sites, to see how things were done. You'd get so far, and by the time I'd caught up with them I'd have to find another building site, because they'd passed me! So what do we do now? And I listened to the building inspectors. And they're very helpful, because they tell you. And if you do what they say you've got to have a chance, haven't you?

D.   They didn't mind you wandering around their sites, picking up tips?

J.   No. I used to tell them. I used to say, I'm building my own house, what do I do here? And they'd say, Oh you just do this, do that. And the beauty of that is, you're not fixing yourself to one man's ideas. Because you're actually picking up different ideas. I think nowadays you need to be working at different jobs. Otherwise you can't draw things together, can you? And I did mail order for two years, as well. In between. Direct mail. That was good. Tools. I designed my own tool. Foundry used to make them in Sheffield, and I used to sell them direct mail. That was a nice business.

D.   So why did it only last two years?

J.   Well, I'd only got one product. They went slower and slower, and the cost of advertising was getting dearer and dearer, and the actual sales were going lower and lower.

D.   And once everyone's got one, nobody wants another.

J.   Not these, because they were indestructible.

D.   No built-in obsolescence?

J.   No, I couldn't build-in any! No. I like inventing things, so.

D.   This was an idea you had, and you followed it all the way through, from the idea to the customer?

J.   To the end product, yeah. I made a few bob out of that one. I suppose I could have made more, but . . . It was very interesting.

D.   It's really the story of your life, by the sound of it. I mean, you have taken things from the idea stage in your own head, all the way through to the end product. With your bare hands.

J.   Anything I'm doing, I like to go right from the beginning to the end. It's like the Bed and Breakfast. I build the rooms. Sheril decorates them. And I do all the work. And then I have to actually do the breakfasts, and take them to the airport! See the whole thing right through. I wouldn't advocate it for everybody because . . . I'd say you do need specialist advice on lots.

D.   There's not many people who could turn their hands to so many different things.

J.   Needs must! The secret is, to listen. The only way you'll learn is by listening. You can't learn by talking.

D.   Now all this tremendous development here: have you done all this to a Tatton house, or at some stage did you buy this from Tatton?

J.   Well I own it now. I bought it eight years ago.

D.   Off Tatton? You went to them?

J.   No, they asked me. They were offering, I think they were offering a few, to different people, and just said, These are the ones we're thinking of selling. First to come up and buy, we sell. After that, that's it. So it was once in a lifetime. And I thought, we'll have a go. Not the land. I've got the paddock and the pond, with the fishing. I've got coarse fish in there. At the moment we're just thinking about splitting it into three buildings. Three houses. It's on the market as it is.

D.   I was a bit surprised when I heard what you were asking, I thought it must be worth more than that.

J.   Six-fifty? I think it's probably worth more, but we'd be happy with six-fifty. We could live on that. If someone came along now they could have it for six-fifty.

D.   But if no one comes?

J.   Well you've got to look at the other course, haven't you? It would make three houses. If we sell this house, we move into there. Then we'll move into the B&B and make it into another five-bedroomed house, then we'll sell that one. Then I want to retire and sail round the world. I want to go sailing.

D.   Oh, that's what it is, is it, in the end?

J.   When we travel we don't want property. People say, Invest your money in property. I say, If I can come out with six or seven hundred thousand, why do I want to be investing my money in property? If I can get ten percent, say, on six hundred thousand, what do I want to be doing? I can go anywhere in the world and rent property.

Stay there as long as I want to. When we've had enough we can just pick the bags up and go. I'd love to do that.

D.   Any favourite places? Where will you go first?

J.   Want to go to South Africa first, stay there for a month. And then we'd like to sail down the East Coast of America. Or up. Because there's a waterway goes up the East Coast of America, inland waterway.

D.   So when you say sail, you mean in your own little . . .

J.   Oh yeah. Buy a boat. Do the Great Lakes. Alaska, round there. But the beauty of it is it's so cheap, once you've bought your boat. And then we'd like to do the French and German canals. And then we'd like to end up in the Med. That'd be nice. Sail round the Med.

D.   You haven't got down to Australia, I notice.

J.   We've been to New Zealand. I've been there twice. We've done that one. We've done Thailand, we've done Singapore. Done Kenya. Gambia.

D.   So that really is your big thing in life?

J.   Like travelling. And with over sixty thousand a year we can keep travelling.

D.   Where are all your family now?

J.   They're all here! We've got Jo at Cherry Tree. Near Chester Road. Mrs Mason used to live there. Anyway Jo's in there. And then, we've got Heather at Dairy House. Emma's come back from New Zealand, she's at Sainsbury's now, manageress. And Peter's getting married this year, in December. He's a car salesman with Volvo at Pickmere now. And his girlfriend's a qualified teacher now. They've bought a house together.

D.   So you've got bases to come home to?

J.   Well that's the other thing I'd like to do is, in between, we'd like to do house-minding. Which would tie a few weeks up. We've got friends who've got B&Bs, we could run them for them. There's plenty of places to stay.

D.   So you don't envisage any sort of permanent base?

J.   No. I don't want a permanent base. People need a permanent base for security. If I've got six hundred thousand pounds tucked in the bank, I'm secure. That'll do me. I wouldn't be greedy. But it's a lot of work. It's taken a lot of work to get this far. It's taken me thirty years to do.

D.   And that's from the idea to the finished product.

J.   This last seven years has been . . . When we bought this, and then the airport was coming over the top, and I was into the banks for three hundred thousand on a bridging loan. I had all my tenants out. There was nothing coming in. And three hundred thousand at ten per cent. Thirty thousand a year, and nothing coming in. I was suicidal. I was there. And it's not very nice.

D.   How long were you in that position?

J.   Three years. That wasn't nice. I look back now, and I don't know how I got through that. Because I was in negative equity at one time, here. And I was worth half a million when I bought this. On paper. But because I bought it on the back of the other property, which I couldn't sell. So I ended up selling all that other property, up there. And the property in Wales, I had a cottage in Wales. A villa in Spain. And still in debt. Because I bought it just when the value went down. For a long time. Couldn't have been worse. I couldn't sell a thing. Three years, trying to sell it.

D.   I hadn't realised you'd had a patch as bad as that.

J.   Oh that was three years of it. When I started doing these first few B&Bs we had no money. I tried my farm shop. It was getting nowhere. I said, we have to do something with these barns. Dave said, why don't you make a couple of B&B units? And I spent my last £250 on paying the plasterers. We'd got second-hand units out of *Loot*. And I got this boiler and put that in. And I built those two units with my last few pennies. The bank wouldn't lend me any more money. Obviously. And the first night, I'd got two people booked in, and they didn't turn up! I said, Right we're away now, I've got two people coming, we've got fifty pounds coming in! She says, I'll go and buy some food. And they didn't turn up.

D.   It must make it all the sweeter, seeing what you've got now.

J.   Oh it's sweeter now, yeah.

Prill Lloyd. Thorns Green

D.   Prill, when did you come to Ashley?

P.   August 1995, initially to Castle Hill Farm. And then we've just moved recently down here.

D.   What brought you here?

P.   Well, we were over the main road, in Ringway. The property which we rented there was being acquired by the airport, so we had to look for somewhere else. We went along to the auction of Castle Hill Farm, hoping to purchase it, but were outbid by the Davieses. And then we found out that the Davieses weren't intending to use it for themselves, and approached them about renting it from them. It suited both parties.

D.   You'd already been living in a similar sort of place?

P.   We've always been very open space-type people. And although we would probably be looked at as townies by the local inhabitants here, we're not really town dwellers. The country's always held an appeal to us. And since having Thomas as well, we want him to grow up in this sort of environment - the village environment, and the ethos that's held within the school itself. And if we were in a town, I think we'd probably want him educated at the type of school that Ashley is.

D.   How old is Thomas now?

P.   He'll be six next week.

D.   So first you were at Castle Hill Farm. You had Bed & Breakfast, didn't you?

P.   That's right, yes. I did Bed & Breakfast and Simon was working at the airport. And things were going very well there. I was building up the business, Simon was doing very well at the airport. But then unfortunately his father was taken ill and we had to devote a lot of time to caring for him. And Simon was given a choice between looking after his father or keeping his job, and chose to look after his father. So he lost his job. I had to devote more of my time to looking after his father, and then his mother, who was also taken ill. So the Bed & Breakfast business started to dwindle as well. So, after Simon's father died we were left in a situation where Simon hadn't got a job, my business was significantly decreased, and we basically couldn't afford to live there anymore. So hence the move down here. So I've been able to combine what was left of my business with the Williamses' Bed & Breakfast business. I help John and Sherril, and Simon's gone back to his first profession, which . . . So I help John and Sherril out, which gives them some freedom - because it is a very tying business, it is seven days a week, seven evenings a week, because you've got people coming in, and for breakfast in the morning - so I try to help them out at least two or three times a week so that they can have some free time. And we've got a roof over our head. And so it suited both parties again. And of course John's continued to develop the property here. So that's that, really. That's where we're up to at the moment. Tom's very very happy at Ashley School, there's no way we'd ever take him away from there. The education he's receiving is superb and he's developing very very well.

D.   I suppose actually - it was a terrible thing to have to happen - but quite extraordinary that you should have found another roof so near to where you were.

P.   It was beginning to come down to the line. You know, there was a time limit. We approached the estate about taking estate property, we applied for the council house on The Green that Joanne eventually ended up with. It really was coming down to the line. It was very - . We've had a bad eighteen months really, but hopefully this is the turn in the wheel. We've been through worse, and come out the other side. But from John and Sherril approaching us and putting this proposition to us, to us moving in, was ten days. That's how close we were to complete and utter disaster! I must say John and Sherril have been superb friends and neighbours. From when we first moved in, I think they were the - we knew Peter and Hazel Jackson previously, but John and Sherril came round and introduced themselves, and have been nothing but supportive neighbours ever since.

D.   Well this must have been a particularly difficult time for you, then?

P.   Oh, yes. Yes. But, as I say, we've dealt with worse. Thomas is actually our second little boy. We lost our first little boy with meningitis. So we've been through that, and come out the other side. Losing Simon's father was horrendous, but I don't think it can compare to losing a child. We came out of that. So it's sort of like, Well we can deal with anything now. And you do, you've got to. You've got two options, you either deal with it and get through it, or you let it envelope you, and you lose the plot completely. So . . .

D.   Was that before Thomas was born?

P.   Yes. James would have been nine in December. He was three weeks old when he was taken ill, and we kept him on a life support machine for two weeks, until they established that the meningitis had completely killed his brain. Then we had to have the decision of turning his machine off. You'd never wish it on anybody, it was completely horrendous, but it actually made us stronger as a couple, and it made us individually stronger people. It puts things into perspective. Things like having enough money, and being comfortable, just aren't important as long as you've got each other, you've got your family, you've got your house, you can cope.

D.   Looking back, can you think of any particular things that helped you through?

P.   We've got a very strong family. My mum and dad, and Simon's mum and dad, are very very close, we're a close family. My mum and dad are in Wilmslow and Simon's mum is in Heald Green. So we're all close by. So the family were very good. And we had a lot of very good friends who helped us. We also lost contact with a lot of people. But Simon and I were able to talk about it from day one. And we found that talking helped, because we were acknowledging that James had been here, and he was a being, whatever: and it's not something where you say Well that didn't happen. Because it did happen. So that, and I think the family and friendship was what got us through. And we did a lot of fundraising for Pendlebury Children's Hospital from there. So that's what really got me on the fundraising bandwagon. We raised five-and-a-half thousand pounds for Pendlebury.

D.   What a wonderful way of working it off, working something off.

P.   Well that's right, because when we were in Pendlebury it was amazing to see how, I'd say ninety per cent of the equipment that was used had got a little plaque on the back, "Donated in memory of . ." You sort of think, Well, gosh, if these people didn't do anything, what equipment would be here? And then when Thomas was born, when I was pregnant with Tom, - because if I hadn't have gone to James when I did, in the middle of the night, and found him as he was slipping into unconsciousness, and we got him to Wythenshawe: - if Id slept through, he would just have been classed as a cot death. So when I was pregnant with Tom we went into this scheme called CONI, Care of the Next Infant, which is for people who have had cot death children. You get alarms, you get all different things; and everything, again, that we were given - baby alarms, this, that, - had all got "Donated in memory of . . ." again. And you sort of think, We wouldn't have this if people hadn't got off their backsides and fund-raised, and done something. So I think you only get out of life what you put in. And you need to - I think fundraising's a pain in the backside, but if you live in a village environment like this, the village is only a village if it's got it's community spirit. And you've got to pull people together. And fundraising and organising do get people together, it's the way to do it. But it's difficult to try and get every section of the community together! We sit and rack our brains, Who would this interest? and Who would that interest? Things for the kids, things for the older members . . .

D.   Now we're veering onto fundraising, and it seems as if you're saying there are two parts of fundraising: one, the actual funds you raise, and the other, the effect it has, the activity has, on the community. Which do you go for as a priority? Now?

P.   I think they've got to go hand-in-hand.

D.   Well I've been struck by the number of people, as I go round, who have expressed appreciation about the ease with which they've been drawn into, especially people who've come recently, been drawn into the community and feel they belong, through these activities. It's almost converted me, because I'm a very reluctant fundraiser! My attitude is being changed by what I hear as I go round.

P.   Well that's right. If you're willing to do something. It's like the Rose Queen. Last year I was involved in doing the costumes for the children, and it was damned hard work, starting from scratch again, and getting the costumes organised: sewing, and trying them on, and going round the shops trying to get the best bargains for material. The year before that I was involved in perhaps doing eight costumes, that was all. The year before that I did nothing. Do you know what I mean? And I don't feel that, perhaps, Thomas did get so much out of it, because I didn't know what was going on. Whereas this year he was involved in the build-up to it, and it became this fantastic Day, and he came down in the morning and was helping getting the stalls ready, and it's more of an event. Rather than just walk round the road and do this, this and this.

D.   I wonder if we could spend some time, if he's willing, talking about Simon? He was working at the airport. What's his line?

P.   Well, I'll start right at the beginning, because then it makes more sense. When he left college he decided he wanted to work at the airport, that's what he's always wanted to do. And his father said, No. I want you to have a proper job. Playing with aeroplanes is not a proper job. He wanted him to go into the stockbroking market. So there was a bit of toing and froing here, as you can imagine! And eventually Simon agreed to go to a firm called Pilling Trippier, in St Ann's Square in Manchester, and train as a stock jobber, a position that no longer exists, with the change in the Stock Exchange. And so he did this for two years, sat all his exams, got all his papers and was fully qualified as a stockbroker; and then said, Right, Dad, I've done that. I'm now going to go to the airport. Which is what he did. He started as the lowest of the low and worked his way up, with airlines, working with airlines.

D.   Working as what?

P.   Well he started off as what they call a ramp tramp, basically turning aircraft round; and then worked his way up to be station manager. He was involved with a company called Cargolux for a long long time; who used to run the 747s from Manchester and Stanstead down to the Carribean on behalf of Airtours, before Airtours even had their own airline. And that was the forerunner to Airtours getting their own airline, and the position they're in now. So Simon basically set up a three 747 operation from Manchester. He was fully in charge of all the crews. And then latterly he was working for Caledonian Airways. That was his last position at the airport, as Station Manager. He was in charge of Caledonian Airways' operation from Manchester. But, as I say, they made him choose between his job and his father, and there wasn't really a contest. But then of course, he was looking after his dad, he'd always kept a dabbling in stocks and shares after leaving Pilling Trippier. So he was looking after his father, and had a little free time in which to study the markets. So he started using his experience.

D.   So after all!

P.   After all he's back. And that's what he's doing full-time now. He trades full-time, using the Internet, on the stock market. Starts in the morning, in London, and goes through to the States, and then through to Japan. So it's ironic. That it's come full circle.

Enter Simon.

S.   Smoking break.

P.   Oh, right. You've just missed your story.

S.   My story?

P.   Well, about starting up at Pilling Trippier because your dad wanted you to, and then going to the airport, but then coming back to your stocks and shares. It's ironic really, isn't it? Because if your dad hadn't been taken ill you wouldn't have got back into this really, would you?

S.   No. Although I always kept an interest in it. I've banned myself from smoking in my own office.

P.   So he smokes in mine, instead! You should really be outside with that!

D.   He's going, now. Any thoughts about the future of Ashley?

P.   I think the future of the village is going to be rosy. As far as housing coming into the village, extra housing, I would love to see additional housing coming into the village; but, as I have made my views very clear at numerous council meetings, I do not want to see huge great big houses with price tags that look more like telephone numbers. When the planning application went in at the garage for five very large houses - seven - I made the point, if you would like to build fourteen smaller houses that people who perhaps already own their properties on The Green could move into, that people of existing farming families could afford to buy - who round here could afford to buy a house at £325,000? But if it was a house of about £95 - £100,000 it might be more feasible. And allow people, rather than families having to move out. Stay in the village.

D.   And what you were saying would have not actually affected the money that would be made by the people who were selling the ground? Or the developers?

P.   I don't think so. But they told me it would.

D.   They said it would?

P.   But I said, instead of having seven very big houses, have fourteen smaller houses. But the school - have you seen the plans at the school, for the extension? The diocesan people had architectural plans drawn up for an extension to the school, to incorporate a hall that both the village and the school could use. They were smashing plans that they'd had done. Now the gentleman from Cheshire that phoned up and said We've just finished the meeting, you're not going to be closed, go away and educate for the next hundred years: he said, You do realise these plans to extend the school, you can't have them done straight away. They'll have to go in the waiting list, it might be a year or so before you get them done. Now they're talking as if they're going to do them. Cheshire are going to do them. So if Cheshire can build them, and the village can fundraise so that we can kit it out as we would like, rather than as Cheshire would like, then we've got our village hall. So that would be nice.

D.   I think that must be something for the Millenium Committee to think about.

P.   It will still be a huge investment. You're probably looking at £40- £50,000.

D.   If they could give it a start . . .

P.   Yes. But you see the airport have said that they won't fund any capital projects, but if we went to them and said, We've got this hall: we'd like to put curtains in it, and some seats and buy some tables. They have a Community Fund to do that with. So we've got lots of fingers in pies.

D.   Well thank you. I think that's a very good note to end on! Optimism, and based on information rather than wishful thinking.

Peter and Meg Wright. Chinley Cottage

P.   I've lived in Ashley all my life. Third generation. Grandfather lived at Back Lane Farm, where my father was born. He was married in 1926, round about then, and moved up to Little Thorns Green Farm, which is half a mile away, where I was born. We were all educated at Ashley Primary School, and I went on to a private school at Knutsford which I left at the age of fifteen, and went straight into the family business, which was farming and retail milk business. We produced the milk and retailed it from Little Thorns Green Farm. In 1959 I married Meg, who came from Salford,

D.   May we stop and go back a bit, and ask you about life in Ashley as a child? You must have been born before the war?

P.   Yes, I remember the wartime days. I remember we had, at Little Thorns Green Farm, we had an anti-aircraft battery on one of the fields, with a searchlight. As a kid-die, I was only, what? about six or seven, and it was great fun then. I remember the bombing raids, particularly incendiary bombs, they used to drop incendiary bombs looking for the airport. The airport was a military base then, they trained paratroop-ers from Ringway, they used to drop them in Tatton Park and bring them back along the roads past the house, and they used to march them back in those days.

D.   And you used to see that?

P.   Oh, yes.

D.   Are there any of your contemporaries at school still around here?

P.   Yes, Geoffrey Hunt. Geoffrey's younger than me, so his stories will come up pretty well the same. We remember the Home Guard, the real Dad's Army sort of thing, you know, and there was quite a lot of pill-boxes around. One at the end of Brickhill Lane, there's one at Ashley Hall corner. So, quite vivid memories of wartime, but as I say it was very much funtime. School, looking back on school, most of the children from Ashley went on to Bradbury in Hale. But my parents, and I could never know why, because money was very short, they paid for my education. Basically, because the school was very much farm-orientated. All the farmers' sons went there. I don't think I learned any more, though! I left very early, I left before I was fifteen actually, and went straight onto the farm. Worked on the farm and then, probably when I was eighteen or nineteen, I took over the milk round. And that became my pigeon, which developed over all our married life, didn't it? Until eight years ago.

D.   Can I give you a rest there, and ask you, Meg, how you came into this? How did you meet?

M.   We met in the Isle of Man.

D.   Where had you lived before?

M.   Salford. And I trained at Hope Hospital as a nurse. And my father died prema-turely, at forty-eight. And my sister and I took my mother away, to the Isle of Man, and Peter was there. When we got married two years later I did wonder if I was going

48

to be accepted by the farming community, you know? Being a towny. But Peter's father married a towny, didn't he? A butcher's daughter. So she wasn't, you know.

D.   Was she a help to you? Was she able, because of that, to know how you felt?

M.   Yes, she did. I'm sure she knew how I felt. Yes, we got on very very well. But I did find it very strange when I did marry, and move here. After living in a town. I felt very lonely. It was so quiet. And I did find it hard to settle down, and thought I would never be accepted in the village.

D.   Where were you living, when you married?

P.   We moved in here. The whole area were old people then, when we moved in. Arthur and Elsie Sant moved in. They got married just after us. And Meg became very friendly with Elsie. And also my mother took you to the Women's Institute, didn't she?

M.   Introduced me to the Women's Institute. Yes, I had to go along with my mother-in-law.

D.   Did you continue working?

M.   No. When I got married I, obviously, left and came here. And Nigel was born exactly a year after we were married. And then three years after, Jalna, and three years after, Michael. And so I brought them all up, stayed at home, quite happy, getting used to country life. I learned to drive. And they all went to the school. And when Michael went to Ashley School, so he'd be five, then I went back to work. And I went back to Wythenshawe then. And I was there for twenty-two years. Only went for twelve months, to see if I liked it! I said to Peter, I'll give it twelve months. Because I'd been out for twelve years. And I was very nervous.

D.   Was there a lot of catching-up?

M.   Not really. But it was a bit traumatic, going back as a staff nurse, when I'd been out for twelve years. I would rather have gone back as an Auxiliary for a year! It was very traumatic, going back. But I soon got used to it. And stayed for twenty-two years. I did most of the specialities - surgery, medicine - but I ended up on Gynaecology, which is my favourite. So I probably did about twelve, fourteen years on there.

D.   That sounds, actually, a lovely way of coming into the place. Having your children straight away, and growing into it as they grew up.

M.   Growing into it, yes.

P.   And then, together, we started playing badminton. We formed our own club. The Silver Feather Club, which is a big club in Altrincham now, in the leagues. We formed, and we named it, sat round this table. It was a tube of shuttlecocks.

M.   And the name was Silver Feathers.

P.   There were about six of us who couldn't play, and we hawked ourselves around other clubs, and they didn't want to know six people who couldn't play. So at the end of the day we said, Right. We'll do it ourselves. And we formed it and started it at Hale Barns, didn't we?

M.   We can't believe it's still going.

P.   And the Silver Feather is quite a big club. Nobody will remember us, but we actually started the club. Four couples.

D.   Where are your children now? We've got Nigel working next door.

P.   Well Nigel owns next door. I ran a milk business all my life till eight years ago. Sold up. And when I sold up he took the building on, the premises, because he started his business before that. So Ashley Mowers is Nigel's business. And now I work for him. It's quite a big business now, I mean he employs six people now. Nigel lives in Rostherne.

D.   But going back to Ashley Mowers just for a moment: that's really done very well?

P.   Done very well, yes. He's worked very hard, and it's a very successful business. His wife Elizabeth's in with him, she spends a lot of time here. They've got three children.

D.   So that's where Nigel is, and where he's got to. Then Jalna?

M.   Jalna lives in Rostherne with partner Richard and daughter Ellie. they are getting married in June, 2000. She went to Australia between her general training and her midwifery, is that right?

P.   She was qualified, she was a qualified nurse.

M.   Then she took a year off, three of them did, three nurses. And went to Australia. And they worked in St Vincent's, in Sydney. It was much easier then to get jobs. I believe you can't get them if you go abroad now. They all got in the same hospital, got the specialities they wanted. And then they motored round after that, after they'd made a bit of money. Bought an old banger of a car, and had a whale of a time. And then she came back and did her midwifery. And now she lives in Rostherne. She's still nursing, she's a practice nurse now, part-time.

D.   So that's Jalna. And Michael?

M.   Michael's in Bolton. Married in '97 to Laura, who's a teacher. And he's a graphic designer. Works for an advertising agency.

D.   And he's the one who did the Australia trip with Kevan?

P.   That's right, yes. and after their adventures in Australia he came home and went on to study graphic design at Bolton Tech. And he did very very well there. So the three of them, we're very proud of them. They're all doing very well. Nigel's three children, Lucy's 14 now, and Emma's eleven and George is eight. We're very lucky with our families.

The other thing is we've always been very involved in the village. Meg as well as myself. She's been President of the Women's Institute, and always been very active in the Women's Institute. And in Ashley itself, I mean. And that's how I got involved with the Council. I must have been on the Council now over twenty years. And I've been Chairman for the last seven. And when Peter Robinson moved from Midways I think it was on the cards that the rose fête was - nobody was going to do it. Pete Jackson and myself said, We can't let this happen. And of course that's when we took it over, and we've been doing it ever since. I say we've been doing it, we just do a bit of the organising. The helpers do most of it. That's part of us and Ashley, isn't it? And Ashley itself, it's a wonderful place to live. You get help if you ask for help. I mean, fundraising: we've raised so much money. Meg raised £120 for Kosovo at the pub's Quiz Night last week. All those sort of things, where people are supportive.

M.   And very supportive of the rose fête, making clothes for all those kiddies.

D.   One of the impressions that I get, one of the things people really appreciate about it, is that having these things gives an opportunity for people to become involved. Especially at a time like this, when there are quite a lot of new people moving in.

P.   Well we try now to get new people involved.

D.   Any thoughts, since it's the Millennium, any thoughts about the future?

P.   We've just got to, as a village, fight for our village life here in Ashley. It's very special. In the future it's got to stay the same. We've always got to have the school. We've always got to have the church, and the pub and the post office.

Rob and Caroline Davies. Back Lane Farm

R.   I am the youngest of three. I have a brother and a sister. I was born at Cranford Lodge at Knutsford in 1960. My brother's six years older than me, and my sister's nine years older. And they all went to Ashley School, and so did I, at the age of five. I quite enjoyed the school. I thought it was very unnecessary at the time, because I rather liked being at home! Like most children! There was lots of exciting things going on at home. I didn't think school was very necessary. My father always let us have ponies, and that was my main interest at home. And the main enjoyment was being able to tack up and ride the ponies around Ashley. It always seemed a lot quieter on the roads then, I don't know if it was. This was before the M56 was built, and we could ride all over Ashley: round through Ashley Hall, which you can't now, it's restricted to just pedestrians isn't it? And you could go down Clibrans track and come out near Ryecroft Farm. And you could go all the way round in a great big loop. You could ride for about three or four miles without any obstructions. Obviously that's not possible now.

And it was nice to be able to go on my own - I was only about nine or ten, wasn't I? - and you didn't need to worry about being left on your own. So I think everything was a bit more open then. And I enjoyed watching what everybody was doing. I used to go to the village playing field. We used to call it the playing field, it was the field at the back of The Greyhound, which is now built on and is called Egerton Moss. We used to play football there, and meet up with all the other children on The Green. That was good fun, that always sticks out in my mind. There was a row of cottages by the station, which aren't there anymore. They were still there. They were occupied. And I can also remember the cottages at the crossroads, they were there before the road was widened. And also the barn which has been converted into the house. I remember the barn being for my father's turkeys and calves for a number of years.

Mrs Davies Sr. (*Rob's Mum*)   Still smell it!

R.   And I remember herding the turkeys down the road, past the school, back to the farm, ready to be reared on and killed and plucked for the Christmas trade. It doesn't seem that long ago.

C.   You herded them? All down the road?

R.   Yes, you shooed them ahead. Then the barn was empty for a year or two, because I think the Tatton Estate wanted to lease it out and let it as a house, and that's - I saw all that happen. Just while I was at school. From being full of turkeys, from being run down, and then converted to this beautiful house which is owned by Mr Salt. And they chopped a bit of the barn off, to make the road a bit wider, didn't they?

D.   I never realised that y'ur father had that barn. I remember the turkeys outside here. I used to walk past, on the road here.

R.   Mr Salt says he can still smell the calves and the turkeys!

D.   Well thank you. Perhaps we can come to you, Caroline. How did you get to - well, obviously you got to Ashley via Robert! How did you get to Robert?!

C.   Well I first met Robert when we were about aged nine. Because I also used to ride a pony. And so Robert was in the North Cheshire Pony Club, and I was in the East Cheshire. And about three or four times a year they'd have competitions against each other. So I'd go for my Pony Club, and he'd be in his Pony Club. And we used to look at each other, and probably - we never used to say anything, but I used to talk to Robert's Dad. And he used to talk to me. And Robert and I would probably go past each other and have a quick look at each other, and that'd be it. And we did that for about five or six years, I think. We maybe said hello when we were about sixteen, but that was about it. And then, when I was twenty-one I went to a disco with a friend at The Kilton Inn. And my friend, she'd been in the Young Farmers in Leicestershire, and she was very keen to join the Young Farmers at Knutsford. I wasn't that keen on going really, but she needed moral support, so I went with her! And we were standing at the bar, and Wendy was enquiring about the disco, and I suddenly saw Robert, across the bar. I think he'd got somebody sitting on his knee at the time! Anyway, to cut a long story short, I went to the disco, and I think Robert came over and said he recognised me. And it went from there.

D.   Yes. "Across a crowded room . . ."

C.   That's right, yeah! And we went out for three years together, and then we got married, and we got married at Prestbury Church, and we first lived at Great Warford, for six months. And then a house came free, Hough Green Cottages, and we lived there for about -

R.   Number four, wasn't it.

C.   Number four. Yes. For about three or four years. And it was lovely living there, I really enjoyed it, it was really nice.

R.   We were in the centre of the village, and very involved with the village. And we knew everybody, didn't we? Well I knew most people anyway, but it gave you a chance to meet everybody and get to know everybody. You delivered *Ashley News*.

C.   No, not to start off with, I didn't. My job was, when it was the May Day, I was to go round the village, I was given the job of asking people Could they give butter and milk, or tea, towards it? So I'd go round The Green and knock on the door and ask people, Would they be good enough? So I got to know them all. I did that for about three years, I think. And then of course, living there, I'd go to the post office, and go and get bread and whatever. And Brenda was there. And so you used to meet people in the post office as well. And Robert didn't have a car, and you'd go to work from the cottage on a bicycle, and you'd put the Jack Russell in the basket, wouldn't you? And you'd come back for lunch and then you'd go back again, and you'd come back for tea. And then after we'd been married awhile we had Camilla. And I enjoyed living there with Camilla, because people could knock on the door. And you'd take her out in the pram, and people would talk to you. It was lovely. But what we found was that if I hadn't got a car I was rather stuck because I think there was only Warburtons who lived at Dairy House Farm, and they had Amy and Henry, and Vivienne Erlam lived at Sugar Brook. And so Camilla would see Amy and Jessica, but not much. But it was nice, because at Hough Green Cottages we had a garden. There was garden there which - you know, you could open the back door, and they were safe. And the children have been privately educated, they didn't go to Ashley School.

R.   Now, thankfully, she passed her Eleven Plus, so she's at Altrincham Grammar. That's nice, that's not too far away.

D.   So Camilla's already started there, has she?

C.   Yes, she started in September.

D.   And Guy?

C.   Well he goes to a school at Alderley Edge called The Ryleys.

D.   And what do they do when they're at home?

C.   Guy loves to be outside. He's got these pedal tractors that he pedals on. And he loves being dirty. He likes to have his overalls on, and he likes to fork up the silage for the cows. And as soon as Robert goes anywhere with the tractor he's got to be with him. He doesn't like to miss out, does he?

R.   There's a little seat by the main seat, and he can sit there quite safely, pretending that he's driving. He likes to pretend, and makes all the noises. And I think he just likes to be around the farm. He doesn't go into the village to play football, because there's nowhere to do that kind of thing.

C.   No. He plays football in the garden with friends from school to play with him.

D.   His friends of course are school friends.

C.   Yes. They are.

D.   So they get brought in from far and wide?

C.   They do. You have to go and pick them up, and take them home.

D.   And Camilla?

C.   Oh she likes . . . When she's at home she likes to read quite a bit. She likes the television. She does a lot of homework. And she rides the pony. And that's Camilla really. And she likes . . . Upstairs in the attic they've got like a playroom. And she likes playing with her dolls. And Guy's got a farm set-up there. And at Christmastime they've had a table tennis thing, and a snooker table, and they enjoy playing that as well. So really we've had to bring the entertainment here. And let the children play here, really. And we don't like them to go into the farm. Because these children come really from the towns. And they see the cat, and they run after the cat. Well if they run after the cat they can run into a tractor. You know, they're not . . . Because my children are brought up here, they know not to go, or not to tread on this, but . . .

R.   They know the boundaries, where they can't go. They're aware of the dangers.

C.   That's it. Yes.

D.   Yes, it must be quite difficult. And quite a responsibility, actually.

C.   Well, yeah. They want to come, and they want to look round, and some of them, they're giddy, aren't they. I mean your children, you can say *Be careful*.

R.   They think it's an adventure playground.

C.   That's it. And they just want to climb on everything.

R.   They want to go up the bales, about eighteen foot high, and jump down to the bottom, and they think that's fun. You can't let them do things like that. Because they're other people's children. We try to keep them in a confined area if we can.

C.   In the garden. Oh, and Camilla's the Rose Queen. Well, up until May.

D.   Oh, she was last year's Rose Queen? Did she enjoy it?

C.   Yes, she's really enjoyed it. Thank you. And she reads in church. At Christmas. Khanikhah asked her to read quite a bit, so . . . Oh, and they've got a new Sunday School now. Which they didn't have when my children were little. We used to just take them. And Camilla would take a Barbie Doll and Guy would take a tractor. And we'd take a few sweets, and they played with it like that, but . . . They used to go to church quite a lot when they were younger, didn't they?

R.   I think if it wasn't for the ponies, and the competitions which they like to take part in most Sundays, I think we would have been at church a bit more than we have done, unfortunately. You can't do both, can you? And the ponies seem to have got them to ride, and they enjoy competing at weekends. And at Castle Hill Farm we have the Wilmslow Riding Club use one of the fields for a horse show every month, in the summer. And they want to stay with us, they've got plans to stay with us for another four years. They want to build a cross-country course on the land, and try and be permanent.

D.   That'd be wonderful for them.

R.   Well there is the River Bollin in one of the fields. They might incorporate that in their cross-country course.

D.   It just reminds me of what you were saying about your childhood, and riding around. And it's always struck me ever since I've been in Ashley, that it's so sad. There's so many people keep horses here, and yet there's nowhere to ride them.

C.   No, there isn't. We put them in the horsebox now.

D.   Well, I think everyone who can, does. It's the children that can't.

R.   Well my daughter can't do what I did.

Christine Erlam. Hough Green Cottages

C.   I've lived here all my life. Born, I think in a nursing home in Altrincham, but not very far away anyway. And lived at Hough Green Farm: I've been in the cottage now since 1983, but when I dream, it's still always at the farm. I think our family had been at Hough Green Farm for five or six generations. So when Dad died, which was 1986, my brother didn't want to move to the farm, to Hough Green, John wanted to stay at Sugar Brook. I think I had an option to carry on renting it, but it was too big a house for me to live in on my own. So anyway, great childhood. Living on a farm was fantastic. And I was always a bit of a tomboy, so it was nice. But it's a shame that so many of these working farms are now being sold off. But that's the way it goes, I'm afraid.

D.   It must have been a very sad day when you moved out of Hough Green Farm.

C.   Well it was awful, because all the furniture had been in there, not only had we lived there for ages, but this wonderful old furniture, oak sideboards and . . . I think there were a lot of creepy-crawlies, as old as our family, and when the furniture came out all these things peered out, where the furniture had been! Part of the house, was the furniture. Now all that's gone. Yeah, it was awful moving out. But it was one of those things. You come to a crossroad, and there you go. But it was a shame.

D.   When I was talking to John one of the themes running all the way through his childhood was his frustration at not being able to get onto the farm, because it was all the other side of the road.

C.   Yeah. That was the problem. We had so many animals killed on that road, going back and to. All these little Jack Russells we used to have, and they always used to get squashed on that road. We used to have cows down there, and I think Dad got out of milking when I was fairly young, so it must have been in the sixties, and then he started, he did very well, he started doing contracting, and arable. I think he made more money out of the contracting than the farm. I thought the world of my dad, and when he died it was awful because when he died in such a - like these cancer victims do. He suffered an awful lot. But life moves on, doesn't it? So yes, I moved here. Geoff Ware, who used to work for my dad, now does my garden. So it's immaculate. When I first moved in here I think there were more bicycles growing than anything else! And he came in at the bottom of the field with a tractor and ploughed it up. And he's done the garden, and it's brilliant. So I'm quite settled here.

D.   I was talking to Jean and Dave the other day: this row of cottages, the way you share gardens.

C.   Oh yes. I'm the flower, Dave does the veges, keeps us all in veges, because he's wonderful with his veges. So I've got a trayful of courgettes and beans . . . So yes, there are lots of benefits. And of course Sylvia and Ken at the end, they're great because when we moved from the farm I had the dogs, I brought the dogs here. And of course it was difficult looking after the dogs, because I was working every day. And so Sylvia's been walking my dogs for the last ten years.

D.   So what is your work?

C.   I worked initially at Chrysler in Knutsford. I did that for not very long, and then

56

I got a job with IBM in Sale. I worked for IBM for a couple of years on the Sales Support side; and then I wanted to start selling, and making more money. I met a chap in a pub who said ICL were looking for some people, and I went to see the guy who was recruiting at ICL and got a job at ICL. And I've been there since 1979. So I've been there twenty years. And it was supposed to be a temporary job!

D.   And it's lasted twenty years! It's obviously changed a bit, you must have moved around in ICL?

C.   I've always been based in Manchester. The company's changed a lot, because every company's changed a lot. Used to supply a lot of computers to the government. It was very fat and very rich. And then of course things changed with a competitive market. I was doing a lot of travelling, which used to drive me mad, being away from home for days on end, I didn't like that at all. It's all right for a bit, but No. And going up and down the M6 and M40 wasn't much fun. So now I'm pretty well based in Manchester. I was based in the Arndale Centre when that got blown up. Saturday, June the 15th, 1996, it must have been. So we had to be relocated. So I'm working in a grotty part of Manchester, West Gorton, but I quite enjoy the division I'm working in now, I quite enjoy that. It's called High Performance Systems, it's the mainframes division, you shouldn't really call them mainframes anymore, but it's where they develop big systems for big companies. So it's more moving into the solutions and services. And big: supplying corporate computer systems and corporate data storage systems, enterprise storage systems. And we've got a big alliance with Microsoft, so we're trying to get Microsoft into the enterprise at Data Centre level. So it's quite exciting, what we're doing. I'm still on sales. But with big targets. OK. Pays the wages, keeps the horses, keeps the horses in hay.

D.   Is that honestly its main point, or do you also find it fascinating?

C.   I think I've got a little bit more cynical. I was ambitious when I was younger, but I think it was a bit of a crossroads when Dad died, you know. The career . . . The ambition went, and it was more focusing in on home, so . . . I enjoy working, but I'm fairly cynical about it. All these companies now, they say they value people and look after people: I think it's a load of rubbish.

D.   And the point where the ambition really went coincides with the time when your father died?

C.   That's right, yeah.

D.   Is that a coincidence?

C.   Oh no. The two are related, definitely. Well Dad always used to say that when he was sixty five he was going to do this, that and the other. And he was dead before he was sixty five. It makes you think there's got to be a balance in life. Work is important, and it does come first to a point, but I do think you've got to have a balance in life.

D.   So really, the effect of your father's death was to make you reassess what you were doing, and what was important?

C.   That's right. Yes. That's right. And there's got to be other things in life than work. I have seen so many people that worked for ICL all their lives retire, and they're dead within two years. So there's got to be a balance. So I work to live, not live to work. I think that's a good way of summing it up. But unfortunately I've got to work. I thought by my age now I'd be kept in the way that I'm accustomed, and it's a bit of a blow when you have to do it yourself! Bit of a shock to the system!

D.   So the other side of your life has to be a great deal occupied by horses, doesn't it?

C.   Oh yeah, yeah. That's my passion in life, my horses. I've had horses all my life. After the milking cows were sold we went into beef cattle. Dad used to buy cattle from Joe Boyling, a livestock dealer. I remember mithering Dad for a pony and one evening Joe turned up with a wagon full of cattle and on the back was a small grey pony. I don't know if Joe was setting Dad up, but the pony came off the wagon and stayed! That was when I was eight. He was called Silver. I used to go for riding lessons with Miss Barclay at Arden House and it was here I met Angie Simpson (now Levenson) who has been a close friend ever since. I love my horses. It's great. At the back now I've got the two fields, which I have off Tatton, and I've got my stables at the back. And I've got four horses: two hunters that are a bit knackered, but I can't have them put down.

D.   Is Bertie still one of them?

C.   No, Bertie unfortunately has gone to that happy hunting ground! My two old hunters, and another two which I'm getting fit at the moment. And they will go off to livery in another couple of weeks, in time for the hunting season. Which is my passion. And of course I suppose, out of any hobby-horses I've got, one is Tony Blair, and if he bans hunting how it's going to affect the countryside: because I don't think people realise, the urban society now, realise how much rural society will be affected. There's a lot of issues with it. But if they ban hunting I think I'll probably go and live in Ireland, and hunt in Ireland!

D.   That's an interesting point. There might be quite a big emigration. To Ireland.

C.   It'll be a shame, because I do like my fox hunting, and I'm not so keen on drag hunting, because it's all a bit hurry-scurry, and it's a different type of people that go drag hunting. It's farmers that go fox hunting. But yes, that's my passion. I love my hunting. We're coming to this time of year, and I know we've had a lovely autumn, or are having a lovely autumn, but the winter is so grey and awful: if you've got a sport or pursuit, it does make . . . life a bit more bearable. I mean, the Mosedales next door, they go off to Spain for the winter. That's another option when you can't hunt, you go off to the sunshine and get some blue sky.

D.   That's almost exactly what Frank's thoughts are, because he used to hunt.

C.   He did. Yes, actually, he did. He used to hunt with Cheshire Forest. I hunt with the Cheshires, who are based really round Tarporley. The kennels are at Sandiway. I'm on the Hunt Committee, which I was elected to this year. So I'm pretty involved in that side. And it's very sociable.

D.   Is there work? It's a working committee?

C.   Oh very much so, yeah. But I enjoy that. And I enjoy the people. And if I did move I'd move over that way. It's a cracking social life, we have a great time. In fact I should have been going over there tonight, but I'm going to see an old friend in Knutsford. But we have a really good time, and you know it's all involved in the hunting and the point-to-pointing, and we all like going down to Cheltenham, racing. Oh, it's great. It's good fun.

D.   So these two younger horses, is it hard work, bringing them on?

C.   Oh yeah, you have to put a lot of time in. It is difficult, working. It's all right when the nights are long. You have to put in eight weeks' walking, and then you start them cantering, and luckily I can go round John's fields, and do the canter work in John's stubble fields. But it keeps me fit, that's the other thing. I'll get up at six in the winter, muck out, turn them out; come back, bring them in. But it's great, because it's real therapy: when you're with the horses, all you do is think about the horses. And then when you go to work, you think about work. So it's a good balance.
   The main regret round here is the amount of traffic. And there's a bit of a threat with the garage here. You know, if they got planning permission there, the plans were for twenty-odd houses: I think that's been bounced, but I would hate to see that happen, because again I think it will detract from the village. We've got to protect our rural countryside, and we shouldn't let it happen.

D.   It's going to take some protecting though, because they're powerful interests aren't they?

C.   Well they are powerful, and money talks, but you've got people like Walter Wright, who's now mayor of Macclesfield, and he understands. The airport, that was all done and dusted years ago, that it was going to be developed there, because we always had a view that it should be developed over at Liverpool. You do wonder how the infrastructure keeps on growing all the time. But you've got to stand up to these people, there's no question about it. But I think with this government we've got in at the moment, I don't know. I have concerns. We are a democracy. And I sometimes wonder how democratic the current government is. Minorities. Anyway, I rattle on all day about that!

Frank and Pat Mosedale. Thistlewood

D. You must have built this house yourselves?

P. No.

D. That's extraordinary! It seems so perfect for you, I'd always assumed that you'd built it. When was this, that you came?

F. 1980. We'd sold the family house in Brooklands Road, Sale, and we wanted something smaller, and easily managed, and Pat spotted this advertisement in the paper - which was a home-made one, home-drawn and everything, and, er, we fell in love with it, quite rightly. Yes, you were saying it right.

D. When you were leaving Brooklands Road what were you looking for?

P. Well, a smaller house, but something near the country, or as near the country as possible, because of the hunting.

F. And we liked Hale.

D. You were still hunting in those days?

F. Oh yes, yes.

D. Do you still do that?

F. Oh no, no. No, I gave it up shortly after we came, here. It was the Cheshire Forest. I was their Secretary.

P. Well when Philip Hunter retired as the Master of the hunt - Frank and he were both in it - Frank retired as well. Because at that time we had a house in Trearddur Bay. A holiday house.

F. Our holidays were in Trearddur Bay then, not abroad.

P. And that entailed another hobby, if you can call it that. Sailing. Trearddur Bay Sailing Club. So we had twenty good years there, you see, and the children adored it. And Frank was Commodore of the Sailing Club for so long, and when he'd done his stint as the Commodore I said Right! This is where we're going to change. We thought of retiring to Trearddur Bay. Originally. But we realised we couldn't. It was too quiet. Too windy.

F. Too dark in winter!

P. Too boring. So we decided to go to the sun. And that's when we went to live in Spain.

D. And how have you found it?

P. Wonderful! It's a different life.

F.   It keeps us more active there, David.

P.   There's so much going on.

F.   I mean until two years ago we played tennis. All the time. Now we've changed to golf. Which is not so energetic, but it's still good exercise. So that's keeping us going.

D.   That wouldn't have happened if you'd lived here all the year round?

F.   Well the weather prevents you, when you're getting on a bit, from playing too much golf here.

D.   So you think the climate is the main difference?

F.   Oh yes. Grey skies are very depressing. You come home and you see grey skies, and grey people really, for a while. Until you get used to them again.

D.   So you do find that, coming back?

F.   Yes. But after a couple of weeks you become a grey person yourself again!

P.   We met an old friend at the weekend. Tod. You remember Tod Sloan. And we hadn't seen each other for quite a long time. And he said, We spend a lot of time in Greece. Because his wife Anne speaks fluent Greek. And he said, It's wonderful. We love it. We've got so many friends there, and it's a different - I said You're just saying what I always say. He said, Rather than coming back to this - well I won't say what he called it! Grey skies.

F.   I love it here.

P.   But it's lovely to come back.

D.   You see that's what I find so interesting. In spite of all that, you can say that you love it.

F.   We love the summer here. I love my garden in the summer.

D.   Is this in spite of the grey skies?

P.   The temperature, the climate's changing all the time. I mean, two years ago we had a heatwave here when we came back, and it was hotter than Spain. But last year we had no summer.

F.   But if I had to choose I think it would be here.

P.   Well the family's here.

D.   Going back to Spain: are all these people, all your friends, are they English?

P.   Every nationality. There's an awful lot of Scandinavians, especially Swedish.

American. Irish, Scottish.

F.   British. The majority are British.

P.   A lot of Spaniards are our friends.

D.   I was going to ask are they all ex-pats?

P.   Oh, no. We're members of a wonderful golf club, Alloa. A beautiful old Spanish golf club. And we're as friendly with the Spaniards as we are with the British.

F.   But the members are like us, aren't they. Go so often. Some longer than others. You miss them some times of the year, and other times you see them. It's a nice mixture, actually.

P.   And all ages. All age groups. And it's such a wonderful life, there's so many things to do. There's no excuse for people to be bored. I mean, if people get past golf and tennis, there's always bowls. People are mad about that sort of thing.

F.   Eating is reasonably priced. So we eat out a lot.

P.   Practically every day, really.

F.   It hardly pays to cook.

P.   But we've just moved house again, for the fourth time.

F.   And that's it.

P.   And that's it. We've now moved to a house. We were in an apartment, and we had the neighbours from hell. Put up with it for a long time, but we decided we had to do something.

F.   It's a town house. Not detached.

P.   We didn't want a detached house because - you know, security. And you don't want to have to look after your own swimming pool, etc. etc. Maintenance. So you - we're in an urbanisation with eighteen other houses. And it's beautiful. Simply beautiful. So we do love it. We miss it. We miss all the - . I've got a big birthday coming up in November. And I'm saying I would like to have it in Spain. The family come over to us.

D.   Well, that says everything.

P.   That says everything. But if anything happened to either of us, I know we'd come back.

F.   Any real illnesses or anything.

P.   Here. Because the family's here. And this is why we keep this on.

F.   The crux of it is that, I'm sure Pat's the same, I feel ten years younger when I'm there.

P.   Oh yes. I come back here, and I feel . . . I feel my age.

F.   That's the trouble!

D.   Everything you say makes me think, what an extraordinary thing it is that you still come back, and still enjoy being here once you've got acclimatised to the greyness again. And you like it.

P.   But it gets more difficult every time we come back.

F.   It's less grey here in summer, you see. We're talking about mid-summer, you know, July or August.

P.   But we never stay. People who live there never ever stay July, August in Spain. Too hot. Too crowded. Can't get in anywhere. And, er, we like, you know, we love to come back. Christmas. Easter. Whatever. If there's something going on we come back. We're very lucky. We know a lot of people - now - who are saying they are going to do, would like to do, what we are doing. And a couple we're meeting when we get back this weekend, they're going to look around with this thought in mind.

F.   But Ashley's a lovely village. It's part country. We're so lucky to be on the edge of Tatton Park.

P.   We're so lucky not to have a runway at the end of the garden!

D.   Frank, when you stopped hunting, did you also stop riding?

F.   Yes. Yes. I'm that sort of person. When I stop something, I do it altogether. I haven't had my leg over a horse since I stopped.

D.   People say there are two sorts of hunting people, there are people who ride to hunt, and there are people who hunt to ride. Which sort were you?

F.   I think I hunted to ride.

P.   You enjoyed it, didn't you.

F.   I loved the riding. There's nothing in the world like belting across country on familiar land.

D.   And how can you possibly do that without hunting?

F.   You can't. No, you can't.

P.   Last Tuesday he went to the Hunt Dinner. At the Grosvenor. Hunt members' dinner.

F.   And they continue, and you see all the old guys. And every now and then you get a lttle cross against your name, if you've gone.

P.   There's a painting in the dining room of the Hunt club. And Frank's on it. There's a painting in The Arkle Bar of the Grosvenor Hotel, the cocktail bar, and we go there occasionally, we have lunch there when we go into Chester, and the barman always knows that he's on it, in the middle. The moustache on him's rather large, but it's very interesting.

F.   Don't be like that!

P.   Yes, he had to dress up on Tuesday in all this tie, and the pink coat, etc., etc. And he could hardly move.

F.   True. My neck's grown again.

P.   Funny. Putting weight on. Lucky you can still get into it.

F.   But, I mean, I miss it occasionally. And I definitely miss my sailing. I used to love sailing.

P.   We've some wonderful memories. And he was - well, you were a member of an air club - he was a Spitfire pilot during the war. Shot down.

D.   Ah yes. I hadn't realised that's what you did before you were caught. I remember hearing about you as a POW, playing poker, that's as far as I knew. But we must come on to that perhaps another time. But thank you very much.

F.   Did I speak at all? Did I get a word in?

D.   Do you want a last word, Frank?

F.   Not really.

P.   He's not used to having the last word!

F.   And I don't want it now!

Alan and Diane Warrington, Katie and Michael. Ashley Post Office

D.   When did you come here?

Di.   1992.

D.   How did it happen?

Di.   It was a combination of things, really. Michael had been quite poorly with asthma, and I had been trying to hold down a part-time job. And every time he went into hospital I was having to take time off, because I went into hospital with him. So we decided that we'd cut our losses and get a business together, originally. With having our own business it would mean I would be at home, if Michael took ill. I wouldn't have to take time off work. So we started looking for a business together.

A.   In other words, Diane could have a full-time job. With the children. So we looked around: Newsagents, a few other things.

D.   Oh, you'd looked at a number of businesses?

Di.   Because the original idea was, we were going to go into the business together. Alan was going to leave Royal Mail, and we were going to set up a business together. And we were both going to work.

D.   Because then you'd be free to go into hospital if you had to? Yes. Got you.

A.   And we fancied a post office. But the main ones in, like, Hale, Timperley, were way outside our price range. And I noticed an advert for a rural one, near Altrincham. And having been on the post for quite a number of years, when it gave its description I knew it was Ashley. Because I used to come and collect from here in Brenda's time, and Sally's time. And I've always thought, if I'd like to live in a village, Ashley would be the one. Because The Greyhound's only fifty yards away!

D.   And was the training all done *in situ*? Or did you have to go somewhere else?

Di.   No, it was all done *in situ*. I had a week's training, a week's proper training, and then I think he sort of like stayed on for a few days, just to make sure I could do all the transactions, before they actually left me on my own. So I was travelling backwards and forwards from Sale. Leaving Sale eight o'clock in the morning, well before eight, coming here, working here all day, and then going back to Sale in the evening. And I did that for about six weeks, before the actual business went through - as being ours.

D.   And all this started, the whole project really, was to get you the best sort of working conditions to be free to go into hospital with Michael if necessary, is that right?

Di.   Yes.

D.   Have you actually had to go in much, since?

Di.   Well, no. Ironically. Where we used to live used to be not far from the refuse incinerator in Sale. It never struck us at the time that that might have been the cause of Michael's asthma. But when we moved here he had a couple of small attacks, and now he has no problem at all. Well he's still on record as being asthmatic, but since he moved here, touch wood, he's had no problem.

D.   Well, what do you think about it, Katie? How old were you when you moved?

K.   Six.

D.   Do you remember much about it?

K.   I remember meeting Mrs Mason. I remember her giving me chocolate biscuits. I remember my first day at school. I didn't know anyone. I walked into the cloak-room, took my coat off. I knew Sarah Littlewood, I'd met her before I came to school. So I just hanged round with her.

D.   Was it an easy school to make friends in? Because you must have had two starts, not knowing anyone, in two years.

K.   Ashley was easier, because there was less people. And you got to know everyone quickly.

D.   Thank you, Katie. Michael, do you want to give us any memories?

M.   Can't remember anything.

Di.   Of course it's a long time ago. He's at Knutsford now.

D.   How long have you been at Knutsford now?

M.   One year.

D.   Where are your friends?

M.   Most of them are in Knutsford.

D.   Do you see them outside school? Do they ever come here or you go there?

M.   A few.

A.   The difficulty is transporting to and from. The majority of his friends probably come from him playing football. At Egerton.

Di.   He goes round and plays with Sam and that other boy on The Green.

D.   Well they are a lot younger, aren't they? What about you, Katie, with friends?

K.   Oh . . . they live all over the place.

D.   Are they mainly from school?

K. Yes, mainly.

D. What year are you in now?

K. Now I'm in Year Ten.

D. Does that mean GCSE next year? Yeah.

A. Hence the computer.

D. Oh well of course, you've got to have a new computer if you're doing things like that! And what other things - Michael plays football, what do you do?

K. Tennis. After school sometimes.

A. Used to be very keen swimmers, both of them. They swum for Altrincham for quite a few years. Competitively. Trained three times a week. But they found it was getting a bit too much.

Di. Yeah. We had to think about calling a halt with Katie, because the next stage of the training would have been getting down there for five o'clock in the morning.

D. Were you sorry, Katie? Did it hurt, having to stop?

K. It was different. Not getting to the swimming club. It was a bit different, but I soon got used to it. I still miss it, but . . . I get to do it next year for GCSE, so I'm doing it next year.

D. Is sport one of the things?

K. No, I got to choose it. We could do PE core, which is, you get a certificate at the end. It's not a GCSE. But I decided to do it for GCSE as well. So I get to do two lots.

D. Do you choose your games?

K. If you do GCSE you have to do a bit of everything, but for the core you have to choose. An indoor sport, an outdoor sport. Summer, winter. My choice is swimming, trampolining, hockey and . . . I can't remember the other one.

D. And how do they examine it? Do you have practical tests?

K. We have to do sixty per cent practical and forty per cent written work; on, like, muscles.

D. Sounds very interesting. And what's your favourite subject, Michael?

M. PE.

D. PE as well! And what's your favourite sport?

M.   Football.

D.   Where do you play cricket?

M.   Mobberley.

D.   And do they play at school as well?

M.   Yeah, but I'm not allowed to go in the team, because you can't do both.

D.   So what's the rest of your GCSE then, Katie?

K.   Well I'll be doing French, History, Music, Drawing and painting, and PE, five chosen ones. Then I've got my English, Maths and Science. And Social Studies, and PE Core.

D.   Social Studies?

K.   That's dealing with people, the public. Having talks.

A.   Talking to retired vicars.

D.   Yes! Has it been a help, serving in the shop here?

K.   Yeah. Yes, it has.

D.   And do you enjoy it? Or do you just do it for money?!

K.   No, I like to talk to people. I like the money also!

D.   Yes, good! Well we've got off a bit. Can we go back, Diane, to your coming here: how did you get on, when you actually came in and started?

Di. Well having worked for six weeks prior to actually moving in, people - they didn't know the family, but they knew me. We planned to move over the Easter Weekend, because obviously it being a long weekend, we could move in, get ourselves sorted. And I arrived here, and there was like loads of cards, *Welcome to your New Home*. I think there must have been a card from practically everybody in the village. Which really made me feel good. And I'm here in my jeans and my dirty rags, and the phone goes, and it's a lady off The Green saying, I hear you're moving in this afternoon. Can I come down and help you clean your house? As my Welcome to Ashley? So I said Yes, please! So she came down and we both worked in here, cleaning it up, before the furniture arrived. But everybody was really great. They really made us welcome.

Jean Fitzgerald. 1 Egerton Moss

J.   Brian and I were living in Timperley, and looking particularly for a bungalow in this area. We were driving to Mobberley looking at properties when some friends one evening said, They're doing something behind The Greyhound, they're clearing the land. So on the way home we called. We drove round, and saw a builder's sign. So the following morning I rang him and he said he was building three houses. We said we were looking for a bungalow. He said, If you're looking for a bungalow maybe I can build you a bungalow. Actually I think I'd probably prefer to build a bungalow there. And if I can get planning permission, then you can have it. He applied for planning permission and was refused. The planners said that it was a development of houses, and that's how it should stay. He didn't agree. And he and his men spoke to the neighbouring residents, and they said they'd rather have a bungalow there too. Because of course the houses across the road are slightly lower than these, and it was the side of the house that they were going to see, which was just a brick wall. They said, We'd rather have a bungalow. So apparently he appealed to the planners, and they had second thoughts about it and came to the site to have a look. And they changed their minds and agreed he could build a bungalow. So really we felt as if we'd put our mark on this particular spot. Because it nearly was a house. If we hadn't come along and said we'd prefer a bungalow, it would have been a house, I think.

D.   He redrew the plans?

J.   Yes. He said that's how much land you've got. You have a choice of about half a dozen different designs.

D.   So you had a bit of a say?

J.   Yes, we chose the inside design. It feels strange. There was nothing on the land before we came along. Now a bungalow has been built. So we've actually made a mark on the landscape, if you like! And as years have gone by I feel more and more that we were right, and that a bungalow was the right property to build here. And I hope most of the neighbours would agree.

D.   It's always looked so absolutely natural to me, I'd never heard of this. I'd no idea you changed it. I just assumed it was always planned like that.

J.   No, it would have been the side of a house that faced the cottages.

D.   Smack there, against the road. Well this is an improvement.

J.   I would think so, yes. Anyway we've been very happy here. We both loved Ashley so much. So that's how we came to be here.

D.   How long did Brian have in Ashley? Because he died terribly young.

J.   Yes. I guess we'd been here about twelve years when he died in '94. He died very suddenly, at the age of sixty-two. He had a heart attack. But he survived that, and he went into hospital and he was there for about ten days, in Intensive Care for about three days, and gradually he got better and stronger. The specialist said, It's just really convalescence now that he needs. So he came out of hospital on the Sunday. We had a nice evening, and we even walked round to the pub, The Greyhound. After we'd had a meal he said, I'd just like to show my face. I'd like to let everybody know that I'm OK. So we walked round to The Greyhound and there were a few people in that we knew, and he just had a half of bitter and then we came home. He'd had a very relaxing day. The next day he'd had a relaxing day, and was watching the World Cup on TV. I was making the meal and through the hatch I spoke to him; but he wasn't in the lounge, he'd gone through to the bedroom. And he'd had a heart attack, another one. Off the bedroom is a bathroom, and the door was closed. I shouted, Brian? Are you all right? but he didn't answer. I opened the door and he was lying on the floor. I ran outside for help and Kevin and Bob, our neighbours, came in and tried to revive him. They were very good, but it was too late. Even so we called an ambulance and they rushed him to Wythenshawe Hospital, but it was no good. And that was a terrible, terrible shock. I never really thought that he would die with the first heart attack. I thought, you know, He's lucky. Brian's always lucky. Somebody's watching over him. We always used to talk about his Guardian Angel watching over him. Of course when he came out of hospital we were both delighted, and he was delighted to be home. His grandchildren came to see him on the Monday afternoon. And he died about half past six that day. So he was home, he'd seen his grandchildren, he'd seen his family. But none of us were prepared for his death. It was a terrible shock because he was a very busy, active, young sixty-two year-old.

D.   What did he do? Can you tell us more about him?

J.   He was a professional musician, a pianist/musical director, and worked for the BBC for many years. He was the pianist with the Northern Dance Orchestra and later the Northern Radio Orchestra, until he became their conductor towards the end of its era. Because about twelve years ago the BBC finished that orchestra. They cut a lot of orchestras, and the Northern Radio was one of them. He did lots of other work as well. But the Northern Radio Orchestra was a nine till five job really. They'd record sessions for lots of different radio shows, like the Charlie Chester Show, John Dunn, Roy Castle, Les Dawson, I could go on: programmes you'd hear every day on the radio. He also did freelance work, shows and tours of Britain with international stars such as Andy Williams, Johnny Mathis, Shirley Bassie. In his very early days, as a young man, he played for people like Gracie Fields and other famous old-time variety stars. After the Northern Radio Orchestra finished he concentrated on his other work. He did have an interesting and satisfying career. He enjoyed his work.

D.   And he stopped being a nine-to-five man.

J.   That's right, yes. He was here a lot more during the daytime. He did a lot of arranging, and writing music. He loved sitting here in the conservatory working. He also helped a lot of younger musicians in his capacity as Chairman of the Manchester Branch of the Musicians' Union. He used to say he would never want to move again from Ashley. He was a talented musician and such a tragic loss when he died, but I'm grateful that he had such an interesting and happy life when he was alive. When I had to organise the funeral I couldn't think of a nicer place than St Elizabeth's Church in Ashley, as he loved the area so much.

D.   I'm surprised you had room.

J.   Well the church was full, and they also relayed the service to the people standing outside. The following day we buried his ashes in the grounds there. And so, when I go to church now, even when I drive past, now I just know. He's there. And I feel that he's around. Here. In Ashley. And that's so important to me. But life goes on, and I'm lucky because I have lots of recordings of the music, as well as some very happy memories.

D.   What a blow to have to pick yourself up from.

J.   Well I was going to say, there's part of a song which says

"Pick yourself up, Dust yourself off, And start all over again"

A friend said to me, Jean, you either sink or you swim. And you're not going to sink! It's a very basic way of putting it, but you can easily get so withdrawn and full of self-pity: 'Why does it happen to me?' And, 'why did he have to go?' And, 'what am I going to do now?' And just wrap yourself up and hide away and be a kind of recluse. Particularly in a village like this. I mean you've only got to look out of the window, it's so beautiful! You could easily just lock yourself away and do nothing. But I don't think that's doing justice to the marriage we've had. Or to Brian, really. I think he would want me to go on and use the experience and lessons I've learned with him in life to the best of my ability. That's what I'm trying to do. One of the lessons I've learned from this is that we're all mortal. And we're here for such a short time - in the scale of things - that we have to make the best of that time. Try to make people happy; try to do the right thing; with God's guidance, make the right decisions in life.

D.   Thank you for that, Jean. I feel very moved, listening to you say that. You have managed to put into words what I'm sure is the spirit in which we would all like to face our bereavements when the time comes. And as you say, in the scale of things it comes so soon.
      It seems trivial to talk about anything else after that, but I'd like to ask about something I'm sure you were involved in: it must have been while Brian was alive that we had all the drama with The Greyhound. What was the story behind that?

J.   It went on for a long time, this struggle between the brewery, the parish council and the villagers.

D.   The brewery wanted to - ?

J.   Extend the pub to almost two-thirds again as big as it is. To provide a huge restaurant accommodation, and a much bigger bar, and a play area. We didn't feel that there was a necessity or a market for that size of 'Pub restaurant' in this area; having so many restaurants in Hale. And lots of big pubs around that do food. To have one in Ashley, which is a small residential area, we just didn't feel was in keeping with the village at all, and would spoil it. It would alter the look of it from the outside, and certainly alter the view from our back gardens.
      The parish council got together with the people who were directly affected. We had a petition against it that went round the village. Three times they applied for planning permission, and three times they were refused. They appealed against that decision and were referred to an independent tribunal, which went on for two days. The brewery put forward their reasons for wanting a bigger pub, then we - the parish council and the most affected neighbours - put forward our objections to the pro-

posal. We emphasized that we were very close to The Greyhound, and to extend it closer to our houses would be very unsociable and unacceptable. It would take away the view, and be much noisier from the pub garden. Our main point was that the area that the pub occupies is not big enough for that kind of property. If the restaurant didn't succeed it would end up being a huge pub, and then there would not be enough parking spaces. So then there would be parking on the roads around here, which would be dangerous. Bob in particular, who is Manchester City Architect, obviously made a very good case, and knew all the correct terms. So he said his piece, which brought out a lot of technical points, and Brian and I typed out a long piece on how we felt about it. And as the tribunal went on for two days Brian wasn't prepared for this, and he'd had one day put aside for the tribunal. And it took the other side, the brewery, a whole day to get over their side of it. So we went on to the next day, and then it was Ashley's turn to say what we thought. So as Brian couldn't be there, he had an engagement, I had to get up and put across our objections. Fortunately it was all typed out and everything.

D.   So you went without Brian and had to read your piece. How did you feel, going to this thing? Was it very intimidating?

J.   Yes, it was. It certainly was. And they had good lawyers, who made you feel as if you were standing in court, and accused of something.

D.   Did we have lawyers?

J.   We had a lawyer from Macclesfield Council. Provided by the council, I think. We had our parish council, the local people who were going to be most affected.

D.   How many came, in the delegation from Ashley?

J.   From Ashley? I would say about a dozen. To the actual Appeal Tribunal. And a lawyer. And then on their side there were several lawyers. And sound specialists. And experts on this, and experts on that. They really did have a huge back-up.

D.   So how did you feel at the end of it? After the two days, what was the mood?

J.   Well I felt that we'd really done the best that we could, under the circumstances. I felt that they were very strong and very powerful, but I still felt we had a chance. Because we had a valid point. Trying to believe in justice and fair play, and the fact that the chap who was presiding over the tribunal would surely see the sense in what we were saying. But maybe he wouldn't. I don't know.

D.   So what happened then? Did anyone say anything? I mean, to close the proceedings. "You'll hear from us in due course." ?

J.   Yes, he said, You'll hear from us in - probably three months.

D.   And when the news came through, how was it delivered? How did you hear?

J.   I think we all got a letter. After we'd been to the Tribunal the brewery invited us, the parish council and the people involved, to the brewery for a damage limitation talk. Just in case they lost, they wanted to know how we felt about how they should go ahead. We said, We don't want any extensions. By all means refurbish the place, and alter it inside as much as you like, but we don't want the outside to look very much different than it does now, in keeping with the village. We went away, and all waited to hear the result. After the result was known they did refurbish the pub.

D.   More or less exactly how you'd said.

J.   Yes, in keeping with the village, and they made a very nice job of it. In - what do they called it? - distressed walls, where they make all the walls look old, though they're actually new walls. They're actually new walls. So I think everyone was happy.
    We found out in June, as Brian died in the July. I was so pleased that he knew the result of the Tribunal. And it was wonderful, that we'd stood up to this huge conglomerate, with all its power. I think common sense won through. We weren't just saying 'Not In My Back Yard.' We had good, valid reasons for objecting.

D.   So here we are, approaching the Millennium. Looking into the future, do you see anything particular? Any hopes or fears for the next . . .

J.   I look forward to a peaceful world in the future and hopefully good health and happiness. I try to keep busy and do interesting things with my life. Just recently, after giving up my full-time job, I have been helping a friend refurbish and modernise a tumbledown old farmhouse in Tenerife, which has been interesting, and very satisfying to see the end result. But it's good to be home and Ashley is a lovely place to live. I hope it can stay like this and doesn't alter too much over the coming years.

*From the Manchester Branch Bulletin of the Musicians' Union,
11th September 1994;*

Brian Fitzgerald   1932 - 1994

"When Brian Fitzgerald died suddenly on July the 4th he was Chairman of the Manchester Branch, Chairman of the North West District Council and a member of the Union's National Executive Committee. If, as is occasionally asserted, one measure of the quality of a man's life is the number of his friends and admirers who attend his funeral to pay their last respects, then Brian Fitzgerald's life was incomparable.
    "At his funeral, at St Elizabeth's Church, Ashley, on the 11th of July, there were some 250 people packing the church and some 150 people outside the church listening to a relay of the service: and present were two of the multitude of 'names' for whom Brian had acted as Music Director: Frankie Vaughan and Ken Dodd. Indeed, Doddy told me that when things were not going too well during his most recent season at the London Palladium he would look down into the orchestra pit and Brian would be giving me the thumbs up and 'geeing me up'. "I'd have paid him just to stand in the pit" Ken said.
    ". . . Brian's close friends . . . warned him that in the light of his indifferent health - he suffered badly from asthma - he really ought to consider cutting down on his Union duties: but that was not his way, he did not need any help with his musical career but he was all too well aware that so many of his colleagues needed his help with their careers. So he ploughed on regardless.
    "He was a lovely man . . . a great pianist and a superb Music Director. He was that rare creature: an M.D. that musicians actually liked and respected."

Bob and Geraldine King. 2 Egerton Moss

D.   Before you came here you were living in Canada, weren't you? How did it come about that, when you came back to England, you came here?

B.   On our initial return we went back to Devon. Whilst we were in Canada Janis had gained a place at Chetham's where she started in the Autumn of 1985, so it was through her that our connections with the North West started. We were taking a little time out but with an eye on the architectural vacancies - economic realities have to be faced! That autumn, Manchester advertised the job of Principal Assistant City Architect and Janis's presence in the City was undoubtedly a factor which encouraged an application to local government in the North West, both of which represented new departures. The interview was held on November 5th. It was a memorable day as I got the job. We lodged at Glossop while seeking permanent accommodation. A rural situation was our ideal within easy reach of the City, so we looked out along the railways radiating out from Manchester. Geraldine found the development of three houses which completed Egerton Moss and we bought the last one.

D.   How did you find it, Geraldine?

G.   It was advertised in Bridgfords' catalogue.

D.   Was this already built, or was it still in the building stage?

B.   When we first came in February it was a building site.

D.   It must have been quite an act of faith. What on earth did you think of it when you first came to see it? And what you see is a building site?

G.   We had bought two new houses before and so had some idea of what was involved.

D.   So you got here in 1986. Janis had started that year, had she, at Chetham's? So you and Janis commuted in and out?

B.   Janis had been boarding from the previous September and that arrangement continued. What it did mean of course was that we could get to concerts and recitals at the school. And it was easier to get Janis home for holidays and exeats and so on than if we had remained in Devon.

D.   And what did you do, Geraldine?

G.   Working on and off for the Civil Service. I was working just through the school term time. It was short-contract work.

D.   That's interesting to know that you can do that.

G.   Well you could do it then. I don't know that it would be so easy now.

D.   Perhaps the thing to do would be to work backwards, and ask what were you doing in Canada?

B.   After university we'd had seven years in Gloucestershire, where Janis was born.

D.   Were you already in local government architecture?

B.   I was in private practice. I'd become an associate in a progressive office in Stroud which worked thoughout the UK, into Europe and opened offices in South Africa and Australia. But at that stage in one's career it is perhaps too soon to settle. We wanted new experiences, both had family overseas, and there were opportunities abroad. I took a job in Edmonton, Alberta managing a small private office.

D.   Was Canada special for you? Was it definitely Canada when your time came to go abroad?

B.   We had some friends there. Quite unbeknown to us, another chap from our Stroud office had similar inclinations. He and his family had made the move about a year earlier. He started with Alberta Public Works and then moved into the office to which I first went. When I left there I went to Public Works whilst he moved on into another private office. We subsequently worked together on a major project and our paths have criss-crossed ever since. This summer we revisited them in Victoria where they have since moved.

D.   So your first taste of public works was in Canada?

B.   It was, but in a move of greater underlying significance, for it involved my becoming a project manager rather than a drawing board architect. In that environment I developed skills that I can say in retrospect laid the ground for the move I subsequently made to Manchester. Firstly I became a manager and secondly I began to work in a more politicised environment. I do not think I was aware of it at the time, but I was taken under the wing of the wily and astute Irishman who became head of the department while I was there. Under him I received an apprenticeship of inestimable value.

D.   And what were you doing all this time, Geraldine?

G.   Janis was fairly small at the time, and so I was working part-time at the University of Alberta.

D.   And Janis will have had her first experience of school and everything. What was it like there? Did she go to nursery school?

G.   Yes she did, actually, she went to a Montessori nursery school and the elementary school that she subsequently went to was rather different to the normal school over there, as it was very English-based.

B.   And incidentally to that we enrolled her on two music programmes, a Yamaha one which not surprisingly was keyboard based, and a Suzuki string programme which was based on memory work. Her progress on the Suzuki course was meteoric, perhaps twice the normal rate. In a couple of years she was playing well ahead of her age but had learned none of the written language of music. We managed to get her an audition with a very talented American violinist called James Keene who was the concert master with the Edmonton Symphony Orchestra. And he heard her play, and took her on as a pupil.

D.   How old would she have been when she started?

G.   Five or six. Probably six. She became a member of the small "orchestra" at Alberta College. Annually she entered the local Kiwanis Music Festival and won a lot of awards. She was on local television and radio. There was comment on the radio about the little girl who had fought very hard for her place among the first violins, and got it. But her legs were far too short for her feet to touch the floor. I remember the funny remark from the interviewer about the child with her feet on a box; the sort of memories that you take with you.

B.   When some time later we knew we were likely to return, we looked into the four specialist music schools in England including Chetham's. Over transatlantic channels she secured a place there, and so her immediate future was settled before ours.
    I started in Manchester in January 1986. Five months later the then City Architect resigned. It fell to me to run the Department on an acting basis while the position was advertised. I was left to address a question which from choice I would have deferred for a couple of years - whether to apply for a position I felt I was not yet ready for, or stand back and see it go to somebody else, with goodness knows what potential consequences. History records that I applied for it and was appointed.

D.   Yes, that must have been quite a nasty shock.

B.   Certainly it was an unforeseen surprise. But there you are. It worked, and I think my experience in Canada gave me sufficient reserve to get hold of the job and chart a way forward, as a manager more than an architect. The politics of the Alberta I worked in were as far to the right as Manchester then was to the left, but both need effective management to deliver their agendas, and so I found that I didn't change my style one little bit. I tend by nature to be apolitical in party terms. I don't easily run with any particular crowd. So I can deal with a political environment without being coloured by a particular political affinity.

D.   I should think that must be almost essential. It would be terribly difficult if you had strong political leanings yourself.

B.   Some do and seem able to operate from a strongly political conviction. I don't. I care about the job and doing it well, but the motivation lies in the provision of an effectively managed service which provides value to the community which pays for it. Politics in the tribal sense can be very divisive. I feel I can be more effective if I can get on with people independently of political beliefs and the accompanying baggage.

D.   And have you enjoyed the work?

B.   Well, that's an interesting way of putting it! It has been hard and at times extremely demanding, but overall the answer must be yes. There's never been a dull moment.

D.   Have there been sleepless nights?

B.   Oh, there have been a few - from a variety of causes. Manchester is a big city dealing with big issues and challenges. When it has problems they too tend to come in larger than normal sizes. And some of the things I've been asked to take on are a long way from the professional course on which I originally embarked. But that is what life brings. If I look back on my time in Canada, I think I acquired a sort of reputation for being able to face the challenge of awkward problems and get on top of them. To a certain extent, for reasons I have not actively intended, that has happened in Manchester as well. In 1989 I was asked to run the Housing Department, which had got itself into something of a pickle, and I had three years of dealing with that, which was probably the toughest thing I would say I have done in Manchester. In 1993 we again made national news. A faulty gas heater installation put in by the municipal works department led to the death of an elderly pensioner and his dog from carbon monoxide poisoning. I spent the next twenty-one months managing programmes of inspections of similar installations, remedial work, and a major reorganization of the operation and structure of the groups previously responsible for dealing with such work. And the bomb of 1996 caused in every respect the most intense demands and worries, and brought its problems literally to the door of my own Department, whose regulatory role includes responsibility for dealing with dangerous buildings.

[*See Appendix*]

D.   Yes, but again it was another thing that, in a sense like these other two, were over and above your actual routine work, which presumably had to go on, of the Department?

B.   It was here that several years of strengthened management systems returned valuable dividends. The accumulated operational momentum meant that normal routines in other areas could withstand the effects of my having to apply enormous amounts of time to dealing with those technical aspects of the emergency which were my responsibility.

D.   I can see now that your life, Bob, is really work and home. I mean, when you're home, you need to be . . .

G.   Away from work?

D.   Away from work! Which probably means - or it would if it was me - to some extent anyway, being away from people. I'm just wondering how you experience Ashley, as a place to live in? Or is Ashley not even a dimension that exists for you?

B.   I think we all need some sort of hinterland or retreat to which we can turn for relief from pressures of career and the world in general. Moving into a new place you can never be sure whether it will deliver what is needed to make that work on your particular terms, but I guess that Ashley has delivered what works for us. One of the reasons is the diversity of people all mixed in here. There is no stereotype. I said in connection with politics that I run with no particular crowd. So it is socially. When I leave my office it is good to engage with those unconnected with architecture and the environment in which I work. One of the pleasures of a place like this is that at the post office or the pub you meet a range of characters from different backgrounds and circumstances. And what I think is so appealing about Ashley is that it has that mix. There is the farming community which has its own particular character, there is The Green, which has a different kind of ambiance and in the seven houses in this group there are people from a variety of backgrounds. None really dominates. One can be comfortable here, meet people and say hello, and be on good terms with them without getting under each others feet.

D. What about you, Geraldine?

G. Oh yes, I agree with Bob there. You've got the mixture of people. Particularly when I was working, and catching the train. That's how I got to meet a lot of people from The Green. You know, have a good chin-wag at the station. Yes.

D. Some people find that actually it isn't all that easy to meet people. I mean, you mentioned you met people on the station?

G. Yes, I think that's how I first got to meet people, yes, down at the station getting to chat about this, that and the other. Then gradually the network extends - through the fête for example.

B. Yes. The pub was another source, we met a few people there.

G. Yes. And having children, or a child, then the net extends again. Well that was in fact how we met you, through Sophie and guinea pigs. Of course being close to the post office I was always meeting people in there. A centre of activity!

D. So you feel at home here?

G. Yes definitely.

B. Very comfortable. Yes.

Mary Walker. 3 Egerton Moss

D.   You started life in Ashton on Mersey. Where did you go from there?

M.   Sale. I moved just into Sale. But my parents still lived in Ashton Village, right in the village. So all my friends and contacts - I was at school with, at the little village school, and I just grew up in a village community.

D.   And how did you come here?

M.   Here? I used to walk a dog every week in Tatton Park. A well behaved dog in those days, not this one! A very well behaved boy. We used to go to Tatton, and we used to walk across the farm and round about, but mainly Tatton. Gerald always said, I'd like to live in Ashley, and I used to say, Where is Ashley? When we used to come we were through it, we'd missed it. Gone. And then one day I just happened to be driving through, to Tatton Park, and saw this building going on. Right out of the blue. We were ready for ret-, thinking of retiring, and that's it. We really intended to have a bungalow, a small bungalow, but we said, Oh this will do until we get a bungalow. It will let us sample living out here: do we like it? And we're still here!
      I took early retirement. Gerald was still working at the time. We'd mentioned Ashley, we'd always talked about Ashley, because we felt it was not too remote. It was accessible to places we wanted to visit, and it was right for us. The building of the house itself wasn't right, we didn't want a little modern house, but it was just right at the time. So we were just lucky, I think.

D.   And how did you find it, coming to live here?

M.   Erm . . . Very quiet . . . I just didn't know anybody in the village. The only people that I really spoke to were the neighbours on this little block here. People on this block. And Brenda. Brenda at the shop. And that was it. I didn't know any other people in the village at all. I didn't go to the church at that time because I was still teaching. I'd not retired, and Sunday was a schoolwork day . . . A classroom, to me, is a lovely friendly - most of the time! - a lovely friendly place where - I mean, really, if your discipline's right, you've no discipline problems - where there's a lovely relationship between teacher and children. And you're kept busy. And your mind's active, and you enjoy the challenge of the work. So it was just nice to come home and be in a quiet area. I worked in Stretford. So to come from that close, tight, environment, it was just lovely to come home here.

D.   And now, you're teaching again?

M.   Well. A little tiddy bit now.

D.   Before you came there hadn't been a Sunday School at church. You've had about sixteen months now. Has it got established?

M.   I feel it is. But I do have my worries about the future. We've got the youngest children in The Green coming. And as yet we've no more babies in prams. Not that I'm aware of. To come up to us. And I just feel that those children who are, there's a few who are nine and ten years old. And I don't want them to feel that when they get to eleven and they get into secondary school that they're too old for this. I'm trying

79

to think of some way to interest them after they become ten or eleven. Because, the boys particularly, feel it's a bit beneath them, don't they? It's a bit too childish for them.

D.   So that's one of your problems, how to keep them next year when they get into secondary school. And another is the dearth of babies to form your next generation. How about those who come?

M.   The children who are on The Green come. As far as I can see, all the children on The Green come. Parents are very supportive. They're good. They're very nice young supportive people. We just have to keep our fingers crossed, and hope.

D.   Do you have any help?

M.   Yes. Dee Langley and Pat Gregory. Yes, yes. They come as support. Michael our vicar is always there for us. And we get a lot of support from Caroline Holmes. She's very good. She's helped us with the purchase of tables and chairs, she organised the Ploughman's Lunch. We've done two. We went to the pub and they were very good, they supported us. The pub did a Quiz Night, and he channeled all the proceeds to us, about a hundred and fifty pounds. So we've got, we now own, tables and chairs, the Sunday School. That was local help we got there.

D.   Have you any hopes or fears for the new Millennium?

M.   I've been thinking about the actual community itself, here. One or two things I would like to see. Obviously I don't want it expanding. Having come from Ashton on Mersey village, which was a little village, little farms in the middle of the village, and it was very quiet and everybody knew everybody else in the village. And it's expanded and expanded. And it's lost its village status. It's just a rough area, and when I go back to the village I feel awfully disappointed, because this was so - a lovely close community where we played in fields, that is now a housing estate. I'm sure local people feel that about Egerton Moss, because this was an open plot, wasn't it? I'm sure the local people must have been horrified to think they were going to build on this plot. Initially. It's very upsetting to a little village. And this is what has happened in Ashton on Mersey. I don't want this village to . . . I don't want it to become so . . . And yet, saying that, what right have I? Because I do know the garage want to have houses built there. So I'm not saying NO, they mustn't build houses there, I'm not saying that. I don't quite know what I am saying really! I don't want it to lose its . . . There's still a kind of oldness about it, isn't there, in Ashley. It's still got the village quaintness. And I don't want it to go. I don't want the airport to expand any more, I don't want them to start screaming out for a third runway, and expand further. I don't want that to happen. I must admit, when I came to live here I never ever thought it would go for a second runway, and we'd all be frightened that we were going to lose our village then. So I don't want progress made at the expense of the village. I like the friendliness of the people. And I feel - I know we've had some violence in the last couple of years, which when we first came here we none of us would have expected, would we? I think that's happening everywhere, but I don't want to feel frightened in the village. I feel very secure here, very settled and very happy. I feel people are not in each other's pockets, but if you call for help there's always somebody to come and give it to you, without them being in and out of your homes the whole time. I don't see my neighbours - I think I've seen Tim and Suzanne once to say Happy New Year. And I don't think I've seen them since then. But I know they're there. I know that I can call on Geraldine and Bob, and know they're there. I feel quite secure. Quite safe, here. And I think it's nice to feel that on our door we've got this lovely open country. When I'm coming home from visiting my daughter in Sale, or the other one in Stretford, and we're driving home, we often, Gerald and I, we often say to each other, as we're driving along Ashley Mill Lane, or along Ashley Road here, Aren't we lucky? Aren't we lucky to come home to a little, a little peaceful place like this. My friends say to me, Why the dickens do you live in a remote place like that? What on earth do you do with yourself? Well what do I do with myself all day? I don't know. But I know this, when I come home I think, We are lucky! We are lucky, to look over those fields, to look over the farms. When you come out of the church door and you look across, and it's just green, and there's a cricket match going on. It's a bit of Old England, isn't it? We've still got a bit of the Old England left, on our doorstep. And I don't want it to go.

Tim and Suzanne Elliott. 4 Egerton Moss

T.   In 1982 we lived in a flat in Bowdon opposite The Griffin, and it was a small flat, so as Suzanne was pregnant at the time, we decided that we should look for a larger house. And then I saw this - I don't know how - but I saw this house in Ashley.

S.   We'd passed them loads of times, because we often used to go to Tatton Park and seen them and driven past. Then Tim came to have a look at it. And you . . .

T.   I think I bought it.

S.   You bought it, yes, and you came back, and he told me. He said, I've bought us a house in Ashley, and I was . . . I was not best pleased! because at this stage I'd only looked through the windows. And I thought, There's no way I want to live in that. In a beautiful rural location, four boxy houses: it just didn't seem fitting, they seemed totally out of place. Anyway I suppose the rest is history really, we moved in and we've been here ever since! It's been sixteen years. And we love Ashley. I think now the houses are just maturing enough, that they are starting to fit in. Was this once a green?

D.   Well, children used to play football on it. It was that sort of an area.

S.   I'm very much one for keeping things, perhaps, as they should be. But having said that, now that we live in Ashley we love it. We'd like to still move from the house, because I don't particularly like the house, but we can't find anywhere that we like as much as Ashley. So if we could build a house in Ashley we'd be absolutely delighted!

T.   When we first moved here, we'd only started our business in '79. We bought it in '77, in Altrincham, George Street, and we opened up in '79, and we'd very much over-spent on the building, more than treble what we'd expected, so we were into huge amounts of money.

D.   This was your first, was it?

T.   Yeah. Well, it's the one we have now. Same place. But I bought the building, which was a bit ambitious at the time, and decided to gut the place. Because I have an interest in architecture, I'm not best at just letting things go. So I overcooked it.

D.   Just for the record, this is a hairdressing salon?

T.   Salon, in George Street, at the end of George Street.

D.   "New Wave"?

T.   "New Wave", yeah, that's right. So when we moved here in '82, which is only really a couple of years later, we weren't exactly flush with cash! I think we had £6,000 to spare. And so we spent most of it on the garden.

S.   It seemed, for a garden, a huge amount, but we decided that was the most important bit. And I think it was money very well spent, because these flags are just beautiful, that they put down.

D.   So you put down the patio, and you planted the Acer . . .

T.   Well we planted all the trees that are in the garden.

D.   All of them? The silver birches?

S.   Everything.

T.   We bought mature trees, which were quite expensive. They looked quite large, but when we had the old photographs of them, you realised how twig-like they were. They were twelve-year-old trees. So yes, we planted the ones there, and we planted them on the green at the front, and we put the wall down the side, with the curve on it. It just made it look more presentable. But then, when we moved inside the house, I was over-ambitious again. I ripped the whole brand new kitchen out, and I think I ripped the bathroom out, and Josh's bathroom upstairs, didn't I? And I started putting lights in, and - I borrowed quite a lot of money again, and I assumed I could put it all back together straight away. But I hadn't really budgeted on it. I can't remember now but it was a lot of money. So we actually lived in-

S.   We lived upstairs.

T.   We lived upstairs in the bedroom, because I'd gutted the place, and I had no money at all to do it. So we had really cooked our goose this time, which caused lots of animosity -

S.   You cooked it!

T.   Yes, I cooked it! Anyway, in 1999 we're still here.

S.   It's the area. You will not move from the area. It's just very lovely living here. You know, it's close to Altrincham and Hale for work, you go on the train. We run, so to run round here in the morning, I ran yesterday morning about half six, and it was just idyllic. I didn't see a car. I didn't see a person. I could just hear the birds and I thought, This is a very very special place to live. You know, we are so lucky to live here, and yet so close to where we work. We can be in Altrincham on the train in, what, seven minutes? So we manage on one car, because we don't really need the two cars. We can walk back from work, which we often do in summer, or run back. It's just lovely. Near to the shops when you want to be, but right out in the country. We could-n't wish for a nicer place.

T.   I think as a person: I'm fifty-three now, I don't have a pension which is rather stupid. We tend to spend a lot, we like going out, wining and dining, holidays all over the place. I think I'm going to work till I drop dead, I don't want to retire at all. So, where most people have probably committed themselves to a massive mortgage, we've finished up living in something which is well within our means. Maybe I was stupid to do so, but because, again back to Ashley, and I've been running ever since the day I came here. I've always said to Suzanne, I don't want to go further than the distance I can happily run home. I've never, ever, used my car to go to work and it stays in the garage. I think I did three hundred miles in it last year. Because I like to run. I feel really healthy for that.

D.   So do you run into work and back again?

T.   No, I go into work, and then I frequently run home. And there's many ways you can run home, it's lovely. Some of it's on the main Chester Road, but a lot of it's lovely, you're nearly always away from the traffic, the masses of traffic. So that's important for me. The quality of life here is terrific. The other thing I like about it is, too, I work in a very pose-y sort of business. It's a very superficial environment, it's very tense, it's all the other things - not that that bothers me because I don't get tense about anything - but I like to remove myself from that; I don't want to be part of that group. So being in the village is quite nice: the fact, I do enjoy the fact that it's a community, and if things go on you are more connected than if you lived even down the road in Bowdon, where you really didn't know your neighbours. You do know everybody round here. I always think, if there's a crisis around here people will tend to help each other, which is a rare thing.

D.   Now when you came here Josh was a baby.

S.   Six months.

D.   How's it been for him?

S.   He loves it. He just loves it. He actually says he never wants to live in a town or a city. I'm sure it will change as he gets older, but he just loves being out in the country. He'd like to go probably even further out, he'd love to live on a farm.

D.   Has he had, at any stage as he's grown up, friends here, or . . .

S.   He hasn't, no he hasn't actually had friends in Ashley, because he's not gone to school in Ashley.

T.   There's never been anybody here of his age group.

D.   I had a feeling there wasn't. That's really why I asked.

S.   So he'd bring kids, but they didn't just come to play for a couple of hours, it was always a sleepover job! But he loves living out here. I think this summer we're going to invest in a little scooter for him, so that he can get about. Because that is a little bit of a problem. I know there's a train.

D.   That's the other problem for teenagers. At that age they start saying it's too far out in the sticks.

T.   It's funny isn't it, really, because he's lived in remote places, all his schools have been. It's a little bit worrying, because he's not part of the real world. I mean, he does love Manchester. And also, because we've been involved in a - we've got the reverse again, because I'm in the fashion business, he's used to that sort of level of sophistication. So he's not removed from it.

S.   But he's very much a nature boy, he loves animals, he loves anything like that. He has had Tatton Park as his playground really. It's so stunning. You go in there and you think, Gosh! This is just up the road from where I live! This is my doorstep, you know. We lost them once in the woods. Had to call the Rangers out. They were supposed to come back. Because we go to Tatton a lot, or we did do then, I would go to fairly remote parts. But they were off in the woods playing this soldiers game, they were quite young, they were about eight. And they had to come back and report every half an hour or so. I was reading a book. And then they didn't come back. And they were missing ages and ages, and I couldn't find them. So ultimately I had to phone the Rangers. And the Rangers came out and searched for them, but they were completely lost. They were lost for me to find them. They didn't seem to think it was too much of a problem! But it is a wonderful playground for the children, to have that on your doorstep. Absolutely fabulous. So we've been very very lucky. OK, there weren't children living in the area, or very few, when he was small, but he's enjoyed it, hasn't he?

D.   This running: do you both run as keenly as each other?

S.   Well Tim was always the very keen runner.

T.   Yes. I got a back injury when I was playing rugby at nineteen. I bust my back and had a back operation. And the operation didn't work terribly well, and I couldn't walk for a couple of years, properly. It's improved since then, but my back is very prone to going. So as long as I run, just the breathing exercise and added strength to my stomach muscles, that keeps my back in order. Well it keeps everything. It stops me getting stressed and it keeps me very healthy, so.

S.   You're not as keen as me now, are you?

T.   No, well Suzanne's become dramatically, she's really into it now. We did the Great North Run last - October, was it? That's a Half Marathon.

S.   And next year, hopefully, I'm going to do a Marathon. And I'll probably do the Manchester Marathon. Just to say *That's It, I've done it!* But I get quite a buzz from doing it. I'm sure it's not so good for your joints, but . . . And it's lovely running round here.

T.   As a family we're both quite athletic. Josh is very sporty. Always loved rugby at school. He's been a snow-boarder since he was seven and he's been skiing since he was four. We're all very active. The sporting life is very important to us.

S.   Another reason for living out here. We'll probably go out on our bikes this afternoon. You don't have to go anywhere in the car do you, really, you just take off from here.

D.   It's lovely to find someone who does, actually, because most people, in spite of that, are very dependent on their cars. Well is there anything else you'd like to add?

T.   Just to say that, with the area as a time capsule sort of thing: to me, Altrincham has been very good. Recently, in '94, we completely gutted New Wave, and we started again.

S.   Again! Just when most people are planning for their retirement.

T.   But this time we spent well over half a million on it, making it the most expensive fitted-out salon in the country. But on top of that, for me, because I enjoy doing my architectural work, I also became Trafford Architect of the Year in '95. That was a plus for me really.

S.   You'll never be able to retire, will you? It'll take the next thirty years paying off the loan.

D.   But it's what he wanted to do! It must have been what you wanted to do?

S.   He was driven by the design. It wasn't the business, was it, he was driven by the concept of the building, and of leaving a building behind. It's a memorial to him!

T.   We got a few awards for it, it's worked very well. It was designed around Modernism, so we started with Rennie Mackintosh on the outside of the building. So it's got the sort of stonework that you would see in Glasgow. And then the interior is Le Corbusier. Le Corbusier got his ideas from ocean liners. So I took the theme of an ocean liner. High-rise buildings actually have arrived on this planet because Le Corbusier segmented a cruise liner, and noticed that you could live in the compartmentalised living accomodation, people can live close-to, which is the forerunner to the high-rise, that's how it happened, yeah. So. It's a subliminal look of an ocean liner. And we run a theme all the way through it, so it's a very theme-orientated but totally - my whole thing was to build a Millennium Building - and it has furniture which relates to Pugin, who was doing retro-Gothic churches at the turn of the Century: so we have Gothic-looking furniture which is stainless steel and bronze, it's all metal, everything is metal. We've got chairs which look like gargoyle legs, but the chairs themselves are now in the Louvre museum. They won a fantastic award on them. And the cabinets are all, they've got seaweed legs, and sea urchins on them; and a dolphin chair behind the desk. So.

D.   Who designed all this?

T.   A guy called Mark Resley-Jones, he's fantastic. So we've got all the stuff within the salon that runs through this century on design, so it's an accumulation of this century's design. It's worked out really well. But obviously it cost a fortune, because I wanted to build something that was very much going to be - : it's going to stay. So we used all maple woods inside: beautiful maple doors, beautiful birdseye maple on the doors. So we did go overboard. But it has won us plenty of awards, so it's been very good for us. But as I say, it's back to the area, really. If it wasn't for the area we live in I couldn't have done it really, because outside of London you couldn't have afforded to.

D.   Because you'd never get the clients anywhere else, to pay what you'd have to charge to cover those sort of expenses?

T.   No. I have to say we're looking now to Manchester and further afield, to open more businesses up. My great edge is I should be cutting down, and I actually want to go ahead and do more now. Because times have changed, they've moved on really.

D.   Yes. It sounds exactly like you to do the opposite of what most people think you should be doing!

T.   Oh yeah, well that's right, yeah. It's an ongoing thing, you know.

D.   And I notice you're in the *Sunday Times* this week. What's the date? It's the second of May. Sunday, 2nd May 1999. How did they get to hear of you?

T.   They just pick. Every week they have a, they choose a salon. What's it called?

S.   "Cut and Dry"

T.   They say "Each week we put a different hair salon to the test." So somebody comes to the salon. Sometimes it's good and sometimes it's bad. I have to say we got ten out of ten, which is, I don't think we deserved it. She did say, the young lady who came, she loved her hair and everything, but it did take four hours, and she wouldn't mind if we sold some food, because four hours is quite a long time! We have been on TV, and we have had write-ups before, different bits and pieces.

D.   And do you think this extraordinary rebuilding of the building would have had some effect, or is this all done on the quality of the hairdressing?

T.   Well no, she has commented - that Elton John would give his eye teeth for the furniture. He's already got the furniture!

S.   They comment on various things. The actual ambiance of the place, the building, and whether they felt happy with their hair, and the chat, and everything else.

T.   We're probably one of four salons in the North West, who are considered the major salons. Yes, it's a big salon. It's got a good reputation. As for living in Ashley, it's quite nice. You work in one environment which is a bit tense and uptight. Then you come home to something quite different. Where you can slob out!

D.   Well judging by the look of the garden, I don't think you can do much slobbing out!

Pat and Kevin Gregory. 5 Egerton Moss

D.   How did you come to Ashley in the first place?

P.   Well we were moving. Kevin wanted to sell the house in Timperley. I had a vague connection with Ashley, in that my godparents were Reg and Ethel Baker, at The Greyhound. So Ashley had been a place, when I was a child, that we would walk to every other Sunday, to see the godparents. The first time I went to Ashley Church was to Reg Baker's funeral. So I'd had vague connections with Ashley, and my mother had been to dances in the school in the wartime, with the Americans! So Ashley was always a place that in my childhood was being talked about. And I was driving through one day, and saw these houses for sale. So we came and looked at it, and decided to have one, didn't we?

K.   Yes. I was aware of Ashley. I used to come out here before we were married. We used to come out here to the pub for a drink on a Friday night. We'd come to some of the ones in Mobberley, and The Greyhound of course. And I think I'd been aware of it before then, because an uncle of mine who lived in Hale used to walk out here on a Sunday morning. And I think I may have been with him on one or two occasions. So we were both aware of the place, perhaps Pat more so than I.

D.   Had you lived, when you were young, in Timperley?

K.   No, I lived in Sale. And Pat was also living in Sale.

P.   And then when we first got married we lived in Timperley. It just seemed a nicer place to live really, didn't it? Bit more rural.

K.   Well, we were on a very busy road, and it was getting busier as things do. So we thought we wanted to move from there. It was really just getting a bit too noisy for comfort. So we moved here. And it's got a lot noisier here.

D.   Yes I was just thinking, history's repeating itself! Were you the first people into this house?

Both.   Yes.

K.   There was only Bill and Trina Walsh living in the house at the end there when we moved in. They finished, the company that Bill was involved with at the time, they finished them off when the original builder went bust. So they moved in to that one at the end, I don't know how long before us. Not that long. Six months, maybe.

D.   Yes. So it was all still really taking shape. How much of what we have here was in place at that stage? Was the little area of green out there established?

P.   The grass was there.

D.   And these lovely trees, which I've always thought were one of the best features of the whole thing, you and Tim between you did that?

K.   More Tim, really.

P.   It depends. I mean, he put the two big deciduous ones in, and we put the conifers in.

D.   Which are really the ones which are particularly striking. And I suppose, being a hairdresser, he keeps them trimmed! I was just noticing the shape of one: it's absolutely immaculate.

P.   It's a nice place to live, this little close, everybody's friendly, but nobody interferes.

D.   Everyone says that.

P.   Not bobbing in and out of people's houses. And yet it was nice when Nick was young, when we first came here, because the Walshes were here with three kids. And Joy lived next door with two girls. So there was quite a litttle crowd out here. Because it was quite safe then, they used to ride up and down here, didn't they?

D.   When did you actually come?

P.   1981.

D.   So how old would Nick have been?

P.   He was nine. He went to Ashley School for a year, and then to Hale Prep. for a year. And then he went on to William Hulme. He liked living here, didn't he?

D.   What happened after he left William Hulme?

P.   He went to the Xaverian College for a year, in Manchester, then to college at Northwich. That was really probably the start of his illness, although we didn't know at the time. We went to an aunt's funeral at the beginning of 1991, and Nick said I'm not going back to college. I can't hack it anymore.

K.   He was always a bit resistant to doing A levels. I think he thought that once he'd done GCSEs he'd spent enough time at school. Although he was quite bright in that way, he was a bit on the lazy side, you know, I think he thought that he didn't want to spend another two years doing A levels.

P.   He never wanted to go to university. So we gave him a month to sort himself out, and then said we wanted an income from him. So he went and signed on one week, and said he was never ever going to sign on again. And from then on he worked for Martin.

D.   He went straight to Martin from there did he?

K.   He had one or two other odd jobs.

P.   He worked for Herbie Hope, worked in pubs. And in the daytime he worked for Martin.

D.   It was very interesting because - I can't say I knew him terribly well , but - it was perfectly obvious what a transformation, I felt had happened, once he started with Martin. It seemed to me that he was in a different place altogether. He was really happy and satisfied there.

P.   I think the pressure had come off him. He felt school . . .

D.   He loved the work.

P.   Oh yes. The gardening work? Oh he did, he loved the outdoors. And it was the lack of pressure really, wasn't it? You know, he wasn't being mithered to get on with homework. As long as he got up for work every day and gave us his housekeeping at the end of the week! In a way, with his illness, the job he was doing made him fairly strong. So he was able to withstand the operations that he had. When he had his lungs removed he had two operations within six weeks of each other, and because he was physically strong he was able to get over that. And he did go back to work you see, after that.

K.   Oh yes, for about six months. From Easter . . .

P.   From Easter till he collapsed with his brain tumour, he worked.

D.   I can't remember how long it was after that.

P.   Well he had his lung out November/December '91. He went back to work Easter '92. And he collapsed with his brain tumour in September, '92.

D.   When did he die?

P.   January '94.

D.   And all that time he was off, and really ill.

P.   Yes, but he could walk to The Greyhound. And it got to the stage that he had to walk accompanied to The Greyhound. And we could leave him there. Then watch for him coming back.

K.   But I mean once they'd put him on the steroids, which stopped the fits, then he would walk on his own there for quite some time. And we used to walk out of the door afterwards and watch him to the end of the road, but he was perfectly OK. And he used to go in there and play cards, that sort of thing, with Ted Tickle, and . . .

P.   Fred Blain.

K.   And Bernard Dolan.

P.   All dead, unfortunately. They're all dead as well.

K.   Except Ted Tickle.

P.   No, Ted's not. But Fred Blain and Bernard. But a month before he collapsed with his brain tumour he actually climbed - they were doing the spire at St Peter's -

and he climbed up the scaffolding to the top of there. We were away on holiday, and when we came back he said about the wonderful view from the top of St Peter's. And he'd been out with some of the kids from Sprads - you know, the St Peter's youth group - he'd been out with them, and coming back they'd decided to climb the spire.

K.   Up the scaffolding.

P.   And that was a month before he collapsed with his brain tumour.

D.   I say! I bet it is a good view, too.

P.   He said it was fabulous. You could see right across to the Welsh mountains.

D.   I'm glad he got that in.

P.   Yes. Well, he liked rock climbing. Well he never actually did it out in the open, did he, but he used to go to the rock wall. In a way it made him grow up, being ill. He grew up. Very quickly.

D.   Yes, I was wondering what it had done to him: how he'd responded to it?

P.   Yes, he grew up. It did make him grow up, didn't it? And he opened up his feelings about how he felt about other people, and how he understood how other people would be feeling about . . . You know, he asked us how we were coping with what was happening with him. So he was aware that, obviously, we were going to get upset. And that life would be very different for us after he died.

D.   And he would be able to talk about it?

P.   Only when he wanted to. I mean, you couldn't walk into a room and sit down and say . . . But there were times, because he wouldn't go to bed at night because he had these fits. And he smoked. So he had to stay up. And so he'd be awake at three, four o'clock in the morning. And then he'd sit and start talking about how he was feeling, and ask us how we were feeling, and that sort of thing.

D.   He got far enough away from his own predicament to think about yours?

P.   Oh yes, he even sort of said to me that he wanted the funeral to be a party. And that he didn't want me to wear black. He said, I don't want people to wear black. I said, Well most of your friends wear black all the time anyway!

D.   Did his friends keep in touch with him?

P.   Certain ones did. There were some friends who were very good . . . There was Kate who used to come round a lot, and then there was another girl from Hale. They used to come out and say, Can I take Nick into Altrincham? You had to watch him because he'd lost his per . . .

K.   Peripheral vision.

P.   So he would walk off pavements and things like that. And he might have a fit while you were out. But she was able to cope with that, and they used to take him so far, and then she'd give me a ring when they were coming back, and I would go and meet them. And ones used to come out and take him for drinks, didn't they? And another one who, we'd actually banned him, or officially banned him from seeing him because together they were bad lads, sort of thing. But in fact when he was ill he used to come and sit with Nick. And I used to take Nick across to his house and she used to look after him. Because she said she'd banned hers from seeing Nick! They were just a bad influence on each other.

K.   I think they were, yes.

P.   So it was different people really, from different areas, coming to see him. But some people couldn't cope with coming to see him. I mean, at his twenty-first: they said that if he had a twenty-first it might kill him. But he wanted, you know: we invited everybody he wanted, so there was like people off The Green. All different generations really, of people. But we didn't know then, we wouldn't know until the day, whether we had this party or not. But it was fantastic, because everybody clubbed together and made all the food, and Herbie Hope said it didn't matter. So all the pressure was taken off me as well. I'd just buy some chicken legs, and bits and pieces. But everybody else did it. And up till six o'clock that night we didn't think it was going to go on. And he got up at six o'clock, and he stayed up all night. And he had a whale of a time. And it was smashing, because Herbie said I'll arrange a disco - because we didn't want a loud disco, because we knew the music and the flashing lights would have brought on the fits. And people came, and he really enjoyed it. A smashing time. They stayed up nearly all the night. So at least he did have that. And at the funeral Herbie was smashing, wasn't he? because we phoned him up. You don't know how many people are going to come back after a funeral. And we said, could you put us a bit of an awning out here? And he came, and he said Oh I'll put a big marquee up - as you know

D.   I remember. Yes.

P.   And I was worried a bit, about what it would cost us. Do you want tables? Do you want chairs? All this. And he said, Pat don't worry. This is my contribution for Nick. So it brought out the best in loads of people. From one person's illness. It brings out a lot of good in a lot of other people. He had people coming every week. On certain days different people used to come and help. And somebody would bring sandwiches, and somebody would come and take him out. It brought out a lot of goodness in a lot of people. The sort of people you hadn't seen before, or you'd been blind to before. It was an experience I wouldn't like to go through again, but it was an experience that sort of . . . I don't know.

D.   That was now almost six years ago. Nick himself was aware of the problems that were going to face you after he'd died. Can you tell us something about how the process went on, of picking up the threads again?

P.   Yes, well at first it was difficult. We were very wrapped up in what had just happened. But then, with the help of family and friends you pick up the pieces of your life, the things that you were doing before the illness had dominated your life. And you definitely needed the support of family and friends to do that. Its easy just to hide in your own four walls and wallow in your own grief, really. Once you do go out - and always the first time of meeting anybody was very difficult - but once you've made that first step of meeting people, and they've seen you again after it's happened, well then - life isn't easy - but it's easier to meet people again, and I found the more you mix with people the easier it is to continue with your life. So that's basically what I did. I was in a Barber's Shop chorus before Nick was ill, and friends kept in touch with me, and then three or four weeks after he died I went back to it.

D.   You went back to your old Barber's Shop chorus? Where is it?

P.   Well now it's based in Sharston. It was based in Gatley at that time. We rehearse once a week, we do competitions once or twice a year and sometimes a bit more. And we do what we call sing-outs, which is when people ask us to sing at different functions, or shopping centres . . .

D.   This is Barber's Shop, isn't it? Where did it originate?

P.   Well it originated in the States. It was originally men in barber shops, waiting to have their hair cut. Singing unaccompanied, four-part harmony. And I think it came over to this country, in a female form, about twenty five, thirty years ago. And there's now quite a lot of choruses. It's either male or female. You can mix with the odd song, but there's such a range of voices.

D.   You haven't caught up with Unisex barbers! How many parts would you have? Always four?

P.   It's always four-part harmony.

D.   So that's more or less the definition, is it? Four-part harmony, unaccompanied.

P.   Unaccompanied, yeah. Acapulco or something is the correct name.

D.   And what sort of numbers would be involved in a chorus?

P.   It can vary. A good quartet makes a fabulous sound. In the competition we were in last weekend the smallest chorus was about sixteen, the biggest chorus was about seventy six; but I've also seen a Swedish chorus with about a hundred and twenty in it. And the sound is amazing. And the sound of a men's chorus is fantastic. And you don't have to be able to read music to do it.

D.   What you need is a very good ear, I imagine.

P.   Not even necessarily a very good ear. The section leader will sing your part on a tape, and you just listen to that tape, you don't really need the music, you just listen to the tape.

D.   So you can take it home and get to know your part just by listening to the tape?

P.   Yes, you learn your part, and then you put them all together. I mean we learned one - obviously not to a good standard - last week, at chorus. There were about ten or twelve members who had actually done this song before - it's only about thirty lines long - and we split into sections for fifteen minutes, and we sang it over and over in sections, then we put it together. It got a reasonable sound.

D.   What sort of songs do you sing, or can it be anything under the sun?

P.   We have what we call barber shop arrangements. Some of them are pure barber shop songs, others are songs that have been arranged for barber shop singing: so you can sing anything from Beatles songs, or Nat King Cole songs, all sorts of different songs with barber shop arrangements. Some of them come from musicals like *Cats*, we've got barber shop arrangements for some of those songs. Then there are things like *New York, New York!* Because it's good if you're performing to the public, to have songs that they can recognise. You've got lots of different talents within the chorus, some people who are very musically minded, others who just enjoy singing. It brings people together. After the competition last week, our last rehearsal, we went and watched the video, got torn apart about what we'd done wrong: then we all went to the pub.

D.   A video of your performance? How excruciating!

P.   Exactly! Your chorus directors'll tell you where you went wrong, and what we've got to aim for for the next twelve months. And having said that we all went to the pub, had our supper there, and sang for the people in the pub! Like it or not!

D.   This was in Harrogate, did you say?

P.   Yes. The Conference Centre at Harrogate.

D.   A big thing.

P.   Oh, it is. There were two or three thousand people there, attending. Forty choruses. Quartet competition, of course.

D.   Thinking of the men's side and trying to imagine the sound, I'm immediately thinking of these Welsh male voice choirs: are they similar, or is that something quite different?

P.   No, it is similar. The arrangements are different. I think they can use music, where we don't stand with music, and we do silly moves, whereas the Welsh male voice choir stand and sing as a choir. Barber shop choruses actually - try and dance, almost. And do movements.

D.   So you do need to be seen, as well as heard.

P.   Yes. Well, it provides something for people to laugh at!

D.   With all this stress on the visual aspect, is it important what you are wearing?

P.   Oh yes, you all have to wear the same outfits.

D.   And a lot of care goes into the choice?

P.   Yes, that's right. Yes. We wear what they call the full stage outfit, which is usually glittery. We have long flowing purple skirts and purple glittery top, and your make-up is completely over the top, and you mustn't have any hair on your face, because your face has got to be seen for the expressions. And then you have what they call walk-outs, which is for when you're singing in a town centre, or the new Trafford Centre and things like that. If you're going anywhere. Each chorus has its own uniform.

D.   Where might we find you if we wanted to . . .

P.   Join?!

D.   No, no, no! If we wanted to watch you? Do you go busking?

P.   Well we're usually booked. We have agents in Manchester, and also we just phone up to, say, John Lewis towards Christmas, and say Can we have an evening - when they do have people like that there - and we go and spend two hours outside Marks and Spencers or John Lewis, and sing. This agent's got us a booking at the new Trafford Centre, bookings there before Christmas, one or two nights before Christmas. I know it's the last thing you want to be doing two nights before Christmas! We're taking our turkey and our sprouts with us! Yes we do that. And then if the masons are having a dinner, golf clubs, weddings. All sorts of different people ask you. Charity Shows. And we also occasionally put on our own shows as well.

D.   Gosh. And that's in Cheshire. I'd no idea there was anything as near here.

P.   And there's one in Lymm. We're based at Gatley. There's one in Stockport. And those are all the Ladies' ones. Preston. Men, there's one in Sale, there's one in Stockport. In this small locality. How it came about was when Laura used to live here. She used to do it in the States. So she went all over the place trying to find one here. Of course she joined one, and then she asked me to go along.

D.   So it was Laura who brought it to Ashley?

P.   Yes. Because otherwise I wouldn't have known about it. So that's provided, although it was an interest before, it's provided an escape, really. I'm the secretary of the club. It's quite time-consuming. We're always trying to get more members.

D.   And what does Kevin do with himself? Isn't he a diver?

P.   He used to be. He doesn't do it anymore, but he was very much involved in diving - at Macclesfield. He had been their equipment officer, training officer. He was chairman. Used to go off for weekends. We've got a brass porthole which he found off the Scilly Isles; a ringworm ointment jar, found that off the North East coast. It had come from India, Nineteenth Century.

D.   Oh, so you can actually find treasures?

P.   Yeah. And he brought a big cannon ball up one year. But to preserve it you have to keep it in water, and it disintegrated. The porthole was completely encrusted, and he cleaned it and it's a lovely porthole now. It provided an interest for him for twenty-odd years. But he's finding it cold now. So since then really he's not taken up any specific hobby. He's taken over my gardening a bit.

D.   Oh, that's nice.

P.   No it's not!

D.   Aren't you keen to have a labourer?

P.   No, no, no, because he's trying to organise me. He wants to scrap it and start again. He would like everything designed architecturally. Whereas I see a plant, buy it, and find a home for it.

D.   So I can see, in a year or two, this garden's going to be divided!

P.   It is. There'll be His and Hers! Definitely His and Hers. Even with plants, he's telling me what colours we should get. He used to say, Just lay green concrete down, whereas now he's into the planting, and what we should have here.

D.   So he's come on from green concrete! I've got a feeling this conversation's getting very unfair! Kevin's not here!

P.   And a thing like rugby, which at one time he was never interested in, he now takes an interest in rugby and he goes to the occasional rugby match, at Sale. Which at one time I would go on my own.

D.   You were interested in rugby? How did you get interested?

P.   My father played for Sale. So we went as children. We don't go regularly, but we go quite a lot. It's good sport, and you can get rid of a lot of emotional adrenalin. You can shout and scream, and it doesn't matter at a rugby match! Shout, and nobody minds! It's very good really for releasing emotion!

D.   There was a time when there was a lot of streaking, wasn't there, at rugby matches?

P.   In fact somebody did it at Sale Rugby Club last year.

D.   Do you understand that? Can you see that as a logical extension of the emotional release?

P.   I think it's people just having a dare.

D.   It's more that? So we can't look forward to mass streaking at rugby matches?

P.   I hope not!

Jean Bloodworth. 6 Egerton Moss

D.   So, Jean, how did you come to Ashley?

J.   I was divorced, and had to find a smaller place. I was looking, and I couldn't find anything at all. Anything at all. There was always something wrong with it. And just by chance, instead of going the main road, I came the back road home, via Ashley. And I noticed a *For Sale* sign. And I'd always loved these houses. And I got home, and I thought, I'll phone up the estate agent. And I couldn't remember exactly what the estate agent's name was. And funnily enough there was an advert on the television for estate agents, and I thought, That's it! So I phoned up the following morning. So I arranged to come and see it, and from the moment I stepped into this house, I knew it was right. Everything about the house was right. So that was it. That's how I came to be here.

D.   And you've been here now - how long?

J.   It must be thirteen or fourteen years.

D.   Mid-eighties? Yes. You were talking earlier on about your life as a dancer.

J.   Oh, that was long before I was married, and I was married for twenty-five years. But having once danced, I've always exercised.

D.   When did you start?

J.   Since my memory began. Can't remember a time when I didn't. I used to teach my fellow-pupils in my infant school, and charge them!

D.   That's one way of boosting your pocket money! And then from school, how did it develop?

J.   Well I went to dancing school, and then studied ballet. I went to Russia. Then went to a choreographic school. But when I came back my ex-husband was wanting me to get married, and so I got married.

D.   And then you said, at some stage, you went into Flamenco; from ballet to Flamenco.

J.   Yes, I did. Because, again, I've always loved dancing. And so I started Flamenco. There was a Dutch lady who advertised classes, and I went along to see her, and I was her only applicant. And she said, well she'd better wait till she could find somebody else. And eventually this other girl joined. But I happened to know a friend of mine who really was a superb dancer. She's English, but a superb dancer. And she was back from Spain. So I got in touch with her and asked if she would teach this other lady and myself. And we learned a lot from her, she was very very good. She and I went to Cordoba. And that was where I met Brian, who was on the guitar course. And we got on very well. His wife had just left him as my ex-husband had more or less left me. Neither of us were looking for anybody. But it was just one of those things. We . . . Like kindred spirits. You know? And then when we got back to England he sold his business down in Torquay, and moved up to Northwich. It's his base, really, he's got an art gallery there. And he played the Flamenco guitar for me when I was teaching.

D.   And where would you go, teaching?

J.   Anybody who'd ask me. We used to do workshops. In Lancaster, Chester, Handforth, Cheadle.

D.   Do most of you do it for your own pleasure, or do you do it with a view to finding somewhere to perform before an audience?

J.   When I used to teach, I taught performance. Because I cannot half-teach. I cannot for two hours have my ladies having a good time. For two hours they worked hard. And funnily enough a lot of people said to me that they loved coming to Flamenco classes because for two hours they thought of nothing else. And all their worries, all the hang-ups, never even entered into their heads for two hours. And they found it exceptionally good therapy.

D.   That's very interesting. And I'm wondering if it connects at all with what you were saying earlier on: tell me again what you were saying about English dancers, and the difficulty for them of really getting into their passionate feelings?

J.   Well I must repeat that I think English dancers are lovely. I really do. And they're so easy to teach. They're easy to teach, but what is difficult for them is to dance from the soul. They can dance physically, make the movements, make beautiful line. But the soul is missing. And it is the soul, in Flamenco, that makes Flamenco. It generates such an emotion for people watching. Many many times after we've danced people would say, You make me feel exhausted. Which is what Flamenco should do. Exhaust you both mentally and physically. And, you see, this is what I try and get the girls to do. And, bless their hearts, David, they do try. They really really try to give me what I want. But, as we were talking about the anger, I had to make them angry before they realised what anger meant!

D.   I wondered if actually expressing these emotions, or getting to be more free to be able to express these emotions: do you think that was part of the therapeutic effect?

J.   Oh yes. It's a wonderfully therapeutic . . . This is why I love schools who do drama. Because for children to be able to act out fear, excitement, loneliness: for them to be able to act these things out without having to bear the consequences, it's wonderful therapy.

D.   Going back to the Flamenco, you mentioned anger. Is there a lot of anger in it?

J.   You see, it's a gypsy art. You have a mixture of Saphardic Jewish, Gypsies, Indian - you get a lot of the music sounding very Oriental - and the Moors. Now all these were suppressed people in Spain. Consequently they had an anger within that could only be expressed in, I suppose, dumb insolence. And they could express themselves, and get rid of their anger, through their dancing. Because when they do what's known as the *Zapateado*, which is the rapid footwork, I say *Get angry with the floor, Get angry with it! Beat it, Beat it!* You know, To get this . . . *fire* into their dancing.

D.   That might explain . . . All these suppressed minorities. The other thing that I would have associated with Flamenco-style dancing, I think, is a certain defiance.

J.   Well yes, it is. Because you see with these suppressed minorities, the don of the Hacienda would say to a gypsy group, Come and entertain us. While they were drinking. And the gypsies would entertain them. And the gypsies would have these sort of inscrutible, half-closed eyes. And they would dance. And they would be insolent. They would be defiant. They would be *angry*.

D.   They could express all the feelings they had, at these people! At exactly the people they wanted to express it to!

J.   Exactly.

D.   And almost like your schoolchildren. They can do it without the consequences! It's a wonderful thing! I'd never thought of it like that. What a gift it is for the dancers, for those original dancers!

J.   Oh, yes. Oh yes: because when I see old movies of Carmen Amaya, who was a wonderful gypsy dancer, she's got these half-closed eyes, and this real - insolence. And arrogance. And the very walk, you know . . . I teach my dancers to walk as if they owned the place. It's a question of emanating a charisma. And it's the way you walk, and the way you sit. And you can do this, you can actually stand and do nothing: but it's emanating from you. Providing it's from the soul.

D.   I'd absolutely no idea of the power of all this. I mean, it's almost like Gandhi.

J.   Yes. Once you get hooked on Flamenco, that's it. I've never had a floating class. I had my girls with me for a long time. And I got a letter the other day from one of my students, who was at Cambridge and she's now teaching in London, to say she's teaching her sixth formers to Flamenco. It's lovely for me to find that these girls are getting the same satisfaction I got from it. When I used to sit and watch them dancing, I got such a satisfaction out of it. To think that they were really dancing, and that they were really dancing with the soul. And they were really enjoying it. Let me show you a lovely, lovely Christmas present from one of my dancers who had arthritis. Now I don't care whether they are crippled with arthritis, or fat. They are there to learn, and they get my attention. And they will get the same attention as the other dancers. Well, she gave me this present, and she said You can open it if you want to. I said, No no no, it's going to be under the tree and I shall open it at Christmas Day. I expected something like a box, something like that. And that is what she produced. Isn't that wonderful? I was so thrilled. I was so thrilled, I said to Brian, You know, that's one of the best Christmas presents I've ever had.

D.   Now that's an oil painting, isn't it? An oil painting of a Flamenco dancer -

J.   It's me!

D.   It is you! I thought it must be you. With Brian in the background.

J.   Well, it's not quite Brian. But I was so pleased.

D.   Had she painted that herself?

J.   No. She had got a friend of hers to paint it. I didn't know she'd even got a photograph. And she'd sent this photograph to the artist, who lives in Cornwall, and she's never ever done a portrait before, she usually paints still life, and she didn't want to do it, but Brenda said, Oh please do it, it would be a lovely present for my teacher. And she did. And I said to Brian, it's just caught that angry expression! So I've asked her if she will do one of Brian, for his birthday.

D.   What a lovely present.

J.   Isn't it a beautiful present? It's lovely.

D.   Well, thank you very much for all that. That really was lovely to hear about.

Bob and Kath Salt. Ashley Barn

B.   We lived in a house in Lymm. A semi. For twelve years. We wanted to move home. I didn't want to live in another box. We kept looking and looking. And I was driving down this road one night, and saw a sign on the end of the old barn. So we applied - what, twenty-one years ago, isn't it? - It was derelict, falling down, in terrible condition. We applied to Tatton Estate. There was a long list of applicants. Nothing happened for a long time, did it? About six or seven months.

K.   You had two interviews.

B.   Two interviews with them, yes. Because really they wanted to know if you'd got the funding to do it. Because they weren't going to give you any money. And also whether you had the imagination.

K.   And then of course it was conservation property. A listed building. Which we believe goes back, as far as we know, to 1552. The beams in it now are the original beams.

D.   Had you during this process had to submit plans and things?

K.   You had a friend, didn't you, that was in the restoring -

B.   Restoring buildings.

K.   He'd done the Store House at Peover, and he was living in that, this friend of ours, Roger Reeves. And he had done some very good renovations in Knutsford. He's won awards, hadn't he?

B.   Little rows of terraced houses in Knutsford, completely renovated, up to modern standards. But kept the character.

K.   So he gave you some plans and, er,

B.   There was a set of plans originally with the barn. Because Salford University Building and Engineering Department had used them as a, an exercise for students, on what they'd do with it if they could get hold of it. And actually we were given those plans, by Meller Braggins. And also we got some more from the university, the original drawings. Which gave us quite a lot of ideas.

K.   And really we couldn't change it very much at that stage, with it being a conservation property.

B.   We were limited as to what we could do. Like, we could only put on this end what had originally been knocked off at the other end. Now the other end of this barn used to go to the white line in the middle of the road. And this grass verge was the road. Because there was the cottages opposite. But eventually we started on it, and we were quoted, I think, twenty-one grand. Something like that. And that included main drainage, garden, garage,

K.   And then we had the front of the house bowing too much. So we had to have all that front taken out, and replace some of the oaks. The timbers. At the front. That cost two or three thousand.

B.   The front, the extra front, cost six K. Twenty-one years ago that was a lot of money.

D.   How long was it from start to finish?

B.   You may not believe that: it took us six months.

K.   Well we didn't do it, did we?

B.   A lot of money, and six months.

K.   So with all this extra money being spent, we ended up with having no landscaping, and no garage.

B.   We cut back inside, as well.

K.   So we had to battle along, and do the rest ourselves, after we'd moved in. So we were . . . You built the garage, didn't you. The first garage.

B.   Yes, that might be interesting. We had a major fire.

K.   An arson. An arson attack on the garage. Completely burnt out.

B.   Ten years ago. Nine years ago. Five o'clock in the morning.

K.   February, it was.

B.   Six cars in there. Five. Five cars, yeah.

K.   Unfortunately we had rather a lot of cars here at the time.

B.   Because I had a rep's car, that had just left. I had two classics. My car. Kath's car.

K.   That's it, five.

B.   Woken at five o'clock in the morning, thought it was heavy snow. It was bits dropping off the roof! Off the garage onto the roof here.

K.   Flames, flames, a terrific amount.

B.   Cars, the whole lot went.

K.   It was lucky it was a long way from the house. And the fire brigade came out of course.

B.   And the police. Very suspicious.

K.   They were very suspicious of Bob.

B.   *Have you got any money through this?*

K.   And *Why was I so calm?*

B.   Yeah, why was she so calm?

K.   But it was a terrible thing, I was frightened for months afterwards. Somebody torched the house. Two or three nights later, in the middle of the night, Bob heard this noise again. And he saw this orange sort of flame, or as he thought, or something. Didn't you? We got out of bed to look through the window, and he saw the fire engine, didn't you?

B.   Somebody had set fire to the Robinsons' garage.

K.   At Midways.

B.   So that made them less suspicious of me.

K.   So somebody had tried to set theirs on fire, you see, and of course with the fields at the back they could escape so easily. But the Major, who was living there at the time

B.   Heard a noise.

K.   He heard a noise, and of course they'd known about our fire two or three days before, so he heard the noise, and he's got a little Westie as well, the Westie barked, and then they got away. And they managed to save the garages, because they were really old then. And of course they've had them rebuilt since. So they did think then that it was definitely an arson attack.

B.   They didn't ask me where I was at the time! I could have been down the road setting fire to it!

D.   Well, would've made sense! Did they ever find out what it was about at all?

K.   I don't think they ever came back to us.

B.   They picked some - no they never came back to see us at all - they picked somebody up about eighteen, twelve months later, something like that. In Rostherne. Setting fire to a farm stable.

K.   There'd been one or two attacks in Rostherne. Before ours, actually.

D.   So it did look like someone who was simply, sort of pyromania.

K.   Yeah. But we never got any satisfaction, did we?

D.   Well it must be some satisfaction to know that. I mean, if it happened to me I'd be desperately wanting to know who'd done it - and why!

K.   Well we never found out who'd done it. And it was about three months before I settled. At night, because I was always worried. I wanted to screw the letterbox tight, in case somebody might pop something through the door. It's frightening to think people are wandering about . . . But it's gone very busy. From twenty-one years ago it was really a sleepy backwater, Ashley, and now it's really very busy. This road is very busy. A lot of traffic.

B.   Ashley's changed a lot though in twenty-one years.

D.   What are the main changes?

B.   Noise. Traffic noise. Airport.

K.   We get - oh, it doesn't bother us too much, but there is a marvellous increase in air traffic.

B.   The airport's not that much of a problem

K.   But road traffic's very heavy.

D.   We're talking about late seventies, seventy-six, seventy-seven you came, I suppose? And it was quite sleepy then?

B.   Compared with now. It's still sleepy now compared with lots of places.

K.   We're disappointed that the garage didn't continue to sell petrol, I suppose. Rather than be just a car salesroom. And of course they really want to build on that land. Do away with the garage.

B.   The planning application was rejected. But I think they're determined enough to have another go.

K.   We're against it, really.

B.   I'm not against it, I'm not against it on the principle that there's houses going to be built on there. I'm against it on the principle that if you allow more buildings to go on in Ashley, the next thing you'll find is that we'll be joined to Mobberley and Hale. Because they'll find "There! that piece of land there's vacant, let's build something on it!".

K.   There's just no stopping once they start. So it'll just end up a very big . . .

B.   I'd say, if that piece of land here on the corner went -

D.   You've got the whole thing filled in.

B.   Yep. That's an assumption.

D.   Well that's interesting, because it's the sort of assumption that needs to be made if anyone wants to stop it happening. Somebody was telling me, I was talking to earlier on, who'd come from Sale I think, and was telling the story of the building around Ashton on Mersey.

K.   Well I come from Ashton on Mersey. I was born there. My mother was born there.

D.   And they were all thinking they were perfectly safe there, with Green Belts and so on . . .

K.   A little tiny village, Ashton on Mersey was when I was a girl. Even more so when my mother was. A hundred years ago. You can't stop progress altogether, but . . . This is a nice little place to live. It is so convenient to get into Manchester or - anywhere, really. There's plenty of dog-walking places. It's very handy if you've got animals, obviously. And of course we get the Hunt here occasionally. Twice a year, is it, or once a year? At the pub.

B.   The Drag Hunt. There's been major efforts to change that pub.

K.   It has changed from what it was.

B.   But there was an application to try to make it into a kind of Beefeater type of place.

K.   With a big restaurant on the side.

B.   And there was massive opposition to it. And eventually they didn't get the planning application through. Because the pub - I mean, I use it, is a very important part of the character of the village. And to turn it into nothing but a food house would destroy it. It's not so bad now, it's half ours and half. You can still go and have a drink in there. The reason they got it in check was the parking places. They hadn't got enough parking spaces for the number of customers, and the extra staff. Because if you get extra staff they all need parking places.

K.   We don't have any problem with the pub really, do we? There used to be a lot of parking on the road, on the grass verge, but we don't have any problem with it really. The living accomodation for them is quite small, isn't it, but it's quite a nice little pub. It's very popular.

D.   Well it's quite nice to hear that. I was just wondering how many people who live as near to a pub as this would be able to say the same thing. Because most pubs must get noisy at turning-out time.

K.   We're not. No. It doesn't bother us too much.

B.   Of course they take them all out in wheelbarrows! I think it's a nice place to live.

Roderick Carus. Midways

D.   Why Ashley? How did it all come about?

R.   It came about because, when we first got married in 1972, we lived in Didsbury. And our first two children were born in Didsbury, Alexander, now training to be a solicitor, and Genevieve, who recently married and you've just been talking to. And we moved to Lymm in 1977, and lived there very happily for ten years. Again for similar reasons, there now being four children, Kristina and Dominic being numbers three and four, the house in Lymm was getting to be a little bit cramped. There were no suitable houses in Lymm for us at that time, and as all four children were prospectively moving towards secondary education, we needed to consider where that should take place. And like many parents we thought long and hard about it: and I don't believe ultimately the fact that we selected Catholic schools was necessarily to do with religion although we are a practising Catholic family.

D.   They were good schools.

R.   Loretto and St Ambrose College appealed because they were good schools, they had a good sound ethos, which may or may not have derived from their Catholicism, certainly it derived in part from their Christianity. So ten years after moving into Lymm we moved into Hale, in 1987. It was quite a grand house on Park Road, but I never settled there: not so much the house, but there was a feeling in the area, an ambiance in its various social structures which I disliked: I do not want my children getting involved in the sort of throw-away materialistic society which seemed to be prevalent there. I didn't want them to expect to be bought a brand new Golf GTi when they were twenty one, as of right. I thought the expectations in Hale were unhealthy. And consequently I was looking for a move, almost from the time we got there. In 1990 I took Silk which, if the gamble pays off, does provide you with a greater income. And thankfully in my case it did. So we had a wider range of properties to look at.
    In the meantime, since we'd lived in Hale, we had from time to time come out to The Greyhound, as a break from urbanisation and to get a taste of the countryside, which we'd all missed. And we enjoyed the simplicity of The Greyhound, which was then an unconverted pub, as you know. We enjoyed the lack of affectation in the place, and in the people. They were good honest people, from various walks of life. And we got to know quite a few of them. We got to know in particular Jean Dolan, who was nearly always behind the bar. She got to know that I was looking for a place in the country. I'd seen a number of places, I'd seen a farm down in Warburton and so forth. She it was, curiously enough, in or about September 1992, who said, You know the house I've mentioned to you in Ashley, Midways? It's to be placed on the market. That very afternoon Hilary went to Meller Braggins and got the details, although they hadn't been published yet. When I returned from court that evening she showed me them. I was immediately impressed. As always with a place of this size, we could see things we wanted to do to it; but in essence it was plain that the place was wonderfully preserved. Nothing had been done to spoil it. All the old doors were in, the skirting boards and fireplaces, all the things that really matter in an oldish place, they were all here. And so it was a place I would obviously be thrilled to acquire. Then what happened was that we'd almost come to terms in October when the Manchester Airport authority announced in the *Manchester Evening News* that their second runway was now going to be sited on a line between Ashley and Rostherne. I made urgent enquiries as

to precisely where, and it was very close indeed. So I had to get in touch with Meller Braggins, I didn't deal directly with Peter Robinson about it because that's what estate agents are for, and I said I'm sorry, I'm just terrified of this second runway going ahead. However, when the immediate plans to develop towards Rostherne were shelved, I went ahead and so we moved in on June 11th, 1993.

D.   So for, what, four months you thought it was all off?

R.   Something like that, perhaps three months.

D.   Tell me, how did you find it, moving in here?

R.   It was absolutely tremendous. Very exciting. We moved in, and almost immediately took all the pictures and the mirrors and everything out from their packing cases and dressed the walls with them. And then we had a glorious house-warming. Hadn't done a thing to it, and that was marvellous. People would come along and make suggestions: criticise or congratulate, or whatever, you know. And then everybody settled in wonderfully well. Really no misgivings at all. But then, having moved in, for the first year almost without remission we had builders in. They did it top to bottom. But everybody, all the family, really loved it. And the more I got to know of the property, two things struck me: the quality of the building is really very high; and secondly, as I said before, nothing had been changed. Odd things had been done to it, but they hadn't diminished its value. For example, much had been painted. This fireplace you're looking at was painted. All the upstairs fireplaces had been boarded off. So you'd no idea really what was there. But having said that, it's easy enough to remove boarding. It's laborious, but perfectly straightforward. And what we'd got underneath was a perfectly preserved 1885 example of Arts and Craft architecture. We felt we were bringing the house back to life, in a way. We felt we were taking the shrouds off it, as we peeled away the paint. And we were thrilled with everything we did.

D.   Every new room was a discovery.

R.   Absolutely. We made some additions; we replaced, for example, the wood fire surround in the drawing room: we bought a white marble Italian period fireplace for there. It had been a wooden one. We probably made a mistake. We saw it, knew it was wood, heavily painted, and we got rid of it. It was only later, once we had taken the paint off similar surrounds, that we realised it was a very high quality oak. Perhaps it was nevertheless not a bad thing to replace it. The drawing room is, after all a principal room. In the dining room the original fireplace had been removed, and replaced by a brickette one painted blue. That was fashionable in the Thirties but it didn't work for us. So we took that out and replaced it with a fireplace of the same period as the house. So that and other things we did, for example we put a billiard table in the billiard room.

D.   Oh, good! That was one of the things I found most difficult about this house, to have a billiard room without a billiard table!

R.   Well, we put the billiard table back, a period billiard table, and some chandeliers in there too. We did quite a lot upstairs because, as you can imagine, it was a bit short of sanitary and other plumbing. What we did was to make every bedroom en suite. We've got six bedrooms, plus a lounge upstairs.

D.   So your first year or two here, all the attention must have been focused on all this?

R.   Wallpapers and carpets, wallpaper designs, matching curtains, plumbing, extensive plumbing, acquiring fresh or replacement cast-iron radiators, putting extra ones in and so forth. But notwithstanding all that, we were really just replacing the icing on the cake. The cake itself was in first class condition.

D.   So that was your first concern, but I'm just wondering how you felt in relation to the rest of the village? It must have been an enormous change, coming out of a semi-anonymous dwelling in Hale into what I suppose you'd have to describe as the most prominent house in the village?

R.   Yes, I think that is right. I think from time to time you felt you were under scrutiny. But by virtue of the fact that for at least three years we have been coming out to The Greyhound together from time to time, we really knew quite a lot of people. And the number of people who helped in those early stages, with one thing and another, we really didn't feel like strangers in Ashley. And of course the fact that I was the prospective purchaser was known for at least four or five months before completion. So Ashley had about six months to get used to the idea!

D.   You both did, in fact!

R.   We both did. So when we moved in there was scarcely a ripple.

D.   At what stage did you become aware of Midways having been the venue of the Garden Party?

R.   I was aware of that at an early stage.

D.   Presumably, you had to decide what your attitude to that was going to be?

R.   Yes, but fortunately the decision was taken from me, because by that stage at any rate the Fête Committee had decided that it worked better at the school than it had done here. Largely because they wanted to combine the fête proper with the Discotheque. They wanted to have double use out of the marquee. It made commercial sense. And they knew it wouldn't be right to have a marquee arrangement here. There isn't the room. And so I was teased about it, but in point of fact they'd made their mind up quite genuinely, that it was better all round to have it up the road there, in the school field, and then they could have the disco going till two in the morning if they wanted to.

D.   So the question in the end never arose? Because the Fête Committee had already decided they preferred it down there?

R.   It had already been decided. Just to make it absolutely plain, we became aware of course that the fête had been held here for a long time, and indeed that the house had been associated with the fête for a long time in people's minds. We gathered that there'd been an arson attack on the garages at the bottom, during which much of the fête property had been destroyed. For whatever reason, it was then decided to relocate the fête, and probably at that time it was thought to be merely on a temporary basis. At any rate by the time we moved in, in June 1993, the fête had for some time been held at the school, and it was made absolutely plain to us that the new venue was proving to be commercially more viable, particularly because of the discotheque. Consequently no approach either formal or informal was made to us to permit the use of the grounds for that purpose. I would say that had such an approach been formally made they would have had my permission. Because I was really quite proud of the association of Midways with such an important village occasion and certainly, had it been operating at the time I took over Midways, I wouldn't have dreamed of stopping it.

D.   Well thank you very much for clarifying that. While we're on the garden, it must be pretty substantial: how much have you got here?

R.   Well the land in total has been estimated by Meller Braggins, at the time of the sale, to be slightly in excess of four-and-a-half acres. However within that there are two rough paddocks. If one takes those from the total, the garden itself, including the tennis courts, comprises I should think two acres, or thereabouts. The cultivation of it is still quite a significant item.

D.   Is that a pleasure?

R.   I am a very keen gardener. I don't say that I'm particularly gifted, or for that matter particularly knowledgeable, but I enjoy it. I think part of the enjoyment arises from the fact that it is such a contrast to my everyday career, which basically is a sedentary life with my nose in books of one sort or another, and it is a contrast and a pleasure to get out into the garden and do something physical.

D.   And does Hilary do a bit as well?

R.   Hilary admires my handiwork! And picks the flowers. But we also grow vegetables, we've got quite a successful little market garden there, and a cold frame and greenhouse. And so the usual stuff comes out profusely - peas, beans, potatoes, lettuce and all the salad stuff. There's also a sizeable asparagus bed. Good raspberries amd rhubarb. You can sit down most Sundays and claim the vegetables are from Midways!

D.   Are ours!

R.   Are ours, yes!

D.   Now who have you got here of the younger generation? Genevieve's gone off.

R.   Genevieve lives down Castle Mill Lane, as you are aware. Alex has got himself a house on Bold Street, Hale, a very popular first house location. Kristina is at Leeds University, but only in her first year. If Dominic is successful he'll go in October. So we will have the two younger ones here, almost certainly, for the next four years. And who knows for how long after that? But obviously in the medium term we will find the house too large and we would be looking for a smaller property, preferably in Ashley, but such properties are rare. But here is an interesting aside. When I bought the house I was invited to sign a covenant against developing the paddocks, which I refused to do although then I had no plans to develop. But within the next five years

I will be looking at it. I'll be looking at what the village wants in this regard. I've already spoken informally to Peter Wright about it, just to see what the attitude of the Parish Council would be. I broached that with him some time ago, inspired in part by the plight of the school, being aware that the church could do with more people and that without an influx it may be under some threat, I do not know; but certainly being aware that the post office would benefit and that there may be an argument for saying that the village would be more viable if we could bring ten or so families into it. Particularly if you aimed the development at the younger family: to feed the school and to keep the place ticking over. And so I privately mentioned that to Peter Wright, and I think perhaps Pete Jackson, just for them to think about in the long term, and see where it would slot in.

D.   By Jove, that's a good bit of news! I tend to ask people about their hopes and fears for the future, and there's an extraordinary sort of ambivalence: people say No change! at any suggestion of building. But then they say, in the next breath, all the considerations that you've just mentioned about sustaining the basic pillars of the community. And then, what seems to come out of it at the end and attract almost universal lip service, is this magic term Affordable Housing. "if we could only get some Affordable Housing . . ." I should think everyone would be happy, and go for it.

R.   I can appreciate that.

D.   But that has got stuck, as far as I've been able to understand, on the practicality of it - that you can't expect anyone to let go of any land for less than the most they could get for it. And that would mean putting in the sort of development that the garage wanted. Somebody said to me that if they'd been willing to build twice the number of homes at half the price the council would have been quite happy with it, but they weren't interested. I should have thought that this is exactly what the village wanted - about ten first-time buyers.

R.   Well I only say that because that was the message I was getting back. What they don't want are bijou executive homes, where nobody's going to spend any time in the village, nobody's going to send their children to be educated in the village. And so my attitude really has been, as a first step, I would like to present the sort of scheme that satisfies the needs of the village. That might have to be a mixed development, perhaps - two executive homes, and eight or nine cottagey types. If this came off we could move into one ourselves.

D.   Well that's very very exciting, to know that there's anything on the horizon at all. It's the first glimmer of any hope that I've heard of.

R.   Well you can imagine - I think I can imagine - that a small estate, this side of the road, would make quite a compact village entity. The trouble, I believe, is that you've got a much better chance of getting planning permission the other side of Cow Lane, running down to the railway track.

D.   Between the railway track and Cow Lane? I wonder why?

R.   That's the County's planning structure. This side is Green Belt. But it seems to be the case that the government forecast of housing requirements is going to encourage some limited building in Green Belt land. The point is, and I'm not an expert, that Bob Salt has got the Barn as a residence - and that was a change of use - then you've got my front paddock opposite The Green, and then you've got the big houses running towards the motorway: it's almost an in-fill. It's almost a corridor development. And when all's said and done, the front paddock's neither use nor ornament. It's not an enjoyable amenity for the village. There's no one looking over it. Its development would not be destroying valuable parkland. And Midways itself would be unaffected if there was a decent-sized hedge just beyond the two beech trees. It's quite an interesting proposition.

D.   Well it will be very interesting to watch what happens.

Betty Don. Oak House, Cow Lane

D.   Betty, could you say how you came to be living in Ashley. When did you come?

B.   We came in 1971. I can't remember what time of year it was. That was because my husband was so ill, and our house was so big, and the children had all got married and gone away. So we were sort of rattling about in rather a large house. It took us a long time to find a house. We went everywhere you could think of. And then suddenly we saw this, and we asked Stuart Murray about it. And they said, well just wait a bit, I think it's coming up for sale. So then - I've forgotten who it belonged to - anyway, we came and we liked it, even though the decorations weren't quite what we wanted, we liked it very much, and from then on we came. And then after we got here, of course my husband who was ill got worse. But he was very happy sitting up in the window of the bedroom, watching people go by, and people would wave to him you know, and we did have visitors and things like that. Mrs Harris for instance, and Mr Harris. And from then on he was ill. And doctor friends used to come and see him.

D.   Where did you come from?

B.   Hale Barns.

D.   Your husband had been a doctor before he retired?

B.   Yes. He was a Physician. Consultant Physician. He was born in Jamaica and I think he came to Manchester about 1930, from Sheffield. Before that he'd been to Aberdeen University. And he was on, first of all the Salford Royal, which has gone now, hasn't it? Then he was on at Manchester Royal Infirmary. And he was in John Street. And then of course the PPH came, didn't it, the Private Patients' Home, and he did a lot there. In fact when he was so ill, at one time he had to go in for a transfusion, and they were all very pleased to see him, which was rather nice.

     I think he enjoyed his stay here, because it was nice and he had a nice garden, though he couldn't get out but he could see it. He used to sit at the window and watch me mowing the lawn, and things like that. We gradually got to know the people in Ashley, who were all very kind and nice. In fact I think it's a lovely, happy kind of neighbourhood. I've enjoyed our time here, it's been nice.

D.   He enjoyed looking at the garden: and, just looking out of these windows, I'm not at all surprised! Is the garden your special -

B.   Well, I'm very fond of the garden. In Hale Barns we had a much bigger garden, with a little wood and things like that, and of course he never had much time for the garden. He used to like mowing the lawn, that was about the only thing he liked doing. So he never had much time. But he did enjoy looking at it. And of course when he came here he wasn't fit enough to do any of those sort of things, but he used to watch me through the window when I was doing that. And lots of friends, his medical friends, used to pop in and see him. So I think, I mean he was only here from '71 to '73, a short time. But lots of his friends used to come and see him. That was nice.

D.   I suppose it was nice for them, as it's so near, that you hadn't moved further.

B.   That's right. We did look at places in Prestbury, but we didn't like them. So I'm glad we came to Ashley because we had a very happy time here except for losing my husband, that was the only thing.

D.　And that's a long time ago now.

B.　'73. Yes, it is a long time.

D.　What have you been doing since then? It must have made a terrific change to your life?

B.　Well, I felt quite lost, really. You don't know what to do. But some friends of mine worked for the C.A.B., the Citizens' Advice Bureau, and they said Why don't you try that? So I did. And we were in Oxford Road at that time. Do you remember? Opposite the greengrocer's, which isn't there now. And I really enjoy that. You see, I suppose you have your own troubles, but thinking about other people's troubles helps you in the end, doesn't it? So I really enjoy that. And then we moved to the Town Hall. That was a bit posher. But it was still very nice, and we used to have sort of: a solicitor used to come in, every Thursday evening I think it was, and anybody who wanted to see a solicitor would come and see him and then he would advise them what to do.

D.　How about the rest of your family. How many children did you have?

B.　I had two girls, Diana and Susan. Diana was born before the war, 1936 I think, and then Susan was born during the war. My husband of course was in the army, and he was in West Africa and North Africa and Italy. In fact there used to be a thing where you weren't allowed to stay abroad more than four years. Something like that. So he did four years abroad. So it was quite a thing, not to see your husband all that time. And of course he didn't see the children growing up. I mean, Diana was, what . . . she'd have been about nine, wouldn't she, when he came back.

D.　And I suppose, as far as Diana was concerned, this was a stranger coming in.

B.　Yes, that's quite true. And Susan had never seen him.

D.　She'd never seen him at all?

B.　She'd never seen him, until she was two years old.

D.　That must have been very difficult.

B.　It was difficult. And I felt sorry in a way, because you can't make children sort of take to people, can you? And so they used to, sort of . . . I saw them watching him, you know what I mean? Being quite polite, not exactly staring, but watching him. Yes, it was sad really. On the other hand . . .

D.　How did it develop? Did they get used to each other?

B.　Yes. In the end we had our first holiday. We went to Prestatyn for a fortnight, that was our first holiday we had after the war, and I think then they really got to know him.

D.   So now of course your daughters have been married for ages, and you must have grandchildren?

B.   Yes. I've got four grandchildren. James is Susan's son, she just had the one boy. James is in London. He's got a job in London, has a flat in London. He's now twenty seven. Tall fellow, he's taller than his father - six foot two, I think, something like that -. Anyway he's very happy in London.
    Now then Diana had three children. She had Krista, the eldest girl, and Jacki - whose name is Jacki not Jacqueline. Krista and Jacki live quite near here. One lives in North Road, and the other one lives in Paddock Hill. So I see those quite often. And then there is Paul, Diana's youngest, he's in the RAF. He's married and has two children.

D.   One of them is an artist, isn't she?

B.   Jacki. But she found she couldn't make her living being an artist. When you go out and look in the hall, there are two of her paintings there, she's a very good artist, and she has done - she used to paint people's pets, their children and things like that. But for the hours it took her to do a painting, it didn't pay her. So then she went to Didsbury College and she took a teaching class in art. And she made a great success of that, she's at Beech Hall School, I don't know if you know it, in Macclesfield. She teaches there. And she has Hannah, she's the eldest child, she's coming up to fifteen. She's also very good at art. And Rhiannon. She's also, she's seven. She's quite good at art as well. But it's a pity you can't make your living at it, isn't it? And they have a boat. Down in Wales, Pwllheli I think. They do a lot of sailing in the summer, and that sort of thing. And the story goes that, when Hannah was much smaller, six I think, they were on the boat, but in dock. They had two dogs, and they were in a dinghy, tied to the boat. And Hannah, being a bit mischievous, was taking the rope off where it was tied, and putting it back again and taking it off and putting it back, you know how children do -

D.   Oh, oh, oh! I can see what's coming!

B.   And the rope fell in the water. Well. She didn't tell anybody you see. I mean, she was too ashamed of herself. Anyway some friends of theirs were sailing into the Bay. And they met the dogs sailing out! You'd hardly credit that, would you? So they turned round, and towed the dogs back in again. Hannah has never been allowed to forget that one! Now she's quite a serious little person.
    One day, you know, when the policeman lived opposite, and I was in Switzerland I think, and the family was looking after the house. And so was the policeman. Well one day he saw this person coming in with her husband, and taking out pictures. So he came across to enquire. And she said, Oh I'm allowed to do this. I'm Grannie's grandchild! So he says, Yes, but what are you taking out? So she said, Oh I've got an exhibition of my paintings at the library. So Grannie's got most of my paintings, so they were taking the paintings out. Rather amusing, he thought they were pinching things!

D.   Well it's nice to know you're being so well guarded!

B.   Nice to know, wasn't it? Yes, that's right.

D.   It sounds as if the family is scattered far and wide. Do you ever get enormous reunions?

B.   We had a big get-together for my 90th birthday in January, 2001. All the family came. There were eighteen of us. We went to The Roebuck in Mobberley and had a lovely lunch, and cake and champagne.

D.   So you had four generations?

B.   We did, really, I hadn't thought about that. Yes. It was lovely to see them all. And none of them, I must say, was shy. So that was nice. Including the smaller people.

Jim and Jane Nicholson. Outwood, Cow Lane

D.   Jim, what was it like for you coming into this inheritance when your grand-mother died?

Jim. It was something that I was partly expecting, because I'd recently moved to the area, and I was living with my grandmother in her flat briefly. Then I moved up to this flat, while she was still alive. And it was Eileen Mason who actually - my grandmother was very ill downstairs, and she came to say she was very ill. And of course she was taken to hospital where she unfortunately passed away. And then the decision was, What to do with the house, which is a high maintenance place. So it's whether you want to sell it or keep it, and I was living in the area and looking for a property around here. Quite a few people who've been tenants here have wanted to stay in Ashley, but ended up moving to somewhere like Rostherne or Mobberley. So we felt it was a good location, and it's part of the village.

D.   So when did you move here? Were you always fairly local?

Jim. I was born in Altrincham. And then my parents went down south when I was six months old, and I came back about seven years ago. When I came back to the area I lived briefly in Hale, because the flats were busy. Then I moved in with my grand-mother for a while, and then I came here.

D.   And what do you do? Your day job, as it were?

Jim. I'm a Pochin's Designer Build director, a North West development contractor.

D.   And what sort of things do they do?

Jim. Schools, hospitals, industrial units. I do student accommodation in Manchester, the university.

D.   And presumably that means you've got sites all over the region?

Jim. Yes. Lancaster to Birmingham, and then across to Anglesey and over to the Pennines. But it's all within striking distance from here. It's very central here.

D.   Yes. Perfect. So, getting back to this, you decided not to sell, and to make it your home. Did you have to do a lot then, to make the rest of it as you wanted it? I think you mentioned high maintenance?

Jim. The problem with Victorian properties like this, the roof is full of valleys and hips, the decor outside is quite high maintenance; windows are timber and high main-tenance; there's no double glazing. People these days want double glazing and don't cope with the condensation which you do get in this type of property. No one has real fires, which used to dry the place out. So these older houses have been designed with a different way of living in mind. Nowadays everyone likes to have all the windows shut, heating on, and to walk round in a tea shirt and a pair of shorts. But of course life wasn't like that then. It was a jumper and a proper fire. These flats are there, and they were probably quite a high standard in their time, when they started, in the late fifties, sixties.

J.   I think it would be done quite differently now, because there's quite a lot of wasted space. It gives it character, but there's lots of nooks and crannies, up and down, and steps round the corner.

Jim.   But it does provide affordable housing, which is very much on the parish council's agenda. Whatever affordable housing is, I don't know how that's defined. On The Green there's a lot of housing which isn't in the top bracket, as you get in Hale and Bowdon, and that would be arguably affordable. I think the proportion of affordable to the higher bracket stuff is relatively high, actually.

D.   Actually it probably is. I think when they talk about it, it seems to me going round, because I hear a lot of this sort of language, I think people are referring to what they'd like to see in any further development. Like for instance The Smithy had plans for houses: they were not affordable!

Jim.   That's what knocked it back, wasn't it? Personally I think they should have let them go ahead with it. I don't think the garage now serves a function in the village. When it was a petrol station and a small shop I think it was a good service facility, but now it's just a car showroom, totally out of keeping. I think it's a blight, and I think they should have let it be developed as housing.

D.   Anyway, you were here for some time, and then suddenly Eileen Mason's house came on the market. It was interesting to see you take that.

Jim.   Yes, it - there was no intention to make it into a single complex. We were maintaining this property; next door came up, and at the time I was looking for somewhere to find myself to live, and I bought that. And then once I'd got it I just thought, well: it was a lot of money to put it back into the state it was, and the only affordable way of doing that was to put it into flats, with a view to maybe in the future putting it back to one dwelling. So, as I was staying here, I thought, Hang on, why move over there? I may as well stay here, get some income, pay off the mortgage if you like. And then, if I wanted to, I could move back into it. The fact that these have come into one at the front was because of the planning, with road access. I would have loved to have had access onto the road next door, but when I spoke to Cheshire Highways, the problem is that it's an unrestricted road here, even though it's a village street, technically you can drive at sixty even though it's irresponsible to. They hare round that corner. I've always thought it would be quite nice to park an old car on the side of the road there, and they'd all have to slow down! I thought about that, and I thought, No, if someone came round and hit it and hurt themselves I'd feel awfully guilty.

D.   And your turnover: do tenants come and go?

Jim.   Yes. Tim and Michelle Burgess were in the groundfloor flat for four or five years, but they've now moved to Rostherne. Tim was Chief Inspector at the airport.

D.   So they would have been someone who was looking for somewhere in Ashley?

Jim.   They were looking for a long time. And in the end Tatton Estate came up with one of their properties. He was an interesting chap of course, and with the protest going on at the airport when the runway was to be built, he was the officer in charge. He actually said to me that. Just in case, so that I was aware, if the protesters came here he would move if there was a problem, which I thought was rather decent of him. I had visions of coming back here and finding all these people up in the trees! Swampy. But it didn't happen, and as I say Tim's moved on, but when he was here he was quite active in the village. Jane and Colin Harvey from upstairs, they were there for about twelve months. Colin arrived, and in the time they were here they got married, and now they've had a baby. They moved out because they wanted a garden with the baby, and so they've moved to a house in Altrincham, I think it was. And going back to Tim, he was upstairs for a year when he was a single chap, and then he met Michelle and then he moved down. Once here, people tend to like it. There's Paul Chapman, who's next door, he's an estate agent with Reeds, Raines. He's been here for - six years? Seven years?

J.   No, he's not been here that long. About four years. Five.

Jim. I think once people get here they like it, and they don't want to move. I think one of the great secrets of the place is the railway, you can get a train into Manchester. And people don't realise that. They think it's a bit out in the sticks. But you can get straight into Hale, straight into Manchester.

J.   People as well, people say to me, That must be really noisy in Ashley from the aeroplanes. But we don't hear them at all. I find the motorway tiresome. I've got a book on walks in Cheshire, and I've done quite a few of them around here. But at some point in nearly all of them you have to walk by the side of the motorway, or you come across it anyway. It's a shame.

D.   So Jane, how have you come into the picture? Where did you and Jim meet?

J.   Well I'm a teacher, I used to work in Cambridge, and a mutual friend of a friend was having a party in London, and we were both there.

Jim. Richmond Hockey Club.

J.   But I actually come from Lymm. And when a job came up in Manchester, I moved back here. I teach French and German in a comprehensive school. Which is interesting. In the middle of Manchester: very different from the leafy suburbs. On the edge of Moss Side, Hulme, but it's a Church of England school; so it is that area, but it's the whole of Manchester as well. And generally, ninety per cent of the time, behaviour in the school is good. But sometimes people seem to get out of the door and get on a bus, and they metamorphose! I mean there are problems which affect every school, drugs and things, which is my big worry. It's prevalent everywhere.

D.   So how was it actually moving in?

J.   It was fine actually. I moved in and spent a couple of months; and then went to a Sunday service at St Elizabeth's. And it was one of those things: I'd walked past a couple of times before, and heard this amazing singing! And then I went in and realised it was all the tape recorder! It did make me smile, actually. But I met Mrs Fisher, she was the first person I met, and she was very kind and very welcoming. And there was Mrs Blain, and Mrs Dolan knew Jim's Gran.

D.   Of course she did, yes. Of course they all will have, but Mrs Dolan probably better than most.

Jim. I get the impression my Gran was known throughout the village! We don't talk about it too much, as a rule!

D. She'd be disappointed to hear that!

J. I never knew her. But I hear things!

D. Oh, you missed a treat!

J. Yes, I went across there, and everyone was very welcoming and kind. And then, when we got married, we got married in St Elizabeth's, and obviously Michael was officiating. Quite nice to have a fellow, or ex, teacher. He used to work in inner city Manchester. Oh I like it here, it's nice. That's quite good that this farmer here's grown his hedges high, because my dad sometimes comes with me on these little walks around, and he's very much into bird-watching and things, and he's saying how things have changed, and there aren't half as many birds around as when he was a lad.

D. Well there are one or two of the younger farmers now who are very keen on this, and I think maybe things will turn. The thing that upsets me is that I can't remember how long it is since I knew of any plovers nesting in Ashley: when I first came, only about eighteen years ago, there used to be flocks of plover, like a swarm of insects in the distance when they rose. And they used to nest all over the place. But they don't now. It would be a great day if ever they came back.

J. Apparently the Bollin is cleaner. Because Tim who used to live in Flat 1, he's now moved to Rostherne, he actually went down it in a canoe. And he's always lived round here. And he said when he was a boy it was actually filthy. And now he's seen a king-fisher, and herons. It's a nice little village though. And I think the train is quite a plus.

Jim. The other thing that's quite sad is the number of burglaries and hold-ups, fright-ening things like happened to Khanikhah Guy; and the post office, twice. They never caught them, did they?

D. I don't know. I'm glad you mentioned that, because nobody else has.

J. Do you think the village has changed since they refurbished the pub at all?

D. Only that the pub seems better. It's being used much more by the village. They've started doing things like quiz nights on Tuesdays here. Now loads of people I've talked to mention that.

Jim. You've got to pick a night when the landlord's not there, haven't you, really. His wife's delightful, but he is a bit miserable, isn't he?

D. So it seems, and yet it's he who -

Jim. Starts these things.

D. Yes. I think there must be something misleading in his appearance.

Jim. I think you're probably right, yes.

D. Do you have any thoughts how Ashley is likely to develop, as the years go by?

Jim. Well I think it'll have to take more housing. I think the government plan is that they will have to take a certain number of houses in the area. I would say that Ashley is a prime place to locate some more housing. It's got a railway station, post office, good access. So I would think there'll be more housing coming forward, of whatever nature it may be. I don't know who the lucky farmer will be.

D. I presume that this would come down from a fairly high level in the planning world. I presume, for Green Belt restrictions to be lifted, it's got to be fairly close to the government.

Jim. I would have thought it has to come from there. It's basically for the facilities it's got, it's not for the number of people who support all of it. I think there must be quite a strong case for putting more houses and more people - to run a school, to keep the railway station which is direct to Manchester or Chester, to help the post office's viability. Having the railway station as an access facility when people are trying to get away from cars and driving, means that it must be fairly high on the agenda for somewhere they can put new housing. There is alternative transport. There's a school which is struggling to sustain itself; there's a post office which is doing reasonably well, I don't know, but more people passing the door is always a good thing for that to survive. It's crying out, the village's life and survival, is crying out for more people. I'm not convinced by the argument that it necessarily has to be affordable housing. It has to be sustainable, and I think it wants to be mixed, with houses in each bracket. Otherwise you'll end up with the place becoming like a suburban alleyway. I think you need to have a mixture of housing, to give the right character and blend. So I think the parish council need to address - well I dare say they are -

D. It would be interesting to know where these questions are being considered. As you say, they must be being considered somewhere. Of course the other great fear is the airport. And it might be a question of which gets there first? If more housing gets established here, that might be a better defence against whenever the airport wants to put down a third runway.

Jim. In that case I think a mixture of housing, a lot of it affordable because if you want to sustain the school then we need young families to come in. We enjoy things like the cricket fair. We put a team in. People from the flats, and Tim came from Rostherne and joined us. Good fun. Good day out.

J. Things like that, I think, are good for the village.

D. I think we've got the Millennium Committee to thank quite a lot for that. They seem to be promoting things like that. I just hope it won't stop when the Millennium's over, because everyone seems to enjoy it.

Mark Henderson. Outwood, Cow Lane

D.   Mark, how long have you lived here?

M.   I've lived here since March '99. I previously lived down Bold Street, in Altrincham, for six years. So I've actually been over in this area since August '93.

D.   That's very interesting, because it seems to indicate that you've come here by choice, to come out of Altrincham. And this is one of the flats in Outwood, which probably has about four flats. How did you find it, moving away from Bold Street?

M.   Well I've always lived on a farm before I came over here, so I've always been used to living in the country. I suppose it was partly a move to get back into the country-side. When I started living in Hale I loved having Sainsbury's round the corner, and the pub round the corner, and a corner shop: everything was just there, handy. And it was quite a novelty for me, having always had to either cycle or drive or whatever, to get to a shop or a pub. So the novelty still hadn't really worn off when I moved out. But I love being out here, I love being in the countryside anywhere. I don't miss not being able to walk to the shops; we've got the post office anyway, and the pub. So certain aspects of it are not a problem. And I'm quite often in Altrincham with work and things like that, so any shopping I need from town I do then. It's not actually a problem as it perhaps might be to other people.

D.   You say you've lived on a farm most of your life: whereabouts was that?

M.   I was born in Northamptonshire, lived there for the first five years, on a farm, and then we moved to Lincolnshire and stayed near Grantham for about six years, and then moved to Louth, and I lived there on a farm until I left school and went to Agricultural College, in Shropshire, Harper Adams. It's now Harper Adams University College. I'm not very keen that they dropped the word "Agricultural" from the title, but I think that's the way they had to go, to get the funding and to get the people coming to do the courses.

D.   Yes, everyone seems to have to do it. What did you do there?

M.   I actually studied, it was the first of a new degree course, called Rural Enterprise and Land Management. And it was specifically designed for my job as a land agent. I'm a chartered surveyor, qualified at the Royal Institution of Chartered Surveyors in '95, but my title, when I'm talking to people and they say What do you do? I say I'm a land agent. And so the course I did was specifically designed for that. And it exempted me from certain exams for the RICS.

D.   How do you go on to complete the RICS after that?

M.   Having done the degree, which was four years, then you have to do two years of, in effect, work experience. You join a firm, and I came to Meller Braggins, and you work for two years. You have to keep a diary whilst you're doing that, attend various tutorials. Follow a fairly structured training programme of different specialisations within the job. And then after two years you're eligible to sit the exams. And you either pass or fail, and if you fail them you do them again, which is what I did! And then when you pass you're formally qualified then, as a chartered surveyor.

D.   And all the time you've been with Meller Braggins? At the estate office?

M.   No. I originally came for the job, and was interviewed in the estate office in Rostherne, for a job at Rostherne. And then, a few weeks before I started, the assistant land agent who worked with Peter Chapman at Dunham Massey, from the Stamford Estate Office in Altrincham, he moved to Rostherne, because the variety of work there was greater than the variety of work at the Stamford Estate Office. So I went as Peter Chapman's assistant, in '93, to Altrincham, and was involved with the Dunham Massey Estate for just over four years. And I went to Rostherne in September '97.

D.   I hadn't realised that there was still a Stamford Estate Office. I'd somehow assumed that when the last Lord Stamford died the National Trust just took over lock, stock and barrel.

M.   Yes, the Dunham Massey Estate, when Lord Stamford died in, I think, '76, and then the Trust took over in '78, there was a period when the trustees were involved: one of Lord Stamford's requests in his will was that Peter Chapman, who was his agent then, and had been since about 1966 or '68, continued to manage the estate.

D.   And he continues as the land agent still?

M.   He did until he retired, in March '98. There was an administrator at the Hall, who dealt with the day-to-day running of the Hall, but the role of land agent was taken by him. I think that was about the only National Trust Estate in the country where this actually happened. And it was Peter Chapman that they wanted rather than, necessarily, the firm. So it was always assumed that when he retired the Trust would take over direct management. And when Peter Chapman retired I was actually offered the job, to stay on as assistant land agent working for the Trust. At the same time I was also offered a job to carry on working for Meller Braggins in the estate office at Rostherne. It was a difficult choice in some repects, because obviously having been there for over four years I'd built up a good relationship with all the tenants, and a good relationship with all the people I worked with. So it was difficult to decide not to work for the Trust, and to leave all the people behind. But I think my aspirations, careerwise, are eventually that I would like to be a partner in a firm, whether it's Meller Braggins or another firm. And I felt that my aspirations in that direction would be better served staying with Meller Braggins. And also the variety of work we do at Rostherne: we don't just do estate management, which is what the Trust would have done: we also have a number of private clients who want one-off jobs doing. And it could be a very wide range of work. So I thought that would be better from my point of view, because I would be more likely to get a broader experience, which at this stage in my career I want. So that was the reason for choosing to make the break.

D.   It sounds a very interesting office.

M.   Oh we do a very wide variety of things. Land agents often are called Jack of All Trades, Master of none: I would disagree with the Master of none bit! I wouldn't disagree with the Jack of all trades. Particularly nowadays, with farming being like it is. Obviously the bulk of our income comes from managing agricultural estates. And with agricultural incomes declining we're always having to look, partly for the benefit of our clients, we're having to look at different ways that they can make money from diversification: all the impact on the environment; there's so many things now to be taken into account that we're having to become experts in all those other - for example, planning applications on farm buildings, to turn them into farm shops, all those sorts of things which, fifty years ago, weren't needed to be considered. Now we have to be up with all the latest regulations. It's an ever-changing job, we do do an awful lot of different sorts of work. Anything, basically, in the countryside. I think we do try to promote ourselves as being able to do more or less anything.

D.   Listening to you talking about this - I go back to 1968 in this area - and when we had young children we often used to shop in Dunham, and I know a lot of the people there. And I heard - this is going back a long way - that an edict came down from his Lordship that the farm shops were OK as long as they were only used to sell stuff that people had produced on their own farms. So bananas suddenly had to disappear! And they didn't, of course. And ever since then, I was so amused by this, because it was quite blatant actually, and since then I've always felt that there must be a policing aspect for anyone who has an estate like that to run! It must be ticklish. I can imagine that things like this could terribly easily get miles out of perspective. It must take quite a lot of skill to use the tact and commonsense to keep these things in perspective.

M.   One of the things I'll always remember when I first started work for Peter Chapman, is his saying that being a land agent was fifty per cent common sense, and fifty per cent diplomacy. And I think that's a very true thing to say, and I've always tried to follow that, and I've always tried to be diplomatic in anything that I do, because if you start falling out with people you don't get anywhere. And being honest with people and open with them, and talking things through, that seems to be the best way of resolving problems.

D.   And behind that, I suppose, must be how well you're known, that must affect the situation. I'm thinking of here the number of times that Mr Hall's name - he must be Mr Pike's predecessor, I don't know, but he's played important parts in people's lives and it's remembered, and appreciated: but the point I'm making is that he couldn't have done that if he hadn't been known and trusted in the first place.

M.   I still talk to tenants who say, When we first came here Derek Hall said this to us and that to us, and that he would look after us. I think he was fairly widely trusted and respected.

D.   So that's your work, Mark. What else do you do, do you find time for much else?

M.   I think probably my main hobby is music. Music and sports. I don't get as much time for sports as I used to. When I was at school I used to play cricket for Lincolnshire, which was quite an honour, I suppose. Colts. But I will basically play any sport. I used to do a lot of swimming, I used to play in goal for the school football team. All sorts of things like that. Until really I left school. My other main hobby is singing. I sing in a choir in Manchester called The Manchester Chorale. The choir actually started off as the Radio Manchester Choir. I can't remember the full title, but basically for GMR. That was in 1979. They used to do a lot of what they called *Thank you for the Music* concerts, which was all sorts of light music, like *Love is the Sweetest Thing*: all sorts of easy listening. So we still do quite a bit of that. And those I think are actually the most successful concerts in terms of the appreciation of the audience.

Three or four years ago we did a four or five part piece by Byrd, we sang it in The Holy Name Church, in Manchester. And a handful of people turned up. I think it was perhaps a bit heavy for a lot of people. Although we love singing things like that, and I'm sure the few people who come to listen to it like listening to it, but we get a lot better reaction, a lot better feedback from the lighter music, and it draws the crowds in as well. It seems a shame that the more challenging pieces, and the ones that we have to work really hard to perform, don't always get the appreciation.

D.   How many of you are there?

M.   About fifty five on the books. And I would think when we're at full strength, on an average night, there'd be forty five. We have members from all over Manchester, from Bury down to Ashley, so we come from quite a wide radius, and gather in the centre. We sing probably eight or nine concerts a year, and again we will sing virtually anywhere. We sang in Hawkshead in the summer last year, we went to Northern Ireland the year before that. We've sung in the Ninex Arena with Pavarotti, we've sung with José Carreras in Sheffield Arena, so we've done some quite exciting things. I think I've been on television now five or six times, with them. It's a reasonably good choir. I suppose some of them are semi-professional musicians, and a lot of them are just amateurs like I am.

D.   Do you ever, like cricket teams, go on tour?

M.   We sang in Notre Dame Cathedral and Chartres Cathedral four or five years ago, that was what we could call a mini tour! We sang at the Morning Service in Notre Dame, which will always be one of the highlights in my musical life. So I think singing is probably my main thing outside of work.

D.   Has it always been?

M.   Yes, I started singing when I was ten, in the Church Choir back in Louth.

D.   My godfathers! I wonder if you heard me preach? I preached once in Louth.

M.   1981, I started at St James.

D.   Oh you missed it, then. I had a terrible time. I wasn't used to this halter microphone, and I tend to get worked up and forget what I'm doing, and I must have struck my chest, right on the microphone, and there was a sound like a thunderclap in the choir stalls, right in the ears of the choir!

M.   That startled a few, I should think. Woke a few choirboys! I sang there for ten years. Starting as a treble and ending as a bass. The choir used to go away, the boys, for a week's holiday every year, normally to Devon or Cornwall. Then, through connections in Berlin first of all, we went there for a week, sang in the Cathedral there. And then we went to Sweden the following year, and went to Stockholm and one or two other places there. It was very exciting, at that age, to be going away.

D.   It was always a mystery to me - still is - that ten-year-old boys can voluntarily submit to so much, such a huge commitment as is required in a choir of that standard.

M.   Yes. My brother also sang with me in the choir. When I think that we sang on Monday afternoon at four thirty, sang on a Friday night at seven o'clock, till half past eight, and we were there at nine o'clock on a Sunday morning, six o'clock for Evensong on Sunday evening: and that was, apart from the six weeks we had off for the summer, we were there every week of the year.

D.   It's enormous isn't it? When you think of ten-year-old boys. I find it quite amazing. And yet people are competing to get in, as I expect you did for yours.

M.   And also I marvel at my parents, for taking us three miles in the car every Monday and Friday, and twice on a Sunday. We never went away for weekends, or anything like that. We couldn't, because we were so committed to the - didn't have to be, but we were - committed to singing in the choir. I don't think I could go back to it. I like my Sunday morning lie-in too much! I like singing occasionally, when I go home. But I certainly couldn't do it regularly, not any more. But having said that, I thoroughly enjoyed it. Virtually all the time I enjoyed it. And I think the discipline that it instilled in me was very beneficial.

D.   So what other things occupy you?

M.   I think really my singing and the sport that I do. And I run quite a lot. I'd love to do a Marathon. I actually did the Great North Run, a half-marathon, last time. So that's one of my ambitions. My other is that I would like to sing in every Cathedral in England.

D.   Oh, right. So how far have you got?

M.   I've not got very far. I've done one of the Liverpool Cathedrals, I've done Lincoln, Coventry, Manchester, Ripon, Chester . . . I think I'd got to seven in England.

D.   Of the ones you've done so far, which stands out most?

M.   I think Lincoln is one of the most spectacular cathedrals in the country anyway. It's almost on a par with places like York Minster. It's a very big cathedral. And I think that would probably be my favourite to date.

D.   That's very nice, to think that it's also your home cathedral. That's quite nice. And that it out-does Notre Dame and Chartres, for instance.

M.   They were nice experiences, but I think Lincoln was probably the nicest cathedral. I'm hoping to sing in Salisbury this summer. I'm looking forward to that.

Kay Williams. Redcroft, Cow Lane

K.   I've been here twenty-six years, in a house called Redcroft, which has had a variety of names. Looking at the deeds one day, I found it was called The Wilderness. But I don't think it's a wilderness now, because I'm very proud of my garden, so I don't think we'll call it The Wilderness now!

    Yes, it was twenty-six years ago when my husband and I came, having lived in the colonies, and this was the first time that we'd had an English home. Having had a variety of mud huts, and all sorts of odd accommodation. So it was just a lucky day when we were staying in what was then The Arcot Hotel in Altrincham, when John came up to be interviewed for a job in Manchester. And we asked a house agent, and they brought us here. And so here we have remained. Unfortunately John died fifteen years ago, so I've been on my own, finding it a very friendly, lovely little place to live. Somebody's reminded me that when I first came I said that Ashley is just a crossroads. And I think people would agree with that now, because we have a shop and we have a pub and we have a school. But we've never had a meeting place. So that it's always been meeting people in the church or in one's home which is the way to get to know people. And I find that people are very very friendly. Now, at my age, I'm finding that I don't know so many people as I used to do, because the young ones have grown up, they're having children, and I really can't yet sort out who is related to whom!

D.   Kay can we go back to when you first came, which must have been quite a crossroads in your life, never mind the crossroads outside here! You and John had come back from a life in the colonies, from which presumably John had retired, and he - had he already got a job in Manchester?

K.   No. No, that's when we came up for the interview.

D.   That's how you came to be in Altrincham. You came here you really were starting a new life.

K.   Oh I didn't even know where I was. No. I really didn't know where I was.

D.   Of course you'd been used to going to new places, and strange places, and were probably adept at settling down, but what was it like for you, those early years coming here?

K.   Oh, I loved it. I always said I wanted to come home. You know, a lot of people said when you retire you go abroad - you know, Majorca or somewhere like that - I'd always said No, I wanted to come back to U.K. when we retired.

D.   But some people find coming home a disappointment, because home's changed so much.

K.   No, I loved it. And I got angry with people who used to say, Oh you can't get so-and-so in the shops, and I'd say, You should have lived where I lived, chum, you wouldn't complain then!

D.   So you were a staunch defender of Brenda!

K.   Yes! No, it was just luck that we found this place, because we came up from

Swansea, where John's mother lived, to have the interview, and it was pouring with rain, and we got as far as Altrincham and a bit further, and we said We can't go any further. We found our way into what was then The Arcot Hotel, the little one up The Downs. You know what it was.

D.   I'm trying to remember where it was. Did it later become The Portofino?

K.   That's right.

D.   Not a very propitious introduction to the place.

K.   Well they were such - they were a couple of Italian people, lads, and they were so kind. They were really very kind to us. And they used to take me down to the station, and we were trying to buy this house, and there was a postal strike on, couldn't post letters, so I was up and down, Swansea, Manchester - Oh, dear. And they were very very kind. And then of course just down the road was the house agents, Bridgford's. So we walked in there, when he'd got the job of course, and said, Have you got any property? and they said, Oh there's not much on the books. Then they said, Oh well, there is one. The people are still there, but they're building a house, or they're going into a house,

D.   Where are we? We're about the early seventies?

K.   This was '72, yes. So we saw it, and of course we had Mother at the time, as you know, so it just seemed a house with potential to have another person and give her one room, because this was really her room, in a way. So that's how it was. And we said, Oh we can always think later. Well we never did, we just stayed.

D.   And how did John find it, coming back and getting settled into a -

K.   He hated it.

D.   He hated it? Everything?

K.   Well, the job. Not the place at all, or the people. He just hated the job, because it was so nine-to-five. You know, at five o'clock everybody just said *We're off!* And he'd been used to staying till seven or eight or whenever, finishing the work; or people wanted to see him, and it was always open house when you were in the colonies. Anybody could come and see you.

D.   So that your work was really much more your life, there was much more of yourself invested in the work, it wasn't just a job.

K.   Oh, you were very much part of the whole thing. Especially in Sarawak, where the Rajah had said that the District Officers, as they were called, had to be open house to anybody who wished to come. You'd never have a meal because they'd be sitting around drinking your brandy, you know. These lovely old Dayaks thought this was great. All pile in and sit around!

D.   Ashley, you were saying, coming back to Ashley, that apart from the church, the pub and the shop really there aren't any meeting places. Have you found that you've

127

got to know people? Do you feel that you belong here? Or do you still feel like a stranger at the crossroads?

K.   The older I get the more I feel, No, I'm not part of it. Because, as I was saying, when I came I knew such a lot of people, through the church, and I used to go collecting for Christian Aid and, you know, I'd go to every house for Christian Aid and that sort of thing; then the Conservative Party, I was, was I Treasurer or Secretary? I was something for them; we used to have house meetings and we used to have all these people coming to the house for that, and we'd have our big gatherings at Quick's, big parties. I did feel I knew practically everybody. Now, I hardly know anybody. The children that I knew have grown and they've gone away, a lot of them. No, I think that if it wasn't for the church now I'd be pretty well out of everything.

D.   Of course you used to have the dog as well.

K.   Yes. And I can't walk now. And then I used to do Oxfam all the time, twice a week, and I can't do that now because I can't stand around. So. It's just old age. I mean, you know, you just have to sort of temper your life to what you can do. I've now got angina apparently, this sort of nonsense, so you just have to live to what you can do.

D.   This is the sort of thing that, in a different way, Christine is having to get used to. May I ask you what you find yourself doing? I mean, how do you pass your days?

K.   Well I can drive the car. So I do my own shopping; all right, that's nothing much in its way, but at least it gets me out . And I love gardening, so I go to garden centres. Tuesdays and Thursdays Mrs Bell is here. Wednesday the gardener comes, Friday I go to the school to hear the children read.

D.   Ah, you still do that?

K.   I still do that. So every day there is something to do, really. And then people come, and I go out for meals with Betty or somebody in the area. And I go to the Fine Arts thing, that's only once a month, but at least that's another thing.

D.   The school: has that changed much in the time? You've been going there quite a long time.

K.   It has changed, yes. It has changed a lot. I've found it's come alive again. I think it's a good, friendly, up-and-coming, well-run little school now. It's as neat as a new pin, and I just hope it keeps on. There's a question mark over it, isn't there? Big question mark.

D.   So there is quite a difference?

K.   Oh, there's such a different atmosphere there. There's one little spina bifida boy, well he's a Mongol anyway, and a special teacher comes in for him, and in the early days his mother used to come in in the morning with him. And he's still there. So that was a big thing for a little school to take on. His mother was saying the other day he had said to her something when he got home about, er, something. You know, it was more than he'd ever done before. And he pushed her away and said he wanted Miss

So-and-so, his special teacher, and so, yes, I think he is mixing with the others. So I think that's a big thing for a little school like this to do.

D. And it sounds, from what you're saying, as if this is bringing you into contact with some of the parents, as well as the children?

K. No, I rarely see the parents. Unless there's something, an Open Day and they come, and I haven't a clue who's who. Don't know them at all now. Except one or two round The Green. They're all strangers to me. But I hope it keeps open.

D. When is the decision? Pretty soon now, isn't it?

K. It should be pretty soon. It was some time early May, I think. They had a meeting about a month ago, and that was when everyone thought they were going to say, but it wasn't. They said it won't be until . . . Because they're going to build on the school, aren't they, for the Millennium. They had the plans up when they had the Open Day the other day. The plans have all been done. They were there, and a ramp went up so that elderly people could go up in wheelchairs, and it was going to be built on the side, as part of the school which could be used as the school, but also be used as the Village Hall. Which I think is wonderful. But then of course we don't want it all to get built and then they close the school, because that belongs to Brooks.

D. I should think the fate of the school will have been determined before they start building.

K. Oh yes it will. Yes, it will.

D. And of course once it's there, it will be that much more difficult I imagine to close it.

K. As the Village Hall, to close it. They get so uptight, these poor teachers, I feel so sorry for them, getting so much paperwork to do, and at the same time they're supposed to take on extra this, extra that, and they really are working themselves an awful lot. And Mrs Wakefield takes it very seriously, and the thing that's worrying them now is that they're going to have another Ofsted. Any minute now they're coming round. So that worries them a lot. It's not nice to see men with boards listening to you, writing away! They get very uptight about that.

The Langleys. The Old Police House, Cow Lane

D.   How long have you been here now?

Dee. Since just before Josie was three. August '92.

D.   Why did you come here?

Dee. We knew of this house because, obviously, Pat and Kevin live in Ashley.

D.   Pat is Martin's sister?

Dee. Yes. So we came visiting quite regularly. So we knew of Ashley and its where-abouts, and quite a few of the people. And also we'd courted for seventeen years before we were married, and The Greyhound was one of our haunts.

D.   Seventeen years must be a record! But isn't it the case that you had connections with Ashley going way back, Martin?

M.   Well yes, really. Ethel and Reg were Pat's godparents.

D.   These are the Bakers, at The Greyhound?

M.   Yes, they were landlords of The Greyhound. And we were always walked by our father around this area, every Sunday. He liked to walk, and we were taken on these walks. And also an old aunt who lived in Hale, she used to work as a part of the Land Army. And my mother's brothers, three of them used to be at Outwood, as the - I call it Dad's Army - as the wardens. So we got all these stories of Ashley. That's probably why we've got quite a close link. My mother's family was a Hale family, my father's family was a Hale family: but I was born and bred in Sale.

D.   And where did you come from, Dee?

Dee. I was born in Salford. My dad worked at Lynotype, and we lived on what used to be the Lynotype Estate, because they were obviously houses for the people that worked at Lynotype. And they actually bought one when Lynotype sold out to the Bradford Trust. It's a Conservation Area now. Because they're very different, the houses, to anywhere else. They're slightly Dutch, really.

D.   So how did you two meet, seventeen years before you got married?

Dee. How did we meet? We just fell over each other, didn't we?

M.   It was a party at Didsbury.

Dee. Yes we did. It was a Twenty-first. And that was it. We were married in '87.

D.   You must have met in 1970: it's getting serious, isn't it?!

Bang! Bang! Bang!

Dee. Joe, don't bang! Because it sounds on that cassette recorder.

D. It'll sound like a jungle drum. And I don't know how to spell that sound. We've got to turn it into a book in the end, you see.

M. When Josie came along we decided we needed a bigger house.

Dee. And also for your business really, wasn't it?

M. And we moved out here. It had been empty for five years. I presume they leave it empty for a set amount of time, to see if they don't require it again.

D. Are there any peculiarities about the place?

M. Well, there were. There was was the Early Warning System here. We had it taken out. I wish we hadn't, now. We had an Early Warning System, in case of nuclear war.

D. How quaint!

Dee. It was, rather!

D. Can you imagine Arthur getting out on his bike! *They're on their way!*

M. We were actually asked to keep it. Diane said, No, she didn't want it. So the GPO, they took the Early Warning System out, and that went to - Shrewsbury, wasn't it? Direct to Shrewsbury, so I don't know what's at Shrewsbury.

D. A very important policeman!

M. But it's quite antiquated when you think about it, isn't it? So that's the only history we know about the house.

D. And how do you like it?

M. We hate the motorway, we detest the motorway.

Dee. It's really quite noisy here. You can't really sleep with the windows open.

M. But you can live with the noise from the airport. It's minimal. And I quite enjoy the noise of the trains. I like that.

D. The garden, you must have done an awful lot in the garden?

M. A little bit, but not a lot really.

Dee. Oh you have! It was just like a jungle. When we first came here you scythed it, you couldn't do anything but scythe it.

M. We strimmed it.

Dee. No you didn't, you had a big scythe. I don't know where you got it from.

M.   No, we used two strimmers.

Dee. At the front you scythed it. I remember.

D.   You must have!

M.   You can't argue with these ladies, can you. Eh? "The chat with the Langleys ends up in divorce!"

D.   Josie, how old were you when you came here?

J.   Three. I can remember hiding in the cupboards upstairs the day that we moved in, but I can't remember anything else.

D.   Who were you hiding from, Josie?

J.   I don't know. I think we were playing Hide-and-Seek.

M.   I had a metal-detector, and I've got policemen's buttons from the last fifty years, Cheshire Constabulary brass buttons. Evidently they used to burn their uniforms. So the buttons were brass. I discovered all these, and an early milk bottle - who's the local dairyman? Blockley. I would think it's either a forties or fifties. So I've stuffed it full of the brass buttons, and the date that I found them, and I've put it in the roof.

D.   So you've got a time-capsule.

Dee. Josie started school here. She's in her final year now.

D.   What was the feeling last year when you heard the school wasn't going to be closed? You're the first actual person at the school I've spoken to since then.

J.   I didn't want it to close. It's a very friendly school, and everybody gets on.

M.   But Josie was very apprehensive, weren't you, when they were doing their Ofsted inspection, in case it closed.

D.   What would have happened to you if it had closed, do you know?

Dee. They were going to split the children up. Some were going to Egerton and some were going to Mobberley. Which really just wasn't on. If they were going anywhere they should have gone together.

M.   I still feel it's a master plan for the airport. I still think the powers-that-be want the school out of the way. I think once the school's gone the village will lose . . .

Dee. No, I don't think that. It's because basically the school costs the County a lot to keep it going.

M.   I think they're using that as an excuse more than, well . . . I feel that there's a grand plan for the airport and industry and business. And the people that pull the strings know what's going to happen.

Dee. That's what we thought when we had the threat of closure over the school for three years. I'm on the governors at the school, and have been for four years, and I've been Vice Chairman for two years now. They threw at us in the final year of their decision-making that we were going to be Ofsteded again. And we'd only had an Ofsted inspection the year before they'd threatened to close us initially. Of course they came in and did a re-inspection just before the summer last year, and it was such a brilliant report that there was no way they could say they'd close the school. Because the education there is just so good. So that really put the icing on the cake for us.

D.   So you're very lucky, Joe.

Dee. Josie's done very well at school. You did your Eleven Plus, didn't you. We don't know how well you've done in that. They don't know until March.

D.   When did you take it, Josie?

J.   The last one was in November.

D.   How many of you took it?

J.   Only two.

Dee. The thing is, most children tend just to go to Knutsford High. And unless you want something different yourself for your children there's no need to put them through the exam.

M.   But the school, I think, is quite an important part of the village, I think it's a very important part of the village. And really, if they allowed a bit more land to go for building, and lower-cost housing, if that was ever possible, that would make the village a lot stronger.

Dee. We've got big plans to try and get a hall built at the back of the school. A community hall.

Joe.   And a playground!

D.   And will there be some sort of sharing arrangement, built into the constitution of the hall?

Dee. Well in the plans that are being done, the actual building is connected to the school by means of a small passageway, which the children can use without getting wet. But the hall itself has got a separate designated kitchen area, and a separate designated toilet area. So it can be used and rented out to other people in the community, Brownies or Guides or anything like that. It's been done with the intention of being used by the community.

D.   That looks very exciting, Joe. What's that?

Joe.   A girocopter.

D.   What can it do?

M.   It's got a torch at the front, hasn't it? And what else has it got, Joe?

Joe.   Missiles.

D.   I say! So it's a war weapon.

Joe.   Yeah, but you didn't have things like this in the war. Action Man's more braver than just soldiers, isn't he?

D.   Does this belong to Action Man?

Joe.   Yeah. This is Action Man's.

D.   Where is Action Man? I don't see him sitting in it.

Joe.   He's in the drawer.

D.   Having a rest! Martin, how did you get into gardening?

M.   I didn't want to be anything else. No, that's wrong: I couldn't find a suitable job. I wanted to be -

Joe.   An accountant.

M.   No, not an accountant. I told him to be that, because you make more money! I wanted to be a farmer. My next thing was that I wanted to be an artist.

Joe.   Yeah, and you're not very good at drawing.

D.   You're a fine son!

M.   He's a thug! So I was jobless really, wasn't I? And I just went knocking on doors, asking people if they want their garden done.

Dee.   You were only about - you were seventeen, weren't you?

M.   Yes. Because I've not been employed at all. I've never been on the dole or anything like that. And you've got to live, so that's what I did.

D.   And it just went from there?

M.   It snowballed, basically, yes.

Joe.   I thought Dad wanted to be an accountant.

D.   That's you, Joe. We're keeping that for you.

Joe.   I don't want to be an accountant. I want to be an inventor.

D.   What do you want to invent, Joe?

Joe. A flying chair. Instead of going on an aeroplane.

D. How did it come to be called Sale Garden Services?

M. Because I lived in Sale. That's the only reason. I've been doing that since I was seventeen, and I'm forty six now, so nearly thirty years, I've been doing it.

D. Has it changed much in that time?

M. Totally. It's become automated now, hasn't it? Everything's a machine. And most jobs were done by hand. I mean when we first started, in the autumn I used to buy in the region of eighty birch besoms, for sweeping lawns. Now we don't buy one. It's all these blowers. And that's how it's changed.

D. Does the work vary? I mean, is it all maintenance, or do you do all sorts of things?

M. No, it's nearly all maintenance, around Hale, Bowdon, Sale, Hale Barns. And Ashley, now. Help people out in Ashley. And we do run-of-the-mill garden maintenance, and then on top of that we do landscaping in the winter.

D. I was going to ask how difficult it was keeping a steady workflow, with five of you?

M. The thing is that demand for gardening, now, is massive. I mean, as we turn this century, you said last night, all that's on TV is gardening programmes. Or cooking. But they find a theme, and they drive it down your throat. And we don't get cold winters now. So the interest never lapses at all. And our quietest month now is August. Financially. Because people go away. You get this huge rush between March and July, then you get this cut-off point for the holidays, and then it starts to build from September again. But there's no cut-off point in the winter at all.

D. And is all your work in private gardens?

M. All private gardens, yes.

D. What about you, Josie? You're not going to be an accountant as well, are you?

J. I don't know what I want to be. I'd like to work with animals.

D. What animals do you have contact with now? Apart from your brother?

J. Mostly dogs.

D. Your three, there?

J. And quite a lot of people in the village have dogs.

D. Are there any changes you'd like to see, at the start of the new Century?

M. I think a village hall would be a great start. I'd like to see more building, in keeping with the village. And my fears are that it doesn't get absorbed by the airport.

Dee. I think one of my biggest fears about Ashley is the traffic. The speed along this road is incredible. I mean, in the morning when we walk to school, we're all waiting: sometimes you can wait -

J.   Five minutes.

Dee. A good five minutes. To get across the road. The traffic's almost continual.

M.   And it is in the evening, isn't it, as well. Same again. But I just hope the village doesn't get absorbed into Hale or something like that. Hope it keeps its identity. But my greatest fear is it'll get absorbed by the airport in the future. But I see it being swallowed up. That's my greatest fear.

D.   And the most likely candidate to do the swallowing, you think, is the airport?

M.   Definitely. The increase in cars: whoever travels to the airport's got to park their car. So unless this car society changes, or is forced to change, in the next twenty five years I think half of Ashley is going to be under tarmac. Don't you, Diane?

Dee. Yes, I do really. But I think, what did you say about housing?

M.   I'd like to see more housing - where the garage is, because the garage now is useless. It ceases to be a working garage with no petrol.

Dee. I heard that they wanted to sell in order to build executive homes on that plot. But the Council put their foot down and said No, you're not having executive homes: if you're going to have homes they're going to be low-cost homes, so that younger people can come into the community.

D.   This was what I was going to ask you, Martin, when you started on this: I wondered if you could see any way it was at all likely that anyone who has land could be persuaded to part with it for less than the most they could get out of it? Because that's where you've got to start, isn't it? If you're looking for low-cost housing?

M.   Yes. Yes. Well perhaps when I say low-cost, that is perhaps the wrong . . . Shall we say affordable houses. If you understand the difference between what I call an executive home -

D.   The difference between that and one which a first-time buyer might be able to afford? Youngsters.

Dee. Because I'm involved with the school I think of the school as well as the community: because I mean there's precious few children about, to fill the school at the moment. It makes it very difficult if there's no younger families about.

Update: Later in the year Josie gained a place at Altrincham Gammar School for Girls. She was also chosen to be Rose Queen at the Millennium Fête, where at her crowning she made a very gracious speech which she had written herself. And as part of her entourage in her procession she chose to have Joe in the guise of St George.

Gladys and George Watson. 1 Cow Lane

D.   Where were you born, Gladys?

G.   I was born in Rostherne, Lady Mary's Square. I had two brothers and one sister. I went to Rostherne school, and then I went to work. I was working on penicillin in the laboratories at the ICI at Old Trafford. I was supervisor there, laboratory chemist. And on my days off I used to work in Knutsford Hospital as a Red Cross nurse. On one evening a lot of soldiers had just come back from Dunkirk and were stationed in Tatton Park. And I met George, who I knew for three days. And then he went abroad for five years. He returned. And in a fortnight, we were married.

D.   My word! You must have made quite an impression on each other!

G.   We knew each other seventeen days. Of course my mother said It won't work! And we've been married for fifty three years.

D.   There you are, Mother! Well, George, how did you get into this position?

Geo. I went to France in February 1940, and came back on June 3rd, to Dover, through Dunkirk. And then ended up having a lift, got to Knutsford, and a lift in a fish van, Bailey's Fish Van, to Tatton Park. And two or three nights later I met Glad. And we went away three days later, went down to Yeovil in Somerset, and then after that I was sent abroad again, and I was abroad then until the end of '45.

D.   Had you kept in touch with Gladys all this time?

G.   We could retire on all the money we spent on stamps!

Geo. I'd been writing all the while.

G.   I've got a box upstairs, a leather suitcase, full of the letters which had been - what-do-you-call-it?

Geo. Photostat. There was a big sheet of paper you wrote on, and it'd come back about six by four. So we come back by Lancaster bomber. Anyway, got landed at Peterborough, and the following day I come up to Chester. And they said, Tomorrow you can go on leave home. So I sent a telegram home to my mother, said I'd be home by midnight. I didn't, I come here instead.

G.   And met me. I was in lodgings in Altrincham, I was working at Trafford. And he found out where I lived. And then in a fortnight after that we got a special licence, so we got married.

D.   Just before you go on: did you ever get home to see your mother, or had you not been home yet?

Geo. No, I hadn't been home. We went up home in that fortnight. Then we come back and got married at Rostherne.

G.   And then we went up there for six weeks' honeymoon. And on the way up, he'd been in Italy for so long - he was also a Geordie - I can't tell you what he was talking about, because I couldn't understand this Italian and Geordie.

D.   What a mixture!

G.   And then the day we got married we went up North.

D.   This was in Rostherne Church you got married?

G.   Yes. I was christened and confirmed and got married in Rostherne Church. I was in the choir till I was eighteen. And then we went up North, to Hexham, and the train broke down on the Newcastle Viaduct. Our first night. All night, sat on Newcastle Station watching the Sunday papers come in! And then came back here. We were living in Altrincham, in lodgings, and I was still working on penicillin, and George was working in Altrincham for a while. And then he went to Tatton.

D.   I was going to ask you about that, George. How did you get the job at Tatton?

Geo. Well Gladys come across to her mother one day with Denise. She walked up to Tatton Office and had a word with Mr Wright. And asked if he'd got a job for me.

G.   I knew all the Tatton people, you see.

D.   And who did you go and see? You went to the Office to see?

Geo. Mr Wright, you saw.

D.   Was he the Agent?

G.   Yes. And he said, Send him, and within three days he'd got a job, and a house.

Geo. So I went on the following day, and he asked me this, that and the other: Could I drive? So he said, When can I start? And I said, I can start on Monday. When I started at Tatton I went in the woods as a forester. I'd spent five years doing forestry before the war. That was my job before I went in the Terriers, Forestry Commission. I worked for them for five years. And I went in the forestry when I come to Tatton, and I was in that for about two-and-a-half, three years, then I ended up in the saw mills, as a sawyer. And then, when Lord Egerton died, and Mr Brooks bought the estate, I started working for them. Still Tatton, and ended up as a joiner, doing the windows and doors and what-have-you, round the buildings. I was there forty one years.

D.   So you were there for the changeover. Can you describe what happened after Lord Egerton died? It must have been very unsettling.

Geo. When Lord Egerton died he had a big estate in Kenya. And there was a Dutch chap that managed this for him. And then Brooks stepped in and bought the estate here, through Meller Braggins, which was Meller Speakman and Hall then, and Meller Braggins afterwards. But Meller Braggins was Mr Hall, that's who the boss was. So I started working for them.

D.   Did it make a lot of difference?

Geo. No. No difference whatever. Just went from one to the other. Just change of name, that was all. Wages were different, we got bigger wages, that was all. Not a lot, but a bit better.

G. And we moved from Rostherne to Ashley. Well this house was going empty, and it was for somebody working in the forestry. And this was Lord Egerton's land. As you know, he could walk from his house, Tatton Hall, to Manchester without stepping off his own ground. So when the Council took this he claimed the front two houses. It was on his land. So we came in March 2nd, 1951.

Geo. It was '52 when we come in. The Bells were in next door before us.

G. Yes, they had that house. Walter's father and mother.

Geo. He was pigman, at Tatton farm. Quite a number of people worked at Tatton.

G. When I was a child there was a hundred odd. Just worked on Tatton.

D. Where did you go after the forestry?

Geo. I went into the saw mills as a sawyer. That was in the Estate yard. Tatton Dale. The saw mill was up at the top. I used to do gate posts, field gate posts, fencing rails: all sorts of things. And then I used to do all the signs, you know, these notices, *You will be Prosecuted*. I used to do all them for Tatton. Got another five shilling a week for that! Mr Wright give us another five bob. You also got five bob extra for driving.

D. Did you have to do a lot of driving, because they asked if you drove when you were interviewed?

Geo. Yeah, I used to drive the timber lorry, and a tractor. Used to drive all the trees through. Because where those pylons come through, these electric pylons, we took down three hundred and sixty odd trees, from Mobberley through to Lymm Corner. Sixty yards wide. And I carted all them in to Tatton. All of them. With the timber dobbin, pulled by the tractor. We used to go up the Wall side with the two front wheels off the road. The tractor used to rear up. And we used to go up the road like that, with the wheels in the air. And once you start turning you used to drop it, put the clutch in, they drop down and you started driving. But as soon as you got the power on again they used to come up in the air. That's how we used to go! The weight of the trees. Some of the trees was forty foot long, these pine trees, you know.

D. And what happened to the timber? Was it all used on the estate?

Geo. All of it was used, yeah.

D. Where did Lord Egerton live?

Geo. He used to live here about six months, a wee bit short of six months. Then go back to Kenya. I believe that if he stopped there six months and a day , they were tax-free. Something like that.

D. And did he live in the Hall when he was here?

Geo. He stayed at Tatton Hall, yeah.

D.   And Peover Hall, where the Brookses live, what was happening to that before?

Geo. That belonged to some people called Warings, Waring. It was a terrible long place. There was the old building, and there'd been a piece added on, for some anniversary or other. And when Brooks bought it, they bought Peover estate as well, you see, they had that new place knocked down. And the old place was done up by Browns the Builders, at Wilmslow. They did it.

D.   So they more or less restored it to how it had been?

Geo. That's right, yeah.

G.   During the war Americans lived in it.

Geo. General Patton was there, wasn't he? So they had carbons of any antique furniture that was damaged, or any stuff that Mr Brooks had bought. He'd bring it in and he'd think we could do wonders, you know. Repair a thing like this, you know: a leg would be missing: *I want that replaced*. And we'd have to set to and make that. We didn't have a lathe, we had to turn them by hand.

G.   And this was furniture, hundreds of years old. Also, he didn't have the table Magna Carta was signed on, but he did have the sideboard.

Geo. That's right, yeah. Then he had a big black piece, one was signed with the Magna Carta - two, I think two pieces there. One was all black oak, and that had some things that was missing, beading and what-have-you. All that had to be done by hand. You couldn't buy it. So you have to go and get the oak, and stain and mess around till you got the wood to that pitch, after you'd doctored it up like. There was all sorts of things I used to do there. And then Arthur Sant and me had to split one big room into two, for two children. And Mrs Brooks, young Brooks, the one that's got it now, his wife, she had the far end made into a dressing room. For her clothes to hang in.

D.   So you've been living here since 1951. What have you been doing all this time, Gladys?

G.   I was a caretaker at Ashley School for twenty one years, until I retired, at sixty.

D.   By that time you'd brought up your own family?

G.   Three children. The eldest, Denise, she was born in Altrincham, and then we wheeled her to Tatton. She was one then. She works in an office, shorthand typist. And then Malcolm, he went to college until he was twenty one. He's an artist and a graphic designer. And then Jenny was born last, and she was a hairdresser.

D.   Tell me, this church above the fire here -

G.   Mrs Mason painted that.

D.   Yes, I thought it might be Mrs Mason's work. Which church is it?

G.   That's Rostherne.

D.   And the other thing that's fascinated me, George, is above the - Is that your regimental colours?

G.   He embroidered that himself.

Geo. I drew that, for Gladys to do when she was going to have Denise. And in the meantime I did it myself! It's the cap badge, and it's got a hundred and sixty seven yards of silver thread in there.

D.   Say again how much?

Geo. A hundred and sixty seven yards of that silver thread in there.

D.   A hundred and sixty seven yards! So we've got, what is it? It's George and the Dragon, obviously, and "Royal Northumberland Fusiliers". That's wonderful! I'd no idea you could do things like that.

G.   And material was hard to get. Our landlady gave us that grey material.

Geo. And then I've done ten years in the Special Police.

D.   Oh, how did you get into that? Of course, you were originally going to join the police, weren't you? So when did you join the Specials? This document here is a Certificate of Service, to show that you were serving in the Special Constabulary from February 1968 until April 1978, " . . . and during this period gave good and useful service to the County." There! "Given without erasure." So whose idea was it, George, to do that, in 1968?

Geo. I could have gone in earlier on, you know.

D.   It was your own idea, was it? Here's Gladys shouting from the kitchen it was Arthur's idea.

Geo. Oh it was Arthur's idea, because Arthur was the policeman here.

D.   Did you work with Arthur?

Geo. Yeah.

G.   They give him sixpence for wearing his own boots.

Geo. Sixpence an hour, you got.

D.   Towards your shoe leather! What sort of things did you have to do, what were your duties?

Geo. Well you did the same as Arthur. Traffic control, or used to go to Knutsford.

Freda and Walter Bell and Margaret. 1 Hough Green

D.   So how did you all come to be in Ashley?

W.   Well I came, as near as I can tell you, in about 1927. I was born in '26, and my dad worked on the station here. And we come into the Cottages, the old cottages.

D.   The Station Cottages? The same place as Leslie Jones lived?

W.   That's right. Stonehewers was down there - Joan Blain as you know her - she lived down there. We lived down there. My dad's brother and his family lived down there. Joneses lived down there. Bensons, wasn't it? they lived down there, now in the old Station House. And then I think I was about six when I left, when we left here. Went living at Castle Hill Farm, at Ringway there. Not Blockley's, the other one. My grandfather had that. And we went living there, and my dad worked for him, after leaving the railway. About 1932, roughly, we left here. And with that we had to be moving from there. I forget now where we went to. But we went living at Mobberley eventually.

D.   How old would you have been when you got to Mobberley?

W.   About . . . Well, just before War broke out. 1939. Because I left school when I was just thirteen and a half, because we were farming. And War broke out. I left school to go working on the land. And after that I carried on with my farming, and went living-in at a farm at Lindow End, at Mobberley. Then of course went in Forces. Come back to Mobberley.

D.   The war must have been almost over by time you got into the Forces?

W.   Well it's . . . I forget. I come out about '46, came out, did about two or three years. The latter end of the war, yes. And we came back to in the old cottages, what used to be on the corner there, opposite The Greyhound. In 1946, when we came back there.

D.   Now what were you all doing at that stage?

W.   Farming. My dad worked down the farm down the road for - what was he called? Opposite Williamses, down that drive . . .

D.   What about you, when you came out of the Forces? Was it easy to find work?

W.   Yeah, I went back to farming. I went to Tatton. No I didn't. I went on't railway! No I didn't. I went to Tatton, that's it. Yeah, then went on't railway. Of course in them days you didn't stick in the job so long, you went where the money was. I went where the money was. Went on a milk round. That was when Freda and I first started going out together. Which we'd known one another since we was six or seven year old.

D.   So now that we've got to that point with you, can we go to Freda and hear what you'd been up to?

F.   I was born at Station Cottages, at Mobberley. But we lived at the end, this end, the Ashley end of Mobberley. At Brookside. We went to school at Knutsford though. We had more dealings with Knutsford as regards schooling and that. And then, after we all left school, we more or less went into Hale, for work and that.

W.   You went into the Land Army, didn't you?

F.   Yes, I was in the Land Army. I went when I was seventeen, and came out when I was about twenty one. At Moore, near Warrington. I lived at, went into lodgings with a Scots couple. And used to come home every weekend on my bicycle. I rode all the way, on a bike. During the summer time; I'm not saying during the winter. I didn't work really with the cattle, I worked with the horses. But I had to take my turn with the cattle, when it came winter time. There were three land girls. And the father had died, so there were three young boys that were running the farm, under the eye of the mother, and also an uncle, that used to supervise. It was very good.

D.   And what happened at the end? At the end of the war, did they just say, Well thank you very much, you can go home now?

F.   No, I decided I'd had enough, and was coming home. And that. I'd done five years. And I was coming home. That was it. Well, Mother was taken ill in '47. She had an operation for cancer. And so I more or less came home, because my eldest sister was looking after us all, and she'd a young baby. And then of course after Mother died she got a house at Bucklow Hill, so I stayed on at home. '48 mother died.

D.   And then suddenly you and Walter started going out?

F.   Well he was coming on the milk round. He was coming on the milk round, like, round.

W.   I worked for Bateses. They had the dairy in Hale, and his parents had the farm in Mobberley. So I had this Mobberley round. Round here, and Mobberley. And that's - like I say, we'd known one another from schooldays. We used to go down to my cousin's birthdays, didn't we? Mobberley Station. To my cousin, on her birthday, and parties.

F.   We married in 1950.

W.   Had two years at Mobberley, and then we made an exchange with the people that lived here. Her parents lived next door to us at Mobberley, and my parents lived there. So we made a swap.

F.   And with Margaret being how she was, I had to take her up on a bicycle to school. And myself and another person, she was trying to get a taxi to take them to school. Because we walked from Town Lane, right up by the church at Mobberley. And it was a long way. And I'd got Elizabeth and Margaret and David, and I was having Karen at the time, so it was too much for me to do each day. So, as I say, we changed from there when they decided that she could go to a normal school. While she was at Mobberley she went to a school at Bollington. They used to come every day, and take her to Bollington, to Macclesfield. Near Macclesfield, and that. And when they decided, they did the tests on her, they decided that ordinary school would be better for her. But of course she was getting on then. She was past what we'd call school age.

W.   She was only out of the Infants, wasn't she? When we got her into a Church School, or ordinary school I should say, not a church school.

D.   Do you remember any of this, Margaret?

M.   I can remember moving in 1960. Until then I had to go to a re - what's it?

F.   A rehabilitation centre.

M.   A rehabilitation centre. And of course when they moved here, I didn't move till about the December, to come.

D.   You were still in the rehabilitation centre?

W.   At Lancaster.

F.   No, no. No, not at Lancaster. At Rose Hill, at Marple.

M.   Of course I only saw my parents two days or three days a week. That was like on a Wednesday, and Saturday and Sunday. And it was a bit too much. I was glad to come home.

D.   I bet you were. How long had you been there?

F.   Seventeen weeks. Yes, when they'd operated on her leg, and they put it into plaster. That was it. And she stayed for seventeen weeks. That particular time.

M.   This is why I can't reckon up. You know, having missed school, and what have you. Just pushed from pillar to post, kind of. When my father first brought me here I wouldn't get out of the car. Because I told him it wasn't my house.

F.   She'd not seen the furniture come in, or anything. And nothing meant anything to her.

D.   And your parents were already established next door, Walter? When did they come, were they among the original people to move in?

W.   They were the first. You see when this estate was built, the Police House was the last to be built. These twenty six were built, and them two for Tatton. And then the Police House.

D.   Was your father still working at Tatton?

W.   At Tatton. And that's how he come to get the house. Like George Watson. He worked at Tatton. And they were Tatton houses. Because all this land belonged to Tatton. Two houses were built on the front, to Tatton's specification. And they had to build the two what Tatton said.

F.   And where the police house is was the kitchen garden to Colonel Bentley's. At Outwood. And you see Stan Jones worked as chauffeur. Stan Jones: Mr Jones's brother. He was the chauffeur, for the Bentleys. And Mrs Dean, next door, and her mother, they lived there. She was the housekeeper, the mother was the housekeeper, Mrs Ray. And Gwen was the maid.

W.   And George, did George work for Blockleys, was it? Castle Hill Farm. George went to Lower House Farm while he was here. And then George started up on a milk round, on his own. From there. The milk was from there, and everything. He was based down there, but working from here. Where these houses are at the back, what's the estate?

D.   Egerton Moss? Where the lads played football?

W.   That's right. Also George had some young stock, a couple of young stock on there. Each year. Because the bath was at the bottom of our garden. And we used to carry water up. There was no water laid on, we used to carry water for drinking water. George couldn't get to it from his garden, so he used to get his through this garden, round here. Filled the trough up with water. And there of course it was where the lads used to play football. There was quite a few lads on the estate, wasn't there? at the time.

F.   It was full.

W.   Nearly all the same age.

F.   The two Miss Simcocks had the post office. Which was just like a little room.

W.   It was behind a curtain, they didn't have a door. Living room, just a curtain.

F.   To draw it off. Curtain it off, and that. But you got everything. There were two Miss Simcocks. One used to suffer very much with an ulcerating leg, and she was always kind of "laid up".

D.   Was it their brother who lived over there, at number thirteen?

F.   Simcock? No. No relation. There were a lot of Simcocks.

D.   What about Barry Simcock, who married Fran?

F.   Barry Simcock? His mother and father used to live at the top of the road, just before you go down Breachouse. Where Caleb lives now. It was just a coincidence, the name.

D.   Tell me about your children, because I can never work out what order they come in.

W.   Elizabeth was born - listen - on the 21st April, 1952. Margaret was born on the 21st April, 1954. You got them dates? David was born the 17th December. Karen was born on the 18th December, two years after! And our Joan's the 27th August.

F.   Four years, Karen was.

W.   There's two on the same day, and the next two were one 17th and one 18th.

F.   And then Joan.

W.   She was born in 1960, wasn't she?

F.   Sixty six, Joan was born. And Elizabeth is married to Peter Mottershead.

D.   How was it, moving into here in 1960? And when eventually you agreed to come in, Margaret!

M.   That was when my dad dragged me out!

D.   How was it for you?

M.   Well, I get a bit fed up nowadays.

D.   But then?

M.   But then, like, with my dad being younger, we could get out in the car and go out, and what-have-you. But now, I just find I'm trapped.

D.   You play bowls, don't you?

M.   Oh yes, try to. And I play dominoes during the winter. I always take after my father, or try to! I don't win many games at bowls.

F.   You won a cup.

W.   You won the Shield twice.

M.   The Shield twice, that Ron MacFall used to run.

W.   It's not a local, it's a Wilmslow thing. I think he started doing it when he was in the police, before he retired. That's the Shield.

M.   It's like for the best ladies.

W.   It's just a day out, and having a meal after it. It's a fun afternoon. That was the end of it.

M.   I know when I first started, I bowled for The Bull. The Bull's Head, at Mobberley. Then I come in, and won my first game. And then on the Friday I went and broke my arm. That booked me the rest of the season. So they had to fetch my mum to the hospital. But that's what I find now, that I'm just trapped. Because I won't go on the train.

D.   So what do you do with yourself?

W.   Turn the television on!

M.   Well when my father bowls, and he won't book the car in, and he gets the registration wrong, I always argue with him! I just remember these car numbers. And you can say, like, what's Sheila Norbury's telephone number? and I just reel it off. I'd be good in the police!

D.   And what sorts of jobs have you done since you've been here, Walter?

F.   Since you were here you had the wagons.

W.   No, I didn't. I drove for J & A Jackson, brick manufacturers. Brick wagon. I left them and I went into the works, Broadheath. Overhead crane driver. I left there, and bought my own wagons. Had them for ten and a half years. Then I went working for the Council. I was there for thirteen years, and I retired. It doesn't seem the same now like what it used to be. 'Cause, I mean to say, younger ones are coming in, and that's it.

D.   And you can't replace neighbours like George and Gwen, can you?

M.   But you know like when Mr and Mrs Burdett were living here? Everything they did, my grandparents used to do. Like take the dog for a walk. And wave.

W.   Oh, I mean Alf was my dad to a T.

D.   I hadn't realised they were as similar as that.

W.   His ways, and everything. What he did was my dad to a T.

M.   Well I christened them Nanna and Granddad.

W.   My dad used to be tinkering with making anything. It had to be precise. Tap, tap, tap, he wouldn't hit anything hard. Whereas me, I'd gie it a good clonk wi' hammer. Not my dad. Nor Alf. No. They might have been twin brothers.

F.   They were very alike.

M.   Yeah. It was like having another family.

W.   Alf used to come in, come in on a Saturday morning specially, he used to come in and sit down where you are, "I've come out of her's way." Not her way, her's way!

F.   Oh he was, he was a character, was Alf.

Jenny McKenna. 2 Hough Green

D.   Jenny, you're one of the people who were born in Ashley, were you?

J.   Yes. In that house there.

D.   Where your parents still live? Can you recall your childhood in Ashley?

J.   There used to be a lot of children. It was good. I enjoyed my childhood. School was OK. I was a borderline for the grammar, and I went to Delahays Secondary. So I went to Timperley, an all girls' school. That was OK. Not wonderful, but OK.

D.   So who would have been your contemporaries at school here?

J.   What classmates, you mean? Maureen Norbury. All the Norburys. Andrew Slater; his family don't live here anymore. He was my best friend, really. He was a tall lad. He always didn't want me to be hurt by anybody. But I've not seen him since, for years and years. I never fell out with people. I'll tell who's a good friend to me, Philip Tickle. He was in my class.

D.   Would Kathryn Hobson have been in that class?

J.   Acually I can't remember her at that school.

D.   You remember her more living on The Green, I suppose?

J.   Oh, yes. As we grew older we went out together. Went on holiday together as well. And she was a bridesmaid at our wedding.

D.   Are there any others you remember as children?

J.   Margaret next door.

D.   Oh, Margaret Bell. Yes.

J.   In fact, we used to play skipping, outside. And Margaret could run faster than me.

D.   And she would have lived actually next door to you in those days? Oh no, no, they were here, weren't they, next door to you now. It would have been her grand-parents lived next door to you?

J.   That's right.

D.   So you went here, and went to Delahays: how did you find it, moving from a school with about forty children, to one with - I don't know how many hundreds?

J.   I'd rather have this school! But I settled. And went for typing. Did typing. And when I went to the Yoga class which I do every Monday, somebody came up to me and said, I know you from somewhere! And I still can't remember that girl. Gwen. And I don't normally forget things like that, but I still can't remember it.

D.   And what did you do after Delahays?

J.   Hairdressing. Went to college for two years, South Trafford. I did it for three years, because I started work as well, in Hale, at Pinewood. And I had another job at Hale Barns. Did quite well there, as well. And then I went to Altrincham. So I've met a lot of people in my life.

D.   That's three different hairdressing places. But when I first knew you, I think you were doing it in people's houses, going round to their homes.

J.   Yes, I was. That's when I was quite a bit older.

D.   You were married. You lived over there, didn't you, in Hough Green Cottages? Is that where your children were born?

J.   Yeah, I was in that house.

D.   I can't remember who is the eldest?

J.   Paul. He's twenty now.

D.   And was it then that you decided to do the hairdressing from house to house?

J.   Yeah. My kids have never been squealy . . . I suppose it's a lot for my mum, really.

D.   In what way?

J.   She said a funny thing. We went to Mrs Don's house the other day, and Mum just came out with it, to Mrs Williams. And Kay Williams said to her, Do you think you should be saying that? This was about my catheter. I hated it at first, and I don't really like it now. But I have one at night, and I can sleep right through. Before, my mum had to come and help me onto the toilet.

D.   Have you got a call thing round your neck? Yes.

J.   I used that the other day, when I was going to Mrs Don's house. I only have to speak to it, and they can hear me.

D.   It's a wonderful system.

J.   It is really, isn't it? Mum thinks everyone thinks it's free, and you've got a Red Cross list free. It's not. There's only one person who gets it free.

D.   Can we go on and talk more about the MS, since you've mentioned going to the Red Cross and so forth? When did it start?

J.   I was twenty eight. My eyes started. I went to the opticians, thinking I needed to wear glasses. But they said, No. Go to the doctor's. So I went to the doctor's.

(Enter her Cat)

149

D.   Hallo! I've got a picture of this cat. When we had that party. Right on top of the marquee, in the early morning. Looking as if he owned it as if it was put up for him.

J.   He's quite a character really.

D.   So the vision started going funny?

J.   Yes. But looking back, my feet were sore and stuff like that. I just thought, I'd got new shoes, and they were hurting.

D.   How long did they take to find out what the trouble was?

J.   After I went to the doctor's I went to Manchester Royal, and at Manchester Royal I had some words said to me. I looked in the book. And I knew I had it. I told her, and she agreed with me. Some people don't get told straight away. I think it's the type of person you are. I was twenty eight. I'm forty four next week.

D.   Are you really? You don't look it.

J.   Thank you. It's going to be hard saying I'm forty four. A lot of the girls that come here, said How old is Jenny? They thought I was thirty six. I was quite pleased.

D.   So it's been a long time. How does your day go, now?

J.   You mean a whole week? It's Yoga tomorrow. All for MS people. I've met a good crowd now. That's at Altrincham Sports Centre. I get picked up. That's tomorrow. And then I've got Tuesday: Tuesday I'll just be down at the Centre in Knutsford. Which is quite good really, because we have games. I quite enjoy it. I like winning!

D.   What are your favourite games? Chess, you said?

J.   Yes. I play chess. There's somebody else learning it at Knutsford as well. I don't play chess all the time. My favourite game is scrabble. My brother brought a scrabble game for my mum. I couldn't believe it. Madaline and my mum had a scrabble game last week. So we're back to Wednesday now. Wednesday the Red Cross have stopped doing. It's open Monday, Tuesday and Thursday. So I go on a Thursday anyway.

D.   And Wednesday you don't have anything regular now?

J.   No, it's quite good really. This Wednesday I'm going shopping with somebody.

D.   So that's Wednesday.

J.   Now Thursday . . . I'm not doing anything this Thursday. Then I've got a pub lunch on the fifth of October. That's "Pub lunch for Jenny's Birthday." I mean, they're all nice people.

D.   You're reading all this off what looks like a timetable sheet. Are all these activities organised by the same people?

J.   Red Cross.

D.   And they send the transport to pick you up and bring you home?

J.   Yes.

D.   And there's an activity most days of the week, by the sound of it?

J.   Apart from Wednesday.

D.   Is it based in any particular centre, or do you go all over the place? Yoga is at Altrincham Leisure Centre, Tuesday's in Knutsford . . .

J.   Yeah, Knutsford.

D.   So is it usually the same group of people?

J.   Not every time, no. Because we go out for days.

D.   And maybe different people do Yoga from the games?

J.   It's nothing to do with them. That's the MS people.

D.   It sounds as if you've got quite a wide circle of friends, as well as quite a lot of activities?

J.   Yes. Down the Centre we play bingo as well. And I said to somebody, I don't really enjoy that game. Miss Allen says, It's only because you didn't win, Jenny!

D.   True or false?!

J.   True!

D.   So what are the children doing now they're not children anymore?

J.   Paul's working with his dad. Industrial Roofer. Christine's at the Bowdon Hotel.

D.   Does she like that?

J.   No. But she's good at her job. She's good at it. But she doesn't like other people bossing over her. In that way she's like me.

D.   I have a daughter or two who are a bit like that!

J.   I went to see the Blackpool lights last week. They're good. I went to Jodrell Bank for the first time in my life. It's very good. I think it's good to go and see it once.

D.   And here you are back in Ashley, where you started. So you've come a full circle now. You went off when you moved to Knutsford.

J.   Then we went over Warrington way.

D.   How is it, coming back here? Of course you've been back some time now.

J.   I don't know how many years I've been here.

D.   Neither do I. I only know it's several. But are you glad to be back?

J.   Oh, yeah. It's hard seeing new people come into the village. But there again, I can't go out, to them. But I'm happy in the house. Doing all this sort of thing is good.

D.   It keeps you going, doesn't it? It doesn't sound as if you have all that much time. Hearing you say you're quite glad not to have anything to do on Wednesdays, so that you can go and see that shop.

J.   It's like people at the moment get me up in the morning, and put me to bed at night. Mum thinks that's terrible, but I'm happy. I've got a television upstairs. So I'm happy with life here. I'm lucky.

Cat on a cool canvas roof: "Looking as if he owned it..."
(Photograph, Amanda Ellington)

Peter Turner. 3 Hough Green

D.   How long have you lived in Ashley, Peter?

P.   Fifteen years now.

D.   What brought you here?

P.   I was born and brought up in Altrincham. And I married in Altrincham my first wife, and had three children. And then we divorced, and I met my present wife, who lived in Mobberley, and we applied for a council house, and they came up with this one in Ashley, which was perfect.

D.   Just split the difference.

P.   Beautiful. Couldn't be better.

D.   And how did you find it, moving in?

P.   It's hard work at first. It wanted completely redecorating, and the garden was overgrown. It was hard work, but we got on top of it. We like it now, it's an ideal situation.

D.   What about coming into the neighbourhood?

P.   The neighbours couldn't be better. It's perfect. It's a very friendly place, Ashley.

D.   You came from Altrincham: did you work in Altrincham?

P.   I served my apprenticeship as an electrical engineer in Trafford Park. And then when I was twenty one I went in the RAF, National Service, for two years, which I really enjoyed. And then I came out and went back into electrical engineering.

D.   And you've been doing that ever since?

P.   No, I had a break of seven years when I was a steward of a club in Altrincham, the ASE Club. And it was then when I got divorced, so we left there and I went back into my original trade.

D.   And do you still do that?

P.   No, I've retired now. I retired last Christmas.

D.   How do you find it, retired?

P.   It couldn't be better actually. There's a quote in the paper, a person said The only thing wrong with retirement is that you don't get a day off. Which is true! You can find so much to do. I do a lot of Crown Green bowling, I play five or six times a week. And I've taken up golf. I'm really enjoying that now. I've always been active. I think I've played every sport possible, in my lifetime: cricket, tennis, football, rugby, you name it.

D.   Which would be your favourite of them all?

P.   Bowls, probably.

D.   How long have you been playing?

P.   Thirty years? I play for the Railway Inn at Mobberley. I've played for other clubs. I used to play for the Victory Hall at Mobberley, I played for the ASE Club when I was there, in the Altrincham League. I've played bowls for a long time now. But I'm getting to like golf.

D.   You took that up actually when you retired?

P.   When I retired. I've always fancied playing golf, it appealed to me, but I never had the time. So I talked it over with Jenny and . . . she bought me a set of clubs for Christmas. So I did it the right way, went and had twelve lessons with a professional. And I'm really into it now, it's a good game.

D.   It's fascinating to hear you say that, because my wife happened to be looking out of the window, and I think she saw you chip from outside your garden, over the hedge back in.

P.   I practise chipping from this garden, over the hedge into the front garden.

D.   When she told me I couldn't believe it, I said, You're seeing things! I couldn't believe you'd have the confidence to do that: you could wreak havoc, couldn't you, with your windows and things!

P.   No, no. Not chipping, no. I've been practising it so long now that - it's something you've got to practise, it's the hardest shot in golf, chipping on. To get the distance right.

D.   How do you go on, as a new player and a new member, finding people to play with?

P.   Very easily. The Railway have a golf society, the Railway Inn. They also have one at the Victory Hall, where I play snooker. And since I've finished my lessons and taken up playing there are numerous people saying How do you fancy a round of golf? In fact last week I went and played in a team game at Styal, which I really enjoyed. It was a match against another pub. It's progressing now, I get different people saying Do you fancy a game? The chap from the Garage here, Harold Haddock, he found out I played golf and he said Oh you'll have to come and play with me. In fact he phoned me last week, but I couldn't go because I was going to Chester races.

D.   Yes, I see what you mean about being busy!

P.   Plenty to do!

D.   It sounds as if a lot of your activities are centred round Mobberley?

P.   I play snooker for the Victory Hall, in the Knutsford League. It costs ten pounds to join the Victory Hall at Mobberley. And you can go in every night of the week, and it only costs you 20p for half an hour.

D. And is it fairly easy to get a game?

P. Oh yes. At the weekend you can get a game any time, but during the week, in the evenings, Tuesdays, Wednesdays and Thursdays are match nights. They have four different teams. But Mondays, Fridays, Saturdays and Sundays you can get a game. It's cheap, it's friendly. It's a good club.

D. You mentioned the garden was in a state when you first came. I've always noticed you spend a lot of time in the garden.

P. Well you have to, don't you? Especially this time of year. Look at that hedge now. As soon as it gets dry again I've got to cut the hedge.

D. Of course, being on a corner, you've got garden both sides - or all three sides.

P. Three really. We've got the small one here, we've got the other side, and the big one at the back.

D. What do you do with it?

P. I've got two lawns. Last Sunday I got a lot of flowers: dahlias, freesias. We've got roses at the back, miniature roses at the front. Keeps me busy.

D. I should think so. And what about the rest of the family?

P. There's Jenny, my wife. Victoria, my eldest daughter, she's eighteen. Lindsay, the youngest, is fifteen.

D. What are they doing now?

P. Jenny's working now at The Railway, she does bar work. When she's not work-ing at her regular job, which is a care assistant: she goes to different homes, these old people's homes. Mainly now she's at the David Lewis Centre, probably two or three days a week there. Victoria's just started a job in child care. She's working at Bankhall Lane Day Nursery.

D. How does she like that?

P. She loves it. She always wanted to do that. She tried one place and she didn't like it, and then she saw this advertised, and she got the job. They allow her a day off a week to go to college.

D. What does she do there, is there a special child care certificate?

P. Yes, it's all about child care. And health-and-safety. First Aid, and things like that. All the things involved in child care.

D. So that's Victoria, and then there's Lindsay.

P.   She's still at Knutsford High. She's at that age now, she knows best.

D.   You mean there's an age when they don't know best?! The other thing I associate with you - this is from Ron MacFall: you and he seem the only two people left who know how to dress!

P.   People still talk about me. I went to a race meeting, it was a trip out: twenty fellows from the Victory Hall went to the Haydock races. We hired a coach. And they called me the Master of Ceremonies! Just because I'd got a jacket and tie on! I was the only one with a tie on. I've always done: if I'm going anywhere I put a tie on. People don't do it these days. Ron and Roy and I, and Jenny, all play for The Railway at dominoes. That's another game during the winter, another night gone! It keeps you out of trouble.
      Have you heard about this spur they're putting on this railway line?

D.   Yes. Just this week.

P.   They were all parked up at the crossings at Mobberley, all the workers. They're doing some repairs on the line. One of the chaps who lives in one of the cottages there, they wouldn't let him go over the crossings to his home. Anyway he had a bit of a row with them and they let him go eventually, and he was talking to them in the end, and he said, What's happening, then? and they said, Well eventually, in the next twelve months or so, we'll be putting a spur from between Ashley and Mobberley, over to Ringway Airport.

D.   Well it was an obvious thing to do sooner or later, wasn't it?

P.   It'll be a good thing for a lot of people. I mean, look at people from Chester who'll be able to go on their holiday by train, won't have to get a taxi to the airport, or come by car and park it for a fortnight. Just jump on the train now. Cost a fortune to park your car for two weeks there. Some beggar used to park it here, you know. Did you ever see a Mercedes parked? I thought it had been pinched. But it worked out in the end that it was somebody who'd been abroad for their holidays, parked their car here and got a taxi to take them to the airport. Saved about £100 in parking fees.

Stella and Rafe Grassby. 5 Hough Green

R.   I was born in Hale in 1920. My father bought two acres of land in Mobberley for £50 - you won't believe this - and he built this wooden bungalow with one bedroom, and I think I went there when I was about seven, when we moved there. And then he built another one, a brick bungalow next to it. I reckon that cost him three hundred pounds, it was a brand new one. That was all done with casual labour like.

S.   Well I was born in Over, near Peover. I was brought up with my grandmother. In Ashley. Dairy Farm Cottages. But I went to Knutsford School. My mother didn't live there, she managed hotels. She managed The Angel in Knutsford, then The George. And then a big hotel near Lake Windermere.

D.   Did you often see her?

S.   Oh, yes. I travelled, more than what he did. I went to France. We used to go to London. Brighton, a lot. I had an aunty living in London, and I went to Paris when I was about eight, with my aunt. And she had a big house in Maida Vale. And we went everywhere.

D.   And you mentioned going to school in Knutsford, but did you go to Ashley School?

S.   No. No, I never wanted to leave Knutsford School. Because all my friends were there. First of all they sent me to a boarding school, my father and my mother. But I didn't like it, so my mother brought me back, and she found somewhere for me to stay in Knutsford. And then after a while, when I was ten or eleven, I came to live with my grandmother, in Ashley. And I lived there till I left school. And I left Knutsford School, and, erm, then I met you, didn't I?

R.   Aye. It was only because I'd got a motorbike!

D.   I expect you were good-looking as well, Rafe!

S.   My mother saw me as much as she possibly could, but she had to work a lot, to keep me. She kept me very well.

R.   She was a right Tartar though, wasn't she? Always chasing me, she was. Didn't like me, she didn't like me. *You get away from my daughter!* She once took us to that play in Manchester, Ivor Novello in *The Dancing Years*. And I thought it was a comedy, I burst out laughing. And she played hell with me. He come on in a little pair of shorts, and I burst out laughing.

S.   Yes, well the thing was, that was the way I was brought up. I was brought up to go to theatres, the ballet, and everything like that, you see. Even to learn to speak French, at a school in Knutsford.

D.   How did you meet?

R.   I think she was waiting for the bus once, wasn't you?

S.   Missed the bus. We both of us missed the bus, we'd been to the pictures. I missed the bus and you missed the bus. So we both walked home. From Altrincham. And that's when it started.

R.   And what I used to do, I used to - I didn't dare knock at the door - I used to whistle outside. And carry on up towards the bridge and then walk back again and we used to meet. And this night I was whistling and nothing happened: no Stella, nothing. So I went back, and her grandfather was stood at the gate. He said, *I'll bloody shoot you, you're like a bloody canary whistling*, he said.

S.   And of course we met as we walked back, and that was it, wasn't it? There and then on.

R.   And I've suffered ever since!

D.   Now nobody's going to believe that, Rafe!

Then came the war (see Appendix), during which their eldest, Pauline, was born. After the war:

S.   I went to live with his mother. She had a conservatory, and a room off it. I was in there, you see.

D.   By this time was it still only Pauline?

S.   Pauline, Yes. And Ray on the way. My son. Anyway, there was a little wooden bungalow, where they first used to live. So they gave us that, gave me that. I decorated it all and everything. Pregnant about seven month, and doing ceilings! You had to do in those days. And the rations were still on. Anyway after you came out we put our name down for a house. And believe it or not we had our eldest daughter in a cot, at eight? We had one bedroom and a living room. And we couldn't get a house till we got this. And we were the first to move into these houses.

D.   So there were the two children, eight and six. And if Pauline was in a cot, where did Ray sleep?

S.   He was in a cot. One each side of the bed. And our bed was in the middle.

D.   In this bungalow in Mobberley?

R.   That wooden place we lived in, what my father had built: when we was kids it was fine, we only had one bedroom. The Sunday School across the road, my father used to send us there for Sunday School, to get us out of the way. It was the only time he could get my mother on her own, having only one bedroom. And it's funny, we finished up back there, didn't we? When I got demobbed.

D.   So did you do that as well, send your two to Sunday School?!

S.   No. No we didn't, no.

R.   And that Dr Gatting, he was a smashing doctor. Our Ray, he had trouble with his what'sit, and he come and circumcised him on the table, do you remember?

S.　We scrubbed the table down.

R.　And my father had this brick one built, next to it. And you know Freda Bell? Well her father did all the joinery work on it. We were in bed one morning, and my father had ordered a load of sand. And as he come up the drive the wagon caught the corner of this bungalow. And we was in bed, and all of a sudden it was open at one end. And this face comes through there! I'm very sorry, he said!

D.　So was this more or less still a building site, when you moved in here?

R.　I was the night watchman on this, and I was getting more as a night watchman than what I was doing full-time, gardening. And this big Irish foreman come to the door, he said *Would you like a job, boss?* I said, I've got one. Oh, he said, *Night watchman. Just keep your eye on all this stuff in the midddle of The Green.* Because all the baths and that were there, you know. And I looked out the window one morning, and there was a wagon down there, where Ted Tickle lives now, and they were taking stuff out of the house. And I thought he was one of these workmen. But he was taking stuff out!

D.　So did you go and do your stuff?

R.　I never bothered! And we heard this noise one night, and I looked out and I saw this window frame going off The Green, and I saw him put it on a cart across the road there. So I said, What you doing Fred? He said, I'm trying to finish a job off. I said Put it back. So he went and took it back, but it had gone again next morning, so !

D.　So who came here next? Who were your first neighbours?

S.　Betty Bradley, next door. There was Mrs Roberts, Mrs Laxton, Betty and us, they were the first ones to be finished. We moved in first, and then Betty moved in next, and Mrs Laxton moved in. This is all in 1951. And they all said to us, You're getting a new house, and new babies. I said oh no, no, no. But there was. My youngest son!

D.　And how did you find it, settling in here?

S.　I didn't like it. When I left Mobberley I cried and I cried and I cried. I knew everybody. I didn't know anybody at all when I moved into these houses.

D.　How did the children get on moving here, Pauline and Ray?

S.　Oh fine, I think. There were quite a few children really.

D.　And did they start going to the school here then?

S.　Yes, they went to school here. Then finished off at the other school.

R.　We used to have to walk from Mobberley, when we were going to here, we used to have to walk. When we was kids, 1928, I used to walk from Mobberley to here.

D.　You went to school here? I'd no idea you went to school here.

R.   Oh yes. Our names are on that shield there. If they've still got it. Little shields.

S.   How many children was there? Must have been fifty-odd children.

R.   They all had big families. Mind, there was nothing else to do of an evening. No televisions. All the kids grew with each other. They all had kids didn't they, round here.

S.   Well Peggy and I and Vera, we used to play with the children. We used to play rounders, cricket. And we used to make all the bonfires for them. On The Green, didn't we?

R.   Used to have a blooming big fire in't middle of The Green.

D.   Like they have round the back now? You used to do that?

S.   The three of us did that, yes. One of us would make parkin, one would make treacle toffee. And give them all potatoes, you could put them in the fire, you know. Good days.

D.   Where did you work, Rafe?

R.   I went to the brickyard. Oh no, I went to Clibrans first. No, brickyard first.

S.   Yes, then Clibrans, then to your father's.

R.   Aye. When I went working at the brickyard, that's near the airport, I was there about three years, and I was on my bike. And on a Monday morning, when the clay face was wet, the clay used to be that wet, and he couldn't make bricks with it. We used to tip it in the pan at the top, feed in like a big pan, and it used to be like sludge. So somebody brought a clever idea, We'll put this powder on. And we found out after, it was grey asbestos powder. It used to come in big sacks, and a fellow at the bottom of the gantry, he used to put half a shovelful of this stuff, and we'd tip it in the pan, and it used to all dry up lovely and that. After about two or three month everyone was covered in this grey powder. And the lad who worked with me, his nose started bleeding. And he found out he'd got cancer.

S.   With this asbestos powder.

R.   Shortly after I was getting that short-winded, I'd get as far as Ashley School, and that was it.

D.   I was wondering about your emphysema.

R.   Aye. As far as Ashley School, and then I had to get off my bike. And eventually I packed up altogether, didn't I? I was in bed for quite a while. I think it was that asbestos stuff.

D.   Sounds very likely, yes.

R.   I was under this Dr Fleming for about three year, wasn't I?

S.   Mister Fleming.

R.   I used to go and see him and have an X-ray every two month. And he said, You were very lucky, he said, because all it did, it did the bottom of my lungs. My top half was all right. But it's all dead down the bottom half. And he said I was very lucky. So after that I had to go working for my father. It was the worst job I had in my life, that. They say you should never work for your father, don't they? I mean I watch you and Charlie get on, because you always have a laugh, don't you? But me and my father were always at loggerheads. But it's a good job I had my dad to work for, because I don't think I'd have worked anywhere else. Seven days a week, it was.

D.   What sort of work was it?

R.   Importing animals. He imported everything - snakes, monkeys, parrots, fish. Tropical fish, goldfish. He had nearly four hundred fish tanks. And he had about three big sheds. And he used to have bush babies, snakes, monkeys, parrots. We used to work seven days a week. Our busiest day was Sunday. You know, with the shops being shut. All the shopkeepers used to come and . . .

D.   People coming to buy them?

R.   Mmm. Then he had this agency for a firm in Denmark, birdfoods, dog foods; making a fortune out of that. Paying nineteeen and a tanner in the pound, one time. And I was on ten quid a week.

S.   He used to do some for laboratories, didn't he?

R.   Aye. Oh, guinea pigs. He had about three hundred guinea pigs.

S.   You opened the door, and they were all squeaking away!

Christine and David Ellington. 6 Hough Green

D.   Before we get onto what you want to talk about, just tell us how long you've lived in Ashley, and how you came here?

C.   We came here in 1982 because it was a small parish, and my husband . . .

D.   What are the sort of things that interest you?

C.   Well above all, if I could get a bit better, it would be the privilege of knowing people very intimately which comes with counselling. Because I don't think that I've ever done anything so fulfilling and in every way totally satisfying: because the other person can feel free to say anything they like, knowing that I won't repeat it. The other person can get angry, or cry, or laugh, and be free. And I just feel . . . there's nothing in life I've ever experienced like it.

D.   How did you get into it?

C.   Well my illness goes up and down. And at one of the stages when I was able to get out I did a couple of counselling courses at South Trafford. And should do another one, ideally, but this is sufficient for counselling: which really means not something advising, but listening carefully, and picking up on all the clues. Most of the time is spent in being silent while the other person talks.

D.   It's strange, isn't it? I wonder how many people know that's what it's about, because you hear the word "Counselling", and you immediately associate it with giving advice. "The sort of counsel I'd give my children", usually means fairly heavy-handed advice! The opposite extreme.

C.   I think it's a very bad name, and you're right. Also for someone in many previous jobs, such as the one I was in which was being a GP, it's very difficult to take away the directive aspect, which has to be taken right away. The counsellor has nothing to do with directing and, yes, it should be called something else. I can't think what at the moment, but something to do with listening.

D.   Yes. Yes, it sounds more like a listening service, the way you describe it. But you just mentioned that you were a GP: a lot of people, I think, would be surprised to hear you being so excited by the experience of counselling after that, because a lot of us would think of a GP's job as being one of the most fulfilling and satisfying things that are available. And yet, here you are saying - sounding as if you're saying - that you've found counselling much more so.

C.   You're right. The simplest, most basic reason that comes to mind is that I think the allowance is six or seven minutes per patient at a surgery; and my surgery was at the end of quite a long corridor, and if it was a person who walked slowly the six minutes would probably be gone by the time they'd walked in the door! Whereas with counselling it's near enough an hour per person. What previously someone would have taken to the GP and been allowed five minutes for, they are now allowed an hour for the same -

D.   But then there's the feeling that doctors can *do* something. You know, they can bring some effective treatment to bear on the situation: I mean, What can a counsellor actually do? What difference does it make to the person who comes and spends an hour?

C.   I think I can only put it to you this way. Disregarding the fact that you may have had experience of this sort of thing, if you think of going to someone for an hour, who is going to be listening to what you say, listening to your silence if you don't want to say anything and not interrupting, letting you cry if you want to and not putting an arm round you to try and stop you crying and indicating that's enough: this is entirely the hour belonging to that person, and is actually more confidential than the doctor's, because doctors can write letters to other doctors; they have to, to refer patients. Counsellors may not talk about their . . . they tend to be called clients, not a very nice word - to anybody. And the safety! When someone realises that what they're saying is as tightly confidential as that, they can completely open up with things they've never opened up before. And I testify, not only as a person in the counsellor's chair, but as having been counselled for a couple of years, it's an unbelievable experience, a releasing experience; and to compare that with having a urinary tract infection and taking an antibiotic, is like comparing an angel with a cow.

D.   Dear me! That is strong. So tell me how you felt when you first discovered this? I mean, for someone who's done a six-year full-time training for a professional career, something that is only going to ask of you three hours a week for one year, it must have seemed as you were starting out, Oh, this is second best; it's not what I'd choose to do, but it's better than nothing. At what stage did you discover that there was all this richness involved?

C.   Yes, I can see that you're comparing six years with one year. Although a lot of the six years, I must say, was just straight learning. Memorising. But in that one year, I think for the first time for most people - most people - they were willing in the end to open themselves completely, I think completely. And we all walk about perhaps showing a side of us to the rest of the world; but there's a side, which perhaps gets talked about to our spouses occasionally, but not one hour's listening where nothing is going to be condemned, nothing. It just doesn't matter what the person has done: they will not be condemned. So the process doesn't develop into a sort of family argument, because the focus is entirely on the client and the client's well-being; and they will not, under any circumstances at all, be criticised unless they choose to criticise themselves. And this is an experience that . . . that defies words. It's magic.

D.   May I just interrupt? It sounds as if you're talking about the experience of receiving counselling.

C.   I think what I'm saying really would apply either way, thinking of the way I've been involved in the counselling side, and the person there has said what in everyday life would be shocking. But it wasn't shocking. It was something they said, and went on to talk about it if they wished and, again, at long last, they could talk about something which might have been eating them away for years. I think until a person has been involved in it it's an experience which - like any other experience in life which one hasn't done and which is marvellous, like going through the sound barrier, going round the world in a yacht, - it's not necessarily always relating, but it's releasing. And, as students in that year, we could not wait for Tuesdays to come round, and we used to say, What will we do on Tuesdays after this? What will we do? It will just be a void.

D.   And what was it you actually did do on Tuesdays during that year, that you could-n't imagine yourselves doing without?

C.   It was divided into three bits. One was learning about the theory which we had to do; the next bit was in twos and threes practising for the real thing, and then the last part was to do with being more aware of ourselves, in something called Personal Development: small groups, with a tutor there to make sure things didn't get out of hand, and again more opening up.

D.   Listening to you talking, really it sounded as if it was generating in you, - almost a wonder, this experience. I'm just wondering which of these parts it was: was it the practising? or was it this last bit in the group when you were all talking between your-selves?

C.   I think if anything it was probably the group, because the practising had certain definite aspects which we had to practise, whereas in the group it was quite open. And it was very interesting that we might get to the end of the group, and people would say to the tutor, Please can we go on with that subject next week? And he was a very very wise man, and he said, If you still want to next week, wait till next week. And almost inevitably, when next week came, it was another subject that came up. Whereby one learned, almost so that when the client came in, in real life, what they came in with was not going to be the next chapter in a book. They could want to talk about something completely, totally different: either that had happened to them dur-ing that week, or just out of the blue, or just sit until they were inspired to talk about anything. Because it's open, within the little room where you're sitting, it's open. But that's all.

D.   Again, it strikes me as quite fascinating, for someone who's been a doctor, to be able to live happily in a situation that you're describing, which sounds so unstruc-tured. I mean, it doesn't sound as if there's even any continuity from week to week when you're working with clients. They might come in with anything, at random.

C.   If the situation permits, and unfortunately the NHS doesn't always permit, of plenty of sessions: in the end the whole person will start to knit together. If it's only six sessions, that would be all right for a problem, one problem, but for the person-ality there wouldn't be anything like enough. But I think medicine has a certain deifi-cation that is just not wanted. People have a big red swollen toe and show it to the doctor. Well, a thousand to one you've got gout. I mean, it's as easy as that. Now com-pare that - and there's a treatment involved - compare that with the intricacies of a personality! It's child's play! I've just chosen one instance, I mean some others are very complicated.

D.   So it's the fascination of the intricacies of personality, as they gradually disclose themselves?

C.   AND it's a privilege, and it's very humbling, to have another human being who is prepared to open up their heart and tell you what's inside. Particularly as they've never told anyone else before.

D.   Several of the things you've said have seemed to imply that this opening up brings a great sense of release, relief, to whomever it is who's talking, and who's perhaps never said this to anybody else before; it brings them a feeling of release. That's the impression I get, listening to you.

C.   Yes. I must say I'm not so experienced to comment, probably because I think there will be angry people, and resistant people; and I haven't had the lot.

D.   Presumably they wouldn't be so likely to go and see a counsellor in the first place?

C.   Well, not unless they were sent by the court.

D.   What I'm getting at, and wondering, is whether you feel - whether you regret that there aren't more opportunities for people to open their hearts, if it brings such release?

C.   More opportunities?

D.   For people, in everyday life, not necessarily going to see a counsellor, to speak openly in this manner, and at this level?

C.   I don't think many of us would want to disclose our innermost selves to many others, really. And we certainly wouldn't want to if there was any chance that it might be repeated to someone else. So that's a great factor. And the person to whom you're talking in everyday life may not be trained - because this couldn't be done without training - in how to handle what you're saying. So a counselling situation doesn't arise. I'm so sorry, I've forgotten . . .

D.   No, I think you're answering it, because I was wondering, listening to the enthusiasm you were expressing for the beneficial effects of counselling, I was just wondering if you felt it was a pity there weren't more opportunities for people in everyday life to unburden themselves. And I think you're answering that very clearly, by saying No, because in ordinary everyday life communication between people is a two-way process, and what a person in counselling needs is someone who's going to listen without putting their side of the thing; and this needs a certain amount of training. And I'm curious about that: I'm just wondering how on earth a person can be trained to do a thing like that?

C.   I think we just had an example then. You took a little while, with pauses, to say what you wanted to say. I could have interjected, and say, "Or do you mean such and such?" when you paused. But it was much better that I kept quiet and you found what you wanted to say, rather than I suggested to you what you wanted to say. So one of the main things is accurate, concentrated listening. Without interrupting, or suggesting anything *en route*. And then, inevitably really, the person says what they want to; or if they don't, and you still keep quiet, they'll have another go. Now in counselling you are allowed to just check that what they have said is what they mean you to hear. So you are allowed to repeat, in some way, what they've just said: if they've said *My son is absolutely driving me crazy day and night. He brings in so many girls, and I can't keep up with them. And they're so noisy . . .* This is a deliberate pause in case there was something else coming in, but there wasn't. So it would then be permissible to say,

So it's your son . . . that's nearly driving you crazy . . . Just to focus on what it is that a person is talking about.

D.   Because it might have been the girls that were driving her crazy?

C.   It could have been. Or the noise. So you just want to clarify what she really means. And she might answer, *Oh no, it's not my son. It's the girls with their records . . .*

D.   Yes. I was going to ask if it's important to be right? Be accurate in your reflection? What I mean by that is, is it important to be right in saying "So it's your son . . ." or "the girls . . ." or " the noise . . ." If you say, Oh it's the noise, would that be enough for her to say, No, it's my son, fancy my son behaving like this . . . sort of thing. Would that . . . ?

C.   Well she did start off by saying, My son is driving me crazy . . . And that is where the intense listenings go on, as to *exactly* what she said. She didn't say, The noise in my house is driving me crazy, she said, My son . . . But, when I clarified it, I might well have got back, *"Don't you be rude about my son! I'm not talking about my son!"* I could easily get that tone of voice. Now that's where you have to be trained to just let it come out, don't interrupt, let her say exactly what she wants to say. She's probably going to cry any minute. Let her cry. Don't move. If you put your arm round her, which is permissible in this game, that's a signal saying Please stop crying, we've had enough. All you have to do is have a box of hankies, and let her go on as long as likes. And you don't interrupt when she's stopped crying, because that is the precise moment when she's going to tell you something probably, about this son. So you do have to learn it.

D.   The learning of that must be quite hard. Because, going back to somebody crying, you must feel that you are being hard-hearted by seeming not to be doing anything to relieve the distress. I mean, I would be wanting to say, "There, there, dear, don't cry . . .", and you're having to remain out of it: I would feel I was behaving in a hard-hearted sort of way.

C.   I see, so it's distress. Because if they were laughing, you wouldn't ask them to stop laughing. It's only if they're crying. You're trying to stop them showing the emotion that they're feeling: but if they were feeling happy and tickled and what-not, and they laughed, you wouldn't say, Stop laughing: that would be permissible.

D.   Well, you're probing around inside me a bit now, I feel, and I have to say I would feel definitely instinctively drawn to try to stop someone crying. No, I wouldn't stop somebody laughing, you're quite right. I'd feel quite happy with somebody laughing, but I don't feel happy with somebody crying. Because they're not happy. I'd want to make them feel better!

C.   There are two points. One is that counselling skills have to be learnt. These are the sort of things that partly are taught; but partly - I don't know - they come instinctively with experience.

Len and Bertha Roberts. 7 Hough Green

D.   How did you come to be in Ashley, Bertha?

B.   Father worked at Ryecroft Farm, at Hope's, in Ashley. And put his name down on the list when houses were being built here. Before that we were living in Rostherne. But even then I attended Ashley School, and the church in Ashley.

D.   So when did you come into The Green?

B.   When the houses were first built. 1950/51. We got the bungalow.

D.   Where Trevor lives, Number 16? And your parents were the Jenningses weren't they? Did you have brothers and sisters?

B.   Brother Albert, who lived on The Green as well. When we first came to The Green he lived here. Albert was already here with his family. He'd married. Albert got here first. Then Father and Mother.

D.   Three of you, in the bungalow. And what about you, Len, how did you get here?

L.   I was born in Oswestry, and moved to Mobberley. My father was a farm worker. And then about 1950 he had to give in work because of his health. And being a tied house he had to move out. And we got them a house here, Number 15. Where Albert used to live. Where Pat lives now. And then I came home, 1952, came back from Korea. When we were in Mobberley I joined the army.

D.   How did you come to decide on that? Had you always wanted to be a soldier?

L.   No actually, as a young lad I was always set to go in the Navy. To go straight from school. Sent off to the naval school. But I was leaving school at the end of December '44, or 20th January '45, I would have done; but in September '44 my brother was killed in the Air Force. His plane was shot down. So they didn't want me going into the forces.

D.   Yes, that's understandable. So that was the end of the Navy for you: what did you do instead?

L.   Well my first job was with a clothing manufacturer in Manchester. And then I went in the Rectory Garage, Mobberley. It's now been pulled down. And then when I was seventeen I got fed up with things, and decided I - again I went in and made enquiries about the Navy, but you had to sign on for twelve years. And at seventeen twelve years is a long time. We were wandering round Manchester and saw the Army recruiting office. There you could sign for five years. So I joined the army.

D.   Did you consult your parents, or had you decided to paddle your own canoe?

L.   Well, I signed on and then told them! Mother wasn't very pleased, but . . . One of the advantages of going in as a regular, you could choose your Regiment. I joined the Royal Electrical and Mechanical Engineers.

D.   Ah, yes. And how was it, the five years?

L.   Fine. If it hadn't been for meeting Bertha I'd have stayed.

D.   We must come to that in a minute, but you say you went out to Korea: how long was that?

L.   Eighteen months. I went in October 1950, and came back in May 1952. I was with a small unit attached to an Infantry Brigade, an L.A.D. [*Light Aid Detatchment*]. So that, although you were forward area, being with Brigade HQ you were just far enough back to miss the actual fighting.

D.   And did it live up to your expectations, being in REME?

L.   Yeah. The only regrets are that I didn't take advantage of the opportunities that were there.

D.   Well the Korean War got in the way, I suppose. Was it valuable as a training?

L.   I think it gave you more independence. You had to stand on your own feet.

D.   What about the actual trade? Learning a trade?

L.   Again, I'd have been better if I'd have been in a workshop. I'd have had more training. Because in the Light Aid Detatchment you only did running repairs. Just kept the vehicles going. If there was any major work it had to come back to the workshop. So we were restricted in that way.

D.   By the time you came back it was 1952. What was it like coming out of the army after five years?

L.   It was a bit hard!

D.   Did you find work fairly quickly?

L.   Oh yes, no problem there. I went to Quicks first, in Hale; no longer in existence. But I got fed up with that because I was stuck in the workshop, after being used to outside. And I saw a job advertised for a chauffeur fitter for a builder. So I got that job. And that's what started me in the building trade.

D.   Back now to coming home: what was The Green like, how did you find that?

L.   Well at that time there was quite a lot of children on it, wasn't there?

D.   Everyone had moved in, by the time you got back?

B.   Yes, I think we were the last to come in, on that side. They were all completed. Most of them had children, and the children went to Ashley School. And I was in my twenties, wasn't I? By that time I was a secretary in Altrincham.

D.   And how did you and your parents find it?

B.   Well, quite a vast change, actually. Because we'd been in a house in Birkin Heath with no bathroom; no running water, only recently, about two months before we came; and electricity, we hadn't got electricity at the cottage. So it was quite different when we came up here!

D.   And here you are, with twenty two pairs of eyes focused on your front door! How did that feel?

B.   Well it was quite good, because it was company. We knew quite a lot of people already here. Jean Hobson. Joan Blain was there, she left earlier than we did; and May Fisher, the Fisher children - Mottersheads, they were then. The Hunts, Geoff and Kathleen, were where Geoff lives now. I think Jean was in the house with Ron when we came. But I'd known Joan and her sisters, because they used to live on Station Cottages, and they all came to school at the same time, so . . . And Trevor. he was down Station Cottages as well. He was at school at the same time. Peter Wright was another one who was at school at the same time. Below me, I think! So I wasn't coming to a strange place.

D.   No. More of a strange place for your family, I suppose, Len?

L.   Yes. We were in Wood Lane, Mobberley, shut off now by the airport. Just the two cottages and the nursery across the road. I'd got used to being with different people, but it must have been quite a culture shock for them because, again, at Mobberley we had no electricity and no gas. No hot water.

D.   And that's just after the war? And that was the usual, wasn't it?

B.   Yes, well I was in my twenties when we came here, and that was the first time we'd had a bathroom, an indoor toilet, and things.

D.   And can you remember how you met each other?

L.   On the train going up to Manchester.

B.   We were both going to the pictures, I think.

L.   I was still in the army.

D.   So you were coming and going? And when did you finally come out?

L.   1953. And we got married in March '56. I got called back to the army in August.

D.   I'm trying to think what was happening. Suez?

B.   That was Suez, yeah. And he got his job back when he came out.

L.   Most firms kept your job. I was only in about three months.

D.   So by this time you were clearly established in building?

L.   As a plant fitter.

D.   Yes, I see, yes. So you got married in 1956: where did you set up home?

L.   At first with my parents at Number 15. Rose had got married. Then my father died. My mother decided in the end to go down to Cornwall. Two of my sisters lived down there. She just couldn't get over the loss of Dad. So she moved down there. The council said that we could have the house, on condition that we moved to a three-bedroom. Albert needed a four-bedroom, so we swapped. They just said we must move to a three-bedroom. It was up to us how we arranged it. It worked out very well.

B.   Because at that time Albert had Pat's grandmother, as well as three children. So they needed a bigger house. And the council allowed us to change houses. That was in November 1961, was it? Ian, our eldest son, was born while we were across there, and then Andrew was born over here.

D.   What does Ian do now?

L.   He's with NatWest. No, Royal Bank of Scotland now. PA to the Area Business Advisor. He was eighteen when he went there, and he's thirty nine now.

D.   And then you moved. Andy came: new house, new baby, somebody said to me!

L.   '64, Andy was born.

D.   So what sort of things did they get up to? Was it easy, parenting? Were there always friends, they could just go out of the door and there they were?

B.   They could wander round quite a lot then, because they used to go to the Kellys at Arden Lodge, and they used to go up there and play in the woods at Barclays'. They could always go there if they wanted. Davieses and Daniels, they could wander off up there if they wanted to.

L.   Ian and Andy joined the Boys' Brigade. Kevan and Mark. They were in it. That's how they got there. In Altrincham. Hale never had one. Andy left when he was about fifteen. But Ian's still in it.

D.   Ian went into NatWest: what does Andy do?

L.   He's an electrician, he's self-employed. We wrote off about thirty or forty times, looking for an apprenticeship for him. It was very tight at that time, and apprenticeships were very very rare. A small firm in Knutsford took him on. But he'd only been there a couple of years when they went bankrupt. But two of them set up on their own, and took Andy with them, and he finished his time.

D.   What a difficult apprenticeship! Did he go off on his own pretty soon after that?

L.   Yeah. One the chaps, well the chap that took him on originally, he again had set up on his own, and he talked Andy into going with him. But I suppose it was only about twelve months when Andy got fed up, so he struck out on his own. He's had to struggle. I suppose it must be about ten years. His biggest trouble, as all self-employed people find, is getting the money in. He can get the work.

D.   And what sort of things do you find yourselves doing now?

L.   Well, we're City supporters! That's Saturdays. Well, every other Saturday.

D.   And when I first came here you were at the school, Bertha.

B.   Yes, I was there for twenty-odd years. I left my job in Altrincham when I was expecting Ian, and then when he first started school up here the Education decided that they could have a secretary here. And the head asked me, Would I go there as a part-time, because it was only a part-time job. And so I went, and stayed. It fitted in with the holidays and I was with the children. Had a bit of a trauma when Andrew was five, because he had an accident and lost an eye. When he was five years old.

D.   That must have been terrible.

B.   Yes it was a bit. He was in hospital for two months. Being part-time at the school, I was only there in the mornings, so we used to come home at lunchtime with Ian, and we used to travel up to Manchester every afternoon, practically. We'd stay there the whole afternoon until Len finished work, and he'd bring us home, because he was working in Eccles, weren't you?

D.   Well at least something fitted in. You're pretty active grandparents, aren't you?

L.   You could say that!

B.   Yes, I think that's my main interest, the grandchildren.

D.   Who have you got?

L.   Andrew's got Nick and Jacob.

D.   How old is Nick now?

L.   Nine.

B.   And Jacob's six.

D.   So that's those two, and they're here quite a bit, aren't they? Is Nick a City supporter too?

L.   Oh yes, yes.

D.   And Ian's family came later. Who's Ian got?

B.   Bethany's three in April. She was born on April Fool's Day. And Hannah was born on the 5th November, which is bonfire night. One was April Fools'. the other was Guy Fawkes. They've both got decent homes, haven't they? They've both got nice houses. But they've always been very good together, haven't they? Helping each other out with things.

L.   Well, we've got a lot to be thankful for.

Peter and Kathryn Wright, Anthony and Nicholas. 9 Hough Green

D.   Can we start with you, Kathryn? Tell us about your connection with Ashley.

K.   It started when my grandparents lived at Lane End. That's where my mother's family's from. She was born there, and I was born in the house, at number 21.

D.   Where they are now?

K.   Yes. Actually in the house there. So I grew up there, and I lived there for twenty-three years, until I got married. And just moved back this year.

D.   So, full circle! Can you tell us about what it was like for you as a child in Ashley?

K.   It seemed as though it was always hot. The summers were always hot. And the school was about forty-odd then, with twenty in each class. And they were like all farming families. There's one or two who I still know from school, who are actually still here: the lady at number two, she was there, Jenny.

D.   Oh! Jenny McKenna!

K.   She was there. And the Bells, their children, I remember them. I remember Stephen, he was a couple of years older than me, same age as my brother.

D.   This is Stephen Blackburn, next door?

K.   Yes. And Mrs Walker, Yvonne, she was a bit older than me. So there was all those that are still here. And of course one or two of the older people I actually knew, people like Mrs Fisher, Mrs Dolan, Mrs Jennings, Mrs Roberts, Mrs Grassby, Mrs Laxton.

D.   Have they changed much?!

K.   One or two have! Mrs Fisher's about the only one that hasn't altered really, as I remember her.

D.   How much is she paying you for that?! When there were children in every house it must have been so different from what it is now.

K.   It was. We used to ride on bikes round - a bit like they do now.

D.   Like they do now, except there were twice as many of you!

K.   And they used to play football, but as they got older they had to go on the back field, where there's modern houses now. I think there were a few more girls than now.

D.   Yes, the boys are rather in the ascendancy now, aren't they? So what did you do?

K.   We used to be in the Rose Queen of course. I was always a train-bearer. That's a bit smaller now than it used to be. And of course it was at Midways, not at the school. Always a lovely day. This year was the first time I've been back, and it seemed just as nice.

D.   So what about the school? There must have been crowds going from The Green?

K.   Oh there was a lot more. If you take the Norburys and the Daniels out, the rest of the school was from here, virtually. There used to be twenty or thirty of us.

D.   Did you all go together?

K.   No. Some did, and the younger ones went with their mothers, and the older ones, *Oh I'm not going with my mum*, sort of thing! They used to go on a bit. But the weirdest thing was so many different age groups in the Infants and the Juniors. But, having said that, everybody could read and write and do their sums. They all could do it, even with such diverse age groups.

D.   And how did you get on when you had to change school? Where did you go?

K.   I went to what was Delahays, in Timperley. It opened as I went, and I was the first actual intake. My lot were the first to go all the way through. There was a minibus, or taxis, to take us. And just after I'd left they changed to Knutsford.

D.   What was it like going to a normal school?

K.   It was a big change. There was only three of my year went, so it was a bit hard. I didn't really know anybody, it was like starting all over again. It was a big change, but you got used to it.

P.   Of course both these two went to the same school.

D.   Where was that?

N.   It was Green Lane, but it used to be Delahays.

D.   You were there, were you?

Boys.   Yeah.

A.   Some teachers actually remembered . . .

K.   Yes. The headmistress was my old PE teacher.

D.   Oh of course, it was the same school!

K.   But its name changed from Delahays to Green Lane. They were all at Bradbury, in Hale. Then they split the boys and girls up. And now they're all together again.

D.   So you were at the same school as your mum! Yes, I hadn't cottoned on to that. And somebody remembered you? Somebody remembered your mum when she was there?

K.   Yes, the head teacher.

D.   And what did you do after you left school, Kathryn?

K.   I went to work at Copelands chemists, in Altrincham. Where I trained for my Apothecary Hall in Pharmacy dispensing. I was there for ten years.

D.   And somewhere along the line you met Peter?

K.   Yes. In The Greyhound. Even that's changed in twenty-odd years, the pub. There've been two or three changes from what it was. The cottages have gone. I even remember the Barn when it had cows in it. And turkeys. Especially this time of year (September), they were getting them in for Christmas. The train line's different now, it's not as busy. It used to be a heck of a lot busier. I seem to remember there were a lot more trains every hour, plus there was a lot more goods trains going through, than what there is now. They're heavier now, but not as many.

D.   I don't suppose you've been into the station? You probably know, they've just recently converted it into two separate houses, one with four in, one with two. You wouldn't believe it, it looks so marvellous inside. So there we are, we've got people back beside the railway line again. Another full circle.

K.   In my childhood before the motorway was there fields of corn used to grow in the back. And then in the winter you'd get all the cows in. And sometimes all the cows got out of the field, and were walking round The Green! About four in the morning!

D.   It's funny you should mention the cows, because I've been hearing mooing recently. From Stock Farm, I think. But they're the first cows I've heard for several years. It's sad not to have cows anymore. So if we could come to you two, Nick and Anthony, you started off school in Chorlton? And then there you were, at the school where your mother had been. What happened to you, Anthony, from there?

A.   I applied to do A levels at Sale Grammar.

D.   And what did you do for your A levels?

A.   Chemistry, Geography, English and General Studies.

D.   So that's Anthony. Now you, Nick, When did you leave school?

N.   July. The day I left I went to the garage to ask if I could work there. They said I could come in, and I'd be doing like a valeting job, just cleaning cars really.

D.   I remember meeting you once, as you were going in to work, and you were explaining that you more or less went in on a day-to-day basis, and that it wasn't a regular job. What happened next?

N.   There was a just a little rumour that some guy was going to retire. And they were going to be looking for somebody to take over from him. This started just as we were going on holiday. And I was just about getting offered the job, to take over in the Parts Department and to be moved up into there, but then two or three days later we went on holiday for two and a half weeks. So I had to wait a long time to actually find out about the job. It's a Parts Technician, is the full name of it.

D.   So are you happy with that?

N. Yeah. I've still got a lot to learn yet! I'm learning to put it on computers, and a whole lot of up to date stuff, now.

D. And after two years do you then have some sort of qualification?

N. Yeah, I get City and Guilds Level 2. Then there's other courses you can go on after. Like a receptionist's course, or I could go to a Level 3, then Level 4 and 5.

D. So there's quite a ladder of options, you've got yourself onto a career structure?

N. Yeah. It could actually take you to be a Parts Manager.

D. That's great. And did it feel completely different, going back there now?

N. Yeah. In a shirt and tie! It was like going back to school. I've not been smart since the day I left school. Been nearly three months. That's the last time I looked smart.

D. Well that's great, anyway. Great to have a future like that, I should think.

N. Got to fit in rugby as well.

D. Now then, that was the other thing I wanted to come onto with you two, your sporting lives. What do you all do: what do you do, Anthony?

A. I don't really play a sport for a team, just play it for enjoyment. Football and cricket. But I'm not into rugby. I like staying alive!

D. What about you, Nick?

N. Rugby now. First I started with football. Then out of the blue I joined the rugby, Altrincham Kersall. Went down one Saturday, and started playing. I'm in my third year now. I won a trophy in my first season, as the most improved player of the year. That was in my first season.

D. That's something to live up to, isn't it? What sort of teams do they field?

N. Five. For different age groups. Fifteens, sixteens, and now I'm in the seventeens. Which is the Colts. It's 17s, 18s and 19s.

D. So you're now playing with nineteen-year-olds? A big jump, I should imagine?

N. It is, yeah. There's only a couple who've come up from my team. But the nine-teens are going up to the senior side after Christmas. That'll leave more space for us.

D. So what position do you play?

N. I've been a winger at the moment. On the outside of the backs. The men who run with the ball.

D. The ones who score tries, and get their names in the papers!

Steve and Caroline Blackburn. 10 Hough Green

D. Steve, where were you born?

S. At Stock Farm.

D. And how long did you live there?

S. Until I was twenty, I think.

D. What was it like, childhood on Stock Farm?

S. It was quite idyllic really, I suppose. Although I didn't realise it at the time! It wasn't till I left that I realised how lucky I'd been. Because when you're a teenager, and in your early twenties the city seems more attractive. Other places seem more attractive. So I was glad to get out.

D. This does seem to be the pattern. The people who find it most difficult here are the teenagers, I think. But before that, obviously, you went to the school here?

S. Ashley School, yeah.

D. Have we got any of your contemporaries still around?

S. John Erlam. Jeff Warburton. Daniels; Jean Daniel is the same age as me. Norburys. Philip Tickle. He went to school with us, he's a few years younger than me, that's another contemporary. Who else is there? Peter Sant. He's the same age as me, although I don't think I've seen him since I've come back, actually, Peter Sant. He was in the army wasn't he? Colin Hobson, he's the same age as me. Jenny McKenna, she's a couple of years younger than me, and Malcolm, I think he's one year older than me. He lives in Cornwall. The Blains. Grassbys, Diane and Gary. Brian Bowyer. Jenningses. Yvonne's back, I think she's one year older than me.

D. That's interesting. The first four families you mentioned are in farming. Of course, you were farming, as well. Was that your family's living, Stock Farm?

S. Yes, my grandad was the tenant. When my grandad died we didn't renew the tenancy. Dad had to leave the farm. So my dad bought a milk round somewhere, and moved into Timperley.

D. And that was when you were twenty? When did you get back here?

S. Was it '80 or '81? something like that. I think it was '81.

D. And that's when you came into this house?

S. Yes. As children we used to play on The Green here.

D. Here? Or where Egerton Moss is?

S. Well, we used to come down here, but they got fed up with us making a noise and kicking the balls into the gardens, so we'd end up on Egerton Moss, we used to play football and muck about on there. And that was an asset to the Village, which I think has been missed for the kids. Especially for these kids.

D. Well so far, really, since Egerton Moss has been built, there's not been enough kids to miss it.

S. Not until now.

D. And now we're just coming into the stage when we're needing more space.

S. Yeah. I mean I've no problem with the kids playing football on The Green, but in them days there were a lot more kids. Yeah, there was a lot of kids on here. Kids in damn near every house, at one stage!

D. Which shows how difficult it is for the school, doesn't it? I mean it's just beginning to come back now a little bit, but how they've hung on . . .

S. Yeah. As one generation fades away there'll be others with families.

C. New families. You've got a football team already, haven't you? Two here, two at Jackie's, two at Vanessa's, that's six. Two with Tony and Jo, eight. Two with Joanne who's just moved in, ten. In the fourteen or fifteen years I've been round there's never been ten children before.

D. So how did you come on the scene, Caroline? How did you two meet?

S. A mutual friend.

C. Yes, mutual friends. A friend of Steve's lives in Cheadle, Bill. And a friend of mine, she was a passenger on a sidecar, and Bill used to have his own outfit. She used to race with him. Every now and then they got together. Were they living together when we met? Steve used to mechanic for Bill, and I'd sometimes go down to spend the day with Pauline. And we met at a race meeting. I was born and brought up in Lancashire, and was living in Skelmersdale when I met Steve.

D. And did you go straight into nursing?

C. No. No. I don't actually nurse. I've always worked with handicapped children and teenagers, as a house parent. Not actually nursing.

D. So how do you get into that sort of work?

C. Experience, I suppose. My interest came via the family. Mum's an occupational therapist and has worked with handicapped children all her working life. She was a paediatric occupational therapist in Preston when she retired. So it's something that we've always been involved in. I started in that line, and then I was in Lancaster as a house parent. In a Community Home. They were teenagers, they were moving from the "mental hospital" into the community, it was when the fight was on to get them all out of the hospitals.

D.   Halfway house? So how many did you have?

C.   We had four in the house there at Lancaster. I then decided to go back to college. I wanted to do my occupational therapy, follow mother. But despite the fact that I had my A levels and qualifications, because I'd been out of college for so long, I had to show sign of recent study. So that's when I left and went back to Skelmersdale to do another two A levels, didn't I? So I was there part-time, and just transferred with work to the Lancashire Health Authority, and worked part-time as a house parent there. To keep me while I was at college. And from there I met Steve, and came down here. About fourteen years ago.

S.   '86, something like that.

D.   I'm trying to remember whether Karen was still living here?

C.   Yeah. She was eleven.

D.   So you came in -

C.   To Steve and a stepdaughter.

D.   Who is just about to enter her teens.

C.   Yes. Yeah.

D.   That's sounds like a highly tricky situation.

S.   Yeah. Not easy.

C.   It was all right, wasn't it? until she hit fourteen, fifteen. And she's ended up buying a place at Winsford with her boyfriend. And she's still there, isn't she?

S.   She's done all right.

D.   And at what stage in this, I can't remember, were your own children born?

C.   Thomas is nine. So we were living together for about three years.

D.   Was Karen still here?

C.   Oh yes.

D.   How did that go?

C.   Oh very well initially. She doted on Tom. But he was still quite young when Karen actually moved out. About five. And so Robert was here, but Karen only really knew him as a baby. They are both at Ashley School.

D.   How do you find it, this school?

C.   The school seems great. The standard of education seems very good.

D.   Is the school, from the consumer's point of view, affected by the uncertainties about the future?

C.   No. People are still bringing their kids in. The projected figures for September [1999] are higher. They've got the projected figures for the year after, and they're going up all the time. The Rationalisation Panel is supposed to have made a decision two months ago, but the school was picked up for an inspection to be done in May. So the Panel said, Right, we'll wait until the Inspection's over and then make a decision. When the HMIs came in to do the Inspection, before they started they had a meeting with parents, and they did say they could tell us there and then that the school would not reach a satisfactory standard on the value-for-money aspect. It costs too much to run the school. The Inspection went ahead and, Lo and behold! the school got "Satisfactory" for value-for-money.

D.   That's quite dramatic, isn't it?

C.   Yes. How it does, I don't know. Mrs Wakefield must be very good at her finances and what-have-you. So now it's just Wait and see.

S.   There'd never been enough children for that school, all the way. I think when my sister was there they talked about closing it. And there was quite a lot there then.

C.   It's the mix of kids, isn't it? There's a little boy there with Down's Syndrome who actually has a one-to-one assistant with him all day, which to an outsider might seems as if there's two teaching staff, two teachers there, and there isn't actually. There's a classroom assistant who's there part-time, and parents go in and they're very supportive and they go in.

D.   Steve, what are you doing now?

S.   I've got a half-share in a garage in Timperley. It's a modern industrial unit. Before we had a little shack on a farm in Bowdon Vale. We built the place in 1974 or 5, out of an old army hut. We used to work for my partner's father weekends and nights. Did all the work that he didn't want to do. And it built up from there. We had to get off the farm as Walter was retiring. So when we bought this place there was just the two of us. Took us about a year to actually buy it. We found the place, and it was two units made into one, and we couldn't afford both of them, didn't want to take off more than we could chew. And in the end we bought half of what they had to sell. We managed to get the bit that we wanted. Reuters were there before us, the newsgathering people.

D.   And has it settled down?

S.   Yeah. We've never looked back.

Joyce Rowland. 11 Hough Green

D.   Joyce, why did you come to Ashley?

J.   Because Reg had to have a leg amputated. And so he lost his job. He drove farm machinery. He had several operations on the leg, but eventually he got gangrene, so then they took it off. We owned our own mobile home. And we had to sell it and move here, because it was on the boss's land. We'd been on the council list for years, even though we had the caravan. They ask you which areas you want to go to. And we put down Pickmere and Ashley. And as it happened this one became empty because the lady went into a nursing home.

D.   Can you remember what it was like coming here? How did you find it, as a neighbourhood?

J.   I liked it, because I knew of the neighbourhood. So when we knew we'd got the bungalow we were quite pleased. It's a nice area.

D.   But at the same time you, and Reg especially, you both really, were still having to get used to his only having one leg. Which must have made it even more difficult.

J.   It did, because he lost his job, and he had to give the car up because we couldn't afford to run it. But on the other hand, it was just one of those things that happen, and we just had to get on with it.

D.   Do any parts of the Getting-on-with-it, looking back, strike you as having been most difficult?

J.   No. There was the hospital visits and things, but you just have to get on with it.

D.   As simple as that?

J.   That's it. I always remember one of the times he went back for a check-up, the specialist asked how I was. And I couldn't make out why, but they said that some people can't handle it. But both Reg and myself, we're not like that, we're not that sort of person. I mean, it's a bigger problem for him than it is for me, and if I . . . If he can cope with it, it would be a poor show if I couldn't. You just take it in your stride. You have to, no matter what's thrown at you.

D.   It sounds like that's the attitude that's really enabled you both to survive it as well as you have.

J.   That's it. Because some people might crumble, mightn't they? We never have been like that.

D.   What's Reg found to do with himself? Would he mind us talking about him behind his back?!

J.   No, not really!

D.   I mean, he started from scratch, really. There he is, no job, one leg, nothing to do. How did he start building up his life? It must have taken some time?

J.   To be honest David, I don't think it did. I think he just got on with it. He's always liked making things. He's never been one that can't find anything to do. He made all the garden furniture, literally out of old wood that he'd had given to him. He always finds something to do. And the garden, until I took over! He's been demoted to the hedges, and I do everything else.

D.   When did you decide to step in, Joyce, in the garden?

J.   When he wouldn't do it right! You'd better cut that bit out! No. When I started deciding where things went. You know, when I put the roses in, and different things. I let him build the trellises, and he cut the hedge.

D.   Was it a sudden thing? Was there some change?

J.   When my parents died I started putting roses in the garden, because my dad always had roses. And we always had a lilac tree in the garden, as a child. And it's just things that I associate. Memories.

D.   So it was really triggered by your parents dying?

J.   Well, the things that I put in the garden were. And only I know where things are. So that's why I do it. You know, it would be more than Reg's life is worth to break a rose tree! I think it stems from putting a particular thing in, like the rose trees in, and the lilac tree. Getting it how I wanted.

D.   I might be reading too much into what you've just been saying, because you're the third person I've spoken to who's had quite a definite change in their lives as a result of parents dying.

J.   Yeah, as I say, I think it started off when my mother died, five year ago. And then my dad died ten month after her. So I just started putting bits and pieces in. Mainly I took over . . .

D.   Well it sounds as if you knew what you wanted, and where you wanted it.

J.   But I suppose it did stem from my mum dying. Like the lilac tree: when we were children at home, at Aston near Runcorn, there was a beautiful big lilac tree down there. It's just an association. Putting them in to remember them. That's why I took over.

D.   Yes. I shall look at your garden in quite a new light, now. What about the latest member of the family, Jessica: when did Jessica come?

J.   It'll be a year September.

D.   Where did you - *perhaps I should point out Jessica is a dog!*- What is she, Joyce?

J.   A Labrador/Retriever cross, but the vet has her down as a Labrador. I'd say she's ninety five per cent Labrador.

D.   Yes, she looks very Labrador, doesn't she? How old was she when she came to you?

J.   About seven months. She was brilliant. She's never touched anything in the house. She's never made a mess in the house. So we didn't have all that to contend with.

D.   So you can forgive her if she pulls you about a bit on your walks! Or in The Greyhound!

J.   Into the odd tree! She's partial to the privet hedge! You probably hear me screaming at her.

D.   But she's not a threat to the garden? The roses and the lilac?

J.   Well she's not allowed in the garden. She goes on the bit that's flagged, but she's not allowed in the garden. She's very well-behaved in every other respect, never touches anything. But we got her because we'd lost the old dog. If she'd have lived two weeks longer, she'd have been eighteen.

D.   By Jove, I'd not realised. She kept well, didn't she? And she's buried in the back there, isn't she?

J.   Yes. With a rose tree on top! We built a wall round the grave.

D.   Now that's another thing. You might not want to talk about this, but one of the things I always associate you with is your window-dressing for Christmas and so forth: but you did something really moving and spectacular when Princess Diana died, didn't you? Can you talk about that?

J.   It was just something . . . . I did it for the actual day of the funeral. Put a poster of her in, one that I liked. And I think, if I remember rightly, I put flowers, and *Rest in Peace*, I wrote on it. But it was a sort of tribute to her, because I liked Diana. It was just my little piece. I taped it, taped the funeral on television. I taped the Queen Mother's tribute, did you see that?

D.   Do you stand up for the National Anthem, when you're here watching it on television?

J.   No! Not that mad!

D.   You don't go quite that far! My brother would, I think!

J.   No, I thought it was quite nice, but I wouldn't go that far, David! I'm not that patriotic! It was bad enough when you had to do it at the Pictures when you were younger.

D.   Well that was a bit different, there were other complications then, weren't there! So how did the Christmas window start?

J.   There again, it stems back to when we were children. My mother always used to

182

have a tree, and there used to be a big sideboard with a great mirror on it and she would make a scene on that. I think it just stems from your childhood. I like Christmas. It's the best time of year. I like it. I think the children on The Green like it.

D.   I think everyone looks forward to seeing what's going to happen next year.

J.   Little Jordan Williams, Joanne's little boy, said last year that it was like being in Fairyland!

D.   Ah! What an accolade! And that was the Millennium one, wasn't it?

J.   I enjoy doing it. I've got another little treat in store for this year. Something different! Again!

D.   So there's a terrifically strong creative side to you.

J.   Art was my best subject at school. Didn't like anything else, but art. Same as the cake decorating, that stemmed from creating things. Did you see Mrs Mason's?

D.   Oh I heard about it. It was a model of The Smithy, wasn't it?

J.   Yes. I've got a photograph of it somewhere. I made it like an old-fashioned smithy. The only thing she couldn't eat was the dog, the horse and the chickens. But everything else, the steps and everything, was made out of icing sugar. I just like creating. It all stems back from childhood, I think.

D.   This was when Mrs Mason was a hundred, wasn't it?

J.   Yes. She did have an official birthday cake. Mine was just a bit of fun.

D.   Joyce, do you want to say a bit about the fostering? How did that start?

J.   We did intend going into fostering with a view to adoption, but it didn't get that far. We just got into the routine of looking after the two little girls, Tania and Stacey, on the respite scheme. To give the parents a rest. Every third week. It started out every four weeks at the beginning, then it went to every three weeks, and a week in the summer. There were four disabled children in the same family.

D.   The same family? *All* disabled?

J.   Yes. And we used to have the two youngest girls.

D.   How old were they when they started coming to you?

J.   Thirteen month, and three.

D.   And how long did you have them?

J.   About ten years. But we don't see them anymore. Social Services asked us to take both of them on, because apparently there's not many places that will take two sisters together, and they didn't want to split them up. So that's how we got into it.

D.   How did you find it, doing it?

J.   Very rewarding, but very hard work because you had to lift them everywhere. They couldn't walk. You had to lift them everywhere - onto the floor, into the settees, into the beds. And if you took them out you had to take them out in a double buggy, and it was a bit awkward trying to get in most places. Because I don't think the people that build shops think of wheelchairs and buggies. When they first came to us they'd never seen a horse, or realised that there was more than one sort of bird. Us lot in the countryside take it for granted. They enjoyed coming, and we enjoyed having them.

D.   They always looked very happy. The thing I remember - Reg must have built it - was that train.

J.   Yes, Reg made that. There again, out of old scrap wood. And a bit of imagination. And me, to pull them round The Green! I was the engine! I told him many a time to get an engine put in! But the girls enjoyed it. He made swings for them. And an ambulance, he made an ambulance for the Rose Queen procession once, and we dressed them up as nurses. For the Rose Queen.

D.   Did they make friends around here?

J.   Oh yes. There weren't many then, of their age. Because it's going back ten years now. The little ones that are on The Green now, they'd only have been about three. They were only babies. Whereas Stacey and Tania now would be . . . Stacey I should imagine would have left school now. But I didn't realise, when I stopped having the girls, that if you've not worked for Social Services for the best part of twelve month, then you have to go through all the interviews and everything again.

D.   Is that why you stopped?

J.   No. I stopped doing it in the beginning because I couldn't lift them. That was the end. You need to be young and fit, because it entails a lot of hard lifting and carrying round.

D.   Yes. Well it must have been a tremendous help, both to the girls and to the family.

J.   I think for the time they did it it eased their problems a little bit. They liked it round here. When it was the Rose Queen, they used to love that. And they used to like going round to The Greyhound, to the beer garden! Occasionally! But that's about all we've done since we moved up here.

D.   It seems extraordinary to me that you've only been here twenty years. I think of you as an institution! At the back of this book we've got the institutions - there's the church, the school, the post office. Ought to add Joyce! So it's extraordinary that it's only twenty years.

J.   It's just that all my neighbours think it's longer! Life's never been the same since!

D.   And how's it been for you? Are you glad you got to be here?

J.   Yes, it's nice. I like it round here. Well, we both do. You've got most things, haven't you? There's the trains. You're not far from any main shopping areas, are you? They're gradually taking different things away from the post office, aren't they? But Mrs Mason said to me, when Brenda passed on and the post office moved on to new people, Mrs Mason said to me that they wanted to keep that post office in the village. So I should imagine they'd try their best, wouldn't they? The trouble is, same as the post office has got that computer now, technology's taking over, isn't it?

D.   Well, maybe the computer will help to keep the post office here. It cuts down the paperwork.

J.   And I imagine they wouldn't invest in anything like that if they weren't going to keep it open.

The cake Joyce made for Mrs Maison's 100th birthday
"The only thing she couldn't eat was the dog, the horse and the chickens"
(Photograph courtesy of Mrs Joyce Rowland)

Pat and Sam Armstrong. 12 Hough Green

D.   How did you come to Ashley in the first place?

S.   I was working for Mr Warburton, and we were living in Wythenshawe, with Pat's mum and dad at the time. We were looking round for houses, thinking of buying.

P.   And we had two children. There were already four of us in the one bedroom.

S.   And Number 10 came empty. So we came and viewed it, and we decided to come. Pat wasn't too keen, so we thought we'd come for a while, and see if we could buy a house somewhere else.

P.   Oh, I'd no intentions of staying! I'm glad we did now, for the children's sake. I'm not a very good traveller. I was born in Longsight, Manchester. And my mum always wanted to travel, and the next best thing, every couple of years we moved! And ended up at Woodhouse Park, where I met Sam.

D.   How did you meet?

P.   Blind date. It was my friend at work. She'd been out the night before and met these three men. Sam was on his own. No, there were six of us. And I said, No. I'd no intentions of going. But we broke up that day, that Friday. For the holidays. And right up to me getting on the bus I said No. She said, Oh please, Pat. Just to keep him company. Oh, I said, all right, then. So that's how it worked out.

D.   And you've been keeping him company ever since! Who got you in on this, Sam?

S.   I was out at Carrington Power Station at the time, working for a firm by the name of Gleesons, contractors. And I was in the same digs as these two lads from Stoke, doing some work around Urmston. They were going to a club at Wythenshawe, the Yew Tree at Wythenshawe, and they asked me if I wanted to go with them. I went out with them, and that was the next night after that -

P.   The following night I went, and he didn't know anything about it until I rolled up, and that was it!

S.   Joined on from there, then.

D.   Had you always lived in this part of the world, Sam?

S.   Oh no, no. I came over from Ireland to Bedfordshire when I was seventeen. My brother had a boarding house in Bedford, so I came there and worked at different places round Bedford. Then I got a job with Gleesons on contract work and travelled round with them. I went to London, and then I came up to Manchester with the firm. And, as I say, I met Pat. I moved then down to Burton-on-Trent. And I used to get one weekend off every three weeks, and I used to go up and see Pat. And we got married while I was there, and then they moved me down to Maidstone, in Kent. So I decided to pack it in.

D.   So that was end of Gleesons. What was your work with Gleesons?

S.   Machine driver, machine operator: 'dozers and diggers.

D.   Was it easy to get another job? I'm trying to think what the work situation was like then.

S.   It wasn't too bad. Motorways were being built. But I just happened to get a job with Mr Warburton, he had advertised for a driver. I was with him fourteen years.

D.   And when did you get married?

P.   '58.

D.   And moved in with your parents? And who were your first two children?

P.   Stephen and Paul.

D.   So there were the four of you, in the one room. But you still didn't like the idea of moving, Pat?

P.   I don't know what it was really. I think because I'm not a good traveller. And we used to have to go on the bus. And then the train, but I'd no intentions of staying. That's thirty seven years ago!

S.   She's always been used to being around shops. Me, I like it, I'm a country fella.

P.   But I was glad we came here as the children got older. Because when they got into their teens they had to be home, and that was the quarter past ten train then. At least we knew where they were. And they were a grand lot of kids round here, you know.

D.   What did they think of it?

P.   They liked Ashley. Oh they all still like Ashley. In fact there used to be a disco in Hale, and Stephen used to go, and one particular day he missed the train. And he ran all the way home. Because him and Paul were fast runners, and Stuart. Paul had a chance of going into Sale Harriers, but he didn't. But he never missed it again. They were very good kids. We said they had to be here at a certain time, and they would be. If they went out, let us know where they were.

D.   Stephen, Paul: who did you have next?

P.   Then Neil, when we were at Number 10. And the twins, when we were at Number 10.

S.   "New house, new baby". We'd just moved in, hadn't we? He was born the following year.

D.   And then the twins, Lorraine and Stuart? All at Number 10. How long did you stay on there?

P.   Until I think Lorraine was about seven. And Stuart and Lorraine were in a box room, on bunk beds. And I decided she needed a room of her own. So we did look round, trying to buy. But we were either pipped to the post or they were no good. And then Mr . . .

S.   I forget his name, who lived here. Just him and his daughter.

P.   Anyway, he wanted a smaller house, but he didn't want to leave Ashley. And we talked it over, and we decided to exchange. Sam didn't want to, he wanted to build a bedroom over the garage.

S.   I wanted to buy that one, you see. I wanted to buy it and build an extension.

P.   But all the rest of us wanted to move.

S.   So I lost out!

D.   Well it was convenient that it suited both of you to do a swap like that. Most of you, anyway!

P.   Yes, it was. The day we moved, some of the neighbours emptied one of our rooms and others emptied one of their rooms, and we changed over that way. It was marvellous, they were very helpful. And when Mr and Mrs Jennings moved from Robertses, we all did the same thing.

D.   It's one of the great attractions of living here, that spirit between the neighbours.

P.   You're not in each other's pockets, sort of thing, but you know they're there if you want them. Like Mr and Mrs Bowyer, they were marvellous. I really miss them. She misses Ashley. They were here forty nine years, or something. But no they are, they're very good neighbours on The Green.

D.   And where are all your children now?

P.   Stephen, he lives in between Bournemouth and Southampton. He's done very well for himself, he's got a good job in computers, works for an American bank. They like it down there, although they like Ashley when they come. They love it down there. And their children, they've got the accent. We must sound proper common to them, you know! They've got a really posh accent!

D.   So that's Stephen, Number One. Then comes Paul?

P.   They live at Partington. He's a postman. But he's also in the TA.

S.   In the Medical Corps. He's just had a bravery award. Three of them had.

D.   There must be a story behind that?

S.   Well it was just outside the barracks at Stretford. And there was a car, crashed just outside. Two fellas test-driving this car, speeding, knocked two pedestrians down on the side of the road. She was a foreigner. Two students, they were, knocked down. Paul and some of his friends went to help them.

P.   The girl had actually stopped breathing, and he brought her back again. But she died in hospital. The lad, there was no hope for him, because was in such a mess.

S.   But the bravery award was because the car was leaking petrol. It could have blown up any time.

P.   Because they couldn't move her. So they stayed with her.

S.   So we went to the presentation there, last year.

P.   We were very proud.

D.   Yes. You must be very proud of him. And next we come to Neil? Did he work for the Smithy?

P.   He worked at the garage, yes. They're at Reddish, near Stockport.

S.   Yes, he works at Grahams now. Parts Manager now.

D.   And then we come to the twins. Where's Stuart?

P.   They live at Knutsford.

S.   He works in a warehouse at Tesco's. He was in electronics. Made redundant - well, they left before they were made redundant. I think it's his sister-in-law works for Tesco's, in the office, and this job came up in the warehouse. So he decided to go there. And he does shiftwork as well, and a lot more money now, so they've decided to buy their house. They couldn't have afforded it before.

D.   So it's been a good move. And Lorraine?

P.   She lives in Stretford. She works at Knutsford. It was Gallery, it's Liberty now, Liberty have taken over. She's in the office. It's a cosmetics firm. And she's married to Mark, and lives in Stretford.

D.   Sam, where did you go after the Warburtons?

S.   I went to a building firm in Lymm, by the name of Mr Bennett. Building houses. Excavation, footing, and so on; roads, stuff like that. I was with them twenty years.

D.   You went on to retirement with them? How was retirement, after all that time?

S.   Very hard. I didn't retire, we were made redundant from there. While I was there I'd damaged my arm, while I was there, but I carried on working. And then he went into liquidation. Oh I got another job after that, with a plant hire firm in Manchester, after that. But then the arm was getting worse. So I went to the hospital, and they decided to operate on the arm. And after that I couldn't work with it. So I went on invalidity. I didn't work after that. I was sixty then, I think. Sixty. It was very hard, very hard. I used to be very depressed, not being able to go to work, with working all my life like that. I'd been working since I was, what, ten. I couldn't settle for that. Couldn't settle at all. The doctor had to put me on anti-depressant tablets.

D.   How do you find it now?

S.   I've got used to it now. I can keep doing a bit in the garden and stuff like that now, and keep myself pretty occupied. But it was quite a dip at first. It was terrible.

D.   It is a lovely garden. Did you just pick it up as went along, how to do it? Because it's really really beautiful. And the way you've changed the front from grass to pebbles, Japanese type of thing.

S.   I saw it on television. You get ideas from it. Gardening World, stuff like that.

D.   Yes, there's almost as many gardening programmes as there are cooking ones! Which is the other thing I always associate with you, about your Christmas. What happens at Christmas?

S.   Yeah, well I usually take over at Christmastime. The family come down. I do the Christmas dinner, the turkey, and get it all prepared. I do the tea as well, the trifles and the buffet for the tea.

D.   It must be a tremendous party when they're all here! Do you get them all here?

S.   Not as much now, but up until a couple of years ago they were all here. And we used to have your mum and dad here, didn't we? There used to be about twenty.

D.   How do you actually do it? How do you sit them down?

P.   Oh we have a buffet. At dinnertime there wasn't as many.

S.   There were fourteen. I think there were about fourteen or sixteen for dinner. We've got a big table and chairs in there, we can sit ten around the table. And then we've got another small table. We used to have that in the kitchen.

P.   That table in there is what Mum and Dad had during the war. When the bombs were coming down, instead of going in the shelter, we used to sit under the table because it's a very heavy one. We used to sit under that.

S.   It's quite nice to have all the family down, at Christmastime.

P.   When the others started having children, and the children got older, they decided to have Christmas Dinner at home. And they'll come down on Boxing Day then.

S.   And we have a buffet then.

P.   But when Stephen and Pam are coming down we try to get them all down, because it's the only time they see them all. This is the first year I didn't have a buffet. Because Mum was in hospital nine weeks, you see. So I couldn't do it. They all saw each other, but we didn't have the buffet.

D.   Well I think it must be wonderful to have a family gathering like that.

Jason and Sam. 14 Hough Green

J.   We were on the Council list, and we were actually offered two both at the same time. I had a bit of prior knowledge of Ashley, through drinking partners who originate from the village, and it just seemed right. Peter's youngest son Mike and I go back a long long way. Football, first and foremost. And then the social side: a game, a shower, a couple of pints in the clubhouse, watch the results, a couple more pints, three kit bags wherever you thought you were going to end up that evening; at the time they had a bar, so if a table wasn't available you could carry on drinking; something to eat; a couple more beers, and then out into Knutsford. Unless someone had had the bright idea of *I've got a minibus: let's go into Town!* and you'd get sixteen or seventeen of us just sort of fall into Manchester, into a club, and fall out at two in the morning. So Mike and I had been a Terrible Twosome.

D.   This is Mike Wright?

J.   Yeah. Oh yes, same as Kevan Gibbons. We all played together, and we mixed as a crowd a lot.

D.   Which team was this at that stage?

J.   We played for Knutsford Motors. Knutsford teams.

D.   Because Kev still plays, doesn't he?

J.   Yeah, Kev he's just gone back to playing. He took a bad bang on the head a couple of years ago. So I think he's just getting back into the swing of it now. Playing again Saturdays and Sundays.

D.   And you played with that lot? And now, what's your interest in football now?

J.   I still play occasionally, although not at the moment. I coach kids. Egerton Club.

D.   Perhaps the thing to do now is ask you about your family, because that's probably what got you into coaching kids at Egerton, or were you doing that already?

J.   I got more into the coaching side I suppose, as I got older.

D.   Well let's go back: when did you come here?

J.   I moved up to Cheshire in '85. From London. My dad's Mobberley born and bred. And all his side still live in Mobberley. I wasn't that long since finishing, because I worked on the M25. And we were in between contracts, working for Laings. I decided to come up for a couple of days, see the old pals I had not seen for years, see the relations, and go back, ready for the next contract. I came up, and two days turned into a week, and a week turned into a fortnight. And a friend of mine's father has his own transport business, and he was desperately looking for someone to spanner for him, and I said, Oh I'll come along and give you a lift. And so two weeks turned into two months, and after about six or eight months I phoned home and said Well look, I've got a job. And that was it, I've just been here since.

D.   At what stage did you meet Jackie, how did all that happen?

J.   Fate's a funny thing, isn't it?

D.   And you needn't say any more about it!

J.   This is a question with a double edge! Well I knew her before. From my visits up, visiting relations. But I knew her better. I knew her brother very well. As kids we used to bounce around, there was a big group, up to no good. Yeah, I knew her elder brother very well.

D.   Were they from Mobberley as well?

J.   Yeah. I had to drag her kicking and screaming into Ashley! And if we go anywhere now, and they say where do you live? I say, just south of Manchester. And she growls *We live in Cheshire!*

D.   Is she here yet, or does she still think of herself as living on the west side of Mobberley?

J.   I think she still hankers to move back. A lot of people she grew up with have stayed in Mobberley. They are the same age, with families much the same age as ours.

D.   And who lives here?

J.   Myself, Jackie, Sam and Charlotte.

D.   Sam, being here, aged nine.

S.   TEN!

D.   Ten! When were you ten, Sam?

S.   Feb. the first.

J.   And Charlotte soon to be seven.

D.   And what about the subhuman part of the family? There is a subhuman element, isn't there?

J.   It seems to be a disposal ground for animals. Two cats, two dogs, four rabbits, one guinea pig. One hamster. God knows how many stick insects. They keep escaping, we keep on finding them. Your mother thought she had one in her hair tonight.

D.   Who is the great animal fan? Or are you all animal fans?

S.   Jackie!

J.   Yeah. Jackie. Undoubtedly. She'll get them for the kids!

D.   Aha, yes, any excuse! You're very useful, Sam! Tell us about yourself.

S.   Well I like collecting Pokémon cards. They're like little monsters, and there's a TV programme. You have to capture these animals, but they're not like animals out of here: you have like dog Pokémon, which grow and evolve into different things, they can evolve. And you need to catch them.

D.   I'm lost!

S.   There's one called Piggot, and it goes *Ergobergotyoo*. I like one called Yalf.

D.   No wonder you think you can see aliens' hands floating about around your den!

J.   Makes *Lucy in the Sky with Diamonds* look like real life, doesn't it?

S.   There's a place I like in Ashley, and it's got lots of traps. I was telling you that I saw the alien down there, didn't I? And a hand was moving about, and an eyeball was peering around.

D.   What did you feel like when you were being looked at by this eyeball?

S.   We just legged it. I got goose bumps, Tom got goose bumps, and we just legged it off. But it wasn't an alien, it turned out to be, it was a piece of twig that looked like a hand going over like that, trying to nick the wood. And then there's this hole in the tree that looks like an eyeball. So it's spooky.

D.   I went down there once, and there was a notice saying . . . What notices have you put up there?

S.   "NO GIRLS ALLOWED"

D.   That's it! No Girls Allowed. I was with a girl at the time, and she saw this notice.

S.   What did she say?

D.   She didn't say anything. But I saw what she was thinking, behind her eyes. And I think the sort of thoughts that she had might have been to do with nicking bits of wood . . .

S.   Now we've found her! I'll have to tell Tom tomorrow. I like building things down there. Pieces of wood with nails in come in handy, you can just stick them in the tree.

D.   So what sort of things have you done?

J.   Well, he nailed a piece of wood to the bottom of his foot. With one of those nails that was sticking through that's dead handy.

S.   I like playing on The Green, football.

D.   Who do you play with?

S.   Your grandson, Michael. Nicholas. And there's a boy from the post office called Michael. And there's these two big lads, and they're called Nick and Anthony. They come and play. And my dad comes and plays. And your grandson's dad, your son, he comes and plays. And we have a big match. But your granddaughter comes and plays too. And then we have like tea breaks, having biscuits. Someone brought, I think it was your son, Charlie, he brought some drinks and biscuits out, and we had some shandy, and orange juice and everything. And then we started again.

D.   Playing even better. But you also play proper football, don't you?

S.   Yeah. I played for school, and I scored three for them. Egerton. I've scored about thirty for them.

D.   When does Egerton play?

S.   Saturdays, but we've got a break this Saturday. But we really haven't got a break actually, because we've got to do training.

D.   Do you have a training day every week as well?

S.   Yeah. Mondays seven till eight. We've got two hours on Saturday morning. But then we're back to playing some matches. I'm left winger, me. I set up most of the goals. I head in most of the goals.

D.   Jason, is this how you got roped in for coaching at Egerton?

J.   Not really. The group that Sam's attached to are basically the cast-offs from another group. One of the other parents thought this was grossly unfair, so he decided he'd start training with the boys and possibly run two teams. By this time I'd done a couple of my coaching badges, and after about seven weeks he said, Would you fancy coming down and giving me a hand? And what we did was we just stripped them all the way to basics, and started right off back at the beginning again.

D.   And how are they doing?

J.   They're doing very well now. The pleasing thing is, we've had a couple of kids picked up and taken away. We've had one go to Liverpool. We had a couple taken down to City a couple of times and invited back. Which is nice, because it proves that we're doing things the right way.

D.   I say! I'd no idea that these clubs were looking around at people as young as this.

J.   They're at Egerton Club every weekend. I know two guys from Blackburn that come down. A fella from Liverpool that comes down every week. I know two blokes that come from different areas, both affiliated to Manchester City, come down. There's guys from Stockport quite regularly. The most encouraging thing, I was talking to one of the scouts from City, and he was saying his grandson plays in the Stockport & District League. He said, but we don't go and look there generally now, he says, because the standard over here in mid-Cheshire is so much higher.

S.   The school's pretty small in Ashley, isn't it, Dad? It's got an Infants and a Juniors classroom. I'm Year Five and it goes up to Year Six. And it's very small, about only thirty six in the school.

D.   What do you think about that, having a school that size?

S.   Oh, it's good. I think it will be better than big school. You get more attention and everything. And you don't get bullied in that school, because it's small, and you've got no bullies there. Three new people have just started, from Wharton, called Harry, Cayley and Natasha. My sister was the only girl in her year, but now this Natasha that's just come, she's the same age and in the same year, so there's two girls in her year now. And the boy, Cayley, is in Year Four, and the boy Harry is in the same year as me, Year Five. He's the second oldest now.

D.   And do they like it better in this school, do you think?

S.   I think so.

D.   So how much longer have you got at this school, another year after this?

S.   Yeah. And then I'm going to Knutsford. All the boys from Ashley are going, aren't they, Dad? But I probably won't be in the same, what do you call them? They split the year into groups, don't they? And hopefully then I'll get scouted for a team, and become a good football player.

D.   That's your main ambition, is it?

J.   What if you can't do that?

S.   Oh . . . Mechanic. I'm good at fixing things. I fixed the CD player at school, it wouldn't work so I soldered these buttons on it. I fixed the telly. I fixed this CD player upstairs, of mine. If you don't believe me - you probably don't, do you, Dad?

J.   I didn't say a word.

S   I wish that in Ashley there would be an aquarium in the middle of The Green. And then a big football stadium down near the den. And waterworks, so we could have Alton Towers and everything.

D.   Oh Alton Towers as well?   An aquarium, Alton Towers, and perhaps Old Trafford.

S.   And I'd get a job there. I'd be a man that works on machines, and on this runaway train at Alton Towers I'd put it on top speed and it would go upside down and they'd fall out, but then land on this trampoline, but then the train goes under, but the trampoline makes them jump so high that they land back in their seats, and then you go on and on.

D.   Well thank you both. I've ample to be working on, lots will have to be cut out.

S.   Well the school is really good. Oh, yes. . . . The teachers are nice.

J.   I wish you'd be taping this when he comes home from school sometimes.

S.   Er, could you cut that off the tape, please? Cut the tape while I bat him one!

Jim and Yvonne Walker. 15 Hough Green

D. How do you come to be living in Ashley?

Y. I was born here.

D. Of course. Your parents are Pat and Albert Jennings.

Y. Yes, that's right. We lived at Number 7. Bertha lived here.

D. Number 7 . . . That's where Bertha lives now, next door to us.

Y. Yes. We did a swap. We had three bedrooms. When we first came there was my mum and dad, my grandma on my mum's side, and my two brothers. And we only had a three-bedroomed house, which was a bit cramped. I think my mum and dad used to sleep downstairs. Nanny had a room upstairs. And we used the other rooms. Bertha had four bedrooms here. They had one of their relatives living with them too. And one of them died. So we did a swap then. That's why we swapped, because they'd got the extra space, and we needed it.

D. So, Yvonne, have you got any particular memories of childhood here?

Y. We used to like the village school. It was like a family. There was forty of us, I think, aged four to eleven. And the juniors used to help out with the infants. We'd listen to them read while the headmistress did whatever - clerical work. I can remember games, we used to have a bar in the playground, that's all we had, and hopscotch marked out. And we used to play games like bean-bags and rounders. And I can remember I passed my Eleven Plus and went to the Girls' Grammar, where one class had forty children, the same as the whole school here. And probably out of this forty about thirty seven of them came from Altrincham Prep. It was very very hard - I hated it - going from a tiny school like this to a school like that. That's the only set-back, I think, with a village school. And such things as lacrosse and netball, I'd never heard of them! I felt such an idiot! Geography classes at Ashley used to be a walk down to Tatton Park. It was good, I did enjoy the school, I must admit. I hated secondary school. And being at a girls only school, I missed the fellas, you know!

D. I bet you made up for it!

J. Our boys were the same, weren't they? The two youngest went to Ashley School, and they really loved it there, didn't they. We used to end up, about half past three, four o'clock, with the whole school on The Green, playing football. A daily function that was, even at the weekends. They'd come from all the farms and the out-houses round Ashley. But as soon as they went to Knutsford . . . It was going from this little small school to the huge, where you have thirty, forty kids in one class all the same age. After that it's such a big place, isn't it?

D. And as you say, it's got such a friendly, family atmosphere, it's not like a school at all. Suddenly to find you're having to sort of fight for your ground, the way schoolkids do, assert yourself against so much competition: I should have thought it would be terribly difficult. You say your youngest two, what happened to the eldest?

J.   Before we came up to live here the boys went to Stamford Park, in Altrincham. And when we moved here we left the eldest one at Stamford Park, because he was in his last term you see.

D.   Of course. It wouldn't have been worth it at that stage. Perhaps we ought to go back a bit in that case, because we've got now to moving here. How did you meet, you two?

J.   We met in 1968, on the funfair in Altrincham. It was a friend of 'Vonne's, who I knew and grew up with where we lived in Oldfield Brow, Jill Slaney, and we'd gone to the fair with our friends from Oldfield Brow, and Jill met up with 'Vonne. That's how we met. Not straight away, if you see what I mean, but it was a contact between her friend and me, and 'Vonne and her. So she was like a go-between. And then it just went from there. 'Vonne was fifteen and I was sixteen. I'd just started my apprenticeship as a decorator, at Whipp's in Hale.

D.   One last question about youth in Ashley, Yvonne: it seems a difficult place for teenagers?

Y.   Oh, yes it is now, but when we were young it wasn't. Because when I came in, the whole Green was families of the same age. And we all grew up together. That's why I enjoyed it so much. We all went everywhere together, we went to school together, we went to church together: everybody went to Sunday School, eighty per cent went to Sunday School on a Sunday, we all got confirmed together. We used to go to Blackpool.

J.   There were thirty or forty kids living on The Green. I think all the people really, as well, they were the same age, the parents. And they all grew up the same. And they all got old the same.

D.   And I only came in at the stage when they were all getting old: your generation had gone. All that was left was the parents' generation. And I felt quite a sad feeling about this place, this Green at that stage: because there were no young at all, or there didn't seem to be. Just these empty nests. That was the feeling I had as I visited in The Green. And I've so often tried to imagine what it must have been like when it was teeming with children.

Y.   One big family! We used to do trips together. We had coaches and we'd to go to Blackpool together, families. And in the summer, to the Bollin, everybody would move off, mothers with all the kids, we used to go to the Bollin. The big field, where the new houses are [*Egerton Moss*] opposite the post office, every night my dad'd be down there when it went dark, *What you doing in here!* - there'd be all of us sat in the dark, talking. *Oh! What you doing!* It's like the kids, they go on about them now collecting round the train station, in Hale, and things like that: they're only doing what we used to do, but they've got nowhere to go. There's more people, they can be a bit frightening. But I suppose we were probably the same, we just didn't have other people to come past. It was our own little area.

D.   And you'd just started work, Jim. Did you say you were apprenticed to Mr Whipp?

J. I left school at fifteen, and I started apprenticeship as a decorator for C.M.Whipps on Hale Road. It was one of the places to be an apprentice, in that line of work. In Hale and Altrincham. There's only a few. Because it was a big firm when I started. Twenty, thirty men. There was an apprentice of every age. It was very good. I was taught by the best, at the time I was fortunate to have that privilege.

D. I'm interested, having been vicar of St John's, and they're just up the road, in the parish.

J. Well that was my school, St John's. I was born and bred in Altrincham, until I was about eleven or twelve, then it was brought down. Where those flats and Sainsbury's are now, that's where I was born. But my first school was St Elizabeth's. A teacher came to Ashley from there. Mrs Eaves. She still comes to Ashley. She goes to Mrs . . . Is it Mrs Laxton? And they go out together. She's not changed!

D. So C. M. Whipp was the obvious choice for you. I don't suppose you got accepted automatically, if it was as good as that. They were more expensive than any other decorator, that's why we never had them in the Vicarage, because of their prices!

J. Well I moved to an even pricier one, Batemans. And then I went self-employed.

D. It must be one of the most nerve-racking changes to make, to leave employment and go out on your own: what were the factors that made you decide to do it?

J. A friend was an accountant, and he said, Why don't you go self-employed? I can give you so much work. And that's how it started.

D. So what really sparked it off was this accountant saying he could give you work.

J. It's being taught as well. I think what happened is, you were taught well. And it stays with you. There's not many people these days who'll go in somewhere, and prepare a room thoroughly, properly. But regarding the areas, I just do Hale, Bowdon, Hale Barns. I have work in High Legh, places like that. I do have customers who have lived in Bowdon and now live in places like that. The furthest customer I have got is in London, and I go there now and again quite a lot, for a long period. Like weeks, a couple of weeks, a month at a time. I like it a lot actually, because it's the excitement of the place. But after a week, and you're in the house, which is a town house in the middle of Knightsbridge, it's very lonely. Very boring. And very very noisy. There's no rest in London. Police sirens and all sorts going off all the way through the night. Just like New York. But it's nice, because it's right across the road from Harrods. Spend all my money!

D. Everything on your doorstep! Do you get a chance to go down, Yvonne?

Y. I'm his secretary!

D. So you have to go! Can't do without his book-keeper! Do you have people working with you, Jim, or are you absolutely literally on your own?

J. I'm literally on my own. The only person who's ever worked with me properly, full-time, and that was my middle son, Stephen. I took him on from school, and gave him the apprenticeship. With the understanding that when he completed his apprenticeship he could do exactly what he liked.

D.   Now we've got onto Stephen, and missed out on the others. Can we talk about them for a bit: who came when?

Y.   Paul came '75, Stephen in '77 and Richard in '79.

D.   And where were you living?

Y.   Sinderland Road in Broadheath was our first house, we were there for eight or nine years. Then we moved to Ashfield Road in Altrincham when Richard was three months. And moved here when Richard was five. We got married, by the way, at Ashley Church. I'd just like to say, about the atmosphere of Ashley being so nice when we were growing up: we had, from the village here, we had a wedding present from every family. That's how close it was. And everybody knew Jim.

J.   It was like a box, wasn't it? And it was all like washing-up liquid, Flash, you know. Things like soap, a toilet roll, a dishcloth. What when you first got married and first moved into a house, it was a thing like that, a present like that. Which I thought was nice. It wasn't just like a kettle, or. That's the type of things they used to do.

Y.   Everybody putting something in.

D.   How did the move come about, bringing you back here?

J.   Where we actually lived on Ashfield Road, it was at the bottom, where there was no parking outside the house because we were so close to the junction, it was a very bad junction there. And with us having the kids, we used to be in fear of them having an accident there. So we put the house up for sale, and within a fortnight it sold. We'd never expected it to go so quickly, and hadn't even started to look for a house. And it was 'Vonne's dad who suggested that we come and stay here and have a good look, and make sure you get what you want. Not just rush in because you've got to have somewhere. So we came here, and we were here for six months, and we've been here ever since!

D.   Fantastic. There must be skills needed, to live in a house with three generations; teenage boys.

J.   They weren't teenagers when we came.

Y.   When we came back, Ashley was completely different.

J.   It was like what you said before, all the children had gone and it was just the parents that were left behind. When we came I think there was only two children on The Green, and that was Victoria and Karen. And then our three boys, thrown in. They got to know people once they got to school, there were people living on the outskirts.

D.   Yes. Who were very pleased to come and play football!

Y.   Actually we used to get comments from the older ones, when we came back.

Like Mr Hobson, saying Oh it is nice to see kids back on The Green again!

J.   I think Stephen and Richard did like it. Because they had so many friends at Ashley School, that used to come and play every day, and weekends. They had a very very good football team while they were there, at Ashley, and it was Barbara Littlewood who used to coach them. They won loads of trophies. And they got their picture in the *Manchester Evening News*. And she really was very dedicated as well. Very good, she was. For a lady, she was a good manager!

D.   So what did they do after that, when they left school?

J.   Well Paul left school and, while he was at Knutsford, he did a work experience, at McDougall and Rose. And they were so pleased with him that they asked him if he wanted to come back in the summer holidays, and they would pay him. So he did. And he's been there ever since. And the next one, as you know, was Stephen. He's now a decorator in his own right. He can do what he likes. But the big young one, Richard, he works for Robinsons, the builders and timber people in Salford. They renovate old buildings. Not like joinery, putting in doors and windows, they cut more into the joists and the big roof timbers. He does lots of churches and colleges, and all these very old buildings.

D.   And is he the only one left here now? Where's Paul?

Y.   Paul lives in Brooklands Road with his girlfriend. They've been together for seven years.

J.   Stephen as you know lives in Urmston, he's got a little baby boy, called Callum.

D.   I've met Callum here, yeah.

J.   Our first grandchild. We're very proud of him.

Y.   They've all got steady girlfriends. Richard's been going out with his girlfriend for three years.

D.   Yvonne we've been talking about everyone else, what have you been doing all these years? You were at the grammer school and hated it all the time. Then what did you do?

Y.   I went to college for a year, South Trafford, then I worked for an estate agent, followed by a place called RTR, which was a television firm, head of all these shops like Martin Dawes, Rumbelows. They got me into book-keeping. When they moved to Bolton I went to Atlantic Rubber, a group of three companies, to do their books. Which I really enjoyed. I was there about a couple of years, and stopped to have Paul.

J.   The babies started to come.

Y.   Twelve years ago I started working for an accountant in Altrincham, John Sheehan, and I'm still there.

Pat Jennings. 15 Hough Green

D.   Pat, where were you born?

P.   Where was I born? I was born in Altrincham.

D.   And how did you meet Albert?

P.   Dancing. We used to go dancing. Dance mad! St Baldred's in Hale. And the big one in Altrincham, what's it called? Stamford Hall. Sequence dancing and that sort of thing. Ballroom dancing.

D.   So that's how you met. And where did Albert come from?

P.   Rostherne. I'm not sure where he was born, but he lived in Rostherne.

D.   So that was quite a trek, into Altrincham, he must have been really keen. How did he come?

P.   Peddling along, peddling along on a bike! Hail, rain or snow!

D.   Good for him! And where did you settle first?

P.   When we first got married? With my grandmother. She lived on her own, she lived in Altrincham. We joined her for a few months. Then we went to Sunny Bank Farm, Ringway. We lived there for a while. And then these houses were built. We were one of the first in these houses. Then came along the children. Born in Ashley. Brought up in Ashley. Philip was born in Number 7.

D.   Of course, that's where you lived first! Was that as soon as these houses were built? Were you the first into your house?

P.   Mmmm. One of the first in that block. Number 7. Eight of us, I think there was. Would be eight, wouldn't it? In that top stretch.

D.   Yes it would have been eight of you, yes. And of course the place was more or less a building site, I suppose. It must have been an awful mess. How did you find it, moving in?

P.   Traumatic! (*laughs*). That's as best as I can say, I think.

D.   Well that's a very good word for it, I should think! Did it take long to settle down?

P.   Not really. I used to say that I would never live in the country. Milk came in bottles! I wasn't going to stay in Ashley, no way! How long have I been here now? It must be nearly fifty years.

D.   Very nearly. It'll be fifty next year, won't it? What do you think made you change your mind about staying?

P.   Oh, it was lovely for the kids. Plenty of places to roam. They had plenty of space. They loved it.

D.   And loads of other children to play with of course. So who came after Philip?

P.   Yvonne. Yvonne was four years after Philip. Then there was Alan, he was two years younger than Yvonne.

D.   So there you were in Number 7, with Philip and then having Yvonne and Alan: Albert meanwhile, was he still working on the farm?

P.   No, he took up a contracting job. Made it his own business. Hedge-cutting.

D.   This was with the tractor that I remember?

P.   Hedge-cutter. Don't go too close or you'll have no head! And then of course he was made redundant. Oh no, Albert had his first heart attack, that was it.

D.   Ah, that was it, rather than being made redundant: because it was his own business, wasn't it?

P.   Yeah.

D.   How old would he have been when he had his first heart attack?

P.   About sixty-four, I think. Perhaps a little bit less than that.

D.   We're jumping ahead a bit: some time between the children being born and Albert having his first heart attack, you moved from Number 7 up to here. How did that come about?

P.   Well, it was bigger. This was bigger, because we had the three children. And that one suited Bertha.

      [Bertha Roberts, q.v., was Albert's sister]

D.   Who was living here at the time?

P.   The Robertses. Mr and Mrs Roberts, Len's mum and dad. And then they passed away, and we swapped with Bertha. Because that was big enough for us.

D.   The change really came with Len's parents dying?

P.   Yes, I suppose so, really. Suited us all round.

D.   Suited everyone. Yes. It's good to hear something like that happening, that suits everyone.

P.   You don't get many of those, do you?

D.   There's one or two now who could do with that, I should think. And then gradually the children grew up and left. Was there a stage when you and Albert were the only two here?

P.   Yes, but not for long, I don't think.

D.   And then Yvonne and Jim came in, is that what happened? I'd love to know if you've got any memories of what it was like getting used to having a houseful again. A lot of people would have felt, perhaps, that that might have been a bit much, suddenly to go from two to seven!

P.   Well we've got the two halves, you see. You can shut that half off.

D.   So that it worked quite easily?

P.   Yes. So far.

D.   So far, she says! Well I think it was terrific, it was lovely. And it was lovely having the boys here. Because they were about the only youngsters around. Which was a pity for them, I should think. Compared with how your children were, when they were being brought up on The Green, and there were children in almost every house.

P.   I think Albert counted seventy-two at one stage. That was the Queen's Coronation. All the young kids there. All dressed up in fancy dress. It was here on The Green. We had big long tables all down The Green.

D.   They did it again at the Silver Jubilee, I believe.

P.   That's right. yes.

D.   So that's two big parties the Queen's managed to give to the children on The Green. Is there anything else you'd like to talk about? When were you married?

P.   '47. Same year as the Queen. We helped her celebrate!

D.   You went? To the Garden Party?

P.   We went, yes. We enjoyed it, we loved it.

D.   Tell us about it, Pat.

P.   There's not a lot to tell, really. We went into the Palace itself.

D.   How did you get there?

P.   Our Philip, the eldest lad took us. We spent the weekend there. The four of us, with his wife.

D.   So you made a weekend of it. How did you get from the hotel to the Palace?

P.   Philip's car.

D.   Philip drove you up to the Palace gate?

P.   Yeah. We had sandwiches, and cakes, and ice cream.

D.   But before that, what happened? You'd driven up to the Palace gates.

P.   Down The Mall.

D.   And did you just walk in? Or is there a sentry?

P.   Oh there were sentries. They were Ghurkas, I think. There were no cameras, of course, nothing like that. Videos. We spent the whole afternoon there. The bands played. I didn't count them, but there must have been more than one.

D.   And I suppose a huge garden?

P.   Oh, huge. There were one thousand six huindred people there. Or one thousand four hundred.

D.   And you say there were refreshments?

P.   Little cakes with the year on.

D.   And who did you see?

P.   Prince Philip. And the Queen Mother, of course. And the Queen. There was too many to see everybody. But you got a glimpse of everybody.

D.   Did they look any different from how you expected?

P.   No, not really. I thought the Queen was shorter. She's not very tall. And the Queen Mother of course, she wasn't very tall.

D.   It must have been quite tiring?

P.   For them?

D.   Yes, and for you I should think. Were you able to sit down?

P.   Well we walked around for about two and a half hours, and then we found a chair and somebody sat on it, quick! That sort of thing! They didn't have enough tables and chairs, I must say. You had to be quick.

D.   So you were quite footsore by the time . . . Did Philip meet you at the end, or how did you get back to the hotel?

P.   In Philip's car.

D.   He was there, waiting for you?

P.   Is it The Mall? The other side of the Palace? All the cars were parked along the right-hand side. You had a green, I don't know what you'd call it. A ticket, stuck on your windowsill. Telling you where to park.

D.   Of course you've got this beautiful invitation here in a frame, haven't you?

P.   I had that framed, yeah.

D.   May I read it?

> "The Lord Chamberlain is commanded by Her Majesty to invite
> Mr & Mrs Joseph Jennings
> to a Garden Party at Buckingham Palace
> on Tuesday the 15th July, 1997 from 4 to 6
> as part of the celebrations of the Golden Wedding Anniversary
> of the Queen and the Duke of Edinburgh."

Not Albert Jennings? I never knew his name was Joseph. What an exciting thing to happen.

P.   It was an experience, yes. It really was. And the inside of that Palace . . . Out of this world!

D.   So you got to see the inside, as well as the garden?

P.   Oh, yeah.

D.   What was the most exciting thing you saw?

P.   The Throne Room. It's out of this world. Beautiful colours, gold, all sorts of colours. A golden staircase, that really was a beauty. They had a staircase going right round in a semicircle.

Trevor Jones. 16 Hough Green

T.   I was born in Manchester, and I went to live with my grandparents for a few months, in Byrom Street in Altrincham. And then I moved here in about May or April '37. And I've been in Ashley all my life, first down at Station Cottages for forty years, and the remainder in Hough Green.

D.   And next door to you, I suppose, in Station Cottages, you had Joan . . .

T.   The Stonehewer family.

D.   You were born shortly before the war. Can you remember much about the war?

T.   The only thing I can remember about the war is sitting on the doorstep, looking up at a Spitfire and a German Heinkel or whatever it was, fighting. And all bits and pieces were falling all the way round me, and I wasn't aware what it was at all. They were pieces of metal off the planes. I was fascinated by these planes. And of course during the war there was a bomb landed the other side, where the motorway is now, and it damaged all the chimney pots and most of the windows in the houses. And there was another one, the other side of the school. The indentation you can see today. The other thing I can remember about the war is that Earl Egerton of Tatton came for some sort of drive to get money for the forces. And I can always remember outside the school we had tin cans, we placed them on the edge of the curb, and also pennies. But I can't understand what, how far these pennies went. But there was pennies on the curb as well. And of course I used to see the paratroopers coming over to Tatton Park. They trained there. Firstly with, I think they were Wellington bombers. And then it became the Dakotas. But then of course they had the balloons, which was better, because they didn't have to transport the troops back and to all the time. They had big buses, used to take them back and to to the airport. I can remember one balloon getting away, but I didn't know the circumstances until I see the books years later. I found out afterwards, there was two that got away. One got into the Midlands before it was shot down, and the other one was in Chester. But as for the war, of course, I was still at the Ashley School, and I went to Bradbury Central in Hale, which is no longer there now. Knocked down, and I think there's a housing develpoment on there.

D.   And I suppose your father worked on the railway, did he?

T.   Oh no. He worked for Clibrans, the nursery people. He worked at the one down in Ashley at Birkin, Birkin Farm. But he also, at times worked in The Coppice, and the one in Hale, and probably Timperley. No, he didn't work for the railway.

D.   I was just assuming that, living in Station Cottages. But they weren't just for railway . . .

T.   Oh no. Most of them were, but some weren't. How he come to get in Station Cottages I would not know.

D.   Did you enjoy it, living there? I mean, did you develop a great interest in trains?

T.   Not really, because they were that close, you ignored them. I mean I was only perhaps eight feet from the actual running rail. And people would ask you if a certain train had gone through, and you couldn't remember. And of course in those days there was a lot more goods traffic going through. We had a station yard, which was quite well-used.

D.   So stuff was loaded here? What sort of stuff would that be?

T.   Well you've got your farm produce. I can remember, during the war, Mr Walkden from Ashley Hall Farm, put a lot of potatoes on the train. And he used to put dye on them, because they were going to be used for animals, you see. I can always remember them loading them up, and getting this watering can and putting this purple dye all over them. And of course the farmers' produce used to come, and fertiliser, and all sorts. Even machinery came. I can't remember, but during the war there was one farm, Back Lane Farm, a name of Robinson, moved the whole farm to a different part of the country. And it all went on the train. The cattle, everything. Sheep, horses, everything. Machinery, everything. Went off by train. But I can't remember that. It was during the war, but I just don't remember it.

D.   What sort of things did you get up to as a child?

T.   I used to do a lot of farming. I used to go to Hough Green Farm an awful lot, almost lived there through the school holidays. Fred's father first, Arthur. And then Fred. He took over in about '48. He married a girl from near where my mother came from, in Aston-by-Budworth . . . my mother went to school with her father, Mr Ford. So it was a bit of a small world, really. The same when my father eventually moved fom Clibrans, he went to work at Midways, first the Boltons and then the Robinsons. Another coincidence, when the Robinsons moved in, because my mother was in service, and she'd worked for Mrs Robinson's parents, at High Legh. So there's another small world there.

D.   And what did you do when you finished at Bradbury?

T.   I worked with a joiner in Hale for about four years. Then he died, and I moved to another company in Sale, and was there about two years and went to a company in Knutsford for a short time. And then I had a problem with one of my arms, and I didn't work for nearly two years. I had this operation, and one thing and another. Then I went to a rehabilitation centre, a government place, in Leicester for six weeks. And then I came home, and they couldn't find work for me straight away, and I went to another rehabilitation centre, at Horsham in Sussex. And I was there about eight weeks. And then I got a job at the Lyntoype, in Altrincham. And I was there going on sixteen years. And that was one of my first places for redundancy. I finished there, and then I went to Banners Textiles, and I was there nearly six years, and I was made redundant again. And I eventually fetched up at the Ashley Smithy Garage.

D.   Had it been difficult finding work, after the two redundancies?

T.   The first redundancy, I think it was about eight weeks before I got work. And then the second time it would probably be about seven weeks, something like that. But as I say I went to the garage, and at first I started on cleaning cars. In them days I hadn't got a licence for driving cars, although I'd had a motorbike licence ever since 1954. And by this time it was '82. I took a driving test in '85, and subsequently used to go up and down the country, exchanging cars for them. Any model they hadn't got, get it off another dealer. Some weeks I would do over two thousand miles.

D.   So you've had a very varied working life: were there any particular jobs you enjoyed most?

T.   I think the driving, going up and down the country, because at the time I was helping to look after my father. And when I went away the garage used to say to me, Are you going on your holidays this week? Because it was a standing joke that when I was away it was my holidays, basically. Getting away from the environment I'd got at home! Which it was. He used to say, Where are you going this week, for your holiday? It was a standing joke. And of course I had to go and rescue people that had broken down, that sort of thing. Used to get some funny antics with them. Once I went to one lady. I said What's the matter? I tried the oil, and the dipstick come out perfectly dry, and I jokingly said to her, *You want a longer dipstick!* And she believed me! And as I put the dipstick back I noticed something sticking out of the side of the engine. And the piston had come out through the side of the engine! Completely wrecked it.

D.   So she's been running without oil for . . .

T.   Oh yes. She'd never bothered. She'd done about ten thousand miles since its service, and it wasn't a new car. And she said, I've been topping the water up. But she didn't bother about the oil. It's obviously the lifeblood of a vehicle.

D.   You want a longer dipstick!

T.   Oh yes, we used to tell that to quite a lot of people if they were a bit low on oil. They say, It's a bit low on oil. We'd say, It's either oil, or you want a longer dipstick! And of course some of them couldn't see the joke. Of course I've been motorcycling since 1954 all the time. I started off with one of those Cyclemasters, with the engine on the back wheel of the bike. Then I went on to a small, I think it was a James, motorbike. And of course since then I've had a total of about eight vehicles. Eight motorcycles. Nearly all BSA. There's only been the James; and the Triumph. The James was a brand new one. And my first BSA, which was a 500, that was a new one, in '57. But since then they've been secondhand. I mean, the Triumph is an ex-Lancashire Police bike. The problem with police bikes of course is they aren't the same specifications as civilian bikes. One or two things that are subtly different.

D.   Why would police require different specifications?

T.   Well you see, on the electrical side, it's because they've got a wireless on the back. And of course in them days it was still six volts, but they wanted a bigger battery and all that. That was it. And of course the style of the thing was different, because the one I've got, which is 1963 but the actual model came out for civilians in '64. But it was still painted in the original colours, it wasn't painted white, like they did two or three years later, it was still in the colours of the manufacturer. And then the BSA sidecar, I didn't have that very long. And the other BSA, the B31, which I've got now, that is an ex-auxiliary fire service.

D.   How strange. Is that a coincidence, or do you tend to get ex-service bikes?

T.   It was advertised by a company in Bedford. And it was nineteen years old then, but it had done only eight thousand miles. Because the Auxiliary Fire Service was disbanded in '68. So from '68 till '75 it was stored. They didn't release it until then. I've had it for twenty three years now. And maybe different things go wrong, but you expect that. I mean this has now done probably eighty thousand miles. Whereas the Triumph, in the time I had it on the road, it did in excess of two hundred thousand. I suppose it's a lot of mileage, but I suppose when the police had it it never stopped.

D.   What's the attraction, Trevor, of this biking? Is it the actual riding, or is half the fun in the maintenance of the machines?

T.   It's a combination of both. The maintenance of the old machines, and the style of riding. I mean the modern ones would be no good to me. Of course I get round to a lot of these rallies.

D.   What goes on at these rallies?

T.   It's basically displaying them. You go round the arena and they ask you questions about them, but it's mostly gathering for a run there, and then that's it.

D.   So it's for bikers to meet and compare bikes?

T.   And cars, and steam. You see all these come from them. [*Indicating a collection of small oval brass discs balanced in the picture rail all round the room*] Well you see if you're an exhibitor, that's what you generally get. A plaque. Sometimes it'll be a cup or mug, like that [*indicating one*]. I've got quite a few mugs. There's some up there that came from Denbigh flower show. Them stone ones. Various things, you get.

D.   But mainly they're these brass plaques? And I suppose you get to see the same faces?

T.   Oh yes. I don't travel as far now as I used to do. I used to do quite a lot in Sheffield, that area. I still go into Lancashire, Cheshire, Shropshire, Staffordshire, and into Wales, I do three or four in Wales. In springtime I generally do the first one, which is at Urmston. That's on a Saturday. It's a three-day event, but it's the Saturday I go. On Sunday I go to the one at Llandudno. And then back to the one at Urmston on the Monday. The rallies I do like is where they're in parkland. It seems to be a more natural setting. A place like a park that is used for caravans for the rest of the year is not the same. Just a straight piece of grass, sort of thing. Whereas if you get them dotted around among trees, it breaks the whole system up. There used to be one at a place called Harmer, in Clwyd, used to be Flintshire. That's in beautiful parkland. And I do one, right at the end of the season, at Llangollen Railway. The Vale Vintage Machinery have their end-of-the-season rally, and they have it at Carrog, which is as far as the actual steam line goes at the moment. And that is a very nice setting. It's on the bank of the River Dee. But getting back to Ashley: over the years I've seen an awful lot of changes. I mean, we've got now the motorway, which annoys me because of the noise it makes, especially when the wind is in a certain direction.

D.   When did you move here from Station Cottages?

T.   About 1977.

D.   How did you find that? It must have been quite a change from Station Cottages.

T.   Well it was in one sense a change, because down there you wouldn't see anybody other than on the train. Also I missed the trains, although I'm back to them on the opposite side, but further away.

D.   You can't reach out of the bedroom window to pick up your coal!

T.   Oh no, you can't do that! It took a bit of getting used to, because you'd hear a different sound from the trains. You're further away.

D.   And how did your father find it?

T.   I think he settled down quite well, with being involved in the church, and all the people that he knew, and all that sort of thing. It helped. He was with the church for quite a number of years. He started off blowing the organ and looking after the boilers. Bell-ringing. All sorts of things. Odd jobs. When we moved he was seventy seven then. And he lived for another eighteen years. He was ninety six when he died. He was the oldest person in the village at the time. Closely followed by Mrs Mason, who's about two months younger.

D.   When did he die?

T.   July '96.

D.   And you looked after him quite by yourself, you didn't have any help?

T.   When I was made redundant from the garage, in '92, I tried to get other work which would tie in with looking after him, but wasn't successful. So then I became a permanent carer for my dad.

D.   Are there any changes over your time in Ashley you are particularly aware of?

T.   The major change was the motorway. Of course these houses where we are now, in Hough Green, I can remember that when it was just a field. I think about thirty houses have been built here. The airport doesn't make much difference. There's a lot of talk now about this second runway, but I don't think it will affect us much. But the biggest change here is the farming methods. Some of them I think are retrograde steps, because you see some of these that are using quite big vehicles, it's breaking all the drains up. You see how waterlogged the fields are. I mean, we know this particular winter has had a lot of rain. But there never used to be as much as this, because I'm sure they're breaking these drains up, because when these drains were put in it was horses. There was no weight. I think the farming methods today are not conducive to looking after the ground. They say that we're only custodians of the land for the next generation, but I'm afraid the way it's going on there'll be nothing left for them. I mean, they take everything out of the ground, and they're not putting anything back. Unless it's out of a bag. I think the natural humus and that sort of thing is much better, because it was natural.

Brian Clarke. 19 Hough Green

D.   Brian, how long have you been living in Ashley?

B.   Well I'm going back now to the 1950s. I came to live here in about 1949,50. We came to see the house. At the time it was being built, I'd be about seventeen. My father brought me down to have a look round, because he'd been told that he may have a chance of getting one of the houses in Ashley. So we came down on one Sunday morning. And my father had been told that if he was going to get a house at all it would be Number 19. So we came down and had a walk round the estate, which was only partly built. In actual fact the road was only part-adopted anyway, the road to the place. Anyway we found us way round, round the bricks and mortar, and concrete mixers, and what-have-you, and eventually found Number 19.

D.   You managed to find which was to be 19?

B.   Number 19, yes. So we came in. And there was a night watchman who'd been there all night, chap in his eighties. And we sat down and we had a cup of tea and a talk.

D.   So the house was up?

B.   It was up. It was built, but it hadn't been plastered. There was quite a lot of work to do. And we had a chat with the night watchman. And I remember my father saying, Well, it's Number 19. I wouldn't mind this place. I would love to get this place off the council. With the back and side it made a nice garden see, so it would be a nice place to have. So we went back home, which was High Legh. Moss Lane West, High Legh, a small cottage down a by-lane, which was going on to two hundred years old: we drank from a well; paraffin light, you know; flag floors. All prehistoric, you could say! Going back in time. And the fact was that the Admiralty were going to demolish the place.

D.   The Admiralty?

B.   Yes. On account of the fact that the runways weren't long enough, and we were on the apron of the main runway, number 28 runway, which passed the control tower. And we were on the apron, the cottage was on the apron of the runway.

D.   I didn't realise there were runways at High Legh.

B.   Oh yes. So we had notice, to either find your own place, private, or rely on the council. And we come to Ashley. The only houses that were on allocation were the houses that were being built at the time in Ashley. In the Macclesfield Borough. So within weeks of being down to Ashley my father got notice to say that he'd got a chance of getting Number 19, and in the near future he would be told. So it was just a matter of time, waiting. Within nine months of being told we were on the housing list for Ashley, my father was told that he'd got Number 19.

D.   Good! You must have been very pleased, all of you!

B.   We were very pleased. Especially my mother and my sisters, because where we lived at High Legh we'd no bathroom. We had to do a bathtub job on a Friday night, in front of the fire. Well, it was from one extreme to the other, you could say. We didn't have to chuck a bucket down the well, we had taps to turn on. So it was a vast difference. Turning a tap on was a luxury.

D.   And electricity.

B.   And the electricity. To turn it on, whereas you had to rely on paraffin lamps. You know, paraffin. And not only that, the fact was that we were two miles in between, in actual fact, between Appleton and High Legh.

D.   How many of you were there?

B.   It was a full family. Before anyone was married. That was my parents, my two brothers Ron and Billy, Rosemary and Christine, my two sisters. There was five of us children. And with mother and father, that was seven.

D.   And how was it when you all came in? How did you find it, settling in here? Were you one of the first to come?

B.   No, I would say there were in the region of four to five before we came, actually living here.

D.   So it wasn't a complete wilderness?

B.   No, no. It was getting civilised! The gardens were in a state, because - this in particular, this house where I live now, with it being a corner house it was a central point for the rest of the estate. So the concrete mixer had been here, and the actual garden was solid with bricks, and mortar. It all had to be dug out, and fresh soil brought in. Which was no problem.

D.   Did the builders do that, or did you have to?

B.   The builders did. So it was no problem for my father. With him being a landscape gardener. So he understood the fact that the surface rubble would have to be moved. Dug out and replaced with fresh soil. Which he did.

D.   And you were nineteen, did you say, when you moved here?

B.   I was seventeen when I first came to see this place. I'd never been in Ashley before. As a matter of fact I'd never seen a bus or a train till the age of seventeen. It was like living in the Outback, living in High Legh. You went to school, you walked to school. Walk everywhere. You never went into a town or anywhere.

D.   And where was school?

B.   The nearest school was Appleton. That was two miles, towards Warrington.

D.   So what were you doing? Had you found work by now?

B.   Yes, I was working. I worked for High Legh Estates. I started there on the

Monday. I left school on the Friday, and I started on the following Monday. I was on maintenance, which covered quite a series of trades. I was very fortunate. I was an apprentice. The chap that I was working with was a qualified bricklayer. And I was apprenticed to the chap in question. I learned all the trades, I was very lucky: the bricklaying, the plastering, joinering, roofing. We covered a great series of maintenance. We covered everything. So I was very fortunate. I stuck it out till I was eighteen, about three or four weeks before I was called up for the Services, and then obviously I had to finish, you see, for the Services. By then we'd moved to Ashley.

[*For Brian's account of his National Service, see Appendix: The Virgin Soldiers*]

D.   What happened when you came back home after National Service?

B.   Well the first thing, obviously, was to have a break. From everything. Get my bearings. I'd got to think about things now: what am I going to do with the rest of my life? So I did a lot of thinking, and I did a lot of drinking as well! And I finally decided that Yes, I was going to get a job. So I went and I got a job. I started with British Rail. I went for the interview at Crewe. It was the P-way Department, that was working in a gang of four, or you could work on a construction gang of about seventy or eighty chaps, re-laying tracks. Maintenance. So I said, Right, well if you've anything to offer local, I live in Ashley. They said, Oh yes, certainly. We do have a post at Hale. There's a gang there that works from Hale to Mobberley. He said, You'll be the youngest chap on the team. If you're interested, the job's yours. And I started off with a gang of chaps that had been on the railways all their lives, since leaving school. There was a ganger, assistant - there was four in the team altogether. We had two miles of track up, what we call up-road and down-road, to look after. Maintenance-wise.

D.   What sort of things need to be done to a railway line?

B.   Well firstly you have to walk all the length, that's the first thing in the morning. That's walking the length, which means the actual distance you have to cover from one station to another. And that means checking all the crank plates, joint plates, loose bolts, broken plates, of which we had cabins at varying distances along the track, to do the job. Keys had to be knocked in; with the heat in the summertime, the keys do get loose and fall out. So they have to be knocked back in. And this is all done whilst you're walking the length. Tightening bolts. The fish plates. And putting the keys back which have been pushed out.

D.   All these technical words are part of the equipment that keeps the rail stuck to the track?

B.   To the base plates.

D.   Stops the line working loose?

B.   Stops it working loose, yes.

D.   And that needs a daily inspection? You'd usually find there'd be something that would need tightening?

B.   Oh yes. Without a doubt. You'd got what were called joints that were working, with the weight of the traffic - we call it traffic, it was the ICI hoppers, you know? Each of the hoppers weighs about a hundred tons, loaded with stone, the limestone going to the ICI from Buxton -

D.   Which we still have going past here twice a day?

B.   Yes, that's right. As a matter of fact they pay about two million pound a year compensation to British Rail, you know. For the damage that's done.

D.   Damage to the track?

B.   Right. To look after the maintenance of the track. Well I stuck this walking the length in the morning - there's two of you, see - and the job, it was very interesting. Because at weekends, Saturday, maybe Sunday sometimes, you'd be called out to help with a re-laying gang, which meant double time, you see. You always got double time for working with a re-lay gang. You learned more with a re-lay gang than what you did in your own time.

D.   Because yours was more a routine job?

B.   Yes. Because they shut an area down on a Sunday, while it was very quiet, and take a couple of miles of track up completely. Rail, sleepers, everything. You renew it completely. Have a hundred odd, two hundred, chaps working. It's an engineering feat. You have to take it out and put it back within, what, twenty four hours. So you're working to time, you've got all the elements against you weather-wise, you see. So it was quite a job.

D.   Quite a job. Need a good team.

B.   A team that's working together, you've got to work together to get this done.

D.   Brian, I guess we're probably getting pretty short of time. Is there any other part of your life you'd like to talk about?

B.   Well when it comes to interest, interest in the actual community where I live. It isn't so much interest as the fact that I've always been sort of, when it comes to inter-est, interested in characters. People living around you. I've always found that people are very quiet, don't say a lot. They're just classified in my book as a neighbour. But people talk in the local pub - you go for a drink and a laugh - are sort of characters. And I think the characters, you've only got to go back forty years - that's quite a few years - the characters were here when I first moved here. And since then the charac-ters, or people I call characters, have died off. Gone. Which used to go into The Greyhound, and they were characters, there's no two ways about that. Since these people have gone - it's either that or it's me that's getting older - I've found that it's gone very quiet. And people that have gone, and they've died, and people have taken their place over the years: sometimes I feel I'm a stranger in my own village, where I live.

Ron and Joan Reanney. 20 Hough Green

R.   I had an accident in High Legh, where an apple tree fell on top of me, while I was trying to get some apples off the tree. I'd tied the ladder to the tree, for security's sake. If I hadn't done that I'd have been all right. But because I was fixed to a fixed ladder, the top of the tree snapped and it came on top of me, pushing me down onto the ground. It was only about fifteen foot, wasn't it?

J.   Of course it was that bad weather.

R.   Bad weather, November, and I managed to hit onto a paving stone, of all places in the garden, I managed to fall onto a bit of a paving stone. I broke my back in two places. And it started to pour down with rain. I was shouting. She came down running to me. *What's the matter? I've hurt my back and can't move.* So in an hour of wisdom she said, *Don't go away! I'll get a blanket.* So she goes running up to the house, phones for the ambulance, comes down and covers me up with a blanket. So now I look like a dead dog in the garden, with a blanket over. Still raining of course. She goes in.

J.   Yes. It was one of my best blankets. I should have taken an old one really!

D.   This was in your garden, it was your own apple tree?

R.   No, no. It was the employer's apple tree.

J.   I heard him calling and I thought, there's something wrong. And saw him on the ground. He couldn't move his feet. I went to the hospital with you, didn't I?

R.   How long was I in hospital? I can't remember the time.

J.   It must have been twelve weeks.

R.   Just laying there, feet tied together. I wasn't allowed to move. I broke my wrist as well. To be honest, I had more problem with my wrist than with my back. The back heals itself in its own time. You just lay still for as long as you can, and let it heal.

J.   You had to learn to walk again, didn't you?

R.   Had to learn to walk, I couldn't walk. Had to learn to walk again.

D.   How long did that take?

R.   Three months, four. I was on, what do you call those things? A frame or something.

D.   You were three months on your back, and then another three months learning to walk again?

R.   Yes, yes. getting around. Yes. I was off work well over six months in the end, wasn't I? But fortunately we managed to get back and started working again. I changed to a senior horticultural instructor. I founded a horticultural training centre which I started to run from a little field with a gate, started it from the word Go. They just give me money, the government gave me a lot of money to start it off. We had forty-odd trainees in the end. Three instructors. Under the Youth Training Scheme.

D.   And where was this?

R.   In Moore, in Runcorn. I was there for about six years, wasn't I?

D.   And how did your back stand up to all this?

R.   Well I wasn't doing any manual work. Only the blackboard and classrooms. Lectures and things like that. It wasn't too bad. I did it for six years.

D.   How did this get started?

R.   There was an advert in one of the national papers. It just said *Horticultural Supervisor to start Centre*. So I wrote to the one in Runcorn. And they wrote to me and just asked if I'd come along and go and see them. So I went. It started from a little shed in a field with an acre of land, and finished up with a building that would occupy fifty people, and two acres of land.

D.   And you built it up from that to that in six years?

R.   City and Guilds. Everyone had passed the City and Guilds horicultural certificate, Part One.

D.   Are you still in touch with any of your students?

R.   No. I did have one chap who wrote to me asking me for a reference. That was about three years after. But you're inclined to forget people.

D.   If they don't cross your path again.

R.   And some of them you don't want to cross your path again! I did find that the intake: when we first started we had twenty-year-olds, they wanted to learn. But as the intake got a bit younger, to seventeen, all they wanted was to get paid the weekly money that they got, and be out all day away from their parents, you know. It was sad, sad to listen to the things that were said. The person going to my centre was the only person working in the house. And he upset the whole household, because he was getting up. To go to work. All the rest were still in bed at eight o'clock.

D.   And cursing him.

R.   Yes, well he was going in despondent, because he was getting shouted at, *What are you making that noise for at this time in the morning?!* And it put a lot of people off. I found, towards the end of these six years, they were getting younger and I was getting older. It's as simple as that. It was time I went. Anyway after six years, and travelling every day to Runcorn, that was enough, here to Runcorn.

D.   Oh, you were here by then? So when did you come here? After the accident?

R.   Yes. because they thought I wasn't going to work again. We had a choice of a flat in Knutsford, or Ashley. Now I'd never heard of Ashley, so I said We'll go to Ashley.

J.   I said to Ron, It'd be nice if it's a little village, with a church, a post office and a garage. So we came, we came right to it, didn't we? There were no messing, we came right to the house.

D.   When would this have been?

R.   About twenty year ago.

D.   How did you find it, moving in here?

R.   Oh, excellent. They were very good neighbours. They still are!

D.   You must have had the younger generation still living with you?

J.   Janet and Linda. Michael was married.

R.   Our Linda was working in Blackpool, wasn't she, she had a flat in Blackpool, she worked up there until we moved. She liked Blackpool, but as soon as we moved here she moved back.

D.   Then she met Paul?

R.   She met Paul then, yes.

J.   She joined the W.I. I joined the W.I. with her, but it wasn't my scene. So she went with Jenny.

R.   Jenny Watson, as we know her. Jenny McKenna.

J.   And of course they stayed at the W.I. And Linda plays darts, she's very good. And of course Elsie, Paul's mother, they were all in a team. They used to take it in turns, going to different houses. Of course she used to go to Sants'. That's how she met Paul.

R.   And Janet worked at Shearings.

J.   And then she worked at Hale, as a barrister's secretary. And then she married from there.

R.   She married Mark. Schoolfriends. Mark used to come to High Legh on his bike.

J.   And take her to the Young Farmers.

R.   So Janet's only had the one boyfriend.

J.   And she gave him a good hiding, at school.

D.   Oh, they were made for each other, obviously!

R.   He's been all right since! So anyway, after six years at the training centre there was a job going at Tatton. So I thought, that'll do me. It's near home. So I went as a garden warden, my title was called. Which hides a multitude of sins, but that was my title, Garden Warden.

D.　*The* garden warden?

R.　The only garden warden. It was my job to be there at weekends. Two days off in the middle of the week. But to be there at weekends. Anything that went wrong, Go and see Ron. Ron was the only one there for anyone to see, anyway. The rangers were there, of course, about a couple of rangers.

D.　So that's where you finished: where did you start?

Both.　Liverpool.

D.　So Joan, how did you meet this guy?

J.　Well we used to work in Woolton: Bear Brand stockings, they used to make stockings. Ron's sister-in-law used to work there. And one time we went to Ireland, we were about nineteen. Right after the war, wasn't it? And we went to Ireland, so we had to have these photographs taken, passports. And you know the way you used to have to sit, po-faced. And I took them for a laugh to work, you see. And my sister-in-law said, Oh I'll have one of those! Took it home, he's seen it, and he says, I'd like to go out with her!

R.　Love at first sight. We had a blind date, didn't we, love?

D.　Well not completely blind: you'd got a passport photo. So you'd seen the worst!

J.　So every time we did anything wrong he'd phone my sister-in-law and say, It's your fault!

R.　That was about forty eight years ago wasn't it, love?

D.　At what stage were you doing this knitting?

J.　I'd had the three children.

D.　I suppose you've always knitted, but you had a shop at some stage, didn't you?

J.　Yes. Selling baby linen. A wool shop. At the time The Beatles were going very strong. And the young ones, teenagers, used to come in just to get me talking. It was the accent. And they used to ask me all about Liverpool: *Did you live near Paul McCartney?* Not very far away. And of course they'd come in for any little thing, and chat me up, sort of thing!

D.　What a spin-off! I wonder if many people found this spin-off from The Beatles?

R.　They all assumed that because you were Liverpool you knew them, you had something to do with them. The only thing I ever knew was Rita Tushingham. And Cilla Black. Her mother had a flower stall, didn't she, in the Market. She used to have a flower stall on there. Priscilla White, her name was. And she called herself Cilla Black. But they were the people I knew. Oh, Ken Dodd. Everybody knows Ken Dodd! We used to knock about with him, when he was a lad.

D.   Now you went to another Knotty you were living at, at one stage?

R.   Knot End on Sea. We sold the wool shop to go and live at Knot End. Lovely sea coast and everything, you know. You could see all the Lake District, on the other side. Beautiful area, wasn't it?

J.   Oh yes. We used to call it Dead End, there wasn't anything there! It wasn't even as lively as Hale.

D.   But if you're saying that about Knot End, how is it in Ashley for you?

J.   Well we've got used to it, because we lived in a place called Satterthwaite. And that was twenty two miles to the nearest shop. So we were always . . . Actually we quite like it quiet.

R.   We're what is known in Liverpool as Woolly Backs, now. Anybody that lives in the country is a Woolly Back. Sheep.

J.   I didn't think I'd settle here, because I thought the houses would be too close. If the Green hadn't been there, in the middle, I might have found it overcrowded.

D.   I agree with you. I was quite anxious about it when we moved here. It's not just that they're close, it's that they can all see you. You've got everybody's windows looking at you. So going back to coming here, did it take you long to get used to living here, with all these houses around you?

J.   No, not really, no. Because there was that much space. Everyone has been nice. We've never known anyone nasty, or anything like that, you know, argumentative, or anything like that.

D.   What was that story you had about the neighbour with a vacuum cleaner?

R.   Oh yes. We had a neighbour who was using her vac. And she was pushing it to and fro very lightly, no problem at all. And I noticed that it wasn't picking any bits up. So I said to her, Is that working all right? Oh it's fine, she said, it's always been like this, lovely and light, it's no problem at all, you just push it as easily as anything. Look! she said. It wasn't picking up the bits, but she was still whizzing up and down with it. So when she stopped I had a look at it, and there was no belt on the bottom. The brushes weren't going round, just the motor. So I said, I'll have a look at this for you. So she said, All right, she said. So I take it home to my workshop, cleaned it all out. There was no dust bag in, so all the dust had got inside, so you can imagine what it was like. I had to borrow a hoover to clean the hoover! Anyway we flushed it all out, got a new bag and a new belt, brought it back reconditioned and ready to go. I took it in and said Try this now, I think you'll find it'll pick things up better. A bit later she comes round here with the vac, in a storming rage and practically throws it at me. *What have you done with this?* she says, *you've completely ruined it! I can't even push it across the carpet now!*

Ron and Jean Hobson. 21 Hough Green

D.   Jean may we start with you, as you were born in Ashley? Where were you born?

J.   At Lane End Cottages. The one nearest to Tanyard.

D.   Where the Hugheses live now? And did you go to the school?

J.   Yes.

D.   You must have been one of the nearest?

J.   Yes, we could leave home at five to nine and be there at nine o'clock! And home for lunch, of course. Most children, who were too far, had to take sandwiches. There were no school dinners.

D.   Is there anyone still around who went to school with you?

J.   Mrs Blain, Joan Blain. She was in the same class actually. Mrs Fisher was older, she was there at the time. I can't think offhand of any others.

D.   Well that's quite a good vintage, isn't it? And extraordinary that three of you should be living within a hundred yards! And where did you go from here?

J.   Stayed till I left school. It was a few years after that they changed it to a Junior only school. You could take the exams and leave at eleven for the grammar schools, which my brother did.

D.   Have you any particular memories of what life was like as a child?

J.   Well quite, I don't say idyllic, but certainly happy. And we could ramble any-where, and we did, in a gang of us. Through the woods to the Bollin in the summer. And we made bonfires and baked potatoes, and so on. Played cricket! We had a long garden. So there was room there.

D.   And what did you do after you left school?

J.   Started as an office girl at Clibrans, you'll have heard of that. Stayed there for three years, learning shorthand and typing at night school. And then went into a sec-retarial job, in Altrincham.

D.   So how did you two meet?

J.   At the cinema, wasn't it?

R.   One or two of us were together, and a couple of them were going out with the girls Jean came round with. And I was footloose and fancy free, we'll say, about six-teen. And this girl came round the corner with them, and I says can we make a four-some or something, and that was it!

D.   So where had you started life, Ron?

R.   I was born in Bold Street, Altrincham. I started work at Ainsworths, which was a cobbler's. And then moved on to Hale Cinema, to learn projection. This was the Elite of the cinemas in Altrincham. Saturday night at this cinema, Hale Cinema, the circle was practically booked solid, of people who were turning up in dinner jackets and dicky bows. They were regular bookings each Saturday night. George Formby and his wife used to come; and the biggest and the richest one was a millionaire called Berry. Now his daughter or niece was married to Trevor Howard. And they owned Cherry Blossom boot polish. And they lived at Parklands, on Dunham Road, on the corner of Charcoal Lane.

D.   I know their grave, in Hale Cemetry, still immaculately kept, with wonderful flowers, gladioli, cut gladioli, always the same pinky orange colour.

R.   He used to come in, and if he saw you about, or a member of staff, a couple of bob was put in your hand. And at the afternoon shows, if you asked for it, you were served with afternoon tea on trays, while you were watching it. And at the back of Hale Cinema there was a spring. And as you know, opposite is Spring Road. In heavy thunderstorms or torrential rain they had to set a pump going, because the water was rising into the orchestral pit. Presumably they've got it under control now. And from there, after the war, we were married at the Unitarian Church, in Hale Barns. The very old one.

J.   Yes, my family were from Ringway, well my mother's family. And they were Unitarians of course. I was baptised there. So that's where we were married.

D.   And ever since you'd been sixteen you were going out together? All that time. So how was it for you, Jean, during the war? What did you do?

J.   We went to lectures on First Aid. And gas mask things. My dad was one of the Wardens, and had to list everyone, which I wrote out for him on the forms. From Coppice to Castle Mill was his beat. The chief warden was the chap who had The Greyhound, of course! So they could meet up there!

D.   And where were you working by now?

J.   The war started while I was still at school, so I was at Clibrans for the first part, and then it was an engineering firm, who'd been bombed out from the Manchester office and moved into Altrincham. And I stayed with them for the rest of the time. Until Colin was on the way.

D.   Did you manage to keep fairly well in touch with Ron?

J.   Yes. Letters weren't too bad, were they? Everyone was in the same boat, of course.

D.   So tell us about your bit of the war, Ron. Where were you when war broke out?

R.   I was in Bradbury Central School. They tried to get me into Army Cadets, but it was useless, because we were working evenings. In this area at the time were the Royal Artillery Portsmouth Division, in Hale. Of course they used to flock to the cinema and the cafe.

D.   So what happened? Did you go through the rest of your schooldays normally?

R.   No, it was absolutely cut down because of the evacuees. You did mornings one week, and afternoons the next week, and alternative with the evacuees from the Stretford area. After that was the fateful day when the letter dropped on the mat saying *Report to HMS Collingwood, Fareham*.

D.   And did the Navy choose you or had you chosen them? Or was it just pot luck?

R.   I think it was pot luck. Because I originally registered for the RAF! And along plopped "Report to the Navy"! We put it down at that time to, they were after crews for landing craft, with D Day coming along. And I'd never heard of Fareham at that time. And from there we got sorted out a bit. I was then sent on a gunnery course, billeted at Fareham, to Whale Island. Which, according to all sailors, the treatment you received, and what you did, they reckoned the convicts were better off, on Dartmoor! It toughened us up. And from there I went up to Campbeltown, in Scotland, to learn anti-submarine warfare. Although I passed the gunnery course I was turned down because of the spectacles. And yet I was still classed as A1. And then from all that, back to Portsmouth, and then joined HMS Ursa, a destroyer. I came back, and came out in '47. [*See appendix*]

D.   Where were you between the end of the war and '47?

R.   Well the war ended when we were in the Far East. We were the first ship to take the surrender off the Japanese, in Hong Kong. And, with being the newest ship, we ended up taking the Commander-in-Chief, Admiral Fraser, all round his final command. Visiting General MacArthur and all these. It was a marvellous trip. Back to Portsmouth, and we did the Armistice Sunday, our dispersal group, the Armistice Sunday 1946, in Trafalgar Square, London. The day before, the Lord Mayor's Show. The Saturday night before the Sunday, the Festival of Remembrance at the Albert Hall. And then the Cenotaph of the Sunday morning. And then I had this job to wait demob, which came four months later, marching boy seamen between classes.

D.   How did you find it, coming home? Did you have a job to come back to?

R.   You were guaranteed that. Firms, if they would not take you back, were fined rather heavily. So I went back to the Cinema, but I had the feeling, It's a lazy man's job. After being so active. For instance, I swam over the Equator. We presume it was the Equator.

D.   You saw the line!

R.   We tripped over it! Of course the war was over. And it was that flat calm in the Indian Ocean. They put a boat out with a couple of men with machine guns, because of sharks, and we jumped over the stern and swam for'ard and up on deck, and they said you'd swam over the Equator. And the final thing, when people think of the Bay of Biscay being rough: it was a Sunday afternoon, and it was flat calm, there was no danger, so we had ten minutes' swim in the Bay of Biscay. When we went out it had been horrendous. Really rough.

D.   So you came back. And how was Jean, how did you find Jean?

R.   It's a funny feeling. You don't know how they're going to react.

D.   And how did he seem to you, Jean? Was it a big shock?

J.   He'd altered, of course. And he sounded like a cockney. Because most of the rest of the crew were cockneys, and he'd picked up their . . . And it took him quite a while to lose it, and get back to normal. And that's when we got engaged.

D.   He must have changed over all that time. And you must have as well, for that matter. It must have been quite difficult, getting used to each other again.

J.   Yes.

R.   She was the one earning the money!

D.   So then you decided to get married. When was that?

J.   1950, we married. Living at Lane End.

D.   Did you know that The Green was going to be built?

J.   Oh, it was being built. And we didn't get one at first. Someone else lived here for a couple of years. So it wasn't until Colin was on the way that we got a chance. So here we are. There's an old saying, Friday flit, uneasy sit. We moved in on a Friday, and here we are!

D.   Where were you working now, Ron?

R.   I moved around, didn't I? Where the better money was.

J.   You were at Lynotype when we moved in here. And for several years afterwards.

R.   And at the RAF camp at Sinderland Road. And then at the Minster Insurance, ended up there.

D.   And Colin was born first?

J.   Then Kathryn. She was born here. In this house. They encouraged home births at that time.

R.   Half past one in the morning I went to phone, and it was tippling down and thundering.

J.   In June!

R.   And the nurse turned up on a motorbike.

D.   And I suppose The Green was teeming with children?

J.   Well that's it. Everyone had small children at that time. There must have been forty, fifty children.

R.   As the boys got older and started playing cricket, Fred Blain and myself took the lads down there, out of the way of the little ones, and we progressed them to the hard ball down there. And I think the only window we ever broke was one of Blain's! But they used to spend hours doing that, didn't they?

D.   And eventually you were working for The Smithy, weren't you, Jean?

J.   Well I first of all went back part-time, at Clibrans. And I went back there when the children were at school. Because my parents, you see, could have them after school.

D.   Of course! They'd do the same walk home as you did.

J.   Yes. And then when Mr Clibran died I went bureau working. And you can choose your hours then, so that fitted in nicely. And then I got the job at the garage. About thirty years ago.

R.   She's been retired ten years.

D.   You had double glazing put in, didn't you, about a year ago: how's it been?

J.   Oh it's made a lot of difference.

R.   After it was put in, it was a sort of coolish morning, and I came down and opened that door, and I thought we'd left the fire on all night. And it wasn't! It had retained that heat.

J.   Yes, it really does. And the noise, of course.

D.   Yes, because the motorway at the back must be, what, only about two hundred yards away.

R.   When he slipped that in, that window in position there, the noise just went, and it wasn't even sealed around the outside at that time. Myself and Ron next door, we feel as though we were responsible for getting them to agree to double-glazing. They were coming round doing a pre-painting check. And he was saying it's noisy like, and we said, Well we tried to get at the Council to consider double-glazing. Oh, he says, we'll get someone to come out and monitor the noise.

J.   Well he came round the back, didn't he, and said, Oh yes. The noise. Definitely.

R.   It didn't need monitoring. It was there. I suppose now we're getting on a bit, it would be nice to have a bit of central heating. Going in to such like your house, and Colin's, there's that warmth all round. But we're all right, we survive.

D.   And now, your latest venture is editing the *Ashley News*. How are you finding that?

R.   I like doing it, and co-operation between myself and the type-setter is excellent.

Ted and Philip Tickle. 22 Hough Green

D.   Where were you born, Ted?

T.   Congleton. Hulme Lane.

D.   And when did you get to Ashley?

T.   Oh, years and years after that. I was about, what would I be? Forty five, or some-thing like that. I worked for Joe Davies, Back Lane Farm. Bill's brother. I left and went working at Challenor's, Toft Hall. Oh wait a minute, I'm telling a lie. I went for Henry Gardner, got that cottage and worked for Henry Gardner. Sugar Brook. And then I left there, and went to Toft Hall. And then from Toft Hall I went back to . . . Joe got me a little house in Knutsford. And I got working for Fred Erlam, and he got me the house carried on, because it belonged to Tatton, you see. And the farm belongs to Tatton. So he got the house through Tatton, and we still lived there. Then Fred got me this house.

D.   That was when these houses were built?

T.   Well he got me that one. [*Number 23*] Next to Bernard. That's the house we got. All the children were born there. Bar the two girls.

D.   And then you moved here for more space? Did you do a swap?

T.   No, no, no. These people left. And we put in for it, and we got it.

D.   How did you find it, moving into The Green, with all this new, with everything new?

T.   It wasn't finished when we moved in. Not quite. Bernard's house wasn't fin-ished. The houses were finished, but they hadn't straightened the garden.

D.   So you've lived here all your life, Philip? Who did you go to school with who are here now?

P.   Only in the farms, same as Danielses. I think it was Eddie, about my age. Jenny McKenna (Watson). We went to school together. Norburys, they lived just down the road. I think that's about it.

D.   Are there any other things you remember about life as a child in Ashley?

P.   Only when we used to play football on the back field, where those houses are. Used to enjoy a game of football up there. Or climb the trees.

D.   Where are they all now, all the rest of your children, Ted?

T.   Oh, all over t' place. Flixton. Stretford. Shropshire. And I don't know where Linda lives.

P.   Glossop.

T. Glossop? Aye, Glossop, yeah. Wendy's at Broadheath. Not far away.

P. None of us work. My two brothers are both disabled. You know, they can't work because of their disability, like. Same as myself.

(Miaow! Miaow! Miaow!)

P. I'm just going to let the cat out. I'm just glad I've had my knee done, my knee sorted out. It locked up on me. I was going to the doctor's. And I got up to get ready to go, and it wouldn't let me get up. I couldn't move it. In agony. So I struggled to go to the doctor's, and he wrote a letter out to take me to the hospital. He said, Try to get someone to take you. So I got my brother that lives at Sale and he took me down there, and they plastered it up for me. Just bandaged it up. I was due to see the specialist on the Tuesday. The cartilage had torn and it had folded over on itself. And they just cut it off. I'd been under him for my hip for five years. I'm too young to have an operation on my hip.

D. Oh, are you? I didn't realise there was an age limit.

P. Yeah, well they only last so many years, don't they? The replacement hip. So I've got to wait till I'm old and can't enjoy myself. Before I can have an operation you see.

D. The Green must have changed enormously in the time you've been here.

P. Oh yeah. I remember when we used to have bonfires on The Green. On the actual Green itself. Don't do that nowadays.

D. For the kids? Well at least they still have it, but round the back now.

P. Well it's better round the back, I suppose. It's out of the way.

(The terrier interrupts here, wanting us to play with him.)

T. He's spoilt, that's the trouble with him. How many balls do you want? You've got one there!

P. I remember when I was first learning to drive, and my mum taught me to drive first go off, then my elder brother, and I bought myself a little van. And he pinched it off me. My brother. And he was using it, and I couldn't do anything because I wasn't driving at the time, I was only learning. He was using it while I was learning, sort of thing. I try to keep off the motorways. I don't like motorways.

D. This one here must have been a devil of a nuisance, mustn't it?

P. It was before we had double glazing put in. You can't hear it at all when the windows are shut.

D. I can't hear it now, sitting here. That was a rum business, when your car was stolen.

P. Oh, what? That's what made mother poorly first go off, I think. She was upset about that. That's what started her off, I think.

D.   It was upsetting. You must have heard of the two - was it? - two of the younger ones were coming back home, they'd been out for the evening, only about midnight: and they actually saw your car being driven round The Green and out. And one of them said to the other, That doesn't look like Philip's driving. Because it must have been careering about a bit. And that was it. They were actually watching the thing being stolen. And didn't realise.

P.   It doesn't click when it happens, does it? I didn't know someone had seen them. They'd broke into Jean's as well. And of course they'd been in this garage and dismantled the ignition on his bike.

T.   And they pinched the pushbike, and left it round at Mrs Dolan's. Decided then to take the car.

P.   And the police were taking the bike away, and I just happened to see the bike in their van.

D.   They were probably taking it thinking it was the thief's. You still use your bike then, Ted?

T.   Oh, yes. Haven't used it for a bit because it's been so cold. I will do, again.

(A white cat has jumped onto David's knee)

P.   That one'll let you stroke her, then she'll take a chunk out of your hand.

D.   Thanks for the warning! I'll go!

T.   She's not too bad. She's not bad at all now.

P.   I think it's affection with her, though.

D.   It's a love-bite!

T.   If you started playing with her she'd have you. She was very bad-tempered when we first got her.

P.   Oh she's settled in very well. But the cats don't get on, these two. The black'un's gone out now.

T.   This dog hates the sight of her. Doesn't like her at all. He likes black'un. He'll eat wi' black'un. But he won't have that one. If she jumped down now he'd jump after her.

D.   I heard someone the other day saying they thought it would be a good idea to have some trees on The Green. Nobody official, it was just somebody I was talking to.

P.   I think it would spoil it, myself. I mean if they had some maybe down the sewage on the edge of the field down there. Between the path and the field, at the back there.

T.   We had a little dog drowned in t' sewerage. Very much like this one.

D.   Where did it get in?

T.   Under t'gate. It must have been chasing a rat or something. Rat's gone in and it's dived in after it.

P.   And it couldn't get out.

T.   We couldn't find it. I searched all over t'place. It never yelled. If it had been this one he'd have soon have told you where he was. But it never yelled, it was a very quiet dog. That was a stray. You'd let it go out, and it'd be out for about an hour, and then it come back again.

D.   You're the one who summons them back with a police whistle, aren't you?

T.   Yeah, this one comes back with a whistle.

P.   And the last one we had.

D.   I remember Whisky used to. He used to be miles away sometimes. I don't know how far he went, but I'd see you whistle, and several minutes later Whisky would amble up from somewhere.

P.   I think he used to annoy people when he did it on a Sunday morning! Or last thing at night.

T.   This one come back to a whistle. Mind, he's learned it off Whisky you see. He's been hit with a car once. Very lucky. Got his leg broke. All his back leg was red raw. Had a night in th'hospital. I think what happened, he was across the road, and I blew my whistle. And he was coming home, and never looked, you see. Straight bang into a car.

D.   Don't I remember you having something to do with that barn?

T.   Yes. I gardened there. I had hens there. Reg Baker had the pub, he had the pub then: and the cockerel got out and went in t'pub and flew onto t'bar. Reg said I don't mind treating Ted to a pint, he said, but I'm blowed if I'm treating his cockerels!

D.   He ought to have had a Courage house. That's their sign, isn't it?

Miaow! Miaow!

D.   There we are, wants to come in now. You can hear it, can't you?

P.   That's only a mild one. Wait till he gets going!

T.   She lets you know when she wants to come in.

Enter black cat, backwards through the window Philip has opened.

228

T.   She backs up. Then we lift her off, when she gets through window.

D.   Yes, here she comes! In reverse.

Miaow!

P.   That's a girl.

D.   *Thank you*, she says. What an extraordinary operation! You clever cat!

*The dog loses interest in the balls he has been playing with,
and starts digging among some material in the corner of the room.*

T.   He's got another one there.

D.   It's not one of those two balls, it's something else he's after. He's not half having to work for it!

P.   Find it! . . .What are you after? . . . Have you found it? . . . Get it! He's got it, he's got it.

T.   Another ball! That's the one he wants!

P.   That's a harder one, he can chew at that, you see. When he gets a bone he's got to sit on Father's lap here and eat it. Hasn't he? [*Shouts:*]. When he gets a bone he's got to sit on your lap to eat it.

T.   Or a bone. Eats everything on my knee.

D.   So you have to put up with being used as a dinner plate!

T.   Aye. We miss the missus with no cleaner-up, now.

D.   Who does the cooking?

P.   Me. Mind you, he did himself yesterday dinner.

T.   You'd think they'd build a club in Ashley, wouldn't you? Everywhere else has got a club. A club for somewhere to go at night. Play bowls. Snooker.

D.   There's a lot of talk now about a village hall.

T.   Yeah that's it, village hall. Yes.

D.   With the Millennium and so forth, there is some talk about there eventually being a village hall, attached to the school, I think, so that both would use it. So perhaps it'll come.

T.   It probably won't be in my day.

Joanne Williams and Jonathan Everson. 23 Hough Green

D.   Joanne, your parents were - are! - John and Sherril Williams of Little Thorns Green Farm, and so I suppose you were born in Ashley were you?

Jo.   Yes, I was born in Wendy Hughes' house.

D.   Oh yes! Lane End.

Jo.   I was born there. And then we moved away when I was very small, and came back when I was five. And then we were at Little Thorns Green Farm for my child-hood. It was fantastic! It was just freedom. We just used to be outside all the time. We used to have ponies. I was never much of a rider. Everybody despaired of me!

D.   That's very interesting. You've got two very horsy sisters. And you managed to escape that?

Jo.   Mmm. Bikes were a lot easier! I used to get on the back of a horse, but only if someone brought it to me. Then I used to ride, and then my sister used to put it away for me. Dreadful! I used to get out like the Queen! I go out with Heather very occa-sionally. But she still tacks up, gets it ready, does all the work! It's nice to spend time together, but an expensive hobby. My sisters used to go to horse shows, that sort of thing. We used to go to Wilmslow and Mum used to spend a lot of money on show things, and she took me into a bookshop one day and said, Buy three books - now! And I used to buy books, and sit in the back of the horsebox reading, while they were showing.

D.   Where do you come in the batting order? Heather came first?

Jo.   And then I came two years and two months later. Six years later Emma came. And then Peter. So there's a gap of six years, and then a two-year gap again. Quite nice really, because it was nice having a big family. I don't think I'd like to be an only child.

D.   Jonathan, how did you two meet?

J.   We met at a cricket match. I play for Mere Cricket Club, and that's where we met.

Jo.   We didn't actually meet at Mere. Because I didn't see you at all. I met you later.

J.   Oh you went down there, that's right, and I saw you, and - made enquiries, shall we say? And then I think about two weeks later we were invited to a party, and Joanne was there. And about two weeks later I had a few friends from cricket over, and Joanne was invited. And we took it from there, really.

D.   Where were you living?

J.   I was in Styal. I was actually born in Flixton. And then, for my sins, went to Staffordshire, and then came to Grappenhall, near Warrington. And then to Lymm, then Mobberley, and then to Styal. So I've been not far from the Ashley area, except for my short stay in Staffordshire. I used to go to school at a place called Ellesmere, in Shropshire.

D.   So here you are now in Hough Green. Can you tell me anything about how you come to be here?

Jo.   Well I was living in Rostherne, with Sam and Jordan. We'd been on our own for about two years. And I really really loved the house, but it was a big house. And everybody kept saying to me that it was too big. And when I spoke to May Fisher and said, I'm thinking about moving, she said, You don't want to be living in that big house. You've got to come and live here! I loved Cherry Tree Farm, but the roof was dangerous. If the wind blew the slates would come down. And then Caroline said one of the houses on The Green had become available. And I said, Oh I would like to live there. It was so quick, because I hadn't actually much time to think about it. And on the Monday I spoke to Jackie, and she said, Oh you must apply today. And after I spoke to Heather I phoned up and spoke to the woman, and she said, Oh we haven't made a decision yet. I said I wanted to apply. And she said, You haven't applied? Well go to Knutsford now. And I went to Knutsford and applied, and she came round on the Thursday and handed me the keys. It was all so quick. And it frightened me at first, because it is a lot smaller. It is cute, but it's going to be very crowded.

D.   It's very difficult, compressing everything.

Jo.   It's hard going from nine bedrooms. We just had a massive clearout. We've gone from three houses to one house, and gradually we're settling in.

D.   How many have you got here, now?

Jo.   Sam and Jordan. But in May we're going to have another baby. But it's lovely here and you can't take a step back. But it is fantastic for kids. It's like a great big ball park. Sam and Jordan love it. And it was quite funny when I was moving in, because this house was in such a state, I'd done a lot of the work beforehand, I was down here for four weeks, and for those four weeks I hardly saw them. We'd get here and they would just disappear. And then the girls would come acrosss and sit and talk to me. It was quite handy really, because I always had an extra scraper! Just in case! and it was really funny, because Jackie used to come and say, I'm not going to pick a scraper up today! But they always invariably got a scraper and started picking at pieces of wallpaper.

D.   Trouble with Jackie is, she can't reach very far!

Jo.   You've got to put that down in your book! Jackie and Vanessa! The pair of them! And Jackie can't go up steps. She can't cope with any heights. But that really sealed it for me. Because I was very very worried about the whole thing. The changes, and the fact that we were going to such a different environment and we had to start from scratch all over again. It was a bit daunting. We just haven't managed to get as far as the outside yet, there's a lot to do in the garden.

D.   I noticed things are beginning to appear, window boxes and pots and things. So Jonathan, how long have you been here now?

J.   I actually moved in here just after Christmas.

D.   So how have you found it, Jonathan? To some extent Jo knew where she was. What was it like?

J.   It's super. Again, I've come from a fairly large house to something slightly smaller, shall we say.

Jo.   He's integrated himself into the community!

D.   Do you want to say more about that?

Jo.   He has a permanent little place at the bar! Between Ken Pimlott and Simon Lloyd!

J.   Shall we say, They're very friendly in the local pub! I've met most of the people there. And it's great. They're all nice and friendly, you seem to be accepted. Jo's got a lot of friends. Where I was before, in Styal, it was a little bit more in the open, the nearest neighbour was a mile away from us.

D.   That's what I was wondering. And I dare say you were the same?

Jo.   Both of us found it quite hard at first, having people all round. But they're very friendly.

J.   Yes. It's not that they're nosey or anything, it's that I'm just not used to it. I've always lived in the country and away from being overlooked by neighbours.

D.   Well now that is quite an ordeal, it really is; especially the way this Green is organised, so that you feel you've got twenty pairs of eyes trained on you from all the way round. Like a goldfish bowl.

Jo.   Having said that, those twenty pairs of eyes make it a lot safer for Sam and Jordan. At Cherry Tree Farm they had almost the same freedom as I had as a child. Not so much going down to the fields, but they could wander about any part of the farm. And I was worried when I first came here, because the actual area of the house is so much smaller. But because they can go to other children's houses and other children can come here, it completely evaporated all my worries, when I came here. And quite often you don't know you've got someone else's child with them upstairs. They'll come and say, Have you got Adam here? No, I don't think so, but I'll just check! And he's been up there for half-an-hour.

D.   Matthew, with you now: does he come here quite a bit?

J.   Yes. he probably comes once a weekend.

Jo.   He plays with Adam a lot, doesn't he?

J.   Yes, he's been playing with Adam.

Jo.   He's really good with him.

J.   He's fitted in very well with Sam and Jordan. He loves Jordan, Jordan and he get on really well together. It's just unfortunate sometimes we get the timing wrong there: he arrives when they go to their dad. Matthew's just slightly younger than Jordan.

Jo.   He's been a bit on a limb today, hasn't he, because he's been on his own. And sometimes you think, Oh it's quite nice to have Matthew on his own, because Jonathan spends an awful lot of time with my two, and he doesn't have his children here. So he's like a second father to them. And they think the world of him, and he's brilliant with them. But then I think sometimes it's quite nice just to have a bit of pay-back, and have Matthew on his own. Instead of just saying, Oh we'll have Matthew when Sam and Jordan are here. I think sometimes it's nice to spend just a bit of time with just Matthew. But I think he finds it quite lonely.

J.   The other nice thing is that James, my other son, the eldest son, who now lives with the Crawfords at Ashley Hall there, gets on his bike and comes down and visits.

Jo.   Oh, he comes down, and Sam will say, Oh can I just go down the road with James on a bike? They go and get a bottle of milk for me, it's a real exciting thing! But James is that much older, whereas Sam's not got a great deal of road sense. Because we come from real country, it's taken me a while to get him used to, you don't just go anywhere you please, it is a road. He's getting used to it, and it's very good for Sam. It's just spreading his wings a bit.

D.   James must be very good with them, by the sound of it.

Jo.   Sam's funny. I suppose it's a hero thing, Sam absolutely adores James. So he flies round him, like a fly buzzing round him. So James teases him. He's lovely with them. There's not many boys of his age would put up with small children the way he does. He's excellent.

D.   Do you get time for anything else, Jonathan?

J.   No, I'm working all day, and at weekends we tend to have Matthew or James, or both of them. In the summer obviously I will enjoy my cricket. That tends to take most of the weekends.

D.   You're going to stay with Mere, are you? It's rather a long association isn't it: how many years?

J.   Seventeen seasons now, yes. Two seasons ago we were actually in the same league as Ashley, so we did do a couple of visits down here. We came up into Ashley's league, and then we've gone up another league. Ashley stayed where they were.

Jo.   You've got some fantastic players. It's really funny, because the rest of the team are so young. They wheel Jonathan out! Every year he says, this is my last year, this has got to be my last season! He says they'll be taking him out in his zimmer frame!

D.   Can you see any of the younger generation playing cricket? This lot around here? Or James?

J.   Well James is very much interested in cricket. He's actually played for Mere sometimes, with me. But he plays now for his school, he goes to Manchester

Grammer School, he plays for the school on Saturdays. So it's only when they break up in the holidays. He played last year for Joanne's father's side in the Bank Holiday cricket game.

D. Well is there anything else that anyone would like to say? Any more views about Ashley in general?

J. It's a very pleasant place to be. I can't really see it changing that much. It's a nice little close-knit community, everybody gets on, and knows each other. It's far enough away from Hale, Altrincham, places like that, to be as it is. As far as I can see it'll carry on like that.

D. Well lets's hope you're right. A lot of people have their worries.

Jo. I worry about it, because I think Ashley needs to develop to survive. I think if it was left the way it is now, you would endanger it. To continue to get use out of the facilities, Ashley has to have more people living here.

D. Yes, the post office and the school are the prime examples of that.

Jo. Because there used to be a garage. They used to sell petrol. It's just another thing that's been taken away. And if we're not careful we're just going to become a short cut on the road to Manchester. Rather than being a community. I think there is room for other people to live here.

J. I think once they started building we'd eventually become an extension of Hale.

Jo. It is a fine line, isn't it? If you built big houses they would end up as just the latest from Hale, who wanted a bit more space. And that would lose Ashley's charm. And if you had smaller houses . . .

D. Well most people seem to like that idea, because the chances are you'd get younger families, and also families who are more likely to send their children to this school, rather than some private place.

Jo. Peter Wright was saying something about building retirement bungalows. And I said, Well what good will that do? You're trying to infuse young life, rather than bring in old people. He said the idea is to provide for the old people off The Green. I said, That doesn't actually work, because to get younger people on The Green you'd have to get the older people to move out of their houses here, which they won't want to do. So why not build houses for the younger ones, rather than expecting the older people to move out of their homes? I think there's a lot to be considered. It needs to move on.

Jean Dolan. 24 Hough Green

D.   How did you come to Ashley, Jean?

J.   Well I came down here on 25th January - about now - in 1945, from Arbroath. That's where I was brought up, in the Braes of Angus. It was Angus and Mearns when I was a little girl, but it's the Braes of Angus now, in the borders of the Highlands. I came down here with my sister when she asked me, Would I like to come to England with her? Now there was an adventure which I couldn't miss! I'd been ill, and I was at home recouperating. And the war was just beginning to come towards the end. I came down here, and we went to live, came down here with a man called Lieutenant Horsley. He was in the Navy, and he had two children, a boy and a girl, and a small baby called Anthony. And my sister had been in sole charge of the baby. So I was coming down because my sister's husband was coming home from India. She came with me for about six weeks, but I'd been here about three of four weeks in South Downs Road, the Lieutenant's home, and about the fourth week I was here I took the little baby for a walk round the Bollin. And there was this group of lads all larking about, you see. And one of them said, *Oh, I wouldn't talk to her, she's Welsh!* Because he'd been doing a bit of work in the house, and he'd come to the door and he'd asked me for a brew. And, David, I hadn't got a clue what a brew was! And I think he thought I was a bit mad!

D.   And Welsh!

J.   Anyway I ended up with these two, I ended up with two boys walking up the road. And one of them said to me, Would you like to come out tonight with me? And I said, Well I'll have to ask my boss. And he said yes. There met me at the gate this most handsome young sailor! Quite different to the young man I'd met in the afternoon. In uniform! Oh well, of course that - I fell hook line and sinker, David! Never looked back!

D.   Slain by the uniform!

J.   Slain by the uniform! And he went off, I presume to be demobbed. And we met up again. I said I was going home in three months' time, because I was going back nursing. However at the end of the three months he'd come home, and that was it. I was still with Mr Horsley, still stayed there, stayed there till I got married, in 1947. I've never regretted a day of it, David. And we were married, 1947, and we stayed in Bold Street, which is the yuppie street now! which I hated when I lived there. Nine months I lived there. Bernard was born there.

D.   How many of you were there in that house in Bold Street?

J.   There was only Bernard and I, and his mother. Bernard was working back at Ashley Station - as you know, he started at Ashley Station when he was sixteen; went away to the war, came back and his job was waiting for him. And he used to do the garden acrosss at White Gables. But they were emigrating to Canada, and they said to Bernard, they said, Do you think your wife would like to come and stay at White Gables and look after the animals, while we go to London? He said, Oh I'm sure she would, because she loves the country, she comes from the country. And we were waiting to see if we could get a station cottage. So up I came for the weekend, very heavily pregnant with Kathleen, and stayed the weekend. Enjoyed it, and going back to Bold Street with a groan. And when the people came across, they said Would you like us to ask the new people if they want a housekeeper? So Bernard said, Well my wife's having a baby. So they never said any more about it. I had Kathleen, 28th August Kathleen was born; and they went to the station and they went to Bernard, and they said to Bernard, I believe your wife would take a job as housekeeper? He said, My wife is in hospital, she's just had a little girl. They said, Oh that's all right. She's a Scottish lass, and that's all we want to know. They'd never even met me, David. And I was brought from the hospital to White Gables, and I was there for three and a half years. Until I came across to this house.

D.   Well! Perfect!

J.   With the Currys. And they were artists, and they had two little girls - no they didn't, they had one little girl then. So I looked after the little girl, and did the cooking, and looked after my own little girl. Kathleen and Lesley were sort of brought up together.

D.   Were they a similar age?

J.   No. Lesley was three when I went there, and Kathleen was the baby, it was just right, and it was lovely. When we came in, Bernard was at Ashley Station. And then, three and a half years later, we got this house. We were hoping to get a station cottage, but Bert Mottershead got in before us! He got in first. Anyway, we got this house: we got the house on the 29th April, and Johnnie was born on the 3rd May. That was 1951. And of course that's how I come to be in Ashley, and I've stayed ever since.
   The Currys were fascinating people. She was a portrait artist, and he was a landscape artist. But of course they couldn't make their living at that, so they did commercial art. And they did Kendals catalogue - they were all hand done in those days. I mean I was Kendals' model, you know! Oh, I was the model, you've got no idea, I've got pictures. My bedroom there, I can see it now, this gorgeous lemon dress, black velvet gloves. I stuffed my bust with hankies, because they weren't big enough then! I mean, these are the little things that you remember, you don't forget. I mean, standing in the garden at White Gables modelling a fur coat in the boiling hot summer!

D.   Did you keep in touch with the girls when you moved here?

J.   Oh yes. Oh yes. Until they left. Lesley used to come and see me - of course I haven't seen them for years now - but Lesley used to pop in and see me. Because when we first came across here - and I'd looked after Lesley for three and a half years. And apparently she'd said to her mother one night that she wanted Jean to put her to bed, not her mother, and the mum said, Well if you want Jean you'd better go - and I was bathing Johnnie, and there was a little knock on the door, and there was Lesley in her nightie, with a toothbrush! Well I had to take her home.

D.   So, Jean, may we go through your children? We've got Kathleen first.

J.   Kathleen was born in 1948. She's a sister in the Coronary Care at the North Manchester, that's the old Crumpsall Hospital. She works in the Coronary Care. That's Kathleen. Then there's John. John lives in Timperley, he was born in 1951. And he married Carol, who came from Timperley, and they've got Lindsay, who's twenty one next month, and Stephen. And then Michael, who lives down in Weaverham, he was born in '54. Michael works for British Telecom. He's worked with them since he left school. He's in Northampton at the moment, he goes all over the place. Their home's in Weaverham. So that's them all.

D.   And you must have had your Golden Wedding?

J.   We had our Golden Wedding in '97.

D.   '97. So you also were married in the same year as the Queen?

J.   Yes we were, we were married on the 4th July. We have a letter from the Queen.

D.   Oh, there it is!

J.   Yes, I framed it.

D.   May I read it?

J.   Of course you can. Somewhere I have the invitation to Manchester Cathedral. Of course we missed that because we were both ill. That was very sad, I really missed that.

D.   The letter says:

> "This is a special year for you and for us, and we are sorry
> that you cannot be at Buckingham Palace on the 15th July
> to celebrate our Golden Wedding.
> We hope that you have a very happy anniversary, and send
> our best wishes and congratulations to you both."

And that's signed by the Queen and Prince Philip, dated the 3rd June.

J.   It's a wonderful keepsake, David.

D.   "I'm sorry you couldn't be at the Garden Party . . ." I suppose they just put a pin in the list.

J.   Well they had to choose, didn't they? We weren't disappointed - well, I suppose we were, but . . . As I say, we got this lovely gold-edged invitation from the Lord Lieutenant to go to Manchester Cathedral, a time we were really looking forward to. But we never got there. We'd got plans to do that, but . . . However, we had our Golden Wedding, David. We were married fifty one years.

D.   Where were you married?

J.   Arbroath. We were married in Arbroath because Bernard was a Catholic, and I was a Protestant. And all was organised for me to be married in the village church. Then all of a sudden the Minister decided that he couldn't marry a Catholic in his Kirk. There was no getting away from it, and I won't tell you what my father called him! Anyway I was up there, and I rang Bernard up and talked to him about it. So he had to go to get a dispensation from St Vincent's. And I had to go and see the Catholic priest in Arbroath, at St Thomases. And he was a most wonderful Father, I saw, and he understood, and he made all the arrangements. He didn't ask me to change to a Catholic, but he asked me, Would I bring any of the children up Catholic? and I agreed to that. And all my children were christened in St Vincent's. And then I never saw a priest, a priest never came near me, until about six months before Kathleen was due to go to school. And I said, There's no way my daughter's travelling on the train to Altrincham when there's a school up the road. I know I was breaking all the laws of . . . Anyway, she went to Ashley School, and when it came time for them to be confirmed they were all confirmed into the Church of England. It was Mr Henshall that sorted all that out. Because you see I had to be confirmed, because I could only take Communion in the Kirk. I couldn't take it in the Church. It's all changed nowadays, but that worked out quite well. I was confirmed at Little Budworth. I could go and take Communion in the Catholic Church, but I couldn't take it in the English Church.

D.   Make sense of that, eh?!

J.   On our Golden Wedding year we went back to St Thomases. We thought we'll go and visit St Thomases, and we rang the bell, because it's open, the church, and I rang the bell and the housekeeper, I said to her, We'd like to come into church if we could because we were married here fifty years ago. So we were in the church when the - what do you call them? Monsieur?

D.   Monsignor.

J.   Monsignor appeared, and he went and he got the books out, and showed us where it was written into the Register. Which was really wonderful. And when Bernard took ill my sister went and told him. And I had the most wonderful letter from him, saying that prayers would be said for both of us, and his name is in the book. And I was going to write, you see, for the 21st February, and ask them, Would they light a candle for him? Last year or the year before they had their 150th anniversary, at the Catholic Church. I think it's the only Catholic Church in Arbroath. It's right at the top end of a street, but it's got a lovely view. And it's a beautiful - well, they always are, aren't they? But it seems to be stuck at the end of a street. They must have built round it. But he's awfully sweet, the Monsignor, he sent me a postcard of the Altar of the church. It was lovely to be able to go back.

D.   And to be welcomed like that!

J.   Oh, he was so thrilled, and he was so sweet.

D.   Jean, how many different landlords did you work for at The Greyhound?

J.   There was Reg, George Dean, Les, Andy, August, Tony and Shaun. That's eight landlords.

D.   And now you've got Tony living next door!

J.   My next door neighbour. And Tony always treats me with great respect. I mean, he treats me with great respect. His father-in-law says, Tony thought the world of you. Well I didn't have any quarrels with any of the landlords I'd worked for. I put long hours in there, believe me. I really did. I used to look after the place, I used to move in.

D.   I often wondered why they didn't make you the landlord! You must have known all there was to know about it.

J.   I could run that pub better. And there was one of the Brewery reps who was called Johnny Walker, way back in the early days of George Dean, he wanted me to go in for relief work. I said, Oh no, I couldn't do that. Bernard's job: when he was on nights at Trafford Park I was alone in that pub. And there was no alarms. Les used to have a shotgun at the end of the bed, it used to frighten me to death, that! The bed-rooms were very old-fashioned, with the big thick old-fashioned doors. And they had hooks on the outside. And you automatically go out of your bedroom, and you hooked the door. And Bernard had gone off to work one morning at six o'clock, and I was hooked in the bedroom! I couldn't get out, and there was no telephone in there. And one of the cleaners came, and she says Where are you? And I said, I'm locked in the bedroom! Bernard just automatically hooked the door as he went out of the bedroom. And they were big thick doors.

D.   So it was Bernard who did it!

J.   It was Bernard who locked me in. There again, you see, it saved. Because when thieves took the window out the bathroom - the bathroom was like a bedroom in those days, - and they were trying to break into the pub - during pub hours - and they took the complete window out. But they couldn't get out because the hook was on the door. That was the reason why you get the hooks. And I remember Les had gone up. I was clearing up behind the bar, and Les had gone up to change, to go in the cel-lar. And he went in the bathroom, and he thought, It's draughty in here. And he come down and said, Come and see this! He said, What a damned good job, because we'd have never have heard him. Upstairs. So really, you could go on with The Greyhound. All sorts of funny stories. But I might end up in gaol if I started telling them! One per-son, I always remember one funny story, David, when I first started. This gentleman used to come in every night with this lady. And about a fortnight later he came in on the Saturday night, and what do you think I said? You haven't got your wife with you tonight! And of course the person that was with him was his wife! And I had black and blue shins. My landlady said to me, You don't ever, ever say to people who they're with. So I had more fellas came in with their nieces, David . . . ! We had one man, who lived in Ashley: I think he had more beautiful nieces . . . Have you met my niece, Jean? It was that sort of pub. I mean, I'm not saying it was a naughty pub, but it was the sort of pub that men brought their lady friends to, not their wives! Oh I got many a whisky, I did, to keep me quiet! I remember the night when the fella threw a pint of beer over me. Bernard was working at Trafford Park, and Les was away in Spain. We were very busy, and these two fellas came in, very drunk, very obscene language they were using . . .

239

Tony Diggle and Jo Horobin and Laura Horobin. 25 Hough Green

D.   When did you come to Ashley?

J.   It'll be a year ago in February. I'd applied for a council house. For a long time I'd had my name on the list. And Kev Gibbons, as you know, is my ex brother-in-law. I had a conversation with him and he mentioned that there were a couple of houses empty on The Green. So I made enquiries with the Council and pushed it a little bit further, and here we are. We know a lot of people in Ashley.

T.   I'd been working in the area for about three years, gardening. Mobberley, Ashley.

D.   This is part of your gardening beat? So you know it from that point of view.

T.   Yeah. And before, I had The Greyhound pub. I used to work for Greenall's. They asked me to come down and run the pub.

D.   Now when was that, Tony?

T.   '92, '93. Before the alteration, after August and Maureen had it.

D.   You were the one who came after August? Difficult act to follow, I should think?

T.   Yeah, it was a difficult act. Also there was a lot of local feeling about not wanting to change the pub. With the alteration that Greenalls had put forward.

D.   Had Greenalls already got the plans out for the big one?

T.   They'd got the plans out, but they'd been knocked back. And they were deciding at that time what to do. They drew up a few plans; and then the final plan, because of their being knocked back for planning permission, was just to pinch some of the accommodation from behind the pub. There was a lot of accommodation upstairs and round the back. So they moved the accommodation all upstairs.

D.   So you were there more or less when this dispute was at its height, all the furore - all the panic more like - round here about the possibility of that extension?

T.   Yeah. They didn't want it due to traffic congestion, noise and smell - you know, for the food, the catering side. There was a petition that went up and voiced this opinion. So obviously -

J.   You were both on separate sides on this one, weren't you?

D.   Well, funnily enough, No. I think I was about the only one who wouldn't sign that petition. And the reason I didn't was that I was afraid we'd lose the pub. I proved to be wrong, but my fear was that neither Greenalls nor anybody else would find that it was profitable to go on running it as it was. So I was inclined to think it ought to go ahead, rather than lose our pub altogether and become like Rostherne, which would be a fate worse than death as far as I'm concerned.

T.   Yeah, it was running at a loss. And Greenalls couldn't understand, with all the number of business people in the area, and they wouldn't let their businesses run so low and not want to improve them: they couldn't understand why people wouldn't think on that line, as a business opportunity for Greenalls. But like you say they have chosen another alternative which seems to have worked out.

D. Yes. Amazing really. I wouldn't have thought that was predictable at all. But it does seem to be working.

T. Yes. The last year I had it, after the alterations, the pub was doing fine. It met all its expectations, and Greenalls were happy, and all the locals seemed happy.

D. Were you actually the sitting - what, tenant?

T. Manager. Yeah. With the new foundations having to be put in, because it's a listed building. And waiting for the planning officers to come round and OK everything. We shut for seven weeks.

D. I thought that was amazing, that they did it so quickly.

T. The chaps that did it, they just worked non-stop. They were on a time scale, they were on a certain budget. It was just *Bang, bang, bang, bang!* Straight in.

D. I keep hearing this expression from those who talk about it, those walls that are on the inside, stressed: stressed walls, to make them look old. I thought that word was very appropriate, Stressed walls! Stressed manager as well, I should think! Stressed brewery! Everyone stressed, even the walls.

T. We came in at the time when Greenalls said it only needed rubber-stamping, they presumed it only needed rubber-stamping. When we got there we found it was like Custard's Last Stand behind that bar. Jean was working as well, she was in the thick of it, next door, she used to bottle up for me.

D. It must have made it very unpleasant for you.

T. It was hard to be there. It was my livelihood at stake.

D. And it wasn't your idea to extend. But I bet you got the flak! Anyway that's that little chapter. And after that you started gardening: did you start that straight away?

T. Not straight away no. With my divorce I moved into hotels. And then, I'd got to know Jo's dad while I was in The Greyhound, and then I got to know Jo. So on my days off and half-days I used to work for Jo's dad. This give us time to decide whether to go and work for him full-time, or to stay in what I was doing. I chose to do the landscape gardening. I've always had something in me about working outdoors, I always liked the outdoors, fishing and rough shooting, and clay pigeon shooting. So I think I found my patch. I moved to full-time with Bill, met Jo, moved in at Mobberley with her for a couple of years, then moved here, and things have just got better.

D. Of course I'd quite forgotten you're Sally's sister, Jo. I'm sure everyone knows her from when she and Kev had the post office.

J.   I suppose it was quite nice in a way being known as Sally's sister, because Sally was well liked in the post office. And what nicer area to child-mind in?

‚D.   Well yes. Have you been a child-minder for long?

J.   I've been doing it for, what, four years now. I did work in the Alldays shop in Mobberley for a long time. But it just doesn't work with a family. So I chose to child-mind, so that I could be at home for my own children. Because between us both we've got four children.

D.   All living here?

J.   Not Mark and Amy. But when we go on holidays we all go together.

D.   So here we've got Jessica and Laura?

J.   Yes. Jessica's three in April. I was at a play group in Mobberley before I had Jessica. In the day.

D.   Do you have to do some training to be a child-minder?

J.   There's courses and things to take, but as a child-minder, a registered child-minder, you don't actually have to go and take a lot of training.

D.   But you have to get registered? How does that happen?

J.   Through Social Services. They come to your house and make sure it's safe for children. Police checks and things. They ask you all sorts of questions. It's a lot general knowledge really. And then if everything's OK you get your registration. Legally you can't child-mind without your certificate.

D.   And are you given a limit to how many children you can mind at a time?

J.   Yes. It depends on your house space. At Mobberley I was registered for four. Here I'm registered for five, because we've made the extra room. I probably have three or four. But I don't always have the same children at the same time. I have some during the day, and also at night, after school.

D.   That must be a different age-group? So different equipment as well, I suppose?

J.   Oh yes, a lot of different things. I've got toys for all ages, really from babies onwards. I was asked not so long ago to child-mind overnight. I didn't take that one on, because I feel that from about six o'clock I think it's important to be with my own family. I think you need your time.

D.   So, Laura, how's it been for you, moving in here?

L.   I've enjoyed it, yeah.

D.   It was Mobberley before, wasn't it? So it's not a terribly different type of place.

L. I prefer it here though, because it's more exciting. There's more things to do.

T. It's closer to the stables, isn't it?

L. Yeah. It's a case of jumping on my bike and going there.

D. Which stables?

L. Do you know the Patersons? There. Although I don't have all my friends here I've got the stables.

D. Do you go up there every day?

L. I do, yeah. I've got a horse that I look after up there, and I have to go and settle it every night. So if I can't go it's a struggle to get someone else to do it. Because I work as a helper, doing things up there for Louise, like mucking out other stables, I get the use of the horse in return.

D. And if you can't get up there you've got to find someone else to do it for you?

L. Yes. I actually share it. So if I can't go he does it for me. One of Louise's sons.

D. Oh right, yes. Ben. And does it work out that you have it about half and half?

L. Not really. He's got another pony, but this pony's quite big, more my size than his. I don't really go on Thursdays, so he's got him on a Thursday, but that's really the only day I can't go.

D. Is Thursday a day off for you, did you decide this, on principle?

L. Louise is not there on a Thursday, but it doesn't matter to me because I don't need them there for my thing. We go to Pony Club and we do, is it Triathlons? we do them - swimming, running, shooting, with the Pony Club. And they have special swimming lessons for that on Thursdays. I have them with the school, my school. So she does that on a Thursday night, and I choose to get all my homework updated on a Thursday. And then on a Friday night I stay late and mess around in the arena. So Friday night is a messing round night. Basically I go every night, but I have to be home at a certain time so that I can do my homework, so it's a pain really. In the holidays I'm there all day, every day, but since I've gone to High School there's a lot of home-work on your back all the time.

D. This is at Knutsford? The High School. What year now?

L. Year Seven. I much prefer it at that school, but the times you have to get up aren't very good! Another pain! But I prefer that school.

D. Did all your friends move with you, to the High School?

L. Our year-group was very big at Mobberley, there were twenty six of us. Because such a load of people went, three or four went to another school, but the rest of us went to Knutsford High, yes.

D.   Do you get any spare time, Tony, after your day's gardening?

T.   In summer it's hard, because I work six days a week. I used to play football on a Sunday, but now Sunday's like a family day. Because Mark and Amy, they sleep over sometimes on a Friday night, sometimes on a Saturday, Sunday. And now we've nominated Sunday as a family day. We may go to Garden Centres, cycling, stay at home just taking it easy. It's hard in summer, but winter, you haven't got the light in winter. But Sunday is the family day. Jo does the shopping on a Saturday, and the housework, so that just leaves Sunday.

D.   I think a lot of families don't quite make it, always intend to spend more time together.

T.   I feel, through my past experience, that if you do work too hard it affects an awful lot of people. You've got to make that decision to make yourself a day: it doesn't work the other way.

D.   You mentioned fishing and rough shooting: is there any time for that?

T.   I used to do an awful lot, but now I very rarely touch either of them. I used to do a lot when I had the pubs, because I could allocate myself a certain day off. But as it stands now, no, not really.

D.   Well there'll be time for things like that when the family are grown up. If the government hasn't forbidden and banned every single field sport in the book by then. So how are you finding it here? It's the second time round for you, it must have felt strange coming back?

T.   It was, actually, because when I was at The Greyhound and knew everybody, and had a busy life, with people coming in, and I was always there: you're up front all the time, on show all the time, everyone talks to you. You get to hear a lot, people know about you. Then when you move, and I changed my life round to being quiet, with gardening and everything. Then coming to live here, and I knew a lot of people from when I was at the pub. And I never liked to be the centre of attention. I just liked my job at the time. So when we came here I'd come back in myself to how I would have been if I hadn't had a pub, with my family and a quiet life. And I looked forward to it. Especially moving into the house, we enjoyed it. They're nice solid houses, insulated upstairs, cavity wall, double glazing. And it's good to be in a cul-de-sac as well, for the children. And everybody in the square's aware of the children. It's not as if you've got a passing-through road. Everybody knows how many children live in someone's house, and they all go past it slowly. And there's the Green for the children.

D.   And how strange to find yourself next door to Jean!

T.   It is. Yeah. It's like another world. As I say, I'd no idea that I would come back.

D.   Well it's good that you've found you can. A lot of people might have felt just too uncomfortable with the change of role. So it's really good to hear that that's worked out all right.

May Fisher. 26 Hough Green

May chose not to record a conversation (*she was afraid that she might be rude to me: Again*), but instead she has given us this photograph of herself (*seated*) with her two sisters, taken while serving in the Land Army in 1945.

(Photographers: Barns and Dunsmuir, George St Altrincham. Courtesy of May Fisher)

Jane Bennett and Noel Beresford. New House by Station

D.   Jane, how did you come to find Ashley?

J.   I used to live in Hale, and Noel's from Hale as well, and about five or six years ago we saw this plot that was for sale then, and - Noel's always been in the building game - he really wanted to come and live down here, and live in the countryside, with no hassles or anything like that. So obviously at that stage we couldn't afford to purchase the land as it was, there. And then about three years ago we were driving past one day, and we saw that it was up for auction. So we thought, Well, let's give it a go. We were only twenty nine or whatever we were then, twenty eight, I think; and we thought, well why not? We had a house that was up for sale and had a purchaser, and we thought well we'll go for it, and let's see what we can do. And went to the auction, very nerve-racking. It's horrible, I wouldn't advise it to anybody. Anyway we went to the auction, and we ended up getting the plot of land. Which was just, like, Oh, fantastic!

D.   Magic! And the price, when you got to the auction, was it more or less what you expected you'd have to pay for it?

J.   Well, yes. I'd been to auctions before, and you set yourself a limit. It's no good going over that. Then obviously after that you have to go through planning. So you employ an architect. And obviously, with this being a Greenbelt area, it's important to have everything in keeping with the rest of the properties. Because I suppose if we were going to build something like Art Deco style it just wouldn't fit in. And Noel I think met with the Parish Council as well. As well as Macclesfield Borough Council, had a few meetings with them. And the plans went through first time. Which we were very pleased about. It was great.

D.   Did you have to modify what you wanted to do, very much?

J.   Not really, no. Everything that we put down on the initial drawings went through. And then it was just really internally that we wanted to change. One of the rooms and what have-you. So it was fine. And it's a slate roof, not covered with tiles. Just to keep in keeping with the rest of the area.

D.   And Noel built it, I presume?

J.   Yes. I helped! I made the butties!

D.   I was going to ask what part you made! It's been eaten, your part!

J.   No, I did help a little bit. Not a lot.

D.   Was it as informal as that? I mean, spare time and weekends, sort of thing?

J.   No, for six months we had a caravan down here. And a lock-up to put the tools in, everything. Noel stayed in the caravan virtually from when we got it - I think we had it in November, and he stayed over sort of November through to February, the very cold months. And I moved into the caravan about May, when it was nice and sunny, warm. And that was it, really. It was quite interesting, living in a little caravan.

D.   Were there any problems in the building? As you went on?

J.   No. No. We took the embankment back a little bit, here, and we put the walls in, so that shores up the embankment so that there was more room, really. Because with Railtrack owning the property down here, we have to be so far away from their lines. We couldn't have windows opening onto the railway, so we couldn't have a living room there, so that's why the kitchen's at the front of the house. And the living room's on the other side. There was just one or two things, but nothing major.

D.   So he came down in his caravan in - November, did you say?

J.   We bought it in November. It may have been December. '97. And we started work in the February, '98.

D.   And when was it finished?

J.   Probably about the September of that year, it was up.

D.   And when did you move in?

J.   Roughly round about then. We were living in the caravan, and we moved in once the floors were down upstairs. So we lived in the bedroom for a bit. I think we're still moving in really, because there's so much to do.

D.   And have you got plans for beyond, the other side of the house?

J.   That's just going to be the garden.

D.   I can't quite visualise how far you go on, beyond the end of the house?

J.   I think it's about another hundred foot, but it goes to a point, where the garages are at the top. It just goes a bit further on past there. It's very wild at the moment. No lawns or anything like that. One of these days!

D.   Something's gone up. Is it a greenhouse?

J.   Greenhouse, yeah. and we've dug a pond in, a little pond in. We bought some fish, but we think they're all dead. But we've got frogs. Quite like those. It's lovely round here, because we put birdseeds out, and just to sit at the back window and watch all the different birds throughout the year. And you don't really see those when you live in a town. It's nice. It's very tranquil.

D.   And you were both in Hale before?

J.   Yes. Hale, and Altrincham. Not too far away. But the plan was to - we've always bought a house and done a house up, - and it's always been Noel's ambition to build a house. His father was a builder as well, and it was his dad's ambition. And he's done it now. He's quite happy.

D.   It must be very satisfying. It's one of those archetypal things, really, to build your own house.

J.   Yeah, and I think he's very proud of what he's done.

D.   Good. So he should be. And what do you think of it?

J.   When we first came down here I thought we're going to be living next to a railway, I was very apprehensive. But I've got used to it, and I really enjoy it here now.

D.   And the house?

J.   The house, I love the house. I think it's possibly just a bit too big for just the two of us. So hopefully, you know, a couple of years' time, we'll have some children or what-have-you. I think it's a family house rather than just a couple's.

D.   Well, you've done it. That's the great thing. You've done it, and you're here!

J.   I know!

D.   And how have you found it, since you've been here? Are you settling into Ashley?

J.   We don't, because I work very long hours.

D.   Sounds as if you both do.

J.   Yeah, we both do really. So we don't have a lot of time to go out socialising. Otherwise I think we'd be absolutely shattered. And the other thing is, I think, because we haven't got children, and are not at the school, you don't get to meet other people. That's the community bit, round the school there, getting involved in that. So I think that's the other thing really.

D.   What is your work?

J.   I work for an advertising agency. In Wilmslow. So it's not too far.

D.   What does that mean you do?

J.   I deal with the media. I deal with the newspapers, magazines and what have-you, and I place advertisements on behalf of various clients.

D.   Do you find it's the sort of thing you go on learning more about as you go along?

J.   Oh, yes. With the advent of things like the Internet, and all the different types of media, it's just a growing market. You've got digital TV now. And so it's just expanding all the time. But I deal with press mainly. Press and print and radio. the Internet is mind-blowing, but I think everybody should know how to use it.

D.   I was going to say, it must mean you don't half have to be on your toes.

J.   Yeah. Yeah, you do. Definitely. You've got clients constantly who ask you, Can you find out about this new medium? and you've got to know it all. What the circulation is of the AA Magazine! You've got to know. It's very interesting, I do enjoy it. I like getting the deals at the end of the day. It's all a lot of negotiating. And spending your clients' money wisely.

D.   Do you do most of that from an office?

J.   Yes. I go out and see clients, and visit places. Conferences and things like that. I enjoy it. I love it, actually. Quite stressful sometimes.

D.   You mentioned this mind-blowing Internet: it's too early, really, to know how much it's going to change everything else?

J.   It is, a little bit. It will do, definitely. People will be able to buy things from home. I think you can even, in some places, get your groceries now. And they've got like supermarkets on the Internet. And everything's delivered. So I think it would help people considerably. And I think teenagers, they're all taught computing at school, which is brilliant because they can then show their parents how to use it as well! You've got this precocious kid saying, Dad you've done it wrong! So I think it will be quite interesting. One of my clients is Sir Clive Sinclair, the C5. He once said Everybody will have a computer in their home eventually. In every home. And he's quite an interesting man. Very interesting man. Knows what he wants. And he's very nice.

D.   I had a C5 once, because I don't drive and I thought it might be a way round it, but it didn't really work out very well.

J.   His latest one's the Zeta. Which is a battery pack thing you can put on your bike. So if you're going up a steep hill . . . !

D.   I don't suppose you really get much in the way of spare time?

J.   Not really. Noel doesn't have holidays. It's like seven days a week. I'm off this week, so I've had a nice break this week. Went up to the flower show yesterday. It was good.

D.   We came back as they were spilling out. It was quite extraordinary, the traffic.

J.   Oh, it's fantastic! They've got everything. I've been to Chelsea, quite like gardening, so I've been to Chelsea. And it's quite nice, I think they should have something in the North, really. When we go down to Chelsea I take my mum, and we always buy plants, we go on the last day. When we found out they were coming to Tatton Park we said, Oh, we won't go to Chelsea, we'll go down there. We had a lovely day yesterday.

D.   How did it compare with Chelsea?

J.   Well, it's the first one this year. Actually, I thought it was a lot better, because they have more - they've got lots of tents, everything's spread out. There's more land, there is more space. Because when you go to Chelsea it's just a sea of people, and people are jostling around, and you have to know where you're going, to see the exhibits that are there. But this one, I think it was just as good really, I think it'll get better. As time progresses, I think it will be something to shout about, definitely. And there were thousands and thousands of people there yesterday.

D.   Was yesterday the first day?

J.   Yesterday was the first day. It was really interesting.

D.   Do you know anything about how it came about? I mean, it really is quite a dramatic move.

J.   I think we went to Chelsea last year, and we were talking to one of the nurserymen that had a display there, and my mother's very much like, "Why haven't we got one of these in the North?" And he said, Well actually the RHS have decided that they want to do something in the North, and it's going to be at Tatton Park.

D.   Does it look like being permanently here, or will it move round?

J.   Yes, I think it will be here. They've got the layout there.

D.   Aren't we lucky!

J.   We are, yes. I think we're very lucky to live in this part of the world. Don't tell too many people about it, though! Keep it very quiet!

Matthew Hargreaves. Ashley Station

D.   What I'm longing to hear is the story of this station, and how you came to get the idea?

M.   I'd just returned back to Sale from university in Sheffield, living with my parents, looking for a place to live. So I drove round all Mobberley, and all the area. And Ashley Station was derelict, very derelict. Overgrown. And I thought it looked a nice place, arranged to get the keys off Railtrack and viewed it. And it just went on from there. I was expecting at every step for some obstacle to come in the way and that would be the end of that, I'll go and get a terrace somewhere else. But it just kept on going. I looked at it first of all, and I walked into the old ticket office as it was. And just standing in that ticket office, booking hall, with the old corniced ceiling still in place, I thought This would make a great place to live. Put in a split-level floor. Fantastic! And that was it. So as soon as I walked in through the door I realised that this was the place to live. Great! And the place where we're sitting here was in a state of total dereliction. The actual main house section, the old Stationmaster's House, was perfectly sound. But the real bonus was when I got the architect down here, Adrian Usher from Sale, and he presented me with a set of plans which confirmed, which just laid out, my initial plans for the flat next door - because as you know we've got two properties here. And he really scored by saying, Turn the staircase around. The staircase we've got in here: turn it round, we've got an extra attic room, made it into a really nice little house. And to punch a door through the trees that were here where we're sitting, which was all overgrown with trees, to create a nice unusual gully. So that was it. At every step it was, Right, get the architect in, see what he thinks of this; the planners, see what they say. We got nice letters from the parish council saying We support this scheme, which was great to hear.

D.   I should think the parish council were delighted. There have been some fairly hairy schemes.

M.   Quite a lot of people seem to have looked at it, and didn't realise quite what you could do with it. I think now that we've finally got the hanging baskets up outside

D.   - and they've stayed!

M.   Yeah well, that's true. Yeah. It was such a nice old building. 1864, I think it was built. We tried to have everything in keeping. Matching the original front door, the width of the arches.

D.   The shape of the arches. Yes. It really is extraordinarily satisfying that it's been preserved - better than preserved, been given a new lease of life. It's enhanced its attractiveness.

M.   I kept a notebook of how much money I was spending. It started to worry me, so I stopped!

D.   Stopped spending, or stopped keeping the notebook?!

M.   Keeping the notebook, yeah. But it's worth it, because I'm living here. That's why we perhaps went over the top on - just cobbling, putting new cobbles down. But that was in keeping. There was a swathe of cobbles around the original building. We tried to copy it. Having said that, it's not quite as nice yet, perhaps, as Mobberley Station down the road - but maybe he has a bigger notebook!

D.   Was it a surprise when that well was uncovered?

M.   The well, outside? Absolutely, yeah. That was a JCB driver, a local guy, who was putting in the gas and water, putting in the services. Lifted through the drain cover, lifted up some old sandstone flags which is now the front doorstep, and there was this old brick well, which I pumped out, forty foot deep. And as I'm leaping round taking photographs of this well, he says to me, Have you never seen a well before? No I haven't. I've never seen one uncovered on this site. So initially I thought, What can you do with it? The JCB driver said, Just fill it in. We come across them all the time. No, we're going to keep it as it is. It's a feature, whatever that might mean! But there was a really nice chap, Bernard, Bernard Dolan, who during the building process regularly came down. And I'm sure you know he used to work here, started to work here when he was sixteen, and he had such a wealth of information. He used to come down regularly to get the train, I think it was every day, and he'd survey the building works, and he'd point out little details, features. And he said, Oh I'd always wondered where that well was, because there used to be a water pump on the wall here, on the inside. I really valued the time that we spent speaking together, because he was such an interesting chap. No one else had that. I don't think anyone else had that information - to say That was the Lamp Room, and That was the room we used to work in, This is where we used to do that. I think they finished using it in the sixties. It changed into offices in the seventies, and fell vacant in the early eighties for ten years.

D.   Yes. This is about the only way you could use it, I think, with people living here.

M.   That's what the planners said. There was a couple of small objections - how can you live with a hump-backed bridge, trying to get out of the access point? But they took the view that we've got a building, and if we don't allow it to go to residential use it's going to sit empty. No one else is going to use it. It's a last-ditch attempt at getting it used. And it seems a shame that you've got a building that is constructed to such a high standard - I mean, the Victorian builders didn't mess about, they didn't skimp on anything, I mean it's two-foot thick walls - so it certainly taught me a lot more about building. I've done other building projects in the past. In Sheffield I got involved in renting properties and doing them up, but that was just knocking terraced houses together, which is a bit of a different thing. I don't think I realised how much I was taking on, when you actually take on a project to turn trees into bathrooms and shrubs into kitchens! But it's coming along. Obviously now we've got to look towards the gardening outside. I've planted quite a lot of trees. Keep on sticking trees in there. Heard a nice one about planting as many trees as you have years, on your birthday. Which is quite a nice one. Not got quite enough land for that, but - ! The odd one's going in. From the building side, it was just a pleasure to be associated with a building that was nice, that had a bit of character to it. It was good.

D.   Well it was terrific. There is just one question that I'm dying to ask, because it gives me such grief: there seems to be an enclosure there that has no exit or entrance, no door at all, just four walls.

M.   That's right. Well - this is the final bit to finish off. We've got a budget to spend on it. Let's get the main house up and running. And that's just an extra utility room.

D.   One day it will be given a door . . .

M.   And a roof. Yeah. At the moment it's only a partial success as a utility room. But there's a group of us living in here, it's a shared house, which I think most people are doing now, I don't think - my mother was saying, When I was your age I was married with two children. And I said, But this is a different generation. I'm twenty six, twenty seven. None of my friends are married, they all live in shared houses. Which is what this is. Young professionals, if they can call themselves that, living in a shared environment. It's just that for young people it's somewhere a bit different, rather than your run-of-the-mill flat or whatever it might be. What I like about it is that we're still in the countryside here. I'm quite into all this walking and climbing fun and games. And it's just a real pleasure being able to have a stroll down the paths. I had a real vivid experience the other night. I was out - it was a cycle ride, but we were going down a footpath, so we were pushing the bikes across the field, and there were three of us, Kathy and Ross who live here as well: and then - absolutely vivid, it was one of the best experiences of the year so far, thundering down the bank towards us, it looked like two bars about to take off, with their head black and white striped - two badgers. They came right towards us until they got within six foot of us - because as you know they have quite bad eyesight - and the wind was blowing down onto us, so they hadn't picked us up. And they were within six foot, and they were just rolling and playing and fighting - I don't know if they were fighting or courting, I'm not quite sure what, this was June. And we were standing there timing it, five, six minutes.

D.   And they were completely oblivious?

M.   Completely oblivious. And went thundering off again up the bank, up the hill and away. So that's just a real pleasure, knowing that you've got not just the house martins. It's a real pleasure to know that you can go out and see wildlife, which is a real plus point for me. I really enjoy seeing that. There's not too many times you see a couple of badgers coming running towards you, of an evening. Literally on your doorstep. Unfortunately you normally see them as road kills, on the latton Mile. Which is a shame. Nice to see them alive, nice to see them about.

D.   Not only alive, but playing! I don't suppose many people see them playing, above ground like that. So it didn't worry you, the number of negatives, the number of friends who said, Nobody's going to be able to live here with the trains?

M.   Yes, of course I worry about that. That was a concern, but I take the view that the environment that we're in, the setting of the house, it outweighs the couple of seconds when a train's going past. Coupled with the fact that you can jump on a train and have a day at Chester Races! Wish more people would use it.

D.   That's right, yeah. Literally on your doorstep.

M.   Exactly. It's just a bizarre situation. But all the way through the building process, as we were putting it together, I did actually spend a bit of extra money on padding the walls. This wall in particular. But I don't know if it did any good whatsoever, because the sound comes through the weakest point, which is probably the glass. And it just comes straight through. There were bits added on - this is all tacked on. And from the bulding side it's interesting to see the decline of building standards over time. The reason why we had to rebuild that utility room was because it didn't have any foundations at all. It was just tacked on, and the whole wall had bowed with the, probably with the thundering of trains going past. You can see. They were on really nice black bricks, and then Staffordshire Blues with plinths. And the walls got thinner. and then without foundations. Over fifty odd years. You can spot it on the brickwork, outside.

D.   Had you been reading anything associated with this at Sheffield, while you were also concerned with revamping old buildings?

M.   No. I did a degree in Geography and Geology - rocks and rivers. OK, it's got an outdoor bent, which comes back to the walking and climbing interests, but No. I think you just fall into things, you just drift. I don't know how many people make a conscious decision to go down a particular route. No, I had a great time in Sheffield, it was great. I think you can't go wrong with any Northern industrialised city, to be fair. Sheffield was great. That was three, four years - I stayed on and did an extra year, did up a house there. So all that was, was just a subject that was of interest to me. I was up in Torridon recently, and walking on the Isle of Skye a few months back, and you're there trotting over the rocks and you think, Ah . . .

D.   Now you know how they got to be how they are.

M.   Well you look at them, and you think, I must do a course on rocks, to find out what they're all about! You know the basics, obviously, you know the glaciation. Out walking with my father I can bore for Britain on that . . . "You realise there were two thousand metres of ice here . . ." if you're in a quarry or whatever glacial feature it might be. So yeah, that was Sheffield.

D.   Yes. I should think that's a bit different. But it's interesting that you should know about geology. There's some very interesting contours I've always wondered about, round Ashley.

M.   There's hardly any contours around Ashley that I can see!

D.   Well. All of a sudden you come across a dip. And what I'm beginning to think is that they've been excavated for bricks and things for the estate from time to time, and that sort of thing. But there are some very sudden, and not natural-looking - not the course of a river or something, much more abrupt: really as if it was man-made. But it was your talking about ice.

M.   There's not a lot of hard rock geology around here. But what is a shame is that the last of the ponds for the wildlife are finally being filled in. But an old chap who had a wander down here was saying that they used to cycle out here, and steal his mother's clothes prop and put a spoon on the other end, and steal the eggs of nesting birds and take them home for breakfast. Now there's not many of these ponds left, so just from a bird, wildlife point of view, you're actually destroying the last of the natural habitat. It's a bit of a shame really, that all these areas where birds, all these hydroseal stages where you get all these marshes and nice wetland area - there would have been hundreds and hundreds of these in local fields - they're finally now being filled in. There's a bit of a blandness about the landscape, which is a shame.

D.   I was only talking a couple of days ago to one of the farmers round here, who quite surprised me by saying that they had dug out quite a number of ponds. They'd actually dug out new ones.

M.   Why were they doing that, then?

D.   For wildlife.

M.   Ah, that's brilliant. That's absolutely brilliant! Stopping the rot.

D.   Two farmers have talked about what they do for wildlife - by growing their hedges and so forth.

M.   Just this local footpath here, behind the cricket ground. Lovely hummocky terrain and loads of ponds. Last year there were two big ponds, and they've gone now. Big piles of rubble. Certainly the one on the left has definitely gone, and there's a big pile of bricks ready for when they get enough just to fill it in. Which is sad.

D.   The other sad thing is, Dave next door was talking to me about landfill sites for garbage, and one of the reasons why he's interested in doing the job that he's doing is that he says there's a mounting crisis because we're making more rubbish than there is room to tip it into. And here they are trying to think of things to throw in, instead of using them for garbage.

M.   That will be local buiders that tip it. I mean, just from a small point of view, we've got a compost heap, and all our food, everything that's even vaguely grown, goes in there. So we get a host of birds feeding off our banana skins, etc. OK, that's probably only a ton less rubbish a year, but I wonder, if everybody had a compost and threw away their . . .

D.   Gardeners tend to.

M.   Well if you look at that overgrown patch covered in weeds over there, you can hardly say I've got an interest in gardening! Well that's the next stage, the next step is the landscape here. The building process is still ongoing, we've still got little scraps of roofing to cover over there, which gives us another little room, and we're still going to maintain the garden, but, you know, as time goes on.

D.   Yes, as time goes on, that's the thing. It's an evolving thing. I suppose Bernard will have told you that the station used to win the prize -

M.   Best Kept Garden! For a couple of years in the sixties, yes.

D.   So you might find, once you've got the weeds cleared, that it's quite conducive.

M.   The soil, yeah. When we turned the soil over I wondered what might come up. But no, we've got to start again now and say, Right, let's see how we can garden it.

D.   Well it's early days. But it'll be jolly interesting to watch.

Carol Brown and Dave Murphy. Ashley Station

D. How did you come across this place?

D.M. Well actually I was looking on the other side of the track, at the piece of land that was up for sale. And I noticed, obviously that there was a *To Let* sign on the station. Half of it had been renovated, and the other half needed some work doing, and to get somebody in it. So on speaking to the chap on the phone, I more or less knew his voice, but wasn't too sure. So I made an appointment to come down and have a look at the station, and on Thursday morning when we rolled up, on Carol's birthday, Matthew Hargreaves came walking out the door, which I'd worked with him about four or five years ago! So that's how we came to move into the Station.

C.B. The funny thing is, it turned out that I knew him as well, through school friends. So we both knew him from different . . .

D.M. We were on the way to see Carol's Gran at the time, in Glasgow. So we got halfway up the Motorway and I said to Carol, What shall we do? Because when we saw the building, no windows in it, no floors, nothing. And we said, Yeah, we'll take it. So when I phoned Matthew up and said We'll take it, he said Are you sure you'll take it? It's not liveable. And from November 7th, from then on till March, wasn't it, we worked fairly closely with Matthew to try to get it how we wanted to live in it. So that's how we came across the Station.

D. Which year was this? November to March . . .

C.B. November '96.

D. Did you say you both worked on the market?

D.M. Yeah, Matthew is a market trader, and I was a market trader. I worked here locally, in Altrincham for, oh, thirty four years. My parents had a stall on the market, and obviously I took it over when my parents had had enough.

C.B. He is thirty four. He's worked it all his life!

D.M. From being in a pram I was the CCTV camera. Making sure nobody stole anything.

D. What sort of stall was it?

D.M. We used to sell hosiery. Socks, underwear. And a lot of other things as well, as the years have gone by.

D. Was it just Altrincham, or did you move around?

D.M. No I travelled all over. As far as France. Holland, France, I've been all over the place. Paris. Yeah. Liverpool, closer one! Yeah we used to do them seven days a week.

D. And you say you've stopped doing that now?

D.M. Yeah, the market itself, no disrespect to Altrincham, the clientele and people use different ways of spending money now. You know, people obviously spend it on their credit card, and would rather go into Marks and Spencers, Asda, Safeways. The big multiple stores have taken over now. So the markets have gone down.

D.   Is that true of the market world in general?

D.M. Absolutely, yeah.

D.   It's plastic, isn't it?

D.M. It is, but in different parts of the country, such as Newcastle, Liverpool, the markets are still very good. People who've got the cash go out and spend it on the markets. Scotland. We were up spending a bit of time up in Scotland, even up there the markets are still good. It's just round here: not just in this area, but the whole of Greater Manchester, they've just changed. And the biggest thing is, in Altrincham itself, they just charge too much for parking. So by the time people have paid to park they just don't want to go round and shop. So consequently it's made a difference on everybody's business.

D.   There's quite a little clientele gathers outside these windows on market days! They'll be very sorry, because they're regulars. I think it's entertainment.

D.M. It is. It's entertainment. I mean, I've been stopped the market now for - four years?

C.B. You stopped '95. We went to Spain for a year. We worked in Spain.

D.M. We worked in Spain. And I can still walk round Altrincham now, and people will still call me The Sock Man. They still bump into me and say, How are you doing? And people might have bought only a couple of pairs off me, you know. I was actually coming back from a holiday, and I was in Chicago, and somebody came up to me in Chicago airport and said, I bought some socks off you in Altrincham Market! In fact I've got them on! It used to be good, because I travelled down south a lot, we used to do like the Coastal Run, as we call it, in the holiday season, and there were crowds of people I used to see from up in Altrincham. It was good, I enjoyed it. I do miss the interaction with people now, because after all them years of chatting to people, it's hard to find another job where I could talk to a lot of people. That's why I talk to Carol!

D.   Does she listen all right?

D.M. No, no. That's why she's got cotton wool in her ears!

D.   So what do you do now?

D.M. I work for a local firm actually, in Ashley here. And they're into recycling. And I just work as a solely self-employed for a small recycling organisation. So I'm really lucky to live and work in Ashley.

D.   What does it actually involve you in doing?

D.M. I just work in the Trafford area. Every lad has got his different area, where he goes. We go round on a circle of just collecting, week to week. Basically, the English are very very wasteful. They'll buy something and wear it once and think, Oh I don't like that, and they'll sling it. They'll throw it away. So obviously there's another market for somebody who wants that type of clothing. The thicker type of clothing goes to Bosnia and places like that, where it's a lot colder. The thinner stuff goes out to South Africa, where it's very hot. And the clothing what can't be sold is shredded and sold to Slumberland Beds, to make new beds. Or new car carpets, chairs, you name it. It can be recycled.

The challenge what's going to happen though is, with the countryside, the landfills themselves are filling up. And they're running out of space for dumping rubbish. We collect two hundred tons of clothing a week. And there's still a million tons of clothing goes on the rubbish tip every year. So you can imagine. And we're still collecting it. And we're not the only company that's doing it, there's sixty other companies.

D. And Help the Aged and all these other charity shops where my wife dresses.

D.M. That's it. That's it! And that's just textiles. You can imagine paper, glass, bottles, everything.

D. So that it really isn't just for saving materials, it's saving the dumping places?

D.M. It's the landfill. They've got to change.

D. Carol, I first met you going on the train, when you were going to university.

C.B. Yes. That was last year, when I was doing my postgraduate diploma in Information and Library Management. That was a one-year course. I'd already done my degree, at Sheffield. I was there '91 to '94. Then had a couple of years working. We went to Spain for a year, David and I, working in Spain. Then I came back. I already knew that I wanted to work in libraries. So then I did a traineeship at Manchester Business School for a year, as a library trainee. And then I went to the Library School. I went there for a year.

D. It's always surprised me how much time librarians have to spend qualifying. What goes on in libraries behind the scenes, that we don't know about?!

D.M. People just think it's "Shhhh!" and a quick stamp of a book!

C.B. A lot of the work now -. Unfortunately there's a bit of a divide between professionals and non-professionals. Non-professionals do a lot of the work, I mean really.

D. They do the stamping?

C.B. Yeah, they do the stamping. They stand behind the counter. You don't do that. You don't do what people think you do. You work on Enquiry Desks, answering reference enquiries, business enquiries, family history. Most of the day-to-day enquiries about Maeve Binchy's latest novel, can be answered by Library Assistants. We get involved in ordering stock. Promotions, displays. Liaising with schools, businesses.

D.   Do you get enough people asking these questions? Information questions?

C.B.   Well I've been working at Chester Central Library, which is a really really busy library. It's on three floors, and there's different enquiry points. The reference library is very very busy, yeah. I mean, you can get phone calls from all over the country. People tracing the address of relatives. There's business enquiries, although the main business information service is actually based at Ellesmere Port, that's a separate place on its own, it's a constantly busy library.

[*A very heavy freight train goes past, two yards from the window.*

D.   How do I reproduce that noise on a word processor?

We have to wait until it has passed.]

C.B.   We've got a bit of technology now on my course. Use of computers, the internet, websites, databases. That's a huge chunk of my job now. I mean at Chester, when I started, they'd opened a computer centre. Fifteen computers in a room. People can do courses there, and use a tutor as well. They can get qualifications. People come in in their own time, it's open learning.

D.   It is an amazing service. I mean, how on earth is it paid for?

C.B.   Well there is a certain amount of income generation. Fines and charges. Not a lot.

D.   They are going up. My wife had to pay 80p the other day!

C.B.   There's a lot of going in for partnerships now. I mean, computers are part of a Wolfson bit, which is a government funding. It was actually set up by somebody years ago. It's been maintained, so it's like a charity. You put your bid for it. And that's how we got the computers. And they're funded for a year. That year's past for Chester now, it's self-sufficient, it's earning enough money to keep open, and will be kept open and will be expanded. But, yeah, you're looking for like partnerships. There's a lot of bidding going on.

D.   And all that you have to be equipped to do, as a librarian?

C.B.   Yeah. I mean, I like the technology aspect.

D.   So what did you do in this year in Spain?

C.B.   I worked for a communications company. It was interesting.

D.M. Very interesting. The culture was fantastic. And every time it rains we wish we were still there!

C.B.   Yeah, we absolutely loved Spain. The people: wonderful. So laid back, they've just got a different approach to life. It took us a while to get used to it. It's very family-orientated, as well. We were based in Alicante, but we went all over the place. Went to Madrid once a week, Valencia, travelled round.

D.M. We didn't mix with the other English. We did at first, didn't we, we mixed with other English people, then we more or less made our own way into the Spanish quarters. It was more interesting. It was great, really really good. We do miss it a lot. We do miss it.

C.B. It was our dream that we would buy a holiday home in Spain. And spend half our time there.

D.M. And half our time tidying the Station up!

D. And these hanging baskets that have suddenly appeared, did you put them up?

C.B. Oh yeah. Yeah. We got those put up on Sunday. I think they're petunias. We were worried that they might disappear, because things have a habit of disappearing from round the Station. So I was a bit concerned. So we thought we would put three out and see how they get on, before putting up any more. I'd love to have all pots on the Station, but things have been vandalised in the past.

D. Even since you came here?

D.M. Yeah. More so, I think!

C.B. When we first came it was a problem. We did have to call out the police one night. It's not so bad now, but I think things do still get damaged. Because we had a bicycle outside, and that's completely ruined.

D.M. I bought a shed about a week ago. I brought it on the Friday, it's not put together yet, it's laid on the floor out there. I picked it up on the Friday, when I went out on the Saturday morning, somebody had put the windows through on it.

C.B. But we never see anybody. I don't know where they all come from.

D.M. It's been painted at the front as well, so it looks really nice. He's done it really good. We just hope that the train drivers might say something, you know, now it does look quite good.

C.B. It's surprising. I don't know where they all come from. It's not as bad now as it used to be. A lot of people used to hang around at weekends, but they've stopped.

D.M. Well obviously, I think it was for ten years or so, there was nothing here. So the children did have a playground. Or a meeting-place, whatever. So when we moved in we might have spoiled their little bit of fun on a Friday evening. It obviously was going to take time, just to get the children back to know about it. They're OK, aren't they? I don't think it's kids, really.

C.B. I don't know, because we never see anyone.

D. Well anyway it's lovely. I hope you'll go on enjoying it. And the baskets survive!

Chris Stanion. The Downings

D.   Can you tell us a little about how you came to Ashley?

C.   We lived in Sale. And at the time the boys were five, six. Young. And we'd driven down to Tatton Park a lot, and seen the village and liked it. And we just saw this house up for sale, at the same time as our house was sold. Just everything at the right time. And Tom, the eighteen-year-old, was particularly interested in animals, and rotting things off: skeletons. He used to go and collect owl pellets from the church. And he'd bring them home and mount them on pieces of card, and work out which animals they'd come from. Peter Jackson found him a dead fox which he rotted off somewhere or other, and, er . . . So we thought it would be nice for the boys. And because I work for Cheshire, my base is in Knutsford, it's convenient. So it felt as if you were a little bit outside the suburbs, but very convenient for everywhere else.

D.   Yes. And how did you find it, moving in?

C.   Fine. The boys loved it. Particularly when they were little. They were very friendly with Tim Crawford. Tom and Tim were great friends, and they used to spend days together. The three of them got on very well indeed. So that was excellent.

D.   And what stage are the boys at now?

C.   Tom's just started at university, went last Saturday. He was back this Saturday, because he was ill! He's all right, it was just a cold. He came back to his nest. He's at Liverpool, John Moore's, doing a degree in Construction Management. He went from North Cestrian to Mid Cheshire College, and did an NVQ in building. And Oliver is doing the same course. He didn't know what to do. He thought of doing an audio-visual design course at Art College. But in the end he opted to do this, because at least he knows what it entails. He doesn't know what he wants to do, and it's a very broad course. It's quite good, because you sample all different aspects of building - architecture, quantity surveying, electrical work, carpentry - a bit of absolutely everything. And it also gives you the option of university, so it's a really useful course. And there are just so many opportunities for jobs in the construction industry.

D.   And where is it?

C.   At Mid Cheshire College, in Hartford. He gets the train.

D.   I'd never heard of that course before.

C.   It's called *Building and the Built Environment*. They do environmental science and all sorts of things. They go on field trips to Anglesey, where they actually measure a house and work out how much it would cost to build, and survey the land around.

D.   How do they go on for friends?

C.   Tom made a lot of friends from school who lived in Hale. They weren't all from school, some of them were from Cheadle Hulme School, but most of them lived in Hale. So that was easy, he used to go on his bike. But Oliver's friends all live in Cheadle, which is a real nuisance. I spend half my life on the motorway between here and Cheadle. He can get there, but only by getting the train to Altrincham and a bus out to Cheadle. And so that has been difficult.

D.   Do they ever come here?

C.   Oh yes. This house has been very quiet since Tom's gone, because I've always said to them that their friends could come here. A lot of Tom's friends can drive. So we had a fleet out here sometimes. I liked that. I knew they were safe. I knew they were in the house. And this house lends itself well to teenagers, because you can close off that door down to the bedrooms down there, and I can go to sleep up there and we don't disturb each other. So Oliver has his Cheadle friends staying quite a bit. But now they're saying that there's more to do in Cheadle. So he's tending to want to go there. And with Tom gone, that makes it a lot quieter. Sometimes I feel I'm feeding half of Cheshire. Tom said to me, It's going to cost a lot of money for me to go away to university. And he said, Well Mum, you'll save money on food!

D.   And what do you do?

C.   Well I've been a teacher of the deaf for the last twenty-odd years. I started off working for Trafford, and then started working for Cheshire about nine years ago.

D.   How did you get into that?

C.   When I was about sixteen I saw a programme about teaching deaf children, and I thought that looked interesting. So I went to university and I did a degree, and I did an end-on postgraduate certificate at Manchester, which is a centre for training to teach hearing children and deaf children.

D.   Both? As part of the Certificate course?

C.   Yes. And then my first job was with Trafford.

D.   So you've always been teaching deaf children?

C.   Yes. In my first job I had - it was a big secondary school, Sale West, there was a unit there for deaf children - most of my time was with them, and part of my time was with the mainstream, so you did a bit of both. And then I left and had four years off when I had the boys, and then I went back to Trafford as a peripatetic teacher. And then I left Trafford to have a bit of time off. I think I had two days off! We're very short on the ground, teachers of the deaf. And a colleague from Oldham rang me, and could I help her out? I said I can't possibly get back from Oldham, I've got to be back for the children. She said, You come whenever you like, and you can leave at three. So I did a couple of terms there, and then similarly a couple of terms for a colleague in Salford. And then I started working for Cheshire eight or nine years ago.

D.   So do you teach all age groups? Or is it all secondary?

C.   No, no. Since they're diagnosed, from a baby, up until sixteen. And then I pass on to one of my colleagues who deals with Colleges of Further Ed.

D.   So would you be likely to have the same child from the start?

C.   Yes. It's strange, because I've recently, I've gone part-time since September, I'm doing three days a week instead of full time. So we've had to re-organise the way we operate. My colleague who is working in Chester has taken on the majority of my school-based case load. And some of them I've had from being babies, and it's so hard to say to them, It's not going to be me anymore. And the parents have found it hard. And I've tried to say, Well, you know, it's not normal to have the same teacher for eight years, you're passed on. But I've been in their homes when they were little, and the parents say, Yes, but we know you. You've seen us through the diagnosis, and all that difficult time. And I say, Well Rosemary's very nice, you know. So that's been quite difficult, these last few months.

D.   I bet it has. It's probably difficult even when they graduate out of your range in the normal course of things.

C.   Yes. But to leave them mid-way through is different. But the main part of my case load at the moment is pre-school. I kept the pre-school case load. When I went back to Trafford as a peripatetic teacher I very much enjoyed the parental guidance side of things. I find it very interesting when I get a new family, and I've got to sort out all their problems: hearing aids and caring for the baby, and coming to terms with it. And then once I get into just the weekly teaching mode it becomes very routine and repetitive. And so that part of the job's what interests me most, which is why, when I asked to go part-time they said, well what would you like to keep? I said I'd like to keep the babies.

D.   So that you've got the work with the parents? Because I was just thinking that there must be a lot of work to be done with parents, in those circumstances.

C.   Oh gosh yes, because to come to terms with having a severe or profoundly deaf child in the family, and the difference it makes to the siblings, and family life. It's hard work. Because we don't sign with them, we use the residual hearing, with hearing aids, and teach them to speak. And I've got quite a few children on cochlea implants, which has been wonderful. So that's the part of the work I like.

D.   And how's it been, going part-time?

C.   Well it's only since the beginning of September, and I've got to be careful because on Friday, which is one of my days off, I had to go into work for three hours, because one of my babies had to go into hospital for a hearing test, and the audiologist likes me to be there to help. And I can't say No, you see. So I've got to be very careful not to end up working full time for part-time money. One Thursday, which is another day off, I went to help my mother-in-law move into a flat in Solihull, so I'm not really appreciating it yet! But I'm looking forward to just pottering, having a day to potter.

D.   I was just wondering if you had anything specific in mind, when you decided to go part-time?

C.   No. I just wanted some time when I didn't have to rush. That's the trouble with the job, you're rushing from one appointment to the next. I just wanted a less rushed and stressful life. I shall just potter. The dog'll like it. This cat here, by the way, is profoundly deaf. Trust me to get a deaf cat!

D.   How strange! How long did it take you to discover?

C.   Three minutes. As soon as I got him into the car. I started the engine, and he didn't flinch.

D.   But you didn't until you'd got him in the car? You'd no idea, or the people where it came from?

C.   I was supicious when I went into the house. And there were two - I wanted a white kitten - and there were two white kittens. And the young man who was trying to find this one said, he was calling for him, he said to me, That one's always very difficult to find. And it was because he was asleep and he was deaf. But he's two now. He's only started going out this summer. I was so frightened of him on the road. But so far he's all right. We found him on the other side of the platform the other day.

D.   Now it's funny you should say that, because I saw two white cats together, in the field the other side of The Green. And I only know of one white cat on The Green.

C.   I think Tim the hairdresser has a white cat.

D.   Yes he does, you're quite right. Not that I've ever seen their cat stray very far.

C.   Well he's absolutely ruined, our cat, he's spoilt silly.

D.   Well he's a very lucky cat, I think, to have found you. Because it must have been easier for you than it would have been for most people. Do you have much garden?

C.   I think it's about a quarter of an acre. It's a funny shape, the garden. The house has been placed so that you get the view over the field that way, and the view down the lane this way. This was the room that sold us the house, because it was so nicely placed. But I've noticed over the years the motorway's got a lot busier. I don't notice it in the house. I notice it when I'm in the garden. You get used to it, it's not something you think, How awful. Trains don't bother me in the slightest. But I think over the ten years the motorway has got worse. Especially the bit where it flies over the railway line, I think that's the source of the noise. I keep meaning to write and say would they consider putting down that, there's a new tarmac, that reduces the car noise on the surface; they have apparently devised this new tarmac that reduces noise.

D.   I think everyone says that about the motorway compared with the railway: that whereas you can get used to the trains, you don't get used to this. Certainly we find, for instance, we can't really sleep with the window open. If we were fresh air fiends we would find that quite troublesome. Do you notice any other changes in the time you've been here?

C.   Not really. In the village things are pretty much the same. The post office, the pub. The petrol station's a nuisance, not selling petrol. That's a real bind. You get quite a lot of change with the Old Vicarage, because there's constant change there. New neighbours to get used to.

Peter and Eve Robinson. Highley House

P.   When I retired from the Navy I came to work in Manchester in Eve's father's family company. And we settled on The Firs, in Bowdon. That was in 1948, and we lived there for eight years. And one night we went to a cocktail party. We'd been wanting to move out into the country. And I met a woman, and the usual sort of topic of coversation, Where do you live? and she said, In Ashley. I said, I love Ashley, I'd love to go and live there. She said, Well our house is for sale. So we got in touch with the agents right away and were round next day, and we fell in love with Midways. Actually what had happened was that it had already been sold, but the person who had signed the contract wanted to go back on it. And so it was not quite on the market, but it was actually up for sale. That's how we got it, and we moved in March 1956. And never regretted it.

D.   How many children did you have at that stage?

E.   Three. Henry was born in 1955. We carried Henry in a carry cot in '56.

D.   And Jilly and Michael?

E.   Ten and eight. We had quite a gap because Peter kept thinking he'd have to go back to the Navy.

P.   Yes. Cold War. Korean War. Then Suez. Because having just left the Royal Navy, as opposed to the Reserve, I was very likely to be called back. And so it rather interrupted our . . . plans.

D.   You must have felt you were more or less on stand-by for years, with one crisis after another.

P.   Yes, because Suez was 1956. So even then one was worried. But after that it was all right.

E.   Then we'd only just arrived, and they were going to have a fête. And it was going to be in the Vicarage garden. Actually it was wet and it was in the school but they grabbed me to open it, having only just arrived. And we thought, really Midways would make a jolly good place for it. So we said, Why don't you have it with us? and they said, Oh marvellous! And the first year we didn't really organise it, in '57.

P.   Not properly, no. Just gave the site.

E.   But in '58 we did.

D.   So that's how it came about! By their being shrewd enough to ask you to open the fête at the Vicarage: I wonder if that had been at the back of anyone's mind - *well perhaps they might ask us to have it there!* Now I'm betraying my own devious way of doing things, aren't I?!

P.   But I should think that's very likely!

D.   Anyway so there it was, and there it stayed. Are there any particular memories you have of it?

E.   Too many, I think.

P.   It was just a most wonderful family house. It looks enormous, but it's not all that big when you get inside it. It was very easy to run.

E.   There's no third storey.

P.   It was really all centred round the hall. No, it was a wonderful place.

D.   And the garden: were you already as keenly committed to gardening?

P.   I was beginning to. But I never took any interest in gardening before I came out of the Navy. My father used to be terribly keen, and I think I was rather naughty that I didn't help him more.

D.   That's interesting, because that was my experience exactly. I never took the slightest interest in my father's garden, or in gardening, until I had one of my own, that I jolly well had to look after.

P.   That's the answer, I think. And I got more and more interested in it.

D.   Eve, what sort of thing did you get involved in? You had the children during the holidays, and then they grew up . . .

E.   I kept on being grabbed for various committees and things. And I always decorated the house and sewed and things like that. I couldn't garden, but I did other things. Then you see the house was used for many things. We started having the Mothers' Union there. And then it changed to the Fellowship. It was very flourishing actually, because we had that billiard room and so we could have lots of people. We used it for quite a lot of things. Charities and various things.

D.   It must have been very tempting for the church, not having any rooms of their own, suddenly to find you there at Midways with rooms that could be used.

E.   Mrs Henshall when she was here, they were marvellous hosts, she used to have Mothers' Union and things like that there. But it never worked after that.

P.   Well this bungalow wasn't very suitable.

D.   Of course, then it was this bungalow, wasn't it? The Henshalls were the last in the Old Vicarage.

P.   Yes. The bungalow was built in 1970.

E.   And the Taylors were here.

D.   So you have been at the heart of the church here for this whole generation, haven't you?

P.   Well, yes. We were put on the PCC almost the day we moved into Midways. Old Charles Smith, he knocked on the door the day we actually moved in and said, Would we join the Parochial Church Council? This was in 1956, and the very next year Robbie Barclay handed over the Treasurership to me, and I've still got it.

E.   During all those years people kept saying, Would we be Wardens? both of us. And I said no. I was on the Synod and that sort of thing, and we thought it was much more important to get other people in Ashley involved. Then you rang me up when I was languishing in the BUPA hospital.

D.   Have the fortunes of the Church fluctuated in this period, or stayed rather steady?

P.   In the early days they were steadily very bad. If we hadn't had the fêtes I honestly don't think we would have survived. We still need the fêtes, because to keep up with the repairs on a building like that is jolly expensive. We've got a beautiful organ which needs thousands spending on it. But the finances are much better now than they've been for years. And going in with Hale, you see. That was the crux, that was one of the best things that ever happened to Ashley. Because we were having to meet the cost of the vicar ourselves until 1985 when it became a Joint Benefice, and then we shared it with St Peter's, Hale, and it was apportioned according to the gross income of the two parishes. So very roughly speaking we were suddenly only having to pay about a tenth of what we had been paying, and St Peter's putting in the other nine tenths.

D.   Another thing I was wondering if you'd like to talk about was this house, and moving here? At what stage did you make the move from Midways?

E.   This came up. What happened was that Noel and Angela had it on a five-year lease.

D.   This was after there was no longer a resident clergyman for Ashley?

E.   Yes. When we went in with Hale. Noel Vincent was a Canon of Derby. He was head of the BBC Religious Programmes in the north of England, based in Manchester. He did lots of *Songs of Praise* and those things. And after five years the Bishop said I think we should sell that now. Luckily he said that Noel and Angela could have another year. The BBC were changing things, and Noel and Angela were moving down to London anyway. We knew this. So I said to the Diocesan Secretary, What do I do? We might be interested. And he said, Oh we'll talk to the Diocesan Surveyor. They said, If you'd like to have it valued and surveyed we will too. And then they said, Would you like to put in an offer? Because they didn't want the hassle of auctioning it. So that's what happened.

D.   And St Elizabeth's House became Highley House: is there a story behind that?

P.   My parents' house at Upton upon Severn was called Highley House, and it's quite a sentimental thing for the family, because first of all Michael went to boarding school within six miles of it, and then Jilly went to a school within about twelve miles of it. Henry also went to the same school as Michael. And then Henry and Michael both went to Marlborough, which is only about fifty-odd miles away. My mother, bless her, was simply wonderful and always had us to stay. She didn't mind how many boys or girls the children asked out. And so it's a very strong family connection. That's why we called it Highley House. We didn't like St Elizabeth's House.

E.   It's a bit of a mouthful, don't you think?

D.   And in a sense, being in civilian hands, it gives a slightly false impression as well. All sorts of people call at the door of places called St Elizabeth's House, thinking it has something to do with the church. I don't know if you still find that?

E.   We have awful problems with the Old Vicarage and things like that, don't we?

D.   Because people assume that this is the Old Vicarage?

E.   I don't know what they think. Because it's next door I think.

P.   But we talked about Midways being bliss: this is utter bliss. I mean it's one of the best things we ever did, to move here. Did we tell you about the fire in the garage at Midways, and Bob Salt's fire?

D.   Bob talked about it a bit.

P.   It was quite clearly an arsonist.

E.   The police think they know who did it.

D.   Did they never catch him?

P.   They apprehended somebody in a car with stolen goods, and they put various fire things to him. He admitted entering one place in Mobberley with the intent to set fire to the garage. They asked if he'd been to Bob Salt's and Midways and he wouldn't admit it. But I'm quite certain it was the same chap.

E.   The one at Mobberley was the first one. Bob Salt was about ten days later, and we were about ten days after that. You know what happened? PP was with us.

P.   Peter Poncia.

E.   He had insomnia, so he'd turned on the World Service to listen to the cricket from Australia or something. And he thought there's a light in the garage. And then he realised it was flames, and so he woke us up, and the fire brigade. It was freezing cold.

P.   It was 18° Fahrenheit on the thermometer. And I was out there in my pyjamas and dressing gown. But I wasn't cold. It was the adrenalin.

D.   How did you feel afterwards?

P.   It was quite nasty after it. I think one wondered whether the next thing wouldn't be the house. But actually that old garage was in a pretty bad state. It had dry rot in it and woodworm, even though I'd treated it for woodworm.

D. And was it completely gutted?

P. Pretty well. We lost all the fête stuff that was stored up in the loft. All the machines - well no: funnily enough my old mower, which I love, has been resuscitated and I'm still using it here.

D. And did that really mark the end of the fête at Midways?

E. No.

P. No, we still had one.

E. David [*Ashworth, the vicar*] let us borrow things from St Peter's. Tables and chairs, etc.

P. That had no effect on our decision not to run the fête. That was purely the fact that we'd done it for thirty five consecutive years, and we'd had enough.

E. We said we'd give the Parish two years.

P. Two years' notice. So we did the '90 fête and the '91. And that was the last.

D. Looking ahead, are there any things you'd like to say about the future of Ashley?

E. Well the only thing I'd like to say is that I wish we could get more younger people involved with the church.

P. Yes, I'd second that.

D. Well, I suppose a start has been made, with the Sunday School?

E. Yes it has. Oh, Mary's doing terribly well with it.

P. David there are eight, ten, sometimes twelve little chaps there, you know. I wish the families would come. As you know, we don't have the Sunday School on the first Sunday in the month, there's Family Communion with the express object of hoping that they'll bring their children to that. It's a very simple, told-to-the-children, service. And only forty minutes or something.

Khanikhah Guy and Jolie. The Croft

D.   Khanikhah may we start with you? Where do you come from?

K.   I was born in Kent, but my parents were northerners and we were just down there for three years. I actually grew up in Sale, when Sale was green fields and cornfields. Not like that now! But I've known Ashley all my life, and always loved it. Even as a child, driving out here. And for many years I wanted to live in Ashley. And finally made it, about six years ago.

D.   So you were in Sale during your schooldays. What did you do then?

K.   I went to Drama School and went into the Theatre, as an actress and a dancer. And then I went to live in Dublin, where I did more theatre. Came back - actually, to nurse my father who was very ill - and got married, and went into psychotherapy, started to study psychotherapy, for six years.

D.   How did you get into that?

K.   I'd always been interested, from being a child. And then at drama school - it was the sixties, and Jean-Paul Sartre, existentialism, André Gide. Coming from a very religious background on my father's side as well, there was always a fascination with the human condition. And I've lived with a discontent all my life. That pushes you to search for answers. So that's how I got into it. The human condition.

D.   And how did you find it, when you got into it professionally?

K.   Well it answered all the questions that I had searched for in religion. And hadn't found the answers. Having said that, leaping over about twenty-odd years: having found answers, I could then come back to the church and accept in a simple way the things I'd accepted as a child. Now I had the form, the philosophical understanding, I could tear up the textbooks and return to this simple faith. It's very interesting. It was a very lengthy procedure, but one I found necessary to go through.

D.   Yes. Thank you for that. Did you practise, have you been going on practising psychotherapy?

K.   For twenty years, on and off. I worked in a psychiatric centre for a number of years, Toft Hall. And then I worked independently, privately. I had rooms. Park Road.

D.   So there you are, doing these sort of things in Hale, and then - you came to Ashley.

K.   Well I was living in Hale, but I never really wanted to be living in suburbia. And when the opportunity of a house came up in Ashley we grabbed it. And Jolie had associations with Ashley because he worked at Ashley Mowers. I already knew people in Ashley. And we felt very welcomed, and we settled in very easily. The nicest thing anybody said to me was Sheila Norbury. And she turned to me after we'd been here a little while, and she said, *You know, Khanikhah, it's as if you'd always lived here*. And that was the greatest compliment. I was thrilled when she said that.

D.   What have you been doing since you've been here?

K.   Well obviously we immediately went to the church, St Elizabeth's Church. And loved it. I mean, really loved it, from the minute we joined. I was asked to join the PCC after a while. Oh, prior to that David Ashworth of course had been my vicar in Hale. And he asked me to do various things for the church - like, Would I organise the readers? and so on. Then the PCC, and ultimately Church Warden. But it's . . . it's the atmosphere in St Elizabeth's I find quite extraordinary. There's only one other little church I've been in has moved me quite the same, and that was in the Lake District. And again it was a tiny rural, simple church, that has that same prayer-soaked feeling about the walls that St Elizabeth's has. Quite unspoiled by attached kitchens and . . . community centres and . . . It's been unspoiled. It hasn't been interfered with. Hence there are powerful energies in that church. Mustn't say any more. But we love it. And there is a lovely spirit there.

D.   Why mustn't you say any more?

K.   Because I shall never stop! Because I can foresee snooker tables and all sorts being put in there. Pews being ripped up and put outside. And I don't think it should be touched at all. Because I think it will ultimately become a haven that people will want to come back to. A real place of worship. We're also extremely welcomed. Very well welcomed. Made so welcome by people there. And it struck me that the longer we lived here, how refreshing people were, because they're individuals. How politically incorrect everybody was. And I just love them for it. And how, on the whole, completely non-judgmental. Tolerant. Just accept people. For what they are, warts and all. By and large I think they do. And I think that's wonderful. And they're characters.

D.   Thank you, Khanikhah. Jolie, how old were you when you moved here?

J.   When we first moved to Ashley I was about fifteen. I'm in an in-between age-group in Ashley. There's a lot of people younger than myself, and there's a lot of people older than myself. So I've had to mix with people of completely different age-groups to myself. Which I've found very easy.

D.   You didn't mind that, even at the start?

J.   No, not at all. No. Because at the start I was at school, I was at William Hulme's Grammar School, and I had lots of friends there. So I've always had quite a comprehensive range of friends during my life in Ashley, which I've thoroughly enjoyed.

D.   And what sort of things have you done, since you've been here?

J.   Well, if I start with my music background. From the age of about five, I've always played the piano. And my piano tutor Robin Coultard was organist at Ashley. And I carried on my music tuition in Ashley. And he slowly but surely introduced me to playing in the church. And after about a year of sharing the services with Robin he left, and passed it over to me. And for six years now I've been the organist at Ashley Church. And because Robin was also resident organist at St Peter's Hale, I'm now second organist there. I do weddings and funerals, and odd services at Peter's. Which is very good, and I think at my age, as a teenager, I think I did quite well to get up Sunday mornings to play there!

D.   And St Peter's adds quite a big range of experience for an organist, doesn't it, because you've got a choir and all sorts of things.

J.   Absolutely. It certainly keeps me on my toes, playing at St Peter's, yeah. Now the other things that I do in the village: I've always been a keen lover of machinery. Many people will remember me driving round the village on an old grey Fergie tractor, which I got when I was fifteen, and got it roadworthy for my sixteenth birthday, and I used it as a car until I could drive. I went on to work on a number of farms around Ashley, but most importantly Peter Jackson's, Tanyard Farm. I started off doing the baling, bale carting, during the harvest, and then I progressed up the ranks to plough- ing and combining. Many of the major jobs on the farm. I've also worked at Tattondale Farm with Richard Reeves, and carted potatoes for Ian Crawford at Ashley Hall. I originally wanted to carry on in farming. So I went to Harper Adams Agricultural College, in Shropshire, and I did a foundation course in Land and Farm Management. As I was at college, farming sort of went down. Farmers were losing a lot of money, and of course the BSE crisis came in, and as I watched farmers around Ashley, and saw how farming was going I decided not to pursue my career in farming.
   So I left Harper Adams and did an apprenticeship with a tree surgeon who I'd known for many years. And then I worked with him for about six months, and did a lot of training - tree-climbing, chain-saw use and goodness knows what. Safety. And sure enough, round Ashley people got to hear about it, people started asking me to do little jobs for them, and I decided to go into it on my own. Branch out on my own, if you like! And I started my own business in tree surgery. Which has gone from strength to strength. I do a lot of work for the Woodland Trust now, and Tatton Estate. It's mainly forestry work - woodlands and stuff - which I prefer. But I do do a number of private jobs as well.
   Then unfortunately my father died last November. And ever since he went I've had sort of . . . My outlook on life has changed. Dramatically, actually. I suddenly decided that pruning trees for the rest of my life was quite a dim outlook, and I real- ly wanted - I had an adventurous streak in me - I wanted to make my mark on life. During this time I saw a video of Andrew Lloyd Webber's *Cats*. And something clicked in me. And then I thought, What a wonderful thing to do! to go into Theatre. I'd never really thought about it before, and I never realised I had such a love for it. And with my musical background I knew I would have, like a head start, if you like. Not having any dancing experience, but with a musical background it really would help. So I thought about this long and hard, and I decided to ring the Northern Ballet School up in Manchester. Whereupon I had a couple of lessons, with a third-year under- graduate in teaching, and they've given me a place, and possibly with a scholarship. That's for a three-year professional dancer's course. It's quite a contrast, but with my two loves in life, the machinery and the music, I've always had that contrast. And at one time I did think about going into the music world in quite a big way. But I actu- ally, living in Ashley, I couldn't keep away from the machinery. So I sort of pursued machinery and farming. That's about where I'm up to at the moment with sorting my life out, really. As far as earning money's concerned, anyway.

D.   It's very interesting the way that's developed, isn't it? And that the death of your father should suddenly have revealed to you where your real heart lay.

J.   It was. It was. I found it fascinating myself, and I can see the change in me. I'm utterly amazed really. From starting at Harper Adams, and then working through the tree surgery, I never really knew if this was the right thing for me to do. But this, actually, I felt that there was nothing I wanted more than to to go into the theatre. And of course my mother was in the theatre as well. It helps quite a lot.

D.   It certainly comes across, listening to you saying that. You're speaking with much more conviction than I've ever heard from you before. And I suppose you'll be able to do this from here?

J.   Absolutely. Yeah. Yeah, I can just get the Metro from Altrincham.

D.   Will you do that?

J.   I'm going to commute, I think. I don't like living away from home. Really.

D.   Of course you've had your taste of being a residential student, at Harper Adams, haven't you?

J.   Yes. And I enjoyed it. But I missed the village life in Ashley. I really did miss it. I used to come home at weekends and do the rounds, as it were. Go round all the farms. Because Ashley is such a close-knit community, and there being only just over two hundred and fifty people in the village, you can't sneeze without somebody else knowing about it. Which may seem a bad thing, and in one way it is really. But I think the big plus is that, it is, it's like a family. It's just like a big family.

D.   Have you yet got any sense of what people in Ashley think, how they've reacted to this quite dramatic change in your career plans?

J.   From what I've heard - I mean, I've taken a lot of stick about it in the pub, for example, - but I think that most people are saying to me, That's great! You're still quite young, and yet you've found these pathways to go for what you really really want to do. I think people in Ashley are mostly saying, All power to your elbow for doing this. The majority of people that I speak to in Ashley, and I'm very friendly with, are quite a lot older than me. I'm not saying they're all old, but I mean I'm only twenty now. And they've given me a lot of guidance while I've lived here. Working at Ashley Mowers from a very young age, I think about ten I used to work on Saturday mornings, I used to get a lift in on the milk float, it used to be the old dairy of course, and the likes of Peter Wright and Nigel, in quite a big way they've helped me along. And of course Peter Jackson.

D.   Yes. So it really does sound like an extended family.

J.   Yes. I don't think there's many villages around nowadays like Ashley. It's like a storybook village. But come true, you know. I mean, living here you forget about it. You don't think about it, it's just a way of life. But when you stand back and look at it, you can understand how people from outside - we do Bed-and-Breakfast, for example, get people from all over the place staying with us - their mouths fall open when we tell them what the village is like.

Arthur Lamont. South Lodge, Ashley Hall

A.   I was born on the 3rd July, 1934, in a village called Cotar Bridge, near Lockerbie in Dumfriesshire. It's just a small little village, about the size of Ashley: church, did have a shop, post office. And a pub. I went to school in the village school. We walked four miles to the school, uphill going there, so it was all right coming back. And then I went to Annan Academy, which is the nearest town, about six miles away. When I left there I worked in the village shop for about two years, and then I did my National Service in the Royal Air Force. I did three years, in the medical branch, and I was stationed in various parts of Britain: Cardington, Bridgnorth, Lytham, Inverness, Ely. And finally Hooton Park. And that's why I came into Cheshire. Now back home in Scotland our village policeman had always said to me, When you come out of the Forces you come and see me, and I'll get you in the police force. But of course I stayed in England. So the next step was to apply to Cheshire. I remember going to the interview with the Chief Constable, and I remember him saying to me, Could you be a servant of the public? So I said, Yes, sir. So he then said, Oh you're an ideal type we're looking for. Young fit man. Disciplined. It wasn't an interview at all, he just gave me the job. So after I came out of the RAF, two months later I was in the police force, and went to Crewe. I was only there a short time, and then I went to Chester. And I was at Chester five years, and I got married when I was at Chester, and we had two children there. And after leaving Chester I went to Congleton, and I was there for about six years. In the meantime I'd applied for various things, driving courses and so forth. I'd also applied to get a rural beat. And I got offered Ashley. I still remember the day when I came over to have a look at it, coming over the railway bridge from Mobberley, seeing there's the garage and the church, and the cricket pitch. I came to Ashley on the 4th April, 1965, and moved into the Police House. And at that time I was responsible for Dunham, Ringway, which included the airport, Ashley and Rostherne. The airport in those days was policed by a security force, not a proper police force. So I was the only policeman. It was a lot quieter in those days.

D.   Did you liaise very closely with the security force there?

A.   Oh yes. They were, when I say security, they had no training whatsoever. Odd ones were ex-policemen who'd come out for various reasons. Most of them were just gate-openers and closers, and that type of thing. Any criminal matters I had to deal with, so I spent quite a lot of time going up there. And because of that they changed my beat. They took away Dunham and Little Bollington, because Ringway was getting so busy. So up to 1976 I think it was the boundary changes came in, I was up at the airport every day. Of course we also had the swimming pool at Castle Mill, the famous swimming pool. You see there's some double yellow lines still, round there, which I had to get put down because the traffic was just chaotic. You just couldn't get through on a warm Sunday afternoon. The airport work was interesting. Used to see all sorts of people there, Royalty. Once I actually looked after King Hussein one night. He was going to London and it was fog-bound, so he had to come in to Manchester, and stay there overnight. And he actually invited me to sit down on the settee with him, and speak to him. What a charming man! I was there to guard him.

D.   So you were standing outside the door?

A.   Yes. He had a man in there in the Jordanian Army, a colonel, his aide. And they must have said, Oh, there's a policeman going to be outside all night. And the colonel came out and said, Oh the King would like to speak to you. So I said, the first thing I said was, How do I address him? And he said, Oh just call him Sir. So he invited me in, told me to sit down. I sat down on the settee with him. Started talking about - I remember he mentioned Manchester, and that it never stopped raining! That sort of thing. Just everyday chit-chat. And then he just said, Thank you for looking after me. And now, I've got to go and make some telephone calls. I was very impressed by him. And I sat outside the room all night. But there was no armed guards or anything like that, like there would be now.

D.   It's hard to believe. Only about thirty years ago, and only one policeman!

A.   Yes. It's incredible how things have changed. I was the only uniformed man anywhere near them. Harold Wilson, remember him. He sort of said Hallo and Goodbye type of thing. So there was a lot of that. And then we had the famous Moors Murder, which I got involved with. They needed some search teams to search the moors. There was a specific search team for the whole of the Force, and I was one of them. So I went up on the moors, for about six weeks. Probably five days a week. Searching the moors. Prodding with a cane. Sticking a cane into the ground for about four or five feet, pulling it up, and sniffing the end. The theory was that if it went into any rotting flesh you would smell it.

D.   What was that like?

A.   Well. . . I suppose we just took it as part of the job. When I was there we actually did find one of the bodies. The arm was sticking out of the ground. But I only just saw the arm, and the hand sticking up. And then we got some diggers in. The weather was dreadful sometimes. Late November time. Some days we could hardly see each other, it was so misty up there.

D.   Were you close to each other, sort of arm's length?

A.   Yes, in line, fifty yards at a time. About fifty of us in a line. So that we didn't miss any ground.

D.   What was the atmosphere like?

A.   Well when we found the body, it was terrible after that, really. We had to listen to the tapes that they made. It was all part of the identifying thing. It was horrific.

D.   How do you cope with a thing like that? Does it haunt your dreams?

A.   Yes. It would give you a sleepless night. And after a time you forget about it. You have to. A lot depends on the type of person you are. It hurts at the time. But you realise that you must get on, and you've got a job to do. Which was one of the things here, with knowing people so well. If it was somebody dying or something, you had to be careful and not let - although you felt it inside, you'd end up crying as well. And you mustn't do that. You can do that when you take the uniform off.

D.   Yes, it's not much good having a policeman in tears, is it?

A.   No. No, that's right. Although you maybe felt like it sometimes. As a matter of fact I did. So I was here from 4th April 1965 until the 3rd July 1989. It's a long time in one place. It was partly due to my domestic circumstances. I got divorced about a year after I was here. So I was left with two children to look after. It was easier to bring up two children here than to go into a town and work night shifts and things. Lots of neighbours helped. It worked quite well. Unfortunately my son John died. He died from a heart attack. Twenty four. Well it was a total shock of course, at that age.

D.   Did it just come out of the blue, like that?

A.   Totally out of the blue, yes.

D.   What had John done?

A.   Well he was a gamekeeper at one time, as a youngster, which I got him into.

D.   Here on the estate?

A.   No, he was down in Shropshire. That's another thing I was involved in here, the shoot in Tatton. I used to go every Saturday. Yes it was totally out of the blue, John dying. After he died, I decided to get back to work straight away. Some people took time off, but . . . I still miss him. But I've put it down as one of those things in life that happens. I try to keep a hard exterior most of the time. But it's hard. I remember going up to - you remember Nick Gregory died. I was walking up the road, I thought I must go up and see them, as I'd been through the same thing as them. And I got to the railway bridge, and I couldn't do it. I sort of broke down, and had to come back. Went up there gaily for about two hundred yards thinking, Oh I might . . . And then when it came strongly into my mind, I couldn't cope with it. Though the uniform of course helped a lot. It does put that shield up. You put that on, and you seem to have something to help you get through the harder times.

D.   Did you ever notice any other effects the uniform had?

A.   Well I always thought it was good the way there was obviously respect for the uniform, even though they didn't know you as an individual. That was in the initial stages. It did change as time went on. But here it wasn't the same as going into a town. The attitude of people was different. And I'd go out of my way to, particularly with the elderly people. There was a period at Christmastime, I had fourteen elderly people, and I used to take them Christmas presents. I can't remember how it started really. I think it was my neighbour, the policeman at Mere, he mentioned it once, and I thought, Oh I'll do that, that's a nice idea. Elderly people on their own. And Christmas morning I'd go round, take them a box of biscuits, or a bottle of sherry, or whatever was appropriate. And this went on for quite a long time. And it continued after I retired. And now there's only two of them left.

D.   It sounds as if it was a most satisfying job to have.

A.   Yes. It wasn't totally idyllic, because I was putting in a lot more hours than other policemen were. A lot of time that I spent working was my own time, when I should have been off.

D.   But when the children were young it must have been more difficult?

A.   Yes. There was one or two people who were very good. Eileen Mason was very good to me. Of course she lived opposite. So I knew that there was always . . . But I could fit my everyday sort of work into times when they were at school. They both went to the village school. Katherine, my daughter, she was one of the bright ones of that era. And one of Mrs Eaves' protégés. There were three or four very bright girls at the time. And she's now teaching in a school out in Northumberland. They're expelled children. So it's quite hard. And I've got four grandchildren as well.

D.   Do you still shoot?

A.   Not so much nowadays. I was very friendly with the old gamekeeper, Jack Armstrong. And I used to go out with him, doing things like long-netting. And occasionally it was a question of stopping work and putting a pair of his wellingtons on and an old jacket, and going out into Tatton Park. Rabbitting. And then of course I'd go out with the shoot on Saturday. Because I had a good gundog in those days. In those days a lot of the men that were shooting were ex-army colonels and the like. Military men. Totally different people. He was a character, old Jack Armstrong.

D.   He would have been Arthur Savage's predecessor, would he?

A.   Yes. He came to Tatton, he was one of Lord Egerton's keepers. Before the war.

D.   Is that how your son got interested in gamekeeping?

A.   Yes. John would go with me, when he was at school. And the days I was working he would still go. And all the men would keep an eye on him, obviously. One particular man especially. He used to pick him up, take him there, make sure he'd got something to eat. And through that, through the gamekeeper, we heard about this job for my son, and we went down to Shropshire. But he got a bit homesick, I think. But I very rarely shoot nowadays, unless I get invited.

D.   When did you retire, did you say?

A.   The very last day I could stay on to. I had to retire when I was fifty five, so that would be 3rd July '89. The event of my retirement, it was a wonderful time really. Some people said, You're not much of a policeman, you didn't know what was going on! I didn't have a clue really it was going to happen. You know, the band, the weather. Concorde flew over. And I've actually got a bit of video of it. A lot of the souls that are on it are not with us any longer. Like Tommy Molloy and so forth.

D.   So you really got a royal send-off! Can you tell us more about it?

A.   I'll just mention the Rostherne one first, which was an arranged thing where I was presented with an inscribed beer mug. And the local press came, and it ended up in the *Knutsford Guardian*. Then as time was going on I thought, Surely Ashley isn't going to let me go without doing something! And nothing was coming through. There was someone gave me a clue once, which I wasn't bright enough to pick up on. Anyway, this particular day Eric Cox, who's the policeman at Tabley, said to me, How do you feel about having a game of golf? I thought it was a bit of a funny time to have a game, but I said Oh, fair enough. So he came and picked me up. And of course from the Police House, after going a hundred yards to The Greyhound, he said, This is as far as we're going. And I could see a bus outside, and all lots of people. And then I twigged. And then the Greenall Whitleys Band struck up, and there was all these - I don't know, probably two or three hundred people from far and wide. People who I hadn't seen for such a long time, they'd left the village and come back for it. My goddaughter and her family had come up from Derbyshire. My own daughter and grandchildren had come from Northumberland. And I hadn't known about it. So somebody was very good at keeping it all very quiet. It was a real surprise. I have got a video of it, about ten minutes, which Nick Turnbull arranged. And looking at it now, there's so many people who've died since then. Which is rather sad. But it was a lovely time. Quite an emotional time, obviously, as well. I was delighted that they'd done that. It went way beyond what I was expecting, really. They'd gone to a lot of trouble.

D. And did you mention Concorde?

A. Oh of course, yes. During the afternoon Concorde took off from the airport, and of course the story was that they'd arranged it for me! But I don't think I had so much influence as that!

D. Nice timing, though!

A. Yes. And of course I had a lovely cake, an enormous thing. And then of course the Brass Band played all the appropriate tunes. It was lovely. I think it was Maureen at The Greyhound in those days; and Jean Dolan, and one or two others who were the main leading lights.

D. I wondered, yes. I wondered if you knew who they were.

A. Well, I worked that out. But it was a lovely time. It was a nice end to my service.

D. Also an indication of how much you are appreciated, I think.

A. Well, I was here a long time, of course. They get to know you. Sometimes it can be a disadvantage! But to be fair I don't think anybody took advantage of that. I enjoyed doing it, I think that was a lot to do with it. It suited me, the country life, my temperament and everything else. That's why I was here so long, I suppose.

D. Well I think it suited everyone. It suited you, and it suited everyone else.

A. It's just sad that it's all gone now.

D. It is sad, yes.

A. People are still ringing me now. After all this time. But it's nice that people still hold me in that regard, I suppose. So after I retired I got the chance of coming here, to South Lodge. Joe Mercer was moving to the Lake District, so I took the lease on after him. And when I retired I'd just started to take on a bit of golf. That's my main sporting thing now, golf. Two or three times a week. And the garden, of course, which is quite enjoyable. It's a bit of a slog, it's a big garden. I enjoy growing vegetables. Giving them away.

Peter and Rosie Raven and Matt. Willow Cottage, Lane End

D.   You weren't born here, were you, Peter?

P.   No. I came down to Ashley when I was about nine, having been brought up in Cumberland. My parents moved down to a bigger farm, and that was it. I left school and came down, about six months later. I came down, and I went to APS. From there I went to North Cestrian. I was still at school when I met Rosie.

D.   How did that come about?

R.   We met at . . .

P.   Oh, there was a local disco in Willowtree Road. Burrow's. And as it turned out Rosie went to school next door to us. To the convent next door, Loretto. But that was a coincidence.

D.   Convenient!

R.   Convenient, yes, because then we could meet up at lunchtime.

P.   We'd have been all of about fifteen.

R.   When we first met, yes.

P.   So that's . . . a long time ago! '73, '74. We didn't get married till we were twenty-four.

R.   1980.

D.   It just lasted, just like that? No on-off, nothing stormy? Just all . . .

P.   Lovely.

R.   Just the same, always.

P.   We gelled, didn't we? We gelled. So we got married in 1980, and came here.

D.   So you'd really been together about eight years by the time you got married?

R.   I was twenty-one when I got married.

P.   So I was twenty-two.

D.   So it was seven years? So you'd had a fairly good chance to get used to the family, Rosie?

R.   Yes. Yes, and I'd helped out on the farm. It was something completely different, not something I'd done before, even considered. In fact, I didn't even know Ashley existed! That's a terrible admission!

P.   Can you believe that, living in Hale?

R.   A lot of people don't know Ashley exists.

D.   I am the same. Nobody else has said that yet, but I was going to say it, and I'm glad to hear you saying so, because I lived around Hale and Altrincham since 1968, and I didn't know where Ashley was. We used to go to Tatton Park -

R.   So did we, we used to go to Knutsford to the May Fair!

D.   All it was to me was The Smithy. Turn right at The Smithy to get to Tatton.

R.   So it was something I'd never even considered, that . . . But you don't really. I'd never considered a rural setting at all.

D.   So what was it like, Rosie, when you actually moved in here?

R.   It seemed very quiet, dark at night. It took some adjusting to.

P.   It wasn't as busy then.

R.   I'd been used to a street lamp making my bedroom light. So it seemed very dark. And if we ever stayed at the farm, that seemed very dark and quiet. And yet you wonder really, because we have aeroplanes, and trains and cars.

D.   How did you spend your days?

R.   When I was first married I was working in Manchester, for an insurance company. I still used to help on the farm at weekends, used to do silage. And I liked my garden. That was it really, until I had Laura, which was 1982. And then it's been busy ever since!

D.   How did you find it, deciding what to do about schools?

R.   It wasn't a problem. It wasn't anything to worry about initially, because Laura went to Ashley School, although it didn't work out very well. So she left there when she was seven. It was then we re-thought our plans, really. We had Caroline by then, didn't we? Because of our experiences with Ashley, unfortunately, we didn't want Caroline to go. So Caroline went to Elmridge, where Matthew is. Now Matthew's gone to Elmridge. We tried to support the local school.

P.   We did try. The people who were then running the local school made life very difficult for Laura. There was no tolerance. I believe it's changed now.

R.   But apart from the teachers, with her peer group she had a nice time. And it was very sad that she left them. And when they all met up again at Knutsford High it wasn't the same, and she lost the links.

D.   That's really sad.

R.   It was sad. But with hindsight, she went to an excellent school, in Knutsford. It is nice. And she started again and made new friends, some of which she's still with now at college. So she made some very good friends. But it was sad, and we did enjoy the bits that we could enjoy at Ashley School. And the community. Because when Laura started it must have been a bumper year, I think there were seven or eight of them, all started together, all local, and it was nice.

D.   Then she went from Bexton to Knutsford High? How did she get on there?

R.   That was OK. And she's now at Mid-Cheshire College, at Hartford.

D.   That's a long way to go.

R.   She wanted to go there. The school encouraged them to go to Mid-Cheshire, they'd formed a link with the college. And in fact she used to go, for the last two years of schooling she was going to the college one day a week, to do a sort of link course. So she knew the college. Everybody else was going, more or less everybody else was going to do the same thing. So that's where she's gone. We did actually get her a place at South Trafford, which I thought might have been a bit handier, but . . . She goes there, and there's a college bus.

Matt.   They're a bit naughty though, because they sometimes turn people off.

P.   Just the odd time.

D.   Then Caroline is much younger, isn't she?

R.   Thirteen, yes. She's in the second year. Or eighth, as they call it now. Caroline's gone to Altrincham Grammar because I wanted her to go to a girls' school. I'd been to a girls' school, and I felt it would suit her. I also was quite keen to get her away from the situation which Laura's found herself in, only worse now, in that having gone to school in Knutsford for all those years, all her friends were inclined to come from Knutsford, so we always have to get in the car and drive to Knutsford. Which is a pain. Whereas with Caroline, on the whole it's a lot easier for me.

Matt.   Her best friend normally cycles round.

R.   Yes. And her friends can cycle out.

D.   I was going to ask: does she tend to go to her friends, or do her friends come here?

P.   She tends to go to her friends.

D.   Can we talk a bit about the farm now? What do you do down there? Are you and your father on your own at Lower House Farm?

P.   Cows, and some wheat.

Matt.   There's a mystery cow at the moment.

D.   A mystery cow?

P.   We got our numbers all mixed up.

R.   They've been looking for a cow for three days.

Chorus. THE PHANTOM COW!

P.   Three days!

R.   And it doesn't exist! This has been done before.

P.   It happens about once a year.

D.   It sounds like a game played for the VAT man or something!

P.   It goes beautifully. You know, we have numbers for here and numbers for there; so many cows over there and so many here. And then suddenly - something will happen. It's like a switch being flicked. Everything goes wrong. Suddenly there's one short in that field - and it's not here, and it's not there, and it's not with those: where on earth is this cow? And then usually, about three days later, we get *Oh hang on, didn't we put it over there?* And in the meantime it's walking up ditches, through the woods . . . So yes, it's mainly milk. We used to have a lot of beef as well, but stopped selling the beef, somehow.

R.   Since BSE. And the arable crops you grow, to feed the cows.

P.   And a source of straw.

D.   Has the herd changed much, over the years?

P.   When Dad first came down he used to have Ayrshires. We're black and whites now.

D.   That's interesting, because what I associate with you is those big white ones.

P.   Oh, Charolais.

D.   Charolais, yes. Do you still have them?

P.   No. No. No. Stopped that.

D.   So you did go through another phase?

P.   That bull, with all those white things, was called Rupert. And we had Rupert for nine years. That's a long time for a bull.

D.   That was when you were still beefing? Because what I can remember was the difficulty of the calving.

P.   That's right. But in the end, after BSE - we rear things cheaply, you know, off the farm if we can - but even so we just couldn't cover our costs. So we decided to use a Friesian bull to rear our own replacements, to try and make the herd -

Matt.   And now I've got a story to tell.

R.   No you haven't, we don't need a story now.

Matt.   Oh, flip! *The Cow that Thought it was a Bull.*

R.   No, no. Don't be silly.

P.   What, that red one? Oh yes, but that was before your time, Matt.

R.   We don't want your farming anecdotes, there's plenty of those.

P.   We were chasing a cow, and it ended up chasing us! It was like something out of a - what are those policemen called? - *Keystone Cops!* They're chasing the criminals, and then suddenly the criminals start chasing the cops. Twenty years ago. It was one of those things you never forget. This animal got stuck in a gutter. It got through the fence: I think it had calved recently and was looking for its calf, and it had gone into the gutter. So we managed to get it out and we thought, Right, well we'll get it out of this field and into, get it back with the cows. So there we are, shepherding it along. Dad had his old yellow car and he comes into the field. It's getting a bit silly, this cow, it's weaving, it won't go where I want it to go. In the end I start shouting at it and getting cross, and he came across in the car, and next thing, the cow turns on us! It's about turn! So Dad turns the car round while I run up to the car, press the button, and I jump into the boot, get carried down the field with this cow chasing after us!

D.   Chasing the car?

P.   Chasing the car! Oh, dear.

D.   It obviously thought its number was 666!

P.   Just minus one six and it would have been true, too!

R.   So you've basically continued the same really, all the time you've been here.

D.   So you stick to keeping a bull on the premises? You don't use AI?

P.   No. You've got to have a good-tempered bull. Because he comes through the farmyard twice a day with the cows. And this Friesian - normally a Friesian is a rather nasty bull - but this one isn't.

D.   Do you think part of the secret is treating them like this?

P.   No. We reared one, and as soon as we put it with the cows it went doolally.

R.   For two years it had been lovely, and it just went completely mad.

P.   We got this one off a chap we often get cows from. And he said It's a quiet one, and it is a quiet one. Never trust a bull, but he is very very quiet.

Matt.   And the good thing is, he can't charge at you because he's got a foot loose.

P.   He's got a sore foot at the moment. He's quieter than the cows. I can say that, because when we walk out of the dairy we actually have to go through maybe ten feet of collecting yard to get to the entrance to the parlour, and he's often standing there, where we walk in. And you just run your hands down his back, and he just stands there.

D.   Have other things changed much? Like the technology of milking and handling?

P.   Yeah. There's a lot more pressure now. Especially since deregulation. Your milk's tested every day now, whereas it might have been tested once a week. So you have to be far more stringent.

D.   Where does it go from you?

P.   Well ours goes to Hyde.

R.   We went with Waterfords when the Milk Marketing Board was deregulated. And then it became Avonmore. And then at the beginning of this year they became Glambia. Which is a new name that they've invented for themselves.

P.   Which is Gaelic for Pure Food. Then we got a letter the other day to say they're moving out of the liquid milk market, so they're going to sell it to Express Dairies. So it's all a huge circle, because I think, if I remember rightly, when we were with the Milk Board our milk went to the Express. Five or six years on, it's going full circle!

Matt.   We don't keep the cows with the calves. We split them up when they're born.

R.   Well that's normal. It's always happened.

Matt.   But some people don't.

R.   No they do, they all do.

P.   Matt, if you don't want trouble with your cow when it calves, get your calf away. The longer you leave the calf on the mother, when the split does come all hell breaks loose.

D.   So you do it as quickly as possible?

P.   We tend to, yeah.

R.   It's the bureaucracy that's changed.

P.   What's expected of you now: the hygiene. Especially since BSE, bureaucracy -

R.   The paperwork is ridiculous.

David Carr and Julie. 1 Lane End Cottages

D.   How did you come to be living in Ashley?

D.C. Well, I've worked for a local farmer, part-time, for the last eight years.

D.   This is Ed Blockley?

D.C. Yes. When we were given the chance for me to go and be his herdsman we decided that I would take the job, and we were offered, obviously, the house in the village, and decided it was a good move. To come more out into the country, because we lived in Alderley Edge before, on an estate. To come out into the country, even though I've been in the country most of my life, it was such a difference.

D.   You say you started, Dave, part-time?

D.C. I started part-time, nine years ago. I was self-employed, I ran an agricultural relief service where I'd go and milk for farmers at weekends, or holidays or whatever. And not long after I'd started, Edward was applying for somebody through a farming magazine. I just happened to ring up, and got the job. I used to do every other weekend, and a couple of times during the week when he needed somebody to . . . And when they moved up to Rostherne he said, Do you want to do a bit more? And would I come full-time? So as I was used to the place, and wasn't coming somewhere that I didn't know, I get on very well with Edward and his family, I just decided it would be a good move to make. And at the end of the day it's something that I've always wanted to do. Even though I'm possibly taking more of a part in farming than I was in previous years - you know, I do other jobs, I do - with being there full-time I get more involved with the cows and with the farm than just going every other weekend and doing the job and just coming home and forgetting about it. I'm more involved now.

D.   Are you saying that it takes more time? Or that it takes up more of your thoughts?

D.C. It takes a bit more thought, obviously, because you're like more responsible for the cows. You feel like they're your responsibility, and you're not just going every other weekend and doing it, and just forgetting about it, really, when you've finished on the Sunday evening.

D.   That's right, yes. So that this is much more now a job you tend to bring home with you, has become more part of your life, would you say?

D.C. Well it is, really, yes. Even sometimes, you come home and you're thinking about something, you know: what you've got to do tomorrow.

D.   Do you notice this, Julie? That he brings his work home?

J.   Yes, he does. Definitely.

D.   Can we turn to you now for a moment, and ask you what you do?

J. I'm a shop assistant in Alderley Edge.

D. Oh, you stayed in Alderley Edge?

J. Yeah. Well I've been there thirteen years, so. Yeah.

D. Did you both come from Alderley in the first place? Or how did you get to Alderley?

J. Well I lived in Wilmslow, and David lived in Mobberley. We had our names on like a housing list. And that's how we came to get the flat in Alderley Edge.

D. And then you moved here at some stage. Presumably this is part of the Blockley set-up?

D.C. Yeah. Yeah. The house is actually an agricultural house, tied in with the farm at Rostherne. It has its advantages, because I think nowadays the majority of people, if they're looking for a job in agriculture, they need accommodation.

D. Especially if you've got hours like that, you really want to be close enough to get home for breakfast.

D.C. And plus the fact, we find it an advantage: where you're not on the farm, you're actually away from the farm. You do get a bit of a break. When you come home, you're home. You're not looking out of your window and seeing the farm, thinking This wants doing, and That wants doing.

D. And every "Moo" you hear . . .

D.C. That's right, yeah! You'd wonder what was going on. It's nice to live away from the farm. But it's close enough to nip back for your breakfast, or make a phone call.

D. Sounds ideal.

D.C. I'm happy in my job. I've done farming since I left school. And I've actually worked on two other farms in Ashley, over the years. When I first left school I did a what we called in them days a YTS scheme, and I worked on a farm for three days and then I went to college for two days. And I actually started to work for Bill Davies, at Back Lane. And that's where I first started when I left school. Things have changed since then, and obviously in them days it was all shippon milking, all the cows were tied up, all the mucking-out was done by hand. It was all hay. It was quite a shock for me, because even though I'd worked part-time on farms while I was at school, actually when I left school and started work - I mean Julie will probably agree with this - after three weeks I wished I was back at school! You know, it was such a shock. I started in about the June time, and of course it was hay-making. And of course there was bales of hay absolutely everywhere. For someone to leave school: I mean, I left school on the Friday and I started work on the Monday. And to see all them bales, and to have to move them all by hand, it was a bit of a shock.

D. So you were really knackered, were you?

D.C. Ye-es, that's the correct word, really!

D. How long did it take you to get used to it?

D.C. A month, two months. It was still very demanding, because it was very labour-intensive in those days. There was a lot of us worked there, but everything was done by hand. We probably milked something like fifty, sixty cows in about three hours. Whereas nowadays I'm milking at the moment about a hundred and fifty to a hundred and eighty cows, in two hours.

D. And how many of you are doing that?

D.C. Just me.

D. And in the old days, when you were milking fifty or sixty in three hours, how many people would be doing that?

D.C. Four.

D. It's amazing, isn't it? And all that's happened in your working life. It's a revolution.

D.C. It is, really. Yes. And that's happened in what, sixteen years I suppose.

D. What about you, Julie? Did you find the transition from college to the shop more of a change than from school to college, or which was the bigger change?

J. From school going to college. It was a long day.

D. I think it is - much more in your case, with humping hay bales and so on - but I think leaving school and starting in a more adult environment, and adult hours, is much more of a shock than people actually realise. So your time is quite limited as far as spare time is concerned. It's not much use asking you what your hobbies are because you don't have time?

D.C. I suppose the only one I do enjoy doing, it's better with the light nights, I enjoy gardening.

D. Yes, I can see that from out here. All these things growing!

J. They're all in pots, aren't they?

D.C. They're all in pots at the moment. We have obviously got some beds round the house, but because we've just managed to clear it, straighten it up, we've not really got to the stage when we've decided what we want to put in. It's just things in the pots really, most of them being grown from seed.

J. Yeah. We've been given some.

D.C. Quick and easy to put it in a pot.

D.   I think it's very clever, all these pots. It looks very clever to me. And you've got this, like a lean-to, at the back, with a beautiful large area under cover: did you put that up?

D.C. Yeah. I put it up for Julie, with Julie's Dad. We cut all the timber, and put it up ourselves.

D.   So you can sit there and soak in the sun, and not get soaked by the rain.

J.   It's nice if you sit there when it's raining, and you can hear the rain coming down.

D.   Are there any other things that you enjoy doing, Julie?

J.   Not really, no. Sometimes I go to my family. In Wilmslow. My mum and my dad, and sisters. One sister lives in Alderley, and the other sister lives in Wilmslow, and my mum lives in Wilmslow. But we don't get much time to do anything else, really.

D.C. Plus looking after me! We've been meaning to go for a walk, just to discover Ashley really, because Julie doesn't know it that well. I was at Ashley Hall for a short time. I know it reasonably well, I know a few people in the village.

D.   Now Ashley Hall, that must have been quite a different sort of job.

D.C. Mainly tractor driving. Which gave me more experience. I don't know why, but I do sometimes get a bit fed up with cows. But I don't think I could be without them. I'd soon want to come back.

D.   Rum!

J.   Yeah!

D.C. Can't help it!

D.   Takes all sorts!

D.C. You're right, yeah.

D.   No! It's nice to find someone who's found something they can put their heart and soul into like that. Julie, I'm feeling guilty because I've been talking all this time to David.

J.   No, that's all right. I've been here about a year. I don't really know much about Ashley.

D.   Of course! I forget it's only a year. But you've been together longer than that?

J.   Yeah.

D.C. We've been together -

J.   A long time.

D.C. Long time. Since we were at school.

D.   You met at school? My word, there's not many that stay together from there!

[*Lots of giggling*]

D.C. Yeah, we met at school. Yeah.

D.   Would your schoolfriends be surprised?

J.   I think they probably would, yes.

D.C. Because some of them have probably been married for the third time! I think some of them would be, yeah.

D.   Yes. You're saying some of them would probably have been married three times by now. You might not want to answer this one, but here are you, who've been together all this time, and not got married once!

J.   We're just happy as we are really.

D.   Are you afraid it might rock the boat?

J.   It can do, sometimes.

D.C. We know each other's habits. I know Julie's moods, when they're coming! I've worked them out now, so that I can keep out the way!

D.   You make it sound quite like looking after cows, really! I don't know if Julie's going to slap me, or you! Do you see your neighbours much?

J.   Wendy and Roy we see quite a lot, don't we really?

D.C. Yeah, nearly every day.

J.   They've got a pair of step ladders they stand on, and we stand on the dolly tub!

D.C. So we can chat over the fence!

D.   It's a nice corner, Lane End. I should think it's a nice place to live.

J.   It is, it's lovely. Yeah.

Peter Jackson. Tanyard Farm

D.   Peter, you've obvously lived here all your life, but Tanyard Farm has been in Jackson hands for ages, hasn't it?

P.   Well, four generations. I'm the fourth. I have a son, Richard, who when he was born I was hoping would take over the farm. And at eleven he decided to be a vet, and I was most disappointed. But the way farming has gone, and the conflict I used to have with my father - you know, the different generations - we were arguing all the time. I loved him dearly, but we were arguing about farming, and he was miserable, and I was miserable. So when Richard decided not to farm I was most upset; but now it is the best thing he has ever done, because we would be in exactly the same position if he was farming. Farming is, to coin a phrase, "knackered", and I can't see any prospects in the future. Here we have diversified and gone into property; we've got horses. And the great thing is, I am master of this ship, what I say goes, there is no conflict. And to be quite honest I am very happy at the moment, very happy.

D.   Yes, that's really good news isn't it, because it could easily have been otherwise. Fancy Richard knowing so early that he wanted to be a vet!

P.   Yes. Now Sophie, she is a different ball-game. She is a fashion designer and travels all over the world at the moment. But you never know, when she has done the fashion bit she might want to come home to the farm, and if she did that I would be over the moon.

D.   Is she still actively horsey?

P.   No. Old Sandy, we had him put down last year, Sophie's first horse, when she was eight. We kept him in retirement about ten years, and I'm the only person he kicked! But we saw him through to the end, and he is actually buried on the field that he lived in all his life. It was virtually the spot where he kicked me, as well!

D.   But apart from old Sandy, horses seem to play a part in the farm here don't they?

P.   Yes, because you see we're near an area of a lot of money, and they don't want food because basically the only time people want food is when there is a war on, when there is a shortage. They don't want farmers at the moment. We're like the miners, surplus to requirements. So it's diversification. We've got eight or nine horses here in stables, and nine or ten for summer grazing.

D.   I suppose you have tried all sorts of things in your time?

P.   No. No, farming-wise I've always been with the pigs. There used to be about five or six people in Ashley with pigs, and I am the only one left. At the moment the pig job is very bad, but because I have got these other things I can afford to see it through a little bit longer. Whether there is any future after that I don't know.

D.   Now I thought there was almost an edge of bitterness as I heard you say, They only want us when there's a war on. Do you feel under-valued by the nation?

P.   Yes. Basically the Supermarkets have stitched everyone up. They get contracts with farmers: they don't pay them for two or three months; they keep altering the quality and standard of stuff they require; and if they can get it from abroad they don't hesitate to do so. The pig job, which you know I have had for twenty-odd years, we have had imposed on us a welfare standard. As I say the returns are very little, but as soon as ours gets too expensive they won't hesitate to go abroad and get it from cheaper sources, where it will be pumped full of antibiotics. They could be kept in the worst conditions out, but because they can buy it cheaper they won't hesitate.

D.   This is the supermarkets?

P.   Supermarkets. And you see, on the property side: we have one or two properties as well, small shops, but the supermarkets have taken them out, they're just no use at all, people can't make a living out of them.

D.   So really you're saying they are the contolling factor of not only the production side, but also the rest of the retail trade as well.

P.   Yes. And, you know, they're not getting it cheaper at all. They're buying pork at about 20p a pound, this is what it works out at when it leaves here, and it's in the shops at £2 and £3 a pound.

D.   And who takes all this?

P.   Well the abattoirs obviously take a certain amount, but mainly supermarkets. And they put it on offer, and it's still about £1.20 - £1.50, and it's supposed to be half price, and it's still five times more than we get. Basically I think farming as we know it has finished, and so the alternative seems to be horses and things like that.

D.   But you hear farmers saying that they came into the world to be farmers and to grow food, not to provide theme parks and leisure activities for the towns.

P.   But this is the way things are going.

D.   So, coming back to you and Ashley: you went to school here?

P.   Went to Ashley School, and then to North Cestrian Grammar School for the Sons of Gentlefolk. Oh, and with about two or three years at Altrincham Prep. School in between. Richard managed to avoid that, he didn't go to APS, he went to Ashley School until eleven. He went to North Cestrian. Peter Morton said that the sons are far cleverer than their fathers, because there were one or two sons of old boys there at the time.

D.   Well that must be a credit to the fathers!

P.   You reckon!

D.   So you went to North Cestrian. And then what happened?

P.   Well I worked on the farm for a year and then went to Reaseheath, did a year there and funnily enough I ended up as head boy, you know, top of the college. Which was a complete mystery to me, because I seemed to do nothing but drink.

D.   Then you came back here, and started quarreling with your father?

P.   Well, I started working. Yes, basically, that was it. I loved him dearly, but . . . Obviously you had ideas about what this should be doing, but obviously someone with a bit of age doesn't want to change. I wouldn't. He was set in his ways, yes, as I am set in my ways now.

D.   The last thing you would want is Richard breathing down your neck and telling you what you want to be doing!

P.   Yes. Oh, there was a lot of conflict. But unfortunately my father was ill, and I had to take over the farm at twenty-two, which was in some ways a little too early for me, but at the time he was ill and I was going to take over the business. And it was my sister's father-in-law, Edwin Stubbs, who said It's no good getting the business unless you get the tenancy. So I approached Derek Hall, and he said, No problem. I thought it was quite commendable of him to let me have the tenancy because there were one or two farmers' sons in Ashley that, once their father had died, that was it. They were off. When he died, oh about two years ago, Derek Hall, I wrote to his widow saying that I appreciated the trust that he had put in me. At twenty-two I had no sort of record of business acumen or success. The only thing that stood me in reasonable stead was that I had been to college. So the conflict in that case really didn't have to go on too long. I know if Richard farmed it would be exactly the same, and you know sometimes you're just not ready to hand over the reins to someone that's willing to take them. So I am very pleased that he's doing well in veterinary, and I am still plodding away without aggro.

D.   Where is he?

P.   He is in London at the moment, but he does locum work and he actually came back about three weeks ago and did locum work in Warrington and stayed at home when he was here.

The phone rings. It is Sophie.

D.   Does she ring in often like that?

P.   Oh yes, she is very close. But she doesn't expect to stay in fashion for the rest of her life. She says she wants to farm, but whether she does or not I don't know. But it's something she has a choice if she wants to.

D.   And Richard, has he settled to what he is going to do, or is he still going round various types of veterinary?

P.   Small animals, he is going to stick to that. Small animals are where the money is.

D.   Is he likely to stay in London?

P.   I think so, yes. I suppose it's where the money is. He's got one or two stars on the books, with their pets. I don't know who they are but TV stars, things like that.

D.   So now it's Darby and Joan for you and Hazel. How do you like that?

P.   It's quite nice to be on our own again, actually. We have a very good social life, we like walking. I used to love cricket when I was younger, and still play the odd game. I've tried golf, but I can't imagine it really getting hold of me.

D.   There is a report in *Ashley News* of a small triumph in clay pigeon shooting.

P.   Oh yes, that's a different story. We had New Year's Eve in The Greyhound. I was thoroughly, obviously drunk. Came home, had to do my work the following morning. Just felt like staying in bed all day, but John Erlam said he had this clay pigeon shoot, and would I come? And he rang twice, and everything was set up. And eventually I went. And shot everything in sight. I think I was very relaxed. Very relaxed.

D.   Do you often have shoots?

P.   Well I go pheasant shooting maybe once or twice a year, but I don't particularly enjoy it. I used to have half a gun in the Ashley Shoot and the trouble is the birds are tame, they don't fly out properly. In fact in one wood the beaters nearly had to throw them out. And when I joined this shoot they put some ducks on the land that we owned, and when we were carting bales these fifty ducks used to follow us into the shed, in a line, in single file. And then, come November, we had to start shooting them. Well, they got up, and they just circled round and round with various guns having shots at them. And I thought, this isn't sport. I couldn't do with it. So I dropped out after that. I've never been able to hit clays before this New Year's Day effort, so we know how to get them hit now!

D.   The social life around here, do you find it's mainly other farmers, or do you go all over the place?

P.   We do have a lot of farming friends, but mostly they are in other professions. I can think of nothing more boring than to go out with farmers all the time. They are good company, but you don't want them all the time. Inevitably you start talking shop, there are too many of you, but you get enough of it while you are working, without talking about it when you go out. I suppose in a sense we are lucky with our position here, because we have got Hale close, and that sort of thing. If you were in the middle of Northumbria you have only got farming friends and it makes quite a difference, to say nothing of not having North Cestrian up the road.

D.   Yes. I suppose Fate dealt you quite a good hand in decreeing that where the Jacksons had farmed for four generations was here, rather than the back of beyond.

P.   Yes. Yes. When the children grew up they weren't really out in the sticks because Hale, Altrincham and Manchester were close to and they are not really, you can't call them farmer's children, because they have been brought up in an environment next to a big city. I've lived in Ashley all my life, and there is a mix of very nice people. I can't think of anyone who really annoys me. There is no attitude of trying to "keep up with the Joneses", because there is a lot of money in Ashley in various families, and there is no edge to them. Which is nice. In some areas they let you know it, and look down on you. So yes, I think it's just like an ideal community.

Jeff and Maria Warburton & Laura. Dairy House Farm

D.   Can we start with you, Jeff?

J.   Good evening! I was born in Sale, but been here from birth. 26th July 1953.

D.   Good gracious! So what was life like as a child in Ashley?

J.   Idyllic. Long sunny summers, and all that. I was the eldest of four. There always seemed to be another baby coming every two or three years. But as a youngster I can remember farming was a much more busy profession than it is these days, because everything was more manual labour. We used to have a grain dryer in the farmyard there, which used to dry corn for local farmers. In those days it was all in bags, you didn't have bulkers, and we used to dry corn for farmers in Ashley and surrounding parishes. There used to be a queue of trucks outside when we were going to school in the autumn, with all these wagons parked up, with five or six tons in each wagon, in bags. And it was fed through the dryer, and you had to keep very close records, as it went through, to see you put the same amount back in as was tipped into the dryer. Otherwise people would feel they got short change. Also in those days there was a pea-viner in the yard, which again was for local farmers. They used to grow peas in those days, and cut the haum and carted the haum in complete with pods. And the pea-viner was static - because these days they're mobile and go into the field, and the pea-viner picks the peas, and it goes all the way through and comes out the back and goes straight for processing. In those days it was all done by hand. And my father used to be up all night on the pea-viner, and when we were kids we used to have to be very quiet in the morning, not to wake him up, because he's probably only come to bed at about five or six o'clock in the morning. And he'd sleep all morning. Because this pea-viner was going twenty-four hours a day.

D.   Is that how the machinery side of the business started?

J.   Well Father also, he was doing agricultural contracting work. Wythenshawe was being developed as a housing estate, with a lot of playing fields and recreation areas to be developed, basically going on from agricultural contracting to make these playing fields - things like ploughing and things; sowing a field in a farm, but doing it on play- ing fields. That's how it started, really. Before that he had a threshing machine, which was steam-powered. In the forties. And he had a big old steam engine, used to pull the threshing machine round the farms. That beam there, over the fireplace, that was put there by prisoners of war. During the war we had four or five prisoners of war working on the land, because there, obviously the men that would have worked the land were away at the war. Two or three of them were carpenters. They fashioned that beam.

D.   How marvellous, yes. Yes. And did they all go home?

J.   No, I think two of them stayed. I don't know if they stayed in this area, but I think there was two.

D.   I asked, because a prisoner of war, or an ex-prisoner of war, ended up on The Green. Must have married someone there. I'm interested, because until I'd started this book I'd not heard of prisoners of war. Not here. I remember seeing them on a farm in Herefordshire, but I hadn't realised . . . Of course it's obvious, they'd be everywhere.

J.   That's right. Well they were the - I suppose slave-labour.

D.   Yes. The thing that's so lovely about it, is that wherever they went there seem to be things like this beam: they actually developed a real affection for where they were.

J.   I suppose for them it was, rather than being sat in a compound, they were out doing hard manual labour, they were out - probably a lot of them were from farming backgrounds in Germany, and they come over here and were doing the same sort of things, and they got some purpose in their days.

D.   Yeah. I mean, better than being banged up in Colditz, like our people were!

J.   I suppose they got a rapport with who they were staying with. And they'd get fed better, as well.

D.   Yes, I suppose so. So it was probably quite a good deal. But it certainly is quite striking how much has been left behind in terms of little things like that, that you never actually hear about till you see it. So did you go to the local school, Jeff?

J.   No, I went to Altrincham Prep. School, and from there to Altrincham Grammar, so I didn't have any association. I can remember going to a - was it a garden party, or a W.I.? at the school. I won a five shilling National Savings voucher, for flower arranging. At five or six. And then they were having an auction, selling off a box of groceries. And it got to twenty shillings, or twenty-one shillings, and I stuck my hand up and I said thirty shillings. That was the first bid I ever made.

D.   And the last one, I should think!

M.   No! It's what he does all the time now!

J.   All our children went to Ashley School.

M.   Well that's what you said, you particularly wanted them to go to the village school because you regretted the fact that you hadn't gone to it.

D.   Of course you were there, Laura. What was your experience of the school?

L.   I think at the time I was there I really enjoyed it. I think it was good. In a bigger school you don't get to know everybody, only the people your own age. But because there were only maybe thirty people in the whole school you were mixing with people of different age groups as well.

M.   Yeah, but when you all got to eleven, or whatever age when you left, I did think to myself, Did we do the right thing? But now that they're the people they are, I think we did do the right thing. Because I'm really pleased with the way they don't judge people by superficial things, any of them. I really like that. Whereas the schools they've gone on to - not Knutsford - King's, or Tom went to Ryley's: it was obvious that a lot of children there judged people by different standards. And so, maybe they would have got better results at certain stages, but in the end I don't think that would have done them the same, as big a favour, as having a more open mind so that they can have the pleasure of knowing more people. I'll never forget Tom going from Ashley, going to Ryley's, and him coming home and saying, Why do they all ask me what sort of car my dad's got? Nobody's ever asked me that before. So I've absolutely no regrets about it now. I think it was the best thing.

L.   Some people when they moved up from Ashley were really shocked by so many people.

D.   That was my worry. But then I heard, later, that actually people settled down very well, if anything better. And Laura, what are you doing now?

L.   I've just graduated from Middlesex University.

D.   What were you reading?

L.   Philosophy, applied philosophy. Instead of Plato and Aristotle it was Ethics. I didn't like London. And you know why? It was because I grew up on a farm in a rural area, and I had big shell-shock at going to Tottenham. Having people shot down the road and things. It was a bit different from here. I had to persuade my boyfriend to come and work in Cheshire, because I can't live in his place.

M.   He'd always said he was going to live in London. But he's had to change his mind.

D.   And you, what are you going to do?

L.   In the end I'm going to hopefully be a social worker, but at the moment I'm just trying to find any job to earn me some money.

D.   So that's Laura. Who else is there?

M.   Jamie's after Laura. He's nineteen. He's very badly handicapped, he's just -

J.   Just finished school at Hebden Green. He's now moved into a home at Sale.

M.   Lil Stockdale's. In Sale. Which is, I think it's a miracle, isn't it? Because it's absolutely everything that I always thought he wouldn't have, he's actually got now. When he was little, very little, and we realised how handicapped he was going to be, my biggest worry about that was that he wouldn't ever have any sort of life of his own; you know, friends, anything like that. And he was pretty miserable here the last few years, wasn't he? Very miserable. I thought he was always going to be unhappy, really. But he's gone to this house, and he looks a different person. He's got this friend, Shaun, who - it's like they were meant to be together, they're just so similar. And he just loves it, doesn't he?

J.   We brought him home for dinner yesterday, and he'd just had a week in Lytham St Anne's, at Pontin's. They'd been out to three shows, they'd been out to the pub, and here there and everywhere, you know. They really lead a very active social life.

D.   What's the nature of his handicap?

M.   Cerebral palsy. He was a twin. Premature twins. And Jamie was the only survivng twin. And there are all sorts of problems that they have after that.

D.   How did you find this place in Sale?

M.   We had to go and see quite a few places, didn't we?

J.   Cheshire Social Services. There was three to choose from.

M.   No, there were about seven.

L.   Dad was probably asleep.

J.   Whoops! We went to one at Cheadle, which was for a lot older people. The main thing was that the children, or the young adults, there are of a similar age.

M.   Between nineteen and twenty-five. They are together in that house, six of them: that's their home for as long as they need it.

D.   And what do they do? Is Jamie likely to have any chance of employment?

M.   Oh, no. I mean, he can't do - anything. At all. He can't speak.

J.   He has to be fed. Has to be changed. Bathed. Put to bed. Got up. He's in a chair.

D.   Can he communicate?

L.   He's got amazing hearing. He hears cars coming over the cattle grid.

D.   So his reception's all right. What about transmission: can he express himself?

J.   Well, he laughs, or -

L.   Screams.

M.   We know if he approves or not. But if you try to find out what he wants, that can be a bit of an uphill battle! But all the things that he may have been awkward about here seem to have disappeared there. Then there's Kate. She's seventeen in August. She's at King's.

J.   She's in The Greyhound at the moment.

M.   In The Greyhound, waiting on, yes! At this moment. She's quite arty, isn't she? That's what she likes to do, really.

D.   What A levels is she doing?

L.   Art, Psychology and Religious Studies.

D. How old is Tom?

M. Fifteen. He's at King's as well. At the moment he's in Spain with my brother.

D. And very rugby-playing . . . Now how did you get into this outfit, Maria, in the first place?

M. Crikey! Shall I tell him?

J. I was a child bride.

M. Well, I used to be a stewardess. And I'd done a night flight, and had a crash when I came off it.

J. Not on the plane.

M. In the car. And I couldn't fly that night, so this friend of mine invited me to a party at a farm. And I said, I don't want to go to a farmers' party! She said, oh, go on. I said, No, they're really cliquey, farmers. But she said, Oh go on, come! So I went. And it was at Jeff's cousin's, in Lymm.

J. Stretton.

M. Stretton. And I saw him, and I thought, Oh, he looks very nice. But then when this cousin brought him over, he was so inebriated you would not believe. I thought, Actually I don't really like him. But he was very - . When he's had a drink he's very, very friendly. And very, Mmm, like soft! Anyway, he kept asking me to go out with him. And I kept saying No, but he insisted. Which wasn't my usual . . . pattern, people insisting. And in the end I thought, He's never going to stop. So I gave him my address. But he was so drunk, I thought, He'll never remember it anyway. So the next day, on a Sunday, I went to Mass about half past six, came home, and *West Side Story* was on, and I was really looking forward to it. And I sat down to watch it, and my father said, Do you know anybody with a green Range Rover? I said, Oh, No! Anyway, he was sober. And very nice. Different person altogether.

J. And it's all been downhill since!

M. So that was how that happened really, but I'd never really known any farmers before that. A completely different breed altogether.

J. Just flew over them. At a great height.

D. So how did you find it? It must have been pretty daunting, moving here?

M. Well by the time I was getting married and moving into the Cottage, it wasn't. But I remember when I first came into this house, I'd never seen a room as big as this apart from in an hotel. Or an Aga. The Aga was a monster. And when Jeff asked me to make him some cheese on toast I'd only been going out with him a fortnight, I'd thought I'd never see him again after this. But I did like the fact that everybody was very friendly. And then when we got married it was suggested I really want to join the W.I. I really didn't want to do that! But his mum kept saying to me, in the nicest way,

Aren't you going to come this month to the meeting? Anyway in the end, he didn't put pressure on, I don't think he did that, but he just looked so forlorn when I said, Well, no, I don't think so, that in the end I did it. And it was great. It was the best thing I did. I got to know all the people, and it was great.

D.   In what way was it the best thing you ever did?

M.   Well, because I think if I hadn't done that I would always have felt that, whenever we went to all these gatherings, I just felt that "Oh, this is that townie that Jeff's married to", you know. And then, when I was by myself with all these people I found they were just really nice. I think because they were always very interested in what you were doing. It was very genuine, you know. And because they all knew Jeff so well.

D.   The thing that's intriguing is, how similar that is to the story of Meg Wright, who married Peter and she was more or less - I won't say frog-marched! - but Peter's mum was one of the pillars of the W.I.; and I don't think Meg was at all reluctant, but I got the feeling - you know, young wife coming in, from town: not really much choice if you've got any sense.

M.   No, you feel in the end you're letting loads of people down.

D.   Jeff, one last thing: people often find themselves greeted outside Dairy House by what from a distance looks like a mating dinosaur, but actually turns out to be a JCB rampant.

J.   It's usually at Christmas or over the New Year. To liven things up. Put a bit of spark from Ashley into peoples lives.

D.   It certainly does that! How did it start?

J.   I think it must have been someone's fortieth birthday . . .

D.   Oh yes, and I remember one for Laura's 21st.

J.   And then there was Father's 80th last year.

D.   We've come to expect one for Christmas - but we had three this year!

J.   It's being innovative is the problem. But I rise to the challenge!

D.   It must be quite a rise to paint that message onto the shovel! But the most dramatic was the one that greeted the year 2000. It was on a blue background.

J.   That was just an old van I picked up from a scrapyard.

D.   And then painted it blue?

J.   No it came like that, I just did the signwriting. *Bye Bye '99, Hi 2000*, something like that. Just a bit of fun. We're the Blotts. Blott on the Landscape.

Ian and Heather Warburton. Dairy House Cottage

D.   Ian, where was your home?

I.   Here. On the farm.

D.   And have you brothers and sisters?

I.   Two older brothers and a younger sister. My two brothers, they have a separate business they run, and they buy, sell and break JCBs. On the same site. We all work on the farm. I run the farm and I'm the tenant of the farm. And it's a purely arable farm. We grow oilseed rape, we grow wheat, we grow barley, and we have set-aside. And we also have an agricultural merchant and a farm shop.

D.   How much land have you got here?

I.   There's approximately a hundred and fifty acres.

D.   And what seems to me like miles of fences. How much fencing is there?

I.   I don't know: enough, anyway. Maintaining them isn't too bad because, apart from cutting hedges, we put stock fencing round them all when I'd just left college, that was about twenty years ago, and they haven't needed a lot of maintaining. That should give about a thirty-year life.

D.   The other thing I associate with your stretch is cars going through the hedges.

I.   Quite right. We did have a problem. And I'm quite keen on conservation, and I know that the first four foot in height of a hedge, is of no significance to wildlife - because of how high foxes etcetera can reach up. So I decided that I would grow my hedges higher, which I have done across the whole farm. And also, in doing this, it has led to a reduction in the number of accidents that we have. I didn't realise this at the time, but what's happened is: on the bad bend in front of the house where ninety per cent of the accidents happened, people could drive over the railway bridge and they could see, when they were going at speed, right round that corner, they could see nothing was coming, and they would speed accordingly. And we were getting an accident about once every two months on average. But now, since the hedges have been higher, they can't see round the bend. And that slows the traffic, and we get about one every two years.

D.   That's absolutely fascinating, isn't it! Because it seems to be exactly the opposite of conventional wisdom. You know, people tend to blame hedges for reducing visibility, whereas actually what you've done is to reduce visibility, and that's reduced speed, and that's reduced accidents.

I.   It has. We didn't do it for that reason, but that's what's happened. And also, on the hedges side of things, we now cut the roadside hedges later.

D.   So that the nesting's over?

I.   That's right. And we also now cut the inside of the hedge bi-annually, in that we cut half the hedges inside one year, and the other hedges the other year. That means that the flowers which are produced on the hawthorns are allowed to set and have berries. Whereas in the past we used to cut them all every year.

D. Do you actually yourself notice the difference this has made to the wildlife?

I. We've not noticed, because we've only been doing this cutting for two seasons, I think the increase in songbirds that we've got, and wildlife generally, is more to do with the extra planting that we've put in. We've planted about four thousand trees over the last ten years, and I think the increase in wildlife habitat there has probably contributed more. And also, over the last fifteen years, we now use probably a third of the agricultural chemicals. And we accept a slightly dirtier crop, in that there is more weeds there, and we accept more disease than we did.

D. But it is acceptable? It doesn't stop the thing being an economical proposition?

I. It isn't economic anyway, I don't think, on the size we've got.

D. How many thousand trees did you say?

I. About four thousand.

D. Because there's a strip along the road I've always watched with great pleasure. And at one stage you had pigs running in there.

I. We did. Yeah, that was a more environmentally-friendly way of keeping the weeds down until the trees got going.

D. Have you ever thought of going full-blooded organic?

I. At the moment the system doesn't suit me, to go organic. To be organic you've really got to have it tied in to a livestock system. You've got to be a mixed farm. You've got to get your fertility from somewhere. And if you haven't got the farmyard manure to put on, from the livestock, you're going to struggle. And although I do the vast majority of the farmwork myself, with running the shop I haven't got a lot more time to go into the livestock side of things.

D. Do you have any help, or do you do it all yourself?

I. We contract out certain procedures. When we lost a member of staff we went to contract combining, and various other jobs. The rest we do ourselves. Or myself.

D. Just one last question on the farm, a thing that intrigues me: you're the youngest, and you've got the farm. Conventionally, the youngest takes third choice!

I. I'm not sure how that came about, but I think I was probably the one who was most interested.

D. I always noticed your father on his headed notepaper is "Eric Warburton, Farmer." Rather than "Eric Warburton, JCB Breaker." or whatever! As if that's where his heart is as well.

I.   I think Dad has many interests. Farming's just one of them. He's here every day. At eight o'clock!

D.   Thank you very much for that, Ian. Heather, can we come to you? Where did you start life?

H.   Well I started out in Godley, in Hyde. But we moved - actually it's a very complicated story,

I.   Keep it simple!

H.   When I was about four. Because my dad came to work for Ian's dad. So I lived here until . . . we moved to Timperley, and came back when I was nine.

D.   So you probably didn't actually go to school here?

H.   No. I went to Heyes Lane, Timperley. And even though we moved here, we still carried on at the other schools.

D.   So you moved here from having grown up in Timperley. You came to a completely different environment: what was it like for you?

H.   I think I just lived in a field with a horse! I don't think I knew anybody when I first moved here.

D.   So what was it like?

H.   I don't recall actually. Just going back to school, and living on the farm. And going out in the fields a lot. I think I was meant to live in a field, actually!

D.   And suddenly you find yourself with a field to live in?

H.   Yes. That was me. In fact, I think my life started when I moved here. I don't recall much before. I remember walking to school, which I didn't do when I lived here. But I always feel as if I actually . . . you know, life started when I moved into the countryside. I don't really recall it being very exciting, living in a town.

D.   So what sort of things excited you, in the countryside?

H.   I think I was a tomboy. You know, climbing trees and making wooden huts! And playing. I think I was probably very immature compared to today. Nine-year-olds today wouldn't be doing that sort of thing.

D.   Some nine-year-olds wouldn't be. I know one who would! My granddaughter would be doing that, for one! So when did horses come on the scene?

H.   As soon as we moved. I think actually I'd lived for having a horse. Even though I'd never seen one or ridden one. I think that's what life was meant to be for me, because I always used to be horse mad, before I'd ever even seen one.

D.   Did you find yourself riding naturally, or did you have lessons?

H.   No, I didn't have any lessons. I had a pony, and that was it. Yes I didn't have any lessons, I taught myself to ride. And Bill Davies taught me to ride. By swearing at me, and shouting at me! "Get your *beep beep* heels down you sack of potatoes, or I'll hit you with this whip!" He was a wonderful, wonderful chap, Bill Davies. I think he was an adopted grandparent, when it came to horses. He always liked to appear quite hard and tough, but underneath he must have been a big softy. Because he was very good-hearted. And he sorted me out with my bigger horse. He got Robert and Michael to tame it, ready for me to ride. Yes, he was a great chap.

D.   Have you gone on with horses?

H.   I still ride. I'm still horse mad, aren't I?

D.   So how did you two meet?

H.   We met at Ian Daniel's twenty-first. And the reason we met was because Mike Davies called Ian across to sit next to him. And I was sat next to Mike Davies. So that's very local, isn't it?

D.   Gosh that is local, yes. So Mike Davies was - had something to answer for!

H.   Mike Davies and Ian Daniel.

I.   Well it was the only empty seat left! I got there late, from combining peas. I actually thought twice about going. I was sat on the combine, I could keep going for another two or three hours.

H.   His mum told him he had to come. Didn't your mum tell you you had to come? I don't think we would have met otherwise, because Ian's not very outgoing, are you? Or you weren't.

D.   Tell me about the children.

H.   Henry is ten, and Amy is thirteen.

D.   What are their interests in life?

H.   Henry's a commando, isn't he? A commando, tree-climbing . . .

I.   . . . normal country lad! He enjoys being in the countryside. Running round.

H.   We asked Amy the other day, actually, whether she'd rather live in Hale with her friends, be in with the crowd, or live here? And she said she'd rather live here. And yet she is very interested in doing everything they do. But she said she just likes living in the countryside far more.

D.   Did that surprise you?

H.   It did a bit, because she doesn't do an awful lot of riding or whatever, and she does do lots of sports at school. You'd think she'd like to be closer to school. She must appreciate living in the countryside. And Henry just loves being in the countryside.

Can't imagine, the amount of energy Henry's got, I just can't imagine him living in a town. There'd be no garden big enough.

D.   And how about when he has his friends here? I mean, a farm is full of all sorts of places where children could be in danger, I imagine.

H.   They know their limits. Yes. They have to learn them quite early. The heavy plant is out of limits.

I.   You have to be very vigilant, though.

H.   We do watch them. Most of the farm machinery is kept on the other side. And the children have free range round here.

D.   And do you find that the visiting children are reasonably obedient, or are they tempted?

H.   They're tempted to want to go and sit on tractors, but luckily they're quite good children. And the first time they come we explain to them that they're not supposed to. We had one child that has tractors and whatever; but I think you've got to be quite firm with them. And it is a workplace as well as a home. And I don't let them run around willy-nilly down the fields. Perhaps I'm quite a, sort of, I don't know . . . I'm very caring over them. If they want to go down the fields, I usually go with them. Because you just don't know who's around nowadays. I mean, there's big woods down there. It's lovely and tempting to go and run around in it, but there could be any person there. I think that's where society is, a bit. It's very hard for children, there is no freedom for them.

D.   But it sounds as if they're happy, and enjoying life.

H.   They are. They're both very happy. I think Amy's probably more academic. She wants to be a vet or a doctor, she's saying at the moment. Whether she'll ever be either of those, I don't know. But she's a very maternal person as well, she loves children. So I can see her just being . . . you know, she'll just be happy. And I don't know what Henry's going to do. It would be nice to think he'd go into farming, but it's not an option, really. It's not a big enough farm. I don't know what he will do. He's very creative. I can see him doing something constructional. Or the army! The opposite!

D.   He sounds as if he might be a bit like your father.

H.   Yes. He's very close to Ian's dad. Ian's dad. Because they're - you know you were saying about your father and Sophie? Well, it's the same with Henry and Ian's dad. He's always going over to Ian's dad, and they spend quite a lot of time together. In his workshop. Build things together. And he is very much into buildings and things. So it could come from both sides. But Ian's dad, I think he has a twinkle in his eye with Henry. Henry wants to be called Little Eric now. He's called Henry Eric Warburton, and he said to Grandpa the other day, he's decided he's going to be called Little Eric. He's changing his name! So I think he must admire his grandfather a bit, to say that.

Ian and Julie Crawford. Ashley Hall

D.   How long have the Crawfords been here? '72 you came?

I.   '72, yes. We came from Carrington. At the time the Shell Oil Refinery wanted the farm. We were only tenants, and were told to leave. So we had nowhere to go; Father always wanted to own his own farm, and looked all over the country, went to Scotland, went to Lincolnshire, Norfolk, all over the place. Nothing materialised. Then out of the blue Tatton Estate phoned him one day to say the Walkdens were leaving. Walkdens had been here for two or three generations. And Ashley Hall was the place. So we came here in '72, took over a dairy farm. We were arable at the time. And we ended only six miles away from Carrington.

D.   What an extraordinary story!

I.   And he'd looked all over the place.

D.   Do you still farm some land over at Carrington?

I.   We still farm the farm, although they demolished the farmhouse, expecting to bulldoze through the whole farm, so that they could keep on building the oil refinery. It was when the oil crisis was at its height, and ever since the factory has gone smaller, instead of expanding. Now there's very little there, there's hundreds of acres of wasteland and the factory fence. So they never needed the farm, and they never needed the farmhouse and the farmyard that they bulldozed. So it was a complete waste. In recent years we've seen Manchester United taking a hundred acres, next door to us on Carrington Moss, the best farmland in the country: taking it for a training ground. Why they couldn't have used land anywhere else I don't know. I'm concerned that they're going to swallow the whole of Carrington Moss, in the near future.

J.   They've got a lot of airport parking as well there, haven't they? At Carrington. Is that the same place? And they've got a huge yard full of cars, brand new cars for garages. Airport parking for people who go away on holiday or on business. It's a real shame, because it is, it's very good farmland.

D.   Is this all on the part that was taken over by Shell?

I.   The airport parking and the car dump is Shell land, and Shell have now sold a hundred acres, another hundred acres to Manchester United, to provide a training ground. Which is only a metre away from us.

D.   How much land have you got, are you farming, down there?

I.   Four hundred and twenty acres.

D.   And what have you got here?

I.   Altogether, about twelve hundred and fifty acres. That's Carrington, Ashley, Knutsford and Mobberley.

D.   Can I ask you Julie, now, how you came onto the scene?

J. I was living in Hale at the time. And funnily enough I didn't realise this was a farm. I could see it out of my bedroom window, but didn't even know it was a farm. Some friends of mine who live in Ashley were having a Sunday afternoon birthday party, and asked me if I'd like to come along, which I did. And I was chatting to a few people at this party and didn't see Ian until the end of the party. He just came across to me and said, You're not horsey are you? I thought, Well what an introduction that is! Anyway, which I'm not. I'm not. And that was the only conversation I had that time. And then next day Ian phoned me and asked me if I'd like to go out to dinner.

D. Having established that you weren't horsey, you were probably safe! Part of the screening system.

J. And funnily enough, now we've got Olivia he's quite into horses, quite keen for her to ride. So I don't know what came over him that afternoon, I don't know why he said it. It was just a chance to get to chat, I suppose. And that's how we met. And we started going out in the April, and then we got engaged at Christmastime, and got married the following year. So that's how we met.

D. And when was this?

J. Six years ago, now. We've been married for five years, and we've got Olivia.

D. How was it for you, coming out here to live?

J. Well, not very different from Hale, really! Very convenient.

D. It's so close that you kept in touch with all your old friends, and things like that?

J. Yes. And James was at school in Bowdon, so it was just a matter of turning the other way out of the drive, really. It's been so convenient, it really has.

I. She missed street lights and ice cream vans.

D. And what do you do, Julie? I mean, you've obviously got your hands full.

J. Well I'm working. I'm a chiropodist. So I do home visits, chiropody home visits. And I've just started working at an estate agents in Knutsford, which I enjoy.

D. Doing their feet as well? Diversifying!

J. No, I really enjoy that. So since Olivia's been going to school more often, because she's four and a half, she'll be in full-time school in September, I just thought it was about time I did my bit. So I'm doing a bit of part-time work. I'm enjoying it, and Knutsford's so handy. It gives me a good insight into the thing which I enjoy.

D. That was the other thing I'd been wanting to ask you about: about what you've been doing inside here?

J. Well we've been trying to put some of the original features back. It's been covered up really. This kitchen, for example, was two rooms. And we've uncovered all the beams, and put it back into one room. This was originally the kitchen.

D.   And so now it's come back to what it was?

J.   It's come back to being the original kitchen, and it's almost as if that little space there was made for that Aga. We just undid the chimney breast, didn't we? and uncovered it. And now we've put the Aga in.

I.   It's a huge hearth there.

D.   It must have been exciting to find that.

J.   And also, not long ago, I had a lady contact me from the Georgian Society, who was looking into the history of people who'd lived here years ago, the Ashetons. And she's done a bit of research into it, and given me all the information she's found about the people who lived here, the Ashetons and . . . Who were the other people?

D.   Breretons?

I.   Breretons.

J.   That was really interesting. She came out one afternoon and we had a chat about that. I'd like to get hold of some of the original information about what happened to the house, because it was a lot bigger, wasn't it? And to see if we could piece it all together, what was built. Some of it was demolished. The ballroom went.

D.   And I was saying to Ian, All these years I've been walking past here, and I'd never noticed until this evening what a beautiful building that is on the left as you approach the house, that Georgian stable block. Absolutely beautiful.

J.   They are lovely, aren't they? In fact we had somebody who came here, and he modelled a new building that he was designing on these stables and outbuildings.

D.   Yes, I don't blame him. And the wall in the hall that's been uncovered, is that your work, Julie?

I.   I was just showing David where we had the flood last week, and uncovered some of the original wall covers which were dark green, very similar to the wallpaper you put on the wall now. It's uncanny how similar it is.

J.   We had a decorator who came round, because you know we had a flood a couple of weeks ago, and he came round today, and he's tapping the walls saying, Is this wattle-and-daub? or is it plasterboard? All the walls are different. Nothing's consistent. So he's going to have a bit of a job trying to patch all that together. But we're pleased with the house, it's really coming on. Getting back to how we want it. We've got a few original features, there's the original Adam fireplace, and I think there's an original fireplace in the sitting-room, which we stripped back to wood.

I.   That was in a panelled room, a panelled bedroom, the Cedar Room, which was upstairs. That was where the priest hole used to be.

D.   What about the garden? Who does the garden?

I.   Well we have a gardener who comes in once a week. We did try to do without a gardener, but we just can't . . .

D.   Who decides what the gardener does? Because it looks very nice out there.

J.   A lot of it's been here a long time. So it's just a question of maintaining it. But there is a little garden we've got, just through the side there, and a friend of mine and I were discussing having a little Italian garden. We're going to try and plant a camomile lawn. Now I know it's a really old-fashioned idea, but we thought we'd try it. Haven't got round to it yet, but it's on the agenda for when we do get round to it. Because apparently the Victorians liked it, didn't they? camomile lawns. So we thought we'd have that, with a little cottage garden with hollyhocks. All the old-fashioned flowers and shrubs. We have a few geese and a few hens, that keep the paddock down there, and a few sheep that keep the paddock down over there. So they're quite useful. Labour-saving, I should say.

D.   I'm glad you mentioned that, because one or two people do that. I'm glad you do as well. But you use geese, as well as sheep?

J.   Yes. And they're good at guarding the house. We have a lot of trouble with foxes here. They come from Hale. So we just have to keep our eye on the geese and the hens. But no, we've kept these for quite a while. But they've even taken baby lambs from here. So they're a bit of a nuisance to us, aren't they?

I.   They're all Hale foxes, you can tell.

J.   Well they're very brazen, aren't they? these foxes. They're not a bit shy or timid.

D.   Probably like these wretched squirrels, I expect people feed them.

I.   And magpies. But our songbirds are definitely coming back. Our bird population has increased tremendously.

D.   Now, talking of bird population: I noticed as I was walking up, your hedge the other side of the motorway seems to be a couple of feet higher than it used to be.

I.   We've been trying to grow the hedges taller, to encourage wildlife. Twenty years ago we used to cut the hedges down to about three feet. Nothing could ever live in there. So they've increased. We cut the roadside hedges twice a year, the field hedges once a year, but we're going to cut the field hedges once every other year. Partly for economy, but also for berry production. Conservation costs a lot of money, but that costs you nothing. Conservation has to be paid for out of profit. There's not much profit in farming now, so conservation has taken a back seat.

D.   What do you mean by conservation?

I.   Planting trees; re-planting hedges; re-fencing. But not cutting your hedges, although it might look a little bit messy, it helps. Years ago we used to dig ponds out and plant trees. We planted wildflowers and all sorts. That's finished now.

Geoff and Betty Platt. Coppice Cottage

G.   With living in Cecil Road in Hale, I always visualised a cottage in the country. We knew we couldn't afford to buy one. And this one, we saw this one. So we got to find out who the owners were, and it was Meller Braggins, the Tatton Estate. Mr Hall. And he gave me the keys and said, Well if you're prepared to do the groundwork. The old Bucklow Council, as it was in them days, had condemned it. And they gave me a list of page after page, of what wanted doing. There was no electric. There was just one cold tap. There was no drainage, the toilets were outside, up garden.

B.   It was, it was condemned, wasn't it?

D.   Was this already - you mention Mr Hall - was this already Mr Brooks, the landlord?

G.   He'd just taken it over. He'd just bought all the estate over. And we just worked on it for about two years, every weekend and every night. To get it liveable. Septic tank, drainage, electric. I did the bathroom myself, obviously.

B.   This was two rooms. Door here. An old pantry there. It was a wall there, there was no bathroom. No other bedroom. There was no porch on. There was no electricity, there was just nothing.

D.   So you've really completely transformed it. Rebuilt it, really.

G.   They've always said we'd get the first, if they put it on the market we'd get the first chance. But they won't. They just won't. He may do now, because he's mellowed a bit, Randy. But old Mr Brooks would never sell anything. Having got in here, Mr Hall said he didn't see why his tenants shouldn't share in the workload. Because none of the farms round here had bathrooms. And we did, well nearly every farm in the Tatton estate, we went round. Bathrooms, toilets, you know. We had a good agreement with Mr Hall. We didn't do all of it by any means, but we got our fair share.

D.   You had already got the plumbing business established?

G.   Yeah, well my boss died. And I was only, what was I? twenty-three. And he died, and we had the chance to take the business over, so we did. And ever since then I've just worked on my own.

B.   So Dale now works with his father.

D.   He's still with you is he?

G.   Yes, he came straight from school to me.

B.   He's thirty-five now. Will be on the 1st July. Ian's thirty-three. Andrew will be thirty-one in September, and Karen's twenty-nine.

D.   Dale, he's the eldest, and he's with you. Where does he live?

G.   Alsager. He comes down here because he's kept on most of my business. I'm semi-retired, but I muck in with him here and there, give him a lift every now and then.

D.   But apart from that, he's on his own, is he?

B.   Oh yes. He's self-employed, yes.

D.   So that's Dale. Next we come to Ian. He's thirty-three. What does he do?

B.   He works for a mobile phone company, Telecommunications in Altrincham. He lives, just moved from here, only a fortnight ago. He's gone to live in Cheadle.

G.   He's renting a house.

B.   And you know where Andrew lives, don't you? He lives in Mobberley. Just off Wood Lane there.

D.   His business looks as if it's doing very well.

B.   Oh, he's never short of work, Andrew. And then Karen, she's twenty-nine, lives in Maidenhead. She works for Lex, the vehicle leasing people in Sale. And she got the opportunity to go to Head Office. So she went. She's been gone now just over twelve month. She's got a boyfriend now. I think if she hadn't had him she's have been back home, but . . . Because she is a home bird. They all are.

D.   Yes, it sounds like it. The cooking's too good!

B.   Ian come round yesterday, didn't he, and he said, What time are you having lunch? I said About half-an-hour, he said Can I have some?

D.   Yes, I told you the cooking's too good!

B.   Yeah. So that's them four. They all went to Ashley School. And there was Ian, Andrew and Karen were all born in this house. The other was born in hospital. And the three were born in here.

D.   And what have you done? Apart from bringing up four children, which is quite enough!

B.   Well, I've got a job. I work in Hale Barns. I'm a housekeeper. And the lady I work for, I've been with her twenty-seven years. On 2nd May I've been with her twenty-seven years. When we first came to live here there used to be a bus stop outside here. And where my washing line is, if you look out there, that was the bus stop. And they gave me the post.

G.   Because she had her washing line tied on it. When they come to take the sign down, Oh I'll leave you this, love, he says, I'll leave you this.

B.   I used to have my own post, but it snapped. So Geoff put it there. It's in the hedge, you see. So with it being a steel one, Geoff put it round and tied it for me. And Dale came in when he was about this big, and said, Quick, Mum! The man's taking the bus stops down! And I had a line of washing out. And he says, It's all right love, he says, I'll leave you the post. You can have it. It's still there now. Because the bus stopped here every two hours. This road was so quiet. And now it's just like the main road through into Knutsford, now. It used to be nice to walk to Altrincham with children in the pram. Into Hale. I didn't pass my test until our Ian's first birthday. I'd already got Dale then. So I had two children. I used to walk into Hale. Those were the days! That's when you could walk.

D.   With a pram and a toddler.

B.   You couldn't do it now. I wouldn't like to do it.

D.   Has your business changed much, plumbing, over all these years? Materials must have changed.

G.   Yes. We've had to adapt in a big way. You've got to be able to master most things within the building trade now. Within your capability. We never take on anything that we're not sure of, as regards brickwork and joinery. Otherwise you'd never survive. People say to me now, when we get a hard frost, Oh, you must be rubbing your hands! All the bursts and all that. But if we had to rely on frost bursts in this day and age, we'd be out of business. Because everybody's got insulation, everybody's got central heating. The odd outside tap gets blown off, but as regards that sort of - that's why we've had to adapt to other things. I've seen quite a few changes in the material-wise. And that's why you get so many people doing it themselves. Well, they try to do it themselves, and I usually get a ring on a Saturday or a Sunday afternoon, "I'm trying to change my washbasin, and I can't get this . ." "I'm just putting a floorboard down, I've nailed my pipes."

B.   On January 7th we'll have been here forty years. In the Millennium. And when I came to live here, with coming from Manchester, people said to me, they give me twelve months in here. It was too quiet. Friends back home. They said, You'll never stay, it'll be too quiet for you.

D.   And how did you find it?

B.   I loved it. From the day I came. I'd never like to live anywhere else. Even when I went back home. It wasn't the same. You got no bus service, and no street lights, and you're miles away from the shops. You're away from town. And I said, Well, you can always go in to town, can't you?

D.   Still, it must have been like another world.

B.   It was. Living in the country, after living in Hulme. And in Partington, I was only in Partington for five weeks. And we moved in here on January 7th.

D.   You used to come down here for your day out?

B.   When I was younger. In Manchester. We used to get the train from Old Trafford. And we used to come down here, in our summer holidays. You know, a lot of us. Go down the Bollin for the day. Never dreamed I was going to ever live here.

G.   You used to swim in the Bollin.

B.   Used to swim in the Bollin in them days, yeah. There was a bit of sand, wasn't there? But never dreamed I'd ever come to live here. Used to get the train from Old Trafford to Altrincham, and get the bus to The Wolf. And then we used to walk it. Round the back there, down South Road.

G.   On a Sunday you'd get, on a pleasant afternoon you'd get forty or fifty families down there. All with their kiddies running about.

B.   And a picnic!

G.   And paddling in and out the Bollin, because the water was cleaner then. It was only since all the factories started pouring, the dye factories from Macclesfield, started pouring all the pollution in -

B.   You couldn't swim in it then, not after that. When we was children you could see your feet at the bottom of it. We wouldn't have gone in if it was dirty, but I mean it was really nice. I was only about, what, twelve.

G.   How it's changed!

D.   Mind you, I'm getting the impression it might be changing back.

G.   Yeah I think . . . The Environment people, they're always up here. Doing tests on the water. Improving the drainage, and checking drainage.

Joan Newton. Coppice Farm

D. How did you come to live in Ashley, Joan?

J. Well it was me dad. He was with Clibrans.

D. Had he always worked for them?

J. Oh no, he was in Staffordshire. He was in the army in Egypt. And it was Staffordshire he came from, Swynnerton. And it was Lord Stafford's. That's where he lived. And he said he wasn't going to go back "behind the walls", working for his lordship. He wanted another place. So his brother had married my mother's sister and had the Nursery up here, you see. That's how he came. My mother and he went on their bikes down to the nursery here and Mum said, Go and see if you can get a job. So that's what happened.

D. Where was the nursery?

J. In Bankhall Lane.

D. And that was before they were married?

J. Yes. Yes, that's right, yes. They didn't marry until 1924. And he had this job, you see, he used to cycle to. He lived in Ringway, you see. Then they got married and then they they went to live in Mobberley. We went to Mobberley. That's where I was . . . No, I was born in Ringway. Because there was a little old school there, that's where I was baptised. There was no church. Because it was Northenden Church, you see, that was too far off, and I was baptised in this school building. Then they moved to Mobberley and that's where my dad got a motorbike, you see, and came to work on a motorbike. We had just rooms.

D. And where did you go next?

J. Frampton Road, in Hale. And that's when he got, he got chargehand, you see. In the greenhouses there. The half-hardy department, it was called. Then when he got foreman we went to Green Lane, Timperley, you see, and he was foreman over there. That's where the trees were. Then my dad's nursery bit was there as well, but then they moved. They had conifers there, you see, and trees and they moved it after because - this was later of course - because there was a gasworks there. Just beyond our house there was the golf links, Timperley golf links, and then there was the gasworks where everybody's gas was made. And it was affecting the plants. So they moved them. He got the Birkin Farm then. They rented Birkin Farm from Lord Egerton you know, it was Lord Egerton. And that's why he went to the Birkin, for the trees.

D. And was your father in charge of all that?

J. Oh no, no, no, no, there was a foreman there then, Mr Kennely. Then Dad got this foremanship of course at Timperley. Then they moved him to here, into what they called the American Department, I don't know why it was called that.

D. That was here?

J.   All those fields there. Forty-odd acres it was. '37 it was he came here, I remember that. And then they got the Mill for the fruit, where Mr Laxton was foreman. That was the fruit nursery.

D.   It must have been an enormous operation.

J.   Oh, it was. When my dad finished as manager he had three hundred and odd men under him. As the manager. There was the tree department, the fruit department, this American department, and the roses at Timperley, that was the rose department because there was no greenhouses there then. And then there was the greenhouses at Bankhall Lane. Then there was the seed warehouse. They had seeds, you see. George Barton, he still lives in Bankhall Lane, he was in the seed nursery. And then there was the other part, they used to call the packing shed. All the trees used to come to the packing shed and were packed. He used to go there and pack the trains, you know, with the shrubs and trees, send them off. Because when he got the Land Rover we used to go all over the place, all over England. Where they used to sell the trees.

D.   Going all over the country?

J.   Yes. Yes. Clibrans did. It was a terrific place.

D.   It seems so extraordinary that there should have been such a huge concern, and now there's not a trace of it left.

J.   Well you see he died in - '67, wasn't it? And my dad had to sell everything. Sold up. He had to do all that. And then he came here. It was Tatton Estate then, what was his name? Hall. And he said Do you want to carry it on? So Dad said, Yes, he'd keep this bit. Not that bit over there, the farm took that. He kept the heathers and the shrubs and conifers. There's about four acres. And this field down there, but we don't use that, Herbert has that with the horses.

D.   And your father held that and developed it as his own business after Clibrans had sold up? I can't remember when he died.

J.   My father was born in 1900. He was as old as the year, like the Queen Mother. He died when he was eighty two, that's when he died. Didn't you take the funeral? Because you wrote a nice bit in the - I've still got it.

D.   He'd done so much around the church. The vicarage that I lived in, he laid out that garden, didn't he? But he'd done more than that. Didn't he lay out the churchyard?

J.   Oh yes, he did those rhodos. And the garden. And then he wrote that thing, I remember, "The Garden of Remembrance", he did all that of course.

D.   Had you been working with him?

J.   Yes. Ever since my mother . . . She was as old as the year as well, she was seventy. So that's when I stopped and started helping him.

D.   You hadn't done it until then?

J.   No. And then I just did what he told me to do. I was a lot younger then, I used to do all the housework and cook, and do everything. He did most of the work outside, I just used to help with the weeding and whatever. He grew everything himself. I still do that, I don't buy in. I grow everything from cuttings.

D.   You must have learned jolly quickly. Because you took over and you've kept it going.

J.   I must have had it in me, mustn't I?

D.   But you'd had no training. Never touched it until 1970, and by 1982 you were taking over!

J.   Oh yeah, well.

D.   Have you been single-handed?

J.   No, no, I have a bit of help. Of course I've got machines in there, you know. But I don't use them, they use them. And then of course you've got to poison things.

D.   And everything you sell, is that to people who come here?

J.   I don't advertise. It's all cash-and-carry. I've got a list that my friend prints for me, and I've got a heather list as well, you see.

D.   And in all this time - you must have been here since the war - what changes have you seen?

J.   Well, like I say we've all got electricity now. But we didn't have water till we came, so nobody else must have had it. And then when we came they put a bath in for us, you know. Of course it was Mr Clibran that did that for us, not the estate, not old Lord Egerton. And of course they had to put water in the barn. Because we had hosepipes, you know.

D.   Tell me about the barn.

J.   It's a crook barn. Have you ever been in it? There's some huge beams, they call them crook beams, they go like that in an arch. That's what they call a crook barn, you see. It has wooden pegs in it, no nails. Wooden pegs. To hold the roof up. It's all wood, you know.

D.   And how old did you say it is?

J.   Four hundred. Four hundred years. First Elizabeth.

D.   And you were saying something else about the roof.

J.   An architect my dad was friendly with said it was three hundred ton, he reckoned it would be, that stone roof.

315

D.   How long's that been there?

J.   Ever since.

D.   First Elizabeth?

J.   Yes. Because - do you want to know this? - They came. They sent me letters, people coming to have a look at it. They wanted to do it, but can't afford it. Nobody'll pay for it.

D.   They wanted to do what?

J.   Renew it. The estate. I don't think they can afford it. And can't get much from the civil people.

D.   It must be listed?

J.   Well it is listed, yes. I've got a thing there now. Because I sent a letter to them that it was a listed building, to Macclesfield Council, you see. And they've replied to it, you know. Because you've got to watch it, haven't you? They don't care. I have polythene all over the floors upstairs to stop the rain. I don't like it to go to rack and ruin. Anyway. It's lasted this long, hasn't it?

D.   And was used as a tithe barn?

J.   It is a tithe barn. Because it was flailed you see. Until the Mill came. The Mill only came in the last century you know, to grind the corn. Until then they had to flail it on the floor. My dad said there was a flail there when he came. Still hanging. Still men-intensive. It wouldn't get much money.

D.   And once the corn was flailed it had to be stored?

J.   Stored, yes. And then it would be sold for the church you see. To pay for the church. Bowdon Church, because no other was here. It was only Rostherne, Bowdon and Mobberley. Then as soon as they made the Mill they made this road, and that's why this road was made. To take the wagons going to the Mill. It would be quite busy, this road. And then the blacksmith. The blacksmith's was still here when we came, I went in it. You could still see the fireplace, and the chimney's still there. But of course it's made into a house now. But it wasn't when we came, no.

D.   And there were millstones, enormous great millstones, in the vicarage garden.

J.   Yes. Oh yes. That came from the Mill. Like that stone in the yard here. That's a cheese press. It's on its side. My dad got the Land Rover and put it there. There's a hook on the side. It should be upended you see. And that would hang on the iron - you know, they used to have iron arches - and they'd hang that on to press the whey out. For the cheese. It's a cheese press. You wouldn't believe it.

D.   So at some stage Cheshire Cheese was made here?

J.   Yes. Oh well everything was. It was a farm, wasn't it? The pigsties are still there.

And the cattle used to come in. There's an arch there, they used to come in through the gate. There's an archway.

D.   You mentioned Fish House Wood?

J.   Yeah, that's down there. He was still doing it when we were here. The old gentleman, he used to walk down.

D.   He was still breeding fish? Trout for the Bollin and the Birkin?

J.   You couldn't go in the wood. There was a gate, you wouldn't go in. In those days nobody trespassed, did they? Not like now. He used to unlock the gate and then he'd walk alongside the river. No it's a brook, I think. And then it was all divided in wood and stones. It was like a dam. That's it, Fish House Wood. And then they'd put the fish into the Birkin and into the Bollin. It was under Lord Egerton you see. "NO FISHING ALLOWED" as it were.

D.   So. That was those days. And now we've got a different world. What do you think of it?

J.   Not much. It's not as good, the law and order. That's what I think. It must be awful in the towns. Because you see when I was a child you had the cane, didn't you. You behaved yourself. But now - ha, ha! I think it's short of that. But everybody's against it, isn't they?

D.   So you think it's down to that?

J.   Oh yes. It's the way people are brought up nowadays, isn't it? That's the world we live in.

Norah Goulden. Sycamore Cottage

N.   I think it was through the German police that I became very interested in dog obedience. They taught me.

D.   Have you always been interested in dogs?

N.   Oh yes. My father had a champion greyhound at the beginning of the century, and I think it rubbed off on me, the love of dogs.

D.   Where did you live then, when you were a child?

N.   In Northumberland. But I was born on the moors in Durham. And my father had a glorious tenor voice, and yet not one of his children could sing! Peculiar. I worked for a shoe firm, and I went around different branches. And a soldier came into the Consett branch. And I talked with him. And at night time he was outside, and I met him again. And we eventually married. And that's how . . . He was from Sale, in Cheshire, and so he brought me to Sale to live.

D.   Which year would that have been?

N.   That would have been '48. And he was interested in dogs, but not as much as me. He loved dogs. He had bull mastiffs. But they weren't very obedient.

D.   Did you have dogs before you were married? Did you both bring dogs into the family when you were married?

N.   No. My first dog was an Italian greyhound, and she was delightful. I used to call her Dainty Dinah. But she was lovely. I'll always remember her.

D.   And did you stay in Sale until 1960?

N.   We went to Mobberley for two years, to a bungalow there. Because then I was accumulating a lot of German Shepherds. And I would take them along Wood Lane to the river, and they would go swimming there.

D.   So how did you come to move along here from Mobberley?

N.   I met the agent, Mr Hall. He was agent for Tatton. And he came to me and asked if I'd like a cottage with three and a half acres. I said, Oh, yes! That would be delight-ful for my dogs. I could just let them out into the grounds, and they loved it. They had free range, you see. And they did do, they loved being here.

D.   Did you know anything about who'd been here before in this cottage? Because it was a gamekeeper's cottage at one time, wasn't it?

N.   That's right. Yes, Mr Hall did talk about the gamekeepers, and that they had the black labrador type of dog. He actually brought his dogs to my class, because I was president of the dog club. And he brought his dogs to join in the obedience training. He managed his dogs very well indeed. I had to say to him, Well done, Mr Hall! You know, he was so much better than the others.

D.   And did you continue your work with dogs when you came here?

N.   Yes. I had classes. On the Sunday afternoon, or Monday evening during the summer. I used to love that. Because they'd bring their dogs to me, you see.

D.   It sounds also as if you think it's very important, the dog training?

N.   Oh yes, I think everyone should train their dog.

D.   A lot of people find it very difficult.

N.   It shouldn't be, you know. All they've got to do is to use their voice. High, with all the love in their voices, for the dog to come. And low when they give the command *"Sit!"* And to stand, drawn out - *"Sta-a-and."* But *"Come!"* with all the love in your voice, to make the dog come to you.

D.   So the secret is in the voice?

N.   I think so. Well, that's what the Germans told me. They said, *Oh, you English! You scold your dogs too much!*

D.   You went to Germany, to see them training?

N.   I went to their trials. And I was so very impressed. Those dogs were wonderful. One man, his dog, a police dog, absolutely wrapped itself round his left leg. But the Germans didn't like that. For a policeman, they wanted the dog to be a little . . . away from them. But that dog was so fond of him that he wrapped himself . . . And that dog knew which way, before the policeman knew, he knew which way he was going to turn - left, right about . . . It was wonderful.

D.   And you had your own dogs here as well, I suppose?

N.   Oh, yes. I had six German Shepherds. I had one, Fels, he was born in quarantine. He was huge, you know. But I followed a lady called Juliet Levy. I call her book my "Dogs' Bible". I followed her teaching in there for diet. And all my German Shepherds lived until they were fourteen years old, and they never went off their back legs. Invariably other people when they have German Shepherds, their dogs go off their back legs when they're about nine, and they die. If only they would follow what she advocates, but . . . She left England and went to America, and then she eventually went to Israel, she had a vineyard there.

D.   Is there a secret that she was imparting? How to look after your dog?

N.   Natural food, I think. And of course, as the Germans suggest, train the dog with your voice.

D.   So it's diet, and good training.

N.   Yes.

D.   Juliet Levy's ideas on diet sound as if they're quite different from the English, usual way of going about it.

N. Oh, yes. She didn't give them tinned dogfood. But then, her mother you see, had a herbal business in Manchester. Her mother lived until she was over a hundred. She was delightful. I used to speak to her on the phone, and she used to say - the greatest compliment that a Jewess could give to a Christian lady - she wished that we lived nearer, so I could visit. That was lovely, wasn't it?

D. So you knew Juliet Levy herself?

N. Oh yes. She was the person who introduced garlic to the animal world. As a safe-guard against disease.

D. And that has really made a difference?

N. Oh yes. And especially she has a formula for tablets. Lark Hall Laboratories have her natural rearing products now. They are still available from Lark Hall. I would advise anyone to use them.

D. Thank you. Can we move on to talk about how you've found living in Ashley? Because you've lived here now nearly forty years.

N. Ashley is a delightful place. A wonderful village. The people who live in Ashley are so caring. As I've said to the Rostherne people, Their motto should be "We take care of our own." And I just love living here.

D. So people, you feel, take care of you?

N. Oh, yes.

D. Because when you came here, in 1960, you were still active, you were taking dog classes, people were coming to you. You were professionally active. And here you are now, having had a stroke, really finding it very difficult to leave your cottage at all. So that you've been through all those stages, of being less and less active. Can you give us an instance of the way people have helped?

N. Oh, yes. For instance, there was a car had pulled up here with a different regis-tration. And my phone went, and it was the local policeman, and he said, Are you all right? I said yes. He said, I noticed there was this car with a different registration. Oh yes, I said, it's a mother and her son who go round the villages selling carpets. And they are delightful people, this mother and son, Lancashire people.

D. And this was Arthur Lamont? Who already was living in the Lodge there?

N. And he keeps an eye on this cottage, in case there is anyone bothering me. So that's wonderful. And I think all the farmers around, as they pass, they look over. And if there's anything untoward they will come in. And there's been a farmer in the next field, and he's jumped over the hedge to see if I'm all right, because he saw me advancing to my five-barred gate. So that is wonderful, isn't it? So you see, Ashley people do "look after their own".

D. It's very interesting to hear that, because I can remember, at about the time when the last of your dogs was going, I remember how much store you placed by the dogs as a protection, and I've often wondered how you are without the dogs barking. But it sounds as if you've got all these pairs of eyes keeping watch over you.

N. Yes. I'm so happy to be here. I don't think I'd want to be anywhere else.

D. You've got three-and-a-half acres here. Has it been very difficult, the upkeep of the place?

N. Well my gardener has wired off the main area. I used to have it cut every week, but now I don't. I have the bulk of it cut for hay, and the local farmer does it.

D. So a local farmer comes in and takes off the hay?

N. Yes. This land here, and also the small paddack there, belongs to Sycamore.

D. That's very useful, having him do that.

N. Oh yes, it keeps the place tidy. And he does trim the hedges as well.

D. You have the cricket club down one side of your paddock.

N. Oh yes, they're very good. At first, the older cricketers were, er, sort of aggressive. But these new cricketers are very friendly. Isn't that surprising? I think it was because of my dogs. I think they were afraid of my dogs. They didn't want my dogs interfering with them. They thought I was the same as my dogs! Whereas actually the dogs protected the Club!

D. Yes, I don't suppose they thought about that. They could be quite intimidating, those dogs.

N. Yes. Because when anyone walked along the path - I wired it off of course, so that their path was apart from my field - and when anyone walked, my dogs would bark at them. You see they were intruders! And they resented that! And one man was, er, lifting his arm. And I said "Leave it!" I ran across. I said, Leave my dogs alone. He thinks you're an intruder. And he's protecting the Club.

D. But now the newer members are different?

N. Yes. Because one or two of them have brought their own dogs. To be trained. One man in particular, a black labrador, and I trained it very well indeed, a lovely dog. Yes, there's a nice selection of men there now.

D. They've got a new pavilion there now. Has that made a difference?

N. I think so. It's attracted a younger type of cricketer. A younger element.

Andy Paterson and Liza Rose. Arden Lodge

D. How old were you, when you came here?

L. Well I was nine. That's about 1979.

A. It was summer of '76, I think it was, and I was ten.

D. That means, presumably, you just missed school here? Ashley School?

L. I was there. I started there the year before we actually moved here. So I was at Ashley for about three years altogether.

D. Are there still people around here who were at school with you?

L. There are still people I bump into occasionally, but I don't think they still live in Ashley. There's people like Richard Jackson, but I don't know whether he still lives round here.

D. No, he's in London. He's a vet. Right, so that was your early schooldays. What happened to you, Andy?

A. I think I was at Ashley for a year. A new boy chucked in on my own. It was a bit nerve-racking, the first day, but they were a friendly lot. I remember sitting with Mark Gibbons and Stewart Calley, Sue McDonald's brother. I was there for a year, and then went to Knutsford. It was only me and Mark Gibbons that moved up, he was the same age. And Mrs Eaves was headmistress, with a big Alsatian dog. And the ladies used to do the . . .

L. Mrs Laxton. Mrs Watson.

A. Mrs Roberts.

D. And then you went on to Knutsford? And where did you go after that, Andy?

A. After Knutsford? I went farming. I did two years' farming, on day release of course, and then I did a full year at Reaseheath.

D. And what did you do, Liza?

L. The year after I left school I went down to London, to train as a dancer. But I had a hip injury, and I was there for about six months and came back. And more or less, I went to work at the airport as a summer job. And then I stayed there for about nine years. Which led me into the job I'm doing now. So I just, like, worked my way through this company at the airport, into the IT department, and that's where I started working with computers.

D. So what is it you're doing now?

L. I train the Flight Information Display System to different airlines and different airports throughout the world. I've just got back from Singapore, doing that.

D. You do what, exactly?

L. I show them how to use the computer system.

D. Which is obviously quite complicated?

L. Yes! It is quite complicated. Plus the fact you've got to know the airport side of things as well. You've got to know how airports work, behind the scenes, and to relate to how they're going to use it.

D. And you got to know all this in the nine years that you were - the six months! - at the airport?

L. Yeah! And then I started working for Ferranti about a year ago, which is more or less training the people who are buying our systems. But also, because a lot of people who are at Ferranti are programmers who don't really know the airport side of things, a lot of my work as well is finding out what the customer really needs, and explaining it to the people back at the office.

D. Your people?

L. Yeah, our people.

D. So that they can provide the right,

L. The right thing.

D. Well thank you for that. We've gone on a bit. I wonder if we could go back, to find out what life was like. You were at Stock Farm, weren't you Andy?

A. Yeah.

D. Have you got any particular memories about what life was like?

A. A lot quieter. We could all ride round on bikes. I used to go to Ashley Primary on my bike.

L. I did.

A. You wouldn't do it now. And then we used to play down in Arden Wood there. And we played football on that green. Where those new houses are now.

D. Oh, you were still in that space?

A. Yeah. Opposite the post office.

D. You must have been about the last generation?

A. Yeah, we were. I remember them digging the foundations out for that. Dug half the football pitch. Then left it for a year. But it was a good sandpit to play in. Then that was it. Gone.

D.   Now, while we're still talking about Stock Farm: you were telling me about that dip.

A.   In the field? Near Arden Wood is a big dip cut out. And someone was telling me that's where they took sand out, to make the bricks for the church. Originally.

D.   And do you suppose they got all the bricks for the church?

A.   There's a helluva dip there.

D.   It is a big dip. A church-sized dip!

A.   It is!

D.   How extraordinary! Of course legend has it there was a brickyard and a tileyard up the Mobberley Road, just the other side of the railway bridge.

A.   It's a pit now, isn't there? Oh yes, I know where you mean. There. Also there was one: you know where the fishing pit is in Mobberley? That was a brickyard.

D.   And yet inspite of that all being available, the church bricks were got out of there.

A.   Yeah. I think it was the colour, or something.

L.   Well I remember the river was always sandy, and there was a big beach at the bottom of our field. There was a really nice sandy beach there.

D.   Is it still there?

L.   No.

A.   It doesn't flood now, as much. But we've had a lot of floods this year. And a few of the beaches have come back. But it was huge, wasn't it, it was a massive big white beach. A whole corner.

L.   And we always used to go and, me and Lisa Batty who I used to go to school with, we used to go down there and make fishing rods. Sticks, and things like that.

A.   Because you could see the trout in the river there. Used to be loads. You could see them, just pointing upstream. In the shallows.

D.   I suppose they still are.

A.   No, there's not now. I walk down there every single day, morning and night, and I haven't seen a fish for years.

D.   There was a wonderful story I once heard from one member of your family, Liza, I can't remember who: about going down onto your beach; and I think one of the dogs was involved -

A.   Pike.

L.   Yes. Yes. That was Rosie. She got this pike came at her in the river.

D.   Yes! That's what I heard, yes.

A.   When did we see it? Only about five years ago. We were down there, weren't we? And still there's a pretty big pike there. You can see it. We used to try and throw sticks at it.

L.   Rosie can't get out of the river now, and she still goes in. She just used to keep on swimming down the river, and all of a sudden this pike - and so she was a bit wary for a while after that.

D.   But it hasn't put her off! Short memory!

L.   I mean, she's really old now, and she still goes in.

D.   Well, it makes a good story!

L.   And do you remember that barn in our field, opposite Crawfords' field? We always used to call it The Haunted Barn. We used to walk halfway to it and then get too scared, and run back!

A.   I remember before they moved in, and Harrisons used to live in the Littles' house. And they left, and everywhere was empty for a bit. It was great, rooting round there at night. Because it was a nursery as well. They used to have trees that had been taken out of the ground, in great big net balls. We used to climb to the top of them, see how high you could get before they bent over. It was good when that was derelict.

D.   I bet you felt quite disappointed when they moved in!

A.   Yeah, I did. A whole lot of Ashley was derelict I suppose, because our house was derelict. Stock Farm was derelict.

D.   Was it?

A.   When we moved in, yeah.

D.   How long had that been empty?

A.   I don't know, but there was hardly a slate on the roof. You couldn't see the cobbled yard.

D.   Good grief! because you see the Blackburns, one of my neighbours on The Green, he was living there when he was young. And that couldn't have been long before.

A.   Well Mum and Dad sold a farm in Atherton. What they sold the farm for, they spent more renovating Stock Farm. It was absolutely knackered. The whole roof had gone. They scooped a big wedge out of the back yard and built a barn, and everything. There was a big pile of soil for years, that we used to play on.

D.   So what have you been doing, Andy, ever since? You went to Reaseheath.

A.   I went to Reaseheath, and then worked at Ashley Hall for about three years.

D.   Yes. I remember that.

A.   And I gave that up. Went to work in Lanzarote for a bit. Then I did a milk round for a year. And then restored Volkswagens for about ten years. And now I'm doing landscape gardening.

D.   How long have you been doing that?

A.   About six months now.

D.   Oh, it's as recent as that? Where did the idea come from?

A.   Just got bored in the workshop. I like creating things. I wish I'd done it years ago. I've always been interested in gardens. I always liked the garden centre, when I was a kid. I like fiddling with gardens, have done all the time.

L.   He used to do Mary's garden, didn't you.

A.   Yeah, I used to work for Mary and Arthur Little. And Norah Goulden, used to mow all her lawns. I used to do quite a lot.

D.   It seems strange, doesn't it, it seems so strange that you spent all that time with Volkswagens.

A.   I know. I just got caught up in it.

D.   Was there a fascination there?

A.   I did like them. I had my first Beetle when I was twelve, thirteen. And then I went in for the Young Driver of the Year competition. I just got interested in driving them. I think basically I did a car, sold it, and got a lot of money off it. I thought, Oh, this is good! I'll start doing that. It just got to the point I'd got bored going to work. So I gave it up.

D.   When was this Young Driver of the Year?

A.   When I was - fourteen? Fifteen.

D.   And how did you get into that?

A.   I think it was just advertised in the paper. They have it now, they still do it. But this was the first ever one. I applied for it and got in. It was a three-day event, and there were seventy-five people in the three-day event. And I come first every day for three days. Then I went in the national finals, and cocked up! And I failed my driving test several times in between! I must have been seventeen. I think I started when I was sixteen. And then I turned seventeen, and failed my driving test! I think that's what really got me into cars. Anyway I wish it hadn't.

D.   So how long did you take, starting up the gardening business?

A.   I said, Right, I'm going to start gardening. So I went and bought a van, bought a load of tools, and I was busy within days, wasn't I? And I've just got big jobs since. I was going to just do gardening. That's what I bought, all mowers and hedge-cutters. And I seemed to be doing this hard landscaping all the time. You know, building patios and features, and designing gardens and stuff like that.

D.   Is it a wide circle?

A.   I'd go anywhere, but it's in Knutsford mostly. The thing is, you park up and do a job, and they see you doing the job. And if you're in Knutsford a Knutsford person sees you. And I actually prefer working in Knutsford. I did a few in Hale, but I prefer Knutsford. More friendly.

Peter Giles. Arden House

D.   Peter, what brought you to Ashley?

P.   Well, if I start with where I began, I was born and brought up in New Zealand; left New Zealand at the age of nineteen, to travel the world; spent some time travelling around Europe and the Middle East. Came to Manchester, to a family who lived in Hale who had worked with my father, and began work with them in the textile industry. I guess that would be in the late sixties, early seventies. Since then I've always had a connection with the North West, although I spent a lot of time based in London, working in America and Europe and other places. I finally came to Ashley because I was married to a girl from Manchester who actually was born and brought up in Wilmslow, my second wife. In about 1987 I took on the tenancy of Hough Green Farm, which had been the family property of the Erlams, following Fred Erlam's death. I spent quite a lot of money refurbishing, and returning the old property close to its original state in terms of exposing beams and stripping back plaster and all that sort of thing. Geoff Ware, who'd been foreman on Fred Erlam's farm, had created the original garden and was very happy to continue as my gardener. He worked with me throughout the four or five years that we were at Hough Green Farm. During that period I had noticed work taking place here at Arden House and the reconstruction of Arden House following its being burned down in the early eighties. It had been a derelict site for about ten years and in the late eighties it was completely reconstructed, and had largely been completed at the time I began to take an interest. I agreed with the estate to take on a long-term tenancy in return for completing the works and undertaking various other rectification work to the outbuildings. The thing that inspired me about Arden House was the fantastic situation and the opportunity to create a wonderful garden over a twenty-year term. It's not something you can do quickly. It's something you want to live in, and feel as you go. I have very extensive garden plans, no expense spared, on the basis that I'd do it piece by piece over a long period and only do what I could do well, rather than attempting to do a whole lot and not really exploit the full potential of the site. It's become a major project for me. In about 1987 I had a major operation on my spine following various accidents, cross-country eventing. I was very keen on horse-riding, which was part of the reason for wanting to have an estate property with land. Fortunately I have the very good services of Geoff Ware, my gardener, who's continued with me here, as I am disabled and cannot do the garden myself.

D.   He's still with you, is he?

P.   He's still with me, and I guess has been now for something like fifteen years. Between us we've created and developed the gardens, and continue to do so. It's become a major hobby for me, in place of the horses. So that's the background, and the reason I came to Ashley.

D.   Actually how much land is there here?

P.   I think I've got approximately twenty five acres. It includes the fields and the wood to the front of the property, and then about ten or fifteen acres to the back of the property, on the Park side. It includes the stables and the walled garden area, which is all part of a longer term project. I've completely restored the stables cottage. It was a derelict building with the front wall collapsing, and I now have a housekeeper living in the cottage. I put in the knot garden and created the avenues and planted hedges, and have done a lot of tree planting; created a conifer garden down the drive, and have plans to restore the lake. It's all part of a long-term project, which is an expensive process.

D.   And the actual garden part, the part that you're working on of these twenty five acres, how large an area would that be?

P.   My view is that it should encompass the whole twenty five acres, in paths and woodland walks. We mow paths now, including the public footpaths running across the front of the property, through the woods; and across the back of the property, to Birtles Farm.

D.   Do the footpaths give you any problem?

P.   No. Fortunately they're not that well known and it is mainly local people that use them. If you're privileged enough to live in a situation like this you've got to be prepared to share it. We keep the paths mown, and most people are very considerate. They keep to the paths and enjoy the environment, without being intrusive.

D.   That's good to hear. It's good to hear, because you don't always hear that from the farmers.

P.   No, well the farmers are in a different situation. They need to make a living out of the land, and it's more difficult for them, if they're producing crops, cash crops, and people are interfering with them by wandering off the paths and so on.

D.   Yes, that's right. That's the sort of thing I hear.

P.   Whereas for me that's not an issue.

D.   Yeah. Thank you, that was a terrific start. Let me just gather my wits, to see where we go now.

P.   Well it might be interesting just to sort of cover the family background. So having been born and brought up in New Zealand as one of six boys, and studied accounting and history at university, I came here and was involved in company doctoring, trouble-shooting: going into businesses that are in difficulty and - here's somebody coming across the path now - have spent the last thirty years in a whole series of troubled businesses. The Banks appoint me and my task has been to restore the businesses to stability, get them back on the straight and narrow and, generally, to sell them. My most recent involvement has been with Riva Group, which is a Manchester-based business with approximately £80 million revenues and nine hundred people, based across Europe in U.K., France, Holland, Denmark, Switzerland, Spain. We've built a very successsful software business which we sold out in the last few weeks, for approximately £42 million. It was a good deal. My first wife, Sheryl, whom you've met here this morning, is also a New Zealander by birth but lived in Manchester. We married and had two children: my eldest daughter Marissa graduated from Edinburgh University with an M.A. in Economics, and is now working with KPMG in Edinburgh, doing an accounting qualification. My son Sam, who's now twenty one, is at Nottingham University, studying Design. Sheryl is now remarried to Paul Higham, and lives at Birkin House. She keeps her horses here at Arden House and uses the stables. So we see a lot of them round here. She has another two sons, Tom and Edward, who are very good friends with my second family. My second wife, Angela, lives in Wilmslow and I have a son of eleven called Ben and a daughter of nine called Isobel who spend a lot of time here also.

D.   And are based in Wilmslow?

P.   They are based in Wilmslow, but are here most weekends. They enjoy the property and the tennis court and the facilities here.

D.   I saw the goal posts!

P.   Isobel, who's a great Manchester United fan, likes to play with her friends. Ben is more into rugby, and roller-blading. They enjoy playing street hockey on the tennis court. Ben is very keen on his scrambler motorcycle, which he rides round the property. Isobel's more interested in horses, and enjoys riding at Joe Gates' and working with Sheryl in the yard here with the horses. I see quite a lot of my brothers, who are located in various parts of the world, in Israel and Paris, and come here quite often. So it's a very extended family!

D.   It certainly is! Just going back though, that sounds a fascinating line of work. Didn't you say you started in something to do with textiles? Or was that your father?

P.   My father was in textiles, and that was the connection with the Normanton family in Hale. As a result of that I started work up here in Manchester, in about 1969/70. I worked with him for a few years before starting my own business, as a trouble-shooter.

D.   Yes. It's the jump from textiles to trouble-shooting that fascinates me.

P.   That really came about when I first started work with Rex Normanton. They'd established a very succesful company in textile processing; but it had grown so fast that it wasn't working and the place was falling apart. He pulled me in and said, Look, go fix it. At the age of twenty one! Which I was very happy to do and believed I could, with no trouble at all.

D.   Well that's the advantage of being twenty one!

P.   And I suppose it wasn't until about forty that I realised that these things were more difficult! By which time I'd been doing it for quite a long time! And continued to. Most of my experience had been in technology-based business: weapons training systems, nuclear engineering, defence industries; electronics, and most recently in software.

D.   You've covered an enormous range of activities, it sounds: is the common factor the way organisations work, and how to get them to work efficiently?

P.   The common factor is companies in trouble: and you start with the critical financial and banking issues; and the issues of a group of people who've lost their sense of direction, and where usually there is a vacuum of leadership and management. It's about going in and re-establishing leadership, authority, management disciplines: giving people a vision of the future; establishing the disciplines of financial controls and cash-flow management; understanding the basics of the business, and re-positioning them strategically. Usually I find it is a three to five year process. My involvement in Riva Group has been five or six years, and it has been a very profitable experience.

D.   And so you'll go from one to another? I mean, the chances are you'll pick up another ailing company?

P.   I'm currently looking at another international business that's involved in the production of films with digital film technology. It's in its early stages. I'm also involved as a shareholder and director of a company that produces speciality materials for the cable industry, low smoke and fire materials.

D.   So how do you choose? A wealth of companies must pass' through as possibles for you to become involved in: in the end, which ones do you choose? Do you become interested in what they're doing, or in the company, or . . . ?

P.   It has to be a situation of reasonable size, to begin with. Anything that's much less than £50 million revenues and four or five hundred people - you have all of the same problems, and nothing like the potential rewards. So the larger situation is more financially rewarding, and in a sense personally rewarding. Size is a factor. Size dictates the degree of concern the bank will have. The larger the banking problem, the more serious and better-quality attention it gets. I like technology-based businesses, because most people are frightened of them. Technology comes down to basic commonsense. As long as you don't let people frighten you with the technology then it's no problem. I can't even tune in a video! This is the curiosity, isn't it? You're comfortable with all these hi-tech businesses, and yet fiddling with gadgets is really not my scene. It comes down to the way you deal with these creative, innovative, technical people. They require a different style of management to your average industrial management. Which I enjoy, it suits me.

D.   What I'm feeling now, at this stage of the conversation is, What an extraordinary thing, that in sleepy little Ashley I should suddenly come across someone like you, who's flying here, there and everywhere, got all these amazing links around the world: and yet here you are with your base in a place like this, and with this wonderful project of creating a garden here.

P.   Yes. It's a super base, very close to Manchester. You've got a very good centre of professional services in Manchester; very close to Manchester Airport, which is good for international communications. Most of the companies I'm involved with have an international aspect. There is a very good motorway network for getting around the country, to the extent that you're dealing within the UK. So that combination is good. We're right at the pivot here of three good centres, Altrincham, Wilmslow, Knutsford, which again suits me well. This particular location is unique. There are one or two other situations south of Manchester which might compare to it: one is Hare Hill, perhaps, in Over Alderley. But I think it's one of the best siutations around, with the views of the Park, the surrounding woods, and so on. To work in a pressurised, stressful environment - where every day is a crisis, and will you survive the next? - to come home to a situation where I'm thinking in terms of a twenty-year plan to develop a garden, has a whole different rhythm. That contrast, and the lack of pressure and any urgency to do anything, and to be able to do it at my own pace in a much more rural environment, is a good contrast.

D.   Yes, wonderful. Wonderful complement. And the other thing I wanted to ask you about this was, I doubt whether a life like yours allows you time to be actually related to the community, as opposed to the place, but do you find any links?

P.   My links to this community are primarily with my neighbours. David Norbury uses the land. The Norbury family is a very nice family. I have lots of links with the community as a sort of local inhabitant - Ashley Mowers, the gardening, various other services in the village. I know the Erlams quite well, because they're my neighbours - John farming, he's my neighbour on this side. And the Erlam family were at Hough Green Farm before. I know and get on well with Christine, and she rides her horses around the property. I suppose most of my social connections are more international in the sense that that's where my business and family connections take me.

D.   Well, thank you very much. That sounds the most wonderful picture.

P.   I think it's a privilege, in this day and age, to live in such close proximity to large urban centres, with all the benefits and professional services that they have, with a large airport on your doorstep; and yet to be part of a rural, agricultural, small community where you still have an identity because you're part of that small community in an everyday living sense; which is in many ways - I won't say undisturbed by the rapid development of a sort of modern urban environment, but preserved because of the estate. The fact that most of the tenant farmers still have to make a living from the land. And it's not been bought up by all your successful local businessmen and just become another dormitory as Surrey is, or the Home Counties have become: invaded by wealthy business people.

D.   It sounds to me, I'm sure you're right, that this mix . . .

P.   Is actually unique.

D.   But the thing which worries me, going round, one of the things that worries me, is how close to the bone all the farmers are. I mean, they're really really struggling.

P.   Yeah, I think they must be. And I think it must be a very tough way to make a living. I don't see it getting any easier, either, unfortunately. As the Common Agricultural Policy comes under more scrutiny I think they will not find it easier. Fortunately I'm privileged not to be in that position.

D.   Yes. I think it concerns you and me in our interests, in that farming is one of the bastions of this type of community, as you mentioned: that we've got working farms around here.

P.   Yeah. I think they'll have to be very creative and innovative, to continue to produce an economic return.

D.   Yes. And all strength to their elbows. That's the only thing that seems to me to disturb the peace of the village, people's peace of mind: people are terrified of the prospect of encroachment, getting overwhelmed by further building developments, and one thing leading to another.

P.   Well I suppose these farm tenancies may well be the best protection against that. I don't think their rights can be readily usurped in favour of development, and I think as Green Belt this is likely to be fairly well preserved.

D.   This is where we get back to the estate, I suppose, and what you say about the estate, which I hadn't thought about.

P.   I think it plays a very valuable role in the preservation of this community, and this neck of the woods really. And so long as it continues to be sustained as an estate I think it's likely to protect the community. If ever it should be sold and broken up, then I think we would expect to see more development taking place.

D.   And presumably that will come down to the economic health of the estate itself?

P.   I think the economic health of the estate, and the particular circumstances of the Brooks family.

D.   So a lot is riding on that.

P.   I think so.

Mary and Arthur Little. Birkin Cottage

D.   How did you come to Ashley?

A.   We used to live in Knutsford. And I used to travel this way to the office - I used to work in Manchester, as an architect. And I always used to drive past this derelict farmhouse, part of the Tatton Estate, and I used to think that would make a smashing place to live. And then, blow me, one day it was advertised, the old farmhouse derelict next door, and this place. And we came here in 1976. I gather it used to be a big garden nursery. And all these trees here are the original arboretum from the nursery. The situation is terrific. I mean, this is the whole point about an estate. They can be considered feudal in many ways, but architecturally estates are good, because they keep the standards of the countryside and the buildings. Far better than any planning regulations. But it was pretty derelict. It had been empty for a couple of years. It suited us because there's just the two of us.

D.   You go down to the Birkin, do you?

A.   Well there's a little stream at the bottom, which feeds the Birkin.

D.   Ah! The stream that you talked about. It's not the Birkin itself, it's a feeder.

A.   The Birkin is just in Jim's field. This feeds it, and comes from Arden House.

M.   It is idyllic. It was a wilderness when we took it over. That paddock there was just rosebay willow herb and brambles. The weeds were five foot high. Fields that aren't grazed become total wildernesses. In fact, we borrowed a couple of donkeys from an animal sanctuary. And they were there for over a year, to get it down, before we could see what was there!

A.   I worked in Manchester when we first came. This was the road through to Princes Parkway, and it was fantastic to see pheasants in the morning when you were having your breakfast, and be in Manchester in fifteen minutes. They say that when Lord Egerton lived at Knutsford, he could go to Manchester in his carriage without going off his own land. Because I did some work in a church in Moss Side, St Mary's, which was one that he'd actually endowed. At that time I suppose wealthy people had developed a social conscience and started putting something back, baths and wash houses, and he actually paid for St Mary's Church. In Hulme.

D.   Did you specialise in anything in particular, in your architectural practice?

A.   No, not really. It was a very old-established practice, a Victorian one, about 1850, one of the first practices in Manchester, and certainly the oldest existing one. But it had always been a relatively small practice. So it was very varied. Everything. We used to do a lot of restoration work, Chetham's School of Music, things like that. A good deal of church work, which could be anything from a plaque on the wall to a new church. But also things like offices, breweries, anything you can think of. It's nice to have a complete spectrum, not to specialise.

D.   Are there any favourites you look back on?

A.   Well the office was well known for things like the Albert Memorial, that was an office job. And in fact it was probably the first practice to restore one of our own jobs! We restored it in the sixties, and that was interesting, because I still had all the original Victorian drawings, to bring out and use. I'm retired now, but it was an interesting job because you see so many different facets of life and occupations. We did the Science Museum. Which was the original station, on Liverpool Road. It was the original railway for Stephenson's Rocket, from Liverpool to Manchester. And the station building in Manchester, down by the end of Deansgate, somehow was just abandoned. So the original station, and all the warehouses, still remain.

M.   The first passenger railway station in the world. *In the world!*

D.   What a wonderful place to become the Science Museum!

A.   Oh it was ideal, because all the big warehouses were there. Also the Station House; some of the bridges, the canal bridges, some of those were done by Stephenson and, I think, his father. The whole of that area now is, well it's converted into a tourist area. Which started with the Museum, really.

M.   The Queen came to open it, and I made the cover to go over the plaque. And that became more important than the building, as you can imagine! She could have been crowned in it by the time it was finished! Blue velvet.

D.   And apart from that and the garden, what other things have you been doing, Mary?

M.   I trained as a potter at Art College and continue it as a gentle hobby.

D.   Going back to your donkeys, another thing I associate with here: every time I come past there seem to be a number of sheep in residence. Are these your sheep?

A.   Yes, they're ours. There's about three acres. And it's far too big to garden. And it's quite steep down at the bottom. After we'd had the donkeys and got it cleared we got a few sheep, and they keep it tidy and well-kept. And I just cut a bit of grass around the house. We have a little electric fence, and I bring the fence closer and closer, so there's less grass to cut, and Mary moves it back again!

D.   Is that true, Mary?

M.   Yes!

D.   And you mentioned the dogs. Now these are Great Danes. It's been - several.

M.   We've had three. We came with a Great Dane. But each one we've had, they've all been quite small.

D.   This is a *small* Great Dane?

M.   Because she's a bitch. A dog would have been a good twelve inches taller. The second one was abandoned on Kingsway, in Manchester. Because some friends took it in, and, you know, there's no way it could have been accidentally lost. It must have been thrown out of a car on Kingsway. This one is our third, Suzi. We've had her seven years, and she was ten months old when we got her as a rescue dog.

D.   Do they need a lot of exercise?

M.   No, as a matter of fact it's a common saying, They sleep their life away. Yes. They're not stupid. They're either eating -

D.   Or sleeping!

A.   We could learn from them!

Dot and Jim Rose. Birkin Farm

D.   Can you tell us about how you came to live here?

J.   Well initially, I think it was you Dot, wasn't it? You were looking through the papers and you saw the advert, Birkin Farm and Birkin Cottage.

Dot. Yes. And we were looking for a house near to Altrincham where Jim had a shop, that had land for the girls' horses. And so we came to see this.

J.   Well before, it was actually a nursery. Clibrans Nurseries. But the house had not been used. I believe it was nineteen years vacant. And in that time it had been quite extensively let go, and in very poor condition.

D.   Did it actually belong to Clibrans?

J.   No, it was part of the estate. Fireplaces were in the middle of rooms, there were fires inside them, graffiti on the walls, ceilings were falling in. It was quite a challenge. The ceilings were quite bowed. But we could see the potential in the property, and the rent was reasonable. So we took up the challenge.

D.   And when was this?

Dot. 1977.

D.   You must almost have had to rebuild the place?

J.   Oh, yes. We had to strip the roof off completely. Refelt and reslate it. We had to take two chimney stacks down from top to bottom. And there were some old buildings which were on the point of falling down, so we took those away, and transplanted some apple trees which were in the back garden, to the side garden; and fortunately they're still bearing very good fruit. In fact one of the apple trees is marvellous, isn't it.

Dot. Oh it's wonderful. Beautiful Bramleys.

D.   How soon were you able to move in?

J.   Well it must have been eighteen months, mustn't it?

Dot. Eighteen months. because Jim was doing this in his spare time.

J.   I think I was starting off at the time - business was poor: I was opening the shop two days. I was doing a rep's job, covering North Wales and up to parts of Lancashire, selling fitted carpets. And the other three days I was working on the house. And so it was quite a struggle. Later on the business . . . I probably would have been better just concentrating on the business. But anyway it pulled through.

D.   Well that's the important thing, yes. Is this the time to bring in the business? What was the situation with the business?

J.   The business is Oriental carpets. And the initial interest was sparked off when my wife's grandmother left us a carpet when she died. It was a Persian Meshed carpet, and at one time she'd been told by a traveller who'd called at the door that he would refit the whole of her house in exchange for this carpet. So she thought it was very valuable. As it turned out in the end, it wasn't that valuable. There are different qualities of Mesheds. But we loved it, and it didn't matter. We really enjoyed it. But that sparked off the interest. And I started going to libraries, to find out all about it, and going to auction sales. And the interest grew. And at that point in time there were very few retail outlets of Oriental carpets. So I thought to myself there's obviously either a great lack of interest, or - because there were no shops about - people hadn't got the awareness. And then my wife spotted a single-column advert in the *Daily Telegraph*, an advert for a freelance Oriental carpet salesman. And at that time I had an electrical business. And I wasn't too enamoured with it. So I thought, Well I wouldn't mind trying this, it sounds fun. So I wrote up to Persian Carpet Wharf, who put the advert in, and arranged a meeting at the premises, which was just off Commercial Road, in London. Caught the train down to London, expected someone to meet me at Euston, which they didn't, so decided to walk. I looked on the map, and Commercial Road didn't seem far, but it was a sweltering hot day. Off I went, to walk to Commercial Road.

D.   This is right down the East End?

J.   This is right down the East End, yes. And I arrived at Persian Carpet Wharf, and I got the job to cover the North West of England. And I would just follow up leads which they got from their advertising. Which was nationwide. And that was successful, and I did one or two promotions for them at Olympia, at the Ideal Homes Exhibition, and also one or two sales from the Channel Galleries, in the King's Road. Which worked out very well. And so we decided that - they had an outlet in Edinburgh, but they hadn't got one in Manchester, which they wanted - and I found a shop for them in Deansgate, fitted it out, and ran it for twelve months for them. So I thought, well it's probably a good time to make a break. So a shop became vacant in Altrincham, on The Downs, which the lease was actually £2,000 a year, and the ingoings were two and a half thousand: which didn't leave me a lot of money to start. The stock which I had at the time must have been thirty carpets and rugs. Because I had become a collector.

D.   And did you stay in those premises on The Downs?

J.   No, strangely enough. I was due for a rent review. And just before then a gypsy came into the shop and said, It won't be long before you'll be moving to a bigger and better premises. And I at the time had no intention of moving. But within about two or three weeks I had this rent review, and they put the rent up about sixty five per cent. At the same time I heard of this shop; which I had previously tried to get for Persian Carpet Wharf, and which was on Church Street in Altrincham. Quite a big shop, and ideal. Then it was for rent, the shop. But the second time round it was for sale. And it was a ridiculous amount, about £12,000. Which was ideal. So it made sense. And there was a nice flat above the shop, which wanted money spending on it, but Dot's mother and father, they'd left a house in Scotland and were staying with her other sister, on the Wirral. And so I said, If you want to put some money into that, to more or less get it fitted out, you've got it there for life, free of charge. And they did, and they lived there happily for about twenty years. Everything just worked in.

D.   And what have your interests been, since you've been here, Dot?

Dot. Mainly animals; and the children and the grandchildren. My main pleasure - I love cooking and doing pots and the gardening and things like that; and I feed the birds every day, and have some remarkable birds coming into this garden. People come, and they see the woodpeckers - there's about six at the moment, they're the great spotted ones, I've not got a green one - but I have to rush to my bird book sometimes, just to see what particular birds are, because there's just so many varieties. At the moment there's three young swallows on the wires above the house, and they've been there for three days. They're flying, but their parents are still feeding them. And it's just absolutely wonderful to watch them. Even we've got starlings - I mean, I know nobody really likes starlings, but the young baby starling, it's there screeching away, and the parents are going and feeding it: it's wonderful to watch.

D.   So what sort of feeding arrangements have you got?

Dot. Well just a bird table in the summer. I soak bread. It's lovely that bread is so cheap at the moment! And they have a block of lard, which they adore. Because I found out - I was buying these fat balls which are about 60p each, and the crows used to take the whole lot. Straight away. But if I put - I've got like a hollow in a tree: if I put a block of lard, that lasts about -

D.   Just simply a block of lard?

Dot. Press it in. They love it. They absolutely love it. It's only the economy type lard, and they absolutely adore it.

D.   And the crow can't lift it all up and take it away!

Dot. That's right. But in the winter we have all kinds of things, don't we? I buy seed, nuts, and it's magic to see them.

J.   There's cats as well.

D.   How does that mix with the birds?

Dot. Yes. Well, luckily the dogs chase the cats off. The dogs don't tolerate the cats. It's quite funny really, because they chase any cat, even the house cat, if it's in this area where they go, out of that door. But if the house cat is there, which she thinks is her territory, and the dogs walk past, she'll run after them!

D.   So they know where they stand!

J.   There's another interesting story. This was when Steve and Julia were getting married in the June, the 25th June. And at the time we had the pool, and also like a walled garden round the pool. And we decided it would be nice, for the wedding, to have it enclosed. This area is about fifty-five feet square. And there were about two or three weeks to go, and we didn't have a lot of time to build the supports, and it was quite a span. So this Wednesday I said to Steve, I'm going to Chelford. Oh, he says, you can't go to Chelford he says, you've got these supports and everything to put up. We just won't have enough time. You're wasting time. But I said, I'm feeling lucky, I

339

think I'll go to Chelford. This is the market where all the farmers sell their goods, and there's hardware and timber and all sorts of things. So I went along. And Lo and behold, in there, there were eight sections which were about twenty four feet long. And I said to myself, It's my day! Whatever they go for, I'm getting them, they're mine! And the bidding started, and I started bidding at a pound each. And in the end I got them for four pounds each, these sections. I mean, it's unbelievable.

D.   Was Steve with you?

J.   No. And fortunately - you know Herbie Hope? - well Herbie had his trailer there. I said, Herbie, can you help me out getting these home? And anyway, he's a great chap is Herbie, he said Yes. We piled them on his trailer, and how we got started I don't know, but we got them home. And then John Williams, he came along. And he's very good on building, he worked it out to perfection. And we got the roof on for the wedding, and so everything was well.

Dot. Put the windows in the day before, was it?

J.   Some other windows. The Quick's building near Manchester Football ground: just below there was a Lex building which was being taken down, and there were some big windows in that. And so I went over with John Williams, and we got those. So everything slotted in within a matter of about six weeks.

D.   Isn't it fascinating, the way that happens if you really go for it.

J.   I mean, that was uncanny, because I hadn't seen those sections before. I'd seen different sized ones, but just for what I wanted, it was ideal. I couldn't have . . . Just to be there!

D.   As if it was made to measure . . . Do you get a lot of this?

J.   I do.

D.   You have these lucky breaks?

J.   I do, I'm very lucky. I could write a book really about it. Takes a while for things to sink through, and then you think, Ah! That's another story!

D.   Before we stop, can we have a quick round-up? I was talking to Liza the other day. Beverley and Julia, where are they now?

Dot. Julia lives at Bucklow Hill. She's got a house with three acres, and she's got three horses at the moment. We were hoping there's going to be another foal this year but it didn't happen. But she's doing very well in her eventing.

J.   She came fifth in the Cheshire Show. In the show jumping. And that's out of how many?

Dot. She was picked for England, cross country - not cross country - the England Clubs the other year. But the horse went lame unfortunately. But she's got a super horse that she does really well on, eventing. Steve goes along with her. He lives for it too. She's very lucky. Beverley lives in Lower Peover. She's got a baby. She's been with this guy about seven years, but she only started to live with him when the baby was born. She had a little place at Rostherne. And the baby was a month away from being born, supposedly, when they bought this house in Lower Peover. A beautiful house, a big place. And the baby decided to come the week before she moved out. So we had to move everything, didn't we, we had to sort the whole house out. And she came out of hospital to Lower Peover. She's very happy.

D.   Is this your first grandchild?

Dot. No, we've got, Julia and Steve have got, two. Holly and Josh. Holly's nine and Josh is seven. And Charlie is, how old's Charlie? about nine months old. So my grandchildren take a lot of my life, I love my grandchildren. I really do. They're lovely children. We do enjoy them, don't we?

J.   The other child we've got is Liza. She'd done very well with Servisair, she'd got as far as she could in the job. And Dot was actually looking in the *Evening News*.

Dot. I do do other things than read newspapers, by the way!

J.   Situations Vacant! But she's never found a job for herself! Anyway, she spotted this job which was with Ferranti. And she's really made for the job. Now for that to be, for Dot to be just browsing through the paper, she sees something: I mean, Somebody up there knows something! We're not churchgoing people unfortunately, but we do have faith, don't we?

Dot. Yes.

J.   And we try to live the right sort of life. Sad to say, when we go to church, it doesn't really get to us, you know?

D.   I do know. Yes.

J.   And yet we try to live a godly life. Which evolves more or less from the family, doesn't it?

D.   It's sad that the church doesn't seem very often to manage to strike the chord which strikes with people like you and me.

J.   Well you were of that nature really. But a lot of the church isn't like that.

D.   But I hated it. My life started when I retired. I didn't realise quite how much I hated it until I stopped.

Dot. But I think it should be more relaxed, and more - not these set prayers. They're not really meaning much, I feel.

D.   I just don't know what the answer is, anymore.

Dot. In Australia I went to a christening, a Church of England christening, an Anglican, and that was just like here. And yet this Presbyterian in New Zealand, I was just so impressed. You could see that everybody knew each other, and they could talk to each other, and it was wonderful.

D.   Of course that's probably half the battle, is that.

Dot. Yeah, could be. Yeah.

D.   I don't understand it at all, I don't begin to understand it, but about the hardest thing I have to do - I often don't do it, but - I don't think I do anything more difficult than going to church. I have to absolutely force myself to go. And I'm always most uncomfortable. Well, part of that is changing roles, it is a bit difficult; but it isn't just that. I think something happens to me when I go inside that building. I don't know what it is, but something comes over me that makes me feel completely different. I don't know what it is, but I somehow think the formula got all wrong somewhere along the line, got onto a completely wrong formula altogether. What the right formula might have been, I haven't a clue. The only thing that picks me up, that saves me from complete despair, is hearing the sort of things you've just been saying. Luckily, everything doesn't depend on the church. There is a spiritual dimension in ordinary everyday life that conveys itself.

Dot. There is. We were just watching birds. It's a miracle to see things like that. I don't know why, but it's only in the last five years I've been feeding them, and when I first saw the first woodpecker, I couldn't believe I'd got this magnificent thing on my tree! Oh, there's so much beauty around.

Herbie Hope. Ryecroft Farm

D.   Herbie, how long have Hopes been around here?

H.   I can't imagine how long they've been around. We've been in and around Tatton Estate for centuries. We're supposed to have been here about a hundred and eighty years, at Ryecroft. And they were at the Rangemoor before that. My great great grandfather was Regimental Sergeant Major in the Cheshire Yeomanry for Lord Egerton in the early early days. I think that's how we came to get the farm in the family. He was nearly hand in glove with Lord Egerton.

D.   This must actually be one of the farms furthest away from the centre of Ashley.

H.   Yes. A little bit of land is in Rostherne as well. The Bollin is the other side in the Manchester area, that'll be the Bucklow/Macclesfield boundary. I should think we've got one of the best farms in Cheshire. There's no hedges, no ditches. A very very small area of clay. We were one of the earliest to have tractors and what-have-you.

D.   Whose decision would that have been, your father's?

H.   Yeah, well I don't particularly say my father . . . Although we don't seem a very big farm, we had like a teamsman that used to look after the horses, and a cowman to look after the cows, and sheep-shearer Harry, he used to look after the sheep, he was the shepherd. And I'm not saying my father didn't do a lot of hard work on the farm, but he was more administrative, as it were, in them days, because there must have been more money in farming. I can remember seven and eight men coming for their wages on Friday night. And I can remember as many as six Irishmen in the shed. So they'd be casual labour. I suppose I would be about ten when we . . . I can never remember not having a tractor. So when we went into hydraulics and had Fergussons I must have been about ten or eleven, I think, the first hydraulic tractor. Then the horses seemed to disappear.

D.   What did you do about school?

H.   Oh well, it was a long way off, wasn't it? My brother started school at Ashley. I don't remember him walking, but I can remember the stories saying he used to walk across the road, down the fields, crossing what used to be Clibrans, which Crawford's got now: come out by Birkin Farm, and all the way down to Ashley to school. Which was a long long way for a little kid. My earliest time at school, we used to ride from here on horseback, same way unless we thought we'd go through the other way: but mostly through Clibrans, we'd always have a good gallop on the ponies! And then we usually unsaddled the ponies at Reg Baker's, which was The Greyhound. And then put the horses where all Hough Green is now, and the other houses built opposite the post office - all that was Reg Baker's field - well, it was owned by Tatton Estate. Lord Egerton, really. Because when Lord Egerton died, that was when everything was sold up. So we used to put the horses on there, and then return on the Friday night - we were boarders at Knutsford College - and return on a Friday night, hopefully trying to catch these ponies. Invariably Dad had to come out with nuts and ropes and whatever to try and catch these little ponies, little demons they were. I think it would have been quicker to take us to school. And then I went to Wadham after three years. That was in cycling distance. And carried on when I left school, farming. Had horses, I did

343

a lot of horse riding as a kid, showing and gymkhana, went all over Cheshire; Liverpool, Southport. We were quite reasonably good at horseriding. And with tractor driving and carrying on the farming, I seemed to do most of the tractor driving, I qualified for the Royal Show, won the All-England Championship, tractor driving, a couple of years.

D.   Is this ploughing?

H.   Tractor handling. That's different from ploughing. You reverse a trailer through obstacles, drive a trailer through obstacles, use a fork-lift, a muck-loader we called it, a fork-lift to move obstacles. It was very difficult. I won the Cheshire championship eight or nine times. Certainly five times.

D.   And went to the Royal as well?

H.   Yeah, well the Royal wasn't at the Warwickshire site like it is now. It was at Cambridge the first year. I won about seventy-odd pound at Cambridge. I went down to what they call the County Championship, which is, you've got to qualify at Cheshire, to represent the county. And I won that in Cambridge. And then, whilst you're there, you play around in the Open. So we'll say the second day was the County Championship, and then the fourth day, the last day of the Show, was the Open Championship. So I won the County Championship and the Open Championship one year. And then the year after, we went up to Newcastle - going back a few years now - Newcastle, and I hadn't qualified with the Cheshire Championship, but I won the Open Championship again. At Newcastle. Then it obviously got a bit keener, and when it was at Warwickshire I went down there a few times at Warwickshire. Whether I won it at Newcastle or whether I won it at Warwickshire, I wouldn't be sure.

D.   You were still doing it, even when they went down there?

H.   Well, it's no further away.

D.   No, no. It's just that that's come to quite recent times.

H.   When I took over from my dad - I can't remember now. I took over from my father when I was twenty five, and I'm sixty two now, how long ago was that, David?

D.   Well, it's a long time.

H.   We had cattle and all sorts, but nobody wanted to work in the agricultural world in them days. Being near to Altrincham, you could earn more money there, in the works. Now the works have all gone. The lifestyle round here is totally different. I can remember when we were sixteen, eighteen, twenty, going down to the old Manchester Ice Rink, it's called Altrincham now, you couldn't get through Broadheath at seven o'clock at night, quarter to seven, you couldn't drive through. There were bikes coming out of Atlantic Street, you can't imagine. There was plenty of work then. It might not seem much money, but they were on two or three pound a week more than the agricultural workers, maybe not working as many hours. It's a whole way of life, agriculture, and it's finished.

D.   So two things seem to be happening: men were choosing to work away from the farms; and the farms, at the same time, were actually becoming less and less labour-intensive?

H.   Yeah, a lot less labour-intensive: as soon as you introduced the tractor you took away two or three horses. And a plough: a plough would plough ten acre in a day with a tractor; with a horse you'd only plough an acre. So yeah, it got very much more revolutionised as soon as you introduced the tractor. I don't know, I can't really say whether I was a good farmer or not.

D.   Were you a keen farmer? Did you enjoy it?

H.   But you never knew anything different, David. I don't know, when you say about being a keen farmer.

D.   Well there must have been some difference, because your brother chose to go out of it.

H.   Well, yeah. I'm not saying it were easier money, but he made a living just the same as I do. In an area the size of this room! Which is the easiest? Which is right? I can't really say what's right and what's wrong. I don't know what people want to be doing in agriculture for, to be quite honest, now. Truthfully, David, most people know the job's gone.

D.   I get the impression that most of the people I've been speaking with, the ones who are farming, are in it for the life: it's the whole package. The independence, partly. The countryside and enjoying the things that they do, perhaps. But what they all have is this tremendous sense of the importance of what they're doing: producing food. The only thing they don't enjoy is the financial side, and all the records and form-filling that has to be done. It drives everyone crazy.

H.   Yeah, nobody likes that, do they? Well, not being funny, agricultural people are hardly pen-pushers, are they? You might say you're a fool to be involved in agriculture, I don't know. I just see different sides. As you know, I do marquees. I can go and take thirty thousand pounds' worth of equipment, put it on the site, do the job, make £2,000 for doing it, and bring everything away from it. I don't say it will always be £30,000, but in an ordinary wedding marquee it might be twenty grand's worth of stuff tied up, with chairs, tables, lights, lining, what-have-you. You bring everything away. You've provided a service and you're paid in hard cash straight away. Where with cattle, you're going to rear a cow, you might rear ten calves: but you don't know whether you're going to get them in calf, you don't know whether they're going to die of disease, you don't know whether they're going to milk well when you've done it. So if you have ten cattle you might have only six or seven that are going to be profitable. The three or four that you've lost or gone out of line, you're struggling with aren't you? Not every cow born is a production cow.

D.   Then there's this time gap.

H.   Yeah. Two years before they know what they get. Take Ian Crawford, planting potatoes: he plants thousands of potatoes, thousands of potatoes. But if he loses them all he hasn't made anything. But the money's been spent just the same, hasn't it?

There's someone else with four hundred acres, and milks a hundred and fifty cows, and he says I'm doing all this and I've lost money. What's the point in doing it? He's sixty. He's not short of money. What's the point in being involved in it? Just rolling money round for other people.

D. So you took over when you were twenty five? Has what you do for your living changed an enormous amount in that time?

H. Tremendously. I've got no cattle, no sheep, no poultry.

D. When you started, you had all those?

H. It was a complete working farm. Now we're just all arable. Everything's done contract. There's no labour. It's like the milk. You can't afford to have labour stood about. If you're growing corn, you sell it: what happens then? It's just not necessary to have labour there. The most expensive thing is labour.

D. How many people were you employing when you started?

H. I had two other lads on the permanent staff.

D. And did you also use casuals for when you needed more?

H. We didn't really need it. Whether we went into cows or whether we came out of cows was really the milking-parlour situation. The estate would invest money, but they wanted a return on the investment. Really you're wondering whether it is right or whether it isn't. I wouldn't say I was a particularly good stockman. I was telling you earlier about labour: I had to do Saturday and Sunday. I had to milk them all every morning, because the men won't start till quarter past eight, so I've done what I call the work before they've got there. And calm anything at night. I was nursemaid to cattle from morning to night. Maybe I'd got two men, I wouldn't say bad men but not the best agricultural workers. They got very Union-minded. I got one fella, he had an accident on the road, he was very very rude and communistic. And I'll not say he run rings round me, because you're in charge at the end of the day. But they didn't do any favours for me. I had two hernias done when I was thirtyish, and these two men looked after the farm while I was six weeks off with the hernias. And there was more rubbish, less done. So I sold the milk cattle when they calved; kept the cows that were in milk, and when they were in milk next year they were sold on. And that was that.

D. That's how the milk round started, is it?

H. Oh, I retailed milk for twenty five years then. That seemed to go bad with the supermarkets.

D. And you stopped the cows here altogether?

H. Yes, after a period of time. It took like three year, four year. Wind down. When heifers came into calf I sold them.

D. And you wouldn't replace them. Had the sheep gone by now?

H.   Oh yeah.

D.   And the poultry?

H.   Yeah. When I said I had two men, I had three men, not two. I had old Harry. The old stager, Harry was, he'd had the sheep from the beginning. But when he retired I didn't replace him. Got onto low-cost milk production, supposedly. Tried to intensify on one line, rather than diversify. I never went for putting parlours in. Maybe if I'd put in parlours I might have saved the milk money. But the more money you've got invested in farming nowadays . . .

D.   What are your children doing, Herbie?

H.   Well Yvonne works, and she's married now, my daughter's married. Works at the airport. Supervises at the airport. And Simon's a pilot.

D.   Oh, so they're both at the airport?

H.   Yeah, Manchester Airport. So don't run Manchester Airport down! We can't have that closing down.

D.   I don't think there's much danger of that!

H.   No, I don't think there is.

D.   So Simon: who's he with?

H.   Well it's J.M.C. now. It was Caledonia. J.M.C., Air World and another all amalgamated. J.M.C.'s like Thomas Cook.

D.   And does he fly from here, or from all over?

H.   At this time of year he flies mainly Manchester to Bristol, Manchester to Birmingham and back. Shuttle, like. He'd like to try on the agricultural side, but the earning ability is - it's more that than anything. His earning ability now is so much further forward. Hard to say what's wrong. We're coming into a different world, ball game. I don't think agriculture's wanted in this country.

D.   This is the feeling that's constantly being voiced.

H.   Transportation's so easy. Have you spoken to Ian Crawford? He reckons he can put barley or wheat into Manchester cheaper out of Australia than he can from Ashley.

D.   And he can get the land.

H.   And the sun.

APPENDICES

1. Farming in Ashley

a) Higher Thorns Green Farm. Irene and Ian Daniel

I.   Well Ian's father, and his father and his father before him, they used to have a lot of shire horses. And all the work in those days was done with shire horses. And my husband Bill, he ploughed all his land with these horses. And he did enter a lot of ploughing matches, and win cups and championships. But of course it's the time, isn't it? You know, gone out of fashion, haven't they? It wasn't quick enough. Everything went mechanical, and . . . It was a terrible thing when we bought the first tractor. My father-in-law thought the end of the world had come. Bill was so insistent we needed a tractor, he didn't know what we needed a tractor for. But that's changing times, isn't it? You've got to go with it. You've got to join them, haven't you?

D.   Did Bill hang onto horses for as long as he could?

I.   Well he kept one on a long time, didn't he? But she was more of a pet then. In the end.

Ian.   It's mainly a dairy farm now. We do have some arable. It's one of the few dairy farms left in Ashley.

D.   What do you grow?

Ian.   Well, we grow barley and wheat. But our farm really isn't arable land, it's grass land. And we are slowly going back to all grass, because it's very heavy clay, not good arable land at all.

D.   Can you see a way in which the farm can develop and prosper for you?

Ian.   I don't know. The way things are at the moment, I don't know what to do. Hopefully farming will improve, and it will continue being a farm, hopefully. Three dairy farms left, now. I think, if you go back thirty years, virtually every farm was a dairy farm.

D.   Yes. Yes. One or two people have said that.

Ian.   I couldn't tell you how many there was, but just about every little farm, at one point, milked cows. And over the years they've gone out of cows. There's more and more horses in the country now. Almost as many horses in Ashley as cows! Dairy farms have diversified. Keeping horses. We're surrounded by horses.

D.   What's the explanation? There must be something going on.

Ian.   I don't know. I suppose all like small herds, and as time's gone on they became unviable. Change of farming techniques. They've gone into other parts of farming. But now most farming's struggling and suffering. So we really don't know what to do at the moment. Things are not very good.

D.   It must be incredibly difficult, because there are so many factors that are quite beyond anyone's control. I suppose there's always been the weather, and nobody can control that either, but now we've got The E.C., Brussels and politicians and regulations which constantly change, and goodness knows what. It must be an absolute

351

nightmare steering your way through all that sort of thing.

Ian. It is. And supermarkets, like you said before.

D. That affects you, does it?

Ian. Yes it does. We sell our milk, which goes to the supermarkets. And the way things are going, they can come at any time to check your facilities and your records. And if anything's wrong they can refuse to take your milk. That's the way things are going.

D. I'd not heard of this happening to milk before. Who do you sell your milk to, then?

Ian. At the moment we are selling to Milk Marque. But we know they're taking our milk to Wiseman's Dairy. And they're very keen. To sell milk to them you've got be what they call - have this "Farm Assurance". Where everything on your farm is up to spec., if you like. And any time they want to come and check your facilities they can do. And if you're not up to spec. you're penalised for it.

D. So who's introduced this? Is it Milk Marque, or is it the next one up, Wiseman? Or is it somebody behind them? Because it's not a government thing, is it?

Ian. No. It's ever since all these food scare stories in recent years. Since BSE and all the rest of it, it's all traced back to the farm.

D. Mind you, I can remember Tuberculin Tested milk coming in, when I was a little boy, I think. This new thing came in - do you remember that starting, Irene? Which was I suppose a similar sort of thing. And that was a public health issue pure and simple, wasn't it?

I. Yes. Oh yes, we've had to have the cows tested for that for years. They still have to be tested now.

D. And this is anti-TB, I suppose? But the extra things that are required of you now are just in case of anything that we hadn't thought of, are they? Just a move to getting more and more sterile?

Ian. All this adds to your costs.

D. And can you pass it on? It adds to your costs, it ought to add to the cost of the milk.

Ian. Yes, but our milk price is dropping. It's dropping all the time.

D. Who dictates that? Wiseman?

Ian. Or it's dictated by the supermarkets. They tell us what they're paying us.

D. Is there no bargaining, no negotiating? I've not had a conversation like this before, and I can't think why not. There must be a bargaining process going on somewhere, you can't just simply be dictated to?

Ian. That's how it is.

D. I can see it must be what it feels like. But, I mean, if you all said, *All right, you needn't have our milk. We'll sell it to somebody else?*

I. You can't do that.

D. If enough of you did it . . .

Ian. Oh yes. But they won't. But then if you did that, they'd import milk. They've got cheap imports, they could import it. But the milk in England is the cleanest in Europe. And we're getting the worst price for it. It's just grossly unfair really.

D. Well, you make it sound grossly unfair. And I've often had this feeling, going around, and I've never actually got round to pushing it this far before. But what I can't understand is why it's not possible to get - . There must be a real difficulty somewhere in getting farmers to agree to act together, to resist this sort of dictatorship.

Ian. Well that's how it is. You've got to do what they tell you, really.

I. Well the milk, it's got to go somewhere, hasn't it? And it's got to go today, it's no good -

Ian. It's a perishable item.

I. It's not as if it's something you could store up till you get a better price. It's got to go.

D. Yes. You can't just suddenly start making butter with it, or something.

I. No. That's how they've really got you, you know.

Ian. This minute in time, it's like the Depression in the 1930s. It's going that way at the moment. Talk to these old farmers, they're all saying that. That's when the Milk Marketing Board was formed, isn't it?

I. That's when the Milk Board was formed. You see a few years ago they did away with the Milk Board. Well I'm sure if your dad had been alive he wouldn't have agreed with that.

b) Sugar Brook Farm. John Erlam

When I was twenty-three I went into pigs. Then as I took more land on I found that, by the time I'd finished my pigs, at ten o'clock in the morning, you didn't have time. You should really have been out in the fields, doing other jobs. And so the pigs went, as they're very cyclical in their financial aspect, they'd had a very bad time in 1983, and I decided that the next time they became good I would get out. So that's what I did. So I went out of pigs and then concentrated on arable farming. Like I said, arable farming then went through a dip. So I gave up the Hough Green lands, which are not really suitable for arable farming, they're grasslands really, they're hay lands. And kept the lighter arable lands going. And then it became time to diversify. As farming income started to dip, I started off being interested in, Viv was very interested, in horses and so we developed the horsefeed business. And then the horse livery business. And so that took it on until, more or less at the moment, it's more or less like a leisure, more a leisure business. More money comes into the farm, comes into the business out of leisure than it does coming out of farming. Which is a sad case, really.

D.   That is selling horsefeed and, do you still do livery?

J.   Yes. And the way farming's going again now, with 160 acres you can't make a living out of it. You know, one family can't make a living out of it. Which is sad, when probably at the beginning of the century there were maybe four families making a living out of the same land.

D.   I think I heard you say half of your income is from leisure as opposed to farming proper. Did you add the comment that this is a sad sort of business? You don't feel good about that?

J.   Not really, because you would have thought - . There's a lot of satisfaction to be gained out of farming. You feel as if you're doing a worthwhile job, you feel as if you're a benefit to the community. Although at the moment the community I don't think - not the local community but, if you say, Britain in general - doesn't look upon farmers very highly at the moment. We've had BSE. Now GM food. People just seem to think we're trying to rip people off all the time, which I don't think is truthful at all. We just seem to get such a bad press - you know you get bad apples in every profession. The other day there was a programme on a farmer who was treating his sheep badly. It's probably five per cent of farmers, but it's what gets publicised. And that's what Joe Public sees in front him. I can remember, five years ago, if you met somebody for the first time and they asked you, What do you do? And you say, I'm a farmer, they're interested in you. You look at them now. You say to somebody now you're a farmer, they look down their nose at you. They think you're a sponger, you're living off government subsidies. So at present with the farm I'm looking to go into organic farming.

D.   Why?

J.   Again, because there seems to be a great demand for organic produce at the moment. Whereas your ordinary produce . . . you know this year I've sold grain at £60, £65 a ton. Organic would be £180 a ton. Now you will not get the same production. You won't get your three tons. But you could at least aim for a two-ton crop.

You might end up with thirty hundredweight. But 30 cwt at £180 is still better than three at £60. And you don't achieve three. If you average two ton you'd be reasonably happy.

D.   And the limitations are relatively easy to cope with, are they?

J.   They're fairly rigorous. You've got a two-year feed-in period, where you're not allowed to use any chemicals or any fertiliser or any pesticides, for two years before you can become organic. So you've got a two-year period. But there is government money coming in to encourage it. Because ninety-five per cent of organic produce is imported. So there's a big shortfall.

D.   So that goes on as long as that is a reasonable proposition.

J.   They give about a five or ten-year period when that's going to be reasonable. Well I think as far as the business is concerned that's as far as you can look.

D.   And then you just have to be ready to jump whichever direction the market seems to be suggesting you jump at the time?

J.   I can remember having an argument, not an argument, a discussion with some-body. We were discussing farms and diversity. And this farmer was saying, No you should just go for one thing. And you should become a specialist at that. Well it's fine, but - look what happened to the pig job. One of the best pig farmers I know in Cheshire has gone bust. Through no fault of his own. It's the market. So I think you've just got to try and keep your options open.

c) Lower House Farm. Douglas and Alice Raven.

Da. How have things developed in the thirty years you've been here? I mean, there must have been a lot of changes in that time?

Do. When we first arrived here there was labour to be had everywhere. Now, you see, over these years we've been here, we've watched labour drift off the land, because other people could offer them more money, and for less hours. So people - . You see, you're right here on the south of Manchester. There's an awful lot of competition for your labour. Here. You're not out in the sticks, where people have got to stay with farming because there's nothing else.

A. But there again, things have been mechanised, haven't they? So you don't need the people.

Do. Yes but we've watched this change. And we've watched it get very competitive, to get labour on the farms, over the years.

A. Well the whole concept of the farm labourer has changed, hasn't it? They are an extremely well-paid man who knows his job. Must do.

Do. That's right. You see, if you have a cowman, you've got a man who is working with a milking parlour that's cost anything from twenty to fifty thousand pounds, which he's got to look after. He's got to look after. Then he's got a herd of cattle as well. So what's your value then? So these men, they're very responsible people, really. They're not like they used to be. Likewise, if you haven't got a dairy herd and you're an arable man, and you put a man on a tractor: a tractor costs thirty thousand. Fifty. That's for one tractor. So they've got to be pretty responsible, these people. You can't just put anybody on them. So yes, that's how it's changed.

Da. Has it been difficult, keeping pace?

Do. I don't suppose farming's ever been easy, because you've got your two main things: you've got disease always, and you've got weather. So it's never been easy. Farming.

Da. On the other hand, those were natural phenomena. But the sort of things that seem to be in the driving seat more and more now are, as you were saying before, the technological changes and mechanisation on the one hand; and I suppose on the other hand, what seems to me to have changed a lot, listening to the farmers around here, is the simple business of selling your produce. Finding a market. Which is not simple at all. So you've got two fronts that are, I should have thought, relatively new. Not the old natural things that every farmer has always had to contend with.

A. I think one of the most unnatural things is all the paperwork. That is phenomenal now. You're always filling in forms. Yes, it has completely changed. Not for the better. Not for the better. There's a lot more stress now.

Da. I can remember first associating you with those large French cattle - Charolais? Limousins? What became of them?

A.   We did have some.

Do. We were Charolais then. But that was crossing with dairy cattle, with a beef bull you see: to get the value in the calves.

A.   But then with the BSE we went pure Friesian. Only to find, now, that they aren't worth anything. So we've gone back to the beef bulls, the Limousin and the Blond -

Do. I mean the beef aren't worth a lot either. We know that. But we're swinging the other way now. We've sold the Friesian, and we've purchased beef bulls. So we've got a Limousin, and we've got a Blond Aquitaine. We have one running with the herd all the time. One or the other. You have to rest them, you see, and . . . The more cattle you get, the more they get work. So they can't do it all the time. Yes, we did have those big white bulls, yes. They were the Charolais.

Da. And now you're back to the larger ones?

Do. We're going back, because we found that these Friesian heifers and Friesian bulls are bad to catch. So, that's the dairy side. But the other way was, those white bulls you talked about, which were Charolais. We brought them up, you see, because there was a subsidy on them. We brought them up and took the subsidy off them, and then sold them in stock. So we were still buying our dairy replacements in, the whole time. And nothing's changed, as far as that goes. Just the bulls, the colour of the bulls. But you would think that, with BSE, and all the slaughterings there's been in the dairy, there would be a shortage of dairy stock. The average person would think that.

A.   But it didn't work out that way. There's so many consolidatings: you know, small farms being taken over by bigger ones.

Do. There's an awful lot of dairy cattle about. Strange, really. So we went in for the dairy bulls with this in mind. And it just didn't work out that way.

A.   We've got to be very careful if we take a bull to the auction, because we've got probably to finish up paying the auction.

Do. A bull calf.

A.   A bull calf, yes, a bull calf. Because you don't get enough to pay the commission.

Da. Oh, it's as bad as that?

D.   Now, at this moment. It wasn't, but it is now.

Da. Is there a reason for that?

A.   Well there was a subsidy on them. And then the subsidy's gone.

Do. The scheme finished at the end of July. And then the Friesian bull calves became worthless.

Da. So yes, that really pulled the carpet out.

Do. The rug out, from underneath us.

Da. And this is CAP, I suppose? Europe again?

Do. Yes, we are controlled from the Continent - we're part of the Continent, we're not controlled from there, we're part of it. It's like a United States of Europe. I know it doesn't sound it at the moment, this beef job and all that, but that's a different thing. That's a different thing, that's scientific isn't it, that. It's the scientists that seem to be the ones that's the stumbling blocks there.

Da. Now you were saying something before we started about, I think it had been leading to the possibility that more is being produced than is wanted. I think we were talking about milk prices at the time, perhaps, and the way that the producer seems to have no control over the price, no negotiating power. You're just told what you get.

Do. You see, it's a funny situation we're in at the moment, because never before in time could you go and buy a farm, and not start to produce what you wanted. As long as you could sell it you were all right. But you can go and buy a two or three hundred acre farm today, and say I'm going to produce milk on that: no. First, find your buyer. None of the dairies wants to know you. They don't want to take it, so you haven't got a buyer.

Da. It's beginning to look like one of the pieces in this jigsaw is simply over-production. I've heard people say - totally mystified - What we need's another war or something, we were appreciated when there was a war. And here we are now wanting to produce food, and nobody seems to appreciate what we're doing.

Do. And yet a part of the world is starving. So is there a solution? The set-up's wrong. I mean you can't produce food and give it away, can you?

Da. Well this is the whole thing, isn't it? It must be years ago now, when that rock singer was concerned with Ethiopia.

Do. Bob Geldorf.

Da. That's right. And there were people starving over there, and it was just at the height of the first we were hearing of butter mountains and wine lakes, all these mountains and lakes of surplus produce. But somehow it was never matched to the need. I never heard of the stuff ever going to places like that, where it was wanted.

Do. Grain mountains. It did. Russia bought a lot of it. She didn't buy it, she was almost given it. It was a way out for us, you see. And it just slid across Europe into Russia. And very little was said about it. And the least said the better, really. Because it would allow the West to carry on producing. As long as we're allowed to carry on producing we'll never say anything.

A. We seem to be getting a long way from Ashley.

Da. Well yes, and yet it seems to be affecting Ashley. All the farmers in Ashley are being affected by this, one way or another. And it's beginning to sound to me as if there is a tie-up, that is a long way from Ashley indeed, because in the end we've arrived at global considerations now. Over-production is only a very local thing.

Do. There's a lot of dairy farmers around here selling their herds. And just getting out of milk. I've been to quite a few sales round here. These are just on our own doorstep. And they won't go back into them again, I don't suppose. It's a shame really. Because, I mean, it's been their way of life. And it's going on all over the country. And that's why there's so many cattle about. I don't know how many dairy producers there were. I think it's about twenty eight or twenty nine thousand. But there were a lot more. Double that. So you see them getting less. And as they get less the herds are getting larger. You see the sheep, they're over-produced as well. You've got to have a quota to keep sheep, now. And you've got to have a quota for sucklers. Suckler cows. Yes. And without it, you see, you can't draw your subsidy. They've got you on how much you're allowed to draw in subsidy. You can keep what you like as long as you don't want any subsidy; but where subsidy's involved, and that is in breeding animals, you claim your subsidy from the government, and that's when they put the checks on. You could say that you're not getting it on your dairy cows, but you are because they reckon that it works in with your milk quota. How much you produce on your farm, and how many litres are sold from your farm, it's all calculated. So it has changed an awful lot. Oh, it has changed. So you ask what changes there are from when we came here up to now, and they're tremendous. Farming has changed tremendously, really.

Da. I think it's quite extraordinary that everyone seems to have managed to keep abreast of it. That heads haven't exploded. My head is reeling, just listening to all this.

Do. Yes, it's not easy. And no one pretends it is easy. You go around talking to farmers, and other people as well, - I mean, it isn't just farming, is it?

Da. No, I must say: often I find myself thinking, as I listen around here, thinking about the mining communities, and how the story sounds terribly similar.

Do. It is.

Da. In terms of what people are suffering. And why.

Do. They suffered a lot, the miners. And also, look at all these clothing firms. There's one for instance now, Marks and Spencers. They just simply throw the towel at people. They thrown it at one yesterday, Daks Simpson. They're going to have to make top side of a thousand people redundant. And there are others. So it isn't just farming that's suffering. We mustn't think we're alone on this, we're not. We've just got to learn how to find a way round it. Whether it's producing less, or getting more for what we produce, how or what I don't know.

Da. Or finding a way of sending it to where it's really wanted.

d)   Back Lane Farm.   Robert and Caroline Davies.

R.   I was born in 1960, so I'm thirty-nine now. I can remember the cows being milked in shippons. And the milk going down a plate cooler, which was water one side and milk the other, and the milk going into churns, through a sieve, and the milk being put on the garden wall ready for the grain man who used to bring the grains to feed the cows, and then when his wagon was empty he'd come back and pick up the churns, and go back to Manchester with the milk. And on his return trip he'd bring the grains. That's how it worked for a long time. And I remember the cows were tied up in shippons and we used to have to take the milking machine to the cow. There was a bucket attached to it and the milk went in the bucket, and the bucket was carried from the cow back to the dairy. And this involved a lot of men, I think there used to be about two or three men working, milking the cows. And I used to get involved as much as I could, I used to wash the udders, or feed the cows. But when I came home from school I used to help the cowman. Mr Evans his name was. He was with us for about twenty years. And he lived in a tied cottage at the back of the farm. So most days I was helping the cowman. And then things started to, obviously, progress thankfully. Then the cows were milked in a line, which meant that they were still tied up in the shippons, but there was like a glass pipeline over their heads, and the milk was taken through this vacuum in units, up into the line and travelled round all the shippons where the cows were and ended up in the dairy. So that was a progress. That meant there was less walking around with bucketsful of milk. Then it progressed again, I suppose twelve years ago, we, when my father retired, we moved the cows out of the shippons when I took over the farm; at the same time we moved from the cottage to the farm. We spent quite a bit of time putting new, modern farm buildings up, and a new parlour, which made all the old buildings redundant, and now we've got like a modern set-up which doesn't need as much labour, we can milk a hundred and twenty cows and look after them with two men. Going back to my childhood, we probably had about seventy to eighty cows with three men.

C.   And all the mucking-out.

R.   Oh we used to do all that with a wheelbarrow and a shovel, and now there's less effort involved. More output. Cows are healthier. Happier. We've got about a hundred and twenty cows. And I've one man full-time. We've got two hundred and sixty acres. And we do all the work ourselves except silaging, which is all done by contractors, - which obviously in the olden days we used to make hay, and do all the work ourselves. So anything which involves very expensive machinery, we use contractors. So we basically, Robert who works for me and myself, just look after the animals. And then any jobs which need big machines, we contract people in to do it for us. Hedge-cutting. Ploughing. So. The way farming has gone is that we've become more specialised. Rather than having a bit of arable, a few cows, a bit of poultry, a few pigs. Everybody's kind of specialised, and we specialise in dairy. We're looking after as many cows as we can, and keep increasing the numbers, and let other people do the work for us if we can. And keep the staff as limited as we can. Rather than having too many people working for you, and trying to keep them busy all the year round.

D.   And what about marketing?

R.   Well the milk used to all be sold through the Milk Marketing Board. But that was disbanded five years ago, four or five years ago, and now we sell direct to a dairy in

Manchester called Waterfords. So they come and pick it up - that's another change as well: the milk used to be collected every day, but now it's collected every other day. And the milk's kept in a vat which is surrounded by ice banks so it will keep longer. We also acquired a farm three years ago, so that will help us expand, that's Castle Hill Farm. So we've got room to keep expanding, and we'll carry on milking cows, and we'll carry on increasing the number, to try and keep where we are.

D.   Have you changed the herd at all?

R.   Genetically the cows are now far more superior than they used to be, due to technology, basically. Better breeding. We're using sires on our cows to get replacements which come from all over the world. Rather than just having a stock bull, and maybe just being limited to going to the bull sale locally and buying as nice a bull as you can get.

D.   Does that mean you can do without stock bulls now?

R.   They still have a place, a part to play, stock bulls, because it's not always feasible to use A.I. all the year round. But we tend to use beef bulls as a stock bull, and try and use insemination bulls for what we can afford.

D.   So in fact the quality of the herd, because of that, it must be in a completely different league.

R.   You can turn over the genetics very quickly, and improve the animals very quickly, in quite a short time . . . Can you think of anything else?

C.   You keep silage now.

R.   Yes, we used to grow hay -

D.   Of course! The first thing I remember about you, before you were ever married, was you two roaring round the field by Midways, making hay!

C.   Oh yes, I remember doing that! Yeah!

R.   A big step forward was going from hay to silage, because we didn't need all the tackle. We aren't reliant on the weather like we used to be, because silage can be made in a day, and it can be carted in very quickly. These contractors cover the ground very quickly, whereas hay-making -

D.   Do you keep your silage here?

R.   Yes, there's a silage clamp which takes all the silage for the year and has a big sheet over it. And that feeds the cows from October to May.

D.   I remember when we lived at the vicarage, that field opposite the vicarage, you used to take about three mowings off a year. Was that already silage? because it didn't look as if it was hay-making.

R.   No, that'd be silage. So agriculture has basically moved away from a very labour-

361

intensive industry to more of a, er, efficient . . .

C.   More business-like now. Instead of Robert being a farmer, he's got to be a businessman now. Haven't you?

D.   It's capital-intensive, isn't it? I mean, the money that must go into all this machinery, and the equipment that you have, must be terrific. I mean, instead of paying out money in wages you do a big dollop and get all the equipment set up, I suppose.

R.   Well the only capital on our farm is basically cows. The milking equipment's got to be up-to-date, and there are ever so many good animals working for me. That's where our money's tied up.

D.   So although you have fewer people working, the person who does work for you, would you say he's more skilled?

R.   More skilled, yes. He's been to college, and gained certain awards. And he's been with me for four years. There used to be more labourers on the farm, but that's more like a skilled operation now.

D.   You said that had left you with a whole lot of redundant buildings. What did you do with them?

R.   Well slowly we converted them to be used for storing things. And some of the buildings have been used for DIY livery. More for our own ponies now than other peoples, but we did go through a stage when we had other peoples' horses, and they used to come and look after them themselves.

362

e)   Ashley Hall. Ian Crawford.

D.   How much land are you farming here, Ian?

I.   Altogether, about twelve hundred and fifty acres. That's Carrington, Ashley, Knutsford and Mobberley.

D.   Oh I see, yes.

I.   All the land. It's very split up.

D.   I hadn't realised that you were in Knutsford and Mobberley as well. It must be terribly complicated, keeping that sort of a show going?

I.   At one time of day you just had a farm, and your land was within a couple of hundred yards of your farm. It was fairly straightforward. But things have changed now, and we have to travel out to get to land, land's becoming so scarce. We have to travel and all the problems with it. Travelling on the main roads with tractors and trailers, and traffic, and safety. Health and Safety regulations. It is a headache. But it's something we've got used to. That's what we have to do if we want to stay in business. Unfortunately we have to keep on getting bigger, to stay viable. And if we don't get bigger, we go under. So Father retired, he was farming about seven hundred acres, and we've tended to grow every year since then.

D.   I see. How do you pick up land? Does it just become available?

I.   All sorts of ways. Some people approach us, we have to go and tender for it. Make enquiries, other agents, landowners . . .

D.   So it may be different parcels of land in different years?

I.   We've got eight different landlords. And trying to keep them all happy is not an easy task, negotiating with them, coming to the right value for the rent.

D.   And presumably this must mean that you have a constantly changing type of soil?

I.   Mmm. Very different. We've got peat land over at Carrington, light sandy land here, to heavy land here, and extremely light land at Mobberley. All different soil types. And we've got to have machines that will cope with all those different soils.

D.   Machines, and I suppose all the other . . . techniques. What you put in, things like that.

I.   Very different. Very different, yes. So that's what we're farming.

D.   What a headache! I'd no idea you were juggling with a thing like that. So are your basic crops fairly constant, or does that change every year?

I.   It's changing.

D.   I mean, I notice you've got broad beans around Ashley: I've never seen broad beans before.

I.   Yes, rather a lot of beans this year. They go to Saudi Arabia, for human consumption. The Saudis grind them down to a paste, add water to it, to make a guacamole. It's a very popular food. Who would have thought, a few years ago, we'd be growing for the Saudis! And Iran, and places like that.

D.   It's hard to credit, isn't it?

I.   We're growing oilseed rape for biodiesel on our set-aside land.

D.   That's on set-aside, is it?

I.   As long as you can't eat it, don't, you can do it. Most years we grow biodiesel. Anything you can't eat, you're allowed to grow. Pharmaceuticals and biofuels.

D.   How on earth do you find out about something like a market for broad beans in Saudi Arabia? Is there a bush telegraph or something?

I.   Trial and error, really. Growing a few different sorts of crops. Lupins will be the next ones we're going to grow.

D.   And presumably it's no bad thing for the ground?

I.   Does the ground good, yes. We've grown a lot of oilseed rape in the past, and the ground's getting tired of oilseed rape. So beans are a different crop altogether. So that's how the beans came in.

D.   And is there a staple? Are potatoes, for instance, a staple thing?

I.   That's our main business, producing potatoes for crisps.

D.   And that does stay constant?

I.   Fairly constant. The crisps, and pre-packing for supermarkets. The beef is nearly finished. We're getting rid of all the beef cattle now.

D.   Is this BSE?

I.   BSE, yes. We started a suckler herd, a Moray Grey suckler herd, outdoor-fed cattle, about three years ago, hoping that BSE would have worked its way out and confidence will have come back. But I've sold all my cows and calves this spring, and the quota, and we shall get rid of the young stock at Christmas.

D.   So it sounds as if, in the time that you've been in the business, you must have seen so many changes.

I.   I suppose so. The red tape and the bureaucracy and the book-keeping and the records, the certificates needed and the - again - health and safety, drives you round the bend. Although everybody agrees that health and safety's a good thing to have. It's everything, compounded.

D.   Where does this come from?

I.   From Europe. And the set-aside business, having to set aside ten per cent of your crop, farmland, into set-aside; and the bookwork again, and the records having to be kept. And the bookwork and records have to be kept for supermarkets. It's getting worse year by year.

D.   Oh, is it? The supermarkets?

I.   Every single thing we do on the farm now has to be recorded, dated, signed and accounted for. And the office is piling up with paper. I love farming, I've always wanted to be a farmer, because I enjoy it. But the fun has now gone out of farming. That's a very sad thing to say.

D.   Yes, it is. Yes.

I.   You get a great kick out of producing a crop, from a little seed to a big truckload of commodity to sell. Big kick out of it. But the regulations and restrictions just very quickly take all the pleasure out of it. Which is something our forefathers didn't have to put up with. There was none of that.

D.   Of course everyone talks about E.E.C., and the bureaucracy coming from there, but supermarkets I hadn't heard of before: how is it that they get a finger in this pie?

I.   They're so powerful, they are the gods of the food chain now. One small example is, we have to cover all our lights, light bulbs or strip lights, with polycarbonate covers. Cost us a fortune to do just that one thing. Yet you can go down to - your local supermarket, and all your food is under glass fluorescent lights. Now if we have to do it, why don't they have to do it?

D.   What's the idea?

I.   So that if the light shatters it doesn't cover your food in glass. That's just one little example. And so it goes, on and on and on. You're not allowed to wear jewellery or watches on the potato grader for fear of one dropping into the potatoes. You're not allowed to eat or drink on the potato grader. And everything has to be recorded: when you start, when you finish, everything been checked. So things have changed a lot.

D.   What about your actual methods? Have techniques changed much?

I.   Traditional farming methods haven't changed tremendously, because grandfather used to plough, used to break the soil down: in probably a different way from what we do, but he still ploughed and sowed and reaped. We're still doing that. But that is changing now. We're going away from ploughing, because of the cost of it. We're establishing crops very much quicker and easier. We're having early varieties, so we can harvest them quicker and earlier, to beat the weather. Usually beat the weather, but the last two years have been the worst, the wettest times we've ever known. Even the old guys you talk to have never known seasons like it. So we've had that to contend with that as well. We've only got to get a week of dry weather, and we're all happy again. Funny how our doom and gloom lifts when we get some decent weather! Whether we've forgotten all the bad weather from years ago I don't know, but the weather seems to have got a lot worse these last few years. Whether it's El Niño or whatever . . . I think he is probably to blame for it. In spite of everything, our yields have gone up. Because we've got a more scientific approach to growing a crop now. We can test everything now in the laboratories - what the plant needs, to grow. A few years ago we hadn't got a clue what a plant needs, to grow. You just gave it the same plant food that father gave, or grandfather gave. Now we know exactly, and are told, what exactly to put on. So it's getting pretty technical. And there are still things ahead that we don't really understand, like global satellite positioning of machinery in the fields, a computer telling you what part of the field to put what plant food. Things are moving very quickly. Technology's racing ahead of us. I'm computer illiterate. I've no interest in computers whatsoever. Which is a shame, because I think it's the way forward.

D.   Has there been a change in the number of people you employ on the farm?

I.   Less now than ever before. We still employ a nucleus of four full-time. But then at harvest time we could be ten. We used to have six cottages on this farm, until a few years ago.

D.   And how many have you got now?

I.   One.

2. War and Peace

a)   Frank Mosedale. Spitting fire

D.   Frank, this was sparked off by Pat's remark, last time, that you were a Spitfire pilot. Can you remember what you were doing before the war?

F.   I was a young lad working on Father's brickworks. Labouring, mainly. In fact I can remember exactly what I was doing the day war broke out.

D.   It's as vivid as that?

F.   I can remember being told that war had been declared.

D.   Had you seen it coming?

F.   Well, I think I was too young.

D.   How old were you?

F.   Well my father died in 1938, at the age of 42. He was in Stretford Memorial Hospital, and he died worrying that the war was coming. I always remember that. But it didn't register really with me at the time, but I can remember him worrying because he flew, and he was worried that they'd want him to go immediately, as a flying instructor. Which I suppose he would, actually. Because there weren't many about. When I eventually got away - and I say got away - to the RAF, I couldn't wait really, because I'd done quite a bit of flying with my father. I was very very keen on flying, and actually I volunteered once, in 1940. And my elder brother had then gone in the Air Force and I couldn't wait, I volunteered and I got home, told Mother, who broke into tears. So I reversed it the next day. But when the time came when I would prob-ably be taken anyway within a few months, I said to Mother, Well I'm not going to be just taken into the Army. I want to fly. So I volunteered again.

D.   And when would this have been?

F.   1941. And that was the beginning of the Air Force for me.

D.   But not the beginning of flying?

F.   No. No. To put it quickly, I was taken in at half a crown a day, I think it was, and shipped to St John's Wood, London. Recruited on Lords Cricket Ground with a lot of other guys, some hoping to be navigators, some rear gunners, some pilots. We spent quite a few months there before being shipped to an initial training unit in Torquay. I'm going very quickly through this. And then the ones who wanted to be pilots, such as myself, were taken to different aerodromes and given initial tests of capability. I went to a place called Booker, which is near High Wycombe. And it did nothing but snow. I was very lucky whilst I was there, I was very lucky to get any flying in at all. But we just got enough in for them to say, Yes.

D.   Now you people who'd been selected to be tested as potential flyers, pilots: had you all had flying experience?

F.   Oh, no. We'd certainly been through a selection committee that they have. And

369

then they had this aptitude test. Which I just got through, I think. Next thing that happened, we were shipped from Liverpool to South Africa, for flying training in Rhodesia. Which made me quite excited. But I'm a bad sailor - on those sort of liners. And I was sick for three days before I got used to it. Then I was fine. But we were ten weeks on the water. It's a long time, I couldn't believe it. In convoy.

D.   So you had to go at the speed of the slowest.

F.   That's right. On a boat called the Windsor Castle.

D.   Oh, yes! Yes. Good gracious, and that was already going then!

F.   And my first sight of Table Mountain was exciting. And the local people were very very nice. They queued up in cars to take us home to dinner. Wonderful people. Then we were put onto the train to Rhodesia, and we went through places like Ladysmith and Mafeking. A new book just come out, hasn't there, on Ladysmith.

D.   Ladysmith? Just this week, yes.

F.   To Rhodesia, to Bulawayo. And consequently I went to flying training there.

D.   How long did that take?

F.   I'm just trying to think. About six months.

D.   That's pretty good, considering it was, by this time, thick into the war. That they gave you as long as that.

F.   And it was a place I quite liked, apart from not being used to living at 4,000 feet, and everybody being black, I enjoyed it. I didn't get a commission there, I was a sergeant. And the outcome of that was, we had our presentation, we got our wings. Then I had what I now know was the most wonderful trip, but I didn't appreciate it at the time, because they sent us on board lorries and train, with wooden seats in the train, and ferryboats, I suppose: all the way to Egypt. From Rhodesia! It was a super trip really. I can't remember how long that took. Certain parts of it are vivid, like Kosumu, I remember very well. And my first sight of fireflies, in the Congo. We crossed Victoria, and Tanganyika in boats. It was some trip, really. Then we flew from Kosumu to Sudan, and then up the Nile on a Nile boat, into Cairo. When I look back on it now, I wish I could do it again! But I didn't appreciate it then, David. Not at all.

D.   No well, mind on other things. So there you are, trained, got your wings, and you land up in Cairo. What happens next?

F.   They had quite a number of pilots. In other words, they weren't waiting for pilots - I don't think they were losing enough at the time! - and what happened was, they had a Mark 5 Spitfire and a Hurricane. And we were all given the instruction books for these two. We'd passed out on flying training aircraft called Harvards. Single engine, nice aircraft. So they had these two, one Spitfire only, and one Hurricane only, and there must have been about thirty of us. And they gave us these books, like you get an instruction book on your car, and then the next day they said, well there's the Spitfire. We'll strap you in, you take half an hour to get used to it, and that was it. It was quite a big jump, because it is a very delicate aircraft, the Spitfire. The Hurricanes, much more comfortable, but not nearly as nice. So we did that. And then I was drafted with one or two others on ferrying duties; and that is picking up aircraft at certain places, and ferrying them to the Squadron. As they lost aircraft they needed new ones. And of course some of them wore out at that stage, but not many. And I did that for quite a while. I thoroughly enjoyed that up to a point, because we were flying so many different aircraft. We had a little book in which was written the type of aircraft you were entitled to fly. And it was very useful, because you could get stranded somewhere, you could take an aircraft to a Squadron, and they would say, Well so-an-so will be going . . . like a DC3 or something: and he'd probably take you part way back to where you want to get to. But then you were stranded. So the more different aircraft you were capable of flying, the quicker you got back again.

D.   Almost like these car delivery people with the red number plates, you see hitching on the road.

F.   Yes, yes. Except that you did it with aircraft. And I remember once, in a place called El Ouina, which is the airport in Tunis, and I'd been stranded there. My base was actually in Morocco. I'd been dropped there in an American DC3, and he was going no further, and I couldn't get out of it. No one was coming or going. Two days then was a long time, seemed a long time. In somebody else's bed. And I kept going to the commander of the station and saying, Haven't you got anything at all? Eventually he said, We've got a Boston which has got to go back all the way to - Syracuse, I think it was. In Sicily. He said, We have this plane, and you're very welcome to try it, if you want to. Have you flown anything like this? I said, Not really. He said, Well we've got full instructions here, you know. So I said, All right, let me read them up. It was a twin engined aircraft, which I'd never flown in my life. To cut a long story short, I read the thing up, and at the same time - I was then a staff sergeant - at the same time there was a Squadron Leader in the same position. And he was trying to get to a place called Blida, which is in Morocco. And he said, I'll tell you what: you fly this damned thing out, and I'll sign your book. And I thought, well if I can get onto Twin aircraft that would be great. So we did. I took it out, and he sat in the nose - it was one of these semi-bomber types - and we made it. And he signed it. He was very trusting. On the way in to Blida, the airspeed indicator was cracking up, it was an old aircraft, and I wasn't very happy about it. So we got down a bit fast. You see if your speedo's wrong you've got to be careful you're not going to stall. So I took it in a bit fast, to make sure. So he looked a bit pale! And then we were stationed in Fez for about a month, and they were bringing in Kittyhawks, American fighter planes, in crates into Casablanca. And so we were shipped in an old Anson to Casablanca to pick up these Kittihawks which had been assembled there, taken out of the crates and assembled, and took them, that was another new one, took them to the Squadron. But I got fed up with this, this ferrying. So one time I'd delivered and, sitting in the Mess tent was the Commodore of 92 Squadron, a fellow called Kingcombe. He was ex-Battle of Britain. I interrupted his lunch, and I said, Look. Any room in your place? For pilots? And he said - such a nice fellow - he said, What do you fly? Do you fly Mark 9s? Mark 9 was the latest Spitfire. And I said, Oh yes. You're just the sort of fellow we want, he said. I said, Are you kidding? He said No. Give me your rank, name and number, and where you are, and that's it. And about a week later the adjutant of our delivery unit called me in and said, What have you been doing? So I said, Why? What do you mean? He said, Somebody's made a very special request for you. He wants you to go with a view to being flight commander, and to be commissioned. So

I said, Well I can't wait! So it all worked out, and I was sent to the unit belonging to 244 Wing for just a week's training. And what they were doing was dive-bombing, with Spitfires. And I really enjoyed doing that.

D.   Where was this Squadron based?

F.   When I joined them they were at Perugia. Italy.

D.   And you were dive-bombing. At sea? Dive-bombing ships, would that be?

F.   No, troops generally. We were support for our troops. In other words, if the Germans were in my garage - it was almost as close as this - and our guys were here, where we are now, and they couldn't move them, they just rang through. And we had to hit that without hitting them. But on other occasions, any tank movements we used to go and bomb. Dive-bomb. It's quite an art really, when you're coming straight down, trying to hit one tank. Although sometimes, if there was a row of tanks, we might go in for the front one, knowing you're bound to hit the back one anyway!

D.   And what were you hitting them with?

F.   500 lb bombs. We had one underneath.

D.   So you only had one shot?

F.   Oh yes. You can imagine you had one on the Spitfire, between the wings. And you couldn't get more than a 500 lb bomb on them. But it was quite exciting. And although the war in Italy was getting towards an end there were quite a lot of troop movements. The other thing we used to do was recce harbours, for the bombers. So that the bombers could go in and plaster it. That was terrible. I didn't like that at all. Because you used to go over a harbour, and if you had no cloud cover you can't imagine the stuff that came up at you from the German navy. Unbelievable. Frightening.

D.   You couldn't get out of range? You couldn't fly high enough to be out of range?

F.   You mean over a harbour, say? I'm thinking of one particular time when we were over a harbour called Hola, on the Yugoslavian coast. It was covered in cloud. There were only two of us. And this fellow was very worried we'd run out of fuel, and he kept saying, How much further? When are we going to find it? It took a bit of finding. And on his last request I just sent him off, Jettison your tank, and go! And I'll spend another couple of minutes trying to find it, before I come with you. I said, Do you know your way back? he said, Yes. Fortunately I did find it, in a gap in the cloud. And I was able to get under the cloud. I had a little chart where you put whatever you saw in there, and you do this swoop, and back into the cloud again quickly. Which I did for a little while. I didn't want to stay too long, because each time I came out of the cloud up comes all this stuff again. So I didn't stay there too long, and the last time I came out of the cloud there were a couple of aircraft on the water. I thought they looked for all the world like Heinkels. And I thought, Oh my God! I've got to go down. So I waited a little while, and went straight down on top of these two. And when I was halfway there, I shouted to base what was happening, and then I realised they were a couple of Beaufighters, our own Beaufighters. They were very much the same shape. So I broke off, obviously. By which time I was almost down to sea level.

And these harbour defence guys, you wouldn't believe it! They used to call them 88 millimetre anti-aircraft guns. And they were shooting at me with these. I was about twenty feet off the water, and these things were coming past and bursting in front of me. So I went down to about three feet above the water, and I had to do that all the way back to base, it felt like, before these things stopped bursting. So that was one I do remember! After which, the end of my day, David, we were called out very early one morning to strafe a train, up north of Venice, near Udine. Between Venice and the Alps. And unfortunately, at deck level, strafing this train, one of the ack-ack fellows got my starboard wing, blew the oil cooler out. I got back up to 6,000 feet and baled out. I was very pleased, because I saw my aircraft actually burst into flames before it hit the ground. I didn't tell you this bit, but they used to experiment with camouflage. And this one was unpainted. All silver, all over. And they'd allocated it to me. This was the one I was flying that morning. They thought, against certain backgrounds, it would be good camouflage. But obviously it wasn't at low level! Consequently, when I was in a place called Dulag, which they put you into before you go to a prison, to be questioned, they wouldn't believe I was flying a Spitfire.

D.   They wouldn't believe you'd been flying a Spitfire? Why?

F.   Because it was silver.

D.   Oh, because of the colour! Yes, I see!

F.   What happened, they take you to a room with a couple of bully-looking boys, as if they're threatening you - they don't touch you - ask you threatening questions, this that and the other. And all I would tell them was my rank, name and number. That's what you were supposed to do. And after about, what? I was there twenty-one days in total; but after I should think about the eighteenth day, I was getting a bit fed up with this; and the fellow was getting used to me, and he said, Just tell me one thing, and you can go! In his broken English. And I said, What's that? And he said, What sort of aircraft was it? It wasn't a Spitfire, was it? Because he knew I'd been flying with other Spitfires. I said, Yes it was. Because what had I got to lose at that point? He looked at me, and whether he believed me or not, I still don't know! So off to prison camp I marched. But the funny story at the end of all that rubbish is that, from me being shot down, I was put into a barn with an American who was shot down as well, and kept there for the night. But between me being picked up: I landed with my parachute, and didn't even sit down, it was a good landing funnily enough, on my feet, got rid of the parachute, pushed it under a hayrick, and round the corner came an Italian with a beretta, you know. And I thought, Oh hell! I wasn't the least bit afraid of him, not a bit. I didn't know what he was talking about. But as he was telling me about something I heard this marching, down the road. And a squad of Gerries came down the road, straight to me, and I didn't like that at all. They were very brusque. And they put me into - I don't know if you remember, but in that war they had a lot of motorbikes with sidecars. And they put me in the sidecar, they put the guy from the sidecar onto the pillion, and he held a gun at me whilst the other guy drove off. And, of all the cheek, they took me to the gun that they reckoned had shot me down. And took a photograph! I'd forgotten all about this. And last summer, after we'd seen you here, we were in Spain. And I received a letter from a Squadron Leader Dunn, a serving historian, to say that there was a fellow in Germany who had something to do with me being shot down, wanted to know if I was still living, and could he trace me? Did I mind if he divulged my whereabouts, and that I was alive and kicking? So I said, No.

And then shortly after that I received a letter direct from this German, who had a copy of a photograph of me on this gun! This is fifty three years later! And he wasn't the guy that shot me down, but the photographer explained that one of them had died, the lieutenant had died, and the sergeant that was with him he hadn't heard from again. But he was the guy that had taken me on the train to Germany. He was my guard. And we're still corrresponding!

D.   And he had the photo?

F.   What had happened was the fellow that died, who'd been in charge of the gun, he died, probably seven years ago, and left this: the funny thing was, it was in an old cigar box, and my photograph was in this old cigar box with my name, date and time down under it. And he'd kept it as a souvenir. When he died, his daughter, who is now a solicitor, sent this to this guy who was a friend of theirs. And he contacted me. And I remember him well because - and I joked about it in my letter, I think he appreci- ated it: I was the only one with him in the carriage of a train going through the Alps. All snow. Which route, I'm not sure, but it was into Austria. And as we got into the train, prior to the Alps, he made me take my shoes and stockings off. Knowing that I couldn't run away in all this snow. So I reminded him of this in my letter, I said Good Thinking! But he was very nice, and so, so pleased I was still alive. And he became, and still is, - oh no he's retired, he's eighty one - the head of some forestry commis- sion in Germany. Quite interesting. So that was probably my biggest wartime shock, to hear from this fellow after fifty three years. It was a pleasant shock.

D.   It sounds as if you'd been doing some very very low flying.

F.   Oh we were, we were on the deck. Yes.

D.   Did planes often get lost doing work like that? Crashing into the ground?

F.   Well it's difficult to say, because if a plane did go in you couldn't swear that it hadn't been hit.

D.   And nobody would go back and look at the wreckage anyway. So that's not the sort of question it's possible to answer.

F.   No. The only thing I haven't asked this fellow yet, and I'm going to: I never knew what was on that train. Who or what was on it?

D.   You never got round to strafing it? You got intercepted before you reached it?

F.   Oh, no. I was actually hitting the train.

D.   You were? You did get a few in before they got you?

F.   Oh, yes!

D.   Where was the gun that got you? Was it on the train?

F.   Oh no, it was aground. It was in a field actually. Oh no, we found the train, and had a good go at it. Quite a few carriages. There were carriages you see, not . . .

D.   Ah. Not a freight.

F.   You know, it might have been Hitler or somebody. Probably not, but I'm curious.

D.   It would be lovely to know, wouldn't it? Yes.

F.   At that level, you see, and there is a train there, they're ready to protect the train. And as soon as you go down it's almost as bad as the harbour. Not quite, but it's coming in at all angles. And it was only a small one that hit my wing. 20 mil.

D.   But it doesn't take much, I don't suppose.

F.   No, it doesn't. If it's an explosive shell, a small one, all it has to do is hit the wing. And as it happened it hit the oil cooler. So the engine was getting hotter and hotter.

D.   You must have been quite pleased to have managed to get your plane back up to 6,000 feet, with that much damage.

F.   Oh, I was. I was very pleased. And I got the voice of my Number 2, who was asking where I was. And I told him as well as I could. I couldn't see any planes at all around me, by then. And I didn't hear from him again, before I got out. I was determined to get out before it caught fire. You see the oil temperature had gone.

D.   So it was not going to be long before it went.

F.   No.

D.   I'm too young to know these things, it's probably an obvious answer: but were you alone in the plane?

F.   In the Spitfire? Oh they are single seaters.

D.   So you never ever have anyone else with you? No, I hadn't realised that. So you have to do everything yourself. Yes, I see now how they have such a reputation. Because you do everything.

F.   Yes, they're built as a single seat, a fighter. Yes. And we were dive-bombing, and this was just another sideline we got into somehow. They did it pretty well. They were capable of four hundred miles per hour. Straight down, you know. They were very strong, very handleable little aeroplanes.

D.   That was their secret, that they were so handleable?

F.   Oh, yes. They felt very delicate after other planes. Very delicate. And if you saw one, and look at the undercarriage, you know, the wheels: they're not very robust at all. Everything was done for weight, I suppose. I got to like them. In Catania, in Sicily, I also spent a while because I was getting sick of ferrying, they were repairing solely Spitfires. And I went as their test pilot for a while. Had quite good fun then.

D.   I've only just started hearing about something I don't understand at all, this G force business. How racing drivers have to have necks like absolute oxen to withstand it. Was there a lot of that? Did you have terrific strains?

F.   Oh yes, you could. If you were in a tight turn, or . . . This was the sort of thing you were getting by dive-bombing, because you've got to go not too far towards the ground before you release the bomb, and then pull up in time. And the harder you pull out, the more G force you get. So you got to know, after a while you got to know, how far you could go.

D.   Because they're saying, I picked up somewhere, they're saying that the next generation of fighter planes will be unmanned, simply because any improvement on the present performance would give G forces that no pilot would be able to take.

F.   Well today's pilot wears a G suit, to offset that effect. So I suppose they're saying that the next stage from that, when it gets beyond the G suit, is no pilot. The modern ones virtually work themselves now, don't they? Not the modern fighter, the modern bomber.

D.   Did you get back to flying at all after the war?

F.   Yes, I did. I joined the Auxiliary Air Force. I transferred to the . . . And I flew from Hooton. On what were then the Meteors.

D.   Oh did you? So you got your crack?

F.   I did fly jets.

D.   That must have been quite fun?

F.   Yes. The only thing I didn't like, they were our first British jet to go into active service, weren't they? I think they were the only ones. Right at the end of the war. The only thing I didn't like about them was the amount of fuel they carried. You didn't normally fly them for more than an hour. The amount of fuel they could carry would only last just over an hour. And if you had a quarter of an hour's fuel left - it happened! - and you thought you were twenty minutes away, you'd had it. And it did happen on the odd occasion. Once to a friend of mine. He had to come down in a field adjacent to the airport. It was everybody's worry, that. At that time. I mean, you could be over Southport - we were at Hooton - you could be over Southport, and it was probably cloudy or something, and you'd hope you could get directly back. But they were fun. So that all finished in 1954, I think. They closed the Auxiliary Squadron then. So that was the end of my flying career. Oh no it wasn't. I was a member of the Lancashire Aero Club for a while. But I had to pay for it then. That's when I used to take Pat over to France occasionally. So there you are.

D.   Well, there's not many people who've flown Spitfires anymore, I don't suppose.

F.   No there aren't. There aren't many still living. I meet an odd one occasionally.

D.   Well thank you for telling us about it, Frank.

b) George Watsons's Desert Campaign

Geo. Well I'd joined the Terriers before the war, the Northumberland Fusiliers. Then went to France in February 1940.

D.   Tell me, just before we get to France; when did you join the Terriers?

Geo. March 23rd, 1939.

D.   So you could see it coming?

Geo. Yes. Yeah. I should have gone in the Police Force the same night - the following night, rather. They came for me the following night, the police. My father had gone to the door to see what these policemen wanted. Anyway, they asked to come in. They came in, Sgt Henderson and Sgt Jack, and said that your son had applied for the police force, and we've come to tell him that he's been accepted. And I said to them, I'm sorry, I've joined the Territorial Army. That was the end of the police force. I'd applied to the police before the Terriers, you see. Then playing football one night, four or five of us decided to join the army, the Terriers. And we all went up there and signed in. Went to the doctor's the following night, the five of us. And it was only me that passed. The other four failed. I went in first, passed, and the other four failed. Two had flat feet, and the other ones had eyesight trouble.

D.   They were all right for playing football, but not good enough for the forces! Did you have brothers and sisters?

Geo. I had five brothers and one sister. My father was in the army, he joined in 1940.

D.   Had he been in the previous war?

Geo. He'd been in the Great War, yes.

D.   So he joined up for a second dollop?

Geo. For a second time, yes. And then my brother John, he joined up the day after me. And then Tommy joined the Navy. The other two lads were too young, still at school. Derek and Victor were only five and three-and-a-half when I left school, when I left home. I remember the first night we were called up, on the Friday night before the war started on the Sunday, or war was declared on the Sunday: and as I come from work, from the factory about half past five, there was a motorcycle and sidecar pulling away from the front door, two soldiers on it, and I thought, Oh that's it. Anyway I got in, got into the house, and there was a letter left there stating Report to the Drill Hall immediately, and bring your uniform, wear your uniform, and that's it. Your civilian clothes will be returned home afterwards. So I had it on for the rest of the time then. Until '46.

D.   But you'd been in the Terriers for a couple of years?

Geo. No no, March. And I was in France in the February. And we only did about three weekends, rifle training. I went to France in February 1940, and came back on June 3rd, to Dover, through Dunkirk. And then ended up having a lift, got to Knutsford, and a lift in a fish van, Bailey's Fish Van, to Tatton Park. And two or three nights later I met Glad. And we went away three days later, went down to Yeovil in Somerset, and then after that I was sent abroad again, and I was abroad then until the end of '45. And went with the Eighth Army into Alamein. I was taken prisoner at Knightsbridge, about thirty miles due south of Tobruk, on June 6th 1942. And on June 11th 1942 we escaped, bringing back about twenty eight Germans and Italians with us: escaped with the aid of the Long Range Desert Group, which was the beginnings of the SAS.

D.   Now can we go back over that? How did you get caught in the first place?

Geo. We put a barage in about half past four in the morning, which lasted about two hours, and then we had to go forward. We went forward, and we were surrounded by about half past four in the afternoon. They took the whole brigade, about four thousand of us. And we were all marched off, like, all your kit had gone, you were just left with what you stood in. I had a pair of shorts on and a shirt, that was it, and your boots. And we had to start marching. We were guarded by Italians in this prisoner of war thing, just barbed wire set up on the desert, and they went around in threes and fours, they were that scared of you! And we had no water given us for three days, nothing at all.

D.   And this is in the desert?

Geo. Yes. In fact we crawled underneath, two of us crawled underneath the wagons and let the radiators off, trying to drink the water out of that. And in the end it got that bad that someone had brought, had a tin of syrup from somewhere, I don't know where they got it from, but they had a tin of syrup. And you spent a penny into the old dixie lid and mixed it with syrup, and tried to drink that. Because there was quite a number of lads on the floor with their lips all swollen, and tongues, which wouldn't have survived, they'd have died. And then we were loaded up, this was about three days afterwards, we were loaded onto these Italian trucks, driven by Italians but guarded by Germans. And there were twenty or thirty of us stuck in these wagons. Anyway they had two Cockney lads in the front of the cab, I don't know how they got there, but two of the lads from my regiment was in the front of the cab. And they directed this armoured vehicle thing '*To the left go, To the left go*' all the time, you see. Of course the fools did that, the Italians did that, and the Germans decided with them. So that was all right, you see. Because the Long Range Desert Group was lobbing these shells over, you know. They were attacking from the rear. And these two tank things, tank transporters with tanks on, had followed us, followed where we were going. Broke away from the main lot, you see. And they went down into this big wadi, we got bogged down and couldn't do nothing else after a few miles. And these Long Range Desert Group shelled us. And there was only myself and Sgt Dodds, which was two of us, left of about two hundred and thirty men. And Ernie Dodds, this platoon sergeant, got shot through the knee, his right knee, with the bullets from a British Bren gun, from these fellows that were firing at us. So I had to help him, to get him back, he couldn't use this leg at all. And he took his shirt off and started jumping around, waving at these fellas, you know. Anyway they did stop firing. But they wouldn't come to us, we had to go to them. And as we went along these Germans all had to come with us, threw their weapons down, what they had, and they all had to come with us. Twenty eight of them. So we got onto these transporters, they had transporters there with them that was bringing some tanks back that they'd picked up, you see, they'd broken down. And they took us down to Sidi Bengala, and from there we went down to a place called Sidi Bish, and on to Cairo. After that we went back up the desert again, and more fighting. We were there till it was finished. Up at Tunis.

D.   Were you fighting tanks?

Geo. No, we were Bren gun carriers. Vickers machine guns. And we were supporting and protection to these carriers, artillery pieces, you know. I was with the Desert Rats themselves, the Eighth Armoured Brigade it was called then. And then we were trans-ferred to the First British Armoured Division, which was a colossal Division really. So we were called the First British because the Americans had a First American Armoured Division, you see. And I fought at Tunis, then they sent us back, after that finished, they sent us down to Cairo, war-weary after two-and-a-half years in the desert. And we went down to Cairo, and then from Cairo they sent us across to Italy, to join the Tenth Army, Tenth Indian Division. So I was in that until the war finished. They sent us to Casino, we didn't get into action.

D.   You missed the action at Casino, did you?

Geo. We were sent there, but we were on standby, they didn't send us in. Our Ghurkas went in, we had five battalions of Ghurkas with us. They were in. And some of the Indian Infantry. And then I came back to England in the August after that war fin-ished.

D.   This is August, '45?

Geo. '45, after the war was finished.

D.   Had you kept in touch with Gladys all this time?

G.   We could retire on all the money we spent on stamps!

Geo. I'd been writing all the while.

G.   I've got a box upstairs, a leather suitcase, full of the letters which had been - what-do-you-call-it?

Geo. Photostat. There was a big sheet of paper you wrote on, and it'd come back about six by four.

G.   I've got a box full upstairs.

Geo. So we come back by Lancaster bomber. Twenty of us in a Lancaster bomber. There was forty of them set off, and only thirty eight got home. One come down in France, the other one more or less ditched in the sea, but near land, you know. Anyway, got landed at Peterborough, and the following day I come up to Chester. And they said, Tomorrow you can go on leave home. So I sent a telegram home to my mother, said I'd be home by midnight. I didn't, I come here instead.

c) Stella and Rafe Grassby's Flying Colours

S.   And then the war broke out, didn't it? And you joined up, didn't you?

R.   I volunteered. I went down Manchester and joined up, and I got called up within a fortnight.

D.   And did you volunteer for the RAF?

R.   I volunteered for air crew, but I was colour blind on green. So I finished up as a despatch rider. It was lovely in the summer, but in the winter, when you were getting wet through -

S.   You went over the cliffs didn't you, once. Well anyway, we sort of were going with each other when he joined the RAF. And then he got posted, didn't you? Abroad.

D.   Where to?

R.   Well I was at West Kirby, at Liverpool. That was the embarkation place. And I got on this boat, it was called the El Bosso. We got on this, and I think there were sixteen ships in this convoy. The next thing I knew, we'd been at sea two days, and this Warrant Officer came in the cabin and he said, Grassby get your kit together, they're taking you back to West Kirby. So I went back on deck, and this corvette had pulled up alongside. And it must have been about sixty foot down. Get down this rope ladder, he said. So I got halfway down the rope ladder, and fell down the rest! Anyway I went back to West Kirby, and Stella had been to see the Padre hadn't you? To tell him you were expecting?

S.   I wasn't expecting.

R.   Well there was something like that, they brought me back anyway.

D.   And had you joined up as well by then?

S.   I was in the WRAFs, yes. To get away from here, really.

R.   It's a funny thing. This boat I was on, the El Bosso: about three or four months after, I was hitch-hiking home, and I was stood near Chester and a fellow stopped in a car and he said, Where are you going? I said, Knutsford, near Mobberley. Oh, he said, I'll drop you off in Knutsford. And he'd got this thing in the car with him, Trinity House. He said, Have you been abroad? So I said No, I said, I was on the El Bosso, and told him what happened, and how they took me off. He said, You were very lucky, he said. It got sunk at Freetown. He said, I work in the place where the convoys are assembled. And that was it. Trinity House. He said, It got torpedoed, just off Freetown.

S.   So anyway you came back didn't you, you got a three-day pass didn't you? So we got a Special Licence, and we got married. The Padre married us. And then where did you get posted after that?

R.   Oh I think it was near Derby, between Derby and Burton-on-Trent.

S.   First of all, after you got over here, I got pregnant didn't I?

D.   Then you really got pregnant?

S.   Really got pregnant, yes. And you were in London then, weren't you? We had that flat in West Drayton.

R.   West Drayton. Anyway Stella went in to this hospital in Middlesex. And she finished up in that - was it Charles 1 had it built for Nell Gwynne? Was it Charles ll? You know Nell Gwynne, the orange lady? And it was marvellous. They brought her out for her recovery. And it was like a small mansion, in all its lovely grounds. And all the stairs were carved with oranges.

D.   Good gracious, Nell Gwynne. Oranges!

R.   It was lovely, wasn't it? I'm not sure if it was Charles 1 or Charles ll. He used to knock Nell Gwynne about. And he had this built for her.

S.   That's right, yes. I'll always remember it, I was on a stretcher. And they took me up this massive, - oh, huge - staircase. Nearly as wide as this room, with thick red carpet on it. And there was only two people to each room, with a balcony. Lovely wisteria growing up the wall, you know. The gardens were beautiful, weren't they? But it was only for members of the Air Force.

R.   Stella wrote me a letter, when I was at West Kirby, going abroad. And I think it must have been at least six or seven months after, I got this letter back, and it had got this stamp, this RAF stamp on the back, "Not known in Middle East Command." "Not known in Chakaradi." " Not known in Freetown." You got about six different places where . . . And it had followed me all the way, and I got it back. I wish I'd kept it now. They won't do that today, the Post.

S.   But if you're both in the Service they looked after you. If I'd been not in the WRAFs I wouldn't have had all that treatment, you see.

D.   What happened at the other end? When the war finished: were you long getting demobbed?

S.   No. 1945.

R.   About six months, wasn't it? I nearly signed on for a bit longer. But she wanted me out.

d) Ron Hobson. The "Forgotten Fleet" remembered

D.   How did it all start, Ron?

R.   It started really because something had to be done during the war. You didn't go on your own, you were pushed in it with the age-groups. I went off, as I said earlier, to HMS Collingwood, known as the Stone Frigate, at Fareham, and started basic training with their parade ground, and seamanship. But on the first Sunday we were allowed ashore and we went down to Gosport, and I saw my first warship. I'd never seen a warship before. I'd read about them in history, but being North of England, there's no naval presence, and this turned out to be the battleship Queen Elizabeth. As we went over on the ferry it seemed so massive! The thought was, How could twenty-odd thousand tons float?! That was my introduction to it. And a bit of naval discipline. I think the naval patrol realised we were youngsters under training, because I got pulled up for opening my overcoat and going for my handkerchief to blow my nose! But we set off, in this seamanship training. In these training camps there was every conceivable thing that could happen at sea, on deck. There were places for anchor work, sea-boat work, wires, fenders, and the general naval life. You were kitted out. On the way along there, some days you were doing seamanship, and other days you'd be doing what we call Parts of Ship, doing all the sweepings up and things like this, and another part there'd be an hour or two in the gunnery department.

A couple of humorous things were, at that time it was November, it was very frosty and cold. And we were to go sometimes in the gym at eight o'clock in the morning: which would normally be six o'clock in the morning, because the clocks were two hours on at that time. Going in the gym there, the PTIs, they came in with their big rolled jerseys there, and opened all the windows: *Right! Off shirts! Still cold are you? Right! All outside!* And we doubled round the parade ground. We come back quite warm! I will give them their due there: when we came back in, us being young, they made sure that we went into that shower, a warm shower when we'd finished. And the other humorous part is, during the mornings you were told that that's the first period of seamanship, working on the boats, and you'd be quite warm after all that working, because you didn't wear overcoats: and for the last series before dinner they'd take you into the cinema for a film. And the cinema was centrally heated. Of course we were young, heads were nodding, and the instructors had great big sticks, poking at you to wake you up! It was quite a good idea. And the final one, you get on the parade ground first thing in the morning, you fall-in, I think in the army they call it in Companies, but in the navy it's called Divisions. And after the morning prayers and the raising of the White Ensign, you left the parade ground at the whim of the Drum Major of the Royal Marine Band. One icy morning there, he struck up double-march, and everyone was skidding and falling over! But you accepted it. And this training, to me, it made a man of me.

I enjoyed the gunnery part, and I was recommended then for the three week gunnery course at Whale Island, which is another part of Portsmouth Harbour, HMS Excellent. We were still billeted at Fareham, in HMS Collingwood, and we were bussed, or lorried, to Excellent where, from the time you step out until you go inside again, you doubled. You ran everywhere. The only time that finished was when you got out of the camp, or when work finished for the day. And it's a place where there were masses of gun turrets. I went along there through all the different turrets: quick thinking, and it taught me to make decisions. I can make a decision and I'll do it. I may make a mess of it, and that's it; but it taught you that, and teamwork. There were seven of you on the gun, and you went all round these positions, and including the different types of ammunition, which you picked up by the coloured bands. All this was also taking part in the middle of some of the major raids on Portsmouth and Southampton by the Luftwaffe. And after we passed out we got a bit of leave.

I was recommended for a gunnery, but it coincided with my eyesight going short-sighted, so consequently I couldn't go on gunnery. So after that I was sent to the anti-submarine school at Campbeltown, in Argyll. And it was a case of an all-night journey from Portsmouth, as far as Wemyss Bay, through Edinburgh, Glasgow, and then of course we had breakfast in the club there, and then to sail to Campbeltown we went through one of the well-known holiday cruises, through the Kyles of Bute, going up to Dunoon, Innellan, Colintraive, then going to Tarbert. And there it was disproved that the Scots people are tight, moneywise: we got off the ferry and into this cafe there, and sandwiches, buns and drinks of tea were absolutely free, provided by the people of Tarbert. And then we were taken by bus. We had to go down the rough side of Argyll, it was a local service bus, where you sat on it with people, chickens, pigs, vegetables, the lot! It seemed that the road was closed because one of the ships had done a practice firing, and used live ammunition by mistake. So some of the roads were closed. And we got to Campbeltown, which was then the home of the anti-submarine school, and we were billeted in the Grammar School. From there every conceivable ASDIC set, it was known as Asdic then, Allied School of Anti-Submarine, now it is known as sonar. And twice, three times a week we went out to sea. And what we went to sea in was a lot of private yachts. All people with loads of money and that, they'd been commandeered, and they were really marvellous things. And funnily enough the skipper on one of them said to me, Where are you from? I says Altrincham. Oh, boody hell, he says, I come from Bowdon! I don't to this day know his name. But of course after this Passing Out from this school we went to the main barracks, again through the Kyles, to Dunoon, and from Dunoon back down to Portsmouth, to join HMS Ursa, a U Class destroyer.

D. How long had you been in by now?

R. From the November to May.

D. Six months, seven. You must have been a different person by now?

R. I was, actually. I went in, I was just over nine stone, and on my demobilisation papers I was twelve stone seven. HMS Ursa used to patrol; and previously to that, I should have remarked, in one of the destroyers that came up there, it was a Free French one, to have a dome change - the dome is where the oscillator is, underneath the ship, from Asdics - we were sent off on this for a patrol of the entrance of the North Channel. The South Channel, St George's Channel, was sealed off at that time because of submarines, and all the convoys came in through the North Channel, for the Clyde and Liverpool. And I had my first bout of sea-sickness! It took me about a fortnight, because it was a ship which, if you dropped a little cork over the side and the cork bobbed, then she moved as well. God she was lively! Especially when she started charging about at thirty knots. And it took that long, then it just suddenly stopped.

D. A fortnight, did you say?

R. Yes, on and off. It was still early spring, about this time of year, working off Campbeltown.

D.   Were many of you?

R.   Yes, quite a lot. Especially on these smaller ships.

D.   This was all prior to joining HMS Ursa?

R.   Yes. And I was never sea-sick again until the day after my twenty-first birthday. Rum-inflicted!

D.   You took the words out of my mouth!

R.   Yes, rum-inflicted! And we were on our way home from the Far East, which we shall come to later, when we left Fremantle, and our first port of call was Colombo. And out of the harbour there, there's quite a groundswell, and as we came out, as usual, *everyone fall-in, Guard and Band*; we came through the breakwater, and only for about twenty minutes she rolled and pitched. We'd just fell-out from leaving, I was walking to the mess, I felt burned from throat to stomach. With the acid, the spirit, I suppose. But as I say, I've got a bit far ahead of myself.

D.   So, back to the Ursa. Named after the Great Bear was she?

R.   Yes. Part of the Twenty-fifth Destroyer Flotilla. And Mr Robinson, when we were talking, remembered when he was on Rodney, being escorted by the Twenty-fifth, about VE Day.

D.   Would that have included you?

R.   Yes. But we used to go on patrol, and block off right across from the Bay of Biscay, to stop any of their E-Boats. And then suddenly we were told, Right, you're going in harbour for a boiler clean.

D.   This is still in Portsmouth?

R.   Still at Portsmouth. Went into Portsmouth, we got three or four days' leave. We went to sea then, to take the old battleship Malaya to Plymouth. Very old, she'd been used at D Day, and I believe she was getting what is called condenseritis, salt was getting into the boilers, which is dangerous. And we took her there, went out the next day to pick up this convoy, and the same thing happened to Ursa. So what they did, coming back to Portsmouth - this was the Sunday afternoon and Southsea beach had just been re-opened for people, and it was a glorious day - we were told to paint red, and leave the boats hanging, and fake bandages were put round us: to give the impression we'd been in some scrap. And we hadn't, it was a ploy or something in case there'd been an agent of some sort watching. Next day we were told to de-ammunition for the refit. They called it the tropicalisation. And we were sent on ten days' leave. After that we did a bit of a work-up, to make sure everything was OK, then straight up to Scapa Flow.
        There, when we got there, the tale went out that the Tirpitz was loose, the German battleship, and we went skating up to Norway with the battleship King George *V*, the aircraft carrier, the whole lot, charging torpedoes at everything. She just moved further up the fjord when we got there. But it had to be done, it's just one of those things. And then they sent us what we call going out on these patrols, because

some of the German ships - there wasn't that many - and their submarines, used to try and sneak out between Greenland and Iceland, to get into the Atlantic. And then we were suddenly told, Right, you can ride home, and when we get, we're leaving with the battleship King George *V* and two more destroyers, because we're going out to the Far East - we'd been warned we were going out to the Far East, to form the nucleus of the British Pacific Fleet. Suddenly we were sent up to Greenock where, on the battleship King George *V*, she was inspected by the King, Queen and the two Princesses. And when they left the KG *V* we were all fell-in as they went past on the way back, with the *Hip, Hip, Hooray!* and all that. Then the signal comes back from His Majesty the King, *God speed on your journey. Splice the mainbrace!* Which was the extra tot of rum. Which I was not entitled to at that time because I wasn't old enough.

D.   How old did you have to be?

R.   Twenty. So you got the same measure in lime juice.

D.   Ugh!

R.   But in the case of emergencies, if it was very cold and that, you were given some. But it was watered to two in one - two parts water in one part rum. And we set off with her then. Going down the Irish Sea there was a swept channel at this time through the St George's Channel which as you know is off South West England. And we were told, You can go on the upper deck and have your last look at Britain. Have a look to port: - Blackpool Tower! And then we set off, and I know we looked brave, brave sailors there: but when we crossed the Bay of Biscay I've never seen a sea like it except later on. There was times when the destroyers were in the trough, and you just couldn't see a thing but a wall of water. Next minute you'd be on the top of it, and you could see all around, and there perhaps the KG *V*, 35,000 tons, was down in the trough. And then the usual ceremony off Trafalgar, bow to Nelson and his whatser-name; but it was a bit of a flop because we'd had such a rough time. And I wasn't sick, by the way. Felt rough, mind you. Felt rough. Because we were down to just dry biscuits and water. Sometimes a weak tea, something like that. They daren't light the cookers, because they were oil-fired in the Galley, the equipment, they're not electric like they are today. And then we went into Gibraltar.
     The same night they left Gibraltar, and it was left to the Captain to decide that ships proceeding East were to be allowed four days, either in Malta or Alexandria. And Commander Wybird chose Malta, on the Saturday night. And as we turned-to the place was lit up: you've not seen lights like it. And then, next morning, oh, half-past five, six o'clock, Malta lived up to its name: The Land of Bells and Smells! That was the nickname among sailors, The Land of Bells and Smells. All Sunday morning they were ringing. But in the afternoon it was a normal day. Because a lot of us went watching a football match at Selina. After that we were in the time when, even though they'd had it rough, at that time all the sailors, and all the servicemen besides us, used to go for one thing: steak, egg and chips. Whether it was old horseflesh, or what! we went for steak, egg and chips. And then some went down to Strada Strata - I don't know if you want that translating?

D.   Yes, I think so.

R.   That is what is known as The Gut. The street of brothels.

D.   I thought we must be getting there soon!

R.   Adult entertainment! Where they said, there, that it's the only place where the sailors are allowed to walk without their hats. Because if the girls come out and got hold of the hat you had to go in for it, and you couldn't get out until you what'sit. I could tell you a joke about that, but it's rude so I'd better not!

D.   I've never known that stop you before!

R.   It'd be censored! And after that we did a night encounter with part of the Med Fleet. And we went on then to Port Said, to go down the Canal. And I don't know who it was, but as we were waiting to go, we were alongside a troopship and some-one kept shouting to me off this, but I couldn't place who it was. And we sailed going down the Canal, and the only thing I realised afterwards was how true it grew, watching the film of T E Lawrence, Lawrence of Arabia, with the sandbanks there. And the stations there, as you go down, is sort of little castles with people looking down. And suddenly the order came down, Change into tropical kit! And, going out from the Med, you can go straight through. Coming back the other way you have to wait in the Bitter Lakes for the stuff to come out. Coming home we did have a swim in the Bitter Lakes. And went right through then to Port Tewfik, Port of Suez it's called, where we fuelled again. Then it was straight across to Trincomalee, in Ceylon. Of course it's Sri Lanka now, isn't it. That was when we started working up into Task Forces, to go and join with the Americans in the Pacific in time. And as the ships came, arriving, we did one minor Fleet Air Arm strike on the oil wells in Sumatra, and we also did destroyer sweeps, and blowing little Japanese boats out of the water between Nikobar Island and the Andaman Islands, to catch anything Japanese there. We spent Christmas and New Year in Trincomalee.

D.   Now which year would this be?

R.   It would be Christmas '44.

D.   And New Year '45?

R.   New Year '45, yes that's right. We had the usual bit of a service on board. The Captain and Officers served us with us Christmas Dinner, then we had a bit of a sods' opera at night. That's not as bad as it sounds: what it means is Ship's Own Dramatic Society! Where anyone can give a turn or anything.

D.   What did you do?

R.   I was in the Corps de Ballet. With big heavy boots on! Had to find us boots out. And grass skirts and things. Some could sing, some was conjurors. It's surprising what talent crops up there.

D.   And you were dancing?

R.   I was dancing, yes. And then we all suddenly left on the 2nd of January, to start the big Fleet Air Arm raid on Palembang, to cut off the Japanese oil supplies which they were using. You know, Sumatra and Java, with all this oil and rubber places for them: destroy as much of this. We were very lucky afterwards: I was still on the destroyer Ursa at the time, and we were summoned alongside the Indomitable, the aircraft carrier, with the Admiral in charge of the whole operation, he's well known, Captain Vian, the Altmark Captain, he rescued the people from the Altmark at the time of the Norway what'sit. According to the history books I've read, the Admiralty liked to keep him at sea, because he was too blunt! Well he was really, because during a raid by the Japanese Kamikazes the Eurylus, which was a cruiser, fired some shells which were not fused, and they landed on the Illustrious carrier, and killed quite a few of our own blokes. What they call friendly fire. Part of the fortunes I suppose. And he came alongside. We were given all the details of the operation to take to the Cocos Islands, the Cocos and Keeling Islands, in the Indian Ocean, where there's a cable and wireless station. We weren't allowed ashore because, to put it bluntly, it was an island free of disease at the time. But the water there was that clear. It's the first time I've seen a massive sting ray, it must be nearly as big as this end of the room, it was massive. And it's the only time I've ever seen swordfish. So, what did we do? Threw a grenade over the side! From the Gunnery Officer, like. Didn't get it. But going back to join the Fleet for another set of operations against Sumatra and Java, we dropped some depth charges on purpose, and had a feed of fish.

D.   It worked?

R.   It worked! And then we did go back again to Trincomalee for a final big session when the whole Fleet what we were going to use for the Task Force, to do a massive raid on Colombo: not with real ammunition. It was just to be approached, and the local defences of Ceylon as it was then, Sri Lanka today, were to defend it.

D.   This was an exercise?

R.   An exercise with what we call from the shore, Throw-off shooting. And they decided that the Fleet could operate as a Fleet, we were trained up enough, and it was decided that we would go to Australia. And on the way, just overnight, we stayed at Fremantle and refuelled. Well it wasn't big enough for the carriers and battleships to get into their harbour, so we went again

D.   May I interrupt? Tell me, when you say you're with the whole Fleet, how many ships would that be?

R.   There was four aircraft carriers, two battleships, eight cruisers, and sixteen destroyers. That was the main Fleet. Plus what they call a Fleet Train, which came into its own when we got into the Pacific, where in a certain area there would have been the tankers, ammunition ships, hospital ships, the Woolworths-type aircraft carriers. A floating base, to be exact. And rotation of ships, to go back for boiler cleans and what'sits.

D.   Yes. And this is called the Fleet Train?

R.   The Fleet Train, yes. When it was first originated the Admiral who was in charge of the whole thing, Bruce Fraser, you've probably heard of him, the Admiral to take over the Fleet Train was presented by Fraser with a green flag and a whistle! A bit of fun.

D.   Where would the Admiral be?

R.   He had his own bridge and quarters. Generally speaking the Fleet was under the command of Bruce Fraser the whole time. His headquarters was in Sydney, for the simple reason he was too senior over these American admirals: because we became under the Americans, and we adopted the American style of signalling, the British did. And at sea we had another chap, a Vice-Admiral, called Rawlings, Vice-Admiral Rawlings. In charge of the aircraft carriers was Vice-Admiral Vian; in charge of the cruisers was a Rear-Admiral Brind, who was Commander-in-Chief in the Far East over the Amethyst incident, after this war. And Rear-Admiral Eddleston was in command of the destroyers. And a Vice-Admiral was in command of the Fleet Train.

D.   And over the whole thing is this chap

R.   Bruce Fraser

D.   In Sydney?

R.   In Sydney, yes.

D.   That's where the headquarters were?

R.   That's where the Headquarters would be. Of course as time went on and we advanced farther, he moved further up, in time. But that was when we sailed round to Sydney. We were arriving at Sydney at five and six in the morning: Keep quiet, no one knows you're coming. They were waiting for us, the people there. My first impression was, all the houses seemed to have beautiful red roofs. This was February, middle of their summer. But when we got there no one had any Australian money. We still had all Indian and Sinhalese rupees. Yet the people knew. As we went ashore, Come in for a feed, Jack! You're all right, we know you can't buy us anything back, we know you've no money till the banks open tomorrow! Of course there was no pubs open. Sunday was dry at that time, in Sydney, Sunday was dry. So we were taken in to these places. *Oh, when you're getting a long leave come and stay! Come in! What do you want, steak, egg and chips?* Even to this day I won't have the Aussies run down, the way they treated me, and of course thousands of the lads. And we were there for about ten days, till the Americans decided we could go up North to join them.
        At that time, I was still on Ursa at that time, and a bloke come up to me, a Geordie, he says, Can you do us a favour? I said, It depends what it is, I thought he perhaps wanted a duty doing. "I can get my brother to join me. No one else wants to do it, and you're more or less the last hope." I hadn't heard anything about this. I said, What's he on? He said, "He's on the cruiser Swiftsure. And if I can get someone to swap with him the same rates we can be together." They were twins, actually. So I says, Yeah, that's all right. Not knowing it, when I got there, it was the flagship of the cruiser squadron, with an Admiral on board! So I went round and joined this cruiser there, and he went on mine.

D.   What's the difference between a cruiser and a destroyer?

R.   About seven, eight thousand tons. The destroyers were carrying 4.7 guns; the cruisers carried six inch. Plus four inch anti-aircraft guns, besides numbers of 20mm Oerlikons, and the pom-poms.

D.   How many crew would be on the Ursa?

R.   On the Ursa was a hundred and thirty five. On Swiftsure was eight hundred, and up to nine hundred when we were carrying the Admiral and his staff.

D.   Which you were.

R.   Which we were at that time, yes.

D.   So this was an enormous change.

R.   Oh, it was.

D.   Was there an awful lot of learning? Everything must have been done differently.

R.   It was. Different again. On the Swiftsure, where I worked was just under the bridge, right down in the barrels under A turret, the first six-inch turret. When they were firing there, it was bloody hot. There was a big change, but as long as you're one of the lads you always help each other out. And it's something that's stuck with me, sort of. I think it's rubbed off a bit on here, by helping people, what I've done. Don't want any war or anything like it, it's just the thought that you're mates, or you're all one. Until they let you down, sort of.

D.   There is that expression, We're all in the same boat, isn't there?

R.   As you will realise as we go on now. After that, I'd been on about five days, and my leaving harbour at that time I was in the Low Power Room, which controlled all the gunnery circuits. Everywhere is manned to leave harbour, which is quite crowded with a fleet of all these ships moving out together. Mind you some went before, and we were all circling.

D.   You are still in the same Fleet, aren't you?

R.   Still in the same Fleet. And Sydney, as you move out, it's like as you come out of Portsmouth Harbour, you turn right as if to go to the Isle of Wight, what we used to call Number Five Buoy. As you go through out of Sydney you turn like that to go out there, what they call through The Heads. You don't see Sydney Harbour Bridge until you've turned to go into the harbour. You can just perhaps see the top of it, but you can't see the bridge until you get into the main harbour. And as we went then we had to stream paravanes, which we never did on the destroyer. It will have any mines in the way. And we were on our way to Manus, in the Admiralty Islands, which was one of the first bases. From there we exercised again, and were waiting for the word then. King, the American Chief, wanted us pushed out towards Burma way, with the Indian Ocean; but Fraser stuck it out. And Nimitz, the American Admiral, wanted us for this main attack on Okinawa. As we left to the advanced base there was a place called Ulithi, it's in the Caroline Islands. It was ten miles North of the Equator. So you can tell when we worked how we sweated there. We'd topped everything up, oil, ammunition, everything, and we were included in the plan to attack Okinawa. We were on the left side in an American battle fleet, attacking a place called Sakashima, which was the base between Formosa and Okinawa, where the Japanese were staging aircraft. It was a bloody battle that, for Okinawa. It was the last stop before the main invasion of Japan itself. And we used to do three days' attacking, back for two days to the Fleet Train, for I think it was eighty to ninety days' continuous steaming the ships were, with a break of seven days at Leyte, where a new Fleet Train was coming up to refurbish us, so there was two fleet trains going. And off we went again for another twenty or thirty days: three days on, two off.

D.   And all this time were you in action?

R.   On the three days you were at action stations from dawn till dusk. And each day you had to have clean underwear on, in case of wounds. And we had blue overall suits, anti-flash gear, - you could take this down until the alarm sounded - that's all you could see. [*demonstrating blinkering effect*]

D.   What does that do?

R.   It's just to stop any burns. Protects your hair. It's like the idea in the Atlantic, where beards were discouraged. Because oil burns on water, you see, this is it. But it wasn't really necessary out there. And the operation actually started on the Good Friday, '45. And on this first phase, Good Friday and the Saturday, we never saw a Japanese plane, our planes came back and off they went again from the carriers. On the Easter Sunday about seven o'clock the first lot came, and they dived into the Indefatigable.

D.   Kamikaze?

R.   Kamikazes, yes. And everyone - you could use a rifle if you wanted, it was not a case of aiming, it was to put a curtain of fire up. You've never seen anything like it, it's hard to describe.

D.   Did many get stopped like that, or did most of them get through?

R.   Oh some got stopped, because you also had what they call a call'em up air patrol, of fighters over the fleet all of the time; plus a destroyer and a cruiser twelve miles from the fleet, ahead, and twelve miles astern: all expert radar ships. As soon as anything showed on their radars they were spotted. But they still got through. And the news came through after that of the death of Roosevelt, President Roosevelt died while we were there. Of course they didn't withdraw, the Americans, because they'd landed on Easter Sunday. They kept going, but it sort of hung over the fleet. And after the first serial we went back and topped up with the fleet train.

D.   This is your three days, you call a serial, is it?

R.   Your three-day operation and your two two-day replenishment, yeah. And we went back to the area, and on the second day it had been quiet. And the planes were just coming back. And the Japs, some of them, had the knack of slipping in between our planes, coming back. And this one - by that time my action station on Swiftsure was with the electrical party on the ten four-inch guns: if any of their circuits went, it would sometimes blow fuses, you had to whip them out and get them wired, to keep the electrical circuits going. And we were stood there watching them come back in - because we'd had no warning -

D.   Of course, they were in with our people!

R.   They were in with our planes. And we saw this one of ours turn off. And we suddenly, Captain says, like, *Stand to!* We thought it was one of our pilots in trouble and he was going to ditch. But he went like that - I'll never forget it - and he come round like that, and it come straight along there, skimming, sea level: he opened fire with his cannons, he was equipped with guns, and he really blasted, you could see it through the smoke. And it went right across our deck, by that window where me and this bloke were standing, three plops in the decks before he went past, machine gunning, and he shot straight up like that and he dived, straight into the Formidable. Mind you, she was operational again within about an hour. We had an American Liaison Officer on board, and he said, Now if that had been an American carrier it would be either sunk, or a dockyard job. The flight deck of the Americans were wooden. Ours were eighteen inch steel. And all there was was a dent. What they did, they come along with the bulldozer, swept it all into the sea, any dents were filled with quick-drying cement, and away they went. It was surprising, as I say, I'll never forget that. The blokes were like me afterwards, we had to keep going to the toilet for Jimmy Riddles afterwards.

Life for a sailor is tough. You meet nothing like it in civvy street. You were called at five o'clock in the morning, Reveille, you had a proper breakfast; and what you got for the rest of the day till the main meal, about seven, eight o'clock at night, and sometimes a night call there, was just by chance. It depended what was happening. Sometimes you'd get a bowl of soup, sometimes you may get a Manchester tart, with jam and custard on top. Plenty of biscuits. Plenty of water, sometimes lots of tea, but you would not get another main meal. It depends what time some of the cooks could get back to the Galley. And this is how you live. You went back at the end of the day, when you'd been secured hopefully; you took off your blue overalls there, and your singlet and underpants are blue with the dye if they were still on the new side. And then it was a case of having your main meal, getting in your hammock; some of you would be back on watch again from, say, eight o'clock.

Jervis Bay, which is the work-up area for the Royal Australian Navy, we were working-up after this refit, and on the Sunday, after the usual routines, we were settled down for the rest of the day to do what we liked, when suddenly came the order, *Special Sea Duty men to close up,* as we were going to proceed to sea, back to Sydney. And the Captain came and spoke on the ship's system that we were going back because the Japanese had more or less decided to accept the surrender terms from the Allies, to end the Second World War. Entering Sydney well after dark, we tied up alongside a caisson really, not a catamaran, and next morning we proceeded up harbour to our usual berth, where we loaded up with extra medical supplies, ship's boat, extra ammunition, food: anything for the relief of Prisoners of War and Internees at Hong Kong.

On the morning of the 15th August, '45, work was proceeding in the morning, till all hell let loose over Sydney, with Church bells, crackers, fireworks, cheering and hooters; signalling that Mr Attlee as Prime Minister had said that Japan had surrendered, and today was VJ Day. Thinking we were going to have, perhaps, a good time, two o'clock came round and we were ordered to get out to sea with this Task Force to go to the relief of Hong Kong. As we went astern out of our berth into mid-channel, the crowds on the circular quay and - I forget what it's called now, it's the site of where the new Opera House is, it was a big park - and the crowds there cheered and waved us on. And we went to sea there with the aircraft carriers Indomitable and Venerable, Venerable or Vengeance, plus the battleship Anson, the Cruiser Eurylus and the Canadian cruiser Prince Robert, plus a destroyer flotilla, to proceed at full speed to Manus again, in the Admiralty Islands, where we could top up with fuel and anything else. After doing this, news came through that we were not to take any surrenders until General MacArthur, the Supreme Commander, had signed the main surrender documents in Tokyo Bay. So we proceeded to Subic Bay in the Philippines, but the Admiral decided we'd go and wait off Hong Kong.

D.   Now this is the Admiral in command of your -

R.   Relief Task Force.

D.   Task Force. Yes.

R.   And we proceeded off the entrance to Hong Kong Harbour until this had happened. And at noon, I think it was September 2nd, the surrender having been signed earlier, minesweepers swept a channel for us, and the Admiral trasnsferred from the Indomitable to the Swiftsure, for the simple reason that carriers were needed for air cover from the entrance into the harbour.

D.   Can I just interrupt? How long did it take you to steam from - where were you?

R.   Subic Bay.

D.   Subic Bay?

R.   About a day and a half.

D.   So that's the sort of time he was saving by coming up there and standing off?

R.   And standing off, yeah. We stood off for about a day. A day and a half sail as well. And as we proceeded, Swiftsure leading the fleet into the harbour, the cruisers and destroyers into the harbour, they kept the battleship until it had been fully swept, and they realised it was deep enough for her to come in, being, with her big guns, if anything really happened she could fire by radar. And we proceeded in, and like I was saying about Sydney, there's a turn in the channel, a turn to get into the main harbour of Hong Kong. Having proceeded through this channel and into the wide open space of the harbour, Japanese motor torpedo boats were seen leaving the harbour at the other side, on Kowloon, which are known as the New Territories. And Captain McLaughlin ordered to open fire with four-inch guns, and we rather splattered them. Then nothing else materialised. After anchoring, the Japanese representative came on board, and the refusal by the Admiral and his staff even to shake hands with him didn't go down well, I presume, with one or two pressmen who were there. And then it was decided that our Commander, who was Number Two on board, should then go ashore. Swiftsure's task was to go and clear the dockyard of all Japanese, that was the main task for that day. In this occupation I was what was known as The Commander's Runner, a sort of bodyguard to him, to take notice all round that there was no treachery going on from the Japanese, with orders that if anyone approached more than arm's length I was to shoot'em. With a revolver.

D,.   How were you armed?

R.   I just had a revolver, with being his bodyguard, like the Officers had. The crew had Tommy guns.

D.   Had you been trained?

R.   Only on the way up from Sydney to Subic. And told to use it.

D.   What's it like having a revolver? What sort of calibre was it?

R.   I think it was 9mm.

D.   Did you feel comfortable using it? Is it an easy thing to use?

R.   I'd been trained to. And it would either have been me or him.

D.   How accurate was it?

R.   The range was more or less two arms' length, as they approached, which didn't really call for accuracy. I was told, like, wherever you hit him, if he does that, it's not your fault, sort of. And I was quite prepared to use it. I think I would have done. I suppose to the Navy he was more, as a Commander, than me as a pure Able Seaman.

D.   So there you were, escorting this Commander.

R.   This Commander who was in charge of what was known as Brown Force. He was Commander Brown. Of course the Captain had to remain on board, in case the ship had to be moved. On the other side of the harbour, at Kowloon, the Commander of the Prince Robert was called Kennedy, and it was Kennedy Force, on the Kowloon side of the occupation. The senior officer ashore, if you landed, the force was named after him. And so we proceeded, and cleared the dockyard. And suddenly the Japanese Chief of Staff came with his sword, to present to Commander Brown, and gave it to him and said to him, Could you please wait a bit, for my General to come? And Commander Brown, in perfect English, said (I won't use the word), *We've no more ******* use for the Japanese. Clear off!* The Royal Marines went and rounded them all up and cleared them out of the dockyard by three o'clock in the afternoon. And we just stayed outside the gates for that day. We were to move into the town the next day. The Royal Marines and some of the sailors were moved into another part of the town. We'd take the Teikoo and Aberdeen area of Hong Kong that day.
   And some of the things that happened after the hours of darkness . . . We were told, Turn your ears off to whatever you hear outside that gate, till dawn. Next morning though there were bodies at the side of the road. Japanese were floating in the harbour. They had a night of what'sit. So the Admiral issued a decree, he was named as the Governor, Military Governor of Hong Kong the next day, and he give them the order, it had all got to stop. And the whole area will now be policed by men of the Royal Navy and the Royal Marines, to await the arrival of some army blokes in about fourteen days' time. So we were constantly on these patrols. But in the meantime between the forces at the Island, Hong Kong side, not Kowloon, the Admiral and our Captain, when it had settled down, went to Stanley Internment and Prisoner-of-War Camp. And the good old British phlegm, I suppose: the Governor of Hong Kong at the time was wanting to take over straight away, back as the Governor. He had to be told that his days of Governor were over and that he had to go back, we're under a British Miltary Governor at the moment. This went on for about fourteen days. When we were gradually being withdrawn, and some army and RAF blokes were there, an epidemic of sandfly fever broke out in the ship. I was one of the lucky ones who did-

n't get it, having been ashore. And in the mess, our twenty-odd mess, there were sixteen of them went down with it. They were in hammocks everywhere. All we had to do was look after, and keep the mess clean. And they kept sending up tots of rum for twenty, and food for twenty!

D.   And only four of you! Oh dear, oh dear! Must have been the hardest part of the war!

R.   I've never slept so much in the afternoon! Having about four or five eggs each!

D.   My heart bleeds!

R.   When you think it was, what is it, one egg a month? So it was decided afterwards, well, being as the Swiftsure crew had been in from the start, the only way to clear this up, they sent us to sea for seven days, just to cruise around and let all the - it cleared it up. After that we went up, what they call a bit of peacetime routine, to relieve another Britsh cruiser as the guardship at Shanghai.

D.   Ah, now before we come to Shanghai, may I come back to one or two questions about Hong Kong? Brown Force: how many men would you have been?

R.   Two hundred and fifty went ashore. Out of six, seven hundred.

D.   With Commander Brown?

R.   With Commander Brown. It was reliefs you see, as well.

D.   Were you his only personal bodyguard, or were there about ten of you?

R.   No, just me. I didn't have him on a dog lead, but I was there with him all the time, yes.

D.   And I couldn't catch what really happened when the guy with the sword came.

R.   With his surrender? The Japanese handed over their swords. I believe all military men do this.

D.   This was to Commander Brown?

R.   Yes. He came out of, as we call it, a caboose. Part of their headquarters in the dockyard.

D.   And what did he say?

R.   Could we wait a bit for his General. He'd been delayed, and would we wait for him to come?

D.   Wait for the General? Because this guy was junior?

R.   He was his Chief of Staff. The General's Chief of Staff.

D.   And was this a message from the General?

R.   The General, yes. Then Brown said . . .

D.   Yes, I got that bit. I wasn't quite sure what the Japanese were asking for.

R.   So they could negotiate, you see. But he wouldn't accept it.

D.   What happened to the General? He came, presumably?

R.   Oh, he came. And the Royal Marines debagged him.

D.   True?

R.   Quite true. They cut all the buttons off his trousers.

D.   I was going to ask how they were treated? It must have been very difficult.

R.   It was, because there was this, sort of, couldn't give a devil what you did to the Japanese, sort of thing.

D.   Well you must have by this time, even though you spent most of the war at sea, you must have heard a lot of stories about what the Japanese had been doing.

R.   Oh, of course you did. It came through that - remember earlier on we were talking about Palembang, and the Java and Sumatra air raids? Some of the pilots who came down and were captured were immediately beheaded by the Japanese, it turned out after the war. Just beheaded. You know, these ceremonies. And another thing there: the Japanese Tai Kei officers, which was their Gestapo, they'd tried to mix with some of the Japanese and Chinese going on one of the ferries. And Royal Marines from, I think it was the cruiser Eurylus, caught him, and he got obstreperous, and I believe they just took his trousers off and smacked his backside with a bayonet scabbard. He really lost face, and he committed suicide. He lost face. And that is marked in the red card, but don't take it as gospel. I suppose they'd be had up for ill-treatment there. Because they were a bit soft towards them.

D.   So did you pick up a lot of prisoners? What did you do with the Japanese? The military personnel?

R.   They were all herded together and locked into one of their barracks. And they were put to work to clear up all the dockyard, and the mess we'd made, and some of the stuff they hadn't cleared. And to clean up in the town. Under the guards, the Royal Marines and the Naval police force.

D.   Right, so that's what's going on there. Have we got to the liberation of our own POWs?

R.   Yes, we're just up to there. They were brought to the ships, and we were told, Don't give them anything above a cup of tea, because they'd been on such low commons that it could risk - especially chocolate and things like that, or cakes and any of the mess food. They'd all be examined, and some of the food we'd brought was this thick gruelly stuff, just to keep them going until they'd been passed. And then they were taken over to a couple of the hospital ships a few days after, they were all taken on there. But some of the kiddies came on board.

D.   While we're still on the POWs: how close did you get to this part of the operation? Did you see them?

R.   I just saw them coming down to the ships as they were taken off these Japanese lorries really, because a lot of ours hadn't arrived. They got them between the British warships. And they were all glad to have a decent shower. A lot were just given these Japanese loincloths. And ships' clothing was passed to them. They enjoyed their cigarettes, but they were told not to swallow the smoke. But then some of the kiddies from Stanley, of course having the Admiral on board, the Governor and these civilians, I think about thirty of the government and their children came on board. They gave the children a bit of a cinema show, a bit of a party. But you couldn't stop the matelots giving them chocolate. Some of them were terribly sick on board. Because their stomachs had never - you see it's just basic rice, isn't it, with these Orientals.

D.   So that was Hong Kong. How long were you there?

R.   Oh . . . Up to about the end of September. And then we moved up to Shanghai, to relieve the Duke of Newfoundland, who was due for a refit at Sydney. We stayed there as guard ship for a bit. But going up the Yantkse to get to Shanghai - it's not on the Yanktse, it's on the Wang Poo river really: as you go up to Shanghai there's what you call the Bund, which is their Stock Exchange, we were in the Wang Poo river, and that flows at an average of fourteeen to sixteen knots, a very fast-flowing river. And it was in spate. It really is a yellow, mucky river, the Yanktse is, itself. It does go a bit better as you get up to the Wang Poo. But it was a case of entering the Yanktse there. Because it was international I think, pre-war, if I remember right. On the way up we'd just called at another place called Amoy, which I think is just North of Hong Kong, and picked some Chinese official up. And he decided, Right: there's trouble happening now further North, with Mao tse Tung and his Communists. And we were sent to two places, Tiensin, which is right in the North China Sea, opposite Korea, and Ching Wang Tao which is nearly at the Manchurian border, to relieve the British Consulate. And there was nearly trouble there with these people who'd come on. They must have been away from everything. They wanted us as their lackeys to carry all, they ordered the crew to *Carry My Bags*.

D.   This is the staff at the Consulate?

R.   The Consulate. You know, the old colonial crowd. I'm afraid they got told what to do. It was the old-fashioned thing, You've got to be looking up to me, sort of.

D.   And they got very short shrift.

R.   Very short shrift, yes. And then we took them back to Shanghai. Then after that it was back to Sydney for Christmas.

D.   Now we're at Christmas '45?

R.   Christmas '45, yes. And then we had to work-up again, at Auckland, New

Zealand, because they wanted some British sailors on a Victory Parade there. And then for the weekend after this working-up he took us round to this Russell, in the Bay of Islands. And funnily enough it was in one of the magazines, as a sort of tour, wasn't it? that tour of the Bay of Islands.

D.   Russell?

R.   In the Bay of Islands. That's a Maori settlement. And we worked-up there, we got fully worked-up, and then we were sent to Townsville, Northern Australia. But the navigator took us through the Barrier Reef. Clear? You could see the coral down there, just like freshwater. It was a marvellous sail. I don't know if he'd been before, but he took us through there. And then the next stop was to see the Wild Man of Borneo - you know the old saying, the Wild Man of Borneo - that was Sarawak, where we picked up at the Cocos again, picked up Viner-Brook, I think the name was, the rulers of Sarawak. But the only way he could get to his place, we had to use the ship's landing craft to take him up the river, it wasn't deep enough. And we were caught on the edge of one of the Trade Winds while we were there, struggling for the anchor-hold while they took him up river. Going further round again, we went back to the usual hunting-ground of Hong Kong, and were told we was going to be the flagship of the Commander-in-Chief, Admiral Fraser, to do his farewell tour of the Command. And we went to all these American bases, Wake Island, Mindanao, all these places, to meet the people there. And then he went up to Tiensin again, in China. The Communists hadn't quite got that far. And some of us, picked out of the hat, went on this special train - I was one of the lucky ones actually - to have a look at Peking, had a look at that big square that's in there, and then we were taken up to the Great Wall. You only just walk along a bit.

D.   What was it like?

R.   Well, you'd think of the outside of a fort, if you know what I mean. But - I suppose I've got to sound a bit rude here - we did the British sailor's thing when he meets a wall!

D.   Like a dog meeting a lamp post? Say no more!

R.   Two hundred matelots lined up there! And then we came back, and we then took him up to Sasebo, one of the American bases in the South of Japan, in the Southern Island. Then round so that he could go and have a look at Hiroshima. It was on the way back that we called at Nagasaki. And we went into the Kure and Kyoto, and then right up to Yokohama, outside Tokyo. Those who wanted to go ashore, we all had a chance to be taken on a destroyer to one of the places in Tokyo to have a look round, a basket of sandwiches there. Took some tins of tobacco which was part sawdust and some tobacco on the top, to sell to the Japanese to get some yen, and disappeared quick! They thought they'd got a tin of tobacco: they got about that much, and the rest was sawdust. It's no wonder we sailors are rich! Oh, the things we get up to! And then there was a big parade in Tokyo, at the British Embassy. And then we came back to Hong Kong.

D.   How long had that taken, that trip?

R.   Weeks. I'd hate to be on a flagship with the Commander-in-Chief all the time.

We couldn't do nothing without what we termed the Guard and Band was needed. Some General would come on board; some Mayor of some city would come on board; all the ladies of the town - no, that's not right! I'm being naughty again! No, anyone posh come on board, there's the Guard and Band. And he left the ship then. And then a bit of animosity crept into the fleet. The battleship Duke of York turned up. Of course Fraser had been on her when they sank the Scharnhorst, in North Cape. And he'd have stayed on her for this tour, but fuel supply didn't allow it, because of the economic situation, so he used this instead. Of course when the paper come it was the Duke of York doing all this, in the local papers. And it caused a lot of animosity in the fleet. The lads who'd been through the Kamikaze attack, she turned up just before the Japanese surrendered, the Duke of York, she never took part, or fired a shot in anger. And this caused a bit of bad feeling. So they decided, Right, we're moving out to Singapore, in preparation for going home. But you cannot leave the Station until the 1st August. Which was '46. So we went round to Singapore, then we entertained an American battleship over a weekend. And then the final signal turned up: *To make it more interesting, instead of hanging around for another three weeks, you're to go to Fremantle to get rid of your ammunition and stock up with food*. And that's what we did, we had quite a nice spell in Fremantle. And this was the time, in Fremantle, when I bumped into Bernard.

D.   Oh, you bumped into Bernard? In Fremantle?

R.   Yeah. They were ready for on the way, they were, for home. And we'd both been on a tour of the Swan Brewery - not together, like - in Fremantle.

D.   Bernard had lived in Bold Streeet, same as you, hadn't he?

R.   That's right, yes. I remember him.

D.   You were neighbours, then?

R.   Neighbours more ar less, at that time.

D.   And there you were!

R.   Yeah. Isn't it funny?

D.   And then, to end two doors away from each other here! For the rest of your lives! Extraordinary!

R.   And then we sailed from Fremantle, to Colombo. Which I mentioned, about being sea-sick again. Because that's where I spent my twenty-first birthday. And from there we just fuelled again at Aden. We were told the rainfall there was half an inch a year. Then straight up the Red Sea. But something I must mention, it was on the way out, on Ursa there: going down the Red Sea, everything went into a purple wall; everywhere went purple. And they told us what it was: the sun, shining through a sandstrom in the desert. It was eerie, if you know what I mean. And then we went up to the Bitter Lakes, when we got into the Canal again. Then we had to wait for the convoy coming down, and they fixed lights on our bows, because we went up in the dark, up to Port Said. And that's where we'd have a swim, and then they'd give us a sticky bun. And they stayed in Port Said again, just overnight. Oh, and it hadn't gone dark when we started up the Canal, and alongside the Canal was one of the army's canteens. They were all drinking beer like, and there was a lot of banter going on from ship to shore - *Where does your girlfriend live?* And *Get your knees brown!* And after Port Said, a straight run through to Gibraltar, where they fuelled again.

When we left there on the Friday we were due at Chatham on the Tuesday, but the first stop was Portsmouth, because Chatham Dockyard is tidal. You've got to go through locks, not like Portsmouth. If the water's right you can go straight in, but to get into Chatham, on the Medway, you've got to go through the locks. And we set off there, and just ahead of us was an American cruiser, I presume they were going home. And it seems when your ship is paying off, I suppose to check the machinery, you've got to get up to maximum speed, and stay at it for an hour. Of course we got her up to 32 knots, and the Yankee cruiser signalled, What's the rush? The Captain signalled back, We're on our bloody way home! On the Sunday afternoon he stopped in the Bay of Biscay, and the contrast from when we went: it was like a millpond. And we all had a swim, all of us who wanted it. And just going further along there, were French fishing trawlers. And we said, have you got any fish? And they said, Yeah, we'll swap! So they got some fresh bread, a deal was done. And that's the first hot meal we got on a Sunday night, except in the operational areas. Nearly everybody got down, peeling spuds. So we had a great big fish and chip supper on the Sunday night. And then half past five, quarter to six on the Monday morning - Reveille wasn't sounded until six because we're near the end there - the old ship's broadcasting came in: The ship is now off Bournemouth, if anybody wants to look. And we came through and anchored off the Isle of Wight, for the Customs men. But we didn't go in Portsmouth harbour, we went ashore with boats there. Then we went round to Sheerness to get rid of some extra oil. Then we went up to Chatham. And then we went on leave, and being a Portsmouth rating it was a case of hanging around until the next March, I think it was,

D.   March '47?

R.   March '47, yeah, when we were thrown out. All through that very harsh winter of '46 I was at Victoria Barracks, in Southsea. And I was marching, training boy seamen to the what's'ername.

D.   It seems an awful long time after the end of the war.

R.   Well my papers were lost.

Jean. They nearly kept him!

R.   They nearly kept me, yeah! They got mislaid somewhere. It was at the time just me and one other fella. He was lucky, he was on the doorstep: he only lived at Bognor. We used to go ashore together. And they spoke to us a few days before, they called us in and said to him, Look. All of your group have practically gone. It's only you two and a couple of others hanging around. What we're proposing to do in the next week, if your papers have not come, we'll send you on leave with a warrant for a month. Then you will come back on that warrant and be demobbed, and another warrant home. But not far from Victoria Barracks, as you went towards the King's Theatre in Southsea, there's a post office. And I went and changed my postal order there, and I came back, and the lad said, Eh, we're both wanted again up there. Are we going home tomorrow for a month? So we went, and they told us - this was the Thursday - I'm sorry lads, he said, you're going through your demob routine at Portsmouth

Barracks, but you've got to wait until Monday before you can go home.

So we went to the demob place, where you could stow your gear. And we said, Are we staying here? How much money have we got between us? So we worked it out we could go ashore Saturday afternoon, watch Portsmouth play in the afternoon - I always remember, because it was against Middlesborough - and we come back to what we call the Two Bob Eat Shop: somewhere opposite that Brickwoods pub, I think it was called The Duke of York, not far from the station. Anyway we went in there, because for two bob you got a couple of sausages, chips, bread and butter and a cup of tea. And it worked out we could more or less do the same on the Sunday, plus a bed at The Sailors' Rest, in Queen Street. So we decided on that. We had a bag of chips between us for us supper, went in The Sailors' Rest - we were turned in by ten - we come out and on the Sunday we went in the barracks, got us breakfast and us dinner. In the afternoon we did the same, said to the bloke Can we have the same bed, we're going out Monday? Leave it with me, you'll be all right. So we went to the pictures. And the only thing we could get to eat that night - the chippies weren't open - was this, not exactly a chippie, but they were selling like sausagemeat burgers on bread. So we had some of them. And as we were going out, Got your gear ready, being as you're going out, he said. I won't let you down, he said, I'll bring you some real hot water to shave, for going home in.

Jean. Big deal!

R.   And we went back in - Yeah! But it was nearly always lukewarm before.

D.   Overflowing with generosity.

R.   . . . And here's some duty-free cigarettes.

D.   Oh, right.

R.   Went in the barracks, got us breakfast, and then we were told to go and take us kit over to the drill shed, and then we had to wait to get paid, stood for nearly an hour to get paid. And they took us up to Cosham, which is where the civilian kitting-out was. There were just four of us. And a bloke on the lorry there - he shouldn't have done it really, like - he offered to take us to the station for threepence. At Portsmouth. His train for Bognor was there, half an hour is it, from Portsmouth? And here was me on the Waterloo. Outside Euston the train was about ten minutes, I thought I'd get something to eat instead of sitting for four hours. And we had there sausage and chips and something like this bread, that dark bread, National Bread, was it? *It's gone manky, this*, I said. Because we had white bread on board. Coming home it was different again. I suppose I got home round about seven o'clock at night. And then I got nine weeks' leave. A bloke give me nine weeks' ration tickets. There were some left, and between the four of us we divided them out. Stocked up with chocolate and that. And that was it.

e)   Ron and Joan Reanney.   Dodging bombs and school in Liverpool 7/8

R.   Born and bred in Liverpool. Raised in Liverpool. 1929.

D.   And what did you do initially, when you left school?

R.   Well the war was on. I was making cycles. For the army and the airforce.

D.   Did you get any choice?

R.   There was a choice, yes. I did a little bit of painting and decorating. Not decorating: painting and making wood panels for aircraft. But I didn't stay long, so I was told to go on cycles.

D.   Before that: what was it like being in Liverpool with the war going on?

R.   Dreadful.

D.   You must have been bombed all over the place.

R.   Unfortunately Joan lived in Cantsfield Street,

J.   That's off Smithtown Road. The houses, where would you say they were like? Altrincham, the big houses. They had cellars underneath them. And every third house had, it wasn't a shelter, it was the roof reinforced with steel, and big posts to keep them up. Everyone had a door put in the wall of the cellar, so you could go through each house, to the cellar that was safe.

D.   And how often would you have to do that?

J.   Oh, often. Lord Haw-Haw, as you might know, he used to say, *And we're going to Liverpool 7 tonight*. And he did. And he threw bombs, and I lost a lot of friends; landmines and what-have-you, took quite a few houses down at the top of the road, businesses. We had all our windows blown in. It was quite bad really. We were playing in the street, and we could see the planes, or you heard the run of them, and at one time, before the siren went, they were shooting, and some of the buildings had bullet holes in. I suppose he could see most people being about, and he just fired. But it was bad.

R.   I lived in the worst part of Liverpool, which was Dingle, near the Docks. My father was an Inspector in the Fire Service, so we lived on the fire station.

D.   So he was kept busy.

R.   And we got bombed like no one's business, with being near the Docks: if they didn't hit the Docks they hit one of us. We lived in the Liverpool 8 area, we used to call it Holy Land, there was Moses Streeet, Jacob Street, Isaac Street. We used to call it Holy Land. There again, Lord Haw-Haw used to say, *We're going to give Holy Land a bashing tonight*. Sure enough! That was near us, because there was only Moses and Harlow Street, and we were the next. We didn't actually get bombed, but we got so badly damaged, we had to leave the house.

401

D.   So where did you go?

R.   We went to live in Childwall then, which was a way out of Liverpool. But that was more or less towards the end of the war, when they finished. Unfortunately for us - when I say for us I mean for all of us - they had an anti-aircraft gun in the yard. And they used to drag it out at night, and start shooting. And of course when Gerry sees the sparks he knows what to aim for. Well if he missed it, we got it. That's how bad it was. Machine guns and everything. Old bullet holes going right over the house.

D.   And did you have a safe place?

R.   Yes, we had our own air-raid shelter. We were posh!

D.   Well of course, being the Fire Chief, I suppose you would. And were you saying something about your school?

R.   Well the school we went to was called High Park Street. I went there before the war. But when the war started, and blitz started coming, they used my school as a mortuary. You reported to school every day, but it doesn't say you were going to go there. Or go in. Because if you went in you'd see loads of bodies covered with white sheets, right up the passageway. Some of your friends, as well, who'd been killed the night before. So we'd just go in, and go straight out again. Back home again. After about two years of roaming the streets -

D.   So you had two years, with no school?

R.   Two-and-a-half years. We went to school, but we didn't have any schooling. You still had to go there, you had to report. And the teacher or whoever was there just turned round and said, We're sorry. No school today. Or there was a big blackboard up, NO SCHOOL TODAY. So you went home and made a nuisance of yourself.

D.   It must have been very difficult to catch up.

R.   It was. Very hard. In fact they even designed an idea where we used to have a school: about six or seven of us who'd never been to school for quite a few months were sent there. And we went one day, and that got bombed!

D.   Nothing to do with you, nothing personal in this, is there?!

R.   The biggest laugh was, I couldn't get home quick enough, to tell my mum it had been bombed! She said, *Get back! It hasn't.* I said, It has! But as I say, we had a rough time really, you know. Towards the latter end, then it quietened down a bit. Of course in them days you only went to the school in the area. You weren't allowed to go, shall we say, to Beaufort Street, or any other school. Till they hit on the idea of sending me to Wellington Road, which was a huge school. The playground was on top of the roof. A wonderful view, smashing view, over the docks and everything. They sent me there for a while. I can remember they had a daylight raid. No sirens or anything: we saw a bomb actually hit a ship and sink it, we were so close to the Docks. I can recall one occasion, we didn't go to school, I used to love ships and boats, and watching them being loaded. So we used to go down, right down to the dock where they were load-ing them. Used to sit on my bike, hold the railings and watch the ships being loaded

402

with coal and tanks and trains and engines, and all sorts of things. And my father used to say, *You shouldn't be sitting there! You shouldn't be going down there watching all that.* Well I've got nothing else to do, what else can I do? But it wasn't till after the war that I found out that they kept ammunition under that road where I used to sit!

D.   Ah! But he never told you that, he just said You shouldn't sit there!

R.   Well he wouldn't be allowed to. War secrets, I suppose. So he always used to say, *You shouldn't be sitting there! You shouldn't be there at all!* I said, Well I like to see the trains being loaded. He said, *It doesn't matter. Keep away from there!* But obviously he couldn't tell me. It wasn't till the war finished that I found out that they kept all the ammunition for boats there.

f)   The Virgin Soldiers. Brian Clarke's National Service

B.   I was eighteen on the 12th July, and I was called up on the 4th August, National Service. I had to go down to Mount Street in Manchester, for the written test and a medical examination. And within weeks I was in the Services. Originally I was sent to Number One Training Battalion, Aldershot, where I did six weeks' training. That was arms drill and marching, and what-have-you. And finally we went for trade training, six weeks after the main training, to a Trade Training Battalion. I passed as a driving instructor.

D.   Did you get any choice in that, or were you just told?

B.   Oh no, we did have a choice. If you passed your test whilst you were driving, you were graded from day to day. It was a three months' course. You went out, and you started on your third class roads, then second class. Finally, trunk roads. With an instructor. And he was the man to say whether you were fit to be moved on or not. Until, finally, you went on your motorways and trunk roads. And then you passed your examinations in the classrooms. Which a lot of drivers thought, well we've passed the test, we've got the certificate to say that we can drive. The fact was that in the army that only counts for so much. After that you've got to learn to understand that if you break down you've got to know what's wrong with the vehicle engine. You've got to be knowledgeable. So you've got to know your engine component parts. So you have to learn this in the classroom. And then once you've done that, you've got learn how to read a map. Because being able to drive is one thing, but going from A to B and not knowing where you're going, you've got to know your road numbers, and be able to understand maps, be able to read a map: otherwise it would be to no avail. Passing any sort of test wouldn't matter. So I was very fortunate, I passed out on all, I got engine component parts, map reading, and I ended up as a driving instructor.

D.   You must have felt pretty pleased about that, I should think.

B.   I was pleased about it. I was very pleased about it. But it all came to no avail, because the draft at that particular time was going out to the Far East, Malaya, and they didn't want driving instructors in Malaya and Singapore. They wanted chaps going out there for work in the stores department. Ordinances. You supply the British Army, Ordinances. With anything from a pin to a Sherman tank. So it was stores, learning the stores business. From then I went out to Malaya. We boarded a ship by name of the Empire of Clyde. It was a cabin boat, twenty eight thousand tons, built on the Clyde, and it was turned into a troopship. And that particular night we set sail, I was asleep, I got down on a bunk, and the following morning I looked out through one of the portholes, and we were out in the Bristol Channel! And that was it, until we got to the Suez Canal, Egypt. Well we went first to Gibraltar, the key to the Mediterranean, and in to Cairo, through the Suez Canal. We waited there for a con-voy, you weren't allowed to go through single, for security you see. And we went straight through there into the Bitter Lakes, and finally out into the Indian Ocean. Stopping points were Aden, Colombo, to take fresh water on. And finally we ended up in Singapore, from where I was posted to a place called Nesoon.

D.   How do you spell that?

B.   N, E, S, O, O, N. But it's spelt different in Chinese! It was just this side of the

Causeway, before you get into Malaya. It was just this small detachment of us there, it wouldn't be a hundred, Ordinance. All the rest were the East Yorkshire Regiment. They were on board. And we waited for days and weeks before we finally found out where we were being posted. And it worked out that we were being posted out in ones and twos for some reason. And I ended up getting my papers, documents they were called, and I had to report to the place called Jardine Steps. Singapore. I had to make my own way.

D.   How did you do that? What means of travel were there?

B.   Well we had transport, but when I say make your own way, there was no one to talk to. There was a driver there to take you, he'd got instructions to take you, you see - to take me - to Jardine Steps. On my own. With my own documents. I could have scarpered. I could have gone anywhere in the Far East. I could have deserted. I could have done that. So I was taken down to Jardine Steps and told to wait for a landing craft to take me over to a small island off Singapore, which was the place where I'd been posted. A place called Blackamatti.

D.   Now, how do you spell that?

B.   Black, B, L, A, C, K. Then A. Then M, A, T, T, I. A small island off Singapore. The percentage of people who lived there were Malay. There was no Chinese, all Malay. And you could walk round the island within twenty four hours. And I was the only white man, apart from the chap that I was taking over from who was white, on the island. And I was lucky, because I landed at a place called Saratong, five hundred feet to the top, over sea level. And I could see right out to sea. And this was called a SRI: School of Religious Instruction. And we used to give film shows, religious film shows, to chaps who'd been up-country, in Malaya itself, on special duties, you know? Our chaps, that were sort of fatigued: not worn out, but fatigued. A rest camp, this was the idea, it was a rest camp for a week, two weeks, maybe three. Sometimes a month. For chaps who were drained out. They were sent to us there to receive this sort of spiritual . . . er, . . . to put them back on the main, sort of path.

D.   So you were sort of, like a padre?

B.   Well, I wouldn't say a padre. We had a padre that was in charge. He was in charge of running the establishment. It was a nissen hut built out of bamboo, and we also had living accommodation. And there was a padre there, a Captain. And I was there as an assistant, if you like. To pick these chaps up, at Jardine Steps, and take them inland.

D.   How did you like doing that?

B.   Well really speaking, it was something new right from the word Go. It didn't have much to do with the army sort of life. It was out of touch with the army in other words, you could say that. It was something else. And I don't know why, what the reason was. It was just something that, someone must have said something about that Private Clarke, he would be fitted for a job like this, and put me forward for it. So I ended up, and that's what I was doing.

D.   It sounds a little bit like *It ain't half hot, Mum!* Do you remember that TV series?

Windsor Davies?

B.   Well, a similar sort of thing. What was it called, the film? *The Virgin Soldiers*. Well I was out there when they were making that film. It's a wonder I wasn't taking part.

D.   I was going to say, You might have been one of them!

B.   I knew more than what they ever knew about that sort of thing, you know? The actual film was quite good. True to life, you know. Because in actual fact the film, if I remember right, was on those lines. The way of life when you're in that sort of a situation, in National Service. And it was all put across the right way.

D.   So did you serve all the rest of your time out there doing that?

B.   I did nine months on Blackamatti. Unfortunately for me I had an accident. I was driving a Bedford three tonner, and as I say it was one of those things. And I was duty driver, and I went under a bridge and got jammed underneath the bridge. It was one of those things. It was a matter of inches, that's all, a couple of inches. And I was stuck, jammed under the bridge. And it was the only bridge on the island! And that was the end for me, because I was up for a sort of enquiry, as regards what happened. It was the monsoon season, and this particular night it was raging. You couldn't see your hand in front of your face. Windscreen wipers were belting away there. I ended up jammed under this bridge. And I openly admitted it to the Commanding Officer. They let me off, and a couple of weeks later I volunteered to be posted out. And I was posted to Tanglin Barracks, in Singapore. T, A, N, G, L, I, N. And I just picked up from there. With my father being a landscape gardener, I was interested in the place where they used to play cricket, it was where the army played cricket, Tanglin. All sports were played there. The hutted area, which was C-in-C, Far Eastern Forces, this was where the establishment bought for the army. They ran it from there.

D.   So this was a bit busier?

B.   Very busy. People walking round there, Generals. Your arms were falling off, saluting, you know, saluting as you were going along. Most of the chaps used a bit of common sense: Brigadiers and below Brigadier, Majors, Colonels, walked around in shorts, you didn't even know their rank. Just walking about with a piece of paper in their hand, you know. But we knew this was a military establishment, and they were all military. We didn't know their rank. But it was a good job really, because security, from a security point of view, you were walking around, with there being terrorists around, you could have been the first to go, you know. But I latched onto this landscape business, and I ended up with a sergeant there, that was in charge of the sports ground. And he asked me if I'd like to join him in the sports stores, issuing the sports equipment. Hockey sticks, footballs, strips for the football teams, rugby teams. So he said, For that, he said, You'll get two stripes. You'll be made up.

D.   So you went back to your two stripes. Because you'd already been . . .

B.   I lost two, and I got them back. Yes.

D.   I wonder how many managed to do that during National Service?

B.   Well there was one or two who were very lucky. And I was one!

D.   Well it sounds as if you were doing a good job out there.

B.   Yes, well the job that I did was, with it being a Corps, the job that I did was one of thousands. There was quite a lot of chaps down in the hutted area. Clerks, you know. Typewriting, that sort of thing. It was similar to what you'd get for a job in this country, really. Even though you were in a zone which was a theatre of war, you could say. At the time. Unless you went what they call up-country, Malaya itself. Then you knew right away that . . . It was single track from Singapore to Kwala Lumpur. It took a week to get there. And what the terrorists were doing was blowing the bridges, you know. To slow everything down. The Engineers had to build a new bridge before they could move, it may take weeks or months to get to Kwala Lumpur. But some of the chaps there, some of the Infantry chaps, they had a rough packet. A rough time of it. The Manchester Regiment, especially, they were out there. And there were quite a lot killed you know. But they were supposed to have shot more rubber tappers than they did terrorists! The Manchester Regiment. Shoot first, and ask questions after. You see the thing was that a place like Malaya is seven times larger than this country anyway. And they could see you coming, but you couldn't see them.

D.   Jungle terrain, I suppose?

B.   Oh, right the way through, yeah. So these people could see you, and you couldn't see them. And then you got the, er . . . wildlife, put it like that! Mostly, the worst were the mosquitoes. At night you know. A lot of people preferred not to have a mosquito net, because at night time especially, it was that sort of . . . lacking of oxygen, atmospheric conditions: you'd got a job to breathe. And if you've got the mosquito net as well, it made it claustrophobic. So they preferred to do without nets rather than have one. And then eventually you were eaten alive with mosquito bites. But at the same time you had cream to put on your skin, that didn't make a lot of difference. Then you had the snakes, what they call bootlace snakes. You'd wake up and find one of those on you, out in a bivouac, on top of your sleeping bag. But they wouldn't attack you, you just had to throw them away. It was adventure. Something you never forget, I'll never forget it. It was there, you were called up to do it, you hadn't got any choice anyway. And I wasn't sent there, I volunteered to go. I was all out for adventure you see. And it sort of fulfilled my sort of life, for me. I was seeing something that I wanted to see, and I was being paid for seeing it!

D.   Best of all worlds!

B.   That's right, best of all worlds, yeah. And I stayed out there till more or less my time was up, and I came back by boat, the Empire Holidale. Same route. Which was like two months off your service time. It was a month going out, and it was a month coming back. It was a sea trip as well, which was something fresh, an experience. And I couldn't complain.

D.   You enjoyed the sea trips?

B.   I enjoyed it through and through. I enjoyed it.

D.   It sounds as if you enjoyed every minute of it.

B.   Every minute of it, yeah. And as a matter of fact, when I came out of the Services I wondered why I came out.

D.   I was wondering that, yes. Were you offered the chance to stay on?

B.   I was offered, yes. I came very close to signing on again, signing on as a regular. When I got back to Feltham in Middlesex to be de-kitted, about two or three days before I came out of the Services, the Colonel there, he asked me. He said, You've got a good record, you seemed to enjoy the army. It seems to have done a lot for you, he said, And I would suggest you make a career of it. Because I think you're the sort of chap that would make a good soldier. You're already a good soldier anyway. What's the reason why you want to go into civilian life? I said, Well I think I've had enough of the army sort of life. I'd like to get back to civilian life. But I'm also tempted. Well, he said, If you take my advice you'll think about it. You've got a couple of days to do that. Which I had, a couple of days, and I did think about it. And finally I made up my mind I was going to come out.

D.   Can you remember what it was, in the end, that swung it for you? To come out?

B.   I think it was the fact that I'd been overseas in Singapore, and I thought that two years was quite an experience. And I was still young. I always had the chance of coming out into civilian life, having a go at getting a job, and if I didn't like it I could always go back in because I was so young.

D.   So you weren't actually burning your boats, you could have gone back?

B.   Not really. I could have gone back. Yes. As a matter of fact I did go back, in a sort of way. I joined the Territorial Army Voluntary Reserve about five years later. At which I did fifteen years. I was with the Royal Army Medical Corps for fifteen years.

D.   Another Corps!

B.   Another Corps, yes. We used to set up field hospitals. We had choppers, Allouettes, Wessex, fetching us patients in. Procedure for a theatre of war, to set up a field hospital. Reception and Evacuation and all this sort of procedure was what you had to learn. Set the whole set-up up. Ambulances in one way and ambulances out another. Nothing getting stuck: one way in, one way out. I learned all that, you see. That was interesting. And we used to go away for two weeks per year. The CO always picked a seaside resort. It was optional I think, but we always seemed to pick a place near the seaside, so that after the duties were finished from day to day you had a place to go and relax. We ended up in Germany, we went overseas from time to time. I can't say a lot more about it, it's just the fact that it was very enjoyable. And we were paid for it. So it was the best of both worlds.

D.   Again!

B.   Again!

408

g) The Manchester Bomb. Bob King

On 15th June 1996 the IRA detonated a bomb in Corporation Street, Manchester, causing serious damage to the Marks and Spencer store, the Arndale Centre and the Royal Exchange, with a range of lesser damage to buildings within a radius of half a mile. As City Architect, Bob King was at the centre of the emergency.

B. Dealing with damaged and dangerous buildings is one element of the regular responsibility of the City Architect's Department, so that part of the City's emergency response which involved the building damage fell to me. All else, whether as part of my normal work routine or personal, was immediately displaced by the scale and urgency of the imperatives facing us. For a while it took over my life.

D. What was your daily routine?

B. In a sense it started at six o'clock in the evening. At that time I had a major daily meeting with the police and, in the early stages, the other emergency services. That involved assessing what we had achieved in terms of removing problems and returning buildings and businesses to their owners, what difficulties we had encountered, what strategies we should pursue in order to deal with them and what were our plans for the next twenty four hours and beyond. Normally we'd finish in a couple of hours, and then I would go into the cordoned area and walk the city - just walk around it; for having heard all the reports and the feedback from my field staff, there was nothing quite like seeing it for myself to get it into perspective in my mind. I would leave for home around ten o'clock or so with a head full of the latest issues. A bad night's sleep usually followed. By four o'clock I would be awake and soon after return to the city, when I would walk it again to check overnight developments before the formalities of the day's new routines kicked in. Firstly there was a review with my senior staff. At eight I met with my Chief and Deputy Chief Executive and the police again, when we coordinated what we were to present at public information sessions which took place daily at 10 a.m. They were enormously important. People who were dispossessed of business or residential property, and in a few cases both, clearly faced enormous problems and needed to have all the information and assistance we could provide them with. During the early stages these meetings were repeated at two in the afternoon following a noon re-run of the eight o'clock review. Some of the meetings were tense and difficult, though a sharing of information on our approaches could defuse most situations. The rest of the day was spent keeping in touch with developments, dealing with problems and anything else that came up, and trying to snatch a lunch break at a nearby hostelry, with the mobile phone for company!

D. Almost I was beginning to envisage you like Winston Churchill, working from his bed! How long did this go on, at that sort of pitch?

B. I suspect it was less grand than Churchill, but it went on for some weeks, though over time the pattern changed. The remarkable thing was that approximately seven eighths of the area which had been put out of commission was actually back in use within about six working days. Everybody worked their socks off. We quickly arrived at the middle of it, the area suffering the worst damage with the most difficult and dangerous technical problems. And inevitably this was where things slowed down. Safety is paramount, so each move and the sequence of activities is carefully planned from a view of the risks it presents. It takes longer and longer to get through. This stage extended over many months. So the bridge had to be taken down before part of the Marks store with loose cladding could be accessed. Records covered with asbestos disturbed by the blast had to be moved and the building decontaminated before work of any other kind could proceed.

D.   I'm interested, going back, in the difficulty of going to sleep, of actually coming down, once you get home, and switching off. Did you find that you did sleep? Those few hours?

B.   Probably not very well is the answer. You eventually collapse from exhaustion but it is not a restful sleep; the body's in a sense giving up but the mind is still churning away. I must have been living on adrenalin or whatever keeps you going. It was many months before I returned to what I would describe as a normal pattern of sleep. I guess that even after the immediate cause of disruption has been removed, deeper layers of the subconscious are still readjusting. We were immensely fortunate. No lives were lost in the blast but I was aware that the risk to those involved in the recovery was enormous as well, and it preys on the mind. The real significance of these things is perhaps only fully appreciated some time later.

D.   Looking back on it now, do you think there were any factors that might have helped you get through it? And get out of it at the other end?

B.   We have an emergency plan - a part of our statutory duty, and we have to test it from time to time in simulated exercises. But none of this can fully prepare you for the real thing on the day. I had excellent staff whose skill, commitment and dedication was exemplary. We developed a real team spirit and productive relationships with others, particularly the police. In the extremes of the situation you have to reach levels of confidence in yourself and others which in normal circumstances we are unaware of - and somehow we did. And we had some luck. The weather was kind to us when we needed it. Certain things that might have gone wrong didn't. We could have killed more people clearing up than the bomb did, and the distances which separate the two are no thicker than a cigarette paper.

D.   That's the sort of thing that must keep you awake at night. So much for the professional level. I'm wondering now about yourself on the personal level, your own life and keeping yourself ticking over. What helped you through it, and this very difficult period you've mentioned, of coming out of a period like that, and returning to something like a normal pattern of life?

B.   Again, all I can think of I suppose is that home has always been an oasis. This is the bit in the background that's always there. The family relationships are always understanding and adjusted to take up the effects and accommodate the consequences without resistance or difficulty. The value of that is inestimable. If there is a solid base at home it is possible to deal with all sorts of problems outside. Without it I don't know how I would have got through.

D.   It sounds like the sort of home where you can shut the front door, and leave things outside. They don't come creeping in behind you.

B.   Sometimes it's difficult to keep them out entirely, but I think that overall there is a control and balance here that makes it possible to deal with the other things more confidently and more effectively. But what about you? You see the other side of this.

G.   I don't think you bring your work home. It doesn't intrude, let's say.

B.   Not too much, no. Again, the odd vacant - er - pause! You know, when the mind is distracted.

D.   I wonder if there is anything that you experienced, Geraldine, now that it's all over, looking back on it from this distance: you must have realised the pitch at which Bob was working?

G.   I didn't see him, David.

D.   Did you sometimes wonder if he still looked the same?! If he'd got more grey hairs!

G.   I saw more of him on the TV.

D.   How was it for you? Was it worrying? Were you wondering how he was coping? What it was doing to him?

G.   Well, he's . . . He's a very capable person. So in that respect I knew this was something he could get his teeth into. Get down to it, and get things done. Is it fair to say that? To say that you were in your element: you were putting your management skills to work, and bringing everything else together.

B.   It wasn't an unapproachable situation. The ones that must be hell are when you know you are in above your depth and either haven't a clue what to do, or the ability to do it. This was an enormous problem. It posed some teasing difficulties, but there was never any doubt about what actually had to be done, and what was needed to achieve it.

G.   So it brought all the skills together. I think that you had a sense of achievement, a great sense of achievement, didn't you?

B.   Yes. We came through very well. Local government is perhaps viewed in some quarters as a bit of a dotard. It is not seen as very fast-moving, or the place where you expect to find examples of great initiative or imagination. But I think here we proved the reverse. It was the private sector that in some ways was like a rabbit trapped in the headlights. Our decision-making structures can be extraordinarily quick when needs must, and they were. An Extraordinary committee meeting is called, the Chief Executive is empowered and we act - immediately. This situation was beyond private sector experience. Their decision-making mechanisms are much more cumbersome and inertia-laden. Initially they seemed blocked. Paralysed.

D.   Well, doesn't that say something about the perception of local government that you were describing - as being the dotard?

B.   Here it was anything but that. The City Council delivered in spades.

D.   Well yes. This just shows how wrong one can be.

B.   I was part of a team effort which worked well and did what could not have been done anywhere else. The Town Hall became the focus of everyone's attention. That is where people turned to find out what was happening and what could be done. It was the Town Hall that called in the agent of the Bank of England to coordinate arrangements through the clearing banks to avoid foreclosure on businesses which suddenly could not repay loans, and set up the Lord Mayor's Fund which raised over two and a half million pounds to provide practical relief for individuals and businesses. We identified premises to enable many of the small businesses displaced from the Royal Exchange and the Corn Exchange to get back in operation. The international design competition which followed made it possible to turn a disaster into an opportunity, and begin to unlock enormous potential for growth and development which is being physically realised now, and which will continue for a generation. Property damage caused by the bomb was valued at half a billion pounds. Reinvestment in new development over the three plus years which have now elapsed exceeds one and a quarter billion. I can perhaps now look back and feel some pride in having been able to make a contribution to the most defining influence in Manchester since the war.

3. Village Institutions

a) The Church in Ashley. Michael Robinson, Vicar

D.   When did you come here, Michael?

M.   I've been in the joint benefice of Hale and Ashley since May 1st 1997.

D.   Where were you before?

M.   Well I was in an outer city council estate, Blackley in North Manchester; where thirty per cent of the population live below an accepted standard of living according to the government's figures. So there are a lot of seriously poor people, relative to our society, living there; huge unemployment, especially among young males; all sorts of social problems, drugs, hence crime associated with that; vandalism, and all the rest of it. Nevertheless it was a thriving church community, and we were able to do quite a lot of useful work with children and young people.

D.   From one extreme to another! And here you serve two communities which are themselves quite a contrast: would you like to just give us a sketch of the two?

M.   Well I was born in Yorkshire, but from the age of seven I lived in Wilmslow, went to school at the King's School in Macclesfield. So I wasn't unaccustomed to North Cheshire! But what did surprise me was that Hale was spiralling upmarket: we've now reached the situation where people in their twenties who have been to university and are in reasonably well-paid occupations, can't afford to live in the place where they were born and bred. We're very fortunate in that a significant number of the parents who bring their children to baptism then start to come to church once or twice a month, to the Family Communion and/or the Toddler Service.

   Now Ashley, two miles away, is a completely different place. It's a parish large in size, but whereas there are about 5,000 people in Hale, within the ecclesiastical parish of Ashley there are only about 330 people. And the roles of the pub, the post office, the school and the church are essential in keeping the community together. It is a very vital community, I have to say. I think that's exemplified by the fact that just before you started to make this recording we were standing outside the church, and you heard the bells ringing and thought you'd been "Summoned by Bells"! But you had-n't, it was me playing the bells for the *Guardian* photographer, because he wanted to take a photograph of people who'd been responsible for putting the sound system in here. And that actually was a present, so to speak, from the Village to the Church, because it was the Millennium Committee whose idea it was, and who paid for it through money raised by events in the pub like Quiz Nights, from the villagers. So there is a real sense of community. The school is where I seem to meet a lot of peo-ple obviously. I'm there later this afternoon. And all the children are very responsive and the parents are very friendly. When we go in to take assemblies, again they're very responsive. The link between the Church and the school, through the support of the present headmistress, Mrs Wakefield, is devloping all the time. And we're very pleased about that. And people of course from the village go into the school, including some of the people who worship here, like Mary Walker who set up a thriving little Sunday School here in the church. Which is one of the ways that St Elizabeth's is moving for-ward. Now we have a monthly Family Communion here. But I have to be honest, and say that it isn't attracting a large number of people. On high days and holy days, as for example the Christingle, probably literally half the population are in church, a hun-dred and fifty or so. So they will turn up for special occasions. The Rose Queen Fête in May, a large amount of that money raised comes to the church. And the fact that so many people support it indicates that although not a lot of people come to church there is a feeling of goodwill towards the church. And people appear to like the Christian influence in the school.

D.   Going back to the fête, is it explicitly associated with the church, is it a Church Fête? Or is it more or less a thing on its own?

M.   Well it's organised by the Village. But a lot of the profit comes towards the church, and I assume people know that, because it's all published in the magazine. Now the magazine's an interesting thing, because of course Ron, who edits that, does make sure that all kinds of local news does go into it. It isn't just a church newspaper, in fact the reason that the photographer was here today to photograph the bells was that the *Knutsford Guardian* had picked up from Ron the fact that this was going on. They're beginning to take an interest, because Ron has broadened the scope of the magazine by trying to encourage as many people as possible to make their own little contribution, whatever that may be.

D.   It's very interesting that, because Ron himself is a new development, isn't he? I mean, he's only been editing it this year.

M.   That's right, yes. And he's not a churchgoer. But I don't think that matters really, I think it's good that people are involved. I mean, obviously all vicars like bums on pews, but the church seems to me to be viable.

D.   Well this is the thing that has to run through my mind, especially having listened to the post office, for instance, the Warringtons at the post office, talking about their show: I think it's a problem for them, to keep that shop and post office viable, simply because there aren't enough customers. And I have been wondering, comparing our 330 with the 5,000 in Hale, if you just get enough people to keep the roof over your head? Because the expenses, just of running the plant must be . . .

M.   Yes, very high. But we get a very positive response from the people of Ashley. When you look at the actual size of the congregation - twenty five, something like that on average over the year - it's small. But on the other hand we're paying our diocesan share, we're paying our way. We have no bills, we have some money in the bank; but we need some more in order to repair the organ.

D.   Well that sounds like the story of Ashley. I mean Ashley has been wanting to build a village hall since Adam was a little boy. And people talk about funds being here and funds being there. So in a sense this sounds like a parallel.

M.   There's a very real sense of community on The Green, I notice. You must be aware of that more than I am.

D.   But you notice, which is interesting.

M.   Yes, I do. I think people really look out for each other. There are all the feudings that go on, of course, something or nothing; but the positive side is that people will help each other: people are aware when people are ill, aren't they, and they give a hand. And they look out for each other and make sure that people's houses are all right. Some silly gentleman made the mistake of trying to break into somebody's house when they were in hospital, and was fortunate not to have his legs broken by a large resident of The Green who nearly caught him. Who shall be nameless!

D.   But very large, yes. Very large indeed!

M.   You don't mess with him. No. And again, people have said to me that they have found the church supportive of them in times of tragedy, and of course as you know there have been some very sad bereavements in the area, and people felt that the church was on their side in those situations.

D.   Do you think that's possibly easier in this part of your united benefice than in Hale? Because it's very difficult to live in Ashley and be anonymous. Which makes it easier for neighbours and for the church to respond, than maybe it is in Hale.

M.   Yes. We all know each other. Ashley is still distinctly different, with the influence of the farmers still as significant members of the community; the fact that it is large-ly rural; the fact that there are people living in council houses, don't own them but are paying rent, as well as people living in much larger houses. But they all mix in together. So I think there's a broader spectrum of the community in Ashley, small though it is, you have a wider range of people and income distribution.

D.   Well I've noticed, in the course of going round talking with people for this book, that there are, as you know, quite a number of professional people living in Ashley: but they live here almost precisely so as not to live in a place like Hale. They choose this type of environment. It's quite interesting.

M.   Oh yes, I know that. Well when the Robinsons came here they very much chose to live here; not in splendid isolation, but wanting to be part of the community. And I should imagine that's what everybody thinks. Like the school, it's very special. I always think that the children who go to Ashley School will look back on it, and realise in years to come what a fortunate experience they had

D.   Oh, they do. You'll get that in the book as well. I speak to people who are now adult, and even grandparents, who were at the school, and it's fascinating to hear what they have to say about it.

M.   And it's interesting that people have come from Hale, people who are grand-parents in our church, St Peter's in Hale, actually wish that their sons and daughters would consider sending their children to Ashley School, because there is something almost tangible about the special atmosphere of the place.

D.   Does that happen? Do you get any Hale children come here?

M.   A few. We are actually trying to increase the numbers, because all schools now have to market themselves. It's a joint benefice - there's no problem between the two communities. People from St Elizabeth's do join in with things that go on at St Peter's, for example when the Bishop came and did a Saturday morning thing for us on the Gospels, some people from Ashley came to that: equally, people from Hale love to come to Ashley from time to time, just to enjoy the more informal worship. Because although the service on paper is the same, in practice it's not - especially if the organ's playing up, or Keith is having to explain to us which verses we should sing or not sing, according to which CD he's playing.

D.   Explain that, Michael. Most people won't have heard about the way the music is done at Ashley.

M.   Well, twice a month we now have Robin Gill playing the organ for us, but the organ really needs some money spending on it. He battles with that, and he does very well. And on the other two Sundays Keith Munday puts CDs on. So if anybody's going by on a summer's day and the church doors are open, because we're singing along with a CD from, say, Lincoln Cathedral Choir, it will sound as though the church is bursting at the seams. And if the passing visitor was to come in in astonishment to join this vast congregation, he would find that there are about twenty five people there, singing along with the CD - which Keith always introduces in his own inimitable manner. He will say, *The first verse has no introduction, we go straight in. Please listen to the third verse, which is a solo. And in the fourth verse the words are completely different, but you sing the words in your hymn book.* But we mustn't call it the Karaoke, because he gets upset.

D.   Does he? I have heard it described as The Karaoke Church! It must be very good equipment.

M.   Yes. Yes. And actually Keith does a very good job. He chooses the hymns, and he's actually put a list out asking people to list their favourite hymns. The mind boggles, if we're going to have *Onward Christian Soldiers* once a fortnight, or *The Lord's My Shepherd*, or *Abide with Me!*

D.   We'll keep that for the Cup Final weekend! But it's an indication of the enthusiasm, certainly. Is the equipment Keith's, or did the church install it?

M.   Oh, the church installed it.

D.   It must actually be quite good equipment, to work the way it does.

M.   Oh it is, yes. The congregation over the years, as far as I can tell, has looked after the church very well. And as soon as the architect reports on anything that needs doing, you can be sure that it's done. And actually the Parochial Church Council do get on with things. They take a lot of responsibility, for example in ensuring that records are kept, ensuring that their returns are sent in, ensuring that applications to the Diocesan Advisory Committee are properly made: they do.

D.   So a large part of the administrative work is done . . .

M.   Yes, by the lay people. Which is very good. Because I'm no good at it!

D.   And you mentioned that we've got the magazine being edited locally. I'm just trying to think if there are any other instances of local, do-it-yourself leadership, rather than waiting for someone to come in and do it?

M.   Mary Walker and her assistants are doing an excellent job with the Sunday School and their work is displayed at the back of church. For the first time, some of the children took part in the Christingle Service, again due to the efforts of Mary and the Sunday School teachers. I feel very positive about Ashley. And I like the *Let's all muck-in together* approach. They're doers, they're not just talkers.

D.   Are there dreams that you have? How would you like things to develop here?

M.   I would like the community not to have just their present sense of goodwill towards the church, but somehow that we would be able to involve them more in the worshipping life of the church. I mean, I know that if I was to say I'm sorry, but I'm afraid this church is going to have to be closed, there'd be an uproar. And they would hate the idea of the church being closed, because it's important to them as a focal point in the community. But I'm a bit puzzled about their positive response to the church as a building, to the church as a place where there's a Sunday School, as a place where they sometimes go: I'm a bit puzzled as to why they don't go more often. Now that's not to criticise them. That is something I'm thinking about. I'm very interested in what you had to say, the other time we met, about the problem of the church as an institution: I think I really need to start to talk to some of the younger families, find out what we can do to improve the way they think we should be doing things. Is the time of the service wrong? Is the way we do the service wrong? I don't mean I'm going to agree with everything they say, but I think they have a right to their input. They're not infallible any more than I am, but I think I need to get a dialogue going about that. And I think the PCC need to be aware of what people think, so that we can then discuss it, and decide a way forward, because we haven't found it yet here.

D.   And it's not inconceivable that that might be the biggest difficulty: you might find that what would be acceptable to the wider community would be anathema to the established churchgoer.

M.   And what works in Hale doesn't necessarily work in Ashley. We're following the same pattern in both places. So I don't know. There's no use pretending, I don't know the answer.

D.   Well you have only been here since 1997 after all. That's not very long

M.   I've been in rural ministry before, and over a period of four years in rural ministry the congregation did begin to build up. But I don't quite know why. If I knew what it was I would bottle it, and pour it out in Ashley.

b)   Ashley School.   Mrs Naureen Wakefield, Headmistress

D.   Just to fill in the background, when did you come here?

N.W. I came here in January 1987, to take over the post of one-day-a-week teacher, so that Mrs Preston could have that day to do her administration. It soon became evident that one day a week for administration was not sufficient, so that very quickly went to two days a week, and then to two-and-a-half days a week, which I carried on doing until I took over as Acting Head, in November 1996.

D.   What had you been doing before?

N.W. I had been doing three days a week at Bexton Infants' School in Knutsford.

D.   I see, yes. And then you came here, and it just developed from there. Can I put it this way: did you choose Ashley, or did Ashley choose you?!

N.W.. I saw the advertisement for this part-time teacher, which asked for someone with an interest in music. Singing is my passion, and as a member of the Hallé Choir I was able to pass on my love of music to the children, and develop their singing potential and their guitar playing. I thought at the time that I was winding down! One day a week would be quite nice, I should be able to see my new grandchildren, and I should be able to have a bit more leisure time. And here I am!

D.   What a wonderful bit of winding down!

N.W. It sort of wound up and wound up, and then suddenly shot up!

D.   What an adventure! I hadn't realised.

N.W. So it was a case of I was the only person here - because Mrs Atherton had then left to have her baby - who knew the ropes and I just had to step in.

D.   Without much choice, as Acting Head. But at that stage, presumably while you were Acting Head, you had a certain amount of space to decide What do I do now?

N.W. I was fortunate, in that we were able to employ very quickly a colleague of mine. She took over what I had been doing, the two-and-a-half days a week, and I took over the two and a half days that Mrs Preston had been doing. And in fact we altered that timetable once Mrs Taylor had started, so that we split the Junior classs on a Wednesday morning, and we were able to give the children some extra individual help, which has carried on. Mrs Taylor now gives the Year Sixes special lessons on Wednesday morning, whilst I take the rest, the years Three Four and Five.

D.   And what happens to One, Two and Three?

N.W. One, Two and Three are the Infants - no: Reception, One and Two, with two teachers who job-share, in the Infants' class. They also overlap on a Wednesday, so that one of the teachers can give the Year Twos, who are the ones at the top of the Infants' class, special lessons, to help them for the SATS exams, which they're doing this week. There are two groups, the Year Twos and the Year Sixes, who have to do the nationwide tests at this time of the year. That's why we overlap with our jobs, so that we can separate these children out, and make sure that they have the best that we can give them.

D.   This is new to me. It sounds as if all this is made possible by the job-sharing.

N.W. It is.

D.   Is that a reasonably new thing, or did I just not know about it?

N.W. We have instituted it here. I was job-sharing with Mrs Preston all the way along, first of all only one day a week, but it soon became evident that you just cannot do the administration that is required of a Primary School head teacher in one day. It just can't be done. And so the Junior class was always a job-share. But then we instituted it for the Infants, and we found that it works exceedingly well - because of this over-lap in the middle. And we feel that the children are at a great advantage, because they have the benefit of the expertise of two people.

D.   And as well as the SATS, haven't you had somebody doing the Eleven Plus as well, going into Altrincham Grammar?

N.W. We have. That is all included in that overlap time. We are able to help children who want to do entrance exams, Trafford Eleven Plus which we can do from this school, and entrance exams to any grammar schools that parents wish us to . . .

D.   That seems quite extraordinary, that you're able to do all that!

N.W. You can't do it unless you've got the bodies. I mean, I go downstairs and I take the younger ones, the Years Three Four and Five. Mrs Taylor takes the Year Sixes, and all this extra work goes on then.

D.   And it's really all thanks to the day overlap?

N.W.. Yes. I have to fight very hard to hold onto that, in the funding. But I say to the people from the Office, I say to them that it is more important for me to have teach-ers in front of children than it is to put money aside for all manner of other things. That is my priority, the fact that we have teachers in front of the children, to their best advantage.

D.   Thank you. Well what shall we go on to now? Can I ask you about the other pros and cons of small schools against normal-sized schools, or would you like to talk about the rationalisation, or shall we leave that altogether?

N.W.. I think that the rationalisation has come and gone. As far as we believe, we are not now under any threat, not unless our figures dropped so dramatically, and we can't see that because our projected figures for the next few years are growing, and are good. So in the foreseeable future that danger isn't there, and I feel now that we're looking ahead very positively.

D.   That sounds to me like far the best thing. It would be very easy to get stuck in playing over old battles that have been finished.

N.W. Yes. I mean, it would be worth noting that we did work very hard from the 1995 Ofsted Inspection, where we got this *Unsatisfactory value for money*, to the last year's Ofsted Inspection, where we managed, by dint of working very hard and raising standards, we managed then to get *Satisfactory value for money*. Which then put us into the realms of Not-Easy-To-Close-Down!

D.   Nice expression! I wonder if you could put in a sentence or so what areas you spent all this hard work in? You must have focused somewhere in those four years?

N.W. The focus was on this determination by me to put teachers in front of children. That was where it counted. So that we could separate out groups of children: groups of children with special needs, groups of children who were doing these seven-year-old and eleven-year-old tests. And structuring the staff so that we could give the children the best teaching that we thought we could give them. There is no substitute for having a teacher in front of a small group of children, doing that work which is specific to them - at a given time in the week; although I do believe that they all gain from being taught "across the board", the Sevens-to-Elevens in the Junior class: because they do gain, the younger ones gain from the older ones, and the older ones gain from the younger ones.

D.   Well there are all sorts of comments like that in the book, from pupils of all ages - I mean people who are almost still at the school, to people who are grandparents. And the same sort of phrases crop up. It's about the different age-groups, and people looking after each other, and the atmosphere of a family.

N.W. You have such a family, caring atmosphere in a school like this. And children are not separated out. The children who are less able, the children who are very able, are absorbed, and can be where it suits them best without standing out. That is the big advantage.

D.   Which enables children to accept each other's differences.

N.W. Yes. And we do make a point of taking the children away for a residential holiday every year, we have done for the past four years. And that is great - it's great for the staff to see the children out of the classroom, to see them in a social surrounding, and to realise what qualities the children have in those situations, which you might not always see here. So that has been absolutely invaluable. And great fun! it really is. They're all absolutely filthy, and tired out when get back, but very happy!

D.   Do you have a tight programme, you have to keep everything moving?

N.W. Yes. We have been, for the past four years, to the PGL camp at Boreatton Park in Shropshire. And this year, in September, we're going to Robin Wood Centre, near Todmorden, which is different. Similar activities, but slightly different. We decided we'd have a different venue this time.

D.   Do you have to do it all yourselves, or is there a residential staff in these places?

N.W. There is, yes. It's very, very well organised. Safety standards are excellent - they have to be.

D.   I'm getting the picture, which I have to admit confirms my observations ever since I've lived in Ashley, that the advantages of a school this size really seem to be very considerable. My idea of a school was where you have a class per year and a teacher per year: and I've never been able to visualise how you do it here.

N.W. Yes, you have to come in and be here for half a day, and see how it works. You have to differentiate the work: what we tend to do is take a topic - be it Maths, English, History, Geography, Science; and you have to do whole-class teaching, because that makes sense. But you must be aware that the seven- and eight-year-olds can't be expected to do as much written work, or maybe give you as much back verbally, as the older ones would. But the young ones learn from what the older ones say. The older ones understand the limitations of the younger ones. And then you have to give them written work that is differentiated.

D.   Appropriate to their level.

N.W. Appropriate to their level. But the subject is a class subject.

D.   Which also gives children at every level a chance to see how a subject builds up.

N.W. And you may have a subject which comes round in a two-year cycle, so that if you get it in First Year you'll do it again in Third Year, and you'll remember a bit and you'll understand more. And so on. Certainly for Science that happens.

D.   Makes it sound very exciting. I should think, from the children's point of view, that could be much more exciting than what I remember of school.

N.W. Just doing a set thing.

D.   A set thing, and closed. But it must be much more difficult for the teacher.

N.W. I think it is difficult, until you are experienced at doing it. And then you really have to have your wits about you, and you have to be aware when a child is struggling. But it's like everything else, the more you do it the more able you become.

D.   I was just wondering, yes. So do you find that this really becomes a speciality within the profession? Small schools?

N.W. I think you would find it very difficult, initially, to come from a one age, one class, teaching to teaching in this situation. You would have to learn how to do it.

D.   How do they go on for inter-school activities, like sports?

N.W. We take part in not only Knutsford school activities, but also there's an Association of Small Schools in the County, which goes out as far as Wincle, Nether Alderley. And they arrange sports, football, netball. We're taking part in Knutsford Schools' Millennium Concert in July; which is the High School plus some of the feeder schools, and we're taking all our children, I hope, to sing and play the guitar.

D.   Now, talking of the High School, that's another thing that I've often wondered about: the contrast, if you're in a school like this, to going into a school like that, where there are probably almost as many people in your class as there were in the whole school, and you've got seven hundred people in the school: the contrast seems hard to imagine. How do they cope with the change?

N.W. I think that they realise as a matter of course, as children do, that they are going to something different. We don't make a big issue of it. We say, This is here and now: that's what you are going to. We've got one of the children going to Altriuncham Girls' Grammar this time, one of them going to Holmes Chapel Comprehensive, which is half the size of Knutsford, and four of them going to Knutsford. So they're going different ways, and they know this is now, that will be different. And they've all got friends, relatives and so on who have gone ahead of them. So they know. We do take them down to the High School on occasions for a joint science day. The children who are going this year had a joint science and maths day last year, and the year before they went and did something else.

D.   And is this an initiative that comes from Knutsford? To help them?

N.W. Yes. The integration. Yes, the headmaster at the High School now is very open and very friendly, and very welcoming to all the children from the feeder schools.

D.   That sounds very imaginative.

N.W. And we also have a Knutsford Heads' forum which we all belong to. So that we go and discuss matters to do with us as part of the feeder school . . .

D.   So that the system is run much more as a whole?

N.W. Yes. We don't feel as if we're isolated out here, as I think used to happen years ago. Now we feel very much as if we're part of the group.

D.   That must make a big difference.

N.W. Yes, it does.

D.   May we come down to Ashley now, and ask how you see the school relating to the rest of the village?

N.W. I would like to see the development of our extension to the school, which incorporates an extension to the Infants' room to provide them with a wet play, sand area; and a door out at the far end which will lead into a small hall, from which there will be an exit to the playground for the Infants, and their own toilets, which they don't have. And then a couple of storerooms, and then an entrance into the hall. That is my plan - well we have the plans drawn up, they are downstairs, we have got that far. And there'll also be cloakrooms in the hall, and an entrance from outside so that outside, village, people can hire it. I really don't know when that will be started. Sooner rather than later, I hope. We are at the moment in the process of having the whole of the school re-carpeted, and the ancient central heating system is to be replaced in the summer holidays. Some very old radiators and pipes are to be taken out. We had no heating in the school house. Peter Morton, our Chairman of Governors, has pushed and pushed and pushed: we got new heating put into here, which rendered it much more habitable; but then we found that this system and the old system didn't run happily together. So we were either absolutely roasted alive in the classrooms to maintain an even temperature here, or if those were turned down it didn't come up here at all. So Peter has nagged, I think would be the word! the powers-that-be who run the works department at Chester, and we are in the planning to have the central heating. So since we had Ofsted we have re-carpeted upstairs, this was the tattiest old carpet you ever did see.

D.   So the hall, that will be a facility that will be available to the village as well?

N.W. Yes. It was commented in the 1995 Ofsted inspection report that we hadn't got enough room to provide all that the curriculum demanded. We can't do dance and PE, much drama, and have any wet games. So we would obviously have first call on the hall, but our intention is that it should be part of the Village community. The W.I. and the Parish Council already meet here.

D.   What about other things? It always strikes me there's a lot of participation in the school - just as a villager, I hear about people coming to the school: not just parents either, people coming in.

N.W. We have. It's always been my policy to have a very open-door attitude, for parents, visitors, governors, and anyone who has any expertise and would like to offer it to the school: we're only too pleased. It is something that you have to think about, because if you indiscriminately open your doors to all and sundry you can be landed with less than satisfactory helpers. I wouldn't like to put it any stronger than that. If you invite people in you have to be prepared to take them, and all that they offer.

D.   That's quite ticklish, isn't it?

N.W. It can be. We now have a PTA. There wasn't one before because there were one or two people who got a bit *peas-above-sticks*, as we say in Yorkshire! A little bit carried away with their own importance, shall we say. You have to be a little bit careful that you, in the nicest possible way, make people realise where their particular place is. And that's a management aspect that we have to think about. But I think if you are generally open and friendly, people respect that, and will offer, because they feel that what they can give is - valuable.

D.   At the same time it does sound as if you've got to be careful that the offers that you accept are going to be useful.

N.W. It's no good having people in to help with a particular thing if you then find that their expertise in that line of business is not what you would want for the children. So yes, you've got to do this very carefully. For the good of the children; that's all-important. But in the main we haven't had anyone who doesn't fit in. I think if you make people aware of what is needed from the beginning, make them feel welcome, make them feel valued, that that is where you gain, and because people feel that what they've got to offer is valuable to you, then they'll give you a hundred and ten per cent, and be very supportive.

D.   Can you give any examples of people coming in doing particular things?

N.W. We have a gentleman who comes in who is a retired headmaster, who comes in because he's a musician. He has offered his services, and he comes in on a Friday afternoon; and the children just sing. And it's wonderful. We have quite a few ladies who come in and listen to children read. We believe here that reading is the most important thing for children to learn to do, and we endeavour to hear all children read every day, because we have found that that really above all things does bring them on. So we have people coming in doing that. We had a lady who came in and did an Art project: all about clothing from the beginning of the Millennium up to the present day. We have people who come in to do Art; games, a lot of parents help with football and netball.

D.   So that's quite a wide range.

N.W. I like to encourage anybody who's got a speciality to come and give it to the children. Because no matter how good a teacher is, there are always areas . . . I mean for me, I can't catch a ball. I am hopeless. I love sports and games, athletics and gymnastics: but I can't catch a ball! So I am very grateful to somebody who's got ball skills, and can teach them to the children. That's just one area. And when we go on these activity weeks, adventure holidays, Mrs Taylor and I take all the Juniors, which is great fun. And we're both good at completely different things. I will climb up things and hang off things. Mrs Taylor will keep her feet very firmly on the ground! She says, You go and hang up, and swing. I'll take them to the woods and for nature walks and so on! So we all complement each other.

D.   What about the future: do you have any dreams?

N.W. I would like very much to see the building of the hall, because I think that would make an enormous difference. I'm not saying that we can't deliver what we have to deliver now. I think we're fortunate that we have very few wet games lessons, very very few. There are aspects that I realise we can't deliver, but I think in the main what we do deliver is quite special. I think what they lose on one side they gain on the other, with small classes and lots of individual attention.

D.   Well it certainly comes out, listening to the children, and to former children here. One thing above all is that it seems to be always a happy school.

N.W. Very, yes. This is what people say when they come in. When people come in for the first time, and in fact the Ofsted Inspectors said: this is such a happy school. And they said, Nothing that we comment on will be used to be able to close the school. They were so complimentary. And then, after we'd had the Ofsted Inspection we have to have a separate RE inspection by the diocesan people, and he again said the same.

D.   Oh did he? I did hear something about that!

N.W. Why, what did you hear?

D.   Michael [the vicar] was very tickled, because some remark was said about how he seemed to have such good rapport with the children. And Prill Lloyd was saying that the obvious reason for that is that he *is* a child!

Laughter.

N.W. That's about right, I would say! He's very good. He's very, very supportive. We're just so lucky with all our governors, we couldn't have nicer, more supportive and hard-working, each in their own sphere. And I know, talking to other Heads who have Boards of Governors who are not quite like ours.

D.   Something that you have to live in spite of, rather than anything more positive.

N.W. We have three parent governors now, one of whom - you know Dee Langley? Now she is absolutely first class. Not only is she such a nice person, but in the last year we worked a whole afternoon every week, updating all the numerous documents required by Ofsted. She worked with me, and she still does. And that to me is worth more than money could ever buy.

D.   So you've got the children; it seems as if you've got a good body of parents, sup-portive parents who are willing to participate, become involved; and the governors -

N.W. - And the staff. We're very, very fortunate. All the staff are very, very supportive. Mrs Barker, who is the cook, has been here for twenty five years.

D.   Yes! I knew Mrs Barker!

N.W. Mrs Barker's still here, and she is *so* good. Mrs Collier who is the Secretary came when Mrs Roberts stopped, she is very very good, I rely on her. When I took over I could not have managed without her. She was, and still is, so good. And the three other members of staff and I share the teaching now. We all get on well, we're all real-ly hard-working - but cheerful with it!

D.   You enjoy it. It sounds as if you enjoy it.

N.W. We do. You couldn't do it if you didn't. You *have* to like it. There are times when the paperwork gets a bit overwhelming, but with the rest of the people, with Mrs Langley coming in to help me, and Mrs Collier who is so excellent, between us we get through it. I'm getting quite adept at binning things! I remember Mrs Preston saying to me, If in doubt, put it in the bin. If it's very important they'll send you another one! I still see Mrs Preston, I go and have a chat with her, I keep up with her. We've always been great friends. I went through a personal crisis when I'd been here about five or six years, and she and Mrs Barker and Mrs Atherton could not have been more supportive.

[The formal interview concluded, we move towards the school's exit,
stopping first by a notice board in the vestibule]

N.W. (*Showing the plans*). We have plans to develop the playground, and the area in front of the school. And two children, Sarah Goulden and Ben Paterson, designed an area of the school here which is going to be developed as a sitting area, as a place for parents to wait, and as a restful area for the children to sit; as well as the development of the field and ground at the side of the school.

D.   And who's planned all this?

N.W. The children had an input into it, and then the architect went away and drew that up for us. The children's idea.

D.   This will include now - because I'm not very good at reading these things . . .

N.W. All the children had an input into what they wanted here, and then the Junior children designed this area here, which is what we just looked at outside there -

D.   The rest area?

N.W. A rest, waiting area: with a bit of shelter if it's cold and so on.

D.   And then on the rest of the playground you've got some bits that are under cover.

N.W. Yes, that's a space with a shelter. These are trees and paths.

D.   As well as just simple concrete - playground.

N.W. Yes. And we have already got some money towards carrying that out.

D.   And this is all going to be done: these trees aren't here at the moment, are they?

N.W. No. There is a tree there, and one or two here; but there are going to be one or two more. And that. of course, that is the hall plan. And this is, as I was telling you, out from the Infants' classroom, a practical area. And then, outside, toilets; and then into the hall.

D.   So that you've got access from inside and access from outside. Yes, that's marvellous, isn't it?

N.W. It could be. It *will* be! And we had this done before the Ofsted Inspection, done by the diocese: the diocese paid for this. They believed in us so much that they paid for that. Over a thousand pounds they gave us, to get that done.

D.   Have you had any comments back from Mr Brooks yet? because he's seen them, hasn't he?

N.W. Yes. Dee has spoken to him, she's in charge of that sort of thing. We haven't had any adverse comments yet.

D.   He was very interested in it when I spoke to him.

N.W. We'd like him to come down actually.

D.   Well, I hope you'll ask him. I think he's quite likely to come.

N.W. It's just a case of getting the whole thing off the ground, really. But we've been concentrating on getting the roof done, which is very much in need of mending. The roof, and the interior, the central heating.

c)   The Post Office/Shop.   Diane and Alan Warrington

A.   So we replied to the advert and we came down one afternoon. Sally was here and showed us round. And we said, *We'll go for it.* That was it, basically.

D.   You were dealing with Sally, not the post office?

Di.   No, I had to get the job. I had to go for an interview, job interview. For Postmistress.

A.   It had to be both. And I did as well.

D.   Which comes first? Do you get the outline of a deal with Sally first, and then apply to the post office for their job?

A.   Well, it was actually Ernie wasn't it? It was his business. Well, Sally was running the shop and everything, with the possibility of her and Kevan taking over, but actually Ernie was the inheritor. Of course. It was his business. So basically we were dealing with Ernie.

Di.   And we told them we were interested in buying the business, and they informed Counters.

A.   The next thing was to apply to become Postmistress.

D.   I see, yes.

Di.   And then dependent on whether I got that job, on whether we got the business.

D.   And so there was a selection process?

A   Yep. And for some reason we finished top.

D.   Whew!

Di.   Actually it was quite funny, because we had to go to - the actual property is rented from Mrs Mason - so when all this was going on we had to go and meet her.

A.   Because she's part of the deal, basically.

Di.   If she'd turned round and said she didn't like us and that we couldn't live in her property, then everything fell through anyway. So an appointment was set up for us to go and meet Mrs Mason, and we hadn't got a clue what kind of person she was or anything. We just got told there was this elderly lady living next door who owned the property, and she would like to meet us.

A.   I suppose the other reason why the post office and shop exist in the village is because of Mrs Mason. Because if she owns the property, which is obviously worth mega money because of the area, if she decided to sell it, to offer it for sale, people that could afford it wouldn't want a little shop and a post office. The people who are willing to run the shop and basically have the privilege of living here, want to run the shop. But it's obviously worth quite a sum, because of the land as well. And if she didn't rent it out to the average person, say, who's willing to run the shop and the post office, the village wouldn't have a shop and a post office.

D. Yes! It never occurred to me. You mean she could replace this with a house that would fetch £300,000 or something?

A. This has got to be worth at least that. Because of the land.

Di. This was sort of like said, at our interview. She basically said that she wanted somebody who would keep the shop alive. And that was one of the stipulations, that it would remain a shop as it is or better: a general store for the village, and post office.

D. So a lot will depend on the attitude of her heirs.

A. Not really. Because I think that you'll find it's written, somewhere.

Di. And we were assured that if anything happened to Mrs Mason we would be secure here as long as we wanted to stay.

A. I think basically the rules are, from Mrs Mason, that the village shop will live on and on. So it's probably been written-in somewhere.

D. That's a thought that had never occurred to me until now.

A. The first interview there were just the two of us. And Mrs Mason, with son William present.

Di. That's right, yes. And we were there nearly two hours. And towards the end she sort of like said to us, Would you like some ginger wine? *Oh yes please, I'll have some!* So we all sat down to a glass of ginger wine. And then eventually the interview wound up and we went away. And then came back here the next day. And Sally was saying *How did it go? How did it go?* All right I think. She seemed a very nice lady, we seemed to get on well. But obviously we'll have to wait and see. So Sally said, *Did she get the ginger wine out?* So I said, Well actually, yes she did. *Oh well you're quids in then*, she says, *She only gets the ginger wine out for people she likes!*

A. Did you ever get any ginger wine there, David?

Di. So that was it, then. Everything gelled together after that. We went back again before we moved in, and took the children.

D. And so how long was it between then and moving in?

Di. Well it was probably about two months in total. Because once they told me I'd got the Counters job it was with a view to me starting within two or three days, taking over. Which I did. I mean we did, prior to coming, wonder whether we would be accepted.

D. I should think you must have. I should think it would be quite nerve-racking.

Di.   The previous Postmistress and her family had obviously been very popular. And when we knew we'd got the post office we obviously had to let the staff know what our plans were. We put them out of their misery by saying if they wanted to stay on, they could stay on. And of course one of them was Brenda's sister Fran. So she made us very welcome even though I was taking over from her sister, basically. She brought me a New Home present, which I've still got, growing on the landing. And all our fears about moving into a small village were completely dispelled, because we were made so welcome.

D.   Mmm. That's nice.

Di.   There was the odd occasion when there was a remark like It wasn't done like that before!

D.   I relate to that, as a vicar! I think little villages like this do tend to be very conservative: *As it was in the beginning is now and ever shall be* sort of thing! Always a dinosaur lurking, not far below the surface!

Di.   Well we haven't made many changes, for that simple reason. We took our time in putting our name up. But when we put some security up in the shop we had quite a few comments like saying, *Oh it's Ashley Prison now, is it?* Because they hadn't been there before.

D.   And that was before there had been any trouble?

[*This refers to two burglaries that had taken place within a week of each other; the first time the window had been taken right out, the second time it had been smashed. The bars must have been effective, as no further entries have been attempted through that window. - D*]

A.   No, after.

D.   And *still* you got comments like that? Even after that?

Di.   Well it was because of the trouble that we put them up.

D.   And even so you had people saying this? Did they know what had happened?

Di.   Oh yes. But we didn't want to spoil the front of the shop and so we didn't want to put the bars on the outside. We wanted it to be discreet. So Alan asked a friend to make the bars to fit the inside of the window so that it wouldn't be too obvious, but it would give us the protection needed. So this friend made these for us. But still we had people saying, *It's Ashley Prison now, is it?*

D.   Dinosaurs.

Di.   You've got to be very careful when you come to make any changes. Even little ones like that.

A.   Mrs Mason, not long after we'd moved in, said that it seemed a bit small. I said We can cope, like. So she said, Well I was thinking about putting a little extension on. So she built us this. It used to finish there. And then after she'd built it she said,

Hmm. Maybe we should have gone two storeys instead of just the one.

Di.   It was quite funny how she did it, because she said to me once, The kitchen's not very big, is it? So I said, Well we can manage. She said, But it would be better if it was a bit bigger, wouldn't it? So I said, Yes, but we can manage. We knew what we were coming into. She said, You definitely need more. And you could do with a dining room as well, couldn't you? So that was the start of the extension.

D.   From time to time there are waves of panic sweep through the village, that the post office might pull out. I think it's a long-standing worry, the first scare was long before you came. And everyone was going round making sure everyone was buying as much as they possibly could - not buying, using the post office as much as they could, because of this threat. And this was back in Brenda's day. So it happens periodically.

Di.   Obviously there'd be nothing that - if Counters decided to pull out - there'd be not a lot we could do about it. But we have maintained the post office, and it is maintained . . .

A.   What tends to happen with, like Dunham, is it becomes what they call a Community Post Office. So the lady who works there gets paid a certain amount, gets paid a wage. Whereas we don't get paid a wage, we get paid on the work we do. Now when an Office gets below a certain volume of work, it's not financially viable. Then it becomes a Community Post Office and they just pay you a small basic wage. And then it doesn't matter whether you sell one stamp in a week or five thousand - it stays there. So that's what happens.

D.   Whereas you're paid on the basis of turnover?

A.   On the transactions that we do.

Di.   I mean, if everybody cleared off tomorrow and wouldn't come in the shop, I wouldn't get any money. We've managed to maintain it. By it being a Community Office it would actually be a part-time Office, it wouldn't be open full-time. It would only be open certain days. But if we can maintain it as a full-time Office, which touch wood we are managing to do at the moment . . .

D.   Is there a known bottom line?

Di.   Obviously Counters have a line.

D.   But you don't know where?

A.   Hopefully we're well above it. We've altered the post office business slightly, through new transactions that the post office do. Probably not increased business, but not lost any either. So we're keeping it constant.

D.   It just suddenly occurs to me that this might by associated with the post office, I'm not sure: there's a good deal of discontent on The Green -

A.   - on the rent.

Di. Well before all this latest episode - I didn't know anything about this until a customer came in and told me. To which I responded by ringing Counters. Prior to ringing Counters I was shown the letter and I said, Well that's ridiculous, what they're saying. Because we are actually going to be - our Office, not every Office at the moment but they eventually will be: but we are -

A. - a selected Office. One of the good ones.

Di. Selected Offices, to be automated. Counters are going to put in a computer into the Office, the idea being that we could actually do more business, because it goes directly through to the central computer. So what is actually said on the letter, about the automation and Giro saying that we can't do it, is nonsense. You see, the rents come in to me and I accept the payment on them. But the only time Counters actually get involved on that side of it is when I send the rent money off. Which is done through the Giro.

D. Not Counters at all?

Di. So it goes on a Giro. So if I can't write out a Giro . . . They are basically saying that we cannot accept a Giro. But we will be able to accept it because we do a lot of business, practically every transaction has a Giro on it. All your gas, your electricity, they've all got Giro payments on them. And that is basically what the rent is. So why they're saying we can't do the rent in that manner we've no idea. I phoned Counters and told them. They knew nothing about it. So they're supposed to be actually looking into it now.

A. So we've sent a copy of that letter off to the person who deals with customer relationships and they're going to look into whether there's any truth in it.

D. There's some hope then, by the sound of it. Because it caused a lot of dismay.

A. Macclesfield have been trying to get people into Direct Debits for years. If they can put them on Direct Debits it's dead simple for them. But people prefer to pay cash sometimes.

Di. You see, my basic thing is, they're using this as an excuse.

D. Macclesfield?

Di. That's my own personal view.

D. But there are people who don't have bank accounts.

Di. Exactly. That's my argument.

A. So they'll have to travel all the way to Knutsford.

D. Exactly.

Di. And my argument is that they can't even travel to Knutsford, because they don't have transport, some of them.

D.   Only the train. If one comes. Then they've got to pay for that.

Di.   So I'm actually still waiting for Counters to get back to me.

D.   So there's quite a strong social case for it, as well as the fact that you'll be auto-mated in the near future and then it will be very much simpler.

Di.   You see, at the moment I get tied down with a lot of paperwork. And we have to balance the post office every week, we have to do a manual balance. Which can take anything from three to six hours. Longer, if you don't get balanced straight away. The idea of this automation is not only that we can do the transactions quicker at the counter, i.e. not keep anybody waiting: but by the fact that everything I do through the computer is being deducted off my stock and added onto my cash, or vice versa, all the paperwork in the actual balancing will take an hour and a half instead of six. So I can actually be still available on the counter instead of being stuck in the back here doing paperwork.

D.   Do you do that? Manage to do your paperwork during shop hours?

Di.   I have to. On a Wednesday I do. The paperwork I do every night, obviously I do when the shop's shut, from half past five onwards, the daily paperwork. But on a Wednesday I have to do it during the day.

D.   Another question I wanted to ask you is, Do you get a sense, do either of you get a sense, of the significance of your role in the community here? And of the extent to which people depend on the services that you provide?

A.   Occasionally you get people mentioning. This week, the fact that we've received so many cards and flowers. Just highlights the fact that, Oh yes, They are actually thinking about us. And you realise that we provide a service.

Di.   You sometimes say you feel as if you're flogging a dead horse.

A.   The other time is, as you said before, when there's a rumour around that some-body's going to shut the post office, and everyone rallies round.

Di.   Everybody comes in then.

D.   Did you realise before you took it on? Had you seen that it was rather different from having a shop in a shopping precinct? Not just the way of life and the environ-ment, but the number of people who actually depend on you?

A.   Well this is why we have certain items that we buy, that possibly only one person buys. Those little sticks you put in an oven, bread sticks, possibly one of them -

D.   Ah, you mean my half-baked bread! That's very good, I'm glad you brought that up! Everyone will be eating them soon!

A.   We do try to provide what we can.

d)   The Greyhound. Shaun Hayes

D.   When did you come here, Shaun?

S.   I came in June 1995.

D.   What stage were things at then? Was the refurbishment complete?

S.   Yes. The refurbishment had been completed for six months when I came.

D.   So it had been up and running in its new guise for six months?

S.   Yes.

D.   There'd been quite a clash between the village and the brewery over the planning earlier on. Were you aware of there still being any feelings about that, or had it

S.   There were a few people who seemed to think that the pub was there purely and simply for their purposes and nobody else's. Only a few though. And the main objectors never used the pub in the first place, so I never came into contact with them.

D.   As usual! And had the pub seemed to have settled down in its new shape? Because the shape was completely altered, wasn't it?

S.   Whenever there are any alterations it takes about twelve months before they settle down.

D.   Yes, I see. For different groups of people to find their different areas for their different activities?

S.   Yes. When they were used to being in one particular area which is now unavailable for one reason or another. They just relocate themselves.

D.   And that was happening when you came in?

S.   That was still going on when we first came.

D.   And since then has it changed very much, in the way that it's being used?

S.   Yeah, I suppose the advent of the Quiz Night for local causes has made a big difference. It brings in people once a month that we never normally see, from the village. I think they realise that although this is a business it is also part of the community, and we try to help them as much as possible.

D.   Well it's been very interesting for me, watching mainly from the sidelines - sidelines both as far as my relations with the pub was concerned, and also as my relations with the various organisations that have done this Quiz Night. To see the place gradually becoming used like that: because I don't think it ever had been before.

S.   Not to my knowledge, anyway. We like to give something back, but they must also realise that we have a business to run. I'm sure that one or two things that we do

435

upset a few people. It's just the nature of the game. We don't deliberately set out to annoy anybody. We try to get on as peacefully as possible.

D.   Of course, yes. And it must always be a problem in any pub. Neighbours.

S.   I wouldn't buy a house near a pub.

D.   Quite. But then there are other people who probably can't get one near enough! How did it all start? Did the initiative come from organisations in the village, for these Quiz Nights?

S.   If I remember correctly the first one that we did was to raise some money for the May Queen. I think someone approached us and asked if it would be possible, and we said, We'll give it a go and see what response you get. If it takes off, fine. But I think all the ones that we have done have had a good success rate. One or two suffered from the time of the year, that makes a slight difference, but there are now a hard core of regulars who go to the Quiz whether it's for the church or whatever. And there are others who appear purely and simply because it's for their cause.

D.   And there is one every month?

S.   The first Tuesday of every month.

D.   So that it's become a regular feature now. Do you notice people coming in again, as a result of that? Has it gained you any more regulars?

S.   In all honesty? No.

D.   So it's not really any advantage to you other than perhaps having a busier night.

S.   Well people think that there's an advantage in having a busier night, but it doesn't increase our trade by a significant margin.

D.   That's very interesting, that was one of the things I was wondering. So in fact this is really giving as far as you're concerned?

S.   Well it just gives an opportunity for them to raise some money for whatever cause they want. Because we never pick the cause, it's always someone's suggestion.

D.   And do you run it yourself?

S.   Unfortunately yes, I do all the questions.

D.   Unfortunately?

S.   It's getting harder and harder to do, now. On the level of questions, you know.

D.   There's only so many questions you can ask?

S.   There is. And not only that, you can only ask them at a certain level. I mean there's no point in having a quiz where everyone sits there scratching their heads. We like the teams to get big high scores.

D.   Are there sources of questions?

S.   I actually just use quiz books from a shop. I pinch one or two questions off the
Internet, but basically I have to sit and go through a book and if I can answer that
question I put it in and if I haven't a clue I leave it out.

D.   I just wondered, because it seems to have mushroomed all over the place, pub
quiz nights. I wondered if it was the sort of thing that breweries produced now, lists
of questions?

S.   There are companies around that will send you a quiz. But you don't know the
level of the questions. At least I know now seventy five per cent of the people that will
be here on a Quiz Night, so I set the questions that I think they'll be able to answer.

D.   Well I think that's much better, yes.

S.   Well it's not much of a quiz for you if you're sat there and four questions have
gone by and you've not had a chance of answering them.

D.   Yes that's just demoralising, yes. I have a lot of trouble with the Bible questions!

S.   Well I set it at their level.

D.   Shaun, now that you've been here quite a long time have you any feelings or
comments you'd like to make about the village? Do you get out much, or do you only
see Ashley from your side of the bar, as it were?

S.   Because I no longer live here I tend to just see the village from here. Before, I
suppose being on a crossroads, we tend to see the village in two halves, that side and
this side. I think there are two sides to the village.

D.   That's very interesting. And it's the road?

S.   The road splits it. There's definitely two halves to the village.

D.   And, from where you sit, how do they seem to relate to each other, these two
halves?

S.   There's no animosity between the two, but I don't think the two . . . Well, in my
opinion they only come together when there's a village thing. They tend to be different.

D.   So normally they just don't actually meet?

S.   They don't integrate, no. Definitely one or the other.

D.   That's very interesting, because it's not emerged anywhere else. I can imagine
that it wouldn't emerge anywhere else. [for further details, see end of this appendix.]

S.   Maybe nobody else wants to actually say it, but I find that there's a definite Us and Them feel to it. Although the two sides do generally get on quite well together. There's no animosity between the two.

D.   What's the balance between locals and people passing through in here?

S.   Our trade is eighty per cent regulars, of which only five per cent at the most would be villagers.

D.   So the trade is eighty per cent regulars, and of that eighty only five per cent are from the village? And the other seventy five, do they come from far?

S.   The surrounding areas. We get a lot from Hale, Hale Barns. In the summer, with Tatton on our doorstep we get a lot of passing trade. People who drive to and from work along these roads and see the pub, they'll stop. We couldn't survive upon the village.

D.   Well that must have been the thinking behind extending the restaurant in the first place. How does the eating side fit in with the more traditional pub side? Are they quite separate?

S.   At night they're separate, we keep them separate at night, we keep the drinkers and the diners apart. But then we tend to make the restaurant more up-market. Whereas during the day you can eat anywhere, people can just sit down and eat in any available space. But there again, our dinnertime trade is no per cent from the village. It's all people who have retired, people out walking, businessmen who work locally or at the airport. You don't see any villagers.

D.   I suppose the ones who'd be able to afford it would be at work somewhere else.

S.   In the fields or at work.

D.   Do you get people using both facilities, come and use it as a pub but also come and eat here?

S.   Oh yes, people who use both sides of the business, yes. There's no problem with that. They mix well together.

D.   That's interesting. I've found, as a customer, that I don't find I can mix the two: if I have a meal I feel very uncomfortable about the people at the bar, because I want to go and join half of them!

S.   And yet you have to stay where you are, yes! At night we keep a definite set area for the restaurant, yes. And we don't allow it to overspill.

D.   It's probably been a matter of shaking down. Time maybe helped?

S.   I think initially when we started to do more food here there was a bit of an adverse reaction from locals who didn't want to be bothered by people. Because most of the diners do not live in the area. The night time diners don't live in the area.

D.   And in time people have discovered that they don't actually get bothered by them? So there's much more tolerance. How do you get on for staff? Is it difficult?

S.   Staffing-wise its location makes it difficult. Any country pub, or any business out in rural areas would find that:
        a) you don't have a big workforce on your doorstep and . . .
        b) transportation to and from here, apart from the train, is zero.
So to work here you have to either:
        a) live on its doorstep or . . .
        b) have a car, and there are not very many.

D.   What sort of proportion of your staff are local?

S.   At the moment the young waitresses tend to be the nearest ones. But even two of those you would say are more in Knutsford than here. There's only one that lives in Ashley, there's only one of our workers who actually lives in Ashley. So that's one in fifteen.

D.   And the cooking: that must be crucial, having a good chef?

S.   Yes, you have to have. The standard of food that you do, you have to have a good chef.

D.   Is that difficult?

S.   Extremely. Again, it's location. Also a shortage of chefs.

D.   There is a shortage of chefs as well? I often wonder about that, because a number of people I know have done catering courses and trained as chefs, and then jacked it in because of unsocial hours.

S.   At the moment, for the majority of chefs, it's unsociable hours, and it's not exactly the best pay in the world.

D.   You mentioned when you were living here, and now you're not: would you like to say anything about that?

S.   Basically the accommodation upstairs is not big enough for my family.

D.   Every landlord I've known has said that. But you found a different solution from any of your predecessors. Was it difficult? Was it your idea? Did you have to persuade the brewery?

S.   Well no, because I don't belong to a brewery now. It would have been impossible while we belonged to the brewery, they would never have allowed it. It was the first priority once we'd taken over the business, purely and simply for ourselves, to find somewhere else to live; because although the area's lovely, you can't wish for a better area to live, the accommodation is just too small.

D.   Absolutely impossible. It's driven at least two landlords out in the time I've been here. But I hadn't cottoned on to this change in your relationship to the brewery.

S.   It's three and a half years now since it's changed. It's not something we shout about or publicise too much. We found that once we'd escaped from the Big Brother breweries we could institute changes much quicker and more effectively. If we saw something that wasn't working we could change it, whereas before we had to ask permission from someone else, who'd ask permission from someone else. Whereas now, hands-on, we can make the changes as and when they're needed, we don't have to wait for anybody to say you can do this, do that, don't do that. Customerwise no one has suffered from losing its big brewery umbrella. The advantages are subtle, so that they don't stand out, but there are several advantages. The customers might not realise, but they do get a wider choice of things.

D.   Well I enjoy the Guest Beer!

S.   Which we wouldn't be allowed to do otherwise.

D.   I should have twigged. I was a bit surprised when I saw there was always a guest beer. It seemed a bit generous of Greenall's!

S.   We get quite a lot of regulars now who come purely for the guest beer.

D.   So you made your move, and you live in Hale,

S.   Well we live in Altrincham now.

D.   And that did the trick for you?

S.   Yes. It's more advantageous for everybody in the family. I don't live over the job, so I'm not on call all the time. If I don't want to be contacted I just turn my phone off. It's much better for the kids because they have more room. Because I live on a fairly new estate there are lots of kids around. I know there are lots of kids on The Green, but at the age they were here it was imposssible for them to say Can I play out? and for them to go to The Green. When they played out they had to play in the back garden. Julie prefers it as well because, although she's not working all the time she'd have the same thing, being above the business restricts what you can do. So all the family are much better for it.

D.   So it's really worked out.

S.   It's the best thing we've ever done. We wouldn't be here now if I was still -

D.   I've never heard of it happening before.

S.   Nowadays you get one or two tenants who don't live on the premises, but yeah, it's still a rarity. You do actually need special permission from the licensing people to do it.

D.   And obviously there has to be somebody living here?

S.   A reliable person.

D.   Do you see anything on the horizon as you look ahead? Are there any things you dread or look forward to?

S.   In this location, here? Yes, I'm not looking forward to the train line going through.

D.   This is the line to the airport?

S.   To link the airport to the Welsh line, or the Chester line or whatever. I think that will cause massive disruption, a lot more than what the second runway has. I'm not sure how many people do know about it. I was originally told by someone who's seen the plans: 2011 is the start date for it. That's ten years away, so it won't be that publicised yet, but I think it's a definite. All I knew is that the crossing is somewhere between here and Mobberley, and I've never been quite sure where it might run.

D.   It's very interesting that so little has been heard. I don't think we've recovered from the second runway yet. Listening to people's comments: so many people are saying *Where's the third one going?* and not noticing the railway.

S.   Well if you have an increase in the airport you have to have an increase in the infrastructure to service the airport.

D.   Yes of course you do.

S.   And the railway, I'm afraid, just happens to be everyone's favourite at the moment. To get the railways going again. Personally I think one or two people in the village should step forward into the present day as well. We've heard of several applications for houses to be built that have been refused for no apparent reason. Now it's only a small village. It's got a small school which has had a fight to keep going. I'd have thought the more people they had in the village, the better they would be.

D.   A lot of people say things like that, but then they go on to say . . .

S.   *But not next to me!* The garage across the way is a prime example. Because it no longer sells petrol, I don't see how it's an amenity to this village.

D.   I think if they hadn't been executive-type houses . . . Well, people say that.

S.   Yes, they would have been high priced, but they would have been nice. But you can never understand their logic: they turn it down to take away a showroom that doesn't want to be there, it wants to move. The builders want to build the houses on it. And they go and give permission to do it, not two hundred yards further down.

D.   Oh I didn't know that.

S.   There's a house being built two hundred yards further down now. And that's one house. We're talking about a million pound house, here. For one person. It's very nice having green belt and everything, but I think the village does need building up a little bit. That field opposite us is hardly ever used. And they used to have three cottages on it. So if they used to have three, why don't they put three back?

D.   The feeling that I keep hearing is that if only they would build them cheap enough for first-time buyers, so that it would benefit the school,

S.   Yes, you have to have families coming in. Young families.

D.   I think that's what they were so much after. And they felt that the Garage proposals were not going to do that. That was the main objection that's come across to me.

S.   That was the objection I heard, that they would not be affordable houses.

D.   That's the magic word, isn't it? Affordable housing.

S.   And what's affordable nowadays? I wouldn't like to be starting up again. I think one or two people just may be realising that it's time to step forward a little bit. The view from the upstairs of the pub is fantastic. But I don't think one or two houses would spoil that. And it would bring more to the village. Whenever I mention this to people they say, Well you're only after their money. But I just turn round and say, My money doesn't come from the village anyway.

D.   Yes. You're in a very good position. It's much more to the point to say that it will feed the school and the post office. They're the two that are under threat, and that'll hurt, really hurt the village if they go.

S.   If they was to lose the post office, the nearest one would be in Hale: again, it's transportation to get there. And if you don't have a car and you have to get the train it's an extremely long walk from Hale station to the post office. I would imagine that it's a fair walk for a few people in the village to Ashley station, as well.

D.   And once you've got to the post office in Hale you've got to wait until the queue's moved, to get to the front of the queue.

S.   I think everything should be done to try and keep the post office going.

D.   People acknowledge that. There's a sort of split thing. They say *Must do that*, and yet any sign of change and they say *Oh no, no.* It doesn't really fit, you're right.

S.   They must realise that villages everywhere are losing their amenities, and to hold on to what you've got should be your number one priority.

D.   And how to play your cards so as to get the best possible compromise is the name of the game, I should think.

S.   Compromise, yeah. Six or seven extra houses in the village would not make a drastic change to the landscape. It might be an improvement in one spot. It would be a vast improvement in one corner. But that's not their fault in the car showroom business, they don't even want to be there.

D.   Yes, that's what's rum about it. But they're sure to put up another scheme, aren't they?

S.   No, they're now extending the garage.

D.   Oh, they've given up?

S.   By all accounts they've decided that as we're here we're here. Or for the time being, shall we say. I suppose money always talks. If there ever came an offer and permission was given.

D.   I didn't know that. I somehow guessed that people were assuming that there'd be another scheme put forward.

S.   No, they've got planning permission now to build on the opposite side. To make it a proper showroom. Pull down some sheds and what have-you, and make it a proper showroom. I suppose the longer you've been in the village, the less likely you are to want it to change.

D.   Well that's human nature, yes.

S.   But they do need to take just a little step forward. Realise that things can't stay the same.

D.   Think what happened to the dinosaurs! Well thank you, Shaun.

S.   That'll get me nicely shot by a few people!

[*Note. It is not possible to tell, from the Contents, who lives which side of the road in question (Cow Lane, the road from Hale to Mobberley). If anyone wants to consider Shaun's statement in more detail, people who live on the other (East) side of the road are to be found on the following pages: 1-18; 33-53; 99-127; 277-302.*]

e)   The Tatton Estate. Randle Brooks Esq

R.B. My father bought the estate towards the end of the fifties, I can't remember the exact date. It's about 5,000 acres.

D.   We in Ashley must be at the far end of the estate?

R.B. It stretches from the far end of Ashley Village to Mere, and through to parts of Mobberley, but Mobberley has always been divided between several estates.

D.   And you took over from your father?

R.B. Yes.

D.   Well can I mention the things that have come up during the course of my conversations round the village? And the first one, that is the most worrying, is the plight of the farmers.

R.B. Well farming is in crisis. They're in crisis because they're not able to get the proper price for what they sell. And the proper price must be based on the cost of production. That isn't recognised by the government. And the government is only interested, to their shame, in joining this Greater Europe. Which is a folly. In my view we're just about to have a crash anyway, a financial crash, when all our plans will become history.

D.   Do you want to say more about that?

R.B. Not really, no. That's only my view. But the trouble is, there aren't any experts on crashes that are in the future. There are only experts on crashes that are in the past.

D.   I'm just wondering if there are any ways in which you see the estate as being able to either encourage or in any other way support the efforts of your tenants?

R.B. Well we do our best, that's all I can say.

D.   Do they discuss it with you, or with the office?

R.B. Yes, they do. Yes.

D.   Because I was struck, and this was another discovery, by how much expertise there is in the estate office in Rostherne.

R.B. They understand the business, and we do actually farm ourselves. So we're aware of the problems.

D.   Diversification seems to be the word on most lips. I suppose it's filtered through from everywhere.

R.B. But diversification into what? The politician talks about diversification: *You should be better at your business*. The politician generally is somebody who's done nothing in his life except shoot his mouth off. So that's wonderful. It's advice from those who have not done it. Usually. And those who have done it, these days of course are excluded from politics.

D.   That's an interesting comment.

R.B. Usually. They're excluded by scandal, which is the most obvious thing. And I think they're excluded usually by the mood of the moment in the selection process. The career politician, the only thing he's done is canvassed, and something in the party's Central Office.

D.   So it's quite refreshing - I suppose you're in the same constituency as we are - to have an M.P. who's come out from somewhere quite different. But would you have an attitude - it just strikes me, this is more my feeling than anything I've heard from Ashley people, but - where we are, so close to Hale and Bowdon and a lot of people who are wealthy and enjoy riding, but have trouble finding anywhere to keep their horses: I've often wondered, when they talk about diversification, whether there is scope for more to be done with horses? But maybe there are reasons why that is not a good idea?

R.B. Well, I don't know what you can do. Cross country courses, stables where you could keep horses. But I don't think you could keep many farms like that. It would be another activity, like keeping hens. And of course farms were based upon diversi-fication, you had some geese and you had some pigs, you had some sheep and you had some cows and you milked a bit, and so on. Farms have tended to be, is the expres-sion monoculture? More and more that way.

D.   It's almost as if the pendulum is now swinging away in another direction: except that I suspect that when people talk about diversification they're not talking about going back to the old mixed farming that you're describing.

R.B. No. They're talking about running seminars in the buildings and that sort of thing.

D.   And golf courses, or something.

R.B. Yes. Which is not to everybody's advantage necessarily, and usually I think it's rather an overcrowded market. Farming prices are the answer. The job of the farmer is to grow produce. To feed the nation. And not to feed the drones in Brussels.

D.   So that's where the effort needs to be concentrated: the real effort in that case is outside and above the concerns of local farmers, really.

R.B. Yes. American farmers are subsidised, European farmers are subsidised. And our farmers aren't subsidised enough. It's as simple as that.

D.   A lot of them complain about the influence of supermarkets, which I can't quite understand.

R.B. I can't either.

D.   Right, well we'll leave that one!

R.B. But traders generally complain about the influence of supermarkets: the small shopkeeper complains about it. Whether that's right or not, I'm not sure.

D. Well it does seem as if they've become a dominant . . . and I suppose any disturbance in the balance of power is going to be disruptive.

R.B. Yes. That of course is the difficulty, and there's always been a change in the balance of power. At one time the man who made the thing had the money; and then it moved on to the warehouseman; and then it moved on to the retailer, and that's where it is at the moment.

D. And then it'll move on somewhere else.

R.B. To somewhere else, and we don't know quite where. Because the retailer at the moment is very much under pressure. If you look at the shares of the big retailers, they're all down. So that is a sign of the times. And I think quite a lot of the money has gone - we're talking about the share market - has gone, appearently from the traditional - Marks and Spencers or something like that - straight into something called The Internet. Or modern technology. And what that means, nobody really knows anyway! It's a marvellous situation. I think the South Sea Bubble.

D. Yes! All over again! Well let's move on. I'll take what might be the most boring thing next, which is the airport. One of the fears in Ashley is that sooner or later we shall just be under airport tarmac.

R.B. Well there is always the danger that that airport, which is in the wrong place, will have to expand, and it will expand where the planners wouldn't have wanted it to expand, if they'd have been asked in the first place. But nobody realised that airports were going to be quite that big.

D. I keep thinking, as I listen to people, that Stansted managed to beat off the Third London Airport for a long time. But it seems to be being developed now.

R.B. It seems to be being developed as if they'd never bothered with the Public Enquiry. So Public Enquiries don't mean anything.

D. So are we up against something here that's too big for any local control?

R.B. Well, if they want to build a runway in the Ashley direction, then Ashley will be under tarmac.

D. Yes. And if they don't go that way there'll be some other Ashley somewhere else.

R.B. It'll either go into Wilmslow or somewhere.

D. So place your bets.

R.B. Unless they move the airport, of course. Which is a possibility.

D. People talk about Speke being an ideal site.

R.B. Well I've always thought that Burtonwood would have been the best site. It will mean putting the motorway under the - which they shouldn't have built there because they ought to have been far-sighted enough not to have spoiled the site for themselves: but on the other hand it means they've got a motorway which goes right through the middle of the airport. It was big enough for American bombers in the war, and evidently it must be high enough for aeroplanes to come in and out, I've never heard there's been any difficulty, and I should think there's probably been - well there were certainly a great many flights in there during the war, of big aeroplanes carrying, probably overloaded. And it's better placed than Manchester Airport, I think. Personally, Manchester Airport suits us round here, as passengers, very well, because it's only ten minutes down the road. It would be half an hour to Burtonwood.

D.   Can we move on to the whole question of development, and by that I mean any future building that is done, any plans that are laid: some people are afraid that we shall gradually get overtaken by creeping suburbia, and that the same thing will happen to Ashley as happened to Ashton on Mersey.

R.B. Well as far as I can see, I think it's generally accepted the Bollin is the - what do you call it, not watermark - the natural boundary. I would have thought that should be the case. And the Bollin Valley, which, if I was a planner would mean the sight from the water, would be the line which I would take into consideration. I know that the planners don't seem to be very good at that. If you drive down the motorway - and millions of people drive down the motorway - you would have thought that the planners would have had the politeness to have protected the skyline. I was thinking in particular - I shall be driving to London in an hour or two - and when I approach Stoke-on-Trent on the left, you almost go past the Potteries without seeing the skyline infringed upon at all, till two or three years ago. But they've come over the ridge. Well they shouldn't come over the ridge. I thought they were a proper profession that would have had for themselves, in-house, proper rules; but evidently they don't.

D.   And when we think about anything that might happen around Ashley, you've introduced now this concept of planners: what people talk about locally is something much more random and piecemeal - like, recently the garage in Ashley -

R.B. They tried to do too much. To develop the site there. And the planners, very sensibly I think, turned it down.

D.   Well who are these people, the planners? The Council did a lot of work on that application from the garage, the Ashley Parish Council. But how far their influence extends, it's very difficult to know.

R.B. Well their influence extends as far as we support them. And if we support them, then their influence will extend a good deal further, that's all I can say.

D.   Right, that's a good point. Thank you. But the other thing which I think is widely appreciated is the way in which the estate's properties have been preserved.

R.B. Well, generally speaking, estates are better, for some reason, the bigger the estate is. I don't say that could really be argued, but it seems in practice that the bigger the estate, the better the planning. You might be able to tear that down if you find it a politically offensive remark! But, for instance, between here and Knutsford there is an estate, quite a big estate: and, if you notice, that's really, considering the area, it's one of the prettiest areas there is. When you leave The Whipping Stocks, until you enter Knutsford, there's more or less just one landowner. There are two other small landowners, but that is a case where a large estate . . . But if you take, say, round Wilmslow and Alderley Edge, the landowners have gone: and it seems to be a sort of free-for-all. And, as a landowner, I must say I feel a certain amount of resentment that individually people can't behave properly. It's in the case of big companies, and big companies take advantage. If we were in Sicily I'd expect it, but not in England.

D.   Because you do take a great deal of care as to what people do, don't you? I'm thinking now of that barn in Ashley. I understand that the people who wanted to convert that into a home had to submit plans, and you chose the one . . .

R.B. Yes. It was empty for years, and rightly or wrongly we had it made into a house, and the planners agreed. And I hope it's not too offensive.

D.   Oh, quite the contrary. I've not heard anyone say other than praise. And it sounded, from his story, as if he had to convince the estate that his plans were acceptable, and better than anyone else's: which an estate can do.

R.B. Well I think, if you just own one or two properties in a district, you don't see the point of doing it. Other people, perhaps, would not be able to see the reasonableness of it quite so clearly as if you happen to own the whole - then you can put it to them that, Really Mr So-and-so, you oughtn't to put on a dormer because the rest of the village hasn't got dormers of that sort. But if there are a lot of dormers just like that, it's very difficult.

D.   Yes, I can see that: you're likely to be able to preserve the character of a place more effectively if your writ runs over a wider area. I think that's covered all the topics that have been raised by people in the book. One small personal thing I'd like to add is how thrilled I was to go to Arden House. Last time I was there it was a tumbledown wreck with cellars filled with concrete, and quite uninhabitable. Now that it has been rebuilt it is an absolute delight, that house now.

R.B. It is, it's very nice. And its occupant is a very nice man, and he's done wonders to it. He's a great asset to the district.

D.   Well that's just what I've been thinking.

R.B. It's rather interesting, just talking about the house: the doors came from the demolished part of this house. There was a huge wing on the right hand side here, and my mother insisted that it should come down, and I think it was probably the right thing, so down it came. But we kept pieces like this fireplace and so on. And the doors were there, and they're quite tall doors, and I never thought that we'd ever be able to use them again. But we put them in Arden House, and really they don't look too big there at all, so Arden House is quite a big building. They're mahogony, at least they're mahogony faced. And the house that was demolished was 1760, so they're after that: I don't know when they were put in. And there are one or two fireplaces that came from another house called Grafton Hall, in Somerton in Cheshire.

D.   Oh next time I see Peter I must ask him to show me things like that.

R.B. It must have been a nice house at one time. And then it was messed about and messed about. And then it had fallen into disrepair.

D.   Yes well I think this one's lovely. I'd no idea we had such a gem there.

R.B. The other nice house is Ashley Hall, which has very nice farm buildings.

D.   That's the best part of it, I think. The farm buildings.

R.B. The farm buildings are really quite splendid, aren't they? And the staircase is very nice. And there used to be a range of rooms on the right-hand side, but unfortunately they had to be demolished.

D.   Yes, I never knew them, they were down before I came into the area.

R.B. That's where the meeting took place. The conspirators must have gone up the staircase, whose portraits are on the staircase at Tatton. Those portraits were in the demolished room, until the Egertons bought it in eighteen forty whatever-it-was, and then they took them to Tatton. About half a dozen local landowners, and they included I think the Leighs from Lyme and Grosvenors from Eaton, so they were quite important. And Mr Smith-Marriott from Marbury. So there was a lot of influence there. If you look in Kelly's Directory you'll see that.
    One of the big problems with Ashley is the traffic. I drove a friend to the airport the other morning, and I came back through Ashley. And it's terribly busy. It really does need some form of traffic calming measures there, I think they call them. They do it everywhere else except Ashley. They put promontories from the footpaths. There's a similar place I know, called Eton Wick, which I used to visit because my son was at Eton up till last year; and that has become a sort of rabbit run, into Eton. Through a residential area a bit like Ashley. And there are notices saying *Give way to oncoming traffic*, which slows people down enormously, and there are several of these things. Those could be considered. The roundabout is a nightmare. Perhaps the roads should be altered so that they're not opposite each other.

D.   Of course everyone's suddenly discovered it's a short cut into Manchester.

R.B. Well the Ministry of Transport's idea of course is, Eliminate the corners and widen the roads. Everybody goes faster. But the local Council I think would have the sense to do the reverse, and make it more difficult!

D.   Well, a very interesting thing happened on the road between Ashley and Hale. Those hedges were constantly being crashed through.

R.B. I know. Because we had to pay for it. A car a week.

D.   Well suddenly these gaps in the hedges stopped increasing. And I was talking to Ian Warburton at Dairy House, and I asked him what had happened? And he said he thinks it coincided with his decision to grow the hedges, which was motivated purely by consideration of wildlife.

R.B. Well it's interesting you should say that, because - I can't remember the corner now, but somebody said they wanted to cut the hedge down, and put railings there.

And my reasoning was that I didn't like that, because it would speed the traffic up! So I'm pleased to have a verification of my idea! If you make it too easy, all you do is that you don't have a smash until you have a very bad one.

D.   Well Ian had no idea it was going to do this. He was only interested in providing safe nesting sites, four feet above foxes and things. But what he realised after a year was, all of a sudden the hedges stopped being crashed through.

R.B. So if you put the hedges round the tarmac at Brands Hatch, I think it would close down, wouldn't it? So there we are. And the other thing is, I don't think there's a village hall at Ashley.

D.   No. But there is talk of the school adding on a hall.

R.B. Well the school has mentioned to us that it wants to expand. And we've said that there is land available. I think they need a bit more space.

D.   Well there is talk that if - when - they do that, it will be available to the village as well. The school is very anxious to increase its ties with the village community.

R.B. That might be the answer. I must have been told that the idea was in the air, although I don't think they've mentioned that to us. But it seems a good idea if it's a building which can be used as a village hall. But it would mean separate facilities, I would have thought.

D.   When it had that close shave with rationalisation last year, and it meant that it might have been shut down: one of the criteria they were looking for apparently was links with the local community, and that started focusing minds.

R.B. Are they preparing plans? I said I wanted the building to look like - because I own the school - and I'd like the building to look the same. Rather than put on a flat concrete roof, or building with a different brick. And iron windows, that's what they used to build.

D.   Well presumably somebody knows about this?

R.B. Yes, they do. We did give some computers to the school.

D.   That's right, yes.

R.B. And they asked me to go round, but I've never been there.

D.   Well I hope you'll find a chance to go some time. It's a very welcoming school.

f)   The Parish Council. Peter Wright

P.   I must have been on the Council now over twenty years, and I've been Chairman for the past seven. During this time I feel proud of all we have achieved on behalf of the Parish.

D.   I stand on a remote part of the touchline watching these things, but even I get the impression of a very effective Parish Council.

P.   You see nowadays we have, as a Parish Council, we've made our mark, because we do demand quite a bit of the higher authorities. And they listen to us.

D.   Well this is what is so interesting. It hasn't always been the case.

P.   I wish people did know more about the Parish Council. You see, Ken Crook is about the only person who comes to our meetings just to listen. People say, What does the Parish Council do? I think you'd be very surprised, the things we do.

D.   Tell me some.

P.   We got the traffic calming done, which we'd fought for a long time.

D.   These bars across the road?

P.   That's right. We wanted more, we wanted a 30 mph limit, but we couldn't get that. We've had a lot of run-ins with the railway over keeping things tidy. That's helped a lot now, with the other development of housing. Fencing up the railway bridges, we've done that. We have a lot of say in planning applications - I mean, we've no authority, but we do put our point on developments in the village. There was a development in the Smithy for seven houses, and I got a lot of phone calls saying We don't want that. And we opposed that, and that's gone by the board now, they've lost that. We were very involved in the airport fight. We were never going to win that one, but . . .

D.   And of course there was the brewery.

P.   Yes. And we liaise with the police all the time.

D.   When we lost Arthur and didn't get another policeman to take his place in the village I can remember how much effort went into trying to change minds that had already been made up. Has it made a big difference, not having a policeman in the village anymore?

P.   Well the police will tell you, No. You look at statistics, the crime rate didn't rise. We feel it did make a difference. But the policeman we've got now is very approachable. We're very happy with Gareth, he's a village policeman, he - obviously he's got a bigger area, but I think he does a good job.

D.   I'm just wondering, from where you are sitting, how much difference it made?

P.   Well we fought for a long time against selling the house. We didn't want the house sold, just in case. But you see the police authorities wouldn't wear that. We tried to reason with them, but they did sell it. Which we've lost forever. The big campaign is obviously for the school. And we ought to be involved more with the cricket club. I think that will happen, because they seem interested in bringing the village back into the cricket club. Arthur is their president, but there's no village members there now. I think we should be involved in that. But I think we have interesting nights in The Greyhound on Fridays now, as you were introduced to last week. I mean, people do get together, and we do talk. More people seem to know who their councillors are now than they did some years ago. And we do get hassle. Not hassle, but we get comments. Can you do this for us? And we try to.

Meg. You would like more people to attend the meetings really, wouldn't you?

P.   Yes we would, yes, just to know what goes on. But the actual Hough Green itself, we've been very involved with Walter Wright, he's a borough councillor, and Albert Turner who's just recently died, he was a county councillor, and they have both said what a credit The Green is to Ashley. How tidy it is; there's no problems, you get no complaints from neighbours; it just seems to be a very nice estate. I mean, all right, it's half privately owned and half council now. But it's a little bit of a showpiece around Cheshire, as a council estate. There are nice things done, like Bill Davies used to bring a load of muck for the gardens. And the skip's there every so often, and that helps. There's no rubbish about. Kept very tidy.

D.   Has that always been done, the skip?

P.   No, we initiated that originally, because people were saying, What do we do with the rubbish? That sort of thing we do. We got all the bulbs, all the bulbs along the roadsides, we planted those. Those have been free. You've got to apply and everything, but the councillors have done the work, they've actually planted them themselves. We developed the car park at the school. The estimate for the car park from Cheshire County Council was £22,000. It cost £2000 in the end. Because of the work of the Parish Council, we did all the work. We did all the planting. Jeff Warburton got his machinery in. That's the sort of place Ashley is. And I think Ashley has got to stay that way.

D.   It's a really hands-on Council, then.

P   Yes. It shows what can be done.

D.   Yes, and what could easily not have been done. It's not your usual idea of a parish council, being prepared to roll up their sleeves and do a back-breaking job like that!

P.   Yes, well you see that was why we went into it, we needed it there and then, as we said. And they were going to have it put on the list, and they couldn't promise it, and they said they certainly couldn't afford that sort of money. The latest scheme, the big one at the moment is, Ashley's had a complete new water system. That's the Parish Council: we've been banging the drum on that for the last seven or eight years. And when we went almost public about it, about the number of bursts and how much it was costing, at the end of the day we got the full system renewed. And that was really the work of the Parish Council. This is what the villagers don't see, which I wish they did.

We have made inroads. We've got a very good clerk now, Mollie Woodbine, who looks after the paperwork and everything. And we've got great support from Walter Wright. He's no relation but he's our borough councillor, he's actually going to be Mayor next year. And Albert Turner, who was a county councillor, was wonderful. Albert used to come to our meetings, and if we had any real problems he would carry them to Cheshire. He was a great help. But I think, by influencing these people - and they liked Ashley, didn't they? they loved Ashley -

D.   I think that might be the secret.

P.   And I think they saw in the Parish Council, they saw a group of people who loved their village. There's all sorts of little things that happen. We used to have heavy lorries coming through, and we stopped that. You know, we got onto Esso and they fully agreed with us, they were very cooperative. Lesser councils - I was talking to a councillor from somewhere else and he asked, How does Ashley get so much done? We can't. It is that. It's just the group of people.

D.   How often do you meet?

P.   Six times a year, plus extra planning meetings. Probably about twelve in all.

D.   Looking at the list of councillors, I notice that all the old Ashley families are there: do you think that's part of the secret?

P.   Yes.

Members who served on the Council during 2000

Peter Wright, Chairman
Jeff Warburton, Vice Chairman
Ed Daniel
Christine Erlam
John Erlam
Peter Jackson
Prill Lloyd
David Norbury
John Williams

Clerk: Mollie Woodbine.

g)   Ashley Smithy and Marjorie Mason

Thirty years ago the best-known landmark in Ashley was probably what was affectionately known as 'The Smithy'. Ashley Smithy Garage, to give it its full title, occupies the corner of the crossroads the other side of The Greyhound, and had the franchise for selling Toyota cars - one of the first to be established in England. This brought people into the village from far and wide, but here in the village The Smithy is better known as the birthplace of our Centenarian and undisputed Senior Citizen, Mrs Mason. Marjorie Ellison was born there in May 1900, "on the same day," she says, "as the Relief of Mafeking!" Educated at Altrincham Grammar School, she returned here and was a teacher at Ashley School before marrying George Mason and moving to Rostherne, where they farmed. On their retirement they moved back into Ashley, by the post office, where Mrs Mason still lives.

Mrs Mason chose not to record a conversation for this book, but she wrote the notes on which is based this reminiscence of The Smithy as it was for most of this Century.

William Ellison, her father, came to The Smithy in 1890 'with £20 and a good character', having been recommended to the Tatton Estate by Naylors the timber people, of Warrington.

Most of the work was shoeing heavy horses from the farms, and in those days there were few other horses. Light horses - ponies and hunters - only began to occupy more of their time after the introduction of tractors started the gradual decline of the heavy, working horse.

The Smithy had three hearths or fires, employing six men.

In 1962 trade was so diminished that they turned to petrol sales and to repairing tractors. They started selling cars in 1970, first British Leyland, then Toyota.

EPILOGUE

It is Sunday afternoon, one of those peerless January days after a frosty night, when the air is as clear as crystal and the sun barely clears the rooftops: and people, even today, go for walks. I too have just come in from my walk; not a very adventurous one to be sure, just the Ashley ring: out of The Green, left at The Old Police House (but you can do it clockwise if you like), past the large Victorian villas, mostly flats now, Outwood, Ribbledale, Redcroft, White Gables; under the motorway and into the open country towards Hale, past the Warburtons' stronghold at Dairy House (no dinosaurs today, but last month there were three to wish us Happy Christmas); over the railway and on to the next bend where the road goes right and we turn left into Ashley Hall's drive, a right of way for people on foot. These large flat fields on the right still have skylarks nesting here every year. Past the farm buildings and the Hall, set back behind its own lawn-lined drive and the magnificent eighteenth century farm buildings mentioned by Randle Brooks; more, and more modern, farm buildings and down into the dirty bit, wooded on the right, where there always seems to be a drainage problem whatever the weather; then up, stamping and scraping our feet to get the mud off, as the drive rises to the little bridge taking us back over the motorway and down to the end of the drive, which comes out on the road leading to Knutsford, having neatly by-passed the village.

This Lodge is where Arthur lives, our retired policeman. Turn left here for the homeward stretch. Over the road on our right is the path leading down to Ashley Cricket Club's ground which we can see the other side of the field by the road: convenient for Arthur, who is currently its President. Now we pass the church and its two former vicarages, the bungalow now called Highley House where the Robinsons live, and The Old Vicarage, a much more substantial Victorian affair, which is let. There are two more houses on our left before we approach the railway bridge, with a drive leading down this side of the track to the old station building, now so imaginatively converted by Matthew Hargreaves. This is one of the places where the traffic is most difficult, it being almost a hump-backed bridge, so that traffic is lost from view within yards either side of it.

From the crest of the bridge we can look down and see Mrs Mason's house, the Post Office, Thistlewood and the row of Hough Green Cottages on the right (the horses in the field behind there will be Chris Erlam's), with Egerton Moss on this side of the road. Before reaching there, turning left down the other side of the railway line, is the track leading to the house recently built by Noel Beresford. Past Egerton Moss is the crossroads, with Ashley Smithy Garage on our right and The Greyhound on our left. On the corner opposite is the Old Barn converted by Bob Salt and beyond that, Midways, the school and the lane leading down to Back Lane, Lane End and Castle Mill. Here we turn left past The Greyhound (well all right, then. A quick one!) and left again, back into The Green.

It is tempting to think that this walk has taken us through a little piece of Old England so unchanging as almost to be sacrosanct, but that wouldn't be true. We have heard from two farming families of the fateful decision to get a tractor. It is hard for us now to imagine what Ashley would have looked like, sounded like or even smelled like before then, with teams of horses at every farm, and every farm a working farm, at least two working smithies - and how many families being supported by all this? I have laughingly referred to the erections by the roadside outside Dairy House as dinosaurs, but of course what they symbolise is exactly the opposite: adaptation to change; pieces of equipment our great-grandfathers couldn't even have dreamed about, capable quite literally of changing the face of the earth. And above us, never out of sight or earshot for long, those men in their flying machines, each carrying hundreds of passengers in and out of the airport now threatening our backyard.

How many people assume that the dinosaur implies an attitude of entrenched hostility to change? And of course at one level it does, hence my comments in the post office and the pub. But a portrait of Ashley, or of any other community still enjoying the privilege of being set in the countryside, would not be complete without the other sort of dinosaur, the one on our cover: symbolising, not necessarily progress, but rather a creative response to the stern demands of evolution.

David Ellington. January, 2001.

(Photograph, David Ellington)

INDEX